Business Services, Pa
Outsourcing Contracts: a Practical Gu

Business Services, Partnering and Outsourcing Contracts: a Practical Guide

AMANDA LEWIS
Dentons

SWEET & MAXWELL

THOMSON REUTERS

Published in 2012 by Sweet & Maxwell, 100 Avenue Road, London NW3 3PF

Part of Thomson Reuters (Professional) UK Limited
(Registered in England & Wales, Company No 1679046.
Registered Office and address for service:
Aldgate House, 33 Aldgate High Street, London EC3N 1DL)
Typeset by Thomson Reuters (Professional) UK Limited
Printed and bound in Great Britain by CPI Group (UK) Ltd, Croydon, CR0 4YY

For further information on our products and services,
visit www.sweetandmaxwell.co.uk

No natural forests were destroyed to make this product;
only farmed timber was used and re-planted.

A CIP catalogue record of this book is available for the British Library.

ISBN: 978-0-414-02433-5

TITLE HISTORY

| First Edition | 2004 | by Amanda Lewis |
| Fourth Edition | 2012 | by Amanda Lewis |

For Howard, Sivanne, Benjamin, Annabel and Rebecca

Preface

Intended audience

This Guide is aimed at in-house legal counsel, finance directors and senior management at both customer and supplier organisations, and at government legal departments who are dealing with services, partnering or outsourcing projects and commercial lawyers, accountants and consultants who advise customers or suppliers on procurement.

Business and legal issues

A major reason for writing the Guide is that I feel that there is inadequate business and legal guidance for parties entering into services arrangements. Business books on services or outsourcing arrangements often omit important legal issues that could have profound business implications. Legal textbooks are not designed for business people and do not put legal issues in the business context, without which it is impossible to truly understand services arrangement.

In addition, legal textbooks usually fail to address all of the legal issues relevant for services agreements, for services arrangements usually involve contract, employment, pensions, data protection, property law, corporate, finance and insolvency issues. They may also, however, involve many other areas of law such as regulatory, competition or environmental law.

This Guide describes all of the relevant legal issues in simple terms that should be clear to lawyers and non-lawyers. Strategic issues are dealt with in the main text of chapters whilst detailed legal and business issues are set out in tables. Senior business people can read the main text of the book to understand the strategic issues without being bogged down in the details contained in the tables. As the Guide is intended as a practical handbook and not a legal textbook, it contains summaries of relevant legal issues, not detailed expositions. Cases and statutes are not referred to unless they are useful to illustrate the points being made.

There are highlights of some of the more general taxation issues that could arise in England and Wales. However, both customers and suppliers are strongly recommended to obtain specialist taxation advice on specific projects both prior to and during the negotiation of the arrangement, and indeed where substantial variations to existing transactions are proposed.

The Guide reflects the legal position as at 1 November 2012 (other than the foreign chapters, which reflect the position as at 1 August 2012)

Best practice and innovation

Another reason I initially wrote the Guide was because I wanted to describe, develop and encourage the implementation of best practice and encourage innovation. I have, over many years, taken the time to interview leading individuals in the sourcing industry about: their experience, what they regard as best practice, what they learned from their projects, what they wish they had done differently and any creative and innovative ideas they have employed in their projects. There is a lot of knowledge about sourcing which has not been included previously in any written articles and books on sourcing.

I would like to thank, in particular: James Adamson and Gina Gill of the FSA, David Gittings of Lloyds of London (LMA), Mark Thomas and Claire Royal of Standard Chartered Bank, Jeremy Barden of HBOS, Tony Brown previously of Barclays Wealth, Carolyn Fiddes of Friends Life, Brian Wilson of Northern Rock, Gry Gundestrup and Jesper Christensen of Nordea Bank, Mandy Caller of Svenske Handelsbanken, David Casement of Mitsui, Ian Seagrave previously of Deutsche Bank (now at Novartis), John Roome of Mitsui, Ranald Munro of Chubb Insurance of Europe, Markus Eckert of Cigna, John Rixon of Prudential, Amanda Wright of Standard Life, Magnus Koch of Volvo, David Wilde of Essex County Council, Christine Peacock of London Borough of Hackney, Alan Baxter of the Highways Agency, Linda Bonner of the London Borough of Enfield, Mike Whay of RSRL, Steve Alexander and Les Bond of Southern Water, Nigel Annett of Welsh Water, Mark Richards previously of EDF Energy, Andrew Phillips and Dave Copeland of Wessex Water, Heather Rogers of Centrica, Guy Muir of BAE Systems Detica, Mark Williams and John Ashworth of Pearson, John Seglias of Ipsos Mori, Keith Marriott of the NEC Group, Tim Cowen previously of BT, Paul Woodward of Telefonica 02, Dean Francis of BAA, Chip Nazmi of Kimberley Clark, David King of Boots, Jane Kimberlin of Domino's Pizza, Stefanie Neuhierl of Intel, David Eveleigh of BT, Scott Hamilton of IBM, Jonathan Stevens of Atos, Victoria Proctor of Serco, Charles Lilley of Steria, Robert Dunk of CBRE, Soren Lundsberg of G4S, Geoff Smith of Getronics, Martin Hobbs of Morse, Charlie Goddard of Navigant; Ian Reeves of Gartner Consulting, Tony Rawlinson of EquaTerra, Tony Dyhouse of QinetiQ, Lulu O'Leary of Blue Moon, Charles McLachlan of Amsphere, Dan Derry of OPS Logistics Consultancy and Peter Higgins of PD Consult.

Lessons learned from different services and sectors

The Guide also describes best practice with regard to different types of services and in different sectors, so that customers and suppliers can apply best practice from other services or sectors. I certainly find this very helpful in practice in assisting me to find creative solutions to business issues. The solutions to the problems of one sector or service are often to be found in the tried and tested solutions employed in another sector. For this reason, for example, the chapters in the Guide on the public, utility and financial services sectors address the question as to what customers and suppliers in other sectors can learn from the experience and regulations in that sector.

Extension of the Guide to cover services and partnering contracts

The first, second and third editions of the Guide focused on outsourcing. I have decided to extend the scope of the fourth edition of the book to cover services and partnering agreements. There are various reasons for this decision:

(a)   Growth and move up the value chain – As outsourcing has continued to grow, there has been an increase in business process outsourcing.(* According to Ovum (the independent technology analyst) - The global business process outsourcing market will reach revenues of $93.4 billion in 2015, a compound annual growth rate of 5.4% from the $71.92 billion it hit in 2010.) Some business process outsourcing agreements are better described as partnering agreements due to the close relationship between the supplier and the customer. In addition, as some customers become more experienced at outsourcing, in attempting to get the best out of their arrangement and out of their supplier, the arrangement becomes more of a partnering arrangement.

(b)   Move towards multi-sourcing in IT outsourcing – One of the long-term trends over the last seven years or so has been an increasing commoditisation of IT with a corresponding move in IT outsourcing towards multi-sourcing, with customers entering into multiple agreements with the various different IT suppliers rather than entering into one agreement with a prime contractor who then enters into subcontracts with other suppliers.(* According to KPMG (Sourcing Advisory 2012 Global Legal Pulse Survey) – over 40% of respondents identified that outsourcing contracts were becoming more complex (only 5% surveyed said contracts were less complex). The report identifies multi-sourcing as one reason behind increasingly complex contracts.) The effect of this trend is that the value of services outsourced has reduced and the distinction between outsourcing and services agreements has become blurred. I note that, during the recession, there has been a short-term trend, in some sectors, for customers to enter into larger outsourcing deals, in the hope that this will assist them achieve cost savings quickly – the Guide already covers these arrangements.

(c)   Move towards commoditisation and utility models – Another long-term trend is the tendency for services (including some services that are business critical) to become more commoditised over time with a growth in utility charging models, where services are made available to customers on a rental basis. This has contributed to the cloud-computing phenomenon. This trend means that the distinction between outsourcing and services is becoming less important. I do not feel that it is helpful to devote time and effort to deciding whether specific arrangements can properly be called outsourcing arrangements or not.

(d)   Increasing politicisation of outsourcing - During the recession there has been a tendency for the term "outsourcing" to be equated with offshoring or to be associated with redundancies, particularly in the United States, and hence to acquire an emotional edge to it. For this reason we detect a trend for people to use the term "services" rather than "outsourcing", in some circumstances.

(e)   Relevance of the book to services – Because of the close connection between outsourcing and services, many of the chapters of previous editions of the book were already relevant to services agreements. This was particularly true of the chapters on the law and practice in European jurisdictions, China and India, which were added in the third edition. As part of the process of writing the fourth edition of the book, I have reviewed all of the chapters to ensure that they cover issues relevant to services agreements. This does not mean that all issues mentioned will be relevant for all services agreements (any more than they are relevant for all outsourcing agreements). Services agreements cover a wide variety of arrangements on a spectrum ranging from strategic services agreements to low value, commodity arrangements. Some of the issues will be less relevant for lower value arrangements.

Changes in the fourth edition

The desire to ensure that the Guide comprehensively covers the various different legal and business issues relevant for services, partnering and outsourcing agreements has meant substantial changes in the fourth edition of the Guide. I have reviewed the whole of the Guide and updated all sections, including, in particular:

1. adding a new chapter on the implications of a breakup of the Eurozone;
2. re-writing the chapters on supplier models and joint ventures;
3. adding a new chapter on different customer models and shared services arrangements;
4. re-writing the chapter on data protection and security and strengthening the other sections in the Guide on data protection and security, to reflect the increasing importance of these topics;
5. adding a definition of cloud computing and ensuring that the various chapters deal with specific issues relating to cloud computing, where necessary;
6. explaining the new emphasis on the service integrator role and the various service integrator models;
7. re-writing the chapter on dealing with disputes and adding a section on common problems that lead to disputes;
8. re-writing and updating the chapter on Competition Issues;
9. re-writing the classification of services, in the light of the extension of the book to cover services and partnering arrangements;
10. re-writing the chapter on Pensions in the light of recent case law, legislation and changes to guidance;
11. updating the Guide to deal with the great expansion of regulation in the financial services sector, so that there are now five chapters on financial services;
12. updating the chapter on competitive dialogue in light of recent government guidance and including a section on the future of public procurement;
13. replacing the chapter on the public sector to cover the material changes in policy in the public sector;
14. reviewing the chapter on the Private Finance Initiative in the light of the current change in government policy in the UK, whilst highlighting the adoption of the PFI model outside the UK;
15. expanding the guide to consider environmental issues in greater detail where relevant;
16. updating the chapters on the procurement and utilities directives;

17. updating the chapters on due diligence by the customer and the supplier;

18. updating the Guide in the light of recent cases, including Uniplex (UK) Limited v NHS Business Services Authority [2010]; BSkyB Limited and another v HP Enterprise Services UK Limited (formerly Electronic Data Systems Limited) and another [2010]; GB Gas Holdings Ltd v Accenture (UK) Ltd and others [2010]; AstraZeneca UK Limited v Albemarle International Corporation and another [2011]; AXA Sun Life Services plc v Campbell Martin Ltd and others [2011]; Compass Group UK and Ireland Ltd (t/a Medirest) v Mid Essex Hospital Services NHS Trust [2012]; Odeon Cinema Holdings Limited v BFI IMAX Cinema, 16 July 2012 ME/ 5482-12; Shared Network Services Ltd v Nextiraone UK Ltd [2012]; and The Procter & Gamble Company v Svenska Cellulosa Aktiebolaget SCA and another [2012];

19. updating the Guide in the light of recent legislation and regulations, including the Localism Act 2011; the Bribery Act 2010; Commission Regulation (EC) No 1998/2006; National Health Service Pension Scheme (Amendment) Regulations 2009; The Local Government Pension Scheme (Administration) Regulations 2008; Alternative Investment Fund Managers Directive; Directive 2009/ 138/EC; Solvency II Directive 2009/138/EC; UCITS IV Directive 2009; Public Procurement (Miscellaneous Amendments) Regulations 2011; the Alternative Investment Fund Managers and amending Directives 2004/39/EC; and

20. updating the foreign chapters to account for changes in foreign legislation and practice.

Extension of foreign law chapters to cover US and UAE law and best practice

In the fourth edition of the Guide, I have extended the Guide to include additional chapters that cover the US and the United Arab Emirates. The chapters have been written by experts in the relevant jurisdictions, John Funk, Ross Docksey and Joby Beretta, who are partners at Dentons. In addition, I have worked as editor with experts in other jurisdictions and other law firms who have updated the chapters on the law in their specific countries. I am extremely grateful to all of them for their contributions. In particular I would like to thank:

(a) Germany – Prof. Dr. Peter Bräutigam / Dr. Thomas Thalhofer, Noerr LLP ;

(b) Spain – José Ramón Morales, Partner, Garrigues;

(c) France – Mary-Daphné Fishelson, Partner, La Garanderie & Associes

(d) Italy – Gabriele Capecchi, Partner, Legance;

(e) Sweden – Jörgen Axelsson, Partner, Setterwalls;

(f) Switzerland – Michele Bernasconi, Partner, Nicola Bernardoni, Associate and Philippe Fuchs, Associate, Bär & Karrer AG;

(g) Ireland – Anne-Marie Bohan, Partner, Matheson Ormsby Prentice;

(h)   India – Sajai Singh, Partner, J.Sagar Associates; and

(i)   China – Anthony Chan, Partner and Lawrence Cheng, Dentons.

The main chapters in the book cover EU Directives and their implementation in the UK. The EU country-specific chapters cover the implementation of the relevant EU Directives in the relevant country. The chapters on China, India, the US and the UAE cover specific legal issues in these countries.

I would like to thank all of my colleagues at Dentons who have helped me with this Guide, including in particular Dan Burge, Mark Bassett, Thomas Leyland, Nick Graham, Jan Willem van den Bos, Sam Szlezinger (essentially rewriting the chapter previously written by Adrian Magnus), Angelique Bret, Jeremy Cape, Richard Barham, Sarah Dyke, Pauline McArdle, Emma Radmore, Michelle Grudzinski, John Funk, Ross Docksey, Helen Dayananda, Nisha Darbari, John Woolley, Elizabeth Elliot, James Borshell and Sam Oustayiannis.

Lastly, I would like to thank my publisher, Nick Bliss, for his help and support.

If you have any comments on the Guide, you can email me at amanda.lewis@snrdenton.com.

Amanda Lewis is a partner in SNR Denton UK LLP and John Funk, Ross Docksey, Anthony Chan, Lawrence Cheng and Joby Beretta are partners in SNR Denton, Dallas, US, SNR Denton/Brandt Chan & Partners and SNR Denton UAE, which has voted to combine with Frasier Milner Casgrain LLP and Salans LLP to form Dentons, a unique global law firm with more than 2,500 lawyers and professionals in 79 locations in 52 countries across Africa, Asia, Europe and Central Asia, the Middle East, North America and the UK.

Amanda Lewis
1 November 2012

TABLE OF CONTENTS

Part 1

Introduction

Chapter 1

Scope and purpose of this Guide

1.1 Outline

This Guide covers outsourcing and services contracts. This chapter explains the relationship between services and outsourcing arrangements and explains the different types of services arrangements. It also describes the purpose of the Guide, defines successful projects and explains some of the reasons why customers enter into outsourcing or services arrangements. Lastly, it explains the difference between contracting for business outcomes, services outputs or inputs, a distinction that will be used throughout the Guide.

There are references to "suppliers" and "customers"; the intention is that the Guide should assist both public and private sector customers and also suppliers. Customers of the customer are referred to as "clients".

1.2 What is the relationship between services agreements and outsourcing?

Outsourcing agreements are a type of services agreement. The Financial Services Authority (FSA) provides a useful definition of outsourcing, defining outsourcing as

> "an arrangement of any form between a firm and a service provider by which that service provider performs a process, a service or an activity which would otherwise be taken by the firm itself".[1]

The FSA definition clarifies that outsourcing involves the provision of a service that is not a commodity service which the customer can turn on and off at will (unlike, for example, the provision of standard stationery). There is a level of dependency upon the supplier. This could arise, for example, because people or assets needed for the provision of the service are transferred to the supplier. It could also arise because elements of the service are tailored specifically for the customer.

From the supplier's perspective, there is a level of interdependency between

---

[1] See *http://www.fsahandbook.info/FSA/html/handbook/Glossary* [Accessed 1 November 2012].

the parties in an outsourcing arrangement as the supplier depends upon the customer's ability to pay the supplier its fees. In addition, if the customer is satisfied with the supplier's performance, it is more likely to increase the services provided by the supplier. Lastly, if the customer's business or reputation suffers in the market, this may affect the supplier's business.

Services arrangements cover an extremely wide variety of transactions, and as an industry, the services industry is continually changing and developing to satisfy customer needs, as market conditions change and technology develops. They include some arrangements that are designated as "shared services", "managed services", "strategic partnerships" or "partnering arrangements". They cover the recent developments regarding "mutuals" in the public sector.[2] They also cover cloud computing (both public and private).[3]

1.3   Classification of services arrangements

1.3.1   *Sector*

One way of classifying the wide variety of services arrangements is by sector. There are specific laws and regulations that apply to customers entering into services transactions in certain sectors, notably the public sector, utilities and financial services sectors. For example, firms regulated by the FSA will be subject to its rules and guidance on outsourcing. Chapters 38 to 42 covers some of the regulations that relate to the financial services sector.

---

[2]   See section 17.5.
[3]   Cloud computing reflects two long term trends in IT:
    (a) **Commoditisation** - it reflects the trend towards the commoditisation of IT services.
    (b) **Utility computing** - it reflects the movement towards the provision of IT services on a utility mode, with the customer paying for the IT services on a pay-as-you-go basis. This payment mechanism is particularly useful for customers who experience seasonal variations. This development has been supported by the development of virtualisation software. Virtualisation software enables the creation of a large virtual machine that acts like a real computer with an operating system comprising various physical machines. Software executed on the virtual machines is separated from the underlying hardware resources. Hardware virtualisation software can be used to improve scalability and overall hardware-resource utilisation, thus supporting utility computing models.
    There are three types of cloud computing:
    (a)   **Infrastructure as a Service** (IaaS) - this involves users renting the use of servers.
    (b)   **Platform as a Service** (PaaS) – this involves users renting use of servers and the system software to use on them.
    (c)   **Software as a Service** (SaaS) – this involves users also renting application software and databases. The supplier manages the infrastructure and platforms on which the applications run.
    There are four basic deployment models for cloud computing:
    (a)   **Public cloud** – this involves services being provided by the supplier to various customers over the Internet. This has security and data protection implications.
    (b)   **Private cloud** – this involves the provision of infrastructure solely for a single organisation, whether managed internally or by a third-party supplier and whether hosted internally or externally.
    (c)   **Community cloud** – this involves the sharing of infrastructure between several organisations from a specific community, whether managed internally or by a third-party supplier and whether hosted internally or externally. In this model, the costs are spread over fewer users than a public cloud, but more than a private cloud, so that some of the cost savings potential of cloud computing are realized, whilst avoiding the security and data protection problems caused by the provision of services over the Internet.
    (d)   **Hybrid cloud** – this involves a composition of two or more clouds (private, community or public).

Chapter 43 describes some of the laws, policies and guidance, which apply to the public sector. Chapter 47 deals with the regulations affecting the utilities sector. All three chapters also highlight lessons that bodies, which are not in these sectors, can learn from the purpose and nature of the regulations.

1.3.2   Nature of the service

A second way of classifying services is by the nature of the service being provided, as listed in Table 1.

This Guide deals with the key issues relevant to all of the listed types of services (for example service descriptions and charging). It does not describe in detail specific issues relating to one particular service (for example telecommunications regulatory issues).

Table 1 Classification of services

Category of services	Subcategories	Examples
IT and telecommunications services	IT	Desktop services Printer services Videoconferencing services Applications management and support services Database administration service Server hosting services Server support and maintenance services Information security and business continuity services Application development and projects services Computer management services
	Telecommunications	Provision of data or voice network systems services Engineering works services Support and maintenance services Telephony services Unified communications services
Business process outsourcing and services	General back office and middle office	Human resources services Pensions administration services Training services Finance and accounting services Audit services Procurement services
	Industry specific back office and middle office	Insurance claims processing services Credit card processing services Lease payments processing services Custody services Fund administration services Derivative processing services Transfer agency services Underwriting support services Claims management services

		Cash pool services Trade finance processing services Mortgage processing services Cheque processing services Life policy administration services Local authority revenue and benefits processing services
	Sales and front office	Call centre services Customer services Sales services
Knowledge process outsourcing and services		Sales research services Market research services Drug trial data management services
Legal process outsourcing and services	Core legal services	Due diligence services Legal research services Discovery and litigation support services Contract review services
	Legal support services	Document management services Paralegal support services
Facilities management and property	Facilities management	Logistics services Fleet management services Vehicle supply and servicing Health and safety management Environmental management services Facilities helpdesk services Mailroom services Administration and supply of stationery and computer consumables Printing and reprographic services Document scanning services Courier services Storage services Meeting room booking services Reception services Travel and hotel booking services Building services Space planning and relocations Security services Energy conservation and management services Catering and vending services Cleaning services Grounds maintenance services Janitorial supplies Office furniture Lift maintenance services Health and safety and environmental management services Engineering consultancy services
	Property	Property management Serviced accommodation "Total property solutions"

1.3.3 Commercial structure

Services contracts can be classified by commercial structure. Thus, services arrangements can be distinguished depending upon whether, for example, they are executed by way of a services agreement between the customer and supplier or whether they involve the parties entering into a strategic partnership or joint venture. Commercial structures are discussed in Chapters 17, 18 and 19.

1.3.4 Onshore/offshore

Services transactions can be divided into those that are onshore and those that are offshore. Most of the chapters in this Guide are applicable to both types of outsourcing. Chapter 47 deals with some of the additional issues that are relevant for offshore outsourcing transactions and Chapters 48 and 49 deal specifically with issues affecting outsourcing to India and China (respectively).

1.3.5 Value

Lastly, services arrangements can be distinguished by value. A low-value transaction will often be simpler than one that is high value. Accordingly, some of the issues raised by this Guide may not be relevant for a low-value project.

1.4 Purpose of this Guide

Despite the differences between the various types of services arrangements, many of the fundamental challenges presented by them are similar. The aim of this Guide is to give the reader an insight into a range of tested solutions so as to enable the parties to a services arrangement to find the most appropriate solution for their particular set of circumstances. It will accordingly enable best practice in one area to be applied in other areas. Chapters 2 to 38 describe the general issues that arise in most types of services transactions (for example service descriptions and charging) and possible ways of dealing with them.

This Guide also describes the key commercial and legal success factors relevant to the various types of services arrangements. In order to keep the Guide short and readable, it is not designed to cover all relevant provisions that need to go into a services agreement, but it focuses on fundamental issues that the parties will need to consider in order to ensure that their project is successful.

1.5   What does it mean to be successful?

A services arrangement can only be regarded as successful if it satisfies the business objectives of the parties entering into the services arrangement.

1.5.1   Customer's perspective

From the customer's perspective, the services arrangement must satisfy the following three types of objectives:

(a)   it must satisfy the customer's original business objectives;
(b)   it must fulfil the customer's future business objectives, which the customer needs to satisfy during the term of the agreement; therefore, the agreement must be flexible and must include adequate change management measures; and
(c)   it must satisfy the customer's objectives on termination. On termination, the customer may want the flexibility to migrate the service back in-house or to an alternative supplier; it will not want to be locked in to receiving the services from the previous supplier.

1.5.2   Supplier's perspective

From a supplier's perspective, the services contract will be successful mainly if it is (or can contribute towards) the supplier obtaining a profitable piece of business.[4] In practice, a services contract is unlikely to be successful from the customer's perspective if the supplier is not making any profit, as, in this situation, the supplier will be tempted to cut corners and the service will suffer.

In addition, even if a services contract is profitable for the supplier, if it is unsuccessful from the customer's perspective, then the supplier may find itself the subject of unfavourable publicity, particularly if the customer is in the public sector or has a public profile. This may cause damage to the supplier's reputation and adversely affect its ability to win new profitable business.

1.5.3   Advantages of understanding the other side's perspective

It is an advantage for each side to understand the other side's perspective.

---

[4]   See Chapter 6, which describes other possible business objectives of the supplier.

If the customer has a greater understanding of the supplier's viewpoint, then it is likely to prepare its initial services offering in a manner, which is attractive to suppliers. This will avoid the need to modify the offering in order to attract sufficient levels of interest from suppliers, thus saving time and money. If the customer can increase the attractiveness of its project to suppliers, then it will improve its bargaining power.

If the supplier has a greater understanding of the customer's perspective, this should enable it to make itself more attractive to customers in what is an increasingly competitive marketplace. Thus, for example, suppliers endeavouring to break into the public sector or utilities market need to understand the specific needs of public sector and utility customers, as described in Chapters 43 to 46.

It is in both parties' interests to understand the other side's concerns so that contractual negotiations proceed smoothly and efficiently. Therefore, this Guide presents both the customer and the supplier perspectives.

1.6 Why customers procure services

The success of the services project has been defined in terms of satisfying the different business objectives of the supplier and customer.

The supplier's business objectives are discussed in greater detail in Chapter 6, which describes the preparation that the supplier will need to carry out before it enters into a services arrangement.

There are various different business objectives that motivate customers to enter into services agreements. The reasons evolve to fit the times. This Guide does not cover the validity or appropriateness of different reasons for outsourcing or entering into services arrangements. There are plenty of books on this subject. For example, in his book *Strategic Outsourcing—a structured approach to outsourcing decisions and initiatives*, Maurice F. Greaver II[5] highlights various reasons for outsourcing. These are listed in Table 2. Greaver's book is quite old now, however it is useful in highlighting the wide variety of reasons why people outsource or enter into services agreements.

---

[5] Maurice F. Greaver II, *Strategic Outsourcing—a structured approach to outsourcing decisions and initiatives*, (Amacom, 1999)

Table 2 Possible business objectives[6]

Reduce costs through superior provider performance and the provider's lower cost structure
Generate cash by transferring assets (such as equipment or premises) to the provider
Turn fixed costs into variable costs
Commercially exploit the existing skills[7]
Increase flexibility to meet changing business conditions, demand for products, services and technologies
Improve risk management
Improve management and control
Improve operating performance
Enhance effectiveness by focusing on what you do best
Increase commitment and energy in non-core areas
Improve credibility and image by associating with superior providers
Enhance product and service value, customer satisfaction and shareholder value
Transform the organisation
Acquire innovative ideas
Give employees a stronger career path
Gain market access and business opportunities through the provider's network
Accelerate expansion by tapping in to the provider's capacity, processes and systems
Expand sales and production capacity during periods when such expansion could not be financed
Obtain expertise, skills and technologies that would not otherwise be available

It will be clear from the variety of business objectives that the customer may be seeking to achieve, that different approaches will need to be taken and different issues will need to be dealt with in the individual project, depending upon the customer's specific business objectives. This Guide deals with the key legal and commercial issues that the parties will need to consider to ensure that business objectives such as those listed above are achieved.

1.7 Risk allocation

Section 1.6 explains that projects can be classified by reference to the business objectives that the customer is seeking to achieve. Services projects can also be categorised by reference to the extent to which the supplier will be responsible for the achievement of the customer's business goals. A major function of a services agreement is to allocate risk between the customer and

---

[6] The situation regarding local authorities is particularly interesting because, under s.3 of the Local Government Act 1999, they have a duty to ensure best value. Thus they have a duty to secure continuous improvements in delivery of their services, focusing on economy, efficiency and effectiveness. This means that the local authorities have statutory objectives and targets that they must satisfy. Central government also has imposed upon itself a significant efficiency saving target of £30 billion for 2010/11. See *http://www.hm-treasury.gov.uk* [Accessed 31 August 2012].

[7] The customer may have special industry knowledge relating to how a particular business process is carried out (e.g. cheque processing). It may want to exploit that knowledge to provide similar services to other companies in its sector. By entering into a joint venture with an outsourcing supplier, it may be able to gain the marketing support needed to market its skill.

the supplier, and a major risk that needs to be apportioned between the parties is the risk that the customer's business aims will not be met. Depending upon the extent to which the supplier will be responsible for the achievement of the customer's business objective, the project may include "business outcome", "service output" or "input elements". These terms are defined below.

1.7.1 Business outcome

The project will be business outcome based if the supplier accepts a level of responsibility for the achievement by the customer of its business goal. For many business objectives, it will not be appropriate to pass on the risk of their achievement to the supplier. For example, if the customer's business is to sell motorcars and it outsources its human resources function with the aim of enhancing its own effectiveness by focusing on what it does best, the supplier will be reluctant to agree that payment of the supplier's charges will be conditional upon the customer selling more motorcars.

In other circumstances, it may be appropriate for the supplier to accept some risk of the customer's business aim not being achieved. Suppliers will not usually accept responsibility for the achievement of business objectives unless they have control over the manner in which the business goal is to be achieved. Therefore, the approach may be appropriate if, for example, the arrangement involves the implementation of new software or the provision of business process re-engineering services, where the purpose of the project is for the supplier to implement specified changes designed to improve the customer's operating performance.[8] In these circumstances, the supplier may be willing to accept some risk that the particular improvement in the customer's operating performance is not satisfied. It may also be appropriate if the supplier is providing training services. For example, if the supplier takes over responsibility for training soldiers and there is some guarantee of the calibre of the people being submitted for training, the supplier may be able to contract to provide a certain number of trained soldiers.

The manner in which the supplier will accept responsibility for the business objective will usually be through a risk/reward charging mechanism. This risk/reward charging mechanism and the problems involved in using such a charging regime are discussed in Chapter 20. The business outcome based nature of the project may also be reflected in the service levels and service credits - these are discussed in Chapters 9 and 21. Business outcome transactions are often termed "partnering" arrangements.

---

[8] Transformational and developmental outsourcing arrangements are discussed in greater detail in Chapter 24.

1.7.2   Service output

In the past, it has been more common for projects to be "service output" based rather than "business outcome" based. Service output based liability is where the supplier is responsible for the provision of the specified service, the service output, but the customer is responsible for ensuring that the provision of the service satisfies its business objective. To describe it in another way, the customer is responsible for ensuring that the service description describes the service that it needs. The supplier's role is limited to providing the service described in the service description.

Suppliers will not usually accept responsibility for the provision of the services unless they have sufficient control over the manner in which the services are to be provided. This issue is discussed in greater detail in Chapter 8.

Lastly, the customer must bear in mind that it cannot entirely transfer over to a supplier the risk that the services will be provided. The customer must have adequate business continuity arrangements to cover a failure by the supplier to meet its obligations under the agreement.

1.7.3   Input[9]

If the liability profile is "input" based, the supplier's responsibility is limited to the provision of certain resources, for example man-days of consultancy. The customer is responsible for directing the consultant as to what to do and hence is responsible for the result of the consultancy services.

1.7.4   Hybrid

In practice, many outsourcing and services arrangements will be a hybrid of business outcome, service output and input liability arrangements, with individual service elements being either business outcome, service output or input based. For example, the project may involve the supplier providing a desktop maintenance service as requested by the customer (service output based) but with the supplier being asked to prepare an annual service improvement plan explaining how the services can be improved so that they satisfy the customer's business objectives (business outcome based).

The distinction between business outcomes, service outputs and inputs will be used throughout this Guide to explain the risk profile of individual elements of the transaction.

---

[9]   If the supplier is going to provide the services in whole or in part from Spain or France, then see Chapter 53 or Chapter 59 before signing an input-based outsourcing agreement.

Part 2

Preparation

Chapter 2

Preparation by the Customer

2.1 Outline

This chapter describes the first stage of the sourcing process, which involves the customer clarifying its business objectives.

The customer must define its business objectives and support them with a business case. It needs to carry out due diligence to ensure that the business case stands up to scrutiny. It also needs to review the business case on an ongoing basis to ensure that key performance indicators are being met and that the objectives and the sourcing arrangements themselves are changed, where necessary, when the customer's business changes. The customer should prepare a risk register and use it to manage risk during the sourcing project.

2.2 Focus on business objectives

A lack of focus on the business objectives that the customer is attempting to achieve by entering into the sourcing arrangement is a major reason why sourcing transactions fail.[1] There has been a tendency, in particular in IT projects, for the customer to see the implementation of particular technology as an end in itself, for example to see the sourcing deal as "the implementation and maintenance of a new finance system". It is more helpful to see IT systems and services as a means to an end, for example implementing a new finance system to enable more efficient billing.

Focusing on business goals, however, is not a straightforward task. It may involve the customer prioritising or seeking a satisfactory balance between the various aims of different departments or factions within the customer organisation. It may involve the customer balancing different types of business aims, for example satisfying a short-term goal such as reducing costs, and ensuring that it does not cause long-term problems of inflexibility. It may also involve the customer analysing how quickly its current business

---

[1] Good business objectives should be specific, measurable, appropriate, realistic and time bound (SMART).

15

objectives are likely to change and how important it is that its business can respond quickly to commercial opportunities.[2]

In practice, any decision about what the customer's business aims are and how they can be achieved is reached in the context of the individual politics of the specific organisation, and external advisers advising the customer's organisation, in particular, need to be aware of this. For example, in the case of a human resources project, the chief finance officer may initiate the sourcing project as a way of cutting costs. The chief executive officer may support the project if he feels that it will improve the company's share price. The human resources director may resent the sourcing project and attempt to undermine it if he feels that it will decrease his importance within the organisation, for example if some of his staff will be transferred out of the company to the supplier under the Acquired Rights Directive (ARD). The human resources director may also feel that he is letting his staff down if he recruited them and now participates in a course of action, which will lead to them, being transferred to another company.

2.3   Business case

The customer's business objectives must be reflected in and supported by a business case which proves that, out of the various options open to the customer (such as keeping the service in-house, moving to a shared service or outsourcing), contracting out the services is the best way to satisfy the specific goal the customer is endeavouring to achieve. As the sourcing project will only be regarded as successful if it satisfies the customer's business aims over the term of the agreement, the business case should endeavour to address anticipated costs and benefits over this period.

This Guide does not describe how to prepare a business case. There is various guidance on this issue, both in the private[3] and the public[4] sectors.

2.4   Due diligence

The quality of the customer's business case and ultimately the success of the sourcing arrangement will depend upon the thoroughness of the customer's due diligence in exploring and establishing the facts and assumptions

---

[2]   This may determine the optimum term of the sourcing arrangement. See section 26.2 below for a more detailed discussion of issues relating to the optimum term for a sourcing arrangement.

[3]   See, for example Ivanka Menken and Gerald Blokdijk, *Outsourcing Best Practices Step-By-Step Guide on How to Manage the Changes, Challenges, Opportunities and Implement a Successful Outsourcing Process,* (Emereo Publishing, 2008).

[4]   See Healthcare Financial Management Association, *Public Sector Business Cases using the Five Case Model: A Toolkit* (2007). For project specific guidance for local government see the Public Private Partnership Programme's (4Ps) guidance for preparing *Outline Business Case* and *Final Business Case* at its website *http://www.localpartnerships.org.uk* [Accessed 31 August 2012].

underlying its business case. Table 3 gives examples of factors that a customer may need to check.

Table 3 Factors to be considered in due diligence

Business objectives

What are the customer's business objectives?

What are the possible ways that the customer could achieve its objectives?

Is outsourcing the best way of achieving its goals, or could its goals be achieved, for example, by improving performance?

What are the customer's competitors doing?

Will the proposed transaction affect other strategic aims, whether related to sourcing decisions or otherwise, for example the anticipated sale of part of the business?

How are the customer's business objectives likely to change over time?

Will the sourcing project result in favourable or unfavourable publicity for the organisation?

Stakeholder support

Do stakeholders in senior management agree with the business requirements and support the sourcing initiative?

Will users and customers affected by the sourcing arrangement support any resulting change in the services they receive?

If the success of the sourcing project is dependent upon users or clients of the customer using the new services, will they use them?

Current services

What services are currently being provided?

What are the strengths and weaknesses of the current method of providing the services?

What are the stakeholders satisfied with and what are they dissatisfied with?

How are the services being provided?

From which locations or countries are the services being provided?

What service levels are being achieved?

What service levels the customer's competitors are achieving?

What volume of services is being provided?

To which locations are services being provided?

What trends are there regarding the volume of services?

Are the services being provided to other members of the customer's group or to external organisations?

Future service requirements

In what ways do the future services and service levels need to be different from the current services, taking into account the customer's business requirements?

What are the consequences for the business if the supplier does not achieve specific service levels required by the customer?

Can providing the services offshore satisfy the customer's business requirements?

Can providing the services via a cloud model satisfy the customer's business requirements?

Can suppliers suggest alternative ways of satisfying the customer's business requirements?

What steps are needed to effect a transition from the existing arrangements and the existing agreements?

Is any business process re-engineering required and if so, when should it be carried out, as part of the sourcing project or before it?

What will the customer need to do to monitor, control and manage the services during the term of the agreement?

If the services involve IT services, should the customer outsource service integration?

What are the customer's possible future service requirements, taking into account its overall business objectives?

What service levels will the supplier guarantee?

What assistance from the supplier will the customer require on termination?

Current data protection and security requirements[5]

What are the current security risks?

What current security measures are taken to protect the customer's assets and data?

What security policies and standards have been implemented?

Future data protection and security requirements

What sensitive and critical data will be affected by the sourcing arrangement?
Is there an accurate inventory of sensitive and critical data?

What security risks will arise as a result of the sourcing arrangement?
Will the supplier be using a cloud model for any of the services?

What security measures should be taken by the customer and the supplier to deal with the security risks under the sourcing arrangement? What security policies and standards should be implemented?

What steps will need to be taken to ensure compliance with data protection legislation?

What transitional measures will be necessary to implement the new security requirements?

Assets or premises with regard to which the services are provided (e.g. outsourcing of maintenance of equipment or premises)

Where relevant, what assets or premises are covered by the sourcing arrangements?

Are these listed in an accurate asset register?

Operational risk

Are the services critical to the customer's business?

What are the operational risks involved in the transition?

What are the operational risks involved in outsourcing the services?

What are the operational risks involved in transferring the services back in house or to a successor supplier on termination?

What are the security implications of outsourcing, including the initial transition and the transition on termination (including the implications of termination for insolvency of the supplier[6])?

If the customer is regulated by the Financial Services Authority, will the outsourcing or services agreement adversely affect its ability to comply with its regulatory obligations?[7]

Costs and charges

What are the costs of the current service?

What will be the whole-life costs of the sourcing transaction?

What costs will be incurred in procuring the services?

What costs and expenses will be incurred as a result of the transition to the new arrangements?

What charges will be payable for the services?

What costs will be incurred as a result of managing the new arrangement?

What costs will be incurred on expiry or termination of the new arrangement?

What are the tax implications (particularly VAT) of the proposed project?

What are the exchange rate risks and who will bear them?

What are the inflation risks and who will bear them?

---

[5]   See Chapters 36 and 37 for an explanation of the laws on data protection.
[6]   See Chapter 29 for a more detailed discussion of insolvency issues relating to outsourcing projects.
[7]   See Chapters 38 to 42 for an explanation of the regulation affecting outsourcing in the financial services sector.

Funding and structuring the arrangement

What are the alternative ways to fund or structure the new transaction and which is the best way?[8]

Staff and contractors

What staff and contractors currently provide the services?

Will employees transfer from the customer to the new supplier under ARD?

What are the relevant terms and conditions of employment of the transferring staff?

Will employees transfer from the customer's existing suppliers to the new supplier?[9]

What rights to information and other protections does the customer have under its agreement with the existing supplier?

What if any are the health and safety implications for staff and contractors of the proposed outsourcing or services arrangements?

How do any such implications need to be addressed?

Assets

What assets are used to provide the services?

Does the customer own or lease the assets?

Does the customer have an asset register?

Is the database up to date?
Will the supplier be providing any assets?
Who is to maintain the assets and who is responsible for the cost of maintenance?
Will the customer require the assets to be replaced at any time; who will do this and who will be responsible for the cost of this?

Third-party licences and permissions

Will the customer need to obtain permission from its software licensors for the supplier to use its software licences and, if so, will the software licensors demand a fee for granting permission?[10]

Can the customer's current supplier agreements be transferred to the supplier where required?[11]

Will the customer need permission from its landlord or mortgagees to grant licences or subleases relating to relevant premises?[12]

Client relationships

If the project relates to services provided to the customer's clients, is the customer restricted by its contract with its clients from entering into the arrangement?

Will the customer breach its confidentiality obligations to its clients if it outsources the services?

Will the sourcing arrangement damage the relationship of the customer with its clients?

Regulatory requirements

Does the customer require the approval of any relevant regulator before it can outsource the services?
Are there any other regulatory requirements?[13]

---

[8] See Chapter 17 for a description of different outsourcing structures.
[9] See Chapter 31 for an explanation of relevant staffing issues.
[10] For an explanation of issues relating to open source software, see Heather J. Meeker, *The Open Source Alternative: Understanding Risks and Leveraging Opportunities*, (John Wiley & Sons Inc., 2008).
[11] See Chapter 14 for a discussion of software licence and other supplier issues.
[12] See Chapter 15 for further information on property issues.
[13] See Chapters 38 to 42 for further information about regulatory requirements in the financial services sector.

If the customer is in the public sector, does it have the power or "vires" to enter into the sourcing arrangement?[14]

Environmental issues

Do the services require inputs or result in outputs that are subject to environmental obligations such as those on substances, emissions and pollutants, packaging or other waste law?

Is there a risk of any environmental liability arising?

Are the services covered by the terms of an environmental permit? If so, it it lawful to outsource them?

How will any corporate and social responsibility concerns and legal obligations relating to sustainability be met?

Could the customer face responsibility for any administrative or criminal sanctions for breaches of environmental law by the supplier?

How will the sourcing project affect the carbon footprint of the customer? Will the carbon footprint of the sourced service cease to be included in the carbon footprint of the customer? Will the outsourcing or services arrangement introduce complexities for the customer in complying with any emissions reporting requirements?

Does the customer operate an accredited environmental management system such as under ISO:14001? If so does this have a bearing on the choice of supplier?

If environmental taxes are introduced, how will this affect the sourcing arrangement?

Culture and training

How will the project affect the morale of employees providing the services who will transfer to the supplier?

Are there cultural differences between the customer's organisation and the proposed supplier?

What skills will the customer need to manage the new arrangement?

Procurement process

What is the most appropriate procurement process for negotiating the sourcing arrangement?

What is the desired timetable?

Is the desired timetable realistic?

Does the timetable need to be sped up to ensure the quick achievement of the customer's business objectives?

If so, what are the risks of a truncated procurement procedure?

Contractual terms

Will the customer be able to impose its own terms and conditions upon the supplier or will the supplier expect to use its own standard terms and conditions? If the latter, (a) does the supplier reserve the right to unilaterally amend its terms and conditions and (b) what legal system do the terms and conditions claim to be governed by?

Is there a material difference between the liability that each supplier is willing to accept?[15]

2.5   Updating the business case

After the customer has carried out its initial due diligence and prepared a first draft of its business case, it will need to update the business case and

---

[14]   This problem is only likely to increase with the new innovative structures and shared services arrangements being considered in the public sector. Particular care should be taken when the public sector is seeking to contract out a "function" which includes specific legal powers e.g. operation of a local road network.

[15]   See Chapter 34 for further information about liability and risk.

the due diligence as the procurement progresses to ensure that the underlying assumptions in the business case continue to be correct, in particular if details of the sourcing arrangement (e.g. the exact services to be outsourced) change.

Once the agreement has been signed, the business case should be used as a tool for monitoring progress in achieving the business objectives, for example when changes to the services are proposed.

It should also be updated to reflect changes in the customer's business goals. The subject of changing business objectives is covered in greater detail in Chapter 25.

2.6   Risk register and risk management

The quality of the customer's business case depends upon the level of due diligence carried out, so, if the customer decides that in order to achieve a business objective it does not have time or resources to investigate certain factors, it should be aware of the risks it is taking. It may be appropriate to list in a risk register these and any other risks that may affect the project and consider ways in which they may be mitigated.

The risk register should list the individual risk, the likelihood it will occur, the effect of it occurring and the mitigation strategy. It may also be useful to specify who will be responsible for managing the risk, as between the customer and the supplier.[16] The parties should bear in mind the principle that allocation of risk to the party who is best able to manage it tends to provide the most economically advantageous solution.

Like the business case, the risk register should be monitored throughout the term of the sourcing arrangement and should be updated to reflect changes in the risk profile. The parties should review the risk register regularly throughout the project, so that they can consider appropriate steps that should be taken to manage the risks.

2.7   Feedback from suppliers

Before initiating a procurement process, as well as understanding its own business objectives and risk profile, the customer may also want to investigate whether there are suppliers who can provide the necessary services. If

---

[16] See Robert White and Barry James, *The Outsourcing Manual*, (Gower Publishing Ltd, 1996) for a more detailed discussion of risk registers. In the public sector see the Cabinet Office, *Policy and Standards Framework – Best Practice Guidance* on the Cabinet Office's website at *http://www.cabinetoffice.gov.uk* [Accessed 31 August 2012].

there are suppliers available, the customer may (in the private sector[17]) want to decide which ones will be most suitable—this may involve the customer profiling the supplier market, the key players and the drivers affecting the market.

The customer may also want to investigate the suppliers' potential business objectives and risk profile. This will help the customer to understand whether suppliers will be interested in providing the services that the customer requires (taking into account whether demand for services exceeds supply or vice versa, at the relevant time).

It may also help the customer decide how to package the services (e.g. by aggregating services or dividing them up) to attract suppliers and maximise its bargaining power.

Lastly, it may provide the customer with an understanding of the suppliers' perspective that will prevent the customer preparing an offering to suppliers that undermines the suppliers' potential business benefit from the project, hence resulting in limited or no response to the offering.

---

[17] See Chapters 43 and 46 for an explanation of the Procurement Directives that apply to the public and utilities sectors.

Chapter 3

A Competitive Procurement Process

3.1 Outline

Chapter 2 describes the first stage in a sourcing project, namely the customer's preparation for the sourcing transaction. The next stage involves the customer procuring the services, and that is the subject of this chapter. The chapter describes different procurement approaches, depending upon whether or not the procedure involves an element of competition between the different suppliers. It also gives practical hints for preparing an invitation to tender.

3.2 Procurement process

Once the customer has completed its due diligence and come to the conclusion that the evidence supports the business case for outsourcing, the customer will need to decide how to procure the services.

3.2.1 Public and utilities sectors

In the public and utilities sectors, the procurement process used by the customer will be dictated by the applicability (or not, as the case may be) of the EU Consolidated Procurement Directive 2004 or the EU Utilities Procurement Directive 2004 (Procurement Directives) which have been incorporated into UK law by the Public Contracts Regulations 2006 and the Public Utilities Regulations 2006 respectively (Procurement Regulations) . If they apply, the relevant Procurement Regulations set out the procedural framework that the authority or utility must follow and lay down principles for the selection of the supplier. (See Chapters 43 and 46 for a more detailed discussion of the application and implications of the Procurement Directives and Procurement Regulations.)

The interesting point about the procedures set out in the Procurement Regulations is that they are all highly competitive and highly structured. Only two procedures are suitable for high-value and/or relatively complex contracts, the "competitive dialogue procedure" and the "negotiated procedure". The former is now recommended by the government to be used only in limited circumstances by the U.K. government, which would prefer that its central government departments and their agencies rely on the "restricted procedure", albeit with comprehensive early market engagement. Both procedures require that authorities should continue to "dialogue" or "negotiate" (as applicable) with more than one supplier until the parties have agreed all of the key commercial issues.[1] In the private sector, following a tender process, customers often select one preferred supplier or a restricted panel.

3.2.2   Private sector

So, in the private sector, what are the advantages and disadvantages of adopting a procurement procedure that involves competition between different suppliers? From the supplier's perspective the position is clear. Suppliers, not unnaturally, prefer customers to negotiate exclusively with them, so that they know that they are likely to be awarded the contract and do not waste time and money negotiating contracts that are then awarded to another supplier.

From the customer's perspective, the situation is more complex. Table 4 lists some advantages and disadvantages of a competitive procurement process.

Table 4 Advantages and disadvantages of competition for the customer

Advantages of competition
Cheaper charges
Suppliers may be more aggressive in their charging and may charge a lower margin if they know that they are in competition.
Better terms
Suppliers may be more amenable to agreeing commercial and legal terms that suit the customer if they are competing for the business.
More thorough examination of the possible solutions
Negotiating with more than one supplier may mean that the customer examines its business requirements more thoroughly and considers possible alternative solutions. (However, customers should be careful not to breach confidentiality obligations agreed by the parties by disclosing elements of one supplier's solution to other bidders. See section 3.5 below for a more detailed discussion of confidentiality issues relating to suppliers' proposals.)
Innovative solutions
Suppliers may be incentivised through the competitive process to come up with innovative means to provide the services.
Disadvantages of competition
Suppliers drop out

---

[1]   See *The Competitive Dialogue Procedure 2008 – OGC/HM Joint Guidance* at *http://www.hm-treasury.gov.uk* [Accessed 31 August 2012] and similar sector-specific guidance for local government at *http://www.localpartnerships.org.uk* [Accessed 31 August 2012].

Suppliers may drop out of the procurement process if they do not think that they are likely to win.

Charges uneconomic for supplier

In some high-value outsourcing arrangements, where negotiations with two suppliers can continue for two years or more, it has been argued that this can lead to a situation where suppliers have invested so much time and money in the procurement that they feel they cannot afford to lose. Accordingly, or so it is argued, they have been forced to quote extremely low charges to ensure they win. There is a concern that this can lead to suppliers being forced to cut corners in providing the services, so that ultimately the customer suffers. In addition, competition is not the only way of ensuring a reasonable price; see Chapter 23 for a description of other ways of ensuring value for money.

Cost of negotiating with different suppliers

Negotiating with more than one supplier may actually involve lower fees if it enables the customer to maximise its bargaining power.

Otherwise, negotiating with more than one supplier may involve more management time and, if external advisers are being engaged to handle part of the negotiations, more fees being paid to the advisers. In this case, the customer will need to weigh up the possible reduction in the charges and improvement in terms resulting from exerting competitive pressure upon suppliers against the cost of running more than one set of negotiations.

Emphasis on charges

It is sometimes argued that running a competitive procurement procedure results in a particular emphasis in the negotiations on the fees charged by different suppliers rather than, for example, the quality of the different suppliers' solutions or other commercial terms (e.g. risk allocation). An extreme example of this is where a supplier is selected by using an e-auction, where, once the suppliers satisfy certain minimum quality criteria, the preferred supplier is selected entirely on the basis of cost. This may or may not be appropriate, depending upon, in particular, whether:

(a)   the price is the most important factor in the procurement;

(b)   the services are commodity services which can be defined clearly;

(c)   the charges can be determined by reference to a defined service description, without the need to negotiate them to establish the best balance between service quality and price; and

(d)   sufficient suppliers are willing to participate in an e-auction.

Quality of the supplier's proposal

If suppliers know that there are several suppliers being asked to respond to the customer's request for proposals (RFP), and hence that their efforts may be in vain, they may be reluctant to commit substantial amounts of time to developing their proposal. The customer needs to manage this situation to encourage suppliers to invest in the procurement, perhaps by limiting the number of suppliers asked to respond to the tender to two or three, or (in exceptional circumstances) by offering to contribute towards the bid costs of the bidders.

Delay

Negotiating with more than one supplier may delay the commencement of the services. If the sourcing arrangement is designed to reduce the cost of running the services, then the customer may be reluctant to allow any delay in signing the agreement. The customer may feel that any reduction in the charges resulting from exerting competitive pressure upon the supplier will be offset by the money lost as a result of the delay.

Sensitive information

Negotiating with more than one supplier may increase the number of organisations that will have to be given confidential information about the customer's organisation.

Secrecy

The customer may not want its employees to know about the sourcing transaction until it is clear that there is a business case supporting the sourcing proposition. Therefore, it may want to restrict the number of people who know about the project.

Looking at the advantages and disadvantages of competitive procurement procedures, as described in Table 4, it can be suggested that in many cases the most appropriate procurement procedure will be one that reaches a balance which ensures that some of the advantages of competition are achieved without too many of the disadvantages. For example, the customer could maintain a dialogue with two suppliers so that there is competitive tension between the two, whilst in practice concentrating efforts in negotiating with one particular supplier if it was clear that that specific supplier was more likely to achieve the customer's business objectives. The customer would not formally select a preferred supplier until the key commercial issues had been agreed.

However, ultimately, like so many other issues in an outsourcing arrangement, the most appropriate procurement procedure will depend upon the customer's business objectives.

3.3   Preparing the RFP

If the customer decides to adopt a procurement procedure that initially involves negotiating with more than one supplier, it may need to draft a document (commonly called a request for proposals, invitation to tender, invitation to negotiate, request for information or other similar title) to send out to suppliers.

The customer may break down the procurement process into different stages with an initial request for information. This is designed to obtain feedback from suppliers on the customer's proposed procurement and to enable the customer to select appropriate suppliers who will then receive the RFP.[2]

Table 5 includes a description of information which the customer should consider including in its RFP.

Table 5 Checklist for RFP

Background on the customer
What is the relevant background information on the customer's organisation (such as its history, recent events that have affected it, its culture, size and organisational structure)?
Customer's business objectives
What is the customer's exact business objective?
How important is it that the supplier is flexible in agreeing changes to the arrangement?
How important is it that the supplier assists with a smooth transition on termination?
Benefit for the supplier

---

[2]   In the public or utilities sectors, if the Procurement Directives apply, information that can be requested for the purposes of the initial shortlisting is strictly limited. See Chapters 43 and 46 for further information.

What will the supplier find attractive about the customer's project? (This issue is particularly important if the market is such that there are many opportunities for the suppliers at the time.)

Multi-sourcing/prime contractor

Does the customer reserve the right to divide the services up and appoint different suppliers to provide different services?[3]

Current services

What services are currently being provided to the customer?

How are they being provided?

Where available, what service levels are being met?

What volume of services is being provided?

What are the trends regarding the volume of services?

Are services being provided to other members of the customer's group or to external organisations?

Are there any specific problems or challenges currently being faced or which the supplier will need to deal with?

Future service requirements

How would the customer like the services and the service levels to be changed, both after the initial transition period and throughout the rest of the agreement? (The customer may want to give the supplier an opportunity to suggest ways in which the customer's objectives can best be achieved, rather than being too prescriptive.)

What service management and service reporting is the customer expecting the supplier to provide?

What services are excluded from the scope of the outsourcing project?

Is there any potential for the customer to give the supplier additional work?

Are there any quality processes and accreditation that the customer expects the supplier to have?[4]

Would the customer be willing to move to a more standardised or commoditised service?

Current security requirements

What security measures does the customer or an incumbent supplier currently take?

Future security requirements

What additional security measures will the supplier have to take?[5]

Assets or premises with regard to which the services are provided

Where relevant, what assets or premises are covered by the services?

Operational risk

What are the major perceived risks and how will the risks be allocated between the parties?

Staff

What are the current resourcing arrangements for the provision of the services?

---

[3] See Chapter 17 for a discussion of the implications of multisourcing versus single-sourcing strategies.

[4] For example, the customer may want the supplier to hold an ISO 9001 certificate. Such a certificate proves that the supplier has an adequate quality system whose effectiveness is regularly assessed by an independent auditor. The certificate does not guarantee the quality of the services provided, although it is an indication that the supplier takes quality assurance seriously. The ISO 9000 series of standards emphases the ability of the supplier to learn from experience and to implement continuous quality improvement. For offshore outsourcing transaction the customer may want to refer to Six Sigma qualifications or ask suppliers to carry out STAR audits.

[5] See Chapter 37 for a detailed discussion of security issues.

On what basis should the supplier prepare its proposal, regarding the application of ARD?[6]
Assets
Are there any assets that the customer intends to provide to the supplier so that it can provide the services?
Are there any costs and liabilities that the customer intends to transfer to the supplier?

It will be apparent that many of the topics in Table 5 reflect those listed in Table 3 as areas where the customer will need to carry out due diligence before it issues the RFP. Failure to carry out effective due diligence with regard to these areas may make it difficult for the customer to provide sufficient information in its RFP and accordingly undermine the suppliers' ability to provide meaningful proposals.

3.4 Procurement process

The customer should specify in the RFP what information it will need the supplier to provide in its proposal so that the customer can ascertain whether the supplier meets its evaluation criteria. This will include the general information in Table 6.

Table 6 Information that the supplier must provide in its proposal

Background on supplier
What is the supplier's management structure?
What is its customer base?
How large is the supplier's organisation?
How long has the supplier been in business?
Service requirements
What is the supplier's solution?
From where will the services be provided?
How will it manage the services?
What key personnel would be used to provide the services?
What is the staff attrition rate?
What sub-contractors will it use?
How is it intending to implement the transition towards the new services?
What experience does it have of providing similar services?
What experience does it have of providing services in the customer's industry sector?
Can it provide references from other customers?
What is the supplier's track record?
Is any litigation against the supplier existing, pending or threatened?
Is the supplier the subject of any investigation, enquiry or enforcement proceedings by any governmental, administrative or regulatory body?
What history of involvement with relevant regulators does the supplier have?

---

[6] See Chapter 31 for a detailed discussion of ARD. If the customer is advised by its legal advisers that ARD will apply and that certain employees will transfer to the supplier from the customer, then the customer may want to include general details about the employees transferring, including the number of employees and their salaries and other benefits, so that the supplier can include these costs in its charges. The customer will need to ensure that it does not breach data protection law in disclosing information about staff. See Chapters 36 and 37 for a description of data protection law.

Has the supplier complied with its obligations under agreements with other customers?

Security requirements

Can the supplier comply with the customer's security requirements?

Operational risk

How will the supplier manage those risks allocated to it?

Commitment

What is the relative size of the services to the supplier's overall business?

Are there any other factors that influence how important the customer will be to the supplier?

Quality

What quality processes and accreditation does the supplier have?

Environment

Is the supplier's solution environmentally friendly? (This will be particularly relevant for certain public sector bodies and corporates who want to be included in the "FTSE 4 Good Index".[7])

Charges

What are the supplier's charges?[8]

The customer will also need the supplier's proposal to include any other specific information required to enable the customer to evaluate whether the supplier satisfies the concerns specified in Table 6, where relevant.

The customer may want to summarise relevant evaluation criteria in the RFP, and may want to specify whether the supplier can submit variant bids that, for example, represent better value for the customer than the standard bid.

The customer may want to specify the intended procurement process, with details of the procurement team. It may want to explain at what stage it envisages the supplier carrying out its due diligence. If the customer has sufficient information to formulate a draft or outline project plan, it may want to include this as well. Where relevant, the customer will need to specify the procedure by which the suppliers may raise queries on the RFP, the dates on which the supplier will be able to make a presentation (explaining its solution), the date for submission of proposals, together with the number of copies of the proposal required and how they should be submitted. It is advisable for the customer to specify that the suppliers' proposals must follow a particular format so as to facilitate comparison between different suppliers.

3.5 Confidentiality[9]

The RFP should make clear if any of the information that it contains is confidential, from the customer's perspective.

---

[7] The FTSE 4 Good Index lists companies that meet criteria in three areas: working towards environmental sustainability, developing positive relationships with stakeholders and upholding and supporting human rights. For further information, see *http://www.ftse.com/Indices/FTSE4Good_Index_Series/index.jsp* [Accessed 31 August 2012].

[8] The customer will need sufficient information about the charging structure and a breakdown of the charges to enable it to determine its final requirements. See Chapter 20 for a discussion of charging issues.

[9] In certain sectors, the customer will need to ensure that suppliers' staff who have access to the RFP have appropriate security clearance. See Chapter 37 for a discussion of security issues relevant in outsourcing agreements.

It should set out how it proposes to deal with confidential information made available by individual suppliers. If the customer states that it will not disclose details of one supplier's proposal to other suppliers, then the suppliers will be more willing to disclose original suggestions about how the services can be improved. If the customer states that information made available by one supplier may be made available to other suppliers, so that they can provide quotes for providing that solution, then suppliers will be reluctant to suggest novel solutions to the customer's requirements.

A similar concern can arise with regard to questions asked by suppliers. Customers sometimes feel that they will be regarded as acting unfairly unless they give all suppliers the same information. However, if the customer states that all information provided in answer to a question by a particular supplier will be copied to other suppliers, this may deter a supplier from raising questions that indicate the innovative solutions it is intending to propose. A possible compromise is for the customer to state that it will copy answers to all suppliers, unless there is a reason not to do so. It will then explain, when a question is raised, whether it proposes copying the response to other bidders, giving the supplier raising the question the opportunity to withdraw it if it considers that this will be prejudicial.

The approach taken by public sector procurers is slightly different. Due to requirements to comply with the public procurement principles of transparency and equality of treatment, a public authority will share all clarification questions with other bidders unless the bidder raising the query specifically marks the question as confidential and provides sound reasons why revealing the question to others would give away commercially sensitive information particular to that bidder. However, bidders can take comfort that, once the dialogue begins in earnest, the public sector customer is prohibited from sharing one bidder's "solution" with others under the Procurement Regulations.

3.6   Legal terms and conditions

Within the RFP, the customer will need to explain its commercial requirements, for example how long the arrangement will be.

3.6.1   *Full set of draft terms and conditions*

If the nature and structure of the sourcing arrangement is not likely to be fundamentally varied at a later stage, there may be an advantage to the customer in including a full set of draft terms and conditions in the RFP. This will establish that any negotiations will start from the customer's draft terms and conditions and not those of the supplier. It may also mean that the customer can negotiate the terms and conditions from a position of strength before selection of a preferred supplier.

3.6.2   Heads of terms

If the customer is giving the RFP to several suppliers and it is not practical to include a full agreement, it may be possible to include heads of terms, key clauses or key principles and request suppliers to agree to or comment on these so that the supplier is aware of the customer's desired approach to key commercial and legal issues. This is particularly important in markets where there is a wide variation in how supplies approach key issues, such as the fund management sector.

3.6.3   Supplier's response

If the customer does include heads of terms, key clauses or key principles, it should explain how the supplier is expected to respond to these. In either situation, the customer may want to indicate if certain terms and conditions are non-negotiable. The customer should explain whether the supplier must include in its proposal general comments on the agreement or a detailed mark up the agreement. Marking up an agreement involves a substantial investment of time by the supplier and suppliers are often reluctant to commit to such an investment at a stage where several suppliers are being asked to bid for the work. (See Chapter 4 for a more detailed discussion on selecting a preferred supplier.) Equally, from the customer's perspective, it may not want to spend time reviewing a detailed mark up of the agreement from suppliers until it has shortlisted the final two or three suppliers.

3.7   Legal protections

The customer will usually want to include the protections described in Table 7 in its RFP.

Table 7 Legal protection to include in the RFP

The customer does not guarantee the accuracy of information provided in the RFP.
The customer reserves the right to amend the RFP document and the RFP process at any time.
No contract arises until the procurement has completed and the services agreement formally entered into.
The customer reserves the right to disqualify bidders who collude[10] with each other or who submit non-compliant bids or for other reasons.

---

[10] Suppliers should note that collusive tendering is a serious breach of competition law, which could result in fines of up to 10% of turnover; unenforceability of the agreement; action for damages by third parties; directors' disqualification; and imprisonment of individuals involved. See Chapter 33 for a detailed description of competition law and its implication for outsourcing. In a decision relating to the roofing industry, the Office of Fair Trading noted that "there is no reason why undertakings invited to participate

> The customer is not obliged to proceed with the negotiations, so that it can abandon the process if it becomes apparent that the customer's business objective will not be achieved or for any other reason.
>
> The customer will not pay the supplier's costs, whether these relate to the supplier preparing and submitting its proposal, undertaking any tests, demonstrations or meetings as part of the negotiations, participating in the RFP process, participating in the negotiation process or preparing for the provision of the services.
>
> The customer may accept the supplier's proposal in part (where relevant).
>
> The customer reserves the right to select whichever supplier it regards as appropriate, and not necessarily the cheapest supplier.[11]

3.8   Disclosure of information in the RFP

On the one hand, the customer will need to include sufficient information on the matters specified in Table 5 to ensure that suppliers can submit meaningful proposals. It will need to ensure that it attracts the right suppliers and that the supplier will not withdraw from the process as and when they fully understand the requirements. This is particularly important in the public sector or utilities sector, as a failure to describe the scope of the requirements adequately in the RFP or the call for competition could constitute a breach of the Procurement Directives where they apply.

On the other hand, the customer must ensure that it does not disclose in the RFP any information about its organisation that is sensitive, in breach of confidentiality obligations (e.g. in its supply or client agreements), or in breach of competition law[12] or data protection law.[13]

In addition, before the customer provides the suppliers with any information about its possible sourcing project, it must ensure that they sign a non-disclosure agreement agreeing not to disclose any information made available to them. This is particularly important if the customer has not made public the fact that it is considering outsourcing and especially if there is a risk that staff will be made redundant as part of the sourcing arrangement. To safeguard confidentiality, the customer may want to specify that the supplier may discuss the negotiations only with specified members of the customer's negotiation team. In some case, it may also be helpful for the customer to include non-solicitation provisions in the NDA, to prevent the supplier soliciting the customer's staff.

In practice, once a customer commences the procurement process, it must recognise the risk that this fact will become known publicly or by its staff, and should make contingency plans for dealing with the possible

---

in a ... competitively tendered process would need to communicate with one another in relation to the tender before returning their bids" (Collusive tendering for felt and single ply roofing contracts in Western-Central Scotland Case (CE/3344-03) July 8, 2005 at [121]).

[11]   A public sector or utility customer will be constrained in the basis upon which it may select a supplier (see Chapters 43 and 46).

[12]   See Chapter 33 for a description of competition law.

[13]   See Chapters 36 and 37 for a description of data protection law.

implications. In some jurisdictions, national laws relating to information and consultation with employees (e.g. where there are Works Councils) have an impact on the timing of this process.

Chapter 4

Selecting a Preferred Supplier

4.1   Outline

Chapter 3 describes the customer's preparation of an RFP. The next stage is the selection of a preferred supplier or preferred suppliers. This chapter deals with the criteria for selecting a preferred supplier and how the selection or evaluation criteria should be reflected in the services agreement.

4.2   Evaluation criteria

Whether the customer has decided to negotiate with several suppliers before selecting a preferred supplier or to negotiate with only one supplier, it will need to decide upon the evaluation criteria that will assist it in choosing a supplier.

As mentioned at section 3.2 above, for public sector transactions covered by the Procurement Directives, the evaluation criteria will need to comply with the requirements set out in those directives. These are described in greater detail in Chapter 43. Subject to these constraints, the evaluation criteria should ultimately flow from the business objectives which the customer wants to achieve and so will depend upon the individual facts of the case.

Examples of issues that may be relevant in selecting a preferred supplier are listed in Table 8.

Table 8 Selecting a preferred supplier

Business objectives
Does the supplier understand the customer's business objectives and business strategy?
Does the supplier's solution support the achievement of the customer's business objectives?
Does the supplier's suggested method of structuring the sourcing transaction achieve the customer's business objectives?
Does the supplier's track record demonstrate that its solution will achieve the customer's business objectives?
Commitment
Is the supplier committed to achieving the customer's business objectives?

Where relevant, has the supplier shown commitment by its senior management to the transaction?

What commitment does the supplier have to the provision of the services in the future?

Is the provision of the services the supplier's core business?

How important is the customer's industry sector to the supplier?

How important will the customer be to the supplier?

Will the customer be one of the supplier's key clients?

Stakeholder support

Does senior management within the customer's organisation approve of the supplier?

Do users within the customer's organisation approve of the supplier?

Service requirements

Is the supplier's solution sufficient to satisfy the customer's business objectives?

Do the supplier's staff have sufficient skills and experience to provide the solution?

Does the supplier's track record demonstrate that the supplier and its staff have the ability to implement the supplier's solution?

Security requirements

Is the supplier's solution sufficient to satisfy the customer's future security requirements?

Do the supplier's staff have sufficient security skills and experience?

Does the supplier's track record demonstrate that it has sufficient security skills and experience? Has the supplier been the subject of any investigation (formal or informal) by the Information Commissioner's Office or any other data privacy regulator? If so, what was the outcome? Was an adverse finding made or enforcement action taken by the relevant data privacy regulator?

Does the supplier's solution result in any additional security risks, for example because of the location of the supplier's premises or the use of emerging technology such as RFID or facial recognition technology?

What additional security measures will need to be taken to deal with these additional risks?

Operational risk

Is the supplier's proposal for managing risk adequate?

Does the supplier conform to recognised security standards such as ISO 27000?

Does the supplier have an adequate security and data breach incident management policy?

How does the supplier ensure business continuity?

Supplier's resources

Does the supplier have the resources to provide the services?

If the services agreement is a substantial one, are there pressures on the supplier's resources due, for example, to it recently winning other business?

Supplier's other customers

Does the supplier provide services for competitors of the customer?

Does the supplier provide services to those customers from the same site or using the same personnel who would be used for the provision of services to the customer?

Does this cause confidentiality, security or other problems?

Charges

What charging assumptions has the supplier made?

How do the supplier's charges compare with its competitors' charges?

How carefully has the supplier checked its charges?

Will the supplier commit to price protection schemes such as benchmarking or maximum margin?

Have customers of the supplier said that the supplier has been reasonable in agreeing the charge for changes requested by the customer after signature of the agreement?

Flexibility and innovation

Can the supplier provide services that may be required in the future?

Do the references indicate that the supplier takes a flexible approach to agreeing changes in the charges?

Do the references indicate that the supplier expects to increase its margin by levying substantial charges for changes to the services?

Are there any grounds for believing that the supplier will not be flexible about agreeing changes to the agreement?

If required, has the supplier demonstrated that it keeps pace with cutting edge technology and is continually innovative in the services it offers to its clients?

Configuration management

Does the supplier have adequate configuration management processes?

Staff

What is the track record of the supplier regarding managing the transfer of employees from customers?

What opportunities will transferring employees have working for the supplier?

What experience does the supplier have of dealing with the transfer of staff under ARD?

How does the supplier treat its staff?

Does the supplier invest in training its staff?

What are the supplier's staff turnover levels?

How will the project affect the morale of employees, including any staff transferring to the outsourcing supplier?

Independence

If the services are to include consultancy services or the provision of advice, will the supplier be able to provide independent, impartial advice or does it have exclusive arrangements with specific suppliers?

Will the supplier commit to informing the customer of any commissions it receives for recommending certain suppliers?

Termination

What is the supplier's approach to helping the customer ensure a smooth transition on termination?

Can the supplier give examples where it has assisted other customers to effect a smooth transition to a new supplier on termination of the agreement?

Are there any grounds for believing that the supplier will not assist in a smooth transition on termination?

Culture

What is the supplier's culture? For example, have the supplier's customers said that it has behaved in a trustworthy manner and with integrity?

Are the cultures of the two organisations compatible?

Commitment to customer satisfaction

What is the supplier's culture with regard to emphasis of short-term aims (e.g. maximising profit for the relevant quarter) over long-terms aims (e.g. whether the customer will extend the agreement when it expires in five years' time)?

Is the supplier committed to achieving customer satisfaction?

Is the supplier good at establishing and maintaining longer-term relationships with its customers?

Financial stability

Is the supplier financially stable?

How long has it been in business?

What is the financial standing and credit rating of the supplier?

Is it unduly reliant upon certain outsourcing contracts or specific markets?

Is the supplier aware of any pending or threatened claims against it?

Does the customer need to require the supplier to provide additional comfort, in the form of a parent company guarantee or a performance bond?

Management structure

How stable is the supplier's management structure likely to be? Is the company a likely target for a takeover?

Legal terms and conditions

Where the customer has supplied terms and conditions, how do the supplier's comments on the agreement compare with comments from other suppliers?

What do the supplier's comments on the terms and conditions show about its confidence in its ability to provide the services and its confidence that it can achieve any cost savings expected by the customer?

What do the comments show about the commercial prudence of the supplier organisation?

Is it being prudent in protecting its commercial interests?

Bribery and corruption

Does the supplier comply with relevant legislation on bribery and corruption?[1]
For example in the UK:

- Is the supplier an associated person of the customer under the Bribery Act?
- What risks do the arrangement and the supplier present?
- Is the supplier directly subject to the Bribery Act?
- What anti-bribery and corruption procedures does the supplier have in place?

---

[1] In England and Wales, the Bribery Act 2010 will apply to the customer where the customer is incorporated in, or carrying on business in the UK. Where this is the case, the customer must put in place adequate procedures to ensure that neither it, nor any of its associated persons (as defined in the Bribery Act) bribe to get, or keep, business for the customer. The Bribery Act contains a number of criminal offences:

(a) The general bribery offences (ss.1 and 2) - The Act creates two general bribery offences that encompass both the giver and the recipient. The offences rely on the "improper performance" (determined by what a reasonable person in the UK would expect) of a "relevant function" (which is broadly any activity carried out in the course of business – in the public or private sector - where there is a reasonable expectation that the function holder will perform it impartially or in good faith, or is in a position of trust). Note also there is no exemption, or de minimis, for facilitation or grease payments, which are commonplace in many jurisdictions and industries. Any local custom or practice is to be disregarded unless it is permitted or required by the written law applicable to the country or territory concerned.

(i) Bribing another person: A person commits an offence by offering, promising or giving a financial or other advantage to another person, directly or through an intermediary:

- intending that advantage to induce a person to perform improperly a relevant function or to reward a person for so doing (whether or not it is the same person to whom the advantage is offered); or
- knowing or believing that accepting the advantage would itself be improper performance of a relevant function.

(ii) Being bribed: A person commits this offence by requesting, agreeing to receive or accepting a financial or other advantage, directly or through a third party, for his or her own or someone else's benefit: and

- that person intends that, as a consequence, there is improper performance of a function; or
- there is improper performance of a function (whether as a reward, in anticipation of or as a consequence of the request, agreement or acceptance). The request, agreement or acceptance itself may be the improper performance of a function.

(b) Bribing foreign public officials (s.6) - It is an offence to bribe a "foreign public official". Foreign public official is broadly defined to include legislative, administrative and judicial officials and employees, and the law is triggered when a person:

(i)   intends to influence the official in the official's relevant capacity;

(ii) intends to get or keep business or a business advantage; and

(iii) offers or promises, directly or indirectly, any financial or other advantage to the official (or another person at the official's request or with agreement), and the written law that applies to the official does not allow or require him to be influenced.

So local customs and traditions are no defence to this offence.

(c) Extra-territorial effect - As well as catching an act of bribery which takes place in the UK, the Bribery Act catches an act of bribery which takes place outside the UK if the person engaging in it has a close connection with the UK. Having a close connection includes being a British citizen, an individual usually resident in the UK or a body incorporated in any part of the UK.

(d) Senior officer liability (s.14) - There is a specific offence for senior officers. If any of the above bribery offences are committed by a corporate body with the consent or connivance of a senior officer (or person purporting to act in that capacity), that senior officer or person may also be liable for the underlying offence. However, where the corporate body is only liable because it has a close connection with the UK, a senior officer can only have liability if he also has a close connection with the UK.

(e) Failure of commercial organisations to prevent bribery ("failure to prevent") (s.7) - Any organisation (a partnership or incorporated body) formed or carrying on business in the UK commits an offence if it or anyone associated with it bribes another person or a foreign public official intending to get or keep business or a business advantage for the organisation.

Under the Act, an associated person is someone who performs services for or on behalf of an organisation and may include employees, agents or subsidiaries. Under the guidance referred to below, although an employee is assumed to be an associate, a subsidiary may not always be, depending on the relationship between it and its parent. A supplier in an outsourcing or services context will almost always be an associate.

However, it is a defence for an organisation to prove it had in place adequate procedures to prevent persons associated with it from engaging in this conduct. As required by the Bribery Act, the Ministry of Justice has produced guidance (Guidance) on what constitute adequate procedures for the purposes of this section.

The "failure to prevent bribery" offence catches a corporate body or partnership formed within the UK, regardless of where it carries on business, whether within the UK or elsewhere. In addition, a corporate body or partnership comes within the scope of the Act if it "carries on a business, or part of a business" in the UK even if it is not formed in the UK. The Bribery Act and its accompanying Explanatory Notes do not expand on what may be considered to be carrying on a business or part of a business in the UK. However the Guidance anticipates that question will be answered by applying a common sense approach. It is unlikely, for example, that merely being listed on the London Stock Exchange will bring a company within the territorial scope of this offence – but equally, it is not necessary to have a physical presence in the UK to come within it: again, this will be a case by case analysis. The Serious Fraud Office has indicated it will prosecute foreign companies that fall within its jurisdiction if it feels they are acting in a way to disadvantage British business, for example winning business by paying bribes that their UK-connected competitors cannot do.

It is important to note that, for this offence, there is no need for the associated person (who has committed the act of bribery) to have a close connection with the UK. So the associate might make a payment that is legal under appropriate local law but which would be a bribe if it took place in the UK or the associate was a UK national. This would be a bribe for the purposes of s.7 even if the associate itself is outside the jurisdictional scope of the Bribery Act.

(f) Penalties for breach - The maximum penalty for the offences is 10 years' imprisonment and/or an unlimited fine. For the "failure to prevent" offence, the fine alone applies.

(g) Practical implications - The UK already has statutory and common law offences relating to bribery. However, the new offence of failing to prevent bribery combined with the extraterritorial application of the legislation represent a significant extension of the law. It is also important to appreciate the Act is wider than the US Foreign Corrupt Practices Act in several significant respects, including:

(i)   it applies to the private sector as well as to foreign public officials;
(ii) it has no exemptions for facilitation payments; and
(iii) it has the failure to prevent bribery offence.

This is why it is necessary to consider whether one should deal with bribery in commercial documents and to note that because a document may refer to the FCPA this will not of itself address the risks posed by the Bribery Act.

Accordingly, any customer covered by the Bribery Act will need to assess:
- whether the supplier is an associated person of the customer under the Bribery Act;
- the risks the arrangement and the supplier present;
- whether the supplier is directly subject to the Bribery Act; and
- what anti-bribery and corruption procedures the supplier has in place.

Particularly where the supplier is not directly subject to the Bribery Act, the customer will usually require the supplier to represent it has not committed any bribery offences, that it will not bribe within the meaning of the Bribery Act, in the context of its agreement with the customer, and that it will comply with the customer's anti-bribery and corruption procedures. It will also wish to require a right of audit of relevant papers, and have the right to terminate the agreement immediately if it has reason to suspect the supplier has breached the relevant provisions of the agreement.

4.3   Recording the selection process

The customer may want to ensure that its evaluation criteria are objective by listing them in a table and weighting them. The customer will also need to ensure that, in comparing the prices of different suppliers, it is comparing like with like. It will be easier for the customer to do this if it has provided in the RFP a charges template for the suppliers to complete. Some suppliers may state that aspects of the services will be provided at an additional charge and the customer should take this into account.

In the public and utility sectors, the customer will be required to keep records of how it selected the supplier and provide feedback to the unsuccessful suppliers.[2] In the financial services sector, the customer may want to show that it has considered issues set out in the FSA Handbook, relevant to outsourcing.[3] Customers outside the public, utility or financial services sectors may also want to keep records of selection processes to demonstrate the probity of the process followed.[4]

4.4   Due diligence

Before the customer selects a suitable supplier, it will need to carry out sufficient due diligence to ensure that it has collected adequate evidence to show that the supplier can satisfy the customer's evaluation criteria. This due diligence exercise may involve the customer taking account of the sources of information listed in Table 9.

Table 9 Due diligence of supplier

The supplier's proposal including information about the supplier's track record.
A report by accountants on the reliability of the supplier's financial model.
The results of security audits.
Presentations given by the supplier's team who would be responsible for providing the services.
Site visits to the supplier's premises.
The supplier's annual accounts.
Industry reports relating to the supplier or the services.
Searches for newspaper articles relating to the supplier.

---

[2]   See Chapters 43 and 46 for an explanation of the Procurement Directives applying to the public and utility sectors.

[3]   See Chapters 38 to 42 for a description of the regulations affecting the financial services sector.

[4]   US public companies will also need to comply with the US Sarbanes-Oxley Act of 2002. This requires that the principal executive and principal financial officer of an SEC-registered firms sign a statement in its annual filings declaring that procedures and controls are in place and working effectively to ensure accuracy in asset disposals, transactions and internal reporting processes. In short, they must pledge that their company's accounts are "truly presented". If any accounting irregularities are found subsequently, executives face substantial fines and jail terms of up to 20 years. However, a violation of this section must be knowing and intentional to give rise to liability. This Act will apply to any asset disposals relating to outsourcing arrangements. Depending upon the nature of the outsourced services, a customer that is a US public company must evaluate compliance with the Act in determining the scope of outsourcing services and its audit requirements.

> Reports of litigation against the supplier.
>
> Case studies provided by the supplier.
>
> References provided by the supplier.
>
> Feedback obtained from other customers of the supplier as a result of reference site visits.

4.5 Reflecting the evaluation criteria in the contract

A customer will usually select its supplier on the basis of information provided by the supplier. As stated in section 4.4 above, the information may have been contained in the supplier's proposal, or in correspondence, or it may have been revealed during discussions with the supplier. The customer must ensure that it can rely upon this information and has a remedy if this information proves false. There are various ways in which it can ensure this.

4.5.1 Warranties

The customer can suggest that the supplier warrants the accuracy of every statement that it has made in writing or possibly even in conversation before the agreement is made. For the warranty to be useful, the customer will need the supplier to warrant that these statements are still accurate as at the date of signature of the agreement. There are two problems with this approach:

(a) it may be difficult for the customer to prove what the supplier has said; and

(b) the supplier is unlikely to agree to a provision that does not list the specific representations relied upon as it will need to check that they are still accurate when the agreement is signed.

4.5.2 Attaching documentation to the agreement

Rather than warranting the accuracy of statements made before the agreement is signed, the supplier will usually prefer to exclude reliance on such statements. However, if this is not acceptable to the customer, a compromise position may be for the customer to identify the statements that are important and ensure such statements are either set out, or cross-referred to, in the agreement. Save for these express exceptions, the supplier will exclude[5] all other representations made during the period of negotiation.[6]

---

[5]   Entire agreement clauses must be drafted with some care to be effective in this regard.

[6]   Representations and warranties are different at law. Representations are statements that may induce the person to whom they are made to act in reliance upon them in some manner. Representations that are

Such exclusion will only be enforceable if it is reasonable.[7] If this approach is adopted, the parties should consider having someone present at the negotiations who takes minutes of everything that is agreed. The minutes can then be circulated to the other side for approval. Once agreed, the minutes can be circulated to any legal or commercial advisers, who were not present at the meeting, to ensure that any important promises made by either party are incorporated into the agreement.[8]

---

untrue may give rise to a variety of legal consequences, depending upon the particular circumstances. Fraudulent misrepresentations may create a right to action in the tort of deceit. Negligence misrepresentation may create a right of action in tort for negligent misstatement. Any representations which induce the entry of a contract may give rise to rights to rescind the contract or to recover damages, the availability of these remedies being governed by common law in the case of fraudulent misrepresentation and by common law as modified by the Misrepresentation Act 1967 in the case of negligence or innocent misrepresentations. Rescission of a contract for misrepresentation is conceptually quite different from termination for breach of contract. Rescission amounts to setting the contract aside for all purposes, so as to restore, as far as practicable, the parties to their pre-contract position. The measure of damages recoverable for a misrepresentation may differ from that recoverable for breach of a warranty in identical terms to the misrepresentation. Damages for misrepresentation will be based on the "reliance" measure of loss, that is, the loss suffered by the customer relying upon the representation. A warranty has two meanings: (a) a term of the contract, the breach of which may give rise to a claim for damages but not to a right to treat the contract as repudiated. The use of the word "warranty" in this sense is reserved for the less important terms of the contract, or for those which are collateral to the main purpose of the contract, the breach of which by one party does not entitle the other to treat his obligations as discharged. The amount recoverable is the sum required to put the innocent party in the position which it would have been in had the warranty not been breached; or (b) in the context of commercial contracts, (such as services agreements), "warranty" usually refers to particular statements that are incorporated as contractual terms in the agreement, which are identified as being "warranted" by one party and made subject to a special regime. Damages for breach of warranties will usually be based upon the "contractual" measure of damages, as described in Chapter 34.

7 Under s.3 of the Misrepresentation Act 1967. The test of reasonableness is contained in s.11 of the Unfair Contract Terms Act 1977. Provisions excluding liability for fraudulent misrepresentations will not be regarded as reasonable.

8 Entire agreement clauses must be drafted with some care to be effective – see, for example, *Axa Sun Life Services Plc v Campbell Martin Ltd* [2011] EWCA Civ 133, *Quest 4 Finance Ltd v Maxfield* [2007] EWHC 2313 (QB), *Crystal Decisions (UK) Ltd v Vedatech Corp* [2007] EWHC 1062 (Ch), *Inntrepreneur Pub Co Ltd v East Crown Ltd* [2000] 2 Lloyd's Rep 611 and *Deepak Fertilisers & Petrochemicals Corp Ltd v Davy McKee (London) Ltd* [1999] 1 Lloyd's Rep 387.

Chapter 5

The Project Plan

5.1 Outline

This chapter explains how the submission of the RFP and the selection of the preferred supplier fit in with the general project plan for the procurement. The chapter describes the benefits of preparing a project plan for the procurement of the services and provides an example plan. It also highlights the importance of appointing a project manager to manage the project plan.

5.2 Advantages of a project plan

One of the concerns felt by customers is that the negotiation of the sourcing arrangement, particularly if it is a competitive process similar to that described in the previous chapters, will incur excessive amounts of time and (particularly where external advisers are involved) money. For this and other reasons, it may be useful to prepare a project plan and timetable setting out how the negotiations will proceed and issuing an agenda for each meeting on the project plan. Table 10 lists the advantages of working to a project plan.

Table 10 Advantages of a project plan

Realistic timetable

Listing all of the activities that will need to be completed before the agreement can be concluded may assist the parties to determine a realistic deadline for contract signature, together with a realistic assessment of the resources that they will need to dedicate to the project to ensure that the deadline is met.

Dependencies

Listing the activities may assist the customer to identify dependencies upon the other party or upon third parties and ensure that activities are carried out in the right order.

Good preparation

Establishing a time when certain issues are to be discussed may assist both parties to focus on the negotiations and to turn up to meetings well prepared and with the correct negotiating team for that particular meeting. Separating out different issues to be covered at different meetings may avoid a situation where service managers, financial advisers, human resources or legal advisers attend meetings only to find that many of the issues discussed are not relevant to them.

Discourages renegotiation

> Setting aside a particular meeting to discuss a specific issue, which is then resolved at the meeting, may discourage the other side from re-opening issues already discussed and agreed.
>
> **Heightens competitive tension**
>
> From the customer's perspective, structuring a project plan so that it is clear that the same issue will be discussed consecutively with different suppliers may serve to heighten competitive tension between the different suppliers.
>
> **Indication of commitment**
>
> From the supplier's perspective, preparation by the customer of a project plan may be seen as a positive step, explaining to the supplier the negotiation procedure that will be followed until contract signature. It may serve as an indication to the supplier of the commitment of the customer to the sourcing project. For this reason, once a project plan has been finalised, it is important that the customer keeps to it, or, where this is impractical, communicates changes to the plan and the reasons for the changes.

5.3   Example project plan

Table 11 shows an example project plan for a private sector customer. Section 3.2 mentioned that, for public sector outsourcing projects, the procedural framework that the authority must follow is covered by the Procurement Directives.

Table 11 Example procurement project plan

Date	Action
	Establish internal team and project manager
	Customer to carry out due diligence described in Chapter 2
… to …	Prepare RFP
	RFP sent out
	Date by which suppliers must submit any questions on the RFP
	Date by which proposals must be submitted by suppliers
	Clarification meetings with various suppliers (including presentations by the suppliers if required)
	Customer's due diligence on supplier
	Shortlisting of two suppliers
	First day of negotiation of service description with supplier 1
	First day of negotiation of service description with supplier 2
	First day of negotiation of charges with supplier 1
	First day of negotiation of charges with supplier 2
	First day of negotiation of legal terms with supplier 1
	First day of negotiation of legal terms with supplier 2
	First ARD meeting with supplier 1
	First ARD meeting with supplier 2
… to …	Suppliers' due diligence
	Discussion of the supplier's due diligence findings and agreement of changes to the service description or the charges.
	Second etc. day of negotiation of service description with supplier 1

	Second etc. day of negotiation of service description with supplier 2
	Second etc. day of negotiation of charges with supplier 1
	Second etc. day of negotiation of charges with supplier 2
	Second etc. day of negotiation of legal terms with supplier 1
	Second etc. day of negotiation of legal terms with supplier 2
	Second etc. ARD meeting with supplier 1
	Second etc. ARD meeting with supplier 2
	Best and final offers submitted by suppliers
	Selection of preferred supplier
	Consultation with employees, election of employee representatives and holding of consultation meetings
	Final negotiation of service description (including transition plan and service management)
	Final negotiation of charges
	Final negotiation of legal terms
	Final ARD meeting
	Signature of the contract and press release
	Presentation by the lawyers summarising key terms of the contract
	Commencement of transition
	Commencement of service delivery

5.4   Project manager

The customer will also need to appoint a project manager, either from the customer's staff or an external consultant, who will be responsible for ensuring that the deadlines in the project plan are met, that sufficient resources are dedicated to the project and that delays are managed. The project manager's role is fundamental to the success of the project and it is therefore important to ensure that the project manager has appropriate experience and authority.

5.5   Project team

As well as appointing a project manager, the customer will need to appoint other relevant members of the project team to form a cross-functional team who will be able to work together to ensure that the project is successful. This will usually include procurement, finance, operational and legal experts. The sourcing arrangement is more likely to succeed if the members of the project team work together to ensure that all members are aware of relevant financial, operational and legal issues, rather than individual members of the team working in silos.

The project plan should be prepared taking into account a realistic view of the commitment required from and availability of the relevant members of the project team.

5.6   Communication plan

The project team will need to inform the stakeholders within the customer's organisation of progress with the sourcing project. For this reason it is usually useful for the project plan to include a communication plan.

Chapter 6

Preparation by the Supplier

6.1   Outline

Chapters 2, 3, 4 and 5 describe the preparation that the customer will need to carry out for the sourcing project. This chapter covers the supplier's preparation. It explains how the supplier will prepare its business case. It also discusses the due diligence that the supplier will need to carry out and the issues surrounding the question of when the supplier should complete its due diligence.

6.2   Preparation of business case

The supplier will use the information in the RFP (as described in Chapter 3) to assist it in preparing its own business case (supporting a decision to bid for the work). The business case may include the issues in Table 12.

Table 12 Supplier's business case

Supplier's business strategy
How will the sourcing opportunity fit in with the supplier's business strategy regarding the size of the contract, the types of services it wants to provide, the location at which it wants to operate and the types of customers to whom it wants to provide services?
Will the arrangement provide the supplier with a reference site in a sector it is targeting?
Profitability
What will be the supplier's estimated revenue, expenditure and resulting profit over the term of the agreement?
Can the supplier maximise its margin by "sweating the assets" namely using the staff, assets and premises to provide services to other customers?
What are the prospects of receiving additional business from the customer?
Service requirements
What are the customer's service requirements and how confident is the supplier that it can satisfy them?
What service credits are payable if it fails to meet the service levels?
Security requirements
What are the customer's security requirements and how confident is the supplier that it can satisfy them?
Customer's financial standing
What is the customer's financial position?

Will the supplier require guarantees from the customer?
Risks and key legal terms and conditions
What risks is the supplier expected to manage?
How will it be able to mitigate them?
Can it charge a risk premium for accepting the risks?
Bid strategy
What is the supplier's bid strategy?
How likely is the supplier to win the business?
Is there an incumbent supplier?
Is the customer asking for a quotation from the supplier merely so that it can renegotiate the charges payable to the incumbent supplier in line with market rates?
What costs will the supplier need to incur before selection of a preferred supplier?

The supplier's business case will usually need to be approved by the supplier's management before the supplier submits its proposal. The business case will then be updated from time to time until the supplier's management grants final approval for signature of the agreement and the agreement is signed.

The supplier will usually update the profit and loss account for the project throughout the term of the agreement, in particular to ensure that it is making a profit on the individual sourcing deal.

6.3   Types of due diligence by the supplier

Just as the customer needs to carry out due diligence regarding its business objectives and its requirements (as described in Chapter 2) and the supplier's experience and financial standing (as described in Chapter 4), the supplier will need to carry out due diligence to substantiate its business objectives, the details of its solution and its charges. Table 13 provides examples of the type of due diligence which the supplier may need to carry out.

Table 13 Due diligence by the supplier

Customer's business requirements
What are the customer's business requirements?
Can the supplier suggest an alternative way to satisfy the customer's goals?
Current services
What services are currently being provided?
How are the services being provided?
What service levels are being achieved?
How confident is the supplier that the information given about the current services and service levels is accurate?
Does the information provided by the customer show service levels over a full period (e.g. a financial year)?

Is there a backlog where services have not been provided as a result of the impending sourcing arrangement?

Future service requirements

Is the service description clear?

How will the new services differ from the current services?

How similar to the supplier's standard offering are the services?

What improvements in the service levels are required?

What will the supplier need to do to achieve the improved service levels?

Is the supplier confident that it can provide the services to the service levels required?

What is the risk of it failing to provide the services to the required service levels?

What volumes of services (e.g. number of users using the service) does the customer require?

Are the volumes likely to rise or fall considerably, for example due to external events?

Current security requirements

What security measures are currently being taken?

Future security requirements

Are the security requirements clear?

How will the new security measures differ from the current security measures?

What improvements in the security measures are required?

What will the supplier need to do to satisfy the improved security measures?

Is the supplier confident that it can satisfy the security measures?

Assets or premises with regard to which the services are provided

Where relevant, what assets or premises are covered by the services?

Is there an accurate list of these?

How much further due diligence is required on, for example, the state of the assets or the premises?

Risks

What are the major perceived risks?

Will the supplier be able to manage those risks allocated to it?

How will it manage them?

Charges

What assumptions has the supplier made in calculating its charges?

Which of these assumptions have been tested and which are still subject to due diligence?

Are all of the assumptions listed in the proposal?

What opportunities are there for the supplier to provide additional services?

How is the risk of different tax consequences allocated between supplier and customer?

Employees

General

Does the supplier agree that the relevant staff will transfer under ARD?

Which staff does the customer or incumbent supplier maintain will transfer to the supplier under ARD?

Staff profile

How many employees are there?

How long have the staff been employed?

Are there any other employees who are assigned to the business but are on long-term absence or maternity leave and who would transfer under ARD?

What are the employees' ages?

Are any of the employees approaching retirement age?

Have they transferred recently?

Where did they transfer from and what pension entitlements did they have immediately before the transfer?

Organisational

Is there an organised grouping of employees who carry out the services?

How much of the time of the relevant employees is dedicated to providing the services to be outsourced?

At which sites are the employees based?

Will the supplier need to relocate them?

Staff benefits

Has the customer notified the supplier of the salaries and other benefits received by the employees?

Has the customer notified the supplier of any other terms and conditions of the transferring employees (including pension arrangements, special redundancy entitlements, notice period, overtime payments, loans, company car arrangements or parking spaces entitlement)?

Are there any collective agreements that have been incorporated into the employees' contracts?

Have any variations to the terms and conditions been agreed?

Will the supplier need to change the terms and conditions of the transferring staff and, if so, has it checked whether it is legally able to do so?

Do their terms and conditions allow for any potential relocation?

Is there a normal retirement age under the employees' terms and conditions, and if so what is it?

Could any of the employees potentially qualify for enhanced pension benefits during the contract term or at the end of the contract term?

Potential liabilities

Do the employees belong to a trade union? If so, has any industrial action been taken or threatened in the previous two years?

Are there any current claims, or is the customer aware of any possible future claims against it by staff?

What payments have been made over the last 12 months in overtime payments?

What accrued holiday entitlements are owing?

What details are available of performance monitoring arrangements?

What are the staff sickness levels over the previous 12 months?

Are any of the staff subject to disciplinary proceedings?

Have any of the staff raised a grievance in the previous two years?

Staffing and contractors

Is the number and quality of the staff and contractors sufficient to provide the services?

Are specific members of the customer's staff or contractor's staff key to the supplier's ability to provide the services?

Are the key staff transferring?

Are the key contractors willing to work for the supplier?

Is the customer (or incumbent supplier) intending to transfer staff out of the business so that they will not transfer to the supplier?

Is the supplier aware of any staff intending to resign?

What skills transfer will the supplier need and what training will need to be provided to staff or contractors who will provide the services?

Does the customer expect the supplier to change the staff that provide the services?

What are the safety implications of the proposed outsourcing or services arrangement e.g. relating to the interface between customer and supplier staff? How do any such implications need to be addressed?

Assets and premises used to provide the services

What assets and premises would transfer to the supplier?

Will the customer warrant the condition of the assets or premises?

If not, has the supplier been able to check the condition of the assets or premises?

Will the customer warrant that the transferring assets or premises are all of the assets or premises currently employed to provide the services?

If not, has the supplier been able to check the adequacy of the assets or premises?

Will the assets and premises be suitable for providing the services or does work need to be done to make them suitable?

What technology refresh will be required for the assets?

Are there any additional security or health and safety measures that need to be taken at the premises?

Can the assets or premises be used to provide services to other customers?

Are any of the assets required held by an incumbent supplier?

Is the incumbent supplier willing to make these available to the supplier and, if so, on what conditions (financial and otherwise)?

Legal and regulatory requirements

Does the supplier need to comply with any specific legislation or regulations in providing the services?

*For example, if the supplier is to provide call centre services, then the supplier may need to comply with the Data Protection Act 1998 (see Chapters 36 and 37), The Privacy and Electronic Communications (EC Directive) Regulations 2003, The Consumer Protection (Distance Selling) Regulations 2000, Telephone Preference Service, E-mail Preference Service, Fax Preference Service and Mailing Preference Service. If the supplier is required to dispose of electronic or electrical goods, the customer may also want to clarify that such disposal must comply with the Waste Electrical and Electronic Equipment Directive (WEEE Directive). The directive was implemented in the United Kingdom in the WEEE Regulations, which came into force on 1 July 2007. The WEEE Directive seeks to address the growing impact of electrical and electronic goods on the environment by making producers liable for financing the collection, treatment and recovery of waste equipment. The most common and practical means of compliance for suppliers is to join a distributor "take back scheme" which has been set up by the government to establish a network of designated collection facilities for consumers to dispose of their electrical and electronic waste. European Parliament and the Council are expected to adopt a draft Directive to revise and replace the WEEE Directive. This is expected to progress through the EU legislative process during 2012.

Does the customer or the supplier require the approval of any relevant regulator before it can enter into the sourcing arrangement?

Will the supplier be prevented by any laws from providing the services as it proposes?

Environmental issues

Will the supplier be exposed to any environmental liability risk by providing the services?

If so, what is the nature and scale of such environmental liability risk? Is it reasonable for the supplier to assume such risk?

Software licences and other supply agreements

What software licences and other intellectual property rights are needed to provide the services?

Is any open source software used?[1]

How can the supplier obtain the necessary rights?

---

[1] For an explanation of issues relating to open source software, see Heather J. Meeker, *The Open Source Alternative: Understanding Risks and Leveraging Opportunities*, (John Wiley & Sons Inc., 2008).

> Will the supplier need the customer to license it to use software owned by the customer?
>
> Will the supplier need the customer to ensure that it is licensed to use bespoke software created by the previous supplier?
>
> Will the supplier need the customer to ensure that it is licensed to use other third-party software?
>
> What licences, subcontracts and other supply agreements will the supplier need to take out?
>
> **Liabilities transferring to supplier**
>
> What third-party contracts does the customer want to transfer to the supplier?
>
> What are the terms of the relevant third-party contracts?
>
> Do the terms of the third-party agreements permit transfer or are there costs involved in obtaining third-party consents?
>
> Are the terms of the third-party contracts acceptable?
>
> Is the performance of the third-party suppliers acceptable and compatible with the supplier meeting the service levels?
>
> If not, how can the supplier terminate the third-party contracts?
>
> **Property leases/licences**
>
> From which site will the services be provided?
>
> Will the customer make accommodation available to the supplier free of charge?
>
> What will be the terms of any leases or licences between the parties?
>
> Will the supplier need to amend the software licences to use the software at the new location?
>
> **Service dependencies**
>
> Is the supplier dependent upon the customer carrying out certain actions so that it can provide the services?[2]
>
> **Supplier's other customers**
>
> Does the supplier provide services to competitors of the customer?
>
> Is the supplier prevented from providing services for the customer by its agreements with its other customers?
>
> Will providing services to the customer cause confidentiality, security or other problems with its relationships with its existing clients?
>
> **Financial standing**
>
> What is the financial standing of the customer?
>
> **Cultural**
>
> What is the customer's culture?
>
> Are the cultures of the two organisations compatible?

Until the supplier has completed its due diligence, it will need to protect itself in any correspondence with the customer by stating that any information it provides is subject to due diligence or subject to specific assumptions which will need to be investigated at a later stage.

The result of the due diligence may lead the supplier to propose variations in the customer's requirements or the charges or may lead to suggestions as to actions that should be taken to minimise risks revealed by the due diligence. In extreme cases, it may lead the supplier to the decision that the

---

[2]   See Chapter 12 for a discussion of customer responsibilities.

project is unviable or not suitable for the supplier, and hence prompt a withdrawal from the process.

6.4   Warranties

The amount of due diligence required by the supplier will depend upon the thoroughness of the customer's due diligence. This is evident from the similarity between Table 2 and Table 14.

It will also depend upon whether the customer is willing to warrant information that it provides to the supplier. Table 14 lists the type of warranties commonly requested by suppliers.

Table 14 Customer warranties

Sufficiency of assets and contracts

That the assets, properties and contracts are all that is required to provide the services in the same manner and at the same level as for the 12 months prior to the signature of the services agreement.

Condition of assets and contracts

That the assets and properties are in a suitable condition to provide the services.

Title of assets to be sold

That the customer is the legal and beneficial owner of the assets and properties and sells them with full title guarantee free from encumbrances other than those agreed and those existing in the ordinary course of trading.

Information about charges due

That any information provided by the customer about the charges due under the leases, licences and supply agreements is correct.

Information about the customer's premises

That, where the services are to be provided on site, at a customer site, the premises are suitable for the provision of the services, do not have any latent defects, and all appropriate consents have been obtained.

Information about employees

See Chapter 31 for a discussion of people issues relating to ARD.

Laws and regulations

That there are no laws or regulations which the supplier will need to comply with in providing the services.[3]

General warranties

That the customer has disclosed all material information that could reasonably have been expected to affect the supplier's willingness to enter into the services agreement.

If the customer agrees to provide the warranties requested by the supplier, then the customer is taking the risk that its due diligence has not been thorough and that the information that it is warranting is not accurate. The customer will often therefore be unwilling to provide general warranties, such as the last warranty in Table 14. The customer may want to give some

---

[3]   The supplier may be particularly anxious to obtain this warranty if it is an offshore supplier unfamiliar with the legal system in the customer's jurisdiction.

warranties "to the best of its knowledge or belief" or subject to the contents of a disclosure letter.

The customer may also be reluctant to provide warranties where the supplier has an alternative course of action open to it. For example, it may refuse to grant warranties about the sufficiency or condition of customer assets, preferring the supplier to check the assets, unless there are specific circumstances that mean that it is unreasonable to expect the supplier to rely upon its own due diligence. This may mean that the customer will not provide any warranties other than those relating to information about employees transferring to the supplier, title of assets transferring to the supplier or specific contractual liabilities transferring to the supplier.

If the supplier agrees to rely upon its own due diligence, then it is taking the risk that its due diligence has not been thorough and that it has made mistakes. It may be reluctant to accept this risk where it cannot verify information provided by the customer, for example (as explained in the previous paragraph) relating to charges due under supply agreements transferring to it, or information about employees transferring from the customer or an incumbent supplier to the supplier.

6.5   Timing of due diligence

In circumstances where the customer is reluctant to provide warranties and where the supplier has to rely upon its own due diligence, the issue arises as to when the supplier should carry out its due diligence.

6.5.1   Advantages of carrying out due diligence early

The customer may prefer suppliers tendering for a sourcing project to carry out their due diligence as early as possible, so that the customer has a reliable view of the charges proposed by the suppliers and their solutions and hence will be able to clarify whether the sourcing arrangement will satisfy its business objectives.

6.5.2   Disadvantages of carrying out due diligence early

Alternatively, the customer may want to restrict the number of suppliers who carry out due diligence if the exercise involves the customer's staff in dedicating time and effort to assisting the supplier or if the due diligence will interfere with the customer's operation. It may also want to restrict the disclosure of sensitive information so that it is disclosed to only one supplier. Therefore, it may want to delay the supplier's due diligence until it has selected a preferred supplier.

The supplier may also want to delay due diligence. It may need to spend substantial amounts of money and time in carrying out due diligence of its solution and its charges. Therefore, it may also prefer not to invest in due diligence until it been selected as preferred supplier and is confident that the customer will sign an agreement with it or until it has received some reassurance of the customer's commitment. The reassurance may be in the form of heads of agreement, or a letter confirming the customer's intention to proceed, or a lock out agreement in which the customer agrees not to negotiate with other suppliers for a specified period.

Even once the supplier has been selected as preferred supplier, it may be impractical for it to carry out a full due diligence exercise. Thus, if the due diligence effort required is substantial (e.g. the services involve numerous assets at numerous sites), the supplier may suggest that it would be more economical for it to carry out due diligence at each site after signature of the contract, when it rolls out the services to each site. Carrying out a separate due diligence and roll-out exercise may involve duplicating costs that the supplier will endeavour to pass on to the customer. The supplier's due diligence may also interfere with the carrying out by the customer of its business or operations.

6.5.3   *Disadvantages of delaying due diligence*

The problem with postponing due diligence until after contract signature, from the customer's perspective, is clear, in that the customer will not be certain that the solution or charges will not be changed once the supplier has completed its due diligence. It may also be concerned that, when it comes to negotiate these changes, its bargaining power may have weakened following signature of the contract. At its worst, it could mean that the customer would be entering into the services agreement in order to achieve certain business objectives but without sufficient clarity that its goals will be achieved.

For example, the customer could enter into the agreement to achieve certain cost savings that it believes it will achieve. Because the customer is anxious to sign the agreement as soon as possible so as to obtain cost savings quickly, it does not want to delay signature of the agreement so that the supplier can carry out due diligence. The parties sign the contract on the basis of certain pricing assumptions that the supplier agrees to confirm during the first six months of the agreement. Once the contract has been signed, the due diligence exercises carried out by the supplier indicate that some of the pricing assumptions were incorrect and the customer is forced to agree increases in the charges which destroy the benefits which it anticipated receiving.

Accordingly, the customer should think very carefully about signing services agreements or other commitments to the supplier until it is certain that the arrangement will satisfy its business objectives. In most cases, unless there are exceptional circumstances, this will mean the customer insisting that the supplier carry out sufficient due diligence before contract signature so that charges and service commitments included in the agreement are guaranteed and not subject to renegotiation. The supplier may also prefer to have certainty before signature of the agreement as to the charges it will be paid.

6.5.4   *Possible solution—customer carries out due diligence*

It will usually be sensible for the customer to endeavour to carry out substantial amounts of due diligence itself (anticipating the due diligence which the suppliers will need to carry out) to collate the information and to make it available in an electronic or physical data room. For example, this process could be applied in relation to asset or property-related surveys, which can be extremely costly and disruptive to existing operations and can readily be carried out by an independent third party.

The customer can either bear the cost of this due diligence or the costs could be shared equally between the suppliers, possibly with the unsuccessful suppliers being reimbursed by the successful supplier once selected. The first option may be simpler, bearing in mind that the successful supplier is likely to build any resulting cost into its charges for the services agreement.

6.5.5   *Possible solution—customer pays for due diligence*

If the supplier cannot agree a fixed charge or finalise its solution because the customer has not carried out adequate due diligence and is unable to provide sufficient information to the supplier, then the customer may agree to pay the costs of the due diligence exercise if the sourcing project is ultimately abandoned. Otherwise, it may see the costs as part of the supplier's cost of doing business.

6.5.6   *Possible solution—agree variation mechanism*

In exceptional circumstances, where due diligence cannot be carried out before contract signature, the customer may want to consider agreeing exactly how the charges will be adjusted to reflect the findings of the due diligence exercise so that the supplier is not given the opportunity to reopen the negotiations. An example of this would be where the parties agree that, as part of the sourcing arrangement, the customer will transfer to the supplier certain third-party supplier agreements. The customer provides the supplier with information relating to the charges payable under these agreements but the customer cannot be certain that the information is up to date. The customer is accordingly unwilling to warrant the information relating to the contracts. The parties may agree to attach a schedule to the agreement showing what the customer believes to be the correct charges payable under the contracts. The supplier is given six months to check that the information is correct. The parties then agree a specific adjustment to the charges so that if the information is incorrect, whether too low or, for that matter, too high, the annual charges payable under the services contract will be adjusted to reflect the exact change in the annual charges payable under the third-party contracts.

Part 3

Services

Chapter 7

The Service Description

7.1   Outline

Chapters 2 to 6 describe the procurement process by which the customer will select a supplier. Chapters 7 to 10 cover the services to be provided by the supplier. This chapter includes a summary of the purpose of the service description and some practical hints for drafting service descriptions. It also discusses whether suppliers should have a duty to advise the customer of weaknesses in the service description.

In this Guide, the phrase "service description" is used to describe any documents that describe the services, including "service requirement", "service levels agreements", "customer requirements", "statement of work", "scope of services" or any other similar term.

7.2   Purpose of the service description

The business objectives and the business plan referred to in Chapter 2 must feed into a detailed service description. In this way, the customer must communicate to the supplier what its business and service objectives are with regard to the sourcing project.

It is no exaggeration to say that the service description is the key document in the services arrangement and that failure to prepare a clear service description is a major reason why disputes between the customer and supplier occur.[1]

The service description must satisfy various requirements.

7.2.1   *Support business objectives*

The service description must support the customer's business objectives.

---

[1]   In August 2011, the International Association for Contract and Commercial Managers (IACCM) published its 10th annual study results. It reported that the scope of the services to be provided under services agreements was one of the least negotiated areas and one of the most frequent causes of dispute.

For example, if the customer wants to reduce costs, it may consider ways in which it can reduce the service hours without affecting the operation of its business. The customer cannot transfer to the supplier the responsibility for deciding what the customer's business objectives should be. The customer must define its business goals and decide when these need to be modified or superseded during the term of the agreement, although the supplier may be able to advise on alternative ways of achieving the customer's business aims.

7.2.2   *Describe services*

The service description must communicate to the supplier, on a practical level, the services that the customer expects to receive.

7.2.3   *Describe services covered by fixed charge*

If the charges for providing the services are to be calculated on a fixed-price basis, then the service description will also serve the function of defining what the customer gets for its money and what the supplier is obliged to provide in return for receiving payment of the charges. (See Chapter 20 for an explanation of possible charging mechanisms.) Therefore, if the boundaries of the service description are unclear, this is likely to lead to a dispute between the parties, as neither customer nor supplier will be certain as to what is or is not covered by the fixed charge.

7.2.3.1   *Supplier concerns—vague or open-ended service descriptions*

From the supplier's perspective, if it accepts a service description that is vague or open ended, it can find that it has given what is, in effect, a blank cheque to the customer. The supplier will therefore need to ensure that the services are sufficiently clearly defined for it to be able to price them accurately.

Where services are reasonably commoditised, it will be helpful for the supplier to prepare detailed and clear service descriptions for its service offerings, which the customer can use to save both parties time and effort. It may be necessary to include flexibility in the service descriptions (e.g. gold, silver and platinum levels of service) so that the customer can select which level of service particularly meets its requirements.

Unfortunately, this solution will not be practical for services which vary considerably between customers or which are competitively tendered by the customer in circumstances where the customer will expect to go out to tender with a description of its requirements.

7.2.3.2 *Customer concerns—incomplete service descriptions*

From the customer's perspective, if it drafts a service description which omits elements of the services, it may enter into the sourcing transaction assuming that the charges will be cheaper than its previous service, only to find that the supplier can make additional charges for providing the omitted services and that the end result is that the services are actually more expensive than the in-house solution.

7.2.3.3 *Solution to customer's concern—wide drafting*

The risk to the customer may also be mitigated by drafting the service description widely, bearing in mind, however, that the supplier will calculate its price on the basis of this service description so that, if the service description implies a wider scope than the customer requires, the charges may be higher.

An alternative approach, where staff are transferring to the supplier, is to state that the service description is intended to include all of the services previously provided by the employees transferring to the supplier, although this may have an impact upon the price that the supplier charges to the customer if it means that the supplier includes all of the staff costs of the transferring employees in the charges, rather than assuming that staff can be partly deployed in providing services to other clients.

7.2.3.4 *Solution to customer's concern—due diligence*

Neither of the above solutions satisfy the customer's concerns about having omitted elements of the services, as they may lead to the customer paying more for the services than is necessary. The ideal solution is for the customer to carry out adequate due diligence exercises, as stressed in Chapter 2, so that it has an accurate view of the services being provided prior to the sourcing arrangement and of the changes that will need to be made in these services so that they will reflect the customer's current business objectives and service requirements.

7.2.3.5 *Solution to customer's concern—ITIL*

The IT Infrastructure Library (ITIL) can help the customer carry out due diligence and draft complete service descriptions in several different ways, as described below. The UK government developed ITIL. It was designed to codify best practice in the IT services industry. However, some of the concepts may be helpful for business process outsourcing (BPO) agreements, particularly those involving a substantial IT element. ITIL is used extensively within Europe, the US and Japan.

(a)   ITIL emphasis on documentation

ITIL emphasises the importance of documenting key aspects of how IT services are provided. For example, ITIL includes detailed descriptions of documentation that should be maintained as part of configuration management.

A customer who has adopted ITIL is less likely to find that it has little or no relevant documentation showing the services it is currently receiving.

However, the costs of providing an ITIL-compliant IT service (whether in-house or outsourced) may increase because of the level of documentation required and some companies feel that the ITIL approach is too bureaucratic for their specific business.

(b)   Use of ITIL as checklist

ITIL includes a detailed description of IT processes and services that will usually need to be carried out as part of IT service management. A customer entering into IT services agreements can use this information as a checklist to ensure that its service descriptions are comprehensive, even if the specific details of its services and the manner in which they provide the services are different from those suggested by ITIL. For example, ITIL clarifies that business continuity involves consideration of capacity management, availability management, business continuity plan management, risk management and risk analysis.

(c)   Use of ITIL to reflect best practice

As ITIL is intended to reflect best practice in IT service management, a customer entering into an IT services agreement can also use ITIL to consider ways in which its IT management can be improved. For example, ITIL suggests that it is good practice to distinguish between "incident management" and "problem management". Incident management is designed to restore normal service operations as quickly as possible by dealing with the immediate issues causing service failures. Problem management is designed to resolve the root cause of incidents, reduce the number and severity of incidents, minimise the adverse impact of incidents and prevent the recurrence of incidents.

7.2.3.6   *Solution to customer's concern—value for money*

Where the customer is entering into a services arrangement to cut its costs, its due diligence will need to be sufficient for it to have a detailed understanding of the services required to support its business so that it can distinguish between service or levels of service which are essential for it to carry out its business and services or levels of services which are desirable but not necessary. It may be useful for the customer to collaborate with the supplier to gain an accurate understanding of the charging structure for the services and ways in which the charges for the services can be reduced without affecting critical elements of the services. The customer will then be able to make an informed decision as to what services and levels of services it requires.

Unfortunately this may not be practical in all cases, for example if the due diligence would involve considerable amounts of time or if the customer wants to keep the sourcing arrangement confidential until it has decided that it is likely that outsourcing will satisfy its business objectives.

7.2.3.7   Standardisation of services

Another factor which the customer will need to consider, in particular if it is endeavouring to reduce its costs under a services agreement, is the extent to which it can standardise or harmonise the services it requires so that all parts of the customer organisation require the same or similar (e.g. gold, silver and platinum) services.

For IT services agreements, implementing ITIL[2] may assist the standardisation of relevant services and hence help reduce costs. Clearly this will not be so, however, if the standard of service previously required by the customer was considerably lower than that required by ITIL.

Another way that the customer may standardise its services is to accept a commoditised service from the supplier. There is a long term trend in IT services for services to become more commoditised. One example of this is the growth in cloud computing. See section 1.2 for a detailed description of cloud computing. In cloud computing arrangements, the customer needs to clarify and document its service requirements and service levels and evaluate which supplier's offering best meets its requirements, but the customer ultimately contracts on the basis of the supplier's standard service offering (although not necessarily on the supplier's standard terms and conditions).

7.2.4   Legal document

The service description is an important legal document. It must set out the division of responsibility between the customer and supplier. In some cases this may involve describing the boundary between the responsibility of the customer and that of the supplier (e.g. in a telecommunications service, that the supplier is responsible for the network up to a specific point on that network).

---

[2]   See section 7.2.3.5 for an explanation of the background to ITIL.

It also involves defining terms used in the service description. ITIL[3] may be useful in this context for IT and BPO outsourcing agreements as it defines key terms relevant for service management, for example "incident" and "problem". This provides a common technical language for the parties to the sourcing arrangement. This is particularly useful for offshore or near-shore outsourcing agreements, where the ability to rely upon a common understanding of relevant terms may assist communication between the parties.

Lastly, it is important, particularly to the customer, that the service description is drafted so that it is legally enforceable. It must state clearly who is responsible for what action (project plans which include lists of actions without stating who is responsible for carrying out the specific action are particularly unhelpful). The customer will want the service description to be drafted in the form of obligations (e.g. "The supplier will ..."). It is desirable that a lawyer checks the service description to ensure that it is legally enforceable.

7.2.5   Tax considerations

The description of the services will be an important factor in establishing whether the services (e.g. certain financial services) fall within a relevant exemption from VAT. This will be particularly critical where customers cannot recover all of the VAT charged on a standard-rated supply of services. The nature of the services supplied, rather than the way in which they are described in the contract, is the key determination of the VAT treatment. Nevertheless, describing exempt services in terms that suggest standard-rated treatment (e.g. marketing, administration) is unhelpful and should be avoided. Describing the services in a way that is consistent with the relevant VAT exemption, consistent with principles and themes derived from legislation, case law and HMRC guidance, is to be preferred.

7.3   Timing of agreement of the service description

7.3.1   Problems agreeing the service description

Sometimes customers find it difficult to define the services before the agreement is signed. If the customer cannot document the services to be provided, and as a result it is not certain that the parties have a shared understanding of the services to be provided, then it is difficult to avoid the conclusion that the agreement should be input based (with the supplier being obliged to provide resources only) or that signature of the agreement should be postponed until these issues can be clarified, as none of the objectives of the service description have been satisfied.

---

[3]   See section 7.2.3.5 for an explanation of the background to ITIL.

7.3.2   Problems documenting the services

The situation is more difficult if the parties have problems documenting the services to be provided in the time available before contract signature but feel that they are clear as to what services are to be provided. Theoretically, it would appear that one of the functions of the service description has been satisfied in this situation, namely that the supplier understands on a practical level the services that the customer expects to receive. In practice, as anyone who has experience of negotiating service descriptions will confirm, parties often assume that they have the same view of the services to be provided but subsequent negotiations show that each party has made different assumptions as to the exact service to be provided.

However, if the parties do have a mutual understanding of the services to be provided, perhaps because the services are not complex, they are commoditised or because they reflect services currently being provided by the customer, then the question arises as to whether the charges can similarly be calculated and agreed. If the charges can be agreed, then the parties will need to decide whether they want to take the risk of starting the provision of the services without the agreement of a binding legal document. In the short term, the parties may be willing to take this risk if they feel that both parties have an interest in getting the details of the services documented as soon as possible after signature. Naturally, lawyers will usually advise against taking this risk.

7.4   Contents of the service description

Because the service description must communicate to the supplier on a practical level the services that the customer expects to receive, it must address all of the issues mentioned in Table 15.

Table 15 Contents of the service description

Nature of services
What services are to be provided by the supplier?
What is the scope of the services? Are there any particular exclusions from the scope of the services?
Where services are provided by other suppliers of the customer, what are the boundaries of the services and the handover points? (This will be particularly important where the customer has adopted a multi-sourcing approach, as described in Chapter 17.)
Application of services
Where relevant, if the services involve the support or maintenance of assets or premises, is there a list of those assets or premises?
Are any assets or premises specifically excluded?
Recipients
Which parts of the customer's organisation are to receive the services?
Are the services also provided to clients of the customer or any external organisations?
Will this change over the term of the arrangement?

What will happen if there are changes in the customer's organisation, for example a purchase or a sale?

Customer dependencies

What assistance will need to be provided by the customer's organisation so that the services can be provided?

* See Chapter 12 for a discussion of customer dependencies.

What assistance will need to be provided by the customer's other suppliers so that the services can be provided? (This will be particularly important where the customer has adopted a multi-sourcing approach, as described in Chapter 17.)

Transition

Will the services be provided in a different manner during an initial transition period?

Does the supplier have additional tasks that it must carry out during the transition period to ensure that it can provide the services to the contracted service levels?

Can the supplier commit to carrying out these activities in accordance with a detailed project plan?

What are the acceptance criteria that must be satisfied before the end of the transition?

Changes in the services

Can the customer foresee any changes in the services?

Are the services to improve during the term of the arrangement and, if so, how is the required improvement described and how will it be measured?

Will the customer want to benchmark the level of services against the level of services provided at that time in the market?

Will the supplier be obliged to inform the customer of, or make available, new technology?

How will this affect the charges?

Seasonal variations

Is a different service to be provided at certain times, for example the customer's year-end?

For how long will the special service be provided, for example 30 days prior to year-end?

Term

Are all of the services to be provided during the full term of the agreement?

If a particular service is to be provided for a shorter term, will a replacement service be provided when that service ceases (e.g. mainframe services replaced by mid-range service)?

Is the replacement service specified in the service description or will it be agreed through change control, in which case does the business case take into account the fact that additional charges will be payable for the replacement services?

Service hours

During what service hours will the services be provided?

If the service hours are not 24 hours a day, seven days a week, can the customer extend the service hours?

If so, is a particular notice period required and is the extension at an additional charge?

Location

Are the services being provided in respect of assets at particular locations? Do the services need to be provided on site or can they be provided remotely? Can they be provided offshore?

Quality

What quality procedures will the supplier need to comply with?

What quality procedures must be followed to ensure version control of documents?

What inspection, testing and approvals will be needed before new systems are implemented into a production environment?

Industry codes of practice

Will the supplier be required to follow relevant industry codes of practice?[4]

Legislation

Will the supplier need to comply with relevant legislation?[5]

Policies and procedures

Will the supplier need to follow the customer's policies in providing the services (e.g. security or health and safety policies)?

Disaster recovery/contingency?

What force majeure events could affect the services?

How likely are they?

What would be their impact if they did occur?

What measures (including disaster recovery and business continuity services) will the supplier need to take to deal with force majeure events?

What measures should the customer take to deal with force majeure events?

Training

Will the supplier need to train the customer's users to ensure that they can take full advantage of the supplier's services?

7.5   Multinational arrangements

If the customer is a company comprising various different divisions or group companies or is a multinational group of companies, then there may be additional issues that will need to be considered in the service description.

The customer may need to decide the extent to which the service and the service levels will be mandated centrally so as to allow standardisation of the services received throughout the group, or whether the services may be customised to fit local requirements. For example, where the service comprises a telecommunications service, the customer may decide that

---

[4]   Here are a few examples of codes of practice which may be relevant in England and Wales:

(a)   Intellect's *IT Supplier Code of Best Practice* may be relevant for IT outsourcing arrangements. For more information about Intellect, see *https://www.intellectuk.org* [Accessed 4 September 2012];

(b)   the Customer Contact Association's (CCA) *Standard Framework for Best Practice* may be relevant for call centre outsourcing arrangements. For more information about the CCA, see *http://www.cca-global.com/* [Accessed 4 September 2012];

(c)   the Direct Marketing Association's (DMA) *Code of Practice* and relevant best practice guidelines may be relevant if the services involve direct marketing campaigns. For more information about the DMA, see *http://www.dma.org.uk* [Accessed 4 September 2012];

(d)   the International Chamber of Commerce's (ICC) *International Code of Advertising Practice* may be relevant if the services include advertisements for the promotion of goods or services. For more information about the ICC, see *http://www.iccwbo.org* [Accessed 4 September 2012];

(e)   the PhonepayPlus *Code of Practice* may apply if the services include the provision of premium-rate services to customers within the UK. For further information, see *www.phonepayplus.org.uk* [Accessed 4 September 2012];

(f)   the Finance and Leasing Association's *Codes of Conduct* may be relevant for outsourcing of leasing collection services. For further information see *http://www.fla.org.uk* [Accessed 4 September 2012].

[5]   For example, if the services involve the provision of a call centre in England or Wales, the supplier may need to comply with the Data Protection Act 1998, The Privacy and Electronic Communications (EC Directive) Regulations 2003 and The Consumer Protection (Distance Selling) Regulations 2000 (or, in the case of certain services supplied to FSA-regulated firms, the FSA rules and FSA and industry guidance implementing the Distance Marketing Directive). To give another example, if the services being outsourced are personnel services, then it is a fundamental part of the services that the supplier will comply with all relevant employment law.

members of the group must accept a certain minimum level of service, but that group companies will be free to decide that they need (and want to pay for) a higher level of service where appropriate for their particular business.

7.6 Stages in drafting a service description

Table 16 provides a checklist of stages that can be followed in drafting service descriptions.

Table 16 Checklist of stages in drafting service descriptions

Stage 1—list service elements.

Stage 2—consider service elements that need to be included in the service description.

Stage 3—consider appropriate names for the service elements.

Stage 4—decide which documents are going to make up the service description.

Stage 5—draft an introduction to the service description, listing the different service elements.

Stage 6—draft the detailed description of each service element, using precedents where available and appropriate.

Stage 7—add the customer's responsibilities.

Stage 8—add definitions not defined elsewhere in the agreement.

Stage 9—list (and draft, if necessary) documents to be attached to the service description (e.g. lists of assets or premises to be maintained) if not in the rest of the agreement.

Stage 10—consider the term during which the services will be provided.

Stage 11—add details of service hours.

Stage 12—add details of service management.

Stage 13—add service levels and service credits.

Stage 14—proofread.

As the service description defines what the customer receives in return for paying the charges, the service description and the charging schedule must be drafted so that they are consistent. The structure of the service description must be consistent with the structure of the charging schedule. (See Chapter 20 for a discussion of charging regimes.) The customer may want a description of each service element, with a breakdown of the charges for the service elements, so that it can understand the charging implications of changes in the services.

7.7 Supplier's duty to warn

A final issue relating to service descriptions is whether the supplier should be required to inform the customer if the customer has included in its service description requirements that the supplier knows will not lead to the satisfaction of the customer's business objectives or to the provision of an efficient service. This is a way in which the supplier may be asked to accept some form of liability for achievement of the customer's business objectives. This has been referred to, in Chapter 1, as acceptance by the supplier of the business outcome risk rather than the service output risk, and it may or may not be appropriate depending upon the circumstances.

7.7.1 No general obligation

The situation at law is that the courts in England and Wales will not imply a general duty for the supplier to warn the customer about problems with the services,[6] although the position is not entirely clear. [7]

7.7.2 Supplier to advise customer at commencement

Therefore, it will be in both parties' interests for them to clarify exactly what the supplier's responsibility will be in this regard and to document it clearly in the agreement. For example, if the customer has specifically asked the supplier to advise on how its business objectives can best be achieved, then the parties should document this.

7.7.3 Supplier to advise customer on continuing basis

A more difficult situation arises where the customer expects the supplier to warn it on a continuing basis if the customer instructs the supplier to do something, or itself does something that may adversely affect the provision of the services or the achievement of the customer's business objectives.

Instructions as to how to provide the services are limited. It will also be helpful if there is a procedure (such as the change control procedure) that will be followed to ensure that the supplier considers the impact of the customer's instructions upon the services and the customer's business objectives. The procedure should ensure that the customer documents the precise nature of its instructions and that the supplier responds within a specified period of time, notifying the customer of any identifiable problems with the instructions.

The supplier will also need to ensure that agreeing to the obligation will not

---

[6] See Richard Stephens, "Is there a duty to warn" *C&L Computer and Law*, June/July 2003.
[7] In the case of *J Murphy & Sons Limited v Johnston Precast Ltd* [2008] EWHC 3024 (TCC) the judge discussed implying terms into a contract. In particular, the judge found that there is an implied term in supply contracts such that, if a supplier knows, or ought reasonably to know, that a certain material would, or might, create problems when used in conjunction with the supplier's product, they are obliged to warn the customer (in this case the contractual duty to warn continued from the time that the contract was made up to almost a year later). This is the case even if they find out about the proposed use after the contract has been made. The judge noted that the Supply of Goods and Services Act 1982 did not apply to this case, only the Sale of Goods Act 1979 applied. Note that this case did not involve an outsourcing contract and only applied to the Sale of Goods Act and so it is unclear whether it would apply to outsourcing or services contracts. It is also unclear whether the supplier's implied obligation to act with reasonable skill and care implies such a duty.

constitute a blank cheque and that it can evaluate the amount of effort needed to comply with the obligation or make an additional charge for complying with the provision.

Chapter 8

Control Over How the Services are Provided

8.1 Outline

Chapter 7 provides some practical guidance on preparing service descriptions. This chapter deals with the issue of whether the customer should have some control over how the services are provided, including, for example, whether the customer should have the right to instruct the supplier how to provide the services.

8.2 Reasons for allowing the supplier control

8.2.1 Supplier is responsible for the services

In many cases, the supplier will be permitted to control precisely how the services are to be provided. The supplier will not usually accept responsibility for the services (i.e. the service output risk, as described in Chapter 1) unless it has sufficient control over the manner in which they are to be provided.

Allowing the customer to control how the services are provided can undermine the supplier's clear responsibility for the services. If there is no clear division of responsibility between the customer and supplier, this increases the likelihood that any failure in providing the services will lead to a dispute between the parties.

8.2.2 Supplier is an expert in providing the services

It may also make sense to allow the supplier to control how the services are provided, because the supplier, assuming that it is an expert in providing the services, may be best placed to decide how they should be provided and may be able to suggest improvements in the services. This is particularly relevant for IT and telecommunications projects if the supplier is a leading IT or telecommunications provider. The situation may be more complex in business process outsourcing projects, if the customer has more expertise in providing the services than the supplier and the supplier is dependent upon a knowledge transfer from the customer or the transfer to the supplier of the customer's skilled workforce.

8.2.3   Services will be more flexible

In addition, focusing on the service outputs to be delivered by the supplier will mean that the services will be more flexible and that the parties will not need to change the service description when the manner in which the services is provided changes.

8.2.4   Customer benefits from fixed price

If the customer attempts to control how the services are provided, by insisting that changes in how the services are provided are agreed through the change control procedure, this can undermine the benefit of the customer having agreed a fixed price with the supplier. By agreeing that changes in how the services are provided will be approved under the change control procedure, the customer may (intentionally or inadvertently) accept the risk that the supplier will attempt to increase the charges as a result of such changes rather than allowing the supplier to take control of and the risk for how the services are delivered.

8.3   Reasons for allowing the customer control

However, in some circumstances the customer may want control over how the services are provided. These circumstances are described in the following paragraphs. In addition, Chapters 38 to 42 describe specific rules and guidance on this issue from the FSA, which is relevant for firms regulated by the FSA.

Ultimately, with regard to all of the situations described in the following paragraphs relating to the customer concerns, the parties will usually need to find a compromise that provides sufficient reassurance for the customer without unduly restricting the supplier's ability to control how it provides the services. The supplier may need to be informed of the proposed restrictions before it can agree the service levels and the charges.

If the customer concludes that it needs substantial control over how the services are provided, then this begs the question as to whether the customer should enter into an input-based sourcing arrangement (where the supplier provides resources only) or should set up a joint venture with the supplier for the provision of the services (see Chapter 17 for a discussion of joint ventures). In some cases, it may also beg the question as to whether outsourcing is the appropriate course of action or whether the customer should be providing the services in-house.

8.4 Service requirement includes how the services are to be provided

In general, if it is not important to the customer how the services are provided, they should be defined in terms of the services to be provided. If it is important to the customer how the services are provided, then the customer must seek to control the inputs. For example:

(a)   if the customer wants the supplier to ensure that call centre staff are polite, then the customer should specify this in the service description; or

(b)   the customer may want to control or approve the technical architecture and may dictate standards or policies with which the supplier will need to comply. See section 25.15 regarding the implications of changes in the customer's policies.

In addition, if the customer has selected the supplier on the basis that the supplier has undertaken to implement a particular technical solution, then the supplier should not be able to change its proposed technical solution without the customer's consent.

8.5 Inability to operate business

The customer may want to control how the services are provided so that it has the power to act before its business suffers. The customer cannot pass on to the supplier the risk of it being unable to operate its business as a result of the supplier's failure to provide the services. Claiming damages from the supplier after the event may be an inadequate remedy.

8.5.1 Employees[1]

The customer may want the supplier to warrant that it will provide suitably qualified staff to provide the services. In some situations (e.g. where the sourcing is resource based or is a knowledge process outsourcing arrangement) the customer may want to specify the specific qualifications, skills

---

[1]   If the supplier is going to provide the services in whole or in part from Spain or France, then see Chapter 53 or 59 before including provisions allowing the customer control over the employees.

and experience that staff must have. It may also need staff to satisfy security vetting procedures.[2]

In certain circumstances, the customer may want a further guarantee that there will be sufficient staff engaged in providing the services or may want the supplier to commit that employees will be exclusively engaged in providing the services. This latter restriction is usually not helpful because:

(a) it will prevent the supplier from employing specialists to provide parts of the services;

(b) it may have cost implications if the employees could otherwise have been used to provide services to other customers; and

(c) it may also restrict the supplier's ability to deal with changes in the services (e.g. reductions in volumes) where the employees must continue to be engaged exclusively in providing the services even if there is not sufficient work to keep the employees busy.

The customer may want the ability to instruct the supplier to remove an employee or certain listed key employees from the provision of the services, even if the supplier is not in breach of the agreement. The supplier will usually want to avoid abuse of this provision by defining the circumstances in which it will apply and stating that the customer must act reasonably and explain why it is relying upon the provision. The supplier may also need notice of the exercise of this right in order to give it sufficient time to arrange a replacement. Lastly, the supplier must ensure that, whatever the customer's instructions, it continues to respect the employment contracts it has in place with its own employees.[3]

8.5.2 Sub-contractors

The customer may want the right:

(a) to approve the supplier's sub-contractors; or

(b) to instruct the supplier to stop using specific sub-contractors to provide the services.

The first right is less problematic from the supplier's perspective, particularly if it can obtain the customer's approval of the sub-contractor before the agreement is signed.

---

[2] See Chapter 37 for more information on security requirements.

[3] It is worth noting that vicarious liability is not necessarily limited to the entity with which the employee has a contractual relationship. For this reason, the customer may want to seek an indemnity from the supplier for any liability it may accrue for the negligent acts of the supplier's employees. In *Viasystems (Tyneside) Ltd v Thermal Transfer (Northern) Ltd* [2005] EWCA Civ 1151; [2006] 2 W.L.R. 428, the Court of Appeal held that, in considering vicarious liability, the correct question was the measure of control that was exercised over the act in question. In *Biffa Waste Services Ltd and Another v Maschinenfabrik Ernst Hese GmbH* [2008] EWCA Civ 1257; [2009] 3 W.L.R. 324, the Court of Appeal emphasised that control, and not mere supervision, was needed before vicarious liability would be found.

The second provision is more problematic from the supplier's perspective and may mean that the supplier will need to include in the agreement with its sub-contractor a right to terminate the subcontract if the customer exercises its right to instruct the supplier to stop subcontracting the services to the sub-contractor. The supplier will usually want to avoid abuse of the provision by defining the circumstances in which it will apply and stating that the customer must act reasonably. If the customer is unable to define the circumstances in which it will need to rely upon this right, the agreement will be less attractive to the sub-contractor, who may treat the contract as being potentially short term. This may mean that the sub-contractor's charges may be more expensive than they would otherwise have been.

The customer may also insist upon the supplier including certain clauses in its subcontracts (e.g. regarding confidentiality, security, data protection, the customer's audit rights, participation in dispute resolution procedures or the customer's right to step in to the relationship with the supplier).

Lastly, if the sub-contractor is key to the provision of the services by the supplier, the customer may want a direct agreement with the sub-contractor so that it can step in to the agreement with that sub-contractor.

8.5.3   Change of control

The customer may want the right to terminate the agreement if there is a change of control in the supplier. The supplier may be reluctant to grant the customer this right as, in any sale of the supplier company, any long-term outsourcing agreements are likely to form valuable assets which increase the value of the company and the ability of the customer to terminate the agreements may have a seriously adverse impact upon the value of the supplier company. This issue is discussed in greater detail in section 26.3 below.

8.5.4   Location and relocation

The customer may want the right to approve the location from which services are to be provided:

(a)   if the location may have an impact upon the quality of the services, for example if the services involve staff of the supplier travelling from the supplier's location to the customer's site to provide on-site services;

(b)   if the services are being provided by the supplier using customer systems which are made available to the customer or maintained under third-party contracts which restrict the location of the equipment or software;

(c)   if the location may have an impact upon the risk profile of the services;

(d)   if the location may have an impact upon the cost of the services, for example the customer may feel that it should benefit from any potential offshoring of elements of the services, particularly if the offshoring is increasing the risks involved in outsourcing the services;

(e) if any customer data is to be held at the specific location; or

(f) if the location could affect the reputation of the customer.

The customer may also want the supplier to agree that it will not relocate the services after the date of signature of the agreement without agreeing an implementation plan for the move with the customer, so as to ensure a smooth transition during the re-location.

Lastly, the customer may want the supplier to bear any costs associated with the relocation, for example any increased third-party maintenance costs resulting from systems being relocated. The supplier will need to ensure that it includes these costs in its business case for the move.

8.6   Rights other than termination

The customer may want to have other rights to affect the way that the services are provided, short of terminating the agreement.

8.6.1   Step in

The customer may want to have the right to step in and take over the provision of the services itself or via a third-party supplier.

8.6.1.1   Application of step-in rights

Step-in rights are often drafted to apply in circumstances where the supplier is unable to provide the services as a result of it being in breach of the agreement. If the failure of the supplier to provide the services could have serious implications for the customer's business, it is more logical for the step-in provision to apply whenever the supplier is unable to provide the services, whether this is as a result of a supplier breach or a force majeure, assuming that the force majeure event affecting the supplier would not prevent the customer or another supplier from providing the services.

8.6.1.2   Step-in costs

The financial implications of the two situations described above would, however, be different:

(a) If the customer needs to step in because of a supplier breach, then it would normally expect to deduct the step-in costs from any charges due to the supplier for the relevant period. If the charges are automatically reduced when the customer steps in, for example because the payment of the charges depends upon the supplier providing the services, then compensation to the customer should take into account any sums the customer is saving as a result of this reduction. The supplier will be concerned about incurring liability for costs over which it has no control and may either, as a result, refuse to agree to the customer having step-in rights at all or ensure that it is only liable for reasonable costs or costs up to an agreed cap. The supplier may also want reassurance that the customer will "step out" as soon as practicable.

(b) If the customer steps in because of a force majeure event, then the supplier will not expect to be liable for the step-in costs and may argue that it should be paid the reasonable costs of any step-in assistance it provides. See Chapter 34 for a description of the affect of a force majeure event upon the charges due to the supplier.

8.6.1.3   Responsibility for the services

The supplier should not be responsible for services being provided by the customer or a third-party supplier. The supplier may be concerned about ensuring that the customer or third party has not caused problems with the services when they stepped in, for which the supplier will be responsible once they step out and allow the supplier to resume provision of the services. This may result in the supplier refusing to agree to the step-in right at all, requesting an indemnity from the customer or ensuring that the customer or third party cannot step out until the supplier confirms that it is happy to take back responsibility for the services.

The supplier may also be concerned about the customer exercising a right to step in regarding part of the services, in case this adversely affects the supplier's provision of other services. Where the supplier is providing part of the services and the customer is providing another part of the services, this may undermine the clear division of responsibilities between the parties, unless the services are clearly severable.

8.6.1.4   Conditions for exercise of step-in right

As described above, step in raises various concerns for the supplier, in particular because it undermines the supplier's control over the services. Therefore the supplier may suggest that the customer does not have the right to step in until the supplier has been given an opportunity to demonstrate that it can correct the problems with the services. In appropriate cases, the supplier may suggest that it has the right to correct the problems itself or by using third parties. The supplier may use this right to ensure that, where a third party needs to correct problems with the services, the supplier enters into an agreement with the third party instead of the customer. In practice this can be a satisfactory solution for both parties, as the supplier retains control over, and liability for, the services and for the costs involved in remedying the problems with the services.

Any use of third parties would need to be subject to any relevant provisions in the agreement regarding customer approval of sub-contractors or material sub-contractors.

8.6.1.5   Step-in assistance

In practice, exercising a step-in right may be difficult, and its success may depend upon the step-in assistance that the supplier provides. The customer may need the supplier to co-operate with the party stepping in to provide the services and to make available to it any necessary assets and information.

The supplier may be reluctant to make certain information or assets available if the party stepping in is a third-party competitor of the supplier and the parties may need to decide what information and assets will be made available and in what circumstances. For example, the supplier may want the third party to comply with confidentiality and security obligations or may refuse to allow the customer or the third party direct access to its premises and may agree to grant them remote access to its systems only.

Lastly, the supplier may be restricted from making certain assets available to the customer or a third-party supplier, for example third-party software licences, without the consent of the third party licensor.

On termination of step-in, the supplier will usually want the customer to ensure that the customer and any third party employed by the customer co-operate with the supplier in ensuring a smooth transfer of the services back to the supplier.

8.6.1.6   Problems with step-in

It should be noted that step-in may not be the most useful remedy for the customer because of the practical difficulties it involves. In addition the need to effect a transition from the supplier to the customer and back to the supplier may in certain circumstances, where the customer is stepping in to provide most of the services, be more complicated than terminating the agreement.

8.6.2   Requirement for certain actions

Instead of stepping in to provide the services itself or via a third party, the customer may want the right to require the supplier to implement reasonable actions necessary to deal with a supplier default or other problems with the services. This remedy would enable the customer to interfere directly with how the supplier is providing the services and so is likely to be resisted by suppliers. Nevertheless, it may be appropriate in certain circumstances, for example where the customer is a public sector body and the action has been required by the authority's auditors, or the customer is subject to another regulator (e.g. the FSA or the Water Services Regulatory Authority). In this situation the parties will need to agree who will pay for the implementation of the change and whether the supplier will be responsible for the effect of the change.

8.7 Ensure smooth transition on termination

The customer may want control over how the services are provided in order to ensure a smooth transition on termination.

8.7.1 Technology refresh

The customer may want the supplier to commit to carrying out a technology refresh, so that equipment used in the services will not need to be replaced the day after expiry. Another way of achieving a similar result is for the customer to specify that the assets transferring to it on termination must be capable of providing the services for another, say, six months after termination. The customer should bear in mind that the supplier will increase its charges in order to comply with these requirements.

8.7.2 Exclusive assets

The customer may want to specify which assets used to provide the services are to be used exclusively for the provision of services to it, so that they can be transferred to it on termination. This issue is becoming less relevant as suppliers provide services based on the provision of services using virtualised servers. The issue is discussed in greater detail in Chapter 16.

8.7.3 Control over nature of assets used

The customer may want to ensure that the supplier does not make it difficult for the customer to move to another supplier on termination, for example by incorporating into the supplier's services proprietary products owned by the supplier. This issue is discussed in greater detail in Chapter 28.

8.8   Should service descriptions be objective or subjective?

Sometimes a customer includes subjective wording in service descriptions, for example, "The Supplier will provide a service to the reasonable satisfaction of the Customer". The wording is subjective because it does not describe the level of service that will satisfy the customer but leaves it up to the subjective judgment of the customer as to what level of service will be acceptable.

The customer tends to rely upon subjective wording when it is not confident that the service description fully describes its requirements and wants to change the service description once the requirements are clarified.

From a supplier's perspective, subjective wording is unhelpful for various reasons that are specified in Table 17.

Table 17 Reasons for avoiding subjectively worded obligations

Enables control over how the services are provided
They may give the customer the ability to instruct the supplier how to provide the services.
Not descriptive
They do not tell the supplier what it needs to do to satisfy the customer and so, to that extent, they defeat one of the fundamental purposes of the service description.
Unilateral variation
They may allow the customer to attempt to vary the service description unilaterally, instead of agreeing amendments in accordance with the agreed change control procedure.
Retrospective variation
They may allow the customer to vary the service description retrospectively and hence put the supplier in breach of the agreement.
Idiosyncratic behaviour
They may leave the supplier at risk should the party making the decisions behave in an idiosyncratic manner.

8.9   Should the service description include the supplier's proposal?

In some negotiations, the procurement procedure involves the customer preparing an RFP (as described in Chapter 3), which includes a description of the required services. The supplier then responds to the request with its proposal. The question arises as to whether the supplier's proposal should be attached to the contract and form part of the service description. This may sound like a minor issue, but in fact it can have serious ramifications for the services project.

8.9.1   Inconsistent documents

Problems with this approach arise where the proposal appears to differ from the RFP. For example:

(a)   the supplier may not be able to satisfy a particular element of the service description;
(b)   the supplier may propose an enhancement to the service description; or
(c)   the customer's service requirements may have changed and the supplier's proposal may be more up to date.

Including both the service description and the supplier's proposal in the contract can lead to a situation where the description of the services is contained in two inconsistent documents. This will be extremely difficult to manage on a daily basis and stating that, in the event of conflict, one overrides the other does not solve the problem.

8.9.2   Sales document

Other problems with including the supplier's proposal in the service description may arise where the supplier's proposal is a sales document, which includes vague promises, which the supplier is reluctant to include in the contract.

In both of the situations described above, the ideal solution is for the parties to amend the service description so that it contains a comprehensive, up-to-date and clear description of the services. The process of agreeing this comprehensive document may in itself be helpful in enabling the supplier to understand the customer's requirements and the customer to understand the supplier's proposal.

8.9.3   Documents serve different functions

The situation will be different where the service description and the supplier's proposal deal with different issues, for example the service description describing the services and the supplier's proposal containing its solution and explaining how it will provide the services. In this situation, it may be helpful, from the customer's perspective, to include both documents in the agreement. However, both parties should ensure that the service description and proposal are up to date as at the date of signature of the agreement, in particular if either or both of the documents were written several months previously.

The customer may want to clarify that the supplier's proposal does not undermine the supplier's obligation to provide the services and to achieve the customer's business objectives.

Also, the customer may want to clarify that the supplier will not be able to make an additional charge for changing how the services are provided, unless this results from a change in the customer's requirements as documented in the service description.

8.9.4 *Controlling changes to the supplier's proposal*

The customer may want to clarify that the supplier may not change its solution without the customer's consent. In this way, including the supplier's proposal in the service definition is another method by which the customer may seek to control how the services are provided (assuming that the proposal describes how they will be provided).

From the supplier's perspective, this may undermine its flexibility to change how the services are to be provided during the term of the agreement or impose an unwanted bureaucratic requirement that it will need to satisfy before changing how the services are provided. Accordingly the supplier may need to check the details contained in the proposal to ensure that they are likely to apply throughout the term of the agreement and are not unduly restrictive. It may also want to state that the customer will act reasonably in approving changes to the proposal. Lastly, the supplier may want to restrict the areas where approval will be required. For example, it could restrict the areas to those which:

(a) are crucial to the delivery of the services and hence were taken into account by the customer in selecting the supplier;
(b) will result in additional expenditure for the customer; or
(c) would result in a change in the nature or quality of the services or in the risk profile of the services arrangement.

Ideally, the supplier should take into account the fact that, when it prepares its proposal, the customer may regard the proposal as a contractual document. However, if the supplier is in a competitive tendering situation, it may see the proposal as first and foremost a sales document.

Chapter 9

Service Levels or Key Performance Indicators

9.1 Outline

Chapter 8 provides some practical guidance on preparing service descriptions. This chapter discusses the use of service levels and key performance indicators. It applies the distinction between business outcome, service output and input-based sourcing arrangements explained in Chapter 1, by analysing the manner in which service levels support a business outcome, service output or input based risk profile. It includes examples of different service level regimes and analyses the behaviour that they encourage. It discusses exclusions of liability and remedies for failure to meet service levels.

9.2 The need for service levels

The law obliges the supplier to provide the services with reasonable skill and care.[1] The customer may also want to document this obligation in the agreement or specify the standard to which the supplier must provide the services. For example, the supplier may be required to provide the services in accordance with good or best industry practice.[2]

Unless the services agreement is low value the customer will not usually want to rely solely upon this general obligation but will want to ensure that the service description includes specific service levels (sometimes known as key performance indicators) that specify the precise level at which the service must be provided. It may also want to include a service credit regime, with service credits payable by the supplier if those minimum service levels are not met.[3] In circumstances where the management of the services is regarded as particularly important, the customer may want to

---

[1]   Supply of Goods and Services Act 1982.
[2]   The general obligations to provide the services with reasonable skill and care and in accordance with good or best industry practice can, from the customer's perspective, act as a "catch all" provision to create obligations which are not expressly included in the service description.
[3]   See Chapter 21 for a discussion of service credits.

include service levels and service credits for failure to comply with key management obligations, for example the failure to provide specific reports.

9.3 Relationship with the customer's business objectives

The service levels that customers put in their service descriptions should support the customer's business objectives and should be consistent with those that they have in their strategic plans.

9.3.1 Background to the balanced scorecard

One of the most common ways of translating strategic plans into a measurement is through the balanced scorecard. Kaplan and Norton introduced the balanced scorecard in the early 1990s, originally as a means to encourage companies to include non-financial measurement in their accounting:

> "The balanced scorecard retains traditional financial measures. But financial measures tell the story of past events … These financial measures are inadequate … for guiding and evaluating the journey that information age companies must make to create future value through investment in customers, suppliers, employees, processes, technology, and innovation."

Since it was developed, the balanced scorecard has been extensively adopted by companies within Europe.

9.3.2 Balanced scorecard as a strategic management tool

In practice, the customer may use the balanced scorecard to define critical success factors, upon which the future success of the company's business strategy depends.

The principle behind the use of the balanced scorecard is that these critical success factors should not be limited to financial measures but should also include other measures, such as the relationship between the company and its customers, the efficiency of its internal business processes and its ability to learn and change.

It is interesting that the balanced scorecard was developed during the early 1990s recession as a way of enabling companies to understand the types of critical success factors which would be relevant in a turbulent economy, such as the ability to learn and change and the efficiency of their internal processes. As a result, the balanced scorecard seems particularly relevant in today's economy.

9.3.3   Use of balanced scorecard to define key performance indicators

Using the balanced scorecard, companies define key performance indicators (KPIs) that will measure how successful the company is at achieving the critical success factors referred to above, and hence how successful it is in achieving its business strategy and objectives.

9.3.4   Balanced scorecard in the service level regime

In practice, if a customer uses the balanced scorecard to measure its performance, it will be helpful if its strategic sourcing service level agreements are drafted in the light of and in support of the relevant business key performance indicators, such as those relating to the efficiency of internal processes. This will align the customer's strategy with its day-to-day requirements and operations. It will ensure that the supplier understands the customer's business objectives and hence ensure that the services agreement supports achievement of the customer's business objectives. Where relevant, key performance indicators can be used by customers entering into services agreements directly as the basis for contractual service levels, to ensure that the contractual service levels support the company's business objectives.

9.3.5   Contract scorecard

Leslie Willcocks and Sara Cullen[4] have suggested that, rather than using service levels that flow down from the balanced scorecard in sourcing agreements, customers should prepare a "contract scorecard". The thinking behind the contract scorecard is similar to that behind the balanced scorecard i.e. that performance measurement should involve more than financial measures. It should evaluate performance in a holistic and balanced manner, to encourage organisations to think more strategically. They argue that it should involve measurement of the following types of measures:

(a)   financial measures - these will usually be dealt with in the charging schedule to the agreement;

---

[4]   See Sara Cullen and Leslie P. Willcocks, "Measuring Success" in *The FD's Guide to Outsourcing* (Caspian Publishing, 2007) and Sara Cullen and Leslie P. Willcocks, *The Outsourcing Enterprise: From Cost Management to Collaborative Innovation*, (Palgrave Macmillan, 2010).

(b)   service quality - these will usually be set out in the service level agreement;

(c)   relationship - these may be included in a schedule to the contract setting out the relationship charter or code of conduct; and

(d)   strategy - these may be set out in a separate schedule to the agreement.

The contract scorecard is designed to articulate the goals of the contract in a measurable form, providing clear explanations as to what is driving the deal.

Willcocks and Cullen argue that the contract scorecard should include the specific measures set out in Table 18 (classified by the types of measures described above).

Table 18 Contract scorecard—quadrants and contents

Service quality	Relationship
Effectiveness - the degree to which the services produce an end result. For example utilisation, vacancy levels, call reduction and customer retention. **Precision** - the degree to which services are error free. For example accuracy rates, compliance, fit to specification and completeness. **Reliability** - the degree to which services are consistently dependable. For example availability, abandon rates, failure rate, rework and deadlines. **Speed** - KPIs include response rates, queue time, processing time or volumes, turnaround time and backlog clearing. **Satisfaction** - the extent to which customers, users or other stakeholders are pleased with the services.	**Communication** - the degree to which the parties communicate frequently and honestly. **Creative solutions** - the degree to which the parties continuously search for better ways of doing things. **Conflict resolution** - the degree to which there is a focus on solving problems, not apportioning blame. **Fairness** - the degree to which the parties act fairly towards each other. **Integration** - the degree to which the suppliers' value chain appears seamless to the end customer. **Positive interaction** - the degree to which the parties enjoy working together and have respect for one another. **Proactivity** - the degree to which the parties are proactive with each other. **Time investment** - the degree to which the parties provide management time and focus for each other.
Financial	Strategy
Historical/baseline - current cost compared to previous periods. KPIs include maintaining costs to a percentage under the historical baseline, ongoing annual reductions or indexation. **Budget/target** - current costs compared to planned expenditure. KPIs are percentage under/over budget/target. **Competitiveness** - current costs compared to the current benchmarked market rates. **Total cost of ownership** (TCO) - influence upon the cost of the entire supply chain.	**Objective achievement** - the degree to which the strategic reason for the sourcing has been achieved. **Innovation** - the degree to which better practices and assets have been introduced. **Business contribution** - the degree to which the parties have achieved more out of the deal than the fundamental exchange of money for services. KPIs include level of knowledge transfer provided, number of mutual business initiatives created and implemented and royalties earned. **Alignment to customer's business practices** - the extent to which the supplier conducts business in line with the customer's broader corporate goals. KPIs include safety, use of

	SMEs, employment created, positions filled by minorities and environmental benefits.

Willcocks and Cullen state that the intention is that the contract scorecard will be used for drafting the contract documentation, selecting the right supplier and monitoring the success of the sourcing arrangement.

9.4   Relationship with the risk profile

Ideally, the service levels and service credits should support the level of risk that the supplier is accepting.

9.4.1   Business outcome-based service levels

If the supplier accepts responsibility for the achievement of the customer's business outcome (business outcome risk), then the service levels will reflect achievement of the specific business objectives.

9.4.2   Service output-based service levels

Service output-based service levels are usually more powerful than input-based service levels because they relate to the end service being provided to the customer, for example the availability of the services to the customer or end user or the time taken to fix problems. However, care should be taken in drafting the service levels in order to ensure that they encourage the appropriate behaviour. For example, imposing upon the supplier an obligation to ensure that, measured on a monthly basis, all defects are corrected within eight hours, could encourage the supplier to refrain from carrying out preventative maintenance so that small defects arise which the supplier can correct quickly, thus improving the average statistics for the time to fix defects. In this situation, the customer could include additional supporting service levels which ensure that the supplier carries out the corrective maintenance on a regular basis, as agreed, or ensure that there are no more than a specified maximum number of defects per period, if this is acceptable to the supplier.

The supplier may be unwilling to commit to meeting service output-based service levels if it does not have sufficient control over whether the service levels are achieved, for example, if the achievement of the service levels is dependant upon the customer's behaviour or is dependant upon the co-operation of other suppliers of the customer (unless all of the suppliers set up a supplier joint venture to provide services to the customer). If the customer were to insist upon the supplier guaranteeing service levels in this situation, with service credits applying for any service level failure, then the supplier might decide that it was prudent to increase its charges by the amount of the relevant service credits. In this situation, the service credits would encourage the supplier to meet the service levels, as the service credits would operate as a bonus payable to the extent to which the service levels were met.

In an extreme situation, however, where the supplier is unable to influence whether the service levels are met or not, it is difficult to see how the service credits could serve any useful purpose.

In other circumstances, the supplier may be unable to achieve service levels requested by the customer without making substantial changes to the assets used to provide the services. For example, to guarantee certain levels of system availability, it may need to provide a parallel system on which the customer's application will run if the main server is unavailable. It is important in this situation for the customer to be aware of the implications of its decisions. It may be that it is critical to the customer's business that the service levels are achieved, so that the service levels are achieving exactly the desired business objective, namely ensuring that the supplier changes how the services are provided so as to improve performance.

In many cases, however, the customer will need to find a balance between the level of service that it wants the supplier to guarantee and the charges it is willing to pay.

9.4.3   *Input-based service levels*

If the supplier cannot commit to service output-based service levels, then input-based service levels on their own may be helpful. For example if the supplier cannot commit to rectifying defects in a complex application within a certain amount of time, it may be able to commit to commencing work on rectifying the problem within a specified time frame.

In addition, even if the supplier is able to guarantee the service output-based service levels, some of the input-based service levels may be useful where the customer wants reassurance that the inputs will be satisfied. For example the customer may want to ensure that the obligation to fix defects in the services does not encourage the supplier to refrain from carrying out preventative maintenance (as mentioned above).

9.5   Examples of service levels

There are various types of service levels that can be included in a service description. See Table 19 for examples of service levels that can be included in services contracts, classified by the risk taken by the supplier. See also Table 18 for a different analysis of possible service levels.

Table 19 Types of service levels

Service levels that are business outcome based

These will depend upon the specific business objective that the customer is endeavouring to satisfy. For example, if the customer's objective is to improve the speed of its billing process, then the service levels may relate to the time taken to prepare and send out bills.

Service levels that are service output based

Availability: For example availability (or uptime) of a system or service. The parties will need to define when the service will be regarded as being available. The supplier may insist that the services are not regarded as being unavailable during periods of scheduled downtime or scheduled maintenance.

Reliability: For example downtime duration or downtime frequency.

Response times: For example the response time of a system will not exceed a specified number of seconds. This will show how quickly the system is working. If it is slow, it may be unworkable. The supplier may be required to achieve the response time in all cases or in a specified percentage of cases.

Time to fix (resolution time): For example, time within which the supplier will fix incidents, whether measured for all incidents or by the priority of the incidents. The parties will need to decide when the clock starts ticking and when it stops ticking. The customer will not want the period to end when the supplier decides to close the call unless the incident has been resolved. If the customer's representative who reported the fault is unavailable, the supplier will not want the period to continue until the customer confirms that the incident has been resolved.

Capacity management: For example:

(a)   the number of incidents due to capacity issues; or

(b)   the ability of the supplier to meet the customer's demand.

Security: For example:

(a)   the number of security violations;

(b)   the number of situations in which security is not monitored including where events are not detected and logged; or

(c)   the number of situations in which physical access controls or logical security is not maintained.

Backups: For example, all backups are taken as agreed.

Configuration management: For example:

(a)   the number of observed differences between the records and the situation found during an audit;

(b)   the number of occasions on which a recorded configuration could not be located; or

(c)   the time needed to process a request for recording information.

Change management: For example:

(a)   the rate at which changes are implemented;

(b)   the number of incidents resulting from changes;

(c)   the number of back outs related to changes; or

(d)   the number of changes within resource and time estimation.

Service levels which are input based

Service desk or call centre phone answered: For example, the number of times the phone rings or the number of seconds it takes before the phone is answered by the supplier's service desk. The supplier may be required to achieve the service level in all cases or in a specified percentage of cases. The customer should consider whether the service level will discourage call centre staff from dealing with calls thoroughly if they can see that other calls are waiting.

Fault logging: For example, the number of calls not logged by the supplier's service desk. The supplier will usually be required to log all calls.

Time to respond: The time taken from when the supplier becomes aware of an incident or from when the incident is reported to the supplier's service desk until the supplier takes substantial action to correct the incident. This service level may be useful if the supplier cannot guarantee to fix incidents by a certain time.

Call to site: The time taken from when the supplier becomes aware of an incident or from when the incident is reported to the supplier's service desk until the supplier attends the customer's site to fix an incident. This service level may be useful if the supplier cannot guarantee to fix incidents by a certain time.

Utilisation not to exceed specified percentages or cache memory available/unused hard disk capacity to exceed specified percentages: For example, utilisation of the central processing unit (CPU) of hardware or of a telecommunications network over a specified period. This service level may be useful if the supplier cannot guarantee a response time for the system or network.

Service levels to incentivise reductions in repeat calls

Repeat problems: For example, the number of successful security or virus breaches that are exploiting a security or virus weakness previously identified.

Service levels to incentivise first fixes

First fixes: The percentage of calls resolved whilst the caller is still on the line. The customer should consider whether this service level will encourage the supplier to refrain from preventing minor faults occurring so that it can remedy them when the faults are reported to the service desk.

Service levels measuring "soft" factors

Customer satisfaction: Customer satisfaction will often be a key element of the services and the customer may want to measure the level of customer satisfaction as part of the service levels by distributing questionnaires to users. If the users are employees of the customer, however, the supplier may be reluctant to accept the payment of service credits if customer satisfaction falls, because it will be concerned that the customer may be able to influence its employees.

In this situation, the supplier may suggest the payment of a bonus for high levels of customer satisfaction. If the services are being provided to members of the public then the results of any customer satisfaction survey or "mystery shopper" survey may be regarded as being more reliable.

Service levels which can be business outcome, service output or input based

Completion of specified actions within a specified period: For example, acknowledgment of faxes or emails to the supplier's service desk, notification of security problems to the customer, preparation of accurate and complete management reports, printing of documents, updating the asset register, retrieving tapes and restoring data from backups, implementing changes, removal of access to a system, grant of access to a system, completion of monthly financial accounts etc.

Classification: For example, the number of incidents initially classified correctly by the supplier.

Routing: For example, the number of incidents routed correctly by the supplier.

9.6 Defining the service levels

For all service levels, the parties will need to agree how these will operate. Service levels need to be SMART, that is, specific, measurable, achievable, realistic and time bound. Defining the service levels will involve considering the factors specified in Table 20.

Table 20 Definition and operation of service levels

Definition of the service levels
How is the specific service level defined, for example, what is regarded as availability and where is it measured?
Period
Over what period will the service levels be measured: weekly, monthly, eight-week running periods, quarterly or annually? (If the service levels are to be calculated as an average over this period, then calculating the service levels over a longer period will mean it is possible that the services will be extremely bad for a short period and yet that the supplier will still meet the overall service levels.)
Service hours
During what hours will the service levels be measured: over a 24-hour period, seven-days-a-week basis or only during specified service hours?
Transition period
Will service levels apply from the commencement of the services or will there be a transition period during which the service levels will not apply or different service levels will apply?
Will the service levels vary during the term of the agreement, for example gradually improving?
Measurement
How will achievement of the service levels be measured?

9.7   Customer due diligence

Before the customer is able to define its desired service levels, it will usually need to carry out a detailed due diligence exercise, as described in Chapter 2. The due diligence exercise should cover the details of the service levels being achieved prior to the services arrangement and the changes that will need to be made in these service levels so that they will reflect the customer's business objectives and service requirements.

In carrying out its due diligence, the customer will often be dependent upon staff who will transfer to the incoming supplier under the ARD. The transferring staff may be unwilling to co-operate or they may feel a conflict of interest in advising the customer on suitable service-level regimes if they are ultimately going to be working for the supplier. See section 31.9 for a discussion of these and other "soft" effects of TUPE.

Lastly, the customer may want to benchmark the service levels it is achieving against those being achieved by its competitors (if the relevant information is available) to ensure that the customer's business will remain competitive.

9.8   Supplier due diligence and agreement of service levels

The supplier will need to satisfy itself that it can provide the services in accordance with the service levels before it commits to meeting them. If the supplier's acceptance of the service levels is dependent upon an understanding that the customer or previous supplier is meeting certain service levels, then the supplier has two options.

9.8.1 Warranty

The supplier may request that the customer provide a warranty that it has been meeting the service levels. However, the customer may be reluctant to provide warranties of this nature because it means that it is taking the risk that the information is incorrect.

9.8.2 Due diligence

Alternatively, the supplier can rely upon its own due diligence, which means that the supplier takes the risk that its due diligence has been inadequate and that it will not be able to provide the services to the specified service levels.

9.8.3 Advantages for supplier of agreeing service levels after signature

The supplier may prefer to enter into an agreement when the services are defined, but the service levels and service credits are only agreed following due diligence after signature of the agreement. In some situations, this may be a reasonable stance based upon the difficulty that the parties may have in ascertaining what service levels the customer or previous supplier was achieving. Deferring agreement of the service levels may suit the supplier as it means that it does not need to take the risk that its due diligence has been inadequate and that it will not be able to provide the services to specified service levels. It means that the supplier does not have to commit to achieving particular service levels until it has accurate statistics of the service levels it can achieve in practice.

9.8.4 Disadvantages for customer of agreeing service levels after signature

From the customer's perspective, however, this approach is rarely to be recommended. The disadvantage of delaying agreement of the service levels and service credits until after signature of the agreement is that the customer's bargaining power may have eroded after signature and it may be negotiating from a position of weakness. The customer will be dependent upon the supplier to agree to any service levels or service credits and the supplier does not benefit from agreeing any service levels or credits.

The situation is different from that mentioned in Chapter 7, where the supplier starts to provide the services before the detailed service description is agreed, because, in that case, both parties have an interest in ensuring that the service description is agreed. The situation is different here, in that the supplier may be happy to be a party to an agreement that does not impose any service levels or credits upon it and agreements to agree the service levels after signature of the agreement are not sufficiently precise to be enforceable at law. In practice, where service levels and service credits are not agreed before signature, in many cases they are never agreed, and the customer is left without any commitment from the supplier as to the level of service to be provided. It is possible for the customer to reserve certain rights, for example to terminate the agreement, if the service levels are not agreed within a certain period, but the cost and inconvenience of terminating the agreement will usually discourage the customer from exercising the right.

9.8.5   A compromise

Where the customer has not documented the service levels it has been achieving but would like the supplier to commit to achieving the same service levels (where, for example, the customer's objective is to enter into the agreement speedily on the basis that the supplier will provide similar services but at a cheaper price), the parties may be able to agree the principles surrounding the contractual service levels without agreeing the exact availability percentage. This would be achieved by documenting the types of service levels to be measured (e.g. availability) and stating that the contractual service levels will be those achieved by the customer during the period of months after contract signature or prior to contract signature, if this will be ascertainable after signature (e.g. 97 per cent). The parties can specify dispute resolution procedures that will be followed if the parties cannot agree what the service levels were. This approach can be avoided if the customer has been able to carry out the due diligence specified in Chapter 2.

9.9   Transitional service levels

Even where the parties have been able to define and agree suitable service levels in the agreement, the supplier may not be able to commit to meeting the service levels from the first day of the agreement. It may need to make changes to the manner in which the services are provided, for example if the service levels are more exacting than those previously being met. The supplier may suggest that the service levels do not apply or that it will report against the service levels but will not be required to meet them during this transition period. An alternative approach may be for the customer to suggest that the supplier maintains the services at the levels previously being achieved by the customer, until the improvements are made, to avoid a situation in which no service levels apply. The acceptability of this proposal to the supplier will depend upon the exact details of the transition.

The length of any transition period will depend upon the time that the supplier will need to implement improvements in the services.

Where the supplier is initially providing the services using legacy third-party supplier contracts entered into by the customer, the supplier may suggest that the transition period ties in with the period of notice required to terminate the legacy agreements with relevant third-party suppliers and replace them. If the customer is unwilling to agree to this, then the supplier may need to calculate its charges on the basis of a period of overlap between the legacy suppliers and the replacement third-party suppliers. In either case, the customer should understand the charging implications of the different options open to it.

9.10   Restrictions on liability

The supplier will want to ensure that it is not responsible for failure to provide the services or meet the service levels as a result of a force majeure event. (See Chapter 34 for a more detailed discussion of force majeure events.)

In addition, the supplier should consider any actions that it needs the customer to carry out in order that it can provide the services to the service levels. The supplier will not expect to be liable if it is unable to provide the services where this results from the customer's failure to comply with its responsibilities. (See Chapter 12 for a more detailed discussion of the customer's obligations.)

Lastly, the supplier may want to restrict or exclude liability for meeting the service levels if the volume of services exceeds specified limits, for example in a telecommunications agreement if the traffic exceeds the allocated bandwidth or the number of queries to the call centre exceeds a specified number. Where appropriate, taking into account the nature of the services, the customer may want the supplier to take responsibility for monitoring volumes or capacity and anticipating demand, so that sufficient volume or capacity can be provided before the service levels are affected. For other types of services, it may be appropriate for the customer to be obliged to notify the supplier if it takes steps that are likely to increase the volume of services. For example, if the supplier is providing a call centre that takes orders for the customer's products, the supplier may want the customer to notify it if it is planning a marketing campaign that is designed to increase demand for its products.

9.11   Remedies for failure to meet service levels

If the supplier fails to meet the service levels, the customer will want the supplier to commit to correcting the failure, at no additional charge, where the failure can be remedied and to correct the reason for the failure so that the problem does not recur.

The customer may also want the supplier to commit to paying service credits if it fails to meet the service levels. Service credits are discussed in greater detail in Chapter 21.

Some customers feel that service credits are an unhelpful remedy as any reduction in the supplier's revenue is likely to reduce the sums of money which the supplier has available to invest in correcting problems with the services. As a result, they seek creative solutions as to how to incentivise suppliers to meet the service levels. One solution is for customers to define contracted service levels and "performance targets" which measure the extent to which the supplier is supporting achievement of the customer's business objectives, as reviewed and updated by the customer on a regular basis. The supplier is contractually obliged to meet the service levels but not the performance targets. However, if the supplier meets the service levels and the performance targets, it is awarded an automatic extension to the term of the services contract, unless the customer's business objectives make this undesirable. This approach formalises and clarifies the extension process, taking into account that, in any event, the customer is likely to extend the agreement if the supplier is providing a good service and supporting the customer's business objectives. An interesting variation to this approach includes a process for automatically reducing the term of the services agreement if service levels are not met. This approach presents problems for suppliers if they have calculated their charges on the basis that they can spread fixed costs (e.g. transition costs) over the initial term of the services agreement.

Lastly, the customer will want the supplier to be committed to meeting the service levels so that any failure to meet them will constitute a breach of the agreement, and the customer may want the right to terminate the agreement if certain levels of service are not achieved over a specific period or if there are persistent minor breaches of the service levels. Termination rights are discussed in greater detail in Chapter 26.

Chapter 10

Governance

10.1 Outline

Chapters 7, 8 and 9 cover the services that the supplier must provide and the service levels that the supplier must meet in providing the services. This chapter describes the management of the sourcing arrangement by the customer and the supplier. Adequate governance of the sourcing arrangement is a key success factor and the approach to governance has seen some interesting changes over the last few years, with the increasing emphasis, in IT services arrangements, upon service integration.

10.2 Managing the transition

It is important that the transition process between the previous services and the services is managed correctly. This will be particularly important for software development or transformational outsourcing arrangements where considerable change may occur during the transition; these types of arrangements are described in Chapter 24.

10.2.1 Transition team and plan

Managing the transition will usually entail the customer and supplier appointing a transition team who will be responsible for ensuring a smooth transition.

It will also entail them agreeing and maintaining a detailed project plan describing:

(a) the obligations of the members of the transition team;
(b) the interrelationship between each party's obligations;
(c) the key deliverables which will be delivered as part of the transition process; and
(d) the dates by which the deliverables should be completed by the relevant party.

Agreeing a detailed transition plan will ensure that everyone knows what they need to do to ensure a successful transition and by when. It will help each side to allocate the appropriate resources to the tasks for which they are responsible.

One party will need to be responsible for project managing the transition. This will usually be the supplier. If, however, the customer has adopted a multi-sourcing approach (where different services are provided by different suppliers as described in Chapter 17), the customer will usually be responsible for managing the integration of services provided by the different suppliers.

The project manager will need to monitor achievement against the project plan so that he can see where the problem areas are and ensure that any necessary correctional action is taken promptly.

10.2.2 *Communicating the customer's business objectives*

Another important aspect of managing the transition involves communicating the customer's business objectives. This may involve the customer preparing and implementing a communications policy that details how it will communicate the customer's business objectives to staff, users and other stakeholders. Chapter 31 discusses in greater detail the issues relating to the transfer of staff from the customer to the supplier and the importance of consulting with them.

The customer will also need to manage the expectation of users. For example, if the customer's business objective is to reduce costs and hence the arrangement requires the supplier to achieve service levels that are lower than those previously being achieved in practice by the customer or its previous supplier, then unless this is explained carefully to users, they will usually conclude that the supplier is providing a poor service and that the sourcing initiative is a failure.

In appropriate circumstances, the communications policy should also cover how the customer is going to explain its sourcing strategy to the press. This is particularly important, for example, if one of the customer's business objectives is to improve its share price.

10.3   Managing the services

10.3.1   Appointment of managers

The parties will usually want to agree how the supplier will manage the services on an ongoing basis, after transition. This may involve the supplier appointing certain individuals to manage aspects of the services, for example a service manager, project manager, programme manager or account development manager. The customer may want some control over the identity of the individuals appointed to these roles. The customer may also want the supplier to commit to giving a specified period of notice before it replaces the key individuals. Lastly, the customer may want the supplier to commit to maintaining continuity of services when the key individuals are replaced.

The controls mentioned above relating to the key individuals are all interferences with how the supplier provides the services. Nevertheless, they are not usually contentious from the perspective of the supplier. In practice, the customer is unlikely to be satisfied with the services if it is not happy with the supplier's key personnel and so it is in both parties' interests that the supplier's key personnel are respected by and able to work with the customer.

The supplier may be concerned primarily to see that the right cannot be abused (e.g. by stating that the customer must act reasonably in approving or rejecting a candidate for a key role, and must notify the supplier of its reasons for accepting or rejecting a candidate in writing). Second, the supplier will need to ensure that, from a practical and legal perspective, it can comply with the provisions. Therefore, it will want to make it clear that it is not required to give a period of advance notice of the replacement of the key individual if, for example, he is injured.

10.3.2   Reports

The supplier will usually be obliged to produce reports summarising its performance over the previous month or quarter and comparing performance with previous periods, so that the customer can audit the provision of the services by the supplier. Examples of the sort of information that may be required by the customer are included in Table 21.

Table 21 Supplier's performance

Problems
Any problems affecting the services reported to the supplier's service desk including the nature of the problem, the name of the person reporting the problem, the date and time when the problem was reported, the cause of the problem, the action taken to correct the problem and the time and date when the problem was corrected.

> **Complaints**
>
> Complaints made about the services, including the nature of the complaint, the name of the person making the complaint, the date and time when it was received, the action taken to remedy the complaint and the date and time when the remedy was completed. This information may be maintained in a complaints register.
>
> **Service levels**
>
> The service levels achieved by the supplier and any service credits payable by the supplier.

The reports may be collated automatically by the supplier's management systems and the customer may be given online access to the information. The parties will usually meet at regular service review meetings to discuss the service reports.

The customer may want to apply service levels and service credits to the delivery of service management reports by the supplier.

10.4   Managing problems

The supplier may use the reports to analyse the cause of problems proactively and hence prevent their recurrence. For example, the reports may show a need for the supplier to improve the training it has given to users.

ITIL, which describes best practice in IT service management[1] makes a distinction between "incident management" and "problem management". The intention behind the terminology is to distinguish between rapid return of service and identifying and remedying the cause of the incident.

10.4.1   Incident management

Incidents include any interruption or reduction in the quality of a service.

Incident management aims to resolve the incident and restore the provision of services speedily. It includes recording, classifying and allocating incidents to appropriate specialists. Incident progress is then monitored; incidents are resolved and closed.

10.4.2   Problem management

Problems include undesirable situations indicating the unknown root cause of one or more existing or potential incidents.

If a problem is suspected, problem management aims to identify the

---

[1]   See section 7.2.3.5 for an explanation of ITIL..

underlying cause and prevent incidents from recurring. Problem management includes reactive and proactive activities. Reactive activities aim to identify the root cause of past incidents and present proposals for improvement or rectification. Proactive problem management aims to prevent incidents from recurring by identifying weaknesses in the infrastructure and making proposals to eliminate them.

The ITIL distinction between incidents and problems is a helpful one that can usefully be used in situations other than IT services arrangements to ensure that the supplier takes a proactive approach to resolving incidents affecting the services.

10.5   Managing future requirements

The reports produced by the supplier may also be used to carry out trend analysis. Thus the customer may want the supplier to take responsibility for analysing trends in usage by the customer (e.g. an increase in calls to a customer call centre), forecasting future requirements by the customer and proposing appropriate amendments to the services.

10.6   Encouraging innovation

Lastly, the reports produced by the supplier may be used to show areas where the services should be changed or improved so as to improve the scope or quality of the services or reduce the charges.

The supplier may be required to produce a regular service improvement plan (e.g. quarterly or annual). Where appropriate, the supplier may be asked to include in its charges the cost of carrying out a survey of up-to-date technology that may be used to improve the operation of the services and to include recommendations for incorporating the technology in its service improvement plan.

It may be useful for the supplier to be required to carry out a customer or user satisfaction survey before it prepares the service improvement plan, and to use any feedback obtained from the survey and any feedback obtained from the complaints procedure to suggest relevant improvements to the services. The customer may also want to suggest specific concerns that it has, to assist the supplier to focus its attention. Lastly, the customer may also want to benchmark the services against other services available in the marketplace to see if there are ways that they can be improved.

An alternative approach to that described above, could be to use crowdsourcing approaches. Crowdsourcing is defined as distributed problem solving. It has been used by various organisations to encourage innovations and improvement in the organisation by its own employees. It can have a material effect in encouraging a culture of innovation within an organisation. It would be interesting to see crowdsourcing innovation can be used to encourage collaboration between customers and suppliers to effect improvements in services and outsourcing arrangements.

From the supplier's perspective, it is important that any changes to the services recommended by the supplier or proposed by the customer should constitute changes to the services to be agreed by the parties under the change control procedure, so that that supplier has an opportunity to make additional charges for improvements in the services. Assuming that this principle is agreed by the customer, the supplier will often be willing to prepare the service improvement plan itself at no additional charge to the customer, either because it can include the charge for preparing the plan in the charges for the services or because it sees the preparation of the plan as an opportunity to interest the customer in investing further sums of money in the services.

Change management is dealt with in greater detail in Chapter 25.

10.7   Managing the customer's business objectives

The customer must also manage the sourcing arrangement at a strategic level to ensure that it continues to satisfy the customer's business objectives.

10.7.1   Achievement of current objectives

This involves the customer monitoring the arrangement to ensure that it is satisfying its current business objective. In circumstances where the customer is not achieving its business aims, it will want to analyse the reasons for this and what correctional steps will need to be taken to remedy the situation, for example whether training is required to ensure that users take full advantage of the improved services.

10.7.2   Changed business objectives

Managing the agreement at a strategic level also involves the customer recognising when its business objectives are changing and modifying the sourcing arrangement to ensure that it supports the changing business objectives.

10.7.3   *Relationship between technical developments and changed business objectives*

In practice, the processes described in sections 10.6 and 10.7.2 above inter-relate, with the supplier explaining how new technology and new working practices can bring business benefit to the customer and the customer deciding upon its desired business goals in the light of what is achievable, bearing in mind the new technology.

10.7.4   *Partnership board*

The customer may want to establish procedures for ensuring that strategic issues relating to the sourcing arrangement are considered, for example by setting up a joint partnership or partnering board with the supplier.[2]

10.8   Managing the supplier's business objectives

Section 10.7 explains how the customer will need to ensure that it achieves its business objectives. Clearly the supplier will also need to ensure that the services agreement continues to be profitable and to satisfy any other strategic objectives. This will involve preparing and updating accounts that allocate costs to individual contracts and demonstrate the profitability of the arrangement from time to time.

10.9   Managing the customer's obligations

Just as the supplier will need to manage its responsibilities under the arrangement, if the customer has substantial responsibilities, for example in an IT or business process outsourcing arrangement, then it will need to manage these. Sometimes the supplier will suggest that, just as the customer has a right to approve the supplier's key individuals, it should have a right to approve the customer's key representative, on the basis that, if the sourcing arrangement is to be a success, both parties will need to be able to work together.

---

[2]   It is common to refer to the board as a "partnership" board to embody the concept that the parties will be working together to ensure the success of the arrangement. The parties should be aware that "partnership" has a specific legal meaning in English law. A partnership is defined in s.1(1) of the Partnership Act 1890 as "the relation which subsists between persons carrying on a business in common with a view of profit". Therefore, the services agreement will not be a partnership in the strict legal sense.

10.10   Managing security

The customer will want to monitor the compliance by the supplier with its security obligations. It will also need to ensure that its security requirements are reviewed and updated as changes in security risks and solutions occur. Security issues are dealt with in greater detail in Chapter 37.

10.11   Managing risk

Chapter 2 explains the importance of the parties preparing a risk register. The parties will need to review the risk register on a regular basis to ensure that the party best able to deal with them mitigates any risks that may affect the services arrangement.

10.12   Managing value for money

The customer will also need to manage the financial aspects of the transaction to ensure that it continues to provide value for money. This issue is addressed in Chapter 23.

10.13   The service integrator role

10.13.1   *Importance of the service integrator role*

Sections 10.2 to 10.13 have described the importance of managing different aspects of a specific services arrangement. However, particularly in an IT context, it is likely that the customer will have to manage the various aspects described in these paragraphs and the implementation of changes (as described in Chapter 23) across an IT landscape that includes a variety of different IT suppliers and services. This is particularly so with the increasing trend towards multi-sourcing or best of breed supplier models (see Chapter 17 for an explanation of the different approaches), as IT services become more commoditised and the use of cloud computing solutions increases.

Over the last couple of years, there has been an increasing realisation of the importance of this vital service integrator role.

10.13.2   Scope of the service integrator role

Service integrators perform various functions involving the co-ordination of people, processes, tools and technology across the multiple third party suppliers including:

(a)   ensuring that the services provided as a whole better align with the needs of the customer's overall business and end users;
(b)   managing changes to the services provided by the various suppliers to reflect the customer's changing business requirements;
(c)   managing services and collaboration agreements and operational service level agreements between the different suppliers;
(d)   defining and managing a consistent set of processes and procedures (including e.g. incident and problem management and the maintenance of a configuration management database) for the end to end service across all suppliers;
(e)   monitoring and reporting on the end to end service;
(f)   providing a single point of contact for the end user for the service;
(g)   managing the end to end system availability in accordance with the contracted service levels;
(h)   managing the correction of incidents and problems affecting the end to end services, on behalf of the customer;
(i)   managing risk and security across the various suppliers; and
(j)   managing value for money across the various supplier contracts.

10.13.3   Service integrator models

There are various service integrator models:

(a)   **In-house** – the customer can adopt a multi-sourcing approach to its IT suppliers, entering into agreements with suppliers on a best of breed basis and can retain the service integrator role in-house.
(b)   **Prime contractor** – the customer can enter into an agreement with a prime contractor, who then enters into agreements with the various sub-contractors. The prime contractor accepts responsibility for the acts of its sub-contractors.
(c)   **Outsourced service integration** – the customer can adopt a multi-sourcing approach to its IT suppliers, entering into agreements with suppliers on a best of breed basis and can outsource the service integrator role.
(d)   **Lead tower provider** – the customer can adopt a multi-sourcing approach to its IT suppliers, entering into agreements with suppliers on a best of breed basis and then engage the lead tower provider to also act as the service integrator for the other suppliers.

The last two models involve the service integrator managing the other suppliers under tri-partite collaboration agreements and operational level agreements. This may be more difficult to establish if the customer has already entered into the agreements with the other suppliers. The "outsourced service integration model" may also involve the customer outsourcing most of the service management responsibilities. Under the "lead service provider model", the customer must remember that it cannot outsource management of the lead tower provider to the lead tower provider and so will have to retain responsibility for managing that supplier.

Chapter 17 describes the advantages and disadvantages of the various supplier models.

10.14   Audit rights

The customer will want the supplier to carry out audits to ensure that its staff are complying with the agreement and (where relevant, taking into account the nature of the services) are not committing any fraudulent or inappropriate actions.

The customer will also want to reserve the right to audit the supplier's performance and charges.[3]

10.14.1   *Who needs the right to audit?*

The customer and its auditors will need audit rights.

If the customer is in a regulated sector (e.g. the public sector, utilities or the financial services sector) then the customer's regulator may also need audit rights. Customers in regulated sectors must ensure that they have all necessary audit rights under their services agreements—this may include sector-specific requirements.

10.14.2   *What audit rights will the customer need?*

The customer will usually need the right to audit:

(a)   compliance with the terms of the agreement;
(b)   the quality of the services provided by the supplier (e.g. by using a mystery caller to review how the supplier's staff deal with calls to its call centre);
(c)   the assets used to provide the services;

---

[3]   While the litigation process requires each party to disclose relevant documents to the other, audit rights may run wider than this.

(d) any accuracy of any charges payable by the customer;
(e) the reasonableness of any charges proposed by the supplier for additional services or changes to the services; and
(f) the security of the customer's data.

The customer, its third-party auditors and any relevant regulators may also need the right to investigate whether the customer is complying with relevant regulations.

10.14.3   What would the audit involve?

The customer will want the supplier to:

(a) maintain relevant records and grant access to them;
(b) grant the customer access to the assets, premises and staff used to provide the services; and
(c) co-operate with the audit and provide reasonable assistance in carrying it out.

10.14.4   Audit costs

The supplier, at no additional charge, may be able to provide access to:

(a) existing records; or
(b) records that it has a contractual obligation to maintain.

It may want to make a reasonable charge for any additional records that the customer requests it to provide.

It may be willing to provide reasonable access and co-operation if the audit arises out of problems with the supplier's service. Otherwise, it will usually want to make a reasonable charge for any additional costs of complying with the audit.

The customer will not want to pay for the audit if it relates to a failure by the supplier to comply with its obligations.

10.14.5   Confidentiality

The supplier may want to be reassured that any information disclosed during the audit will be confidential and that the audit will not (where this is a possibility because of the nature of the services) be carried out by a competitor of the supplier.

It may want to restrict access to its proprietary materials or to information relating to how its charges are broken down (so-called "open book information"), unless the agreement states that the supplier must provide information on an open book basis.

10.14.6   *Interruption to supplier's business*

The supplier may have security and operational issues that means that it will need to restrict access to its sites. Even where it is able to grant access, it will want the customer to make an appointment before it turns up at a site and requests access. If the services are such that the supplier or its employees may have an opportunity to defraud the customer (e.g. outsourcing of a payroll service, a billing service, a collections service or a local authority revenues and benefits service), then the customer will need special rights if it has a genuine suspicion of fraud. This will include rights of access and the right to demand records without notice. If the customer is regulated by the FSA, the FSA, the customer and its auditors will also need the right to gain access to the supplier's premises.[4]

10.14.7   *Enhanced audit rights*

In certain cases, the customer may want the right to require the supplier to implement reasonable actions necessary to deal with a supplier default. This remedy would enable the customer to interfere directly with how the supplier is providing the services and so is likely to be resisted by suppliers. Nevertheless, it may be appropriate in certain circumstances, for example where the customer is a public sector body and the National Audit Office or other external audit body has required the action or the customer is subject to another regulator (e.g. the FSA) who has required the action.

10.14.8   *Material breach*

From the customer's perspective, co-operation with reasonable audit requirements (particularly if the customer is in a regulated industry), may be seen as being central to the relationship between the parties, and the customer may want to specify that refusal by the supplier to co-operate with audits may constitute a remediable material breach of the agreement which would entitle the customer to terminate the agreement. (See Chapter 26 for a discussion of rights of termination.)

---

[4]   See FSA *Senior Management Arrangements, Systems and Controls Handbook (SYSC)*, Rule 8.1.8 and Chapters 38 to 42 of this book for a further explanation.

10.15   Good faith

In Civil Law countries the concept of good faith has long been used and defined. Recently English lawyers have started to incorporate the concept into commercial agreements, including services agreements. However in English law the term is poorly defined.[5] This Guide suggests that the best approach is for parties to an arrangement to carry out adequate due diligence so that they know exactly what they want from a services arrangement and then document precisely what is expected of each party. Therefore parties should consider carefully what they are trying to achieve before they incorporate concepts of good faith into their agreements and should explain in the agreement what the implications are of the obligation.

---

[5]   See for example *Compass Group UK and Ireland Ltd (t/a Medirest) v Mid Essex Hospital Services NHS Trust* [2012] EWHC 781 (QB). In this case the customer was held to have repeatedly and grossly miscalculated the service credits due under a long-term catering contract. The court held that the customer's behaviour was a clear breach of an express obligation to act in good faith, thus entitling the supplier to terminate the contract.

Chapter 11

Dealing with Disputes

11.1   Outline

This chapter deals with the management of disputes. This includes the day-to-day management of commercial issues that do not rise to the level of formal disputes. This chapter first explains some of the most common reasons for disputes. Second, it considers the various mechanisms for dealing with disputes if they do arise.

11.2   Reasons for disputes

During the life of a sourcing agreement, some level of disagreement between customer and supplier is almost inevitable. In the vast majority of cases, such disagreements will be resolved, in discussion, at a commercial level and this is usually the best way to resolve issues. Parties may not even regard such disagreements as disputes. The reasons that disagreements, and more serious disputes, can arise are myriad.

11.2.1   Lack of preparation

A major reason for disputes is lack of preparation by the parties to a services agreement. It is for this reason that Chapters 2 and 6 have stressed the importance of customer and supplier being clear as to their objectives in entering into the arrangements and carrying out adequate due diligence before signature of the contract.

11.2.2   Ambiguous or incomplete contract

Often the most serious disputes arise between parties where their contractual obligations are ambiguous. This can be a particular problem where the suppliers starts to provide the services before the parties have signed an agreement documenting the exact services to be provided and charges to be paid. It can also arise where the parties sign a specifically negotiated agreement but the parties agree change orders to the agreement and the change orders have the supplier's standard terms and conditions on the back. Lastly disputes are likely where parties use general terms such as "reasonable endeavours" or "good faith" without documenting the specific obligations of the parties in this particular project; in this situation each party may believe that they have agreed something different. Disputes may also arise where the agreement fails to comprehensively document all of the rights and obligations of the parties. It is for this reason that Chapters 7, 8, 9 and 12 have stressed the importance of clearly and comprehensively documenting the services, the customer obligations and the charges.

11.2.3   Poor performance

Disputes may arise as a result of poor governance or poor execution of the services for example as a result of a failure by a party to resource contracts with appropriately skilled people. It is for this reason that Chapter 10 stressed the importance of adequate governance.

11.2.4   Changes in circumstance

Sourcing agreements tend to be long-term contracts often dealing with complex issues. Circumstances may arise that were not anticipated by the parties. The business objectives of one of the parties may change. For this reason, it is helpful for the original agreement to anticipate changes wherever possible and set out how these will be dealt and to include a change control process that explains how other changes will be agreed between the parties, as described in Chapter 25.

11.2.5   Recent increase in disputes

In recent years, macro economic factors have also put pressures on parties and led to an increase in disputes. Customers may put unrealistic pressure on suppliers to reduce charges. With margins squeezed, a supplier may seek to limit the resources available to a particular project or restrict itself to a particularly strict reading of the contractual requirements. These approaches may lead to a breakdown in the relationship and to resulting disputes.

11.3   Importance of documentation

The vast majority of disputes in respect of commercial contracts (whether sourcing agreements or not) are resolved before they ever reach a formal dispute resolution mechanism. That said, when considering the management of disputes, it is important to understand how the formal processes the parties have elected to use will work in the unlikely event that the parties are not able to resolve their dispute through negotiation.

For example, if a dispute does fall for formal determination, the documentary record will be of crucial importance and will help the judge (or other decision maker) decide the case. In the event of a dispute reaching the English courts, a process known as "disclosure" requires all relevant documents (which would include rash internal emails or scribbled notes in a notebook) be handed to the other side. This fact should inform the preparation of all written documents. Parties should also ensure they maintain all relevant documents including change controls, correspondence, complaints and formal notices relating to the sourcing arrangement.

Any disputes with the other side should be recorded in writing (and, if the scale of the potential dispute renders it appropriate, lawyers should be involved). For example, if the service is suffering as a result of the customer failing to comply with its obligations this should be recorded by the supplier to provide a defence to any claim for knock-on failings by the supplier.

11.4   Dispute resolution procedures

The remainder of this chapter describes the main process that parties may choose to use to resolve disputes. As explained above, in most cases the best way of dealing with a dispute, particularly one affecting a strategic sourcing supplier will be to negotiate a commercial solution to the dispute. Resort to any of the more formal dispute resolution processes is likely to have a negative impact on the parties' ongoing ability to work together. Some mechanisms are more likely to be divisive than others. Mediation, for example, often proceeds on the hope that the parties may be able to salvage an ongoing commercial relationship. Arbitration and litigation, as the most formal dispute resolution processes, tend to be the most divisive.

If a dispute arises, there is nothing to prevent the parties agreeing an appropriate mechanism to resolve their dispute at that stage. In practice, however, parties who are in dispute about one thing often have trouble agreeing on anything. For that reason, it is important to ensure that the contract contains a dispute resolution clause providing the mechanism (or mechanisms) the parties are required to use to resolve disputes. The contract often also provides that the parties still retain the ability to obtain urgent relief from the court (for example, an injunction) notwithstanding other mechanisms they are required to use. Mediation, as an extension of negotiation, is routinely suggested by one or other of the parties in the event of a dispute, even though it may not be referred to in the agreement.

11.5   Re-negotiation and internal escalation procedure

Sourcing arrangements often last several years, with both supplier and customer investing considerable time, effort and money in the arrangement. Given the value and length of most sourcing agreements, both parties usually have an incentive to work together to resolve their differences. Often such negotiations form part of the day-to-day management of a contract. Because negotiation is typically premised on the survival of the ongoing relationship, it is often one of the most useful ways of resolving disputes.

Escalation is a process whereby a dispute is referred to individuals (or committees) within the parties with rising levels of seniority. The assumption is that these individuals will be less close to a particular problem, will be able to take a wider view, and will agree a mutually acceptable compromise.

Escalation in some form often occurs as a matter of practice during a dispute. For example, the managing directors of both parties may become involved. In addition, the agreement may specify a defined escalation process that has to be undertaken before a more formal dispute mechanism can be invoked. The involvement of senior executives in the negotiation process may bring an element of detachment that has not been present amongst those involved at an operational level. Where the problems relate to problems with service provision, a resolution may involve senior management agreeing to, and monitoring the implementation of, a correction plan that sets out how any service failures are to be corrected.

11.6   Alternative dispute resolution

The contract should specify the dispute resolution mechanisms to be used if negotiation fails. A number of these mechanisms are known as "alternative dispute resolution" (ADR) procedures. These are so called because they are alternatives to arbitration or litigation.

The most frequently used of these (mediation, early neutral evaluation, mini trial and expert determination) are described in sections 11.7 to 11.11 below. All have value in the right circumstances. However, an important distinction to bear in mind when considering the various forms of ADR is the distinction between those that are aimed at assisting the parties to reach agreement and those where a third party makes a binding and enforceable determination.

11.7   Mediation

Mediation is a consensual process whereby representatives of each party come together for an agreed period (usually one day) and, with the assistance of a trained third party (the mediator), attempt to reach settlement. The role of the mediator is to help the parties reach a mutually acceptable settlement. As such, the mediator does not make any determination on the merits of a dispute. Either party is free to withdraw from mediation at any time. Equally, if the mediation does not result in a binding agreement, there is nothing to stop the parties reconvening the mediation at a later stage.

If terms are agreed, a settlement agreement is drawn up and signed. If the parties cannot reach agreement, they are free to revert to other processes. All of the discussions or negotiations that take place during mediation remain confidential.

Mediation can often be a successful process and it is regarded as an effective way of resolving disputes arising in a long-term commercial relationship. If successful, mediation also has the advantage of avoiding the substantial time and costs that would otherwise be incurred in respect of a dispute. A mediator, in trying to establish some common ground upon which a settlement can be reached, will often try to explore with the parties areas outside the dispute itself to see if there are other commercial matters which may assist the parties in reaching a commercial compromise acceptable on both sides. For example, rather than payment of a large settlement sum, a mediated settlement may require payment of a smaller lump sum with the customer also committing itself to ordering additional services. This type of compromise may well be acceptable to both parties and may allow the parties to preserve the relationship more or less intact.

Mediation clauses in commercial agreements are now extremely common. For example, central government has made it clear that, where the other party agrees, they should be included in public sector contracts. Even if the contract does not contain a mediation clause there is no reason why one of the parties cannot suggest mediation if a dispute arises. Mediation is now widely accepted as a commercial and pragmatic dispute resolution mechanism. Further, if litigation has already been commenced, the court can impose costs sanctions on a party if it is deemed to have acted unreasonably in refusing to mediate.

11.8 Mini trial/executive tribunal

Although not often seen in practice, the mini trial can be a useful extension of the negotiation process. In most forms of this procedure, lawyers or other advisers for each party present a shortened version of their case to a panel made up of senior executives of the parties. A neutral third party is sometimes invited to chair the panel. The objective of the process is to provide a useful starting point from which the parties can attempt to negotiate a resolution.

11.9   Early neutral evaluation

Agreements rarely expressly provide for early neutral evaluation (ENE), but it is an option that can be considered if a dispute arises. ENE is a non-binding process by which the parties agree to refer a particular dispute or issue to a third party (often a lawyer) for an opinion on the merits. The opinion is not binding and the parties remain free to take the matter to litigation or another form of dispute resolution process. In practice, however, the opinion obtained can be very persuasive in causing the "losing" party to rethink its position.

11.10   Expert determination

An expert determination occurs when the parties agree to refer a dispute to a third party with a particular technical expertise. The third party then issues a decision that, with some limited exceptions, binds the parties. In many cases, the expert will have no formal legal background. The exercise is very often paper based without any oral presentation of the arguments. Each party will provide the expert with written submissions setting out its case supported by relevant documents. There may be an opportunity for each party to reply to the submissions made by his opponent and the expert will then make his decision.

The advantages of this process are that, because of the procedure adopted, the cost and, perhaps more importantly, the time involved are likely to be significantly less than with more formal dispute resolution mechanisms. If used properly, it also ensures that an appropriate expert deals with technical issues. Expert determination tends to be used if the dispute is about a valuation or is concerned solely with a technical matter. For example, did work performed comply with a specification? It is important to ensure that the appointed expert has the appropriate skills to decide the specific dispute. The expert may be, for example, an IT expert or an accountant. As such, this procedure is not usually appropriate for questions that can only be answered on the basis of mixed expertise.

11.11   Adjudication

Adjudication is a form of hybrid procedure. It provides for an independent third party (the adjudicator) to decide the dispute within a very short time frame. The adjudicator's decision is binding, but the losing party is free to refer the dispute to a more formal process (litigation or arbitration) if they do not accept the outcome. It can only do this after paying any damages awarded by the adjudicator. Adjudication is used extensively in the construction industry following the introduction of a right to adjudication under the Housing Grants, Construction and Regeneration Act 1996.

In construction disputes, the acknowledged advantage of adjudication is the ability to obtain a quick interim decision and thereby limit the potential for the dispute to hold up progress on the wider project. In this sense, adjudication is effective in quickly producing a "rough and ready" result that meets operational needs. In a significant number of cases, parties decide to live with the adjudicator's decision and never exercise their right to challenge it in another forum. Although still a relatively novel approach, some form of adjudication process is now sometimes included in services agreements. The parallels with a construction contract are obvious: the parties are often working together on a long-term project with a number of critical deadlines for completion of work product. The obtaining of a quick interim decision on a dispute can often prevent time and effort being diverted away from the project.

11.12   Arbitration

In the case of a full-blown dispute, arbitration is an alternative to litigation. Some sourcing arrangements, particularly those involving parties from different jurisdictions, will provide for disputes to be dealt with by way of arbitration rather than litigation.

In arbitration the parties appoint a panel (usually made up of independent senior lawyers) to determine the merits of their dispute. As such, arbitration permits the choice of a neutral jurisdiction to hear a dispute. Very importantly, there is an international regime for the enforcement of arbitral awards that, in many cases, offers significant advantages to the regimes available for the enforcement of court judgments. Another significant advantage is that arbitration is a private process so a dispute will not be aired in public in the same way as it would be if it were dealt with through the courts.

If the sourcing arrangement is a multinational one with a number of subsidiary companies holding separate contracts under the umbrella of a framework agreement, then any arbitration agreement will need to be drafted with particular care.

11.13   Litigation

Like arbitration, litigation should, as a general rule, be the process of last resort in a long-term commercial relationship. Litigation is expensive, can be a slow process and is likely to cause irreparable harm to the relationship between the parties. The weight each party gives to these factors will clearly depend upon what is at stake in the dispute and the extent to which the party needs or values the services provided by or to the other party.

On the other hand, in circumstances where the contract is at an end or the party is no longer concerned with preserving a relationship, there may be little choice but to address a dispute in this way. Where the parties are from different jurisdictions (and assuming that arbitration has not been chosen in preference to litigation) a well-drafted contract will make clear which courts are to deal with any disputes that arise. An express provision confirming the right to seek urgent interim assistance from any other appropriate jurisdiction should also be considered.

11.14   Settlement payments

Both supplier and customer need to consider the tax treatment (e.g. whether the payments are chargeable to VAT and whether and, if so, how they are taxable in the hands of the recipient or tax deductible for the payer) of payments made in settlement of a dispute, or as damages. Where the supplier and customer are subject to tax in different jurisdictions, there may be a mismatch in their respective tax treatments. For example, the recipient may be subject to tax on the damages, but the payer may not obtain a tax deduction. Careful planning can reduce this risk.

Chapter 12

Customer Dependencies

12.1 Outline

Chapters 7, 8 and 9 describe the supplier's responsibility for providing the services. This chapter describes customer dependencies. It discusses first whether the services agreement should document the customer's responsibilities and, if so, how these should be drafted. Second, it discusses the contractual effect of a customer's failure to comply with its obligations.

12.2 Inclusion of customer responsibilities

It is useful to consider whether, from the customer's perspective, the agreement should include a comprehensive list of customer obligations. The customer sometimes assumes that the agreement will be onerous if it imposes too many detailed obligations. Some customers are also concerned that the inclusion of detailed obligations will provide the supplier with an opportunity to evade liability by blaming the customer for failings. For both of these reasons, customers sometimes prefer not to document their obligations in the agreement.

The better view is that to ensure that the agreement clearly delineates responsibility, the agreement should document the responsibilities of both the supplier and the customer. Negotiating the responsibilities of the customer is often given less attention than negotiating the services to be provided by the supplier. Yet, if the services are to be successfully provided, both issues need to be considered carefully. If the agreement does not clearly specify the customer's obligations, then the English courts may imply terms that impose obligations on the customer (see, for example, *Anglo Group Plc v Winther Browne & Co Ltd*[1]). For both of these reasons, it is better to document customer responsibilities in the agreement.

---

[1] *Anglo Group Plc v Winther Browne & Co Ltd* [2000] I.T.C.L.R. 559.

12.3　Defining customer responsibilities

As noted above, the customer will be concerned about how onerous its obligations will be and may worry that the supplier will seek to exploit customer obligations to evade its own responsibilities under the agreement. These concerns can be dealt with by ensuring that customer obligations are clearly defined. This ensures that the customer knows what is expected of it and has the opportunity to ensure that it can comply before it signs. The customer will not want to accept vague obligations.

From the supplier's perspective it is essential that all customer dependencies be dealt with comprehensively in the agreement. This will avoid the supplier being in breach of the agreement as a consequence of acts or omissions of the customer. For example, the supplier may require the customer to commit to providing specific data or documentation in accordance with agreed service levels. The supplier should check all aspects of the services in this regard. In appropriate cases it may be helpful to set the service description out in a series of tables listing the responsibilities of the supplier and customer for each part of the service, side by side. This is particularly so where the end-to-end process requires continual handovers of responsibility from one party to the other.

As explained above customers are sometimes uncertain as to whether they have defined all aspects of the services, and may want to include catch-all phrases to describe the services (section 7.2.3.2 above). Likewise, suppliers may be concerned that they have not anticipated every customer dependency and seek to include general exclusions. For example, they may want a provision that makes it clear that the supplier will not be responsible for failure to provide the services as a result of an act or omission of the customer. The supplier may also seek to include widely drafted customer obligations, such as that the customer will co-operate with the supplier or provide all necessary assistance. Whether or not these approaches are reasonable depends upon the circumstances of the arrangement and, in particular, whether the supplier can reasonably be expected to predict all customer dependencies.

12.4　Obligation to notify the customer of breach

The customer may seek to impose an obligation on the supplier that it must notify the customer promptly if it becomes aware that a failure by the customer to comply with its obligations might have a detrimental effect on the supplier's ability to deliver the services. This notification procedure serves two purposes:

(a)　It ensures that, where possible, the customer's contract manager is informed if customer obligations have not been carried out and is given an opportunity to rectify this before there is significant impact on the services or indeed the customer's business. If the supplier is responsible for managing the overall provision of the services, then it may be reasonable for this to include the responsibility to manage customer dependencies.

(b)   It means that the supplier must promptly state that problems with the services are caused by the customer. This reduces the risk that the supplier will raise such an argument for the first time months after the problems with the services occurred, when it may be difficult for the customer to prove what happened at the relevant time.

The supplier will want to ensure that any notification obligation imposed upon it is reasonable. The customer, however, may want to state that the supplier cannot rely upon the relief until it has served the necessary notification. The parties may want to ensure that they have an agreed procedure for ensuring that the supplier complies with the notification requirement, for example by stating that the supplier must notify the customer of problems at the next service management meeting.

12.5   Service output or input-based arrangement

If the customer responsibilities are so extensive that it is difficult to detail them all, or it is difficult to define the boundaries of the supplier's responsibility, then it may be that the customer will find it difficult to hold the supplier responsible for the services.

12.6   The effect of non-compliance

If the customer fails to comply with its obligations, then the supplier will want to ensure that it is not liable for any resulting failure by it to provide the services. The supplier will also usually want the customer to compensate it for any additional costs it incurs (or, in appropriate cases, damages it has suffered) as a result of the customer breach.

The supplier may want the right to terminate the agreement if the customer fails to comply with its obligations. Whether this is appropriate depends upon the circumstances. This issue is discussed in Chapter 26.

Part 4

Structure

Chapter 13

Existing Equipment

13.1 Outline

Chapter 12 discusses whether customer dependencies should be included in the agreement and if so, how. This chapter deals with one type of customer dependency, namely the provision of assets by the customer to the supplier, usually so that the supplier can provide the services.

Where the customer has previously provided the services in-house, prior to the sourcing arrangement, various assets may have been used by the customer for the provision of its services. The supplier may need these for the provision of the services. Even if the supplier does not need them for the provision of the services, if the customer does not need them after it has entered into the services agreement, the agreement arrangement may provide for the supplier to acquire them and use them to provide services to its other customers, thus reducing the charge to the customer. The issues described in this chapter have become less important over time, as the outsourcing model matures and the number of first generation outsourcing arrangements has reduced.

Chapters 13, 14 and 15 discuss the various ways of dealing with the assets. This chapter covers equipment, hardware, and supply and maintenance contracts. Chapter 14 discusses intellectual property rights. Chapter 15 deals with land.

Where the customer has previously outsourced the relevant services and the current sourcing arrangement constitutes the transfer of the services from one supplier to another, then the customer and supplier will need to negotiate with the incumbent supplier to obtain any assets held by the incumbent supplier that they require (see Chapter 28 for a discussion of the relevant issues).

13.2   Importance of considering taxation issues

Chapters 13 to 15 point out that some ways of dealing with the assets may be considerably more cost effective than other ways. In particular, this chapter includes a very brief, UK-focused list of some of the more important taxation issues.

If the services agreement involves the transfer, lease or license of substantial amounts or values of assets, all parties will need to take specialist taxation advice. These issues will need to be considered both at the time of any initial transfer, on an ongoing basis and on any transfer of assets, or replacement of assets, by the supplier to the customer at the end of the services agreement.

If the sourcing arrangement is multinational, then the parties will also need to take advice on local law. In particular, for UK customers, if there is a cross-border element or the transaction involves procurement on behalf of individual entities, the way in which the transaction is structured may have a significant impact on tax, including VAT costs. At least in the EU, almost all cross-border supplies of services will be treated as supplied where the customer rather than the supplier belongs and, under the reverse charge procedure, the customer will "charge" itself VAT on the relevant supply calculated at the rate applicable in the country in which the customer is based, and not where the supplier belongs.

13.3 Importance of considering ARD

In addition, the customer and the supplier may want to consider the implication of transferring assets from the customer to the supplier or from an incumbent supplier to the new supplier to the application of the Acquired Rights Directive (ARD). This is because transferring assets may increase the likelihood that the courts will decide that the transfer of a business has occurred and that staff employed in the business will also transfer. See Chapter 31 for a discussion of ARD.

13.4 Recommended approach

In deciding between the various options, it is recommended that the simplest and cheapest option that achieves the parties' business objectives should be adopted, unless there are good reasons for adopting another course of action.

13.5 Equipment owned by the customer

Where physical assets to be used by the supplier in the provision of the services to the customer are owned by the customer, there are a number of options. The customer may sell them or loan them to the supplier.

13.5.1   *Selling the equipment*

The advantages and disadvantages to the customer of selling the equipment to the supplier are explained in Table 22.

Table 22 Selling the equipment

Advantages

The customer may receive a cash payment for the assets.

Even if the purchase price is recovered as part of the supplier's cost base for providing the services, the customer will obtain a cash-flow benefit if the cash payment for the equipment is made in advance or over the first few months of the arrangement and the service charges are spread over the term of the agreement.

The equipment may cease to be on the customer's balance sheet.

A sale may be more appropriate if the supplier is to be responsible for upgrading the equipment at its own cost, and the upgrades are specific to the equipment, so that it makes sense for the same company to own both the equipment and the upgrades.

Disadvantages

If the equipment is to be used to provide the services to the customer, the supplier will usually recover the purchase price of the equipment from the customer in the charges.

The sale of equipment may trigger a liability for corporation tax. The nature and extent of any liability will depend upon the specific equipment in question, the amount for which the customer is treated as acquiring the equipment, the amount for which the customer is treated as selling the equipment, and whether the customer claimed capital allowances by reference to its expenditure on the equipment.

VAT is potentially chargeable on a transfer of equipment unless the transfer to the supplier can be categorised as a transfer of a business or part of a business as a going concern. (This treatment is unlikely to apply where the activities and assets transferred have previously been used in-house as part of the transferor's activities.)

In a UK context, stamp duty will not generally arise, although transfer taxes may arise in other jurisdictions, and stamp duty land tax (SDLT) may be chargeable if an interest in land (including equipment fixed to land) is to be transferred to the supplier.

On expiry of the agreement, the equipment (assuming that it is needed for the provision of the services by the customer or the successor supplier) will be owned by the supplier. The customer will need to protect its position by ensuring that, if the supplier has included the purchase price of the equipment in the charges so that the customer has paid for the equipment, the customer (or the successor supplier) has an option to purchase the equipment for a nominal amount.

On early termination of the agreement, the equipment will be owned by the supplier. The customer will need to pay to get it back if the customer or the successor supplier needs it for the provision of the services. The customer may already have paid part or the entire purchase price of the equipment in the charges. The customer will need to protect itself by including in the agreement a right for it (or the successor supplier) to purchase the equipment for a price that takes into account the extent to which the customer has already paid for the equipment. Thought will need to be given to the taxation consequences of such a retransfer. The customer will also need to protect itself against the possibility that the equipment has not been maintained adequately. See Chapter 29, which covers this issue in greater detail.)

The supplier may create security over the equipment, for example by executing a debenture in favour of its financiers. In these circumstances, it may be necessary to have the equipment carved out of any security given by the supplier. The customer may also want a negative pledge in relation to the equipment. This is particularly important where the customer has the option to buy back the equipment.

> There is a risk that the supplier will become insolvent and the customer will find that the supplier owns equipment it needs to provide the services. See Chapter 29 for a discussion of insolvency related issues.)

13.5.2   Loaning the equipment

The customer can loan the equipment to the supplier. The advantage of this approach is that it is a simpler, cheaper option. The term of the loan should match the term of the services agreement so that, on termination, the equipment will return to the customer. The disadvantage is that the supplier may have to ensure that it has an asset register detailing where the equipment is, so that it can be returned on termination.

13.5.3   Recommended approach

As stated above, in deciding between the various alternatives, it is recommended that the simplest and cheapest option should be adopted unless there are good reasons for adopting another course of action. Therefore, the customer should loan the equipment to the supplier unless there is a good reason for selling it to the supplier.

13.6   Equipment leased by the customer

Where equipment to be used by the supplier for the provision of services to the customer is leased to the customer by a third-party lessor then, where necessary, the lease could be transferred to the supplier. Alternatively, the customer could obtain the lessor's consent to sub-lease the equipment to the supplier. In practice, the customer's options will depend upon the precise terms of the lease with the lessor and the extent to which the lessor is willing to agree to changes in the lease.

In any event, as the services agreement is between the customer and the supplier, the customer will need to either negotiate changes in the arrangements with the lessor or assist the supplier in negotiating with the lessor.

13.6.1   Taxation of equipment leasing transactions

The taxation of equipment leasing transactions is complex and beyond the scope of this book. In summary, a key tax issue in any given leasing transaction is which party may be entitled to claim capital allowances, i.e. the depreciation allowance given to a person by reference to the capital cost or value of equipment. Where a lease is not a "long funding lease", that person is generally the lessor, i.e. the legal owner of the equipment. Where the lease is a "long funding lease", that person is generally the lessee. A "long funding lease" is, broadly speaking:

(a)   a finance lease;
(b)   a lease where the present value of the minimum lease payments is at least 80 per cent of the fair value of the equipment; or
(c)   a lease whose term amounts to more than 65 per cent of the remaining useful economic life of the equipment, and in each case the lease has a term of more than seven (or, in certain cases, more than five) years.

As a quid pro quo of the lessee obtaining the capital allowances, the lessor and lessee are broadly taxable as if the arrangement between them were a loan rather than a lease, with the lessor being taxable on its accounting income under the lease.

It can be seen even from the (highly) simplified analysis above that it would be inadvisable to enter into a lease without considering the capital allowance and other tax issues.

13.6.2   Transferring the lease

The advantages and disadvantages of transferring the lease (from the perspective of the customer) are explained in Table 23.

Table 23 Novation of the lease

Advantages
The leased equipment may cease to be on the customer's balance sheet (if it ever was).[1]
Disadvantages
The parties will need to obtain the consent of the lessor to a transfer of the lease. This may take time to obtain. The lease may have been granted to the customer on favourable terms due to the financial standing of the customer and hence it may not be transferable to the supplier on the same terms unless a customer guarantee is produced. The customer may find that the only alternative would be to terminate the lease, exposing it to the possibility of financial penalties.
The transfer of a lease may give rise to a supply for VAT purposes, unless it is part of a transfer of a going concern to the supplier. Even if the transaction is a transfer of a going concern, if the supplier is a member of a partly exempt VAT group, the supplier will be deemed to supply the asset to itself, which may result in a VAT charge that the supplier will want to pass on to the customer in the charges for the services.
On termination of the agreement, the leased equipment (assuming that it is needed for the provision of the services by the customer or the successor supplier) will be in the supplier's name. The customer must endeavour to protect itself by ensuring that the lease can be further transferred back to the customer, or to the successor supplier or the equipment can be purchased by the customer or the successor supplier in these circumstances.. Thought will need to be given to the taxation consequences of such a retransfer. The supplier may be

---

[1]   Operating leases will generally be off balance sheet, although this may change once IFRS proposals for the treatment of leases come into effect.

anxious to transfer the lease to the customer or the successor supplier, so that it is not responsible for making the payments under the lease.

There is a risk that the supplier will become insolvent. The customer may want to protect itself by agreeing a direct agreement with the lessor. See Chapter 29 for a discussion of insolvency related issues.)

There is a risk also that the lessor may become insolvent and, in circumstances where the supplier leases equipment for the provision of the services, it is worthwhile for the customer to consider the creditworthiness of the equipment lessor.

13.6.3   Sub-licensing the equipment

The advantage of sub-licensing the equipment (from the perspective of the customer) is that it is a simpler option. The disadvantage is that it still requires the lessor's consent, although such consent may be easier to obtain than consent for the transfer of the lease, depending upon the terms of the lease. When customers take out leases of equipment, it may be helpful for them to obtain the lessors' approval in principle to granting sub-licenses of the equipment to the customer's suppliers.

13.6.4   Recommended approach

In practice, the parties will usually decide that the customer will obtain a right for the supplier to use the leased equipment, unless there is a good reason for transferring the lease to the supplier.

13.7   Access to equipment

If the supplier will need access to other equipment, whether owned or leased to the customer, which will continue to be used by the customer (for example computer equipment to be maintained by the supplier), then the customer will usually grant the supplier rights of access or a licence to use the relevant equipment. The customer should check the terms of its lease to see whether it needs the lessor's consent before allowing the supplier access to leased hardware.

13.8   Supply or maintenance contracts

Supply or maintenance agreements are not usually personal to the customer and so the customer will have the option of:

(a)   transferring them to the supplier; or

(b)   retaining them in its name and providing for the supplier to manage the third-party supply agreement. This may include the supplier acting as paying agent for the third-party supply agreements by making payments to the third-party supplier on the customer's behalf and recovering the payments as part of the charges.

13.8.1   Transferring the agreements

The advantages and disadvantages of transferring the agreements to the supplier (from the perspective of the customer) are explained in Table 24.

Table 24 Transferring the agreements

Advantages
The supplier may be able to take advantage of corporate arrangements with the third-party supply agreement under which it obtains preferential rates such as volume discounts.
The supplier may be willing to take more responsibility for the actions of the third-party supplier if it is a party to the agreement and has the right to terminate the agreement if it is dissatisfied with the supplier's performance.
Unless the agreement specifies otherwise, if the charges payable to the third-party supplier increase, the supplier will pay these.
Disadvantages
The parties may need to obtain the consent of the third party. This may take time to obtain. The third party may be unwilling to agree to the transfer, for example if the financial standing of the supplier is worse than that of the customer. Until the third party's consent has been obtained, the customer may be in breach of confidentiality obligations in the agreement if it discloses details of the third-party agreement.
On termination, the third-party supply agreement (assuming that they are needed for the provision of the services by the customer or the successor supplier) will be in the supplier's name. The customer may require the supplier to use reasonable endeavours to transfer it to the customer. If the supplier has a corporate arrangement with the third-party supplier, then the charges may incorporate volume discounts that will not be transferable to the customer. This may not be a problem if the successor supplier has similar discount arrangements with appropriate third-party suppliers.
Unless the agreement specifies otherwise, if the supplier decides that it does not need the supply agreement and terminates it, the supplier receives the benefit of the cost saving.

13.8.2   Retaining the agreements

The advantages and disadvantages of retaining the agreements in the customer's name (from the perspective of the customer) are explained in Table 25.

Table 25 Retaining the agreements in the customer's name

Advantages
It is a simpler option—the parties may not need to agree a variation to the supply agreement if the supplier is merely to manage the third-party supplier.
Unless the agreement specifies otherwise, if the parties decide that the supply agreement is not needed and the customer terminates it, the customer will receive the benefit of the cost saving.
Disadvantages

> Unless the agreement specifies otherwise, if the charges payable to the third-party supplier increase, the customer will pay these.

13.9   Defining the equipment

Apart from deciding how the equipment used to provide the services will be dealt with, the customer and the supplier will also need to resolve how the equipment will be defined or identified. In some services arrangements, including simpler arrangements, the customer may have a comprehensive list of all of the equipment, perhaps in the form of an internal asset register.

In other cases, the customer may have an asset register but it may be unclear whether it is up to date or complete. The customer and the supplier may need to decide whether the customer will grant a warranty regarding the asset register, whether the supplier will be expected to rely upon its own due diligence or whether the supplier will get a limited period during which it will not be responsible for problems in the services resulting from assets which are on the asset register not being transferred (for example because they have been destroyed or damaged).

The customer may also agree that, if equipment has been omitted from the asset register that is needed for the provision of the services, then, assuming it is still held by the customer, the parties will amend the asset register so that it is added to it and transferred or made available to the supplier together with the other equipment.

13.10   State aid

Public sector customers must ensure that any assets transferred to the supplier are sold or leased at market value or above in order to comply with the EU state aid rules. The state aid rules are designed to prevent suppliers from receiving public assets at an undervalue. State aid rules apply whether the purchase price is received either as a separate cash payment or incorporated within the overall deal. Where the price is incorporated as part of the overall deal, it is recommended that this be documented. If the transaction is properly tendered, it is likely that the sale of assets will be regarded as an arm's length transaction that does not involve state aid.

Where the total value of the assets in question is less than €200,000, it may be possible to take advantage of an exemption under the state aid rules, provided that the total of any state aid received by the supplier does not exceed that figure over a rolling three-year period[2]. If reliance is being placed

---

[2]   Commission Regulation (EC) No 1998/2006 of 15 December 2006 on the application of Articles 87 and 88 of the Treaty to de minimis aid.

on this exemption, certain reporting requirements apply and reference should be made to the exemption in the transfer documents.

Chapter 14

Existing Software and Intellectual Property Rights

14.1   Outline

Chapter 13 describes the options for dealing with one type of assets, namely equipment. This chapter deals with another type of assets—software and intellectual property rights. It describes the various ways of dealing with software and intellectual property rights that are owned by or licensed to the customer.

14.2   Intellectual property rights owned by the customer

Where the customer owns intellectual property rights (IPR) used to provide the services (e.g. bespoke software developed by the customer), the customer may decide to sell them to the supplier or to license them to the supplier. Thus, the options are similar to those for physical equipment, even if the implications are slightly different for IPR.

14.2.1   Selling the IPR

The advantages and disadvantages (from the perspective of the customer) of selling the IPR to the supplier are described in Table 26.

Table 26 Selling IPR owned by the customer

Advantages
The customer may receive a cash payment for the IPR.
Even if the purchase price is recovered as part of the supplier's cost base for providing the services, the customer will obtain a cash-flow benefit if the cash payment for the IPR is paid in advance or over the first few months of the arrangement and the purchase price is spread over the term of the agreement.
The IPR may cease to be on the customer's balance sheet.

The supplier may be able to exploit the IPR by licensing them to other customers (although this could also be achieved by allowing the supplier to sub-license the IPR).

Disadvantages

The supplier may recover the cash payment from the customer in the charges, unless the supplier has an opportunity to license the IPR to other customers. This may be unlikely if the IPR constitutes software that has been developed for the customer's specific requirements.

Corporation tax liabilities may arise on sales of IPR. Different tax consequences may apply to IPR created after 1 April 2002 when the stand-alone intangibles regime[1] was introduced.

On expiry of the agreement, the IPR (assuming that they are needed for the provision of the services by the customer or the successor supplier) will be owned by the supplier. The customer will need to protect its position, for example by ensuring that it receives a royalty-free licence to use the IPR for the provision of the services by it and a successor supplier.

On early termination of the agreement, the IPR (assuming that they are needed for the provision of the services by the customer or the successor supplier) will be owned by the supplier. The customer will need to ensure that it can continue to use them. The customer may have already paid part of the purchase price of the IPR in the charges. The customer will need to protect itself, for example by including in the agreement a licence for it to use the IPR for the provision of the services by it and a successor supplier. The parties may need to agree a charging mechanism for calculating what licence fee is payable by the customer if it has not compensated the supplier for the purchase price of the IPR. Thought will also need to be given to the taxation consequences of such a retransfer.

There is a risk that the supplier will become insolvent and the customer will find that key IPR needed by it to provide the services are owned by the supplier. (See Chapter 29 for a discussion of insolvency related issues.)

14.2.2 *Licensing the IPR*

The advantages of licensing the IPR to the supplier are that it is a simpler option. In practice, the parties will usually decide that the customer will license the supplier to use the customer's bespoke software, unless there is a good reason for selling it to the supplier.

14.2.3 *Taxation consequences*

If the IPR are either sold or licensed to the customer, then tax issues are likely to arise and so the parties should take specialist taxation advice on this point.

14.3 IPR licensed to the customer[2]

Where software or other IPR are licensed to the customer, in theory:

(a) the licences could be transferred to the supplier;

---

[1] Sch.29 of the Finance Act 2002.
[2] For an explanation of issues relating to open source software, see Heather J. Meeker, *The Open Source Alternative: Understanding Risks and Leveraging Opportunities*, (John Wiley & Sons Inc., 2008).

(b) the supplier could rely upon the customer's licences (with the parties obtaining the licensor's consent for the supplier to use the software or other rights, where necessary, if the licence does not already cover a supplier); or

(c) the customer could terminate its licences and the supplier could be responsible for ensuring that the appropriate licences are obtained.

In practice, the options open to the parties will depend upon the precise terms of the licence with the licensor and what the parties can agree with the licensor.[3]

14.3.1 *Transferring the licences*

The advantages and disadvantages of the licences being transferred to the supplier (from the perspective of the customer) are described in Table 27.

Table 27 Transferring the licences

Advantages
The supplier may be able to take advantage of corporate arrangements with licensors under which it obtains preferential rates when licences are transferred to it.
The licensor may want to transfer the licence so that it has a contractual relationship with the supplier, thus making it easier to sell other products to the supplier.
Disadvantages
The licensor may charge a fee for transferring the licences, but not if the licences stay in the customer's name. The parties will need to agree who will pay the fee.
Signing an agreement to transfer the licence may involve more administrative effort than merely obtaining the licensor's approval for the supplier to use them.
On termination of the agreement, the licences (assuming that they are needed for the provision of the services by the customer or the successor supplier) will be in the supplier's name. The customer must endeavour to protect itself by ensuring that any licences transferred to the supplier can be transferred back on termination without any transfer charge. The situation will be more complex if the supplier has merged the licences in with other corporate arrangements that it has. Before the agreement is signed the customer should check if the supplier will be able to carve the licences out of the corporate arrangement on termination. Usually the customer will not be able to benefit from the supplier's corporate discounts after termination.

---

[3] In addition, if the licences are not to remain with the customer, there are two options: the licences can be assigned to the supplier, or they can be novated to the supplier. An assignment is a transfer of part or all of the benefit of a contract. The other party will still be able to enforce the contract against the original party. Novation replaces the contract so that another party takes the place of the transferring party. Unless the agreement provides otherwise, assignment of the benefit of a contract can take place without the consent of the customer but novation can only take place if supplier and customer agree.

14.3.2   Obtaining the licensor's consent

The advantages and disadvantages of the customer obtaining the licensor's consent for the supplier to use the software or other rights (from the perspective of the customer) are described in Table 28.

Table 28 Obtaining licensor's consent to a right to use

Advantages
The licensor may want to retain the agreement in the customer's name so that it continues to have a relationship with the customer, thus making it easier to sell other products to the customer.
On termination of the agreement, the licences (assuming that they are needed for the provision of the services by the customer or the successor supplier) will already be in the customer's name.
Disadvantages
The licensor may charge a fee for granting the right to use. Note that this could be prevented in the future by the customer ensuring that all new software licences allow use of the IPR by an outsourcing supplier to provide services to the customer. The licence may also be restricted to the use of the software at certain locations. Therefore, if the supplier is intending to relocate the provision of the services, the parties may need to obtain the consent of the licensor for use of the software at the new location. The parties will need to check whether any additional charges are payable for obtaining the consent of the licensor to the use of the software by the supplier or at the new premises, and will need to document whether these will be paid by the customer or whether they are already included in the supplier's charges.
The customer will be liable to the licensor for actions taken relating to the licence, whether by it or by the supplier. Therefore, the customer will need the supplier to commit to complying with the terms of the licence and indemnify it against breaches of the licence by the supplier.

As any IPR licences will be between the customer and the licensor, if the parties decide to adopt either of the above two options, the customer will need to either negotiate changes in the arrangement with the licensor or assist the supplier to negotiate with the licensor.

14.3.3   Taking out new licences

The advantages and disadvantages of the supplier taking out new licences (from the perspective of the customer) are described in Table 29.

Table 29 Supplier taking out new licences

Advantages
The supplier may be able to take advantage of corporate arrangements with licensors under which it obtains preferential rates.
Disadvantages
If the licence fees for the software are payable in one lump sum for a perpetual licence, then taking out new licences will mean the parties paying for licences which the customer has already paid for.
On termination, the licences (assuming that they are needed for the provision of the services by the customer or the successor supplier) will be in the supplier's name.

> Before deciding to adopt this course of action, the customer should check with the licensor whether it will agree that the licences will be transferable to the customer on termination. If the licensor will not approve the transfer on termination, in a worst-case scenario, the customer may have to take out new licences or find another supplier who has the relevant licences. If the supplier has a corporate arrangement with the licensor, then even if the licences are transferable, usually the customer will not be able to benefit from the supplier's corporate discounts after termination.

14.4   Problems with software licences

14.4.1   *Ensuring all relevant parties are licensed*

In considering how to deal with software in an outsourcing arrangement, it is easy for the parties to concentrate on the fact that the supplier will need to use the software to provide the services, and to ignore the fact that the customer may also need to continue to use the software to take advantage of the services or that the licences will need to cover any disaster recovery arrangements.

14.4.2   *Breach of copyright*

Failing to ensure that software licences cover all parties who will need to use the software is a serious mistake to make. Software is protected by copyright. A party will be in breach of copyright to the extent to which it uses software without a proper licence. Software licence agreements may state that software is licensed for use by a specified party, at a specified location, on specified hardware and even by specified listed individuals. Any use outside the specific scope of the licence will be in breach of copyright.

Remedies for copyright infringement include:

(a)   a right to damages awarded on the basis of the loss to the copyright owner. In circumstances where software is licensed, the damages are likely to be calculated on the basis of a reasonable royalty rate;
(b)   an account of profits;
(c)   an order for delivery up of infringing copies;
(d)   an injunction to restrain further or expected infringements; and
(e)   (in extreme circumstances) prosecution for a criminal act.

For these reasons, not only must the parties ensure that any use of the software is properly licensed, but any legal adviser will recommend that they ensure that they take out the proper licences before the supplier starts to use the software.

14.4.3   Due diligence

Before the agreement is signed, the parties may also want to know whether the licensor will be unwilling to grant its consent or will require the payment of exorbitant fees in return for granting its consent to the required use of the software. This is particularly important where it is possible that this will undermine the business case for entering into the sourcing arrangement or may mean that the parties will have to change the services to be outsourced or how they will be provided, for example if it is possible to avoid situations where the supplier uses the software.

Chapter 15

Property Aspects

15.1   Outline

Chapters 13 and 14 deal with the transfer of equipment, software and IPR from the customer to the supplier. This chapter deals with property issues relating to the sourcing arrangement. If the services are to be provided from the customer's site, then the customer can either sell the premises to the supplier or grant it a licence or a lease in respect of the relevant premises.

15.2   Selling the premises

Table 30 explains the advantages and disadvantages (from the customer's perspective) of the customer selling the premises to the supplier.

Table 30 Sale

Advantages
Sale is appropriate where the supplier will be the only party using the premises.
The customer may receive a cash payment for the premises.
The premises (if leasehold, and therefore a liability) may cease to be on the customer's balance sheet.
Any liabilities such as rates, repair and environmental will be passed on to the supplier.
Disadvantages
If the premises are to be used to provide the services to the customer, the supplier will almost certainly include part or all of the cost of purchasing the premises in the charges for the services.
If the property is leasehold, the landlord's consent is likely to be required and the customer may be required to provide an authorised guarantee agreement.
The sale of land may attract corporation tax on chargeable gains, in which case the parties will need to consider what, if any, tax reliefs are available to the parties (e.g. tax reliefs relating to reinvesting in other business premises).
Stamp duty land tax may be payable by the supplier, and so detailed consideration will need to be given to the stamp duty land tax consequences of the purchase and whether any relief is available by reference to the completed transaction (e.g. sale and leaseback relief).
There may be VAT chargeable in addition to the purchase price, depending on whether an option to tax has been made by the transferee in respect of the property. If the customer is exempt or partially exempt (i.e. it can not recover all of the VAT charged to it), transferring the property to a supplier who recovers the cost of the purchase by increasing fees to the customer over the life of the contract may increase the customer's irrecoverable VAT.

> The customer and supplier will need to consider what will happen on termination of the agreement.

15.3 Leasing or licensing the premises

The customer will need to take specialist property and taxation advice on what is more appropriate, a lease or a licence.

15.3.1 Lease

Generally, if the supplier is to be granted exclusive rights to use an entire building, or part of a building, then a lease will usually be appropriate. If the customer does decide to grant the supplier a lease of the premises, then the customer will have to take specialist legal advice to ensure that the lease is excluded from the security of tenure provisions contained in the Landlord and Tenant Act 1954 (as amended). This is a relatively straightforward process.

15.3.2 Specific licence

A licence will be more appropriate if the supplier is to provide the services from part or parts of the customer's premises, shared with the customer, rather than taking over an entire building or defined area from the customer. To be enforceable as a licence, the licence will need to grant the supplier non-exclusive access to the relevant premises and not reserve the customer a right of entry to the relevant premises (which are both characteristics of a lease not a licence). Care must also be taken in ensuring what rights are actually given to the supplier in practice, as whether a supplier is granted a licence or a lease will depend upon the facts of the situation, not just the wording of the agreement. Therefore, whilst a customer may prefer a licence as a simpler document, if exclusive possession is in fact given to the supplier, this could result in the supplier acquiring security of tenure.

15.3.3 General licence

In addition, the supplier may need temporary non-exclusive access to the customer's premises solely to carry out the services. For example, it may need to enter the customer's premises to maintain customer equipment at the premises.

The customer will usually grant the supplier a general licence to enter any of its premises to the extent necessary to provide the services.

15.3.4 *Landlord's consent*

If the customer is not the freehold owner of the premises, then, depending on the terms of its lease, it will need the consent of the landlord to a licence or sublease. The terms of the lease under which the customer occupies the premises will need to be checked to ensure the customer can grant the sublease or licence. Also, the customer should factor into its project plan for the procurement the fact that obtaining this permission may take some considerable time (or, indeed, consent may not be forthcoming).

15.4 Terms of the licence or lease

Once the parties have decided upon the desired approach, they will need to decide upon the appropriate terms of the lease or licence. See Table 31 for a list of issues that may need to be considered in the lease or licence.

Table 31 Licence or lease terms

Outgoings

The parties will need to decide whether the supplier will be responsible for the outgoings (in respect of rates, electricity, telephone, water etc. and the maintenance of the premises) and if so, whether the supplier will be entitled to charge these amounts back to the customer or whether they are already included in the charges payable by the customer. The customer will be reluctant to pay all of the outgoings if the premises are to be used for the provision of services to other customers of the supplier.

Furniture and other facilities

The parties will need to agree whether the customer will make available to the supplier at the premises any furniture or office, parking, meeting-room or canteen facilities.

Security

The parties will need to decide who will be responsible for the security of the premises. They will also need to decide whether the premises satisfy the security requirements necessary to provide the services and if not, whether the supplier's charges already include the cost of improving the premises or whether the supplier will be able to make an additional charge to cover these costs.

Health and safety

The supplier may need to commit to complying with the customer's health and safety, security and access and other regulations at the premises.

Access hours

The supplier will need to know the hours during which it will be able to gain access to the premises and will need to compare this with the service hours during which it must provide the services to the customer.

Non-interference

If the supplier is to be given non-exclusive access to the premises, then the customer may want the supplier to commit to not interfering with the carrying on by the customer of its normal business activities.

Damage to the premises

The parties will want to clarify who will be responsible for insuring the premises and in what circumstances the supplier will be responsible for damage to the premises.

Relocation

145

> If the supplier is relocating the services to alternative premises, the customer and supplier should check if this will result in any additional expenditure and will need to decide who will be responsible for this. An example of a potential problem area is where the supplier is relocating a mainframe computer but the lease for the mainframe hardware and software is remaining with the customer. In this situation, the hardware lessor may make an additional charge under the lease for the relocation of the mainframe.
>
> All of these issues can also affect whether, as a matter of law, the relationship between the customer and the supplier is one of landlord–tenant or licensor–licensee.

15.5   State aid

The transfer of any publicly owned land to a supplier is subject to the EU state aid rules. Under these rules, the transfer of land should be at market value or above. Market value can be determined either on the basis of a tendering procedure or in accordance with an independent valuation. The valuation should take into account conditions attached to the land (such as, e.g., restrictions on use) but not other factors (such as, e.g., other elements of the sourcing transaction).

Where the transfer is part of an overall outsourcing transaction that has been procured under the EU Public Procurement Directives, the purchase price for the land can form part of the overall package.

Chapter 16

Treatment of Assets During Term

16.1 Outline

Chapters 12, 13 and 14 discuss options for transferring to the supplier at the beginning of the services arrangement the assets or rights in the assets previously used by the customer. This chapter deals with issues relating to the treatment of assets during the term of the arrangement. It covers how the customer ensures that it has obtained value for money if it has sold assets to the supplier. It also describes the issues regarding whether the supplier should be able to use the assets for the provision of services to its other customers. It goes on to discuss the replacement of the assets and the funding of new assets.

16.2 Ensuring value for money

16.2.1 Resale of the assets

If the customer decides to sell assets to the supplier, whether physical assets or intangible IPR, it will want to ensure that it obtains value for money from the transaction. For example, it may check the value of the assets and the price payable by the supplier or include a clawback provision whereby it receives, for example, a share of the proceeds of sale if the supplier sells the assets within a certain period of time for more than it paid the customer.

16.2.2 Use of the assets to provide services to other customers

If the supplier includes the cost of acquiring the assets in its charges to the customer, then the customer may want to ensure that it obtains a reduction in the charges if the assets are later used for the provision of services to the supplier's other customers. Therefore, it may restrict the supplier from using the assets for the provision of services to other customers until the supplier has satisfied the customer that it has received a reasonable reduction in the charges to reflect the benefit that the supplier is obtaining. There are two ways that the parties can deal with this situation.

16.2.3 *Approval on a case-by-case basis*

The customer can require the supplier to obtain its approval each time it wants to use the assets for the provision of services to its other customers. The customer could then receive a fixed percentage of the profits (e.g. 50 per cent) or the profits could be distributed in a reasonable manner designed to reflect each party's efforts in winning the new customer. This mechanism can be used, for example, to reward the customer for assisting the supplier in marketing the services to other customers.

This approach will usually be overly bureaucratic unless the amount of money involved is substantial. Even if the amount of money involved is substantial, the supplier will be reluctant to disclose to the customer confidential information relating to its agreements with other customers. In addition, unless the other customers are being granted a licence to use the IPR previously owned by the customer, the contracts with the other customers will not usually involve a separate payment for the use of the specific assets and so it will be difficult to measure the exact benefit that the supplier is obtaining.

16.2.4 *General approval*

In most cases it will be more realistic for the customer to allow the supplier to use the assets generally for the provision of services to other customers subject to ensuring that the customer has received a reasonable reduction in the charges in return for granting this right. This may be the only option regarding premises leased or licensed to the supplier. If the supplier is providing the services from the customer's premises, the only way it can guarantee that the premises will not be used for the provision of services to other customers will be if all of the employees and contractors who work at the premises are dedicated to providing services to the customer. This may introduce a level of inflexibility that will undermine the supplier's ability to provide the services in the most cost-effective manner.

16.2.5 *Residual value*

In appropriate circumstances, even where the supplier is using the assets exclusively to provide services to the customer during the term of the arrangement, the customer may take the view that the supplier should not include the full cost of acquiring the assets in its charges to the customer if the assets will still be valuable on expiry of the services agreement. This is because, on termination, the supplier will still own the assets and will be able to sell them or use them to provide services to other customers after termination. A similar argument may apply where the supplier develops assets especially for the customer if other customers can use the assets after termination. The parties will need to negotiate and agree issues surrounding residual value and who retains that value.

16.3   Use of the assets and premises

Ensuring value for money is not the only consideration arising out of the supplier's use of assets, transferred to it by the customer, for the provision of services to its other customers.

16.3.1   Services not adversely affected

From the customer's perspective, if the assets or premises are to be used for the provision of services to it and to other customers, it will want to be reassured that the services to it are not adversely affected. The supplier may argue that it should have control over how it provides the services and that it is sufficient for it to have an obligation to meet the service levels. In some cases the supplier may use the assets or premises for the provision of services to its other customers and not to the customer. This issue has been discussed in Chapter 8.

16.3.2   Third-party agreements

The customer will need to ensure that it is not breaching any third-party agreements by allowing the supplier to use the assets for the provision of services to third parties. For example, software licences covering the customer and a supplier providing services to it will not enable the supplier to provide services to other customers.

16.3.3   Smooth transition on termination

Lastly, it will want to ensure that the use of the assets by third parties does not adversely affect the smooth transition of the services back in-house or to the successor supplier on termination of the services agreement. This topic is discussed in Chapter 26.

16.4 Damage and maintenance

In establishing a sourcing arrangement, the customer and the supplier usually remember to deal with how the different assets are to be made available to the supplier so that it can provide the services. However, the parties also need to consider ongoing issues relating to the assets.

16.4.1 Damage to the assets

The parties need to decide who will be responsible for damage to the assets and who will be responsible for insuring them. They will need to consider the implications if the customer's users or clients damage the assets and, in particular, who will be responsible for paying any increased insurance premiums and insurance excesses. The parties need to agree the nature of their interests under any insurance policy, and whether they are to be co-insured under it. This may involve consideration of which parties have an insurable interest in the assets in question.

16.4.2 Maintenance and customisation

The parties will also need to decide who will be responsible for maintaining the assets or modifying them so that they are suitable to provide the services.

16.4.3 Replacement of the obsolete assets

The parties will need to decide who will be responsible for replacing obsolete assets used to provide the services if they can no longer be used for that purpose. If the customer retains this responsibility, then it must take this into account in anticipating its expenditure over the term of the arrangement and in building its business case. If the supplier takes over the responsibility, then clearly it will need to include the expenditure in its business case.

16.5 New or replacement assets

If the customer does not have the assets needed to provide the services or its assets need to be replaced, either on the commencement of the services agreement or at a later time, the customer and the supplier will need to decide how to acquire and fund the new assets. There are various options. The most common options are set out below:

(a)   The customer may buy or lease the assets from a third-party lessor, in which case the issues in sections 13.53 and 13.6 above will be relevant. The customer may wish to make the supplier responsible for the selection and suitability of the equipment.

(b)   The supplier can buy the assets or lease them from a third-party lessor. The customer may prefer the supplier to be responsible for acquiring the assets so that it takes the risk as to their suitability for the provision of the services.

(c)   If the assets will be used exclusively for the provision of services to the customer, it may be possible to secure cheaper funding for the assets if the supplier acquires the assets and leases them to the customer on the basis of a lease coterminous with the services agreement.

The parties will need to take specialist taxation, accounting and insolvency advice before deciding upon the most appropriate course of action. Dealing with the various options is outside the scope of this Guide as the issues are not specific to outsourcing or services arrangements.

Chapter 17

Different Supplier Models

17.1 Outline

Chapters 17, 18 and 19 deal with different contractual models that may be adopted by the customer and supplier, including multi-sourcing, prime contractor and supplier consortium models. This chapter deals with contractual models where there are multiple suppliers. Chapter 18 deals with the situation where there are multiple customers. Chapter 19 deals with the situation where the customer and the supplier (or customers and suppliers) form a joint venture.

17.2 Relationship between different suppliers

When a customer decides to enter into a services agreement, it will often find that the service or function will need to be provided by various different suppliers. Equally, when the supplier responds to the customer's RFP, it may conclude that it needs to work with other suppliers to provide all aspects of the services required. The question arises as to how the different relationships should be structured.

17.2.1 Types of relationship

There are various different approaches that can be adopted:

(a)   the customer can enter into multiple agreements with the various different suppliers ("multi-sourcing");
(b)   the customer can enter into one agreement with a prime contractor who then enters into subcontracts with the other suppliers ("prime contractor");
(c)   the customer can enter into an agreement with several suppliers, jointly ("supplier consortium"), and it may be that the suppliers themselves form a joint venture to provide the service;
(d)   the customer and the suppliers can form a joint venture ("joint venture"). This approach is dealt with in Chapter 19; or
(e)   the customer can enter into multiple agreements with various different

suppliers (similar to the multi-sourcing arrangement) but can then enter into a service integration agreement with a consultancy firm or supplier who manages the other suppliers ("service integration"). The service integrator may be a supplier of a lead tower such as IT infrastructure. This essentially involves outsourcing aspects of the governance function. This approach is described in Chapter 10 on governance.

17.2.2   Factors to take into account

Table 32 describes the different factors to be taken into account in deciding which of the above approaches to adopt. In IT outsourcing, there is a trend towards multi-sourcing (and the therefore in the outsourcing of service integration), as IT services become more commoditised.

Table   32   Multi-sourcing,   prime   contractor   and   supplier consortium

Total cost
On the one hand, multi-sourcing may be cheaper for the customer if it avoids a prime contractor charging a margin on the sub-contractors' services and charging for managing the sub-contractors. In this situation, however, someone will need to provide the service integration role. On the other hand, multi-sourcing may be more expensive if it results in one supplier having to test or confirm the quality of a deliverable produced by another supplier.
Multi-sourcing may enable the customer to obtain better value for money for additional services if it can obtain competitive quotations for the services from the different suppliers (although, if a best-of-breed approach has been employed, the other suppliers may not be able to provide the additional services).
Alternatively, under a prime contractor arrangement, the prime contractor may be able to obtain better discounts from its suppliers for bulk purchasing than the customer could achieve in entering into agreements directly with the suppliers.
Transparency of charges
In a prime contractor or supplier consortium model, the customer will not know the sub-contractor's or supplier's charges unless a specific open-book arrangement is agreed. See Chapter 23 for a discussion of open-book arrangements. In the multi-sourcing arrangement, it will know the charges of the different suppliers.
Risk of increases in sub-contractor charges
In a prime contractor model, the charges may be calculated on the basis of a fixed price, so the prime contractor will take the risk of managing its supply chain including the risk that sub-contractors increase their charges to the prime contractor. In a supplier consortium model, the customer will also be able to negotiate a fixed price (which means that it will not take the risk of increases in the suppliers' charges).
Responsibility
In multi-sourcing, it may be difficult for the customer to allocate responsibility for specific faults between the various suppliers. In all of the other arrangements, from the customer's perspective, responsibility for service delivery will be clearer.
In a prime contractor relationship, the supplier will usually expect the sub-contractor to enter into a back-to-back agreement. The sub-contractor may, however, want to cap its liability at a level that is fixed by reference to the value of the subcontract rather than the value of the entire agreement, which will leave the supplier with a residual liability for the actions of the

sub-contractor. If the sub-contractor is an existing supplier of the customer or has been selected by the customer, additional issues arise and these are discussed in Chapter 34.

In supplier consortium arrangements, each supplier will also usually accept joint and several liability vis-à-vis the customer and enter into direct agreements with the other suppliers under which they agree to compensate the other suppliers for losses caused as a result of their actions.

Limitations of liability

Under a supplier consortium arrangement, in theory the parties may be able to use the limited liability joint venture company to limit their liability. However, if the joint venture company lacks the financial standing of its shareholder companies, the customer will usually demand a guarantee from the suppliers.

Setting up the arrangements

In multi-sourcing there will be more work for the customer in negotiating the various arrangements with suppliers.

In a prime contractor model, the supplier will negotiate back-to-back contracts with its sub-contractors.

In a supplier consortium the suppliers will negotiate agreements between each other.
A joint venture could raise merger control issues.

Service integration

In all of the different models, someone needs to be responsible for managing the service integration of the different suppliers. See Chapter 10 for a discussion of the service integration role.

In a multi-sourcing arrangement, the customer will be responsible for managing the different suppliers and (in particular) the integration between the various suppliers unless it appoints an independent supplier or one of the tower providers to act as a service integrator and manage the integration process between the other suppliers.

In a prime contractor model, the customer outsources the management and integration of the sub-contractors to the prime contractor and the prime contractor is responsible for ensuring a seamless service delivery.

In a supplier consortium arrangement the members of the supplier consortium manage the integration of their individual services.

Flexibility

Multi-sourcing may be more flexible than the other options if it means that the customer can replace one supplier without affecting the agreements with the other suppliers. It may also be more flexible if the customer is able to request one supplier to provide services previously provided by the other supplier, or to ask either of them to bid for new additional services. Therefore, it may be argued that the arrangement avoids dependence upon a single supplier. This could be a particular advantage in situations where there is a heightened risk of supplier insolvency.

Multi-sourcing arrangements will, however, not be more flexible if the suppliers are each specialists in specific fields.

In a contract with a prime contractor, the customer may be more dependent upon the prime contractor but can still ensure that it has flexibility with regard to the sub-contractors. Thus the contract with the prime contractor can be drafted to allow the customer to direct the prime contractor to replace a sub-contractor that is repeatedly failing. It may also include a mandatory market testing of sub-contractors on a regular basis, with a replacement of sub-contractors who cannot compete on price or quality with others in the market.

Quality

In multi-sourcing, the customer can select suppliers who are the leading specialists in providing the individual services. However, individual suppliers may be less willing to invest in understanding the customer's business if the value of the individual contracts is less.

In a prime contractor arrangement the prime contractor may subcontract elements of the services to specialist sub-contractors.

A supplier consortium may be established between different leading specialists.

Relationship with end provider

A prime contractor model may result in the customer feeling distanced from the end provider of goods or services, but this can be managed by including regular liaison provisions in the contract or ensuring adequate service integration.
Control
In a prime contractor model, the customer will not have control over the sub-contractors unless specifically agreed. See Chapter 8 for ways in which the customer may control sub-contractors.
In the other models, the customer has a direct relationship with the various suppliers and will be able to decide to replace any unsatisfactory supplier (provided that it has the right to terminate the agreement with the relevant supplier).
Variety
In appropriate circumstances, a multi-sourcing option may provide users with a variety of suppliers to choose from, which may increase support for the sourcing process by users if they feel that they have a choice.

17.3 Prime contractor and Sub-contractor

Sections 17.3.1 to 17.3.3 describe the different issues that the prime contractor may have to deal with in entering into a sub-contractor arrangement.

17.3.1 Due diligence

The supplier may need to carry out due diligence similar to that carried out by the customer with regard to the supplier, as described in Chapter 4, unless the supplier has previously carried out such due diligence because it has a long standing relationship with the relevant sub-contractor.

17.3.2 Teaming agreement

The prime contractor may want to sign a teaming agreement with key sub-contractors. Table 33 explains the types of issues that may need to be covered in the teaming agreement.

Table 33 Teaming agreement

Services - the services to be provided by the sub-contractor.

Dependencies - any dependencies that the sub-contractor has upon the supplier or the customer.

Charges - the charges to be paid to the sub-contractor.

Flow down - the extent to which the subcontract will accept a flow down of the commercial and legal terms in the main agreement.

Collaboration - how the parties will work together during the tender process, the extent to which the sub-contractor will be involved in attending meetings and negotiating or commenting on the main agreement including any restrictions upon the sub-contractor communicating with the potential customer.

Non-competition - any agreement that the sub-contractor will not act as sub-contractor for any other bidders in the procurement. This is unlikely to raise competition law concerns provided it is limited to a particular project. However, any restriction on the sub-contractor could raise competition concerns if it is capable of having an appreciable impact on the market (which would depends on the market power of the parties and the scope and duration of obligation) – see Chapter 33.

Intellectual property rights - the terms on which any intellectual property rights will be licensed to the supplier and the customer.

Liability - liability of each party pending agreement of the subcontract.

Termination - the termination arrangements.

It is important to agree the above issues early on in the procurement process, so that the supplier can ensure that they are reflected in the main agreement, where appropriate.

17.3.3   Subcontract

The supplier will want to enter into a subcontract with the sub-contractor. The main agreement may oblige the supplier to include certain flow downs from the main agreement in the subcontract (for example with regard to confidentiality, security, data protection, the customer's audit rights, participation in dispute resolution procedures or the customer's right to step in to the relationship with the supplier - see section 8.5.2).

In any event the supplier will want to flow down appropriate obligations to the sub-contractor. These may include provisions regarding:

(a)   the exact services to be provided by the sub-contractor;
(b)   compliance with applicable law and customer policies and procedures;
(c)   compliance with any key deadlines;
(d)   the charges to be payable, the payment profile, indexation arrangements and termination payments;
(e)   liability, warranties and indemnities, including intellectual property rights indemnities; and
(f)   rights for the supplier to terminate for cause.

The supplier will need to flow down some provisions in any amended form. For example, where the supplier has an obligation to provide the customer with notice of any relief, the supplier will need the sub-contractor to provide it with notice within a shorter timescale to enable the supplier to comply with its obligations under the main agreement with the customer.

The sub-contractor will usually be unwilling to agree an exact flow down of provisions such as the limit of liability and the amount of service credits, on the basis that such amounts should reflect the benefit of the agreement to the sub-contractor and so the caps and amounts should be lower in the subcontract.

The supplier may want the obligation to pay the sub-contractor to be dependent upon them having received payment from the customer. The supplier may also want the right to terminate the subcontract if the main agreement is terminated.

The supplier will want to get the subcontract signed by the sub-contractor before it signs the agreement with the customer, with the supplier signing the subcontract after the customer has signed. Alternatively the supplier may sign the subcontract but make it conditional upon signature of the services agreement with the customer.

If the sub-contractor is an existing supplier of the customer or has been selected by the customer, additional issues regarding the supplier taking over responsibility for the sub-contractor, and these issues are discussed in section 34.8.

17.4   Supplier consortium

A supplier consortium will usually involve either a contractual joint venture or a joint venture vehicle.

17.4.1   *Contractual joint venture*

If the supplier comprises a consortium of two or more suppliers, then the customer will usually want the suppliers to accept joint and severable liability for their actions under a contractual joint venture.

17.4.2   *Joint venture vehicle*

Chapter 19 describes the different forms of joint venture vehicle and the advantages and disadvantages of each model.

17.5   Mutuals

There has recently been a lot of discussion about mutuals in the context of the provision of services to public sector bodies. There is no single definition of what constitutes a mutual in the context of the provision of services to public sector bodies. No definition was given in the Open Public Services White Paper,[1] and there is no definition in legislation. However, a mutual is generally expected to have the following characteristics:

---

[1]   July 2011, see *http://www.openpublicservices.cabinetoffice.gov.uk/* [Accessed 2 November 2012].

(a) **Purpose**: the mutual will deliver a collective benefit, invariably an improvement in public services;

(b) **Employee ownership**: the employees delivering the service will also, to some extent, share in the ownership of the service provider; and

(c) **Stakeholder involvement**: one or more groups of stakeholders will participate in the governance of the service provider. This could be through their participation in its membership, a right to membership of the board or through advisory committees that advise and support the board.

Any of the vehicles mentioned in section 19.3 can be adapted and used as a mutual.

Chapter 18

Different Customer Models and Shared Services

18.1   Outline

Chapter 17 deals with different supplier models that are relevant where there is more than one supplier, including multi-sourcing, prime contractor, supplier consortium and joint venture models. This chapter deals with different customer models that are relevant where there is more than one customer, including multi-sourcing, prime customer, customer consortium and joint venture models. Clearly services arrangements may involve both multiple suppliers and multiple customers, in which case both Chapters 17 and 18 will be relevant.

18.2   Relationship between different customers

It is becoming more common for various different customers to enter into services arrangements with one or more suppliers, for example as companies and public sector bodies set up shared services arrangements or international companies enter into group-wide arrangements. The question arises as to how the different relationships should be structured.

18.2.1   Types of relationship

There are various different models that can be adopted, but all can be classified into four basic approaches. The classification is similar to that for supplier models:

(a)   the customers can enter into multiple agreements with the supplier or suppliers ("multi-sourcing"). This can include framework and panel arrangements;

(b)   one customer can enter into the agreement with the supplier on behalf of the other customers ("prime customer");

(c)   the customers can jointly enter into an agreement with the supplier

161

("customer consortium"), and this may include the customer establishing a joint venture vehicle; or

(d) the customers and the supplier can form a joint venture ("joint venture"). Joint ventures are dealt with in Chapter 19.

18.2.2   Factors to be taken into account

In practice, customers are often worried about entering into shared services arrangements. In particular they may be worried about whether they will get the services they want or whether they will lose control over the services or their business or they may be concerned about how the collaboration restricts them and how long they will need to be committed for. Table 34 describes the different factors to be taken into account in deciding which of the above customer approaches to adopt to deal with these concerns.

Table 34 Multi-sourcing, prime customer or customer consortium

Control
Prime customer models are particularly appropriate where there is a natural leader among the customers such as where one customer is materially larger than the others or is acting on behalf of the other customers (for example the head quarters of an international company acting on behalf of the rest of the group).
Multi-sourcing or customer consortium models are appropriate where the customers see themselves as having equal control over the arrangements.
Extent of collaboration
Multi-sourcing arrangements are appropriate where independent customers are only co-operating or collaborating during the procurement phase, to save procurement costs. Sometimes customers start out with the intention of collaborating on the procurement only and then develop a closer relationship that results in more collaborative working later.
Prime customer and customer consortium models are particularly appropriate where the collaboration involves the procurement and the delivery phase.
Extent of standardisation of services
Multi-sourcing arrangements are appropriate where there is limited standardisation of the services between the different customers.
Prime customer and customer consortium models are particularly appropriate where the services to be provided to the customers are to be standardised in whole or in part.
Taxation
Customers must obtain expert taxation advice before choosing a customer model, particularly where the customers are in different countries (for example they are part of a group) and the company is deciding whether to enter into one agreement on behalf of the group or separate local agreements between each local customer and each local supplier.

18.3   Services or collaboration agreement

Where the arrangements involve more than one customer, then the parties will need to deal with various additional issues either in the services agreement or (where the issue does not affect the supplier) in a separate collaboration agreement. These issues are listed in Table 35.

Table 35 Services or collaboration agreement

Business plan: How will the parties document the business objectives and measure the success of the collaboration? Will the customers prepare a business plan and benefit realisation plan?

Charges and costs: How will the supplier's charges be divided between the customers? How will adjustments in the charges be divided between customers? What additional costs will the customers incur as a result of the collaboration and how will these costs be borne? What additional costs will the customers incur on termination and how will these costs be borne?

Services: To what extent will the nature or scope of the services be standardised or bespoke for each customer? Will there be a minimum scope or standard of service to be provided. For example, if the customer is a company with different divisions or is a multinational group of companies, will the scope and level of service be mandated centrally to ensure standardisation throughout the group? If different customers require different services, then the customers will need to consider the best way to describe the services. It may be helpful to describe a catalogue of services that customers select.

Transformation: Will the customers agree transformation plans and transformation projects?

Opting out and withdrawal: Will individual customers be entitled to opt out of individual transformation projects and if so, on what grounds? Will individual customers be entitled to withdraw from individual transformation projects and if so, on what grounds?

Governance: Will the customers need additional governance structures, such as a shared services board, to discuss issues that affect more than one customer? What additional records and reports will need to be produced?

Change: How will changes be approved and when will changes need the approval of more than one customer? What will happen if a company leaves the group?

Liability: Will the customers be jointly liable to the supplier or severally liable? What will happen if the actions of one customer cause damage to the other customer or customers? Will there be any limitation upon the liability of one customer to the other customer?

Warranties: What warranties will the customers need to give each other?

Assets: What will be the arrangements regarding ownership, licence and refresh of assets?

Intellectual property rights: Who will own intellectual property rights developed by the supplier as part of the services?

Confidentiality: What information and data will be shared between the parties and what information and data must be kept confidential to the specific customer?

ARD: How will ARD work on the commencement and on termination? The implications of ARD may be complicated in this situation and the customers should ensure that they take specialist employment and pensions advice early on in the process.

Termination: Will customers be able to leave the arrangement before expiry? If so – on what grounds? What will happen on termination? Will customers be able to suspend the participation of one of the customers from the arrangement? Will the supplier be able to terminate the agreement with regard to a specific customer? If so – on what grounds?

Dispute resolution: Which dispute resolution procedures will be appropriate?

18.4   Public sector procurement issues

The public procurement rules mean that there are relatively rigid structures through which shared services can be delivered. The Public Contracts Regulations 2006 (SI 2006/5) (as amended) can apply even when both the supplier of services and the customer are public sector entities – there is no blanket exception to the rules simply because the supplier is also a public body. This strict application of the procurement rules created barriers to the effective delivery of shared service models where one public authority agrees to provide a service to other public authorities. Back office functions are particularly amenable to this form of shared service, for example one local authority might agree to provide the information services functions for its neighbouring authorities but if the authority supplying the service simply entered into a contract with the purchasing authority there is a real danger that this arrangement could infringe the public procurement rules. However, rulings from the Court of Justice of the European Union have recognised two specific circumstances in which public to public contracting is permissible without undertaking a prior public procurement exercise.

18.4.1   The in-house or "Teckal" exception.

The Court of Justice has recognised that where two or more public authorities establish a company, the procurement rules do not apply to the award of the contract to the company by the public authority members if the following three criteria are satisfied:

(a) **Ownership** – The company is wholly owned by all of the public authority members.
(b) **Control** – The company is jointly controlled by all of the public authority members (where the control is similar to how an authority might exercise control over an internal department).
(c) **Services to members** – The essential part of the company's activities is to provide services to the public authority members. The company cannot provide services to other parties.

This exception to the rules is known as the "in-house exception" or the "Teckal exception", after the case where the Court of Justice first established the doctrine.

18.4.2   Co-operation for the benefit of the public

The Court of Justice has more recently also determined that the procurement rules do not apply to the award of a certain type of contract between public authorities, subject to the following two conditions:

(a) **Co-operation** – The "public to public" contract must have as its objective co-operation between the public authorities for the benefit of the public. The contract in question must involve deeper co-operation than simply a contract for the performance of a task in return for remuneration; it will usually involve a common aim and joint performance of the task in question. It may also involve the merging of the personnel dedicated to the service at each public authority.

(b) **Recovery of costs** – Guidance from the European Commission[1] also suggests that such contracts will not generally involve a "profit" being made the supplying authority – the contract would usually simply involve the re-imbursement of costs.

---

[1] *http://ec.europa.eu/internal_market/publicprocurement/partnerships/cooperation/index_en.htm* [Accessed 10 September 2012]

Chapter 19

Joint ventures between the Supplier and the Customer

19.1   Outline

Chapters 17, 18 and 19 deal with different contractual models that may be adopted by the customer and supplier. Chapter 17 deals with situations where there are multiple suppliers. Chapter 18 deals with the situation where there are multiple customers. This chapter deals with the situation where the customer and the supplier (or the customers and the suppliers) form a joint venture.

A structural joint venture, where the parties set up an independent joint venture vehicle, could amount to a concentration or merger subject to the relevant merger control rules. See Chapter 33 for a full explanation of the circumstances in which a joint venture may require clearance from the competition authorities.

19.2   Advantages and disadvantages of joint ventures

19.2.1   Combining strengths

Joint ventures are particularly appropriate for business process outsourcing and partnering arrangements where both sides have skills to contribute. For example, the customer may have an understanding and experience of a sector in which the supplier wants to provide business process outsourcing services and may have a recognised brand in the relevant sector. The supplier may be able to provide technical IT or business process re-engineering skills and the commercial skills required to sell services to other customers. In practice, these situations are rare.

Unless the customer is contributing special knowledge or experience to the joint venture, the joint venture vehicle, which lacks its parent company's track record, may find it more difficult to win additional third-party business than the supplier unless it is able to also use the supplier's branding.

The parties will need to agree whether the supplier can tender for third-party service contracts in competition with the joint venture vehicle:

(a) If the supplier can tender in competition with the joint venture, then this may undermine the ability of the joint venture to win other business and hence its value to the customer.

(b) If the supplier is prevented from bidding for work in competition with the joint venture, then there will have to be a clear agreement as to what type of work the joint venture will tender for in order to avoid a situation where the joint venture fails to win the business and the supplier may have had a better chance of winning the business but is prevented from bidding.

This explains why the arrangement is more likely to be successful if the customer is contributing some special skill or sector-specific knowledge that gives the joint venture an advantage over the supplier bidding on its own.

Competition law advice will need to be taken in relation to any restrictions on the activities of either the shareholder or the joint venture and as to any merger control or other competition issues which the creation or operation of the joint venture may raise. Note that obligations on controlling shareholders not to compete with the joint venture are likely to be enforceable for the duration of the joint venture – this would be consistent with guidance from the European Commission which states that such restrictions are considered as ancillary to a full–function joint venture under the EU Merger Regulation.[1] See Chapter 33 for more information on the application of the merger control rules to joint ventures.

19.2.2 Costs and business case

19.2.2.1 Set up costs

Corporate joint ventures are more expensive to establish than a straightforward services contract as they will involve the negotiation and agreement of a members agreement and articles of association (in the case of a private company).

19.2.2.2 Ongoing costs

Additional legal, administrative and audit expenses will also be incurred in running the corporate joint venture, but this cost will depend on the existing resource and infrastructure which the parties can offer to the joint venture, for example if seconded staff and existing office space is used, costs can be kept to a minimum.

---

[1] Regulation 139/2004 on the control of concentrations between undertakings OJ L24, 29.1.2004.

19.2.2.3   Value for money

The value-for-money argument in participating in a joint venture will, of course, depend on the strength of the joint venture's business plan and the anticipated annual return to each of the partners. Profits are unlikely to be distributed until all of the vehicle costs and overheads have been met.

The parties will need to agree the percentage of profit that will accrue to each depending upon the investment each makes to the joint venture.

Where the customer is VAT exempt, it may be possible to avoid paying VAT on the charges by "grouping" the customer and user in the same VAT group. However, the grouping rules prevent VAT grouping unless one grouped company is controlled by or controls another, or another person controls both of them, and anti-avoidance rules further tighten the requirements to prevent artificial grouping.

19.2.3   Business outcome-based charging[2]

A joint venture approach may enable the parties to link the success of the joint venture business to the service charge that the customer pays to the joint venture for the services that it receives. For example, the customer may extract its profit share from the joint venture by way of an annual reduction in the services charge. However, this can become complicated and it would be advisable to keep the joint venture arrangement and the customer's service contract with the joint venture vehicle at arm's length to avoid conflicts of interest (as customer and shareholder). This is even more important where the customer is a public sector body (see section 19.5 below).

19.2.4   Obtaining funding

Funding arrangements for a joint venture vehicle can be complex. The parties will normally agree the initial funding required for any joint venture vehicle, but funding requirements can often change dramatically during the life of the joint venture vehicle.

It is not uncommon to agree that any further funding requirements, whether equity or debt, are subject to agreement by all of the joint venture partners.

In some joint ventures, there can be quite complex funding obligations agreed by the parties, to the effect that if the management of the joint venture vehicle (who would obviously normally include representatives of the customer and supplier) agree that funding is required, they will ask the

---

[2]   See Chapter 1 for an explanation of the term "business outcome-based charging".

members to provide it. If one of the members agrees to provide the funding they can either bind in the other member or members to provide funding on a similar basis, or if they do not do so, they have the ability to dilute the interests of the member(s) who do not provide the funding.

It is also not uncommon to have milestones against which further funding is committed by the members of the joint venture vehicle.

If substantial investment in the services is required, it may be easier to obtain external finance if the assets and revenue streams are ring fenced in a separate company over which the funder can take security.

19.2.5   *Transparency of charges*

The joint venture approach can result in a more transparent arrangement between the parties. However, the question arises as to which party manages the financial systems and accounts of the joint venture. It is normally the case that all members of the joint venture can ask for copies of any financial information regarding the joint venture. So, a member is effectively able to perform its own audit on the joint venture vehicle.

19.2.6   *Liability*

Responsibility under a joint venture is complicated. It may be more difficult for the customer to enforce its rights against a joint venture that it partly owns then under a standard services arrangement. For this reason it may be seen as a lower-risk approach from the supplier's perspective.

19.2.7   *Conflicts of interest*

If a corporate joint venture is used, conflicts of interests can arise. For example, if a customer (or supplier) were to appoint its contract manager as its nominated director to the board of the corporate joint venture, that can create problems. That individual would, as a matter of corporate law, owe a duty to the company to promote the success of the company for the benefit of its members as a whole (effectively to act in the best interests of the company). That duty will not be mitigated by any duty that the contract manager owes to the customer as its employer. So, a difficult situation could arise if the contract manager/director was required, in his role as director of the company, to approve something (for example, pursuing an action against the customer for an alleged breach of contract) that was obviously for the benefit of the joint venture company even though it was not for the benefit of the customer.

It is therefore advisable for the customer to keep its role as customer and its role as shareholder at arm's length, as far as it is able, for example by ensuring the contract manager is not the same person as its nominated director on the board of the joint venture vehicle.

19.2.8   Management time

Joint venture vehicles may be complicated to establish, as a members agreement (either a shareholders agreement or a partnership agreement as applicable) will need to be negotiated and agreed. It is sometimes argued that this process can divert attention from agreeing the details of the services to be provided to the customer and other key issues. However, this should be taken into consideration when planning the procurement process and timetable. The more effort that is put in at an early stage in agreeing the joint venture arrangements, the more robust the arrangements normally are, and the better the parties understand their role in relation to the joint venture. That clarity often helps to define the joint venture and give it a clear role.

Ultimately, whether a joint venture will represent value for money in the long term will depend upon the strength of its business plan, and providing proper management time and effort to getting this right is often overlooked by both parties in their eagerness to get a deal done.

19.2.9   Control

Joint ventures involve a more collaborative management style. However, one of the parties will usually own a controlling share. Public sector customers will often only take a minority share, limiting their input to significant decisions and not the day-to-day running of the business.

A minority shareholder or member should normally insist upon a number of veto rights being incorporated in the joint venture documentation for the benefit of the minority. So, it would be relatively normal for a minority to be able to veto any changes to the joint venture structure (e.g. the issue of further shares or the transfer out of certain key assets from the joint venture vehicle). It may also be the case that the minority will have a say over key operational matters (e.g. employing senior executives or spending capital sums above a particular limit).

It is also normally the case that a minority will seek protection rights should the majority wish to exit the joint venture. As the minority member has entered into the joint venture agreement with the majority, the minority does not want to find the majority is selling its equity interest in the joint venture vehicle without the consent of the minority. The minority will normally want the status quo to be preserved.

19.2.10 *Termination arrangements*

The parties need to decide what happens on a termination of the joint venture. Termination arrangements are likely to be much more complex where there is a joint venture.

19.2.10.1 *Termination triggers*

As a first step the parties will need to agree what triggers a termination of the joint venture. This would normally occur on the expiry of the relevant project or service provision, and also on a material breach.

19.2.10.2 *Consequences of termination*

Moreover, and perhaps more importantly, the parties need to agree what happens in relation to the joint venture once a termination is triggered. The customer may want the right to buy the shares/interest of the supplier, effectively removing the supplier from the joint venture. It may be that the customer will want to transfer such shares and membership rights to another future supplier. However, this right may undermine the motivation of the supplier to invest in the joint venture; it will not be getting any capital return on the sale of its shares. On the other hand, it may be that the supplier may want the right to buy a customer out in certain circumstances, for example if third party revenue increases.

As an alternative it may be that the parties agree that on termination they take such steps, as are necessary, to liquidate the joint venture vehicle.

The parties will also need to agree what happens to the assets of the joint venture vehicle on a termination. It is not unreasonable for the parties to insist that any assets or rights that they have contributed to the joint venture vehicle on its establishment are returned to them, possibly at no cost or a nominal cost. The parties will need to agree what happens in relation to any assets created or acquired during the life of the joint venture vehicle.

There are obvious additional costs involved in terminating and/or liquidating any joint venture vehicle.

19.2.11 *Staff*

Staff may be reluctant to transfer or be seconded to a joint venture company if they are uncertain as to its future prospects.

19.2.12 Political considerations

A joint venture company may be politically more acceptable to the customer than disposing of its assets.

19.3 Different types of joint ventures

19.3.1 Explanation of different forms of joint venture

19.3.1.1 Contractual joint venture

There are a number of different forms that the joint venture may take. It would be possible, for example, to set up a contractual joint venture. In a contractual joint venture the rights between the supplier and the customer are simply set out in the joint venture contract, and there is no joint venture vehicle involved. Adopting this approach may avoid some of the disadvantages of the joint venture approach described in section 19.2, such as the termination consequences.

19.3.1.2 Joint venture vehicles

If the supplier and the customer decide to set up a joint venture vehicle with each other, this will usually involve the following:

Table 36 Setting up a joint venture vehicle

Setting up the joint venture - The supplier and customer will set up a joint venture vehicle. There are various different forms that the joint venture vehicle can take, as described in section 19.3.2.

Transfer of assets - The customer will transfer the assets (or rights relating to assets) previously used to provide the services to the joint venture vehicle.

Transfer of employees - Employees will be transferred under ARD or seconded to work for the joint venture vehicle either from the customer and/or from the supplier.

Services agreement - The customer will enter into a services agreement with the joint venture vehicle. The customer should consider, where a joint venture vehicle is used, whether guarantees as to the joint venture vehicle's performance are obtained from the supplier.

Supplier's contribution - The supplier may contribute additional assets and investment and may also enter into a services agreement with the joint venture vehicle.

Shares of membership rights - Both parties will have shares or other membership rights in the joint venture vehicle and will agree how any investment will be funded. The precise form of the funding can be complex and will depend upon the structure of the joint venture vehicle, for example, in a corporate joint venture, the funding may take the form of equity (i.e. shares) and/or debt (i.e. loans to the joint venture vehicle).

> **Third party revenue** - In addition to delivering the services to each of the partners, the joint venture vehicle will also then be free to trade and sell services to third parties in order to make a profit for its member partners.

19.3.2   Selecting the right form of joint venture vehicle

19.3.2.1   Taxation implications

There are a number of factors that need to be taken into account when deciding which joint venture vehicle to use, and the rights of the parties in relation to that joint venture vehicle. In particular, tax advice should be sought at an early stage, both in relation to assets going into and out of the joint venture vehicle during its life, and returns from the joint venture vehicle. It will also be necessary for the parties to decide how they are to receive any return. For example, the supplier could receive its return on a particular project through dividends paid by the joint venture vehicle, or through a services contract/sub-contract with the joint venture vehicle.

19.3.2.2   Advantage and disadvantages of different forms of joint venture vehicle

If a joint venture vehicle is used rather than a contractual joint venture, there are a number of different options that are available. The table below sets out some of the options, and the advantages and disadvantages of each (depending on the viewpoint of the parties, some of the disadvantages might be seen as advantages, and vice versa).

Table 37 Advantages and disadvantages of different forms of joint ventures

Joint venture vehicle	Advantages	Disadvantages
Company limited by shares (CLS)	- Limited liability - Flexible governance structure: can accommodate stakeholder participation - Separate legal personality	- Obliged to file financial information and an annual return (associated annual costs) - Termination process/costs
Company limited by guarantee (CLG)	- Limited liability - Flexible governance structure - Separate legal personality	- No share capital, so usually only used where no sharing of profit between members is anticipated - Obliged to file financial information (associated annual costs) - Termination process/costs

Community interest company (incorporated as a CLS or CLG)	- Limited liability - Separate legal personality - Light touch regulation (compared to charities)	- Activities must be carried on for the benefit of the community - An asset lock applies: assets must be transferred at market value, or otherwise to another community interest company or other asset locked body - Restrictions on the ability to pay dividends
Charity	- Limited liability	- Not for profit - Highly regulated - Less flexibility on structure/management
Community benefit societies	- Purpose: benefit the community (both members and non-members)	- Voting is usually on a one member one vote basis - Regulated by the Financial Services Authority
Unincorporated associations	- Limited regulation, e.g. no obligation to file accounts publicly	- No separate legal identity - Personal liability for the management committee
Partnerships	- Flexible structure - Can make profits and distribute them to partners	- No separate legal identity (and hence liability issues)
Limited liability partnerships	- Limited liability - Flexible structure	- Obliged to file financial information and an annual return (associated annual costs)
Charitable incorporated organisations (not yet available)	- Limited liability - Separate legal personality	- Must be a charity (numerous restrictions apply)

In reality, most English law joint venture vehicles take the form of a private company limited by shares (CLS). This is the most common form of company used in the UK, and has the benefit of familiarity. If the company is designed as one that is not meant to make a profit, then a private company limited by guarantee (CLG) may be considered. The other forms of entity (set out in Table 35) can be used from time to time, although they are not as commonly used as a CLS or a CLG.

19.4 Issues to be addressed

Whatever form of joint venture vehicle is used, there are a number of key questions:

(a) What is each of the parties (customer and supplier) proposing to provide to or give to the joint venture vehicle?

(b) How is the joint venture vehicle to be managed?

(c) How is the joint venture vehicle to be funded?

(d) How are returns (if any) to be channelled through the joint venture?

(e) How can a termination be triggered? And what happens on a termination?

(f) Will the joint venture amount to a merger/concentration that is subject to merger control? See Chapter 33 for a consideration of competition law issues.

19.5   Additional considerations for public/private joint venture vehicles

Joint ventures between the public and private sector are becoming more commonplace as the government continues to encourage public bodies to find new ways to make the most of public assets and achieve efficiency saving targets.[3] Local government in particular has been exploiting its powers to trade[4] and invest[5] in commercial activity for some time by taking equity investments in joint venture companies. The Localism Act 2011 gives local authorities even wider powers to undertake commercial activity.

Where one party to a joint venture of this kind is a public body, there are a number of additional considerations that must be taken into account by the parties:

(a) **Procurement law**: the establishment of a joint venture with a private company is not itself subject to the public procurement regulations;[6] however, the regulations will apply to the grant of the service contract to the joint venture and so a procurement which has been advertised in OJEU will be necessary. In practice, authorities frequently advertise seeking a joint venture partner and the award of the service contract in

---

[3] See HM Treasury, *Infrastructure procurement: delivering long-term value* in particular Section 2 "The Broadening Range of Procurement Approaches" at *http://www.hm-treasury.gov.uk/d/bud08__procurement__533.pdf.* [Accessed 10 September 2012]
[4] See s.95 of the Local Government Act 2003.
[5] See s.12 of the Local Government Act 2003.
[6] See the Public Contracts Regulations 2006 (SI 2006/5) and the Utilities Contracts Regulations 2006 (SI 2006/6) as applicable.

the same OJEU advertisement.[7] The public body will not be able to guarantee any future contracts to the joint venture vehicle unless such work was envisaged by the original procurement.

(b) **State aid**: the terms of the joint venture must be structured to ensure that there is no element of subsidy or aid to the vehicle, but rather the agreement is on full arm's-length commercial terms in order to avoid state aid to the vehicle and the supplier partner.

(c) **Powers**: the public sector body must be clear upon the powers on which it will be relying to enter into the joint venture.

(d) **Accounting implications**: the parties will need to understand any regulatory and accounting requirements which may apply to the vehicle as a result of the public sector's involvement.[8]

19.6 Conclusion

The additional expense and effort involved in setting up and managing a joint venture mean that it should only be adopted where substantial benefits can be obtained as a result and those results cannot be achieved by alternative simpler means, (for example, by the supplier investing in shares in the customer organisation or the charges being calculated on a risk/reward basis). A compromise may be to establish a contractual joint venture, where the service agreement includes partnering elements.

---

[7] See Commission Interpretative Communication on the Application of Community Law on Public Procurement and Concessions to Institutionalised Public Private Partnerships (IPPP) 5 February 2008 C(2007)6661.

[8] Consider the application of the Local Government and Housing Act 1989 where the public body is a local authority for the purposes of that Act and also the CIPFA Code of Practice on Local Authority Accounting. If the public body is a non-departmental public body, see relevant guidance from Treasury and the Office of National Statistics which will classify the vehicle as either public or private sector for the purposes of government accounting, depending upon the level of public sector control.

Part 5

Charging

Chapter 20

The Charging Regime

20.1   Outline

Chapters 17, 18 and 19 describe the different structures of the services arrangement, which can have a fundamental impact upon the charging mechanism. This chapter deals with issues relating to charging. It describes common charging regimes for the services. There are various ways in which the charges under a sourcing arrangement can be calculated, determined in part by the extent to which the supplier accepts responsibility for achievement of the customer's business objectives (business outcome risk profile), the provision of the services (service output risk profile) or the provision of resources (input risk profile).[1] This is a crucial area for customer and supplier, as, if they make mistakes, it can have a major impact upon the value that the arrangement has to them.

20.2   Risk/reward

There has been particular interest recently in risk/reward payment structures, as parties seek ways to align the objectives of the parties and maximise the benefits that the customer obtains under the arrangement.

20.2.1   *Appropriate if supplier is responsible for business outcomes*

If the supplier is responsible for business outcomes, then a risk/reward charging mechanism will be appropriate. In this situation, the payment mechanism will involve the supplier being paid charges that reflect the business benefit that the customer receives as a result of the services, for example, that the customer's bills are sent out (and hence are paid) earlier. The charging model must take into account the fact that the customer's business objectives will change during the term of the arrangement.

---

[1]   This distinction is described in Chapter 1.

A business outcome-based charging regime is particularly appropriate for transformational outsourcing arrangements where the purpose of the sourcing arrangement is to effect a change in the customer's organisation. The customer may favour the mechanism, if it considers that it will ensure that the supplier will only be paid if the customer receives the benefit it seeks. It may also be effective in encouraging a closer relationship between the supplier, with the supplier being seen as demonstrating confidence in its services and its commitment to the customer and its business objectives.

20.2.2   *Not appropriate if difficult to measure or demonstrate*

The risk/reward charging mechanism will not be appropriate if it is difficult to measure or demonstrate achievement of the specific business objective that the customer is endeavouring to achieve.

20.2.3   *Not appropriate if supplier lacks control over outcomes*

The supplier may be reluctant to accept a risk/reward payment mechanism if it does not have full control over the manner in which the benefit is to be achieved, for example, if the customer is seeking improvements in its margin—various factors will influence this (e.g. the economic climate).

In practice, it will be rare that the supplier will have full control over the achievement of the customer's business benefit. Usually, external events will affect the achievement of the benefits. At the very least, the supplier and customer will usually need to co-operate to achieve the benefits, for example the supplier will make recommendations that the customer will need to implement. The supplier may suggest that it should receive the payment if its recommendations would have achieved the benefit, but the customer decides not to implement them. This may be unsatisfactory from the customer's perspective if it pays for the services but does not receive the benefit it desires. It also begs the question as to why the customer decides not to implement the recommendations. The customer may want to limit the obligation to pay to circumstances in which it acts unreasonably in failing to implement the recommendations.

20.2.4   *Not appropriate if payment too high*

In practice, dissatisfaction may also be caused even if the customer achieves its desired benefit, if the payment to the supplier is seen as being unjustifiably high. The customer may, therefore, want to cap the potential benefits that the supplier may receive.

20.2.5   Not appropriate during final years

Lastly, the risk/reward payment mechanism may be impractical as a mechanism for ensuring that both parties contribute towards new capital expenditure during the final few years of the agreement if there is insufficient time left during which the supplier will be able to recover a return on its investment before expiry of the agreement. A similar issue arises if the agreement is terminated early. See Chapter 28 for a discussion of this issue.

20.2.6   Appropriate with other charging mechanisms

The risk/reward payment mechanism may be helpful if it is used with other payment mechanisms so that it acts as a bonus and incentivises the supplier to achieve the benefit but does not assume that the supplier has sole responsibility for achievement of the business benefit.

20.2.7   Share of profits on exploiting assets

Sometimes the charging mechanism provides for the customer to receive a share of profits generated by the supplier in exploiting assets or premises transferred to or made available by the customer for a nominal amount. This is properly regarded as part of the arrangement by which the customer makes the assets and premises available to the supplier rather than part of the charging regime for the services. Accordingly, this issue is dealt with in Chapter 16.

20.2.8   Guaranteed costs savings

During the recent downturn, some suppliers have undertaken to guarantee that the charges will provide the customer with a specified cost saving, when compared with previous costs or charges.

20.3   Fixed price

20.3.1   *Appropriate for service output deals*[2]

If the supplier is responsible for the provision of the service (service output risk profile) then a fixed-price charging mechanism is appropriate.

Calculating the charges on a fixed-price basis may be advantageous for the customer and the supplier. From the customer's perspective, this charging regime will mean that the charges it will pay will be predictable. From the supplier's perspective, it will receive a predictable revenue stream; it has control of its costs, it takes the risk that its cost base will increase and receives the benefit if it can reduce its cost base. Because the supplier takes the risk of increases in its cost base, the charges are likely to be more expensive than if they were calculated on a cost plus basis as the supplier will usually increase its charges by a premium to cover the risk of increases in its cost base.

The fixed-price charging regime is straightforward for the customer and supplier to administer for budgetary and other purposes.

The charging regime incentivises the supplier to reduce its costs so as to improve its margin. Therefore, in fixed-price charging arrangements it is important for the customer to ensure that its service description is reasonably complete—otherwise there is a risk that it will not receive the services it needs. From the supplier's perspective, in fixed-price charging arrangements, it is crucial that the boundaries of the services are defined clearly.

The customer does not have price transparency in fixed-price charging mechanisms and so it may want to agree a breakdown of the charges so that it can understand which elements of the services are most expensive and amend the services accordingly or an open book arrangement so that it can investigate what margin the supplier is making.

20.3.2   *Fixed price linked to volume adjustments*

From the customer's perspective, the disadvantage of this charging regime is that it may be tied in to paying the fixed price even if the volume of the services decreases in the future. Equally, from the supplier's perspective, it may be unable to increase the charges if the volume of the services increases.

Therefore, if it is likely that the volume of services will change, the charges should be calculated in one of two different ways:

(a)   On a fixed-price basis *per transaction*, for example per claim processed,

---

[2]   "Service output" deals are described in greater details in Chapter 1.

or alternative methods may be used to ensure that the customer pays for the volume of services that it uses. However, the customer should be aware of the behaviour this charging regime will encourage. Thus, it could be argued that any charging regime which involves the supplier being paid for the number of help-desk calls it deals with relating to problems with equipment or premises being maintained is likely to encourage the supplier to refrain from carrying out scheduled maintenance or problem management/root cause analysis to prevent problems from occurring.

(b) On the basis of an overall fixed charge linked to the provision of certain volumes of services. The parties may agree, in advance, pricing variations that will apply for certain changes in the volumes of the services, for example the number of users receiving the services or number of servers being maintained.[3] They may agree that no changes will occur in the charges until the volumes increase or decrease by more than a specific figure, for example 10 or 20 per cent.

20.3.3   Volume adjustment procedure

If volume adjustments are likely to occur on a regular basis, the parties may agree a procedure for adjusting the charges on a regular quarterly or annual basis. If the parties agree that the charges will be adjusted retrospectively, the customer may ask the supplier to provide regular reports showing the charges it is incurring, so that the customer can budget for the charges. Equally, it may be appropriate for the customer to give the supplier notice of future changes in volumes so that the supplier can plan for these.

From the customer's perspective, it is usually advantageous to agree charging variations for the possible changes in the volumes of services before the agreement is signed, as its bargaining power is usually greater at this stage. (See Chapter 25.)

20.4   Pay as you go

20.4.1   PFI payment mechanism

A related charging mechanism to the fixed-price charging regime is that which was employed in PFI contracts where the charges were payable on a fixed-price basis. However, there were two differences, as described in the following paragraphs.

---

[3]   If the charges are to be varied depending upon the number of servers maintained, the parties need to be clear as to whether they mean physical or virtual servers.

20.4.1.1 Delayed commencement

In a PFI arrangement, the customer does not start paying for the services until the supplier starts to provide them. This means that (unless the supplier is delayed by the customer or other specifically agreed "compensation events") the supplier takes the risk that it is late in providing the services. If the agreement provides for a definite expiry date (rather than the contract expiring a specific period after the supplier starts to provide the services), then any delay by the supplier will reduce the total income received by the supplier. This will be a particular problem where the supplier is spreading capital costs over the term of the contract, as it usually is in a PFI arrangement.

20.4.1.2 Deductions in the charges

Also, after the supplier has started to provide the services, if it fails to provide them in part or totally in a particular month in accordance with the contract requirements, it will suffer deductions in the charges, which means that the supplier will not be paid in full and may not get paid anything that month.

Chapter 44 describes the historic PFI approach in the UK, explains how it has fallen out of favour in the UK, whilst being actively adopted outside the UK.

20.4.2 Non-PFI utility payment mechanisms

A similar pricing mechanism, which may be appropriate for certain types of services (e.g. cloud computing models[4]), allows customers to use services when they need them and to pay only for the services they use. This means that the customer would not need to pay up-front transition costs to enable the supplier to fund the setting up of the services. However, in this situation, customers must ensure that they accurately assess their future needs so that they do not become liable for unexpected increases in charges when volumes increase.

20.5 Cost or cost plus

If the supplier is responsible for inputs only, then a cost plus or resources-based charging mechanism will be appropriate. Cost plus is described here; resource-based charging is described in section 20.6 below.

---

[4] See section 1.2 for a detailed description of cloud computing models.

20.5.1   When appropriate

A cost plus charging regime means that the charges are calculated on the basis of the supplier's actual costs plus an agreed margin, calculated as a percentage of the costs. This may be a particularly useful charging mechanism if the costs of providing the services are likely to change so frequently that it will not be practical for the parties to commit to fixed prices, for example in a vehicle support agreement.

In any event, the parties will need to define which costs will be reimbursed and which will not. For example, the customer will not want to pay additional costs that are incurred because the supplier did not follow agreed service management procedures. This is an important area, as if the costs are not clearly defined, this is likely to lead to disputes throughout the agreement.

The advantage of this charging regime from the customer's perspective is that the customer does not pay an excessive margin to the supplier.

The advantage from the supplier's perspective is that this charging mechanism is low risk, for the supplier, as the supplier is guaranteed to receive charges that cover its costs and its margin.

The disadvantage from the customer's perspective is that the customer may not get value for money, as the supplier has no incentive to reduce its costs. On the contrary, the supplier has an incentive to increase its costs if the margin is a percentage of the costs. This problem may be mitigated by the parties agreeing a capped margin or a fixed margin if this is acceptable to the supplier.

This charging mechanism does not incentivise good performance and so the customer will want to ensure that it includes a suitable service level and service credit regime.

Another disadvantage from the customer's perspective is that it does not have price certainty. To enable the customer to budget for the charges, the supplier may agree to warn the customer when certain spending limits are reached or the parties may agree a target budget and incentives for meeting the target and service credits for failure to meet the target.

The charging mechanism is also not ideal from the supplier's perspective as the supplier has little or no opportunity to maximise its margin.

20.5.2   Use with other charging mechanisms

Even where the cost-plus mechanism is not attractive as a charging mechanism for the overall services agreement, it may be appropriate for certain elements. For example, the parties may agree that the supplier will manage certain third-party contracts on behalf of the customer. These may or may not be transferred to the supplier. In either case, the parties may agree that the fees paid under these contracts will be passed on to the customer. The agreement should state clearly whether the customer is required to reimburse the supplier for the fees or also to pay an administration fee or a margin (in addition to the fees themselves). In this sort of arrangement, the customer takes the risk that the fees charged by the third-party supplier increase, but the customer will benefit if the fees are reduced.

20.6   Resource based[5]

An alternative approach for a services arrangement that has an input-based liability profile is for the charges to be calculated on a resource basis. For example:

(a)   an IT services agreement may include the provision by the supplier of a basic number of man days of software development consultancy services, which will be paid for at an agreed man-day rate, with additional man days of software development consultancy services being charged at that or another agreed man-day rate; or

(b)   an offshore outsourcing agreement may include the provision of certain services, which the parties assume will require a certain number of full-time equivalents (FTEs). The charges will be calculated based on the number of FTEs multiplied by a rate card covering the relevant types of skills.

The parties may want to clarify how many hours or effective hours (i.e. hours at the desk) the relevant FTEs will be expected to work per annum.

The basic number of man-days or FTEs may be fixed over the term of the agreement or notified to the supplier by the customer or agreed by the parties on a regular basis.

The customer should consider its requirements carefully to ensure that it is not tying itself in to receiving services that it does not use.

---

[5]   If the supplier is going to provide the services in whole or in part from Spain or France, then see Chapter 53 or 59 before including resource-based charging mechanisms.

20.6.1 Flexibility to change resources provided

To preserve its flexibility, the customer may also want to consider whether it needs the right to increase or reduce the basic number of man-days of services or FTEs provided.

The supplier may want to limit the customer's ability to reduce the requirement. This may be achieved by capping any proposed reduction to a specified percentage of the original requirement or by increasing the man-day or FTE rate if the reduction means that different volume-related discounts apply. The supplier may also require a specified period of notice before any change in the number of man-days of services or FTEs.

20.6.2 Notice of requirement for resources

The supplier may want to ensure that the customer gives reasonable notice of its requirement for man-days of services.

20.6.3 Use of resources over the relevant period

The supplier may want the customer to commit to using the man-days of services evenly over the contract year, so that the supplier can assign specific consultants to provide those services.

The customer, on the other hand, may want to preserve its flexibility as much as possible so that, if the man days of services are divided up, resulting in the customer having a specific number each month, quarter or year, it can carry forward unused man days to subsequent months, quarters or years.

20.6.4 Payment for resources not used

The customer will want to avoid paying for man-days of services that it has not received. Thus, it may suggest that the charges are calculated on a pay-as-you-use basis. The supplier may not agree to this if it is granting the customer the benefit of certain preferential rates for the services on the basis that the customer will request the minimum level of services. However, the supplier will usually agree that the customer will not be required to pay for services which it has requested but which the supplier has failed to provide.

20.7 Charging assumptions

The supplier may also want to state that the charges are calculated on the basis of specified pricing assumptions. Sometimes the supplier may want to link the charges to pricing assumptions because it has not been given a sufficient opportunity to carry out a due diligence exercise on the services it is to provide. This may arise because to carry out a due diligence exercise would be impractical bearing in mind the scale of the services, or would lead to disruption to the customer's business or undue delay in signing the agreement. This problem was discussed in Chapter 6. In this situation, the supplier will not want to take the risk that information it has been given relating to the services is incorrect or that assumptions that it has made about the type or scope of services it is to provide are inaccurate.

20.7.1   Uncertain charges—the problem for the customer

The inclusion of charging assumptions is a contentious issue. Usually, the customer's business objectives will relate in some form or other to the charges to be payable under the services agreement, with the result that the business case for entering into the services agreement will be undermined if the charges exceed a certain amount—this is particularly true where the charges are calculated on a fixed-price basis. Therefore, the customer will want to know with certainty before the agreement is signed the amount of the charges payable to the supplier. The customer will not want to enter into an agreement where the existence of pricing assumptions means that the supplier can vary the charges payable under the agreement after the contract has been signed. This is particularly so if the customer has enjoyed a good bargaining position before the agreement is signed (e.g. because there are competing suppliers interested in providing the services) which will be reduced on signature of the agreement. There may be a suspicion that the supplier is endeavouring to improve its margin after signature of the agreement.

If this is the case, then it is in the customer's interests to ensure that the supplier is given the opportunity to carry out as much due diligence as is practical and not to agree pricing assumptions that are designed to ensure that the customer bears the risk that the supplier's due diligence has been badly carried out.

20.7.2   When charging assumptions may be appropriate

This does not mean the customer should never agree to link the charges to pricing assumptions. If the supplier is dependent upon information provided by the customer and cannot verify that information independently, unless it can agree some form of relief with the customer then the supplier may be forced to include a risk premium in the charges to cover the additional risk it is taking.

20.8   Risk premium

The discussion about charging assumptions raises the issue of the extent to which the supplier will find it necessary to increase its charges by adding or increasing its risk premium to cover any risk that it is taking, for example:

(a)   the risk that its costs will increase as a result of inflation or otherwise (in circumstances where the charges are fixed price and there is no indexation clause);

(b)   the risk that it will have to pay service credits or liquidated damages—it will assess the risk premium taking into the account its evaluation of the likelihood that it will be able to meet the necessary service levels or implementation deadline;

(c)   the risk that it will be in breach of the agreement, for example because the customer will not agree a reasonable force majeure clause or reasonable limitations of liability—it will assess the risk premium taking into account its evaluation of the likelihood that it will be in breach of contract; and

(d)   other risks that it takes over in signing the agreement, for example the risk that it will have to pay redundancy costs in respect of transferring staff.

"Risk premium" is taken to mean a contingency pool that is added to the charges to cover potential risks such as those described above. The supplier will usually calculate the risk premium taking into account the financial impact of the risk and the likelihood of it occurring.

There are three points to make about risk premiums, from the customer's perspective:

(a)   The important issue is for the customer to understand if the supplier is being forced to add or increase its normal risk premium and to satisfy itself that it provides value for money. In some cases, it may result in the customer deciding that it does not present value for money and that it makes more sense for the customer to amend the service levels or other aspects of the agreement so that they are achievable.

(b)   It highlights the importance of the customer organisation ensuring that its negotiation team operates as a team and not in silos; for example, it would be self-defeating if the procurement department were negotiating the services agreement with a view to achieving costs savings for the customer, but the operations department or the legal department agree unrealistic service levels or liability provisions so that the supplier is forced to increase the charges to include a risk premium.

(c)   Whether the supplier includes or increases its normal risk premium and the amount it includes will clearly depend upon whether it is in a competitive tender with other suppliers to provide the services. The supplier will usually endeavour to negotiate the service levels and the agreement so that they are reasonable, so that it does not need to add a risk premium to the charges, particularly if it is in a competitive tender.

20.9   Expenses

The parties should also agree whether the supplier can charge the customer for expenses incurred in providing the services. There are three possible approaches here:

(a)   **Inclusive** - The parties can agree that the supplier will include its expenses in its other charges and cannot charge separately for them. This will be an appropriate approach where the expenses are predictable or are not substantial.

(b)   **Cost basis** - If the fees do involve an element for expenses, the customer may agree to reimburse the supplier for them on a cost basis. In this case the customer may want to agree the type of expenses to be incurred and may want to give its approval before expenses are incurred. Before refunding expenses, it may want the supplier to produce receipts for actual expenditure.

(c)   **Fixed price** - If the fees do involve an element for expenses, the customer may agree to reimburse the supplier for them on a fixed price basis. In this case the customer may want to agree the type of expenses to be incurred and the fixed price to be paid in respect of these and may want to give its approval before expenses are incurred.

Calculation of expenses on a cost or fixed price basis encourages the same behaviour as payment of the charge on a costs or fixed price basis, as discussed earlier on in this chapter.

Reimbursement of expenses is usually treated as part of the consideration for a supply of services for VAT purposes, so that the person reimbursed would ordinarily charge VAT on the amount reimbursed. In practice, where supplier and/or customer are not in a position to recover the VAT in full, consideration may need to be given as to whether the customer should incur the expenses rather than the supplier, particularly if any "mark up" is or is treated as being charged by the supplier.

Even where VAT is not an issue, it may make sense for the customer to incur the expenses, for example where it can achieve greater discounts for hotels.

20.10   Inflation

The parties will need to agree how inflation will be dealt with. There are three possible approaches that can be taken.

20.10.1   Fixed-price charges

The customer can expect the supplier to include the risk of inflation in its charges. In this situation the supplier will usually build into its prices a figure for anticipated inflation. The supplier will take the risk that the actual inflation over the term of the agreement is more than that anticipated by the supplier. The customer will take the risk that inflation is less than the supplier anticipated.

20.10.2   Charges are indexed

Alternatively, the parties can agree that the charges will be indexed using an appropriate index. The parties may agree to break the charges down into the percentage of costs relating to, for example, salaries, and the percentage of costs relating to assets. They may then agree that the salary costs will be linked to a salaries-based index and the assets linked to an assets-based index. The charges may be directly linked to the change in the index or may be linked to the change in the index less x per cent (or indeed plus x per cent).

20.10.3   Compromise between the two

Lastly, the parties can agree a compromise between the two approaches above, for example the supplier can take the risk of a certain level of inflation, but retain the right to increase its charges if inflation is greater than a specified amount or the parties can agree to index the charges subject to a cap.

20.10.4   The relevant index

When considering which index to use, the parties should bear in mind that, in June 2003, the Bank of England decided that its inflation target is to be set by reference to the Consumer Price Index (CPI; previously the Harmonised Index of Consumer Prices) rather than the Retail Prices Index (RPI) or RPI excluding mortgage interest (RPIX). The CPI measures inflation each month in the European Monetary area as a whole and individually measures and compares each Member State. CPI differs from RPI in several respects. For example, CPI excludes various items of housing costs (e.g. council tax, mortgage interest payments and buildings insurance), which are included in RPI. Therefore, the two indices may well produce different numbers in terms of inflation and accordingly result in different price changes under indexation provisions in contracts.

The Office for National Statistics will continue to publish the RPI. However, as official inflation will come to be measured by reference to CPI, the parties will need to decide which is more appropriate (or indeed whether another index may be more suitable).

20.11   Exchange rate

In addition to considering the implication of inflation upon the charges, the parties will (where relevant) need to consider the currency in which the charges will be payable and who will bear the risk of any fluctuations in foreign currency rates.

20.12   Minimum charge

Section 20.3 above mentioned the possibility that the charges may be reduced if the volume of services is reduced or that the charges may be calculated on the basis of the volume of services used. Section 20.6 above mentioned that the customer may want to reduce the amount of man-days of resources it has ordered from the supplier. Both of these situations mean that the supplier will bear the risk that its income stream will reduce if volumes fall. The supplier may be more willing to provide the customer with this level of flexibility if the customer commits to an overall minimum commitment of revenue.

Another factor that will influence the supplier's willingness to accept the risk that its income stream will reduce if volumes fall is whether it is given the exclusive right to provide the relevant services or resources. It will usually be unwilling to take the risk that the volumes will fall because the customer has ordered the services or resources from another supplier, particularly if it has had to invest in providing the services, for example by taking over staff or assets from the customer.

20.13   Breakdown of the charges

The customer may want the supplier to provide a detailed breakdown of the charges between the different service elements, so that it can reassure itself that the charges are reasonable. This will also be necessary if the customer wants to benchmark different service elements (see Chapter 23 for a description of benchmarking) or to terminate different service elements (see Chapter 26 for a discussion of termination in part). The customer may also want to see a breakdown of the charges to help it to understand how charges for changes in the services will be calculated (see Chapter 25 for details of change management).

20.14   Payment profile

20.14.1   Profiling of the charges

Apart from delaying payment of the charges until the supplier starts to provide the services (as described in section 20.4 above), there may be other reasons why the charges payable by the customer may not reflect the costs incurred by the supplier during the relevant period:

(a)   It is not unusual for the supplier to incur set-up costs at the beginning of the arrangement in preparing for the provision of the services. These fees may be payable in a lump-sum transition, or development charge payable in advance or on completion of the transition or development. Sometimes, however, the making of the transition charge by the customer would result in the customer paying more for the services in the first years than it had previously paid for its in-house services. This may be politically unacceptable for the customer organisation.

(b)   Equally, during the term of the agreement, the supplier may need to make specific additional investment so that it can continue to provide the services, for example if it needs to replace obsolete equipment or to relocate from a particular site on expiry of the lease.

In both of these circumstances, the supplier may agree to profile its payments so that they are spread over the term of the agreement, with the customer paying a similar charge each year of the agreement. If this results in payments being delayed, then the supplier will usually also need to recover the cost of financing the investment. If it results in payments being made early, then the supplier will usually grant the customer a reduction to reflect the early payment.

20.14.2   *Implication for termination or change*

When the agreement is changed or terminated, the parties will need to bear in mind the profiling of the payments. Thus, for example, if the agreement is terminated midway through its term, after the supplier has made an investment in the services but before the customer has paid the charges due for that investment, then the supplier may want the customer to pay a termination charge covering the unrecovered investment costs.

There are two ways that the termination charge can be calculated: on the basis of demonstrable unrecovered investment costs or as a fixed termination charge. The advantage of the latter is that it is a certain amount. If, however, the termination charge is to be calculated on this basis, the customer will need to ensure, if the investment concerned is the investment in assets, that it does not pay for the assets twice. This would happen, for example, if the customer agrees to pay a fixed termination charge but also pays a separate amount to buy the assets from the supplier.

If the termination charge is to be calculated as a fixed charge, then the parties will need to remember to update the amount of the charge if relevant changes to the services and the charges are agreed during the term of the agreement.

The customer may need the right to pay the termination charge, whether calculated as a fixed amount or otherwise, in instalments.

20.14.3   *Payment of termination charge for supplier breach*

In addition, the customer may want to consider the appropriateness of a termination charge if the agreement has been terminated for breach. Thus, if the agreement was terminated because the supplier provided the services with defective assets, then the customer will not want to be obliged to purchase the assets. See Chapter 28 for a discussion of termination charges.

20.15   Payment of the charges

In addition to agreeing the amount of the charges and the payment profile, the parties will also have to agree when the charges will be paid. Charges may be paid monthly, quarterly or annually in advance or in arrears. They may be paid on completion of specified services, for example the transition charges.

20.15.1   *Payment in advance or arrears*

If the charges are paid in advance, then the customer takes the risk that the supplier will become insolvent before it has provided the services. If the customer is paying in advance for software development work to be carried out by the supplier, it may want to have the right to reclaim these amounts if the software development is not ultimately successful and it may want the supplier to provide guarantees or bonds to safeguard any payments made in advance.

If the charges are paid in arrears, the supplier takes the risk that the customer will become insolvent before it has paid and it may want to consider requesting guarantees from the customer.

Each party may also want to review the implication of the payment profile (whether in advance or in arrears) upon the liability levels agreed in the contract.

20.15.2   *Payment period*

The parties will need to specify how long the customer will have to pay invoices. The customer may want to reserve the right not to pay invoices if there is a dispute about the amount covered by the invoice. The supplier will want the customer to pay any undisputed amount covered by an invoice.

The supplier may also require the customer to pay an amount equal to the net VAT that the supplier will have to pay over to the tax authorities on the undisputed amount (or, if the supplier issues an invoice and so creates a "tax point" for VAT purposes, for the full disputed fee) pending resolution of the dispute, so that the supplier is not "out of pocket".

20.15.3   *Reconciliation of charges*

The charges may also need to be reconciled if they have been made in advance on the basis of estimates, for example estimated volumes or usage, and the actual volumes or usage vary from that estimated.

20.16   **Remedies for non-payment**

The supplier may be anxious to ensure that its cash flow does not suffer as a result of late or non-payment by the customer.

20.16.1   *Interest*

Usually the parties will agree that the customer will pay interest on late payments.[6]

20.16.2   *Suspension*

The supplier may also want to reserve the right to suspend provisions of the services if the customer does not pay. This is an extremely powerful, and some would argue excessive, weapon in particular if the suspension may cause interference or disruption to the customer's business. In any event, the customer will not want the supplier to exercise this remedy until it has given the customer notice of its intention and has given a reasonable time period within which to pay.

20.16.3   *Termination*

Ultimately, the supplier will usually want the right to terminate for breach if the customer fails to pay the charges. For more information on termination rights, see Chapter 26.

20.17   Value added tax

20.17.1   *Payments include or exclude VAT*

There may be various payments to be made under the agreement apart from the charges, such as service credits and payments for the purchase of assets. The parties will need to document in the agreement whether the payments are inclusive or exclusive of any VAT that is chargeable. In principle, the consideration is deemed to include VAT unless stated to the contrary in the contract, although if this is the commercial agreement, it is advisable explicitly to state it.

---

[6]   If the agreement does not include a right to charge interest, then the supplier will be able to claim interest under the Late Payment of Commercial Debts (Interest) Act 1998. This Act provides a right to claim interest on late payment in commercial contracts for the supply of goods and services. It applies where all parties to the contracts are businesses or public authorities. In most cases, however, the parties will prefer to include an express right to charge interest in the agreement.

20.17.2 *Supply taxable, exempt or outside the scope of VAT*

Where there is uncertainty as to whether a supply is taxable, exempt or outside the scope of VAT, the parties will need to consider who takes this risk, which may affect the cash flow and profitability of the transaction to the party taking the risk.

20.17.3 *Recoverability of VAT*

Before progressing with the procurement, the parties must also check carefully whether any VAT chargeable will be recoverable, and if there is a possibility that it will not be recoverable because the recipient is making exempt or partially exempt supplies, they should take taxation advice as soon as possible.

20.17.4 *Requirement for VAT invoice*

The parties will usually want to clarify that, where the consideration is VAT exclusive, VAT on any payment made under the agreement (not just payments for the services) will only be paid upon receipt of a valid VAT invoice, or at least that a valid VAT invoice will promptly follow payment of the consideration. This is an important point, as the party paying VAT will ordinarily not be able to recover VAT unless it obtains a valid VAT invoice.

20.17.5 *Timing of payment*

There may be timing issues too. For example, the parties may agree that the VAT element of the consideration charged by a supplier will only be paid over to the supplier (say) two days before it has to account for the VAT to HM Revenue & Customs. (There are detailed rules relating to "continuous supplies" of services which in some cases may mean that issuing a VAT invoice accelerates the date VAT is due.)

20.17.6 *Reverse charging*

With regard to offshore outsourcing, parties need to be aware of the reverse charge mechanism. Very broadly, this causes the customer, as recipient of certain supplies from an overseas supplier, to be treated as making the supply to itself, so it has to account for VAT on the supply. If the customer is able to recover all of the VAT, there is no VAT cost. Indeed the customer may benefit from a cash-flow advantage compared to paying VAT to a UK supplier. But, if the customer is not fully taxable, it will have to account to HM Revenue & Customs for some of the VAT.

Chapter 21

Service Credits and Service Bonuses

21.1   Outline

Chapter 20 describes the various charging regimes and how they reflect the liability profile under the agreement. One element of the charging regime has not been discussed. This is the service credit/service bonus regime, which results in deductions from the charges being made if the service levels are not met and bonuses being paid if specified service levels are met or exceeded. As explained in Chapters 9 and 10, the service levels themselves can relate to the provision of the services or the management of the services. This chapter deals with service credits and service bonuses. It describes the different types of service credit or service deduction regimes, whether service credits should be the customer's exclusive remedy, how the customer may prevent evasion of the service credit regime and how service credits should be paid.

21.2   Types of service credit and service bonus regimes

There are various different ways that service credit and service bonus regimes can be drafted and each one will encourage a different type of behaviour in the supplier. See Table 38 for examples of different approaches.

Table 38 Service credit regimes

Incentive to rectify
The service credit regime could operate over a running three-monthly period. If the supplier fails to achieve the service level in the first month, a small service credit applies or no service credit applies. If the supplier fails to achieve the same service level in the second month, then a greater service credit applies and if the supplier fails to meet the service level after the second month then a substantial service credit applies. This service-level regime is appropriate where failures cannot be avoided and the supplier is incentivised to rectify the defect once it has occurred.
Deter unacceptable performance
The service credit regime could apply so that service credits increase at an exponential rate the greater the failure. This service-level regime is designed to ensure that the service does not reach a certain unacceptable level.

Highlight critical services or service elements

The service credit regime can apply so that service levels for different elements of the services are given a different weighting, so that the supplier can see which service elements are most important to the customer and prioritise its service delivery accordingly.

Transparent service performance

The customer may decide that it wants service levels for each service element (e.g. in an IT services agreement, the desktop service, the telecommunications service, the server service and the printing service) so that it can see the standard being achieved for the individual service elements, but that service credits will be calculated taking into account the end-to-end service for which the supplier is responsible (e.g. availability of the applications on the server at the desktop, or time taken for cheques printed out by the supplier to be delivered to the user).

This example illustrates that it is not necessary for service credits to apply to all service levels. The two regimes can be drafted to achieve different aims. They can also operate over different periods. For example, the supplier may be required to report on the service levels on a monthly basis but (to reduce the administrative effort involved) the service credits may be calculated on a quarterly basis.

Highlight critical periods

The customer may have a period when the services are critical to its business. For example, if the customer is a retail organisation it may be essential that its call centre is open to take orders during the six weeks prior to Christmas. To give another example, if the customer is a body that marks school examination papers, the months of July and August may be critical. If the customer is a water utility, it may need to send out most of its bills over a specific period in February to March. Lastly, it may be particularly critical for a payroll service to meet annual service levels to submit taxation forms on time to the taxation authorities to avoid the customer paying penalties. The service description may require more exacting or additional service levels over this critical period, with substantial service credits for failure to achieve these. Service credits may not apply during the rest of the year, or may only apply for serious failures to meet the service levels.

Deter service deterioration in the final months

The customer may be concerned that the supplier will take less care in meeting the service levels over the last 12 months of the arrangement, particularly if the supplier knows that the customer is not intending to renew the arrangement. Therefore, it may suggest that the amount of the service credits increases over the final 12 months.

Incentivise business benefit achievement

The customer may pay a service bonus if the supplier achieves certain service levels or satisfies certain business objectives. In the latter situation, the approach is similar to having a risk/reward element in the charges. (See Chapter 18 for a more detailed discussion of risk/reward schemes.)

The customer (or indeed the supplier) may pay the supplier's service manager (and possibly other key staff) bonuses that are linked to achievement of certain business objectives or customer satisfaction levels.

As stated in Chapter 9, service levels and service credits should be drafted so that they support the business objectives of the customer. Ideally, each service level and service credit should be justified on the basis that it is achieving a specific business benefit, taking into account the cost to the customer of the supplier complying with the service level, monitoring and reporting upon its performance in meeting the service level.

21.3   Relationship with control

The customer will want to understand and draft the service credit regime taking into account the extent to which achievement of the service levels is within the control of the supplier.

If the supplier is forced to sign up to service credits for specific service levels it cannot guarantee, then it will often increase the amount of its charges by the amount of the relevant service credits on the assumption that it is likely that it will have to pay them every month. In this situation, the service credit regime functions more like a service bonus regime. The supplier is calculating its charges on the basis that it will have to pay service credits. Therefore, when it is successful in meeting the service levels, it will not have to pay service credits and will receive a bonus. Accordingly, the supplier will still be incentivised to take measures to meet the service levels.

In this situation, however, it is important for the customer to appreciate what is happening so that:

(a)   it can take action to reduce any adverse impact resulting from failure to meet the service levels; and

(b)   it can satisfy itself that it is getting value for money by paying the bonus.

21.4   Evasion of the service credit regime

21.4.1   *Gaming*

Another factor which needs to be taken into account in drafting service credit regimes is whether the supplier has any opportunities for gaming - that is, evading the service credits. A good example of gaming is where the supplier has an obligation to rectify defects within a specified period of them being recorded by the supplier's help desk and the supplier avoids the service-level failure by not recording all of the problems reported to it. Another example is where a supplier is obliged to refill the cash in cash machines before they are empty, but the supplier is not responsible for technical defects affecting the cash machine. The supplier avoids the service-level failure by ensuring that the last note in each cash machine is folded so that it creates a technical fault in the cash machine before it runs out of cash. A well-drafted service credit regime should prevent gaming.

21.4.2   *Failure to report*

Another way that a supplier can attempt to avoid service credits is to fail to report that it is not meeting service levels. Sometimes the supplier is the only party who can obtain accurate information about whether it is meeting the service levels. In this situation, there are two ways that this can be dealt with in the agreement:

(a) the customer can ensure that the reporting obligation forms part of the invoicing procedure so that the supplier will not get paid until it provides the necessary information; or

(b) the agreement can provide that, if the supplier fails to submit a report, the customer can require it to produce the report within a specified period, for example 30 days. If the supplier fails to produce the report (other than as a result of a force majeure event or a failure by the customer) then the supplier will be regarded as having failed to meet the service levels.

21.5   Complexity of service credit regime

Penalising the supplier for failure to report on service credits is only fair where the supplier can reasonably be expected to report on them. For this reason, it is important that the amount of effort required to measure and report on service levels and service credits is not burdensome. Clearly, if service levels cannot be measured, then there is little point in including them. Equally, it is not helpful if the service level or service credit regime is so onerous or complex that the service managers from both parties decide not to implement it.

In practice, the right number of service credits should be included in the regime if a focused approach is taken, as described in that last section of section 21.2 above, with each service credit supporting the customer's business objectives.

21.6   Exclusive remedy—supplier's perspective

Service credits or service deductions are amounts that are payable by the supplier without the customer having to prove that it has suffered any losses as a result of a failure by the supplier to meet the service levels.

If service credits are not the customer's sole financial remedy, then, if the customer suffers fewer losses than the value of the service credit, it can recover the service credit or if it suffers greater losses, it can recover the difference between the two. For this reason, suppliers usually argue that service credits are unfair if they are not in full and final satisfaction of the customer's remedies. Limiting the customer's remedies to the service credits also enables the supplier to limit its total liability for failure to meet the service levels.

21.7   Exclusive remedy—customer's perspective

Despite the supplier's argument that service credits should be the sole financial remedy of the customer for breaches of the service levels, in many cases the customer will not want to agree to this, for the reasons described in the following paragraphs.[1]

21.7.1   *Service credits may not reflect the customer's losses*

The first problem with accepting the supplier's argument is that customers usually do not see service credits as liquidated damages but rather as a useful way of incentivising the suppliers to comply with the service levels. Therefore, customers do not usually investigate or quantify the losses they would suffer if the supplier did not meet the service levels and they do not draft the service credit regime to compensate them for losses, except where the losses are straightforward. For example, if the supplier is processing bills on behalf of the customer, it can be assumed that a delay of two days in sending the bills out will cause the creditor to pay the bill two days late and hence result in losses calculated by reference to the amount of the bill multiplied by the agreed daily interest rate multiplied by two.

21.7.2   *Service credits capped*

Suppliers usually endeavour to cap their exposure to service credits to a fixed amount. This amount varies greatly, depending on the type of services arrangement, from 5 per cent to 100 per cent of the annual charge. Fixing a cap (particularly if it is at the lower end of this scale) may mean that the amount of the service credits will be inadequate to cover the losses that the customer will suffer.

21.7.3   *Service credits less than the investment required to correct the defect*

The customer will be anxious to avoid the situation where, because of the cap on service credits, the service credits act not as an incentive but as a

---

[1]   If the parties agree that the service credits will not be the customer's exclusive remedy, the agreement will need to be drafted carefully to preserve the customer's rights. Thus it must be expressly stated that service credits are not the exclusive remedy and are not liquidated damages. In addition, the relationship between service credits and charges will need to be drafted so that it does not appear that the supplier has an option to provide a lesser level of service and receive a reduced charge.

disincentive to rectify defects in the services because the service credits are lower than the amount of investment required to correct the defect.

21.7.4   *Importance of keeping records*

If the service credit regime means that substantial amounts may be payable, then the customer should keep records showing how the amount of the service levels was fixed and that they were not intended to operate as a penalty for breach of contract (as penalties are unenforceable at law[2]).

21.8   Exclusive remedy—possible compromises

In the absence of agreement by one of the parties to accept the other side's preferred position, there are various compromises that may be appropriate in different circumstances.

21.8.1   *Exclusive remedy except for termination*

The parties can agree that the service credits will be the customer's sole remedy unless the customer terminates the agreement or has grounds for terminating the agreement.

21.8.2   *Service credits apply to minor failures*

Alternatively, the service credit regime can apply to minor failures to meet the service levels, with the customer reserving its right to claim damages under the common law if the service levels deteriorate further. The logic behind this regime is that, if the customer is suffering material losses, it should be possible for it to prove them and claim them under the common law.

---

[2]   See for example the cases of *Dunlop Pneumatic Tyre Co Ltd v New Garage & Motor Co Ltd* [1915] A.C. 79, *Philips Hong Kong Ltd v Attorney General of Hong Kong* 61 B.L.R 41; (1993) 9 Const. L.J. 202 and the more recent cases of *Cine Bes Filmcilik ve Yapimcilik AS v United International Pictures* [2003] EWCA Civ 1669, *Murray v Leisureplay Plc* [2005] EWCA Civ 963, and *Alfred McAlpine Capital Projects Ltd v Tilebox Ltd* [2005] EWHC 281 (TCC); [2005] B.L.R. 271. See also *Steria Ltd v Sigma Wireless Communications Ltd* [2007] EWHC 3454 (TCC); [2008] B.L.R. 79, which stresses the point that if a liquidated damages clause is unenforceable as a penalty, the customer will still have an uncapped claim for damages.

21.9 Payment of service credits

The parties will need to agree the mechanism by which service credits will be paid.

21.9.1 Set off

Suppliers prefer to state that service credits may be set off against the charges payable by the customer for the period to which the service credits relate, or if they are not known at that time, by the following period.

If a customer is not able to recover VAT in full, it will usually prefer the service credits to be set off against the charges payable by the customer for other periods rather than recovering them as a debt.

21.9.2 Recover as a debt

This mechanism will not work during the final period of the agreement when, if charges are payable in advance, no further charges may be payable to the supplier. In this situation, the customer may want the right to recover them as a debt from the supplier. The customer may want to have this right throughout the term of the agreement.

21.9.3 Waiver

There is another problem with setting the service credits off against the following month's charges. Often, in practice, the supplier fails to achieve the service levels for several months. The customer does not claim the service credits for the first month, but as it becomes clear that the supplier is not remedying the problem, the customer wants to claim service credits for the current month and, retrospectively, for prior month(s). If this is a possibility, the customer may want to clarify that it is entitled to do this. Otherwise, there is a risk that the customer will be taken to have waived its rights to payment of the service credits for prior periods.

Chapter 22

Contracting out to reduce costs

22.1 Outline

Chapters 20 and 21 deals with issues relating to charging and the payment of service credits and bonuses. This chapter deals with a particular issue, how to use contracting out to reduce costs, an issue that is particularly relevant in a recession, such as the current Great Recession.

22.2 Effectively reducing costs

It is not unusual for customers to question whether it is possible in practice to achieve cost savings in a recession by contracting out services. Many customers have contracted out services hastily in an effort to cut costs but ultimately failed to achieve the desired levels of savings. Whether customers will achieve cost savings in practice depends upon the individual facts of each case. Customers need to prepare a detailed business case based on sound due diligence to investigate whether contracting out services is the right strategy for them. However, there are certain key success factors that customers need to take into account to achieve cost reductions. Section 22.3 describes these key success factors for customers.

22.3 The customer perspective

22.3.1 Supplier market

The customer will need to analyse the supplier market and supplier needs to identify the credible suppliers and increase the attractiveness of its offering to these suppliers and hence its bargaining power, in accordance with Chapter 2. This may include considering matters such as whether services should be aggregated or divided up and what the ideal term for the service agreement is.

22.3.2 *Service requirements*

The customer will need to have a detailed understanding of the services it will require. This is not simple and involves (as described in Chapters 7, 8 and 9):

(a) **Current services**—a thorough understanding of the services and levels of services currently being received by the customer—this will usually form a useful starting point from which to analyse future service requirements.

(b) **Service needs not wants**—an analysis of which of the current services are really required to support the customer's business in the future. This involves distinguishing between services that are essential for the customer to carry out its business and those which are desirable but not necessary. This is sometimes described as distinguishing between "wants" (which may be unaffordable luxuries in a recession) and actual "needs".

(c) **Value for money**—a comparison between the importance of the service to the customer's business and the cost of that specific service. If the service is already contracted out, this may involve the customer having a detailed breakdown of the charges so that it can understand which elements of the services are the most expensive.

(d) **How services are being provided**—an analysis of the manner in which the services are currently being provided, together with an understanding of which elements of the service solution are essential and which services could be provided in another manner, if necessary, for example off-site rather than on-site.

(e) **Cost analysis**—an investigation of the ways in which the service charges can be reduced without affecting critical elements of the services, either by changing the nature of the services or the manner in which they are delivered, for example by standardising the services. This investigation requires the customer to be open minded and flexible in considering creative suggestions so that it can make an informed decision as to what it requires. The process will usually involve "top down" decision making by senior stakeholders who will be required to make difficult decisions about what is really necessary for the business. These decisions will then need to be communicated to users so that they understand and buy into them.

(f) **Sourcing options**—a consideration of the various sourcing options. The customer could, in theory, carry out all of the above steps on its own, whether it is intending to contract out the services or not. However, if the customer is considering contracting out services, it will need to explore the above issues in collaboration with its current or potential service supplier to see what suggestions the supplier has for reducing the charges, for example by offshoring or by the customer accepting the supplier's standard service offering.

(g) **Document the conclusion**—(if the customer decides to contract out its services) documentation of the agreed services and service delivery methods, so that it is clear which specific services are included and which have been deliberately omitted from scope. This documentation must be carefully drafted as, if services are omitted in error, the supplier will not include them in its charges and the customer will have to pay extra for them, potentially undermining the business case for the proposed service arrangement.

Some customers may feel that the above analysis is unnecessary. They may feel that they can reduce costs merely by putting pressure on the supplier to reduce its charges. The problem with this approach is that, unless the customer has tied down the boundaries of the services clearly, the supplier may be tempted to carry out its own analysis (not very different from the type of analysis that it is suggested that the customer should carry out above, but taking into account which services are not clearly documented as being in scope). The supplier will then make unilateral decisions as to how to cuts costs and services, with the resulting impact upon the customer's business.

22.3.3   Risk allocation

The parties will need to have carried out sufficient due diligence to understand the risks that may undermine the success of the project. They will need to agree a sensible and consistent approach to the allocation and mitigation of risk that represents good value for the customer and is manageable from the supplier's perspective.

22.3.4   Charging assumptions

In addition to evaluating its service requirements, the customer should carry out sufficient due diligence to ensure that contracting out services will result in cost reductions in practice (as described in Chapter 4). This includes, wherever possible, investigating all of the information necessary for the supplier to provide the customer with a firm price without either party having to take the risk that the charges are calculated on the basis of unsubstantiated charging assumptions, for example as to volumes of services required.

The customer will also need to be aware of the cost implications of the legal and commercial terms that the customer is proposing, including any provisions transferring risk to the supplier, as described in Chapter 20, so that the supplier will not feel that it needs to include a risk premium in its charges. This means that the customer must employ a cross-functional team comprised of procurement, finance, operational and legal experts who can work effectively together in furthering the joint goals of the organisation. The parties will also need to decide which party will take certain key financial risks, including:

(a) Inflation risk—will the charges be linked to a particular index or will the supplier build inflation into its charges? What will happen if the economy experiences a period of deflation?
(b) Currency risk—in what currency will the charges be payable?
(c) Change in law risk—for example, who takes the risk of future environmental taxes?

The above issues have taken on a new importance, particularly in the current climate of currency fluctuations.

22.3.5   *Flexible arrangements*

Ideally, the customer needs to balance short-term pressures to cut costs against longer-term needs (as described in Chapter 10). This means ensuring that the service arrangement is flexible and sets out how the parties will deal with potential changes to the arrangement, for example when the recession ends, the customer's business starts to expand and the volume of services increases. The customer will then be able to carry out sensitivity analyses for the key drivers and other scenarios that may affect the charges in the future, to ensure that it will continue to receive value for money.

22.3.6   *Efficient procurement process*

If the customer is under internal political pressure to take action to cut costs quickly, it cannot afford to cut corners in deciding upon its services requirements. One area where it may be able to speed up the process is by ensuring that its procurement process is as efficient as possible (as described in Chapter 5).

This will usually involve the customer effectively project managing the procurement, including appointing a project manager and project team with sufficient availability to manage the procurement to realistic timescales in accordance with a well thought-through project plan.

The customer may want to make appropriate use of competitive tension between suppliers, (as described in Chapter 3), for example by carrying out e-auctions where appropriate. Although some customers believe that negotiating with more than one supplier will take more time, this is not always the case if negotiations are handled effectively.

In practice, one way that customers in a recession speed up the procurement process (rightly or wrongly) is by limiting the suppliers they negotiate with to the major suppliers in the particular area. This has the advantage of reducing the need to carry out extensive due diligence on supplier capabilities.

22.3.7   Governance

The customer should not attempt to save costs by reducing the resources allocated to manage the service agreement below those necessary to perform
essential service management functions, including those described in
Chapter 10, such as:

(a)   operational management—monitoring the arrangement on an opera-
      tional level, to ensure that defects are being dealt with and the service
      levels are being met; and
(b)   strategic management—monitoring whether the customer's business
      objectives have changed and if so whether the service agreement needs
      to change, for example as the recession ends and the customer wants to
      take advantage of growth opportunities.

Service management also includes the following elements, which, in a recession, take on a particular importance and the customer must ensure that it
does not cut costs in a manner that undermines its ability to carry out these
roles:

(a)   cost management—ensuring that services are not modified by users in
      a manner that undermines the cost savings and causes cost creep; and
(b)   continuing requirements analysis—carrying out the requirements
      analysis mentioned above on a continuing basis to ensure that the
      customer is aware of and agrees with the supplier what services are
      required from time to time to support its changing needs, the best way
      to provide them and any new ways of reducing their cost.

22.3.8   Whole lifecycle

The customer will need to ensure that, on termination of the arrangement,
there is a smooth transition to another supplier and that the costs of the
transition are reasonable and are taken into account in its business case, as
described in Chapters 23 to 25. Before it signs the service agreement, the
customer will therefore need to consider the specific assistance it will require
on and before termination and wherever possible agree these charges with
the supplier in advance.

22.4 The supplier perspective

22.4.1 *Service obligations*

In any event, suppliers need to resist the temptation to sign agreements with customers before the services have been adequately scoped and to avoid any risk of accepting open-ended service obligations.

22.4.2 *Governance*

Suppliers should ensure that they have sufficient staff to manage the contract from their side and that they do not attempt to save costs at the expense of this vital function. Where service contracts are negotiated with narrow margins, they will need to ensure that they have sufficient up-to-date information about their costs and revenue to be able to ascertain on an ongoing basis whether the individual service contract is profitable. The supplier will also need to ensure that it is appropriately compensated on termination for investments it has made in the services.

Chapter 23

Ensuring Competitive Charges

23.1   Outline

Chapter 23 deals with how customers use contracting out to achieve cost reductions. This chapter deals with how to ensure that the charges are competitive on an ongoing basis.

During the term of the arrangement, the customer may want to ensure that the charges continue to represent good value, particularly if the services arrangements are long term. This concern may be of particular importance where the customer's business objectives in entering into the services arrangements include the achievement of cost savings. The issue also has special significance in the public sector, where local authorities are subject to the "best value" regime.[1] This means that they have a statutory duty to secure continuous improvement in the delivery of their services, focusing on economy, efficiency and effectiveness.[2]

There are various ways in which the customer can ensure that the charges remain good value, apart from relying upon the supplier's goodwill in wanting to satisfy the customer in order to encourage the customer to extend the current agreement and to give the supplier additional business, particularly in a multi-sourcing environment. The following paragraphs deal with the most common mechanisms used, including benchmarking, maximum margin and the most favoured customer guarantee. Each mechanism provides a different type of protection, and the customer may want to rely upon a combination of the various protections.

---

[1]   Local Government Act 1999.
[2]   Local authorities must comply with the Local Government Act 1999, which provides that they must compare their performance with other local authorities and the private sector. They have a duty to ensure continuous improvement in delivery of the services, focusing on economy, efficiency and effectiveness. As a result, they will be obliged to benchmark the charges under the outsourcing agreement. They will be obliged to carry out fundamental performance reviews every five years. As a result, a number of benchmarking clubs have been established.

23.2   Benchmarking

Benchmarking involves comparing the supplier's charges against other charges available in the marketplace. The process can take up to four or five months to carry out (depending upon the services) and may be costly. Accordingly, the approach may not be useful in lower-value services arrangements.[3][4]

There are various different elements to a benchmarking regime.

23.2.1   *Benchmarking methodology*

There are two main types of benchmarking methodology: cost benchmarking and contract benchmarking.

Cost benchmarking involves the benchmarking agent analysing the resources which it anticipates a reasonable supplier would use in providing the services and then building a cost model showing the cost of these resources, taking into account relevant factors relating to the contract being benchmarked. This type of benchmarking is suitable where the benchmarking agent has sufficient information about the relevant costs in the market for it to be able to provide reliable cost information. The supplier may want to state that any cost information must be based on a representative sample of contracts, which may involve information from 10 or more agreements.

Contract benchmarking involves the benchmarking agent selecting a small number of agreements (usually between four and six) which are most similar to the agreement being benchmarked, adjusting them to make them resemble the customer's contract by taking into account relevant factors and making a professional judgment as to whether they are more or less expensive than market value.

Neither benchmarking methodology is a statistical process. Benchmarking does not rely on representative sampling in a statistical sense. This would imply that there is a homogeneous set of prices out there for the same commodity services, but the reality is that many services contract are unique, not homogeneous; although this may change for example with regard to IT outsourcing, as IT services become more commoditised and cloud computing services[5] become more popular.

---

[3]   See Neil Barton, "A benchmark for Benchmark Clauses" *The Magazine of the Society for Computers and the Law*, Volume 18, Issue 1, April–May 2007.

[4]   For a supplier's reaction to benchmarking, see Michael Harvey, "Nobody wants to be average" *Society for Computers and the Law*, 11 April 2012.

[5]   See section 1.2 for a detailed description of cloud computing models.

The only way of obtaining comparative prices for the same arrangements would be to ask other suppliers to bid for providing similar services. This would usually be more expensive, resource hungry and potentially disruptive to the business than benchmarking. In addition, other suppliers are unlikely to take the invitation to bid seriously unless the current services agreement is due to expire or the customer is seriously considering terminating it for convenience.

Benchmarking involves an expert opinion of what would be a fair market price, based on the best available comparative data, adjusted to account for the differences.

23.2.2   *Adjustments*

So what factors should the supplier ensure are taken into account in adjusting the data to ensure that the benchmarking agent is making a like-for-like comparison?

The supplier will want to state that the benchmarking agent should take into account all relevant factors, such as, for example:

(a)   the nature of the customer, where relevant;
(b)   the specific services being provided, in particular any additional security or governance requirements;
(c)   the quality of services being provided;
(d)   the volume of services being provided;
(e)   the geographic area in which the services are being provided;
(f)   the costs and liabilities transferred to the supplier from the customer on commencement of the arrangement. The customer may argue that this should only apply for a certain period and that the supplier should be expected to reduce the cost base over time, where practical. Whether this is reasonable depends upon the particular circumstances;
(g)   whether the supplier is restricted from using certain assets for the provision of services to other customers;
(h)   the terms and conditions under which the services are being provided and in particular the risk profile of the specific arrangement; and
(i)   the size and capabilities of the suppliers.

It should be noted that some factors cannot be benchmarked but need to be considered and removed from the comparison with other contracts. Examples of this include transition charges that are amortised over the life of the contract, and financial engineering schedules of charges that distort the relationship between the cost of delivery and the charges levied (see section 20.11 above). The benchmarking methodology will need to identify these factors and ensure that they do not skew comparisons with other contracts, so that the charges considered relate only to the services being delivered and profiled within the analysis.

The supplier may want the benchmarking agent to explain what adjustments it is making to take into account the relevant factors.

23.2.3   *Benchmarking changes*

The customer will want to be able to benchmark the charges proposed by the supplier for changes to the services arrangement.

23.2.4   *Benchmarking part of the services*

The customer will often also want to have the option of either benchmarking the charges for all of the services or individual service elements (e.g. in an IT services agreement, the customer may want to have the right to benchmark the desktop services separately from the telecommunications services).

In a multinational outsourcing project, particular care will need to be taken in deciding which parts of the services the customer may benchmark separately. For example, the customer may want to divide the services into parts depending upon:

(a)   the branch or country of the customer who is outsourcing to the supplier;
(b)   the country or region from which the services are being provided; or
(c)   the language in which the services are being provided.

For the customer to be able to benchmark the charges for individual service elements they will need to be priced separately. From the supplier's perspective, there is a crucial difference between the supplier providing the customer with some reassurance that the overall price of the services will remain competitive and the supplier providing reassurance that every service element will remain competitive. The supplier may be unwilling to provide this additional level of reassurance. The acceptability of benchmarking in part depends upon the sector and the type of services being benchmarked. It also depends upon the country in which the services are being provided. For example, apparently benchmarking in part for small elements of IT services is more widely accepted in Germany.

23.2.5   *Benchmarking all of the services*

There may be problems with restricting benchmarking to the services as a whole. In particular, the customer should consider whether it will be possible to benchmark all service elements. If it is not possible, then restricting the customer's ability to benchmark the services as a whole will prevent it from carrying out any benchmarking exercises. In addition, this approach may act as a severe disincentive for the customer to carry out benchmarking as, if the customer is concerned that one service element is overpriced, it will not want to be obliged to incur the cost of benchmarking all of the other service elements.

23.2.6   Honeymoon period before benchmarking applies

If the supplier was selected as a result of a competitive procurement process, then the customer may feel that it does not need the right to benchmark until after the first 12 or 24 months of the agreement.

In addition, the information required to carry out a benchmarking exercise may change during an initial transition or transformation period, making it difficult to establish an accurate representative month and so it may be impractical for a customer to carry out a benchmarking exercise until the completion of the transition or transformation.

23.2.7   Frequency of benchmarking

After the initial honeymoon period, the customer may agree not to carry out benchmarking exercises more than once every 12 or 24 months for example. Gartner Consulting recommends benchmarking the total charges every two or three years within the contract (post transition), or carrying out a programme of annual but partial benchmarking (e.g. desktop and help desk in the first year, networks the next year etc.).

The customer will need to ensure that any such restrictions do not apply to benchmarking charges for changes to the services.

23.2.8   Benchmarking agent

Benchmarking regimes often provide for the benchmarking to be carried out by an impartial third party. There are various benchmarking agents who have experience of benchmarking specific types of services, including, for IT services for example, Gartner Consulting, EquaTerra and Compass. Before the agreement is signed, the supplier and the customer may want to agree who will carry out the benchmarking exercise.

If the services are such that some of the benchmarking agents are competitors of the supplier, then the supplier may want the customer to engage benchmarking agents who are not competitors. The customer will need to consider whether this is practical.

To emphasise the impartiality of the benchmarking agent, it makes sense for the benchmarking agent to be appointed by the customer and supplier jointly, with all information provided to or by the benchmarking agent going to the customer and the supplier. The benchmarking agent should be required to show the customer and the supplier how it reaches its findings, giving as much detail as possible without breaching the confidentiality of the peer group companies. Each party should be given an opportunity to comment on the information provided by the benchmarking agent and on the final report. These measures help ensure that the process is fair and hence encourage mutual "buy in" to the process and methodology, and hence greater acceptance of the independent results and conclusions when they are delivered.

The parties will need to agree who will pay the costs of the benchmarking agent. Most contracts encapsulate joint funding, but some contracts insist that the supplier will pay the benchmarking agent's costs if the supplier's charges are found to be expensive and the customer will pay if the supplier's charges are found to be reasonable.

23.2.9 What findings will result in an adjustment to the supplier's charges?

The parties will need to decide when the benchmarking process will result in an adjustment to the supplier's charges. For example:

(a) Will it do so if the supplier's charges are more than the comparative prices?
(b) Will it do so if the supplier's charges are more than, for example, 10 per cent higher than the comparative charges (or for that matter if the supplier's charges are not 10 per cent lower than the comparative charges)?
(c) Will the supplier's charges be compared with those in the marketplace on the date of signature of the agreement to see how they relate to those and to ensure that they maintain a similar relationship with comparative charges?

The customer and supplier will need to decide upon the desired approach when they agree the benchmarking regime.

Some services contracts state that the supplier's charges must be within the top quartile of charges. Benchmarking agents do not recommend this approach if the benchmarking agent is to use a contract benchmarking approach, as this approach inevitably involves a small sample of contracts.

23.2.10 *Adjustments imposed or agreed*

The issue of whether price adjustments will be imposed or agreed is one of the most contentious aspects of the benchmarking regime.

23.2.10.1 *Adjustments imposed*

The customer will usually prefer a mechanism whereby the charges are automatically reduced within a specified period (e.g. a month from the date of the finding) to the market rate or no more than an agreed percentage above the market rate.

23.2.10.2 *Adjustments agreed*

The supplier will argue that the customer should not have the unilateral right to amend the supplier's charges. Agreeing such a change will fundamentally undermine the supplier's expectation that the services arrangement will provide the supplier with a certain level of guaranteed revenue. It may also undermine the supplier's margin and the supplier may suggest that no reduction should be made if it reduces that margin below a specified percentage or if it reduces the charges by more than a fixed percentage.

The supplier will argue, therefore, that it should have to justify its charges and the parties should then negotiate any change in the supplier's charges. This option allows the parties to negotiate other solutions to ensure that the customer receives value for money, such as changes in the service levels. The customer may be concerned that, even if the supplier's charges are too high, any such provision will constitute an agreement to agree.[6] It may be concerned that it will not have the bargaining power to negotiate an equitable adjustment to the supplier's charges.

23.2.11 *Adjustment in the form of a credit*

The parties may be able to agree a compromise whereby, instead of the customer receiving a reduction in the charges, it will receive a credit that can only be used to buy additional services from the supplier.

23.2.12 *Remedies if adjustment not agreed*

If the parties are unable to agree a satisfactory amendment to the agreement within a specified period (usually about a month) after the final benchmark-

---

[6] Agreements to agree are generally unenforceable (see *Walford v Miles* [1992] 2 A.C. 128). However, the case of *Petromec Inc v Petroleo Brasileiro SA Petrobras (No.3)* [2005] EWCA Civ 891 includes some obiter comments regarding circumstances in which agreements to agree, which are of a narrow scope, will be enforceable.

ing report, the customer may want the right to terminate the agreement. This is likely to be extremely contentious and the supplier may argue that the customer should pay the same compensation as that payable on termination for convenience (see Chapter 28 for a discussion of termination rights). The customer will be reluctant to pay compensation if this will undermine the cost benefit it will obtain by transferring to another supplier.

Different considerations may apply in relation to charges for additional services if the customer has an option to ask other suppliers to provide the new services.

23.2.13   *Supplier's right to benchmark*

The assumption so far has been that the customer will have the right to benchmark the services to ensure that they remain competitive in the marketplace throughout the term of the services arrangement. However, in certain services arrangements the supplier may argue that an indexation provision is insufficient and that it should also have the right to benchmark the services and to impose an increase in the charges if they are lower than market rate. In practice, customers are unlikely to agree to this, as it will usually be entering into the services arrangement on the basis that the charges will be a specific amount and it will not be able to increase its budget to cover any increased charges.

23.3   Open book

In certain sectors, particularly the public sector, it is becoming increasingly acceptable for suppliers to be required to disclose information to the customer relating to how its charges are broken down and the margin it is making. Some suppliers are unwilling in principle to do this.

23.3.1   *Different levels of open book*

In practice, much depends upon the level of open book required by the customer. The phrase "open book" can describe a wide variety of different arrangements ranging from one in which the supplier divides its charges into overheads and margin, staff costs, asset costs and other costs to, at the other extreme, one in which the supplier may be obliged to disclose information relating to the salaries of staff and the costs of individual subcontracts and supplier agreements.

23.3.2   Confidentiality problems

There may be various problems with the supplier providing information relating to individual supplier agreements.

(a)   In providing the services to the customer, the supplier may be relying upon goods or services purchased from other suppliers under corporate arrangements, whereby the supplier receives preferential rates that it is prevented from disclosing to other parties such as the customer.

(b)   Most contracts which the supplier enters into with its suppliers to provide the services to the customer will include confidentiality obligations restricting the supplier from disclosing any information about the arrangement.

(c)   The supplier may also be relying upon goods or services provided from other members of its own group, where the internal charging mechanisms under which they are provided are highly confidential.

(d)   Any information provided relating to staff will have to comply with the Data Protection Act 1998 (see Chapters 36 and 37).

23.3.3   Administrative effort

If the customer wants the supplier to disclose information about specific supply agreements, then this may involve substantial work by the supplier in approaching its suppliers and obtaining their consent to the disclosure of the information. Also, some suppliers may not be able to obtain information about costs relating to individual contracts from their accounting systems and may need to get the figures manually for the customer. The supplier may want to charge the customer for any additional administrative effort involved in complying with any open book requirements.

23.3.4   Open book for changes

The supplier may suggest a compromise, whereby information is provided on an open book basis for changes to the charges, as the customer may be particularly concerned about these.

23.3.5   Limitations on value of open book

Customers should also be aware that the supplier has a considerable amount of control over its cost base and over how costs and overheads are attributed to the customer's agreement rather than other arrangements. Therefore, open book arrangements may provide a limited amount of reassurance for the customer.

It is worth pointing out that an open book provision on its own will only enable the customer to receive information about the supplier's cost base and margin. It will not ensure that the customer receives value for money. For the open book provision to have any impact in reducing the charges, it will need to be linked to, for example, a provision restricting the supplier's margin, as described at section 23.4 below.

On the contrary, the biggest drawback of open book arrangements, if not drafted and managed properly, is that, by incorporating the supplier's assumptions about its anticipated margin, the supplier may argue that its charges should be increased if it fails to make that margin and so open book may imply some sort of "guaranteed margin" for the supplier.

23.4 Maximum margin

A maximum margin provision involves the supplier accepting that it will not make more than a specified margin or accepting that, if it does make more than a specified margin, it will share the excess profits with the customer.

The supplier may feel that, as it is taking the risk that it will fail to achieve its margin, for example as a result of unanticipated costs, it should not be required to share any increase in its margin with the customer. It may therefore suggest that the provision only apply if the supplier makes "super-profits".

The supplier may also be concerned that the profitability of the transaction will vary from year to year and that it should not be required to share profits with the customer unless the overall margin earned by the supplier over the term of the agreement exceeds the specified amount. This would be achieved by ensuring that the regime applies to the cumulative profit at the end of each year, with payments of profit shared with the customer being clawed back if the following years are less profitable. Alternatively, the supplier may prefer the regime to operate at the end of the term, when the supplier's profit over the full term of the agreement can be assessed. Depending upon the length of the arrangement, the customer may be unwilling to wait until the end of the term to receive its share, and may be concerned that it will have little bargaining power to enforce the provision at that stage.

23.5 Most favoured customer

Some customers want more protection than that afforded by the maximum margin provision. They want the supplier to agree that the customer will be a favoured customer, in that the supplier will not agree to provide similar services to other customers at a cheaper price unless the cheaper price is also offered to the favoured customer.

Although this may seem like a helpful provision from the customer's perspective, it is difficult to see how it is practical. If auditing the maximum margin provision involves the customer having access to the supplier's books relating to the individual contract with the customer, the most favoured customer provision would, in theory, allow the customer or its agent access to all of the supplier's agreements with all of its customers.

In addition, suppliers will usually be unwilling to agree to this clause because of the manner in which it restricts them from carrying out their business. Suppliers may want to reserve the right to decide what margin they charge on other services arrangements and may, for example, want to reserve the right to enter into other arrangements at or below cost where necessary to break into a new market or where it makes sense for other business reasons.

In any event, a clause that prohibits the supplier from charging another customer a lower price could infringe competition law rules. Such clauses are generally acceptable only if the supplier has the freedom to charge another customer a lower price (albeit that, if it does, it is contractually obliged to offer the same lower price to the favoured customer). These provisions are known as most favoured nations clauses.

23.6   Ensuring value for money for transferred assets

If the customer is transferring its assets to the supplier, it will want to ensure that it obtains value for money from the transaction. This issue is dealt with in Chapter 16.

23.7   Overlap

If suppliers agree charging variations such as those specified in this chapter, it is essential that they consider the relationship between the different regimes. For example, an agreement for call-centre services could include provisions stating that the charges will be reduced in line with reductions in call volumes and that the customer will share any revenue generated as a result of the supplier using the call centre to provide services to other parties. The supplier will want to ensure that the two provisions do not apply at the same time. Thus, if there is a fall in the volume of calls to the call centre, and as a result the supplier is able to use the call centre to provide services to other clients, the customer should be obliged to choose between either receiving the benefit resulting from the reduction in call volumes or receiving a share of the revenue generated by using the spare capacity.

23.8   Multi-sourcing

The concern for the customer to ensure ongoing competitiveness in long-term sourcing arrangements must also be seen in the context of the debate as to whether the customer's sourcing strategy should be one based on a multi-sourcing or a uni-sourcing approach. This topic is dealt with in Chapter 17.

Part 6

Change

Chapter 24

Software Development and Business Process Transformation

24.1 Outline

Chapters 20 to 23 deal with various different issues relating to the charges payable under a services arrangement. A fundamental element of the charging arrangements is the arrangement for dealing with charges for changes in the services. Chapter 25 deals with this aspect (and other aspects) of change management. This chapter focuses on services arrangements whose purpose is to implement change.

24.2 Types of arrangements

Services arrangements designed to implement change can be divided into three categories, business process re-engineering services arrangements, software development and PFI projects. These types of services agreements are described in the following paragraphs.

24.2.1 *Business process transformation*

Business process transformation services arrangements involve the provision of consultancy services to suggest ways in which the customer's processes and procedures may be improved. For example, the customer may engage a supplier to carry out a Six Sigma audit. "Six Sigma" is based on the Greek letter "sigma" which is used in statistical analysis to mean standard deviation. The aim of Six Sigma is to reduce the amount of deviation from standard processes to reduce the variability of performance and hence improve performance.

24.2.2 Software Development

Software development projects involve the development, for example, of new IT systems, their implementation, maintenance and management. Over the last few years there has been a move away from the development of new software, wherever possible and towards the customisation and configuration of existing software. This avoids the need to (and the risk involved in) reinvent the wheel and makes it easier to upgrade the software, as the supplier makes available new releases of the software. However, it involves the customer weighing up the advantage and disadvantages of (a) re-engineering its business processes to reflect the software it is implementing; or (b) modifying the software it is implementing to reflect its current business processes. Even if the customer has a strategic preference for not modifying the software, ideally the customer needs to make a conscious decision, based on an understanding of the business implications of each approach.

With regard to software development agreements, various issues will arise depending upon the development methodology used for the project. There are numerous different types of software development methodologies. Broadly speaking, the methodologies fall into two different types: waterfall methodologies and agile methodologies. These different types of methodology are discussed below. This is an extremely complex (and contentious) topic and, in practice, most customers use a hybrid of the two methodologies. The paragraphs below are designed to illustrate the point that software development methodologies differ considerably and that commercial and legal specialists advising customers on software development agreements will need to understand the specific software methodology being adopted for the particular project before they will be in a position to draft suitable commercial and legal provisions.

24.2.3 PFI

PFI agreements may involve the construction of a school, hospital or other facility, which is then maintained by the supplier and made available to the customer as a service. PFI arrangements are considered in Chapter 44.

24.3 Waterfall methodologies

24.3.1 Description of the methodologies

The waterfall model is a sequential development process in which development is seen as flowing steadily downwards (like a waterfall) through the phases of conception, initiation, analysis, design (validation), construction, testing and maintenance. To follow the waterfall model, it is necessary to proceed from one phase to the next in a purely sequential manner.

If the software or system is to be developed using the waterfall methodology then, as part of the conception phase, the customer will prepare and agree with the supplier a functional specification describing the functionality that it requires. The functional specification may distinguish between mandatory and desirable requirements. (This will be separate from the service description because that will be a description of services and the specification will be a description of an asset and the functionality and operation of that asset.)

The supplier will then, as part of the design phase, prepare a technical specification or architecture showing how the functionality will be achieved from a technical perspective.

The parties will have to agree how the system will be developed or the services provided and in accordance with what timetable.

24.3.2 Advantages and disadvantages

There are various advantages and disadvantages of the waterfall methodology, including the following.

24.3.2.1 Preparation

The advantage of preparing detailed functional and technical specifications is that time spent early on in software production may lead to greater efficiency later on in the software life cycle.

24.3.2.2 Written communication

The waterfall methodology relies upon the agreement of detailed documentation. This can be particularly useful for large projects involving many developers. It can also be helpful if developers leave the project. However, the reliance on written communication can lead to misunderstandings between the parties, depending upon how clearly the documentation is written.

24.3.2.3 Sequential

The methodology assumes that the customer will describe its requirements and that these will be fixed before the supplier develops the software. In practice, the customer may not be aware of exactly what requirements it wants before it sees a working prototype and can comment upon it. The initial specification may include functionality which is not essential or which will not be used in practice.

The methodology assumes that the design is fixed before the programmers start to implement the software. However, it may only become clear in the implementation phase that a particular area of program functionality is extraordinarily difficult to implement. If this is the case, it may be better to revise the design than to persist in using a design that was made based on faulty predictions and that does not account for the newly discovered problem areas.

Because of the problems with the sequential nature of the pure waterfall methodologies, modified versions of the methodology have been developed which provide for overlapping phases so that information on problem spots can be acted upon during phases that would typically, in the pure waterfall model, precede others.

24.3.2.4 Not collaborative

The methodology assumes that the client will describe its requirements and then the supplier will go away and develop software that satisfies that requirement. In practice, the customer may need to work with the supplier to clarify its requirements and the supplier may benefit from collaborating with the customer to ensure that its interpretation of what the customer wants is correct.

24.3.2.5 Inflexible

The methodology assumes that the parties will agree the customer's requirements at the beginning of the process and that the parties will agree any changes through the change control procedure. This may not be a problem where the customer's requirements are stable and where it is possible and likely that designers will be able to fully predict problem areas of the system and produce a correct design before implementation is started.

However, this can be inflexible and unsuited to situations in which the customer's requirements will change during the development process leading to "scope creep" and possibly to disputes between the parties regarding the charging and timetable implications of the changes.

24.3.3 Legal and commercial considerations

24.3.3.1 Business outcome liability

Where software is developed using a waterfall methodology, the supplier will (subject to section 24.3.3.2 below) be responsible for developing software that meets the customer's functional requirements and doing so within the agreed deadlines.

The supplier will therefore want to document any dependencies it has upon the customer.

24.3.3.2   *Acceptance of the technical specification*

The supplier will usually want the customer to accept the supplier's technical specification before the supplier starts developing the software. This will ensure that the supplier fully understands the customer's requirements before it starts to develop the system.

However, if the customer accepts the technical specification, it may take the risk that the supplier's technical solution will not satisfy the functional specification. This will mean that the arrangement will be more of a service output-based arrangement than a business outcome-based arrangement,[1] unless there are other provisions which, for example, state that the acceptance criteria (see below) or service levels will incorporate business outcome-based measures or the charges will be payable on a business outcome basis. Often the customer will be relying upon the supplier's expertise and will not have the technical knowledge to confirm whether the supplier's technical solution meets its functional specification. The customer and supplier need to decide whether the arrangement will be business outcome or service output based. The parties may need to carry out due diligence to ensure that the technical solution will satisfy the customer's business objective. This may involve feasibility studies or pilots.

In PFI contracts, the customer does not usually accept that the system or service satisfies the specification and the supplier retains the risk that the system or services will satisfy the functional specification throughout the term of the agreement.

24.3.3.3   *Payment for development of technical specification*

Developing the technical specification may require extensive work by the supplier, which the supplier will be reluctant to carry out unless it is paid for the work. In this situation, the customer may have to pay the supplier to carry out a scoping study to enable the parties to finalise the specification. The advantage of this approach, from the customer's perspective, is that if the parties can prepare a clear, detailed specification, this may enable the supplier to agree a fixed price for the development.

---

[1]   See Chapter 1 for an explanation of the distinction between "business outcome", "service output" and "input" based arrangements.

24.3.3.4   *Payment for development of software*

The parties may not know whether the software or system works until the whole system is finally tested. This may take many months. The supplier will not want to fund the entire development without any payment by the customer. If the customer agrees to pay in instalments before the delivery of the final system, the question arises as to whether the customer should be entitled to a refund if the system ultimately fails the acceptance tests.

24.3.3.5   *Implementation timetable*

If it is important to the customer that the development is completed by a specific date (e.g. that it is completed before a peak trading period) then the customer may want the supplier to send it reports showing progress made in meeting the deadline, so that problems can be resolved.

The customer will usually require remedies if the system or services do not pass the acceptance tests on time. These may include, for example, liquidated damages payable for each day of delay for the first month or two of delay until the acceptance tests are passed. Thereafter, the customer may want the right to claim damages.

24.3.3.6   *Acceptance tests*

The parties will usually agree acceptance tests that will be designed to ensure that the developed system satisfies the customer's requirements. Both parties will want to ensure that the criteria laid down for acceptance are objectively measurable.

The supplier will want to ensure that it has appropriate opportunities to rectify problems with the system or services. It will also want to ensure that the acceptance tests are not failed where there are minor problems with the system or services.

24.3.3.7   *Remedies for failure to pass the acceptance tests*

The customer may require the right to terminate the software development agreement and recover any investment made in the system if the system fails to pass the acceptance tests.

If the system has been provided in phases, then the supplier may want the customer to pay for phases that have been successfully completed, even if later phases fail, and the customer may want the right to reject earlier phases if they fail the tests as a result of later developments.

24.4   Agile methodology

24.4.1   Description of the methodologies

An alternative development approach is that involved in agile development methodologies, in which the parties develop software in small increments with minimal planning. Agile methods produce completely developed and tested features (but a very small subset of the whole) every few weeks. The emphasis is on obtaining the smallest workable piece of functionality to deliver business value early, and continually improving it and adding further functionality throughout the life of the project.

Using the agile methodology, the parties work in cycles which are time boxed, usually a month long. At the beginning of the process, the parties agree the number of cycles. At the beginning of each cycle, there is a planning meeting to agree the requirements and the goals. The customer also prioritises the requirements. At the end of the cycle, the parties demonstrate what has been built and fully test it. The idea is to quickly develop a product that the customer can use.

Under the agile methodology, the customer has far greater responsibility. The supplier's obligations are to provide resources – the services agreement is an input-based agreement. The parties agree the length and number of cycles and the supplier is obliged to provide agreed resources during the cycles.

The charges for the software developed using the agile methodology will usually be calculated on the fixed-price basis on the assumption that the supplier will work with the customer during a specific number of cycles, where the cycles are of a specific length. The variable factor will be the functionality that can be produced as part of this project, with the customer prioritising the changes it needs.

24.4.2   Advantages and disadvantages

There are various advantages and disadvantages of the agile methodology, including the following.

24.4.2.1   Unstructured

The lack of emphasis on planning may be unsuitable for a customer where the company culture is structured and prefers order. This can be remedied in part by the parties agreeing and documenting iteration goals at the beginning of each cycle and dates by which these goals must be achieved. The methodology is likely to be more successful where the software developers are senior. Also, the lack of planning may be inefficient. If the requirements for one area of code change through various iterations, the same programming may need to be done several times over, whereas if a plan had been agreed up front, the supplier would only have needed to write a single area of code. Lastly, it is arguable that the use of an agile methodology can increase the risk of scope creep due to the lack of detailed requirements documentation.

24.4.2.2   Oral communication

The agile methodology relies upon the running of a series of cross-functional workshops, with representatives from the customer and supplier, to clarify the customer's requirements. Agile methods emphasise face-to-face communication over written documents. Accordingly the agile methodology is dependent upon the quality of the people who attend the workshops and their ability to make decisions on behalf of the customer's organisation. Most agile teams are located in a single open-plan office to facilitate such communication.

The disadvantage of this approach is that it may be more difficult for large software development projects or projects where members of the team are at different locations.

It can also be argued that the large number of meetings may result in the software development project being unduly expensive.

In an agile project, documentation and other project deliverables ("artefacts") all rank equally with working software. Stakeholders are encouraged to prioritise them with other deliverables based exclusively on business value perceived at the beginning of the iteration. This may mean that less documentation is produced as part of the project, creating problems when members of the team leave.

24.4.2.3   Collaboration

The methodology assumes that the customer and the supplier will collaborate in clarifying the customer's requirements and developing software that satisfies them.

This emphasis on collaboration prevents problems being hidden.

24.4.2.4   Iterative process

The methodology is more flexible than the waterfall methodology, as the customer can change its requirements as it goes along, as the implications of different decisions become clear.

24.4.2.5   Incremental

As the system is produced in stages, the customer can use the releases as they are developed. The customer will pay for these releases.

24.4.2.6   Prioritisation

The customer prioritises requirements as the project proceeds.

24.4.3   Legal and commercial considerations

24.4.3.1   Input liability

Because of the lack of a detailed specification that the supplier signs up to, and the collaborative nature of the development process, the use of an agile methodology is likely to lead to the supplier having an obligation to provide resources for the software development project (input-based liability), without the supplier guaranteeing any particular end product.

In this situation, the customer may want to ensure that it has the right to terminate the project for convenience where it feels that it is not obtaining sufficient benefit from the project.

24.4.3.2   Staff capabilities

Because of the resource-based nature of the project, the customer will usually want some reassurance of the abilities and experience of the individual developers who will develop the software and will usually want to include in the contract key personnel clauses to apply to them.[2]

24.4.3.3   Payment for development of technical specification

The customer can pay for the software at the end of each cycle or it can pay for each release.

24.5   Balance sheet treatment

If the software development project envisages significant investment by the supplier, it may be important to the customer to ensure that the assets developed or acquired by the supplier do not appear on the customer's balance sheet. If this is the case, it is important that accountancy advice is taken early on in the procurement.

---

[2]   See Chapter 8.

24.6   Ongoing change

If the services arrangement involves the development of several systems over the term of the agreement, then the parties will need to provide for the development of each system. If the parties are to use a waterfall methodology for developing the new system then the customer may be reluctant to commit to instructing the supplier to develop the systems before the parties have agreed suitable specifications, development obligations, implementation timetables and acceptance tests for each system. In this case, the customer may commit to procuring the first system only and leave it open for the parties to add the development of additional systems once specifications have been agreed.

A similar problem can arise in business process transformational projects, where the customer may not know what services it will require until the business process re-engineering services have been completed. Once again, a possible solution is for the customer to agree individual work packages involving the re-engineering of specific functions. After signature of the agreement, the parties may agree further work packages for the supplier to carry out. These agreements are sometimes called "incremental partnering agreements" in the public sector.

24.7   Transition period

Even in services agreements, whose purpose is not focused on implementing change, the supplier may need a transition period during which it will carry out various changes to improve the services or the assets used to provide the services. It may also need to set up its help desk and establish its service management function and any necessary communications links between its premises and those of the customer.

In situations where there are substantial transition requirements, the customer may require protections similar to those described for software development and business process transformation, for example a transition plan, acceptance tests and remedies for failure to pass the acceptance tests.

Chapter 25

Change Management

25.1   Outline

Chapter 24 describes services arrangements whose purpose is to implement change. This chapter describes other aspects of change management. It deals with how change can be anticipated or, where it cannot be anticipated, how changes to the arrangement can be agreed. It also deals with dispute resolution mechanisms that may be employed where the parties cannot agree changes to the arrangement.

Public authorities and utilities should be aware that they cannot rely on a widely drafted variation clause to bring about endless changes to a contract that was originally tendered in accordance with the public and utilities Procurement Directives. See Chapter 43 for further details of the implications of these Directives upon changes to the services arrangement.

25.2   Anticipating change

In all services arrangements, even those whose purpose is not to implement change, the parties should be proactive about anticipating change. The customer should consider whether its requirements or its business may change.

Before the agreement is signed, the parties should discuss the extent of the flexibility which the customer will have to change the services, so that the customer understands the implications of investments which the supplier will need to make in order to be able to provide the services.

The parties may want to agree the implications of any foreseeable changes. For example, it is often foreseeable that the volumes of services required will change and so (if the charges payable depend upon the volumes of services to be provided) the parties may want to agree in advance the effect of increases or reductions in volumes upon the charges. It may also be foreseeable that the customer will need the supplier to make resources available to it (e.g. man days of consultancy). In this situation, the parties may agree, before the agreement is signed, the man-day rates that will apply.

In most long-term services agreements, the customer will not be able to predict all changes that will occur during the term of the arrangement and the parties will need to agree changes to the agreement.

25.3   Agreeing change—the change control procedure

The second element of flexibility in a services arrangement involves the inclusion of a change control procedure for agreeing changes to the services that have not been anticipated before the contract is signed. Where appropriate, the customer may want to document in the change control procedure that it is a fundamental requirement that the supplier acts flexibly and reasonably in agreeing changes to the services.

The change control procedure also needs to meet various requirements. These are described below.

25.4   Effect of the change upon the customer's business objectives

The change control procedure will need to remind the customer or (where relevant) the parties to consider the effect of the change upon the achievement of the customer's business objectives, so that they are not unintentionally undermined. The nature of this obligation and the party who will be required to comply with it will depend upon whether the supplier is responsible for the achievement of the customer's business objectives (business outcome risk profile), whether it is responsible for the provision of the service (service output risk profile) or whether it is only responsible for the provision of resources to be used by the customer as it wishes (input risk profile). See Chapter 1 for an explanation of the difference between business outcome, service output and input-based sourcing arrangements.

25.5   Effect of the change upon the services

From both parties' perspective, the change control procedure should ensure that the supplier carries out an impact assessment to highlight the effect of the change upon the services and the achievement of the service levels (and in a multi-sourced IT services arrangement, the effect upon the services being provided by other suppliers). The impact assessment should also consider whether the change will affect the security risks relating to the services arrangement and whether the security requirements need to be updated. The supplier may want to specify circumstances in which it can charge for carrying out this work.

The parties will need to consider the best way to implement the change and whether any communications or training will be required to ensure that users are aware of and take advantage of the change.

The customer may also want to consider whether the change will have any effect upon the assistance that it will need the supplier to provide in a business continuity situation or on termination. In addition, it must consider whether it needs to change its software licences or maintenance agreements as a result of the change.

Lastly, the parties will need to document any resulting change in relevant documentation such as the service description, business continuity plan or the exit management plan. In an IT services context, this is part of what is known as "configuration management", which involves ensuring that all information relating to the IT infrastructure is reliable and up to date, including asset registers, software licences and maintenance agreements.[1] However, even in non-IT situations, it makes sense for the customer to ensure that documentation about its services is kept up to date.[2]

25.6   Effect of the change upon the terms of the agreement

The change control procedure should ensure that the parties consider whether any terms of the agreement will need to be amended as a result of the change in the services. It is not uncommon for serious problems to arise, affecting customers and suppliers, where the parties have incorporated changes into the services without taking legal advice and without considering whether the original terms of the agreement are appropriate for the changed services. The moral of the story is for the parties to take legal advice where they want to agree substantial changes to the services or changes in the nature of the services, for example use of the services agreement for the sale of goods.

25.7   Effect of the change upon the charges

From the customer's perspective, often the most worrying aspect of change management is the agreement of changes to the supplier's charges. In some cases, reducing the costs of the services over the term of the agreement is an important business objective of the customer in entering into the services agreement, so this issue is particularly important. Usually, the customer will have entered into the agreement having budgeted for specific charges and

---

[1]   Configuration management is one of the elements of ITIL service management. See section 7.2.3.
[2]   See sections 27.3 and 28.3.

may be anxious to avoid unreasonable and unexpected increases in the charges.

There is a perception that some suppliers enter into services agreements expecting to increase their margin by making substantial charges for any changes requested by the customer. The customer may be particularly concerned about this if it has selected the supplier following a competitive process in which the supplier has been under some pressure to offer the services at a particularly low margin.

There are four main ways that the customer can protect itself from unreasonable increases in the charges, apart from agreeing as many changes as possible during the competitive process where these can be anticipated. These ways are described in sections 25.8 to 25.11 below. Having said this, if changes are inevitable, then it makes sense for the customer to estimate the nature and cost of the changes in preparing its business case, and to include in its budget an allowance for the cost of these.

25.8   Clear definition of changes

It is essential that the parties have comprehensively defined the services to be provided by the supplier so that it is clear what services are included in the charges and which will be regarded as changes in the services, for the provision of which the supplier is entitled to make an additional charge. This is in both parties' interests and will avoid disputes later on. This issue is dealt with in greater detail in Chapters 7, 8 and 9.

25.9   Good bargaining power

Each party will be anxious to ensure that it has good bargaining power when negotiating changes to the services. In practice, any clauses that result in the party having power under the agreement are beneficial to it. For example, if the customer can include a right to terminate the agreement for convenience (assuming that this is cost effective), this may increase its bargaining power.

On a practical level, the customer may find that if it leaves it until the last minute to agree changes, it undermines any bargaining power it has, particularly if the customer has no alternative at that stage other than to ask the supplier to implement the change. (See Chapter 17 on multi-sourcing versus exclusive supplier arrangements.) Providing sufficient notice to the supplier may also enable the supplier to implement the charge over a longer time period, using under-utilised staff and assets rather than having to mobilise additional staff or assets.

25.10 Control over additional expenditure

The change control procedure needs to ensure that the customer has control over additional expenditure.

25.10.1 Prior notice from supplier

This can involve ensuring that the supplier informs the customer before carrying out services for which it claims it can make an additional charge. The customer may want the supplier to inform it that it believes the services are out of scope and to provide the customer with a written statement explaining why it believes the services to be out of scope. It may then want the supplier to comply with the change control procedure before implementing the services, unless the customer requires the services urgently. Some agreements state that if the supplier implements the change before agreeing it through the change control procedure, then it will not be able to charge for the change.

25.10.2 Approval of additional expenditure

The customer may also want to ensure that any changes that result in additional charges being payable by the customer must be approved by specific authorised representatives of the parties. This may be particularly important where the company is a multinational and the agreement comprises a framework agreement with specific agreements or service-level agreements signed between the supplier and the individual members of the group. In this situation, the customer will need to decide the extent to which the members of the group will be entitled to vary the services they receive so that they differ from the framework agreement. In certain circumstances, the customer may want to set minimum levels of service which must be contracted for. The customer will then need to set out who within its organisation has the ability to change the local service-level agreements and who can change the framework agreement.

25.11 Reasonable changes to the charges

The procedure needs to ensure that any changes to the charges are reasonable. This has two elements.

25.11.1   Increase in the charges

First, additional charges quoted by the supplier for changes that involve additional services must not be unreasonable. The customer may want the agreement to provide that, if the supplier proposes charging extra for any additional services, it must demonstrate that the cost is reasonable, possibly by making available information on an open-book basis or by allowing the customer to benchmark. (See Chapter 23 for a discussion of open book and benchmarking arrangements.) The customer may also want to reserve the right to market test the charges for the changes by asking other suppliers to quote for providing the additional services and to either instruct another supplier to provide the additional services, where practical, or to use the resulting information to renegotiate the supplier's charges. If the change is to be implemented by a sub-contractor of the supplier, the customer may want to be able to require the supplier to obtain competitive quotes from other suitable sub-contractors.

25.11.2   Reductions in the charges

Second, the customer may want to ensure that the change control procedure clarifies that changes can result in reductions in the charges as well as additional charges. In particular, problems may arise where the customer wants to make a change that involves a reduction in the services to be provided to it, for example deleting a service that it no longer requires.

Some suppliers may argue that they have entered into the agreement assuming that they have been guaranteed certain revenue and so are not required to reduce the charges at all if the customer decides to reduce the services to be provided. To avoid this misunderstanding, the parties should clarify, in appropriate cases before the agreement is signed, whether the charges are guaranteed, whether there is a minimum commitment or whether the charges may be reduced if the scope of the services is reduced.

If the parties agree that the charges may be reduced in circumstances where the scope of the services is reduced, then the next question is, on what basis should the charges be reduced? The supplier may argue that the services should only be reduced by the amount of cost savings the supplier actually achieves as a result of the reduction in the scope of the services. Where the supplier may not have a financial incentive to maximise the cost savings it achieves, the customer may want to ensure that the charges will be reduced by a reasonable amount, for example by specifying that the charges will be reduced by the amount of the cost savings which a professional supplier could reasonably be expected to achieve or that the supplier must use reasonable endeavours to reduce the costs.

25.11.3   *Relationship between charges for increases and reductions*

In ensuring that the charges for changes in the services are reasonable, it is essential that the customer consider the relationship between the regime for calculating increases in the charges and the regime for calculating reductions in the charges. Customers often fail to notice that there is a mismatch between the two. For example, the charges for additional services may be calculated on the basis of the supplier's additional costs plus a margin and the charges for reductions in the services may be calculated on the basis of cost reductions only. The effect of this arrangement, particularly over a long-term agreement, may be that the supplier's margin gradually increases. Depending upon the specific circumstances of the sourcing arrangement, there are various ways that the customer may avoid this problem:

(a)   Before the agreement is signed, the customer may agree that it will have the right to terminate individual service elements, in which case the charges will be reduced by the amount of the charges for that service element. In this situation the agreement will usually define the service elements and the period of notice required to terminate them and the charges will be broken down so that there is a separate charge for each element. This option will only be acceptable to the supplier if it has priced the service elements on the basis that they are severable.

(b)   The customer can specify that if there are reductions in the services, then the charges will be reduced by the amount of the cost savings plus the margin. The supplier may be reluctant to agree to this unless the parties also agree a minimum charge or a minimum margin.

(c)   The customer can specify that the supplier cannot charge a margin on additional services, although the supplier is likely to resist this approach.

(d)   The effect of change can be fed into a financial model, prepared by the supplier and agreed with the customer at the outset, which preserves the supplier's overall margin.

(e)   The customer may rely upon general protections such as the maximum margin, benchmarking procedures or open book provisions described in Chapter 23.

25.11.4   *Taxation implications*

The parties may need to consider the taxation implications of a proposed change in the services. From a VAT perspective, extending or decreasing the scope of the service may mean that the nature of the supplies changes so that they start or, as the case may be, cease to fall within a VAT exemption (e.g. group 5 of Sch.9 of the Value Added Tax Act 1994 for financial services). The significance of changes to the consumption of services from a VAT viewpoint is that, depending on whether the services are treated as a "composite supply" (so that the VAT liability is determined by the principal component) or a series of supplies with their individual VAT treatment, a change in the components could affect whether VAT is chargeable.

The parties should also consider the taxation implications of any investment to be made by the supplier. For example, additional expenditure may benefit from tax relief. In this situation, the customer may argue that it should only need to reimburse the supplier for the net cost.

25.12   Minor changes

The parties may want to ensure that minor or routine changes do not need to go through a formal change control procedure, to prevent the procedure becoming overloaded or bureaucratic. This would be helpful if the change does not result in a change in the customer's business objectives, does not impact upon other elements of the services and does not necessitate a revision to the charges.

ITIL[3] sets out an arrangement whereby changes that it calls "standard changes" are dealt with via a service request under incident management. Standard changes include, for example, requests to create new user IDs.

25.13   Operational change management procedure

When drafting the contractual change control procedure, the parties will need to consider the relationship between it and the operational change management procedure. The operational change control procedure is the procedure that will be used in practice to deal with such matters as recording, prioritising, planning, approving, implementing, testing and evaluating changes. The operational change management procedure may also involve agreeing and testing (and possibly implementing) a back-out procedure for reversing a change that has been unsuccessful. In particular the parties will need to ensure that the two procedures are consistent and that it is clear when one procedure is used and when the other is used and therefore when changes may result in additional charges. The customer may also want to ensure that the supplier will carry out some form of impact assessments as part of the operational change control procedure.

---

[3]   See section 7.2.3.

25.14 Timescales

The customer may also want to consider whether it needs the supplier to respond to change controls within a certain period and whether it is appropriate to see the supplier's role in dealing with change control requests as part of the services, with applicable service levels and service credits.

25.15 Mandatory changes

Section 25.3 above explained that the change control procedure is a way in which the parties can agree changes to the services. In most cases this is correct and the supplier will not want the customer to have the right to unilaterally vary the agreement without the supplier's agreement.

There are a few instances, however, where the customer may not want the supplier to have the right to refuse to implement the change. The next three paragraphs deal with three such circumstances.

25.15.1 Changes in the law

The first example of such a situation is where changes are necessary to ensure that the services comply with changes in legislation or regulations. In this situation, the customer will need the supplier to commit to complying with the legislation. The supplier will want to ensure that it is protected from any adverse consequences upon the services that arise as a result of implementing the change in law.

The question arises as to when the supplier can make an additional charge for complying with changes in the law. The following paragraphs explain the three different approaches that can be taken to deal with this question.

25.15.1.1 Specific changes

In accordance with the principle described at section 25.2 above, the parties should be proactive about anticipating change. Accordingly, they should endeavour to agree who will take the risk of specific changes in law, for example changes in taxation affecting the customer or supplier. One example of this is changes in taxation resulting from changes in environmental law such as in the rapidly developing field (under international, EU and national law) of climate change.

As the parties will usually be unable to foresee all changes in the law, they will also need to include some general fallback provisions that will apply for unforeseen changes.

247

25.15.1.2   *Customer takes the risk*

Some customers take a view that they do not want the supplier to increase their initial charges to compensate them for taking any risk relating to future changes in law. As a result, the customer takes all of the risk of changes in the law and the supplier is always entitled to make an additional charge for complying with changes in the law. This approach is common in facilities management agreements, where the parties have been influenced by practices in the construction industry.

25.15.1.3   *Parties share the risk—non-PFI arrangements*

An alternative approach, common in the IT industry, is for the customer to expect the supplier, at no additional charge, to comply with general legislation, compliance with which is seen by the customer as part of the supplier's costs of running its business. In this context, general changes in the law refer to changes that do not affect the customer's requirements, for example an increase in the minimum wage. They do not include changes that do affect the customer's specific requirements.

The customer may also expect the supplier to share some of the risk of there being changes in legislation which affect the services, for example by only being able to charge for a limited percentage of the costs incurred. The supplier will usually increase its charges to cover this risk. This approach may or may not represent good value to the customer depending upon whether, during the term of the services agreement, there are actually more or fewer changes in legislation than the supplier anticipated when setting its charges.

This approach may, however, give the supplier an incentive to implement the necessary change efficiently, for example by anticipating changes in health and safety requirements for PCs before carrying out a technology refresh and hence ensuring that all new PCs comply with the change in law before it is introduced.

25.15.1.4   *Parties share the risk—PFI arrangements*

PFI agreements take a slightly different approach, distinguishing between discriminatory legislation, specific legislation and general legislation:

(a)   discriminatory legislation is legislation that affects PFI contracts or the specific customer, but is not of general application;
(b)   specific legislation is legislation that affects the customer's requirements or the particular services, but is not of general application; and
(c)   general legislation is any legislation that is neither specific nor discriminatory.

Under a PFI agreement, the customer will generally be responsible for the implications of any specific or discriminatory changes in law, with the responsibility for general changes in law being shared between the customer and the supplier. The sharing of risk may be by reference to time (e.g. the supplier may be responsible for any general changes in law during the initial five years, such period being linked to the period of initial investment in the project, or for the periods between fixed market testing dates) or by reference to financial caps on any capital expenditure required by the change in law. Tax changes in law (excluding VAT rates) and general operating costs are normally a supplier risk.

Chapter 44 describes the historic PFI approach in the UK, explains how it has fallen out of favour in the UK, whilst being actively adopted outside the UK.

25.15.2   *Changes in customer's policies*

The customer may want the supplier to agree to provide the services in accordance with changed corporate policies, for example its security policy. In this situation, the supplier will have several concerns:

(a)   it will want to make sure that the policy is reasonable and that it can comply with it;
(b)   it will want to ensure that it receives adequate notice of the change;
(c)   it will want to be paid for any costs it incurs in complying with the changed policy; and
(d)   as for a change in law, it will want to ensure that it is protected from any adverse consequences upon the services that arise as a result of implementing the change in the customer's policies.

25.15.3   *Similar services*

The third example of where the customer may want the right to insist that the supplier agrees certain services is where the customer requires additional services which cannot for commercial, technological or other reasons be provided by another supplier without great inconvenience to the customer.

The supplier may want to ensure that it will not be contractually obliged to provide services that it cannot in practice provide, for example by limiting the obligation to provide services already afforded by the supplier to other customers. The customer may want to extend this to cover services that the supplier could provide if it engaged a sub-contractor. The supplier may prefer a general principle that changes to the services must be agreed, but that the supplier will not unreasonably refuse to provide services.

25.16   Project managing changes

The change management procedure should also set out the procedure for recording, agreeing, prioritising and implementing changes. The parties may want to include a post implementation review to obtain feedback on the implementation of the change.

25.17   Resolving disputes about changes

Apart from anticipating change and including a change control procedure for agreeing changes which cannot be anticipated (as described in this chapter), the agreement should also include escalation and dispute resolution procedures for dealing with changes which cannot be agreed by the parties. These may be specifically tailored to suit the particular type of issue and may not be the same as the general dispute resolution provisions described in Chapter 11. For example, a pricing issue may be referred to an industry expert.

25.18   Changes in public sector contracts

The public procurement rules continue to regulate public sector contracts even after the contract has been legally completed. The general rule is that material (or substantial) changes to awarded public sector contracts are not permissible. It can be difficult to determine what amounts to a "material change" but it often helps to look back at the original scope of the tender documentation (including the OJEU notice) to help with this task. The European case law also suggests that if the contemplated change to the contract may have had an impact on the outcome of the tendering process (e.g. other bidders may have been interested in participating; another bidder may have scored more highly if the new requirement had formed part of the original specification) then it is more likely to be material in nature and therefore unlawful.

There is, however, an exception to this general rule. Where unforeseen circumstances arise with the result that a public sector body requires additional services, and those services cannot be procured separately or where the services are strictly necessary for the later stages of the contract, then it is possible to extend the scope of the contract to cover those services. However, the test for what is "unforeseeable" is objective in nature. This means that the authority concerned would be expected to have a reasonable degree of foresight: it is not an excuse for poor project planning. Expenditure using this exception cannot exceed 50 per cent of the initial cost of the contract.

Part 7

Termination

Chapter 26

Term and Termination Rights

26.1   Outline

Chapter 25 describes how the parties manage change in the services arrangement. This chapter outlines how the parties deal with the greatest change in the arrangement, its termination. It includes a discussion of the factors that the parties should take into account in fixing an appropriate term for a services agreement. It also covers the circumstances in which the parties should be able to terminate the services contract.

26.2   Determining an appropriate term

The parties should take into account various factors in determining an appropriate term for the services contract.

26.2.1   Fundamental changes in arrangement

The customer should consider over what period it can realistically anticipate its future needs. Even over a short period, the customer may find that it changes its requirements and has to negotiate changes to the services agreement. This should not undermine the services arrangements. Chapter 25 explains how change can be managed in a services arrangement. However, the customer should decide the term of the agreement taking into account when it anticipates that it may need to re-examine the reasons for entering into the agreement, the current solution or the justification for selecting the current supplier.

As technology is continually changing, customers often find it more difficult to anticipate their technology requirements than, for example, their property needs.[1] This is particularly the case where the customer's technology requirements are affected by changes in the customer's business or

---

[1] The change to virtualised servers and more recently virtualised desktop is a good example of how changes in technology can fundamentally affect the way the technology is used and hence the technology requirements of businesses.

operation. Therefore, it makes sense that, typically, IT services agreements are shorter than business process outsourcing deals, which, in turn, are shorter than property agreements.

26.2.2   *Expected life of assets*

The parties should determine the term of the arrangement in the light of the expected life of the assets used to provide the services. This is linked to the customer's anticipation of its future needs, as the customer may want to reassess its requirements when key assets need replacing.

26.2.3   *Costs saving*

The parties should take into account the financial implications of the length of the agreement.

26.2.3.1   *Ongoing charges*

Thus the supplier may be able to provide the services more cheaply on an ongoing basis.

26.2.3.2   *Transition charges*

However, establishing the sourcing arrangement will usually involve a financial investment. An investment may be required, for example, in implementing the initial transition from the provision of the services by the customer, or its previous supplier, to the supplier. The parties will also need to establish service management structures and processes. The parties may agree that the transition costs will be spread over the term of the agreement.

26.2.3.3   *Termination assistance costs*

Lastly, additional costs may be incurred when the services are transferred back to the customer or the replacement supplier on termination of the arrangement.

26.2.3.4   *Traditional models*

If the term of the services arrangement is too short, the investment needed to establish and dismantle the arrangement will outweigh the savings made during its term. The savings will generally be greater the longer the agreement, unless further investment would be required, for example because the assets will need replacing.

26.2.3.5 Non-traditional models

Not all outsourcing models involve substantial transition and termination assistance costs. Non-traditional outsourcing models such as cloud computing under which IT or business process services are made available to the customer on a rental basis may involve a more straightforward transition and termination, as they involve the provision of a commoditised service by the supplier. Therefore, agreements for these types of outsourcing arrangements are usually shorter (two to three years) than traditional outsourcing agreements.

26.2.3.6 Extensions of the agreement

Whether the arrangement is a traditional or a non-traditional model, the customer may want the option to extend the agreement on expiry if the arrangement is still satisfying its business objectives. The supplier, for its part, may be anxious to retain the business and may therefore be happy to extend the arrangement. However, just as the customer may find it difficult to anticipate its requirements many years in advance, the supplier may find it difficult, when the original arrangement is entered into, to anticipate its cost base in advance and may be unable to commit to a fixed price for the extension. If the charges for the extension cannot be agreed before the original arrangement is entered into, the parties should endeavour to agree an appropriate mechanism for objectively determining the charges at the relevant date. Otherwise this undermines the value of the option to the customer, as in any event (subject to section 26.2.4 below) the parties may agree to extend the arrangement, whether an option was included in the original agreement or not.

26.2.4 Public sector considerations

The term must be consistent with that stated in the OJEU notice and must not be extended otherwise than in accordance with the Public Contracts Regulations 2006 (SI 2006/5) or the Utilities Contracts Regulations 2006 (2006/6) (see Chapters 43 or 46).

If the customer is a local authority, the term of the agreement must be fixed taking into account the authority's obligations to carry out a best-value review every five years.

If the services agreement is, or incorporates, a framework agreement (i.e. those agreements under which a public authority has one or more suppliers on a panel from which it can "call off" contracts for work or services on pre-agreed terms and price) then public sector customers are generally restricted by the Public Contracts Regulations from entering into framework agreements for longer than four years.

26.3 Termination grounds

In addition to fixing the term of the agreement, the parties should also decide in what circumstances each party may terminate the agreement before expiry.[2]

26.3.1 *Importance of agreeing appropriate termination rights*

Termination is an extremely important issue. If the customer has not negotiated the necessary rights to terminate, then it may find that it is locked into an agreement that is not satisfying its business objectives or that is causing damage to its operations.

If the supplier has conceded to the customer extensive rights to terminate, then it may find that it has invested in the contract in circumstances where the customer can terminate before the supplier has been able to recover its investment. It may also find that the customer is able to evade the payment of termination charges for example by exploiting widely drafted clauses enabling it to terminate for breach.

There are various grounds for termination that may be included in the services agreement.

26.3.2 *Insolvency*

See Chapter 29 for a discussion of insolvency issues including termination rights.

26.3.3 *Breach*

Each party will usually want the right to terminate the agreement if the other party breaches it in certain specified ways.

The parties may decide to distinguish between a breach that can be remedied and one that cannot. If the breach is classified as remediable, then the party in breach is typically given a period (e.g. 30 days) to remedy the breach. An example of a remediable breach is non-payment of money. An irremediable

---

[2] All discussions on termination rights within a contract must be linked to the consequences of termination and, crucially, the requirement for compensation payments to be made by either party. These are considered further in Chapter 28.

breach could be failure to carry out a task by year-end when year-end has subsequently passed.

The parties may also want to specify that the right to terminate only applies to certain types of breach, for example material breaches.[3] If the parties do decide to limit the general right to terminate to material breaches of the agreement, then the customer may want an additional right to terminate for persistent non-material breaches. If the supplier agrees to this, the parties should define persistent breach in the context of the particular agreement.

26.3.3.1   Supplier breach

The parties may want to define which clauses of the agreement will give rise to a contractual right to terminate if the supplier breaches them. For example, the right to terminate may be tied in to the key performance indicator regime, so that the customer will have the right to terminate if the supplier's performance falls below a certain level. The parties may also agree that the customer will have the right to terminate if the supplier fails certain acceptance tests, or implementation tests, relating to the transition of the services or the implementation of changes.

The customer will usually want any list of clauses to be non-exhaustive so that it does not take the risk of having to anticipate all potential breaches by the supplier. The supplier will usually want the certainty of having an exhaustive list. In any event, the customer should bear in mind that it will usually want the right to terminate the agreement for reasons other than those relating to performance, for example, a breach of the confidentiality or security obligations or failure to comply with relevant regulatory requirements.

26.3.3.2   Customer breach

The supplier may want to have the right to terminate for a breach of the agreement by the customer.

The customer may argue that its obligations are limited to paying the charges and enabling the supplier's provision of the services. Accordingly it may suggest that, if it fails to comply with obligations enabling the supplier to provide the services, the supplier's remedies should be limited to being granted relief from any liabilities arising out of its own failure to perform

---

3   In the case of *Rice (t/a Garden Guardian) v Great Yarmouth BC* [2003] T.C.L.R. 1 the customer tried to rely upon a express contractual right to terminate for *any* breach. The Court of Appeal held that, as the supplier was required to make a substantial investment so that it could provide the services, the agreement would be interpreted to mean that the customer could only terminate if there was a breach of sufficient seriousness (known as a "repudiatory breach") by the supplier. The parties could not have meant that any breach, however trivial, gave rise to a right to terminate. In *Alan Auld Associates Ltd v Rick Pollard Associates* [2008] EWCA Civ 655, the Court of Appeal found that a persistent and cynical delay in making payments to a party providing consultancy advice amounted to a repudiatory breach.

and compensation for any additional expense incurred in carrying out the services. This is because:

(a) the customer will not want to deal with the disruption caused by the agreement being terminated; and
(b) the customer may consider that the supplier will be adequately compensated if it is provided with the relief noted above.

The supplier may want the right to terminate the agreement if these remedies are not sufficient, for example, if the customer breaches confidentiality or security obligations which cause damage to the supplier's business or to its other customers.

The customer may want non-payment by it to be treated as a remediable breach that it will have a period of time (for example, 30 days) to correct. This prevents the supplier terminating the agreement due to a single administrative error by the customer's accounts department. The supplier may be concerned to ensure that this does not result in the customer deciding to pay invoices late, hence undermining the supplier's cash flow. The agreement may provide the supplier with other remedies to deal with this concern, for example the payment of interest on late remittances.

26.3.4   Force majeure

See Chapter 34 for a description of force majeure events.

26.3.5   Corruption

The customer, in particular in the public sector, will usually reserve the right to terminate the agreement if the supplier or any employee or subcontractor of the supplier is guilty of bribery or corruption in connection with the grant of the contract.[4] Sometimes the corruption clause is drafted quite widely, for example so that it applies if the customer believes that the supplier is guilty of corruption. The supplier may want to amend such a clause. However, the supplier is advised to be extremely careful about negotiating any amendments to the corruption clause. It must avoid giving the customer the impression that it is negotiating the clause because it is worried that its employees may be guilty of corruption or because it has had a problem with corrupt employees in the past.

Sometimes the supplier feels that termination is too severe a remedy and that it should be allowed to resolve the situation by terminating the subcontract or the employment of the corrupt employee.

---

4   See section 4.2 for a description of the Bribery Act 2010.

26.3.6 *Fraud related to the provision of the services*

If the nature of the services are such as to provide the supplier with an opportunity to commit a fraud (for example, payroll services, payment collections services or local authority revenues and benefits services) then the customer may want the right to terminate the agreement if any fraud is detected. The customer may also want the right to suspend provision of the services if there is a suspicion of fraud and this is necessary to prevent further acts of fraud. The supplier will usually want to ensure that it will be compensated if the customer's suspicions later prove to be unfounded.

26.3.7 *Other fraud*

The customer may want the right to terminate if the supplier is guilty of fraudulent reporting relating to its financial accounts, or if it fails to comply with relevant securities law and regulations in the countries in which it is established.

26.3.8 *Change of control*

If the customer has selected the supplier partly on the basis of the particular character or culture of that supplier, then it may want to have the right to terminate the agreement if there is a change of control of the supplier.

The supplier may be reluctant to agree to this, as it will undermine the value of the supplier's business in any subsequent merger or acquisition. In practice, this ground for termination will typically only be relied upon where the supplier is providing the services in accordance with all of its contractual obligations (otherwise the customer would rely upon a right to terminate for breach). Accordingly, the supplier may agree to the right of termination in these circumstances on the basis that it is treated as termination for convenience and the supplier is paid a reasonable termination charge if the supplier would otherwise not be compensated for its investment in the services.

An alternative approach would involve restricting the right to circumstances which the customer is particularly concerned about, for example where the change of control:

(a)   could have a material effect upon the services;
(b)   involves the supplier being taken over by a competitor of the customer; or
(c)   results in a conflict such as where the customer has outsourced its finance function to the supplier and the supplier is taken over by the customer's auditors.

In public sector agreements, the customer may also want to cover the possibility that control of the supplier could pass to an organisation that is unacceptable for political or security reasons.

FSA-regulated firms will want, and sometimes need, to ensure they can terminate agreements where the supplier undergoes a change of control.[5]

26.3.9   Change of organisation or management

In addition, customers sometimes want the right to terminate the agreement if there is a change of organisation or management in the supplier. FSA-regulated firms will be keen to include such a clause in all agreements. Suppliers may be reluctant to agree to this as it may undermine their ability to develop the best organisation or management for their business. The comments on termination for change of control apply equally to this situation.

The question arises as to whether the supplier should have the right to terminate the agreement if there is a change of control, organisation or management in the customer. If the parties have been able to define the boundaries of the services effectively, then any such change in the customer should not increase the burden of providing the services and the parties should be able to agree appropriate changes to the services and charges in accordance with the agreed change control procedure. (See Chapter 25 for a discussion of the change control procedure.)

26.3.10   Loss of licence or approval

The customer (or indeed the supplier) will want to have the right to terminate the agreement if the supplier loses a licence that it requires in order to provide the services, for example a telecommunications licence or approvals from the FSA. The supplier may want to be given an opportunity to rectify the situation before the agreement is terminated.

26.3.11   Termination for convenience

The customer may want to have the right to terminate the arrangement for convenience, where there is no fault by the supplier. The right may be a general right, subject only to the giving of a certain period of notice, or it may only arise in certain specified circumstances.

---

[5]   For further detail on FSA requirements on change of control of supplier, see Chapters 38 to 42.

If the customer wants to have the right to terminate for convenience after an initial period, for example five years, then the supplier may regard the arrangement as a five-year agreement and calculate its charges accordingly. Thus the supplier will calculate its charges so that it recovers its transition costs and fixed costs over the first five years of the agreement. This would mean that the customer would lose the advantage of paying the costs over a longer period. An alternative approach may be to allow for a longer period (e.g. seven years) with the supplier spreading its fixed costs over the longer period. The customer could then have a right to terminate the agreement after the first five years provided it pays the supplier a termination charge that compensates the supplier for unrecovered fixed costs. The supplier may argue that it should also be paid the margin that it would have been paid during the rest of the term.

26.3.12   *Failure to agree*

The customer (or the supplier) may sometimes want the right to terminate the agreement if the parties fail to agree to changes or fail to agree service descriptions, service levels or other details, which the parties were not able to resolve before the agreement was signed. This approach may be helpful if the threat of termination has the effect of incentivising the parties to act reasonably and agree the issues in dispute.

From the customer's perspective, terminating the agreement is not the best way of dealing with such problems due to the costs involved. (See section 7.3 above for a discussion of problems in agreeing the service description and section 9.5 above for a discussion of problems in agreeing service levels.) The customer may prefer that the dispute resolution provisions apply in such circumstances.

From the supplier's perspective, termination will not be acceptable unless it is compensated for any investment it has already made in the services but for which it has not yet been paid.

26.3.13   *Termination under the common law*

Sections 26.3.2 to 26.3.12 cover possible grounds for termination that the parties may want to expressly include in their services agreement. In addition, depending upon the nature of the provision breached, the parties may have the right to terminate the agreement under the common law. In general terms contractual terms are categorised into conditions, warranties and innominate terms as follows:

(a)   the breach of a condition will give the innocent party the right to terminate the agreement;

261

(b) the breach of a warranty will not give the right to terminate (but will give rise to a right to damages); and

(c) breach of an innominate term (a term that is neither a condition or a warranty) may give rise to a right to terminate, depending upon the consequences of the breach.

A misrepresentation that induces the entry of a contract may give rise to a right to rescind the contract (see section 4.5.2).

PFI contracts will usually include a provision excluding any rights to terminate other than in accordance with the express provisions of the agreement. For the sake of certainty, the parties in non-PFI contracts may want to consider doing likewise.

26.4   Other remedies

The customer may want remedies other than a right to terminate if the grounds mentioned in section 26.3 above apply. The remedies could include:

(a) the right to require the supplier to disclose further information;

(b) the right to terminate the supplier's exclusive right to provide the services or the minimum revenue commitment; or

(c) the right to exercise step-in rights (see section 8.6).

26.5   Time limits

Each of the parties may be anxious to ensure that the other party does not abuse its rights of termination. They may therefore agree, for example, that a party cannot exercise a right to terminate beyond a specified period after the event has occurred. Particular thought should be given to how such provisions will apply when small issues, taken together, give rise to a right to terminate.

Whether or not the contract contains such limitations, a party who believes that it may have a legitimate right to terminate should take legal advice promptly. Failure to do so (whilst continuing to perform the contract) may amount to an affirmation of the contract meaning that the right to terminate is lost. It may take the lawyers some time to investigate whether a right to terminate has, in fact, arisen. A party is strongly advised not to terminate the agreement until its lawyers have confirmed that it has sufficient proof of its entitlement to do so. If it terminates in circumstances where it is not entitled to do so, or cannot prove that it is entitled to do so, then the other party can rely upon the purported termination as an act of repudiation. It can then use this act of repudiation to itself terminate the agreement and claim damages for wrongful termination from the (otherwise) innocent party.

26.6 Termination in part

The parties will also need to decide whether the services are severable so that, when terminating for convenience, breach or as a result of force majeure, the customer has the right to terminate one service element and not others. It is preferable for the parties to agree the severable parts of the agreement before signature, if possible.

26.6.1 *Division of services into service elements*

The services may be divided into various service elements that are different in nature from each other (for example, in an IT services agreement, the services may include desktop services and telecommunications services).

The services may also be classified by:

(a)   the branch or country of the customer;
(b)   the country or region from which the services are being provided; or
(c)   the language in which the services are being provided.

These additional forms of classification are particularly relevant for multinational outsourcing agreements. The customer may want the right to terminate the services in part in the above cases.

26.6.2 *Severability of the services*

From the customer's perspective, in drafting the agreement, whether the services are severable will depend on the facts of the individual arrangement. In the case of failings by the supplier, the customer may decide that the failure of the supplier to provide certain service elements would not necessarily affect its faith in the ability of the supplier to provide other service elements. If it is practical for the customer to arrange for another supplier to provide the defective service elements, then it may want to include in the agreement the right to terminate those individual elements. The parties will then need to look at the people and assets used to provide each service element to see if it is practical to terminate them individually.

26.6.3   Severability of the charges

The customer may prefer that the service elements be priced separately, so that the financial effect of terminating any particular element is clear. If the supplier has spread transition costs or other fixed costs relating to the terminated service element over the term of the agreement, it will want to ensure that these are recovered. The supplier will also need to understand how service management costs will continue to be recovered. The supplier may not want to agree to termination in part if it does not want to provide the services in circumstances where the value of the contract is substantially reduced. On the other hand, the supplier may prefer not to lose the entire account if it is having difficulty with one service element only.

26.6.4   Avoiding abuse

If the customer is granted a right to termination in part, the supplier will be anxious to ensure that the customer cannot abuse the right. Hence it will want to clarify that:

(a)   in relation to a right to terminate for breach, the customer can only terminate the specific service elements in respect of which the supplier is in breach; or

(b)   in relation to a right to terminate in the event of a force majeure, the customer can only terminate those service elements affected by the force majeure.

26.6.5   Option to terminate all services

Usually the customer will want the option to decide whether it terminates all of the services or only individual service elements. The supplier may argue that, if the supplier breaches the key performance indicators for a particular service element, or a force majeure event affects one service element only, then the customer should be entitled to terminate that service element only. The contractual provisions dealing with this topic need to be drafted very carefully so that both parties are aware of the precise circumstances in which termination of part may be exercised and the exact consequences.

26.7   Termination of multinational arrangements— right to terminate services to the group

A similar issue arises if the customer comprises a group of companies that have entered into services agreements with the supplier. In this situation, the parties will need to decide whether, if the supplier defaults in providing the services to one member of the group, the customer has the right to terminate the services being provided to the group as a whole.

The parties should deal with this issue expressly. It is likely that, on proper analysis, an agreement between the supplier and a group of companies amounts to a bundle of (identical) parallel contracts. If this is the case then, unless the agreements contain cross-default provisions, the customer's right to terminate may be limited to certain contracts. Cross-default provisions allow for termination of all agreements in the event of a breach of one of the constituent agreements.

Similar issues arise if the customer and supplier have a framework agreement with the individual group companies entering into direct agreements with the supplier based on the framework agreement. If the parties wish to agree wider rights of termination referred to above they will need to think very carefully about the interrelationship between the framework and subsidiary agreements.

Chapter 27

The Termination Decision

27.1 Outline

Chapter 26 covers the circumstances in which the parties will have the right to terminate the agreement. This chapter describes the information and documentation that the customer will need to consider when deciding whether to exercise its right to terminate the agreement with the supplier.

27.2 More due diligence

If the customer has been told by its lawyers that it has the right to terminate its agreement with the supplier, whether for convenience or for cause, the process that it will go through in deciding whether to exercise that right will, in some ways, mirror the process described in Chapter 2, when the customer decided whether to enter into the services arrangement with the supplier. Thus the customer will need to decide what its business objective will be in terminating the agreement with the supplier and whether termination will support that objective. To describe the situation another way, the customer should not terminate the agreement until it understands the resulting business consequences.

A word of caution is needed about termination. The party considering termination for cause may lose the right to terminate if it demonstrates, by conduct, an intention to continue with the agreement. If a party believes that a right to terminate has arisen, then it should work closely with its lawyers to determine what it can and cannot do, without potentially losing the ability to terminate.

27.3 Information and documentation

In order for the customer to understand the consequences of terminating, it will need certain information and documentation to properly understand the costs involved in terminating and transferring the services either in-house or to a new supplier. It will also be necessary to evaluate how difficult it will be, from a practical perspective, to effect a transition of the services.

267

The customer may require some or all of the information and documentation described in Table 39, depending upon the individual circumstances.

This information will also be required by the customer on expiry of the agreement, when the customer will need to decide whether to renew the existing services agreement, enter into another services arrangement or bring the services back in-house.

Table 39 Information and documentation required on possible termination

Current services
What services are currently being provided?
How are the services being provided?
What service levels are being achieved?
What volume of services is being provided?
What trends are there regarding the volume of services?
Are there any specific problems or challenges that are currently being faced or which the customer or incoming supplier would need to deal with?
Is there a backlog where services have not been provided?
Assets or premises with regard to which the services are provided
Where relevant, what assets or premises are covered by the services? Is there an accurate list of these?
Employees
What staff and contractors currently provide the services?
Will employees transfer from the incumbent supplier to the customer or to the new supplier?[1]
How much of the time of the relevant employees is dedicated to providing the services to be outsourced?
How long have the staff been employed?
Have they been transferred recently?
Does the customer agree that the relevant staff will transfer under TUPE?
Are there any other employees who are assigned to the business but are on long-term absence or maternity leave and who would transfer under TUPE?
What are the relevant terms and conditions of employment of the transferring staff?
What are the salaries and other benefits received by the employees?
What are the other terms and conditions of the transferring employees (including pension arrangements, special redundancy entitlements, notice period, overtime payments, loans, company car arrangements or entitlement to parking spaces)?
Have any variations to the terms and conditions been agreed?
Is the supplier entitled to agree variations to the terms and conditions?
Do the employees belong to a trade union?
Is the supplier aware of any possible claims against it by staff?
Over the last 12 months what payments have been made in overtime payments?
What accrued holiday entitlements are owing?
What details are available of performance monitoring arrangements?
What are the staff sickness levels over the previous 12 months?

---

[1] See Chapter 31 for an explanation of relevant staffing issues.

Are any of the staff subject to disciplinary proceedings?

At which sites are the employees based?

What are the employees' ages?

What is the normal retirement age under the employees' terms and conditions?

Are any of the employees approaching retirement age?

Staffing and contractors

Is the number and quality of the staff that would transfer to the customer or new supplier on termination sufficient to provide the services?

Are specific members of the supplier's staff or contractors key to the provision of the services?

Are the key staff transferring?

Are the key contractors willing to work for the customer or new supplier?

Is the supplier intending to transfer staff out of the business so that they will not transfer to the customer or new supplier?

Is the supplier aware of any staff intending to resign?

How difficult would it be to replace key staff or contractors in the time available?

What skills will the customer or new supplier need and what training will need to be provided to staff or contractors who will supply the services?

Assets used to provide the services

What assets are used to provide the services, whether used exclusively for the provision of the outsourced services or not (identified by type, quantity and location)?

Are any of the assets owned or leased by the supplier?

Does the customer have the right to purchase the assets on termination? If so, at what cost?

If not, is the supplier willing to make these available to the customer or new supplier and if so, on what conditions (financial and otherwise)?

Has the customer or new supplier been able to check the condition of the assets or premises?

Would it be difficult to replace any of the assets in the time available (e.g. because they are specially configured)?

Software licences and other supply agreements

What software licences and other intellectual property rights are needed to provide the services?

Are any bespoke materials or software used by the supplier in providing the services? (This applies whether they were developed as part of the services or not and also relates to any modifications made to the customer's bespoke materials or software.)

How can the customer or new supplier obtain the necessary rights?

What maintenance agreements, support agreements and other supply agreements are used by the supplier to provide the services (identified by name of supplier, term of contract and charges payable under the contract)?

Are any supply agreements transferable from the supplier to the customer or new supplier?

Are the terms of the third-party contracts acceptable?

Would it be difficult to replace any of the software or supply agreements?

What is the cost of the customer or new supplier taking out new software licences or supply agreements?

Because the customer will require the above information and documentation before termination, in order that it can make an informed decision on termination, it is essential that the supplier is obliged to maintain such documentation throughout the term of the agreement and make it available to the customer on request. This is explained further in the next chapter.

Chapter 28

Implications of Termination

28.1 Outline

Chapters 26 and 27 describe the circumstances in which each party will have the right to terminate the agreement and the information that the customer will have to consider before deciding whether or not to exercise its right. This chapter covers the implications of termination. From the customer's perspective, this includes a discussion of the termination assistance which it will require, whether relating to information, documentation, data, assets, staff, premises or other assistance. From the supplier's perspective, this includes a discussion of termination charges.

28.2 Consideration of termination before signature of the contract

The customer will be concerned to ensure that, on termination of the agreement, it will be free to move to a replacement supplier or move the services in-house. It will also want to ensure a smooth transition. The supplier will need to ensure that it recovers any investment it has made in the provision of the services before expiry. The rest of this chapter deals with these issues.

The important point to make is that all of these issues will need to be considered before the agreement is signed. Thus, the customer should consider whether adopting a particular solution proposed by a supplier will tie it in to that supplier and hinder a transfer of the services on termination. For example, in an IT services project, adopting proprietary technology may make it difficult for the customer to move to another supplier.

28.3 Information and documentation

28.3.1 *Information and documentation required*

The customer will need certain information and documentation to bring the services back in-house or to arrange for a replacement supplier to take over. This is particularly so for IT and business process sourcing arrangements,

271

where the documentation will usually be one of the most important things that the customer will need to enable transition. The customer may be particularly dependent upon documentation relating to the services where staff who used to provide the services are not going to transfer to the incoming supplier or the customer on termination, for example in an offshore arrangement.[1]

Some of this documentation has already been described in Chapter 27. In addition, the customer may require copies of any documentation that is necessary for the provision of services, including, for example, system design and configuration documents, capacity and performance reports, bandwidth reports and network diagrams. If the documentation has been prepared by the supplier as part of the services, the customer may want to agree that it will own the copyright in this documentation or that it and its suppliers will have a perpetual licence to use it.

28.3.2   *When required*

It is not advisable for the customer to specify that the supplier must simply collate and produce the information and documentation on termination of the agreement because:

(a)   it may be difficult to collect such information at the point of termination if it has not been maintained throughout the term of the agreement;

(b)   if the supplier is to manage the service efficiently, it should in any event be maintaining the documentation; and

(c)   it is likely that the relationship between the parties may deteriorate in the run up to or on termination of the agreement and the supplier will be less inclined to collate and produce the information and documentation than at an earlier stage.

28.3.3   *Who will need the information and documentation?*

The customer is not the only one who may need access to information about the services. Chapter 6 describes the due diligence activities which any supplier who is considering entering into a services arrangement will need to undertake. On termination of an initial services agreement, replacement suppliers will need to carry out similar due diligence activities to those described in Chapter 6. At this stage, the necessary information will often be in the hands of the incumbent supplier. The customer will need the supplier

---

[1]   See Chapter 47 for a more detailed discussion of offshore outsourcing.

to make the information and documentation available to the customer and the prospective new suppliers.

28.3.4   *Co-operation with due diligence*

The customer may need the supplier to respond to any questions which it, or the prospective new suppliers, may have as part of their due diligence activities. The customer may also want the incumbent supplier to co-operate with any due diligence activities which it or the other prospective contractors may wish to carry out. For example, the supplier may be required to provide access to:

(a)   locations from which the services are provided;
(b)   assets used to provide the services; or
(c)   the relevant staff or sub-contractors.

28.3.5   *Supplier's concerns*

The incumbent supplier will be anxious to ensure that confidential information about its business and the manner in which it operates (e.g. proprietary methodologies and its charges) is not passed on to its competitors. It will also want to ensure that its obligation to assist the customer in ensuring a smooth transition does not interfere with its ability to provide the services prior to termination. For these reasons it may refuse to allow competitors access to its premises.

If an agreement has simply come to its end through effluxion of time then the supplier may be asked to submit a proposal for providing the services on a ongoing basis. In those circumstances, the supplier may be anxious to retain any advantage it has as incumbent supplier.

The supplier will also want to ensure that, before it enters into the services arrangement, it understands what information it will be obligated to provide so that it can include the cost of maintaining the information in its charges. If it is difficult to evaluate the amount of effort involved in providing information, or co-operating with due diligence, it may want to limit the number of man days of assistance it will provide or reserve the right to charge extra for providing such assistance.

28.4 Data

28.4.1 *Ownership of the data*

In IT and business process sourcing arrangements, it is often crucial for the customer to have access to its data to allow transition to a new supplier. This means that the customer will want the supplier to agree that all data provided by the customer, or produced by it as a result of the services, will belong to the customer. The supplier must agree to hand a copy of this information over at an appropriate time during the termination timetable to allow a smooth transition to take place.

If the data is held in databases, then it is essential that the agreement clarifies that the customer will own copyright and the various database rights (including the structure of the database and changes in the structure) and ensures that after termination it will be able to use the database containing its data.

28.4.2 *Licence for software holding the data*

If the data held by the outgoing supplier includes archived data held on legacy software which the customer is not intending to run after termination then the customer will need to ensure that it has a licence to use the legacy software to gain access to the archived data.

28.4.3 *Format of data*

The customer should reserve the right to specify the format in which the data will be provided. If this involves the supplier changing the format of the data, then the supplier may want to specify that the new format must be reasonable and that it can charge for converting the data.

The customer may want the supplier to agree to provide it with test data to assist with the handover.

Cloud computing models (depending upon whether the model is a software as a service (SaaS), platform as a service (PaaS) or infrastructure as a service (IaaS) model) provide particular challenges for the transfer of data on termination, although cloud computing suppliers have set up an organisation, "OASIS" (Organization for the Advancement of Structured Information Standards) to establish a standard for enabling portability of cloud applications and IT services technical committee. Customers should check the current progress in developing an adequate portability standard and (once it has been developed) should ensure that their cloud computing supplier agrees to meet the standard.

28.4.4   *Handover plan*

On termination, the supplier should be required to identify all customer data held, agree the method and plan for handover of all customer data and comply with the handover plan.

28.5   Assets

In order to ensure a smooth transition on termination, the customer will need to consider the particular nature of its services and the assets used to provide them and will need to ensure that it will have access to everything that it, or the replacement supplier, will require to provide the services after termination. Many of the customer's termination requirements will depend upon the exact details of the services and the particular assets used to provide them. Sections 28.6 to 28.10 include a description of issues that the customer may need to take into account.

28.6   Assets belonging to the customer

On termination, the customer will want the supplier to return all assets (e.g. the customer's bespoke software), documentation or other property it owns, which it has made available to the supplier (as described in Chapters 13 to 15). The customer may want to provide in the agreement that the supplier will not have a lien[2] over any of the customer's property.

The customer may want the right to come onto the supplier's premises to regain control of its property, including its assets and data.

28.7   Hardware and other equipment

28.7.1   *Customer's dependency upon the equipment*

The customer should consider whether it will need any equipment used by the supplier to provide the services. It may be able to buy replacement equipment easily on the open market. If, however, the equipment is legacy

---

[2]   A lien is a right to retain possession as security for payment of a debt.

kit which is difficult to locate or has been specially configured for the customer, then it may be easier to ensure a smooth transition if the equipment is transferred from the outgoing supplier. The customer may therefore want to reserve in the contract the right to buy some or all of the equipment used by the supplier to provide the services.

28.7.2 Deciding which equipment will transfer— exclusive or non-exclusive equipment

Just as the customer may want to procure the equipment, the supplier may no longer require the equipment after termination if it is being used solely to provide services to the customer. Thus the supplier may want to transfer the equipment to the customer.

The situation is more complex where the supplier has been using the equipment to provide services to other customers. Such equipment may be more than is necessary to provide just the customer's service. Alternatively, the supplier may be unwilling to transfer the equipment to the customer if this will interfere with the provision by it of services to its other customers. For this reason, the customer should specify in the agreement what equipment it will require on termination. The customer may wish to provide that the specified equipment must be used exclusively for the provision of the services to it. If the equipment could have been used for the provision of services to other customers, then this restriction is likely to increase the charges as the cost of the equipment cannot be shared between several customers.

In some circumstances, the parties may be able to reach a compromise whereby the supplier grants the customer a licence to use the relevant equipment after termination until the customer can replace it. However, the customer may not want to rely on a licence from the supplier if it has had to terminate the agreement due to the supplier's breach or insolvency.

28.7.3 Defining the equipment to be transferred

The parties will need to decide how to define the relevant equipment which will transfer to the customer on termination. It will be helpful if the particular items of equipment can be identified when the agreement is signed. However, in many cases it will not be possible to do this because equipment will be replaced during the terms of the agreement as it becomes obsolete or the services change.

In this situation it may still be possible to describe the equipment. For example, in an IT services agreement, the customer may want to purchase any equipment used for the provision of the services other than:

(a)   the service management and reporting tools; and
(b)   common infrastructure at the supplier's premises or help desk.

28.7.4   Sale price of the equipment owned by the supplier

If the equipment is owned by the supplier and is being sold to the customer, what price should the customer pay? The supplier may argue that the customer should pay a fair market-value price, as this is the amount that the customer will pay to procure similar equipment on the open market. However, the customer needs to understand the extent to which the equipment costs have already been included in the service charges. This will usually depend upon two different factors. It will depend upon:

(a)   whether the supplier procured the equipment exclusively to provide the services to the customer; and
(b)   whether termination has occurred on expiry of the agreement or on earlier termination. If termination occurs before expiry, and a termination charge is payable, the customer will need to understand the extent to which any termination charge includes the supplier's unrecovered equipment costs.

If the supplier has used the equipment exclusively to provide the services to the customer and termination occurs on expiry of the agreement, then the supplier may have included the full cost of acquiring the equipment in its charges for the services. In these circumstances, the customer may be able to specify that the supplier will transfer the equipment to it for a nominal fee. The parties may then decide that, if the agreement is terminated before expiry, the customer will pay the supplier's unrecovered costs relating to the equipment.

The parties should also take into account whether the clause will be enforceable upon the supplier's insolvency. A clause providing that equipment automatically transfers back to the customer is likely to be unenforceable whether as a matter of public policy or as a result of a liquidator's right to disclaim onerous contracts.

28.7.5   Transfer of leased equipment

Leases are usually non-transferable. It follows that if the supplier has leased the equipment from a third-party lessor then it may be difficult for the supplier to agree with the lessor on termination that its rights and obligations under the lease will be transferred to the customer. In this situation, if the customer wants to acquire the equipment, it will usually have to require the supplier to terminate the lease. The parties will need to agree who will pay any termination charges incurred in terminating the lease.

The lessor is likely to be more amenable if the supplier requests the right to transfer the lease to the customer before the lease is signed. For this reason, the customer may insist that the supplier ensures, before it enters into any leases for the relevant equipment, that they are transferable to the customer. The customer may prefer the leases to be transferable to the replacement supplier, although the lessor may be reluctant to agree to the transfer of the lease to a company whose identity is unknown.

28.7.6   *Title in the equipment*

The customer will want the supplier to provide appropriate warranties for the equipment, for example, relating to the supplier's title in the equipment.

28.7.7   *Condition of the equipment*

The customer may be concerned to ensure that any equipment that it procures from the supplier is in good condition. One way of doing this is to ask the supplier to warrant the condition of the equipment. The readiness of the supplier to grant such warranties may depend upon whether the equipment was originally transferred to the supplier from the customer and whether the customer was willing to grant warranties about assets transferred to the supplier on commencement of the services arrangement.

The customer may want the ability to require the supplier to rectify defects in the equipment or, if the supplier fails to do so, the right to rectify the defects itself, at the supplier's expense.

The customer may want to ensure that any equipment that it acquires from the supplier will be suitable for providing the services for a certain period after expiry of the agreement. Without such provision the supplier may try to use equipment knowing that it will require substantial replacement at the end of the term. The customer may want to avoid a situation in which it is faced with replacing all of the equipment at the same time as transferring the services to the replacement supplier. If the customer wants the supplier to commit to this, it may have charging implications, with the charges increasing to cover the cost of replacing any equipment that would not otherwise need replacing.

28.7.8   *Option or obligation to purchase the equipment*

The customer will usually want an option (rather than an obligation) to purchase the supplier's equipment. However, the supplier may be concerned to ensure that it recovers its investment in the equipment and therefore may insist that the customer purchases the equipment. The customer may want to reserve the right not to purchase the equipment if it terminates the agreement for breach by the supplier or if the supplier has failed to maintain the equipment.

If the customer has an option to purchase the equipment, then the parties will usually want to agree a period within which the customer must notify the supplier whether it intends to exercise the option. The period may be extended if the supplier fails to provide the customer with sufficient information about the equipment to enable the customer to decide whether it wants to exercise its option or not. An option to purchase on the part of the customer can have tax consequences.

28.7.9   Treatment of assets in cloud computing arrangements

In section 1.2, we explained the long term trend towards commoditised, utility service models, such as cloud computing. The treatment of equipment on termination will depend upon whether the cloud service is a software as a service (SaaS), platform as a service (PaaS) or infrastructure as a service (IaaS) model and whether the parties have adopted a private, public, community or hybrid model (as defined in section 1.2):

(a) **Public** - The adoption of public cloud computing models should mean that the transfer of equipment on termination will become irrelevant, as the cloud computing services involve the provision of services to a large number of customers and the customer is not expected to finance the procurement of specific hardware required to provide the services.

(b) **Private** - The adoption of a private cloud will usually have the same equipment implications as traditional outsourcing models, as the services will be provided exclusively for the customer and the customer will have funded all of the costs of procuring the relevant equipment.

(c) **Community or hybrid** - The situation is more complicated for community or hybrid cloud computing models, particularly with regard to the first customer or customers, as some suppliers endeavour to pass all of the procurement and set up costs of the cloud computing model onto the initial customers, who will in effect have financed all of the procurement costs of the equipment and risk losing their investment on termination. Customers entering into these types of arrangements need to clarify exactly what they are paying for in any set up charges and include suitable protections in the agreement.

28.8 Third-party software licences

28.8.1 Return of customer's licences

In the past, most software has been licensed on the basis of an up-front payment for a perpetual licence, with recurring annual payments of approximately 10 per cent to cover support. Microsoft has changed its pricing model so that the up-front payment is replaced by annual charges for annual licences. It is possible that other suppliers will follow this model in time. For the present, however, the traditional model means that customers must ensure that they do not need to take out new licences for software on termination, thus exposing themselves to the possibility of having to pay the up-front charge again.

If the customer intends to transfer its third-party software licences to the supplier on commencement of the services arrangement, it should ensure that the licensor agrees that the licences may be transferred back to the customer on termination. This issue will be more problematic if, in order to gain a better price for the customer, the supplier intends to merge the software licences with other corporate arrangements that it has with the software licensor. This means that it may not be practical to carve out the software licences and transfer them to the customer on termination, or that if it is possible, the customer will not continue to benefit from the supplier's corporate discounts for the software.

28.8.2 New licences

If the supplier has taken out other software licences for the provision of the services, the customer may want the supplier to ensure that these can also be transferred to it on termination. The supplier will want to ensure that, if the agreement is terminated prior to expiry, the customer has an obligation to pay any unrecovered software licence costs. The customer will want to ensure that it will not be liable to pay the unrecovered software licence costs if it is terminating the agreement for breach by the supplier and does not want to take over the software licences.

28.9 Supplier's bespoke software

The customer should be particularly careful to ensure that it can use any bespoke software developed by the supplier post termination if it is necessary for the provision of the services and there are no ready substitutes.

28.9.1   *Software developed as part of the services*

If the software is developed by the supplier as part of the services, then the customer may want ownership rights over such software or a perpetual licence so that it and replacement suppliers can use it. The supplier will usually want to own the software so that it can exploit it by licensing it to other customers.

Unless the customer has a reason for wanting to own the software (e.g. because it is a modification to the customer's bespoke software, or it wants to control the use of the software so that it is not licensed to competitors), a perpetual, royalty-free licence covering the customer and future suppliers will usually be sufficient.

The customer may want to ensure that it has obtained some financial benefit in return for allowing the supplier to retain intellectual property rights in the bespoke software.

Some customers suggest that they should receive a share of the profits or revenues received by the supplier from licensing the software to other customers. This may appear to be an attractive idea in principle, but it is often extremely difficult to implement in practice. Thus any licence to other customers will usually form part of a general services agreement so that there is no specific charge for the licence. If there is a separate charge and the supplier is providing additional services to the other customers, the supplier will control how the charges are allocated between the licence and the services. Thus determining what other customers are actually paying for the licence is beset with difficulty. In any event, the other customers may want to keep details of the arrangement with the supplier confidential.

Therefore, unless substantial amounts of money are involved, it may be simpler for the parties to agree a reasonable reduction in the charges payable by the customer under the services agreement. (See sections 16.2.3 to 16.2.4 for a further discussion of these issues.)

Where substantial amounts of money are involved, the parties may decide to set up a joint venture company to exploit the software (see Chapter 19 for a more detailed discussion of joint ventures). This may be particularly appropriate where the software has been developed with the customer's expert knowledge of its particular sector and where the customer can contribute to the marketing of the software.

28.9.2   *Other software*

The customer may be concerned about the supplier using bespoke software other than that developed as part of the services. It may want to avoid a situation where the supplier has integrated its bespoke software into the customer's solution in such a way that the customer is locked in to the relationship with the supplier. Therefore, the customer should ensure that the supplier grants it and any replacement supplier a licence to use the bespoke software, so that the replacement supplier can provide the services after termination for a reasonable period until the software can be replaced. If the customer has not requested the supplier to integrate the software into the solution, then the customer may argue that it should not have to pay for the licence, unless agreed by the parties to the contrary. This may act as a warning to the supplier not to integrate its bespoke software into the solution without the customer's consent.

If the supplier develops software that would improve the solution, it could then be open to the supplier to explain the benefits of the software to the customer and agree with the customer a suitable charge. The disadvantage of this approach, from the supplier's perspective, is that there is a risk that its employees will forget to obtain the customer's consent before implementing bespoke software.

28.9.3   Escrow

The customer may want the supplier to deposit the source code of any supplier bespoke software in escrow with a third party. This issue is discussed in Chapter 29.

28.10   Support, maintenance and other contracts

If the customer is procuring equipment and software from the supplier, it may want the supplier to transfer to it any equipment maintenance and software support agreements for the relevant equipment and software.

Whether the supplier will be able to agree to this provision will depend upon the particular terms which it has agreed with its own suppliers. If the supplier has agreed volume discounts with its own suppliers based upon the maintenance and support of equipment and software used for the provision of services to various customers, then the customer will not be able to obtain the benefit of the volume discount after termination. The supplier may be able to carve out from the group-wide agreement with the supplier the maintenance and support of the specific customer equipment and software. However, the charges for the maintenance and support will usually reflect the market rate for such services.

The customer may also want to take over other supply agreements used for the provision of the services, in which case similar considerations will apply to those described above.

28.11   People issues

The people issues relating to termination are discussed in Chapter 31.

28.12   General assistance

The customer may find it difficult to anticipate all of the assistance that it will require on termination. Therefore, it should consider including a general provision, obliging the supplier to co-operate fully with the customer and the replacement supplier so that any transfer of the services on termination is achieved with minimum disruption and requiring the provision of any other assistance that the customer may require at the time. This could cover, for example, training required by the customer on termination.

If the supplier is not able to estimate the amount of effort required to comply with this obligation, it will want to limit it to a certain number of man days of effort or specify that it can charge extra for providing the necessary co-operation. The customer may want the supplier to agree a man-day rate in accordance with which the supplier's charges will be calculated.

28.13   Termination management

The customer should consider how the transition of the services on termination can be effected with the maximum efficiency. This may involve the agreement by the parties of a detailed exit plan. The parties may agree a draft exit plan before signature of the agreement. Usually, however, priority is given to implementing a transition plan under which the supplier will take over the services. As a result, preparation of an exit plan is often postponed for six or 12 months.

The parties may also agree to review the exit plan on a regular basis or when the parties change the services, to ensure that it is still applicable.

The parties may agree on the appointment by the supplier (or by both parties) of a termination manager who will be responsible for implementing the exit plan. The customer may want control over the choice of the termination manager (see Chapter 8).

The customer may want the right to extend the agreement in part for different service elements, where relevant, to ensure that it does not need to effect the transition of the services on termination all at the same time, in a "big bang". If the charges for the individual service elements are specified in the agreement, then the customer may want the right to extend the agreement, for a limited period, at the same charge or another specified charge.

Otherwise, the parties will need to agree the charges to be payable by the customer under the change control procedure (see Chapter 25).

28.14 Termination charges

28.14.1 Supplier's costs

One of the most contentious aspects of termination concerns the payments which should be made by each party and when these payments should be made.

The supplier will need to consider how, in the event of early termination of the agreement under any of the grounds mentioned in section 26.3 above, it will ensure that it recovers its investment in the services once it is no longer receiving revenue from the services arrangement. In some cases, the supplier will have invested in procuring, configuring or customising assets that can be sold to the customer or to the replacement supplier, so that it can provide the services after termination. In other cases, the investment will not have been in assets but in, for example, the training of staff.

The supplier may want the customer to pay a charge if the agreement is terminated early. However, the customer may not want to pay any termination charge or any other charges for termination assistance if the agreement is terminated for breach or insolvency of the supplier. In this situation, it is crucial for the supplier that the agreement includes reasonable provisions relating to termination for breach.

If the agreement is terminated by the customer for breach or insolvency, then the supplier may find itself in a situation where not only has it lost its investment, but it may also be liable to the customer in damages. Chapter 35 deals with ways in which the supplier may want to limit its liability in such circumstances.

In circumstances where the supplier has terminated the agreement as a result of the customer's failure to pay, or insolvency, the supplier may be reluctant to provide any termination assistance unless the customer pays for the assistance in advance.

28.14.2 Payment for termination assistance

The supplier will also be concerned to ensure that it is clear what services it must provide on termination, so that it can ensure that it has included the cost of compliance in its charges.

28.14.3   Agreement of termination charge in advance

Just as the supplier will want to ensure that it understands what services it must provide on termination, the customer may want to ensure that it understands what payments it will have to make on termination. The customer may prefer for these to be provided for in the agreement, except where the customer is unable to specify its requirements in advance.

An extreme approach to this issue was that adopted in PFI agreements where, before the agreement was signed, the parties agreed complex provisions for determining the termination charge that the customer will make upon any early termination. The method of calculation depended upon the grounds for termination. In the case of supplier breach, the termination payments were based upon the market value of the PFI contract if it were sold to an alternative supplier. In the case of customer breach, compensation was designed to ensure that the supplier (and its funders) were fully compensated, so as to be no worse off than they would have been if the PFI contract had continued as expected. These payments were in full and final settlement of the supplier's liability and excluded the customer's rights under the common law. PFI contracts have fallen out of favour in the UK, although they are popular in other parts of the world. See Chapter 44 for a general explanation of PFI contracts. Some other types of services arrangements have adopted this approach, for example some telecommunications or web hosting arrangements.

28.14.4   Retention of charges

The customer may be concerned that the supplier will not co-operate in the transfer of the services to a competitor or back to the customer. Therefore, the customer may want the right to make a specified retention from the charges until the supplier has fulfilled its obligations to provide termination assistance and executed the exit plan. If this is sought, the supplier will be concerned that the customer may never pay the retention, even after the supplier has carried out all of its duties. It may be unwilling to agree to any retention unless the retained sums are held by a third party. It may also suggest that no retention should be made unless the supplier is in breach of the agreement or insolvent and that a reduced retention should be made in other circumstances.

28.14.5   Taxation treatment of termination payments

The taxation treatment of termination charges needs careful consideration. If termination payments replace income to which the supplier would have been entitled, then they may be liable to taxation as income. Otherwise they may potentially be liable to taxation as chargeable gains.[3] The customer may find that taxation relief which had previously been available in regard to payments of the service charges will not be available for termination payments. From a VAT viewpoint, agreed out-of-court settlement payments are not usually liable to VAT unless part or all of the payment relates to services over which there has been a dispute, in which case that part of any settlement which relates to the services will be taxed in the same way as the underlying services.

28.15   Termination in part and step in

The customer should consider the extent to which it will require the supplier to provide termination assistance, of the type outlined above, in circumstances in which the agreement is terminated in part or when the customer steps in to provide the services (see Chapter 8 for a description of step in).

---

[3]   PFI contracts will usually include "grossing-up" provisions for compensation payments made for customer default to put the supplier in a net position. The parties may want to consider doing the same.

Part 8

Insolvency, People and Competition Issues

Chapter 29

Insolvency Issues

29.1   Outline

Chapter 28 describes the termination of the services arrangement whether for breach or insolvency or otherwise. This chapter deals with other issues relating to insolvency. Typically, the insolvency provisions of a services agreement are viewed at the negotiation stage as "standard boilerplating" to which the parties probably pay relatively little attention. However, in the current rocky economic climate, there is an increased risk that the supplier, or the customer to the services agreement, may be in financial difficulty. It should be noted in particular that the number of insolvencies usually increases as a country comes out of recession. Insolvency of a counterparty will always be a potential commercial hazard of doing business. However, adopting sensible precautions alongside a well-planned and drafted agreement will help to reduce the risk of counterparty insolvency and reduce the loss when insolvency does arise.

This chapter covers due diligence that each party should carry out before and after the agreement is signed and guarantees or protections that each side may want to request from the other side. It also discusses issues relating to restrictions upon the transfer of the agreement, and deals with the right to terminate on insolvency-related grounds.

29.2   Due diligence before the agreement is signed

Chapters 2 and 6 describe the due diligence that the customer and supplier must carry out before the agreement is signed. A key element of the due diligence to be carried out by either side relates to the financial standing of the other side. The customer should only be prepared to go forward with the transaction if satisfied that the supplier will be able to perform both operationally and financially.

Each party should consider whether it requires additional protection by way of third-party guarantees (typically from the other side's parent company) and/or performance bonds. Possible guarantees and protections are described at sections 29.2.1 and 29.2.2 below.

29.2.1   *Parent company guarantee*

Either party may request a guarantee from the parent company of the other party. There are two types of guarantee:

(a)   A performance guarantee provides reassurance to the customer that if the supplier fails to provide the services then the parent company will provide them instead. This type of guarantee is appropriate where the parent company has the ability to provide the services.
(b)   A financial guarantee is a guarantee under which the parent company agrees to indemnify the customer or supplier in respect of sums of money owing to it.

29.2.2   *Performance bond*

Performance bonds are agreements by a bank to pay certain amounts of money to the customer if specific circumstances are satisfied. For example:

(a)   if the bank receives a written notice from the customer and the supplier agreeing that an amount of damages is payable to the customer; or
(b)   if the bank is presented with a certified copy of a judgment of a court having jurisdiction or of an award issued in arbitration proceedings under which damages are payable by the supplier to the customer with a statement by the customer showing the amount of the damages which remain unsatisfied as at the date of the claim.

29.2.3   *Payment terms*

In addition to considering whether guarantees are required, both supplier and customer should consider whether the charges should be payable in advance or in arrears. Clearly the customer is taking the insolvency risk if the charges are payable in advance and the supplier is taking the insolvency risk if the charges are payable in arrears.

29.2.4   *Liens*

The supplier and customer may also want to clarify that the other party will not have a lien[1] over their property.

---

[1]   A lien is a right to retain possession as security for payment of a debt. See s.246 of the Insolvency Act 1986 regarding the unenforceability of certain liens.

29.2.5   Source code escrow

The customer should consider whether it needs the supplier to deposit the source code of any software necessary to provide the services in escrow. Software will usually be deposited with a recognised body, such as the National Computer Centre (NCC), who will agree to release it in certain circumstances, for example if the supplier becomes insolvent. It is important that the supplier agrees to deposit up-to-date versions of the relevant software. The customer should also check that it has any necessary rights it needs to modify or support the software after release.

29.3   Ongoing due diligence

Each party should ensure that it investigates the other party's financial standing throughout the term of the agreement. The party may want to include triggers that give rise to additional rights if the other party (or, if a parent company guarantee is given, the guarantor) suffers an adverse event.[2]

29.3.1   Trigger events

Table 40 shows possible trigger events.

Table 40 Example trigger events

Credit rating downgraded and the other side does not provide reassurances that it is able to comply with its obligations.
Adverse decline in the financial ratios below a specified level.
Cash flow deteriorates below specified level.
Late payment of a sub-contractor or a material sub-contractor by the supplier.
Material breach of covenants to its lenders.
Turnover declines below a certain level.
Profitability decreases to a certain level.
Share price reduces below specified price.
Reduction in tangible net worth below a specified threshold.
Commencement of any litigation with respect to any financial indebtedness.

29.3.2   Additional rights

The additional rights could involve:

(a)   the right to require the other side (or its auditors) to provide additional information about its financial standing or evidence that it will be able

---

[2]   A similar approach has been adopted by the OGC in its model IT outsourcing contracts.

to comply with its obligations, including, for example, regular updates on its financial position;

(b) the right to require the other side to provide a plan setting out how the other side will ensure the continuity of the provision of the services in the event that they become insolvent;

(c) the provision of additional financial guarantees or charges over assets. The innocent party must take specialist insolvency advice to check whether the additional guarantees will be enforceable if the other party subsequently becomes insolvent;

(d) the right to terminate if the other side fails to provide the necessary guarantees or reassurances;

(e) the right for the customer to pay charges due under the services arrangement into an escrow account that is used to pay key sub-contractors; and

(f) the right to withhold payments of specified amounts from the sums held in escrow, to cover the cost of transferring the services to a replacement supplier if the supplier subsequently becomes insolvent.

29.4   Assignment or novation of the contract[3]

Before the services arrangement is agreed, each party will generally carry out a due diligence exercise relating to the specific financial standing and character of the other side. Therefore, neither party will usually be willing to allow the other party to transfer their rights or obligations under the agreement to another company without their consent.

The supplier and customer may want the ability to transfer the agreement to another company within the same group (as part of a corporate reorganisation). The other side is more likely to agree to this where the parent company, of the other side, has provided a parent company guarantee and that guarantee will be transferred to cover the liabilities of the group company to whom the agreement will be transferred.

The ability of each party to transfer the agreement in other circumstances will usually be subject to the consent of the other party, although the parties may agree to act reasonably in giving or refusing approval.

---

[3] An assignment is a transfer of part or all of the benefit of a contract. The third party will still be able to enforce the contract against the customer. Novation extinguishes the contract between the customer and the third party and replaces it with a new contract between the supplier and the third party.

29.5   Termination rights[4]

Contracts are not automatically terminated on the other party's insolvency. Each party needs to ensure that there are express terms within the agreement to terminate in the event of the other party's insolvency (unless the other party is a public sector body). The clause needs to be carefully drafted. Naturally the clause needs to give a right to terminate at the very outset of formal insolvency (i.e. liquidation, administration, receivership). However, to maximise the options available to the party, a party may want the right to terminate to be triggered by events that occur earlier in time and which indicate that formal insolvency may follow. Typical examples include the other side becoming "unable to pay its debts as they fall due", a statutory demand being served on it or its credit rating being downgraded.

The corporate insolvency provisions in the Enterprise Act 2002 came into force on 15 September 2003. One of the reforms introduced by the Act was that the administration procedure was reformed and streamlined. Rights to terminate will need to reflect this legislation so that they refer to an application to the court for an administration order and to the giving of a notice of appointment or intention to appoint an administrator.

One should also bear in mind that a party may enter an insolvency process in a different jurisdiction even if it is registered in the United Kingdom. Therefore the termination clauses should be drafted widely enough to capture equivalent insolvency processes overseas. Where relevant, a party may also wish to build in protections giving it rights to receive information regarding the establishment of offices or other operations overseas.

29.6   Direct agreement with sub-contractors or funders

A supplier experiencing financial problems may fail to pay key sub-contractors on time or it may fall behind with repayments to funders. In this situation, there is a risk that a sub-contractor will terminate the subcontract or that a funder will terminate the funding arrangement and repossess the assets which it has funded. Either of these situations could cause serious problems for the customer (although in practice, if the funder knows that the assets funded have been specifically customised for the customer, it may seek to sell them to the customer).

Therefore, the customer may want a direct agreement with the sub-contractor or funder under which they agree that they will not terminate

---

[4]   The parties may want to clarify whether termination of the agreement for insolvency constitutes termination for breach. See the interesting case of *Balfour Beatty Civil Engineering (t/a Balfour Beatty/Costain (Cardiff Bay Barrage) Joint Venture) v Technical & General Guarantee Co Ltd* [2000] C.L.C. 252 in which Lord Justice Walter commented that liquidation is not a breach of contract in most instances.

their agreements with the supplier without notifying the customer and giving the customer a right to step in to the agreement in place of the supplier.

If the supplier has not finalised its funding arrangements by the date of signature of the agreement, then the customer may want the supplier to agree that it will not, without the customer's consent, enter into any funding arrangements or charge key assets used to provide the services. The customer may then make its consent conditional upon, for example, the funder entering into a direct agreement with the customer.

Similarly, in services agreements which are externally funded (and in particular PFI contracts) the funder will usually require a direct agreement with the customer to provide that the customer will not terminate the services arrangement without giving the funder notice, and giving the funder the right to preserve the contract by substituting an alternative supplier.[5]

29.7   Transactions which can be set aside

If the supplier does go into an insolvency process, it is likely to go into either administration or liquidation. Administrators and liquidators ("office holders") have extensive powers to investigate the activities of the supplier in the run up to the insolvency. In certain prescribed circumstances, office holders can lawfully get court orders to claw back assets and set aside security over assets with a view to selling the insolvent estate. Therefore, the customer should seek specialist insolvency advice to ensure the enforceability of particular rights that it will require to guarantee the continuity of its business if the supplier becomes insolvent. It is outside the scope of this Guide to describe this issue further or to cover other issues relating to general insolvency law.

---

[5]   In a PFI contract, where the supplier is generally a special purpose vehicle, which subcontracts all of its obligations to more substantial companies, the funder will also require the right to preserve the subcontracts by stepping in to the place of the supplier.

Chapter 30

Eurozone fragmentation

30.1   Outline

Ever since the euro came into existence, legal and economics commentators have analysed and speculated on the likelihood of an eventual fragmentation of the eurozone, and what the effects of such a fragmentation would be. Since the second half of 2011 this has ceased to be a niche, theoretical exercise: all businesses in the eurozone, or with a direct or indirect connection to it, have had to consider these fundamental questions. This chapter summarises the most likely effects a fragmentation of the eurozone could have on a services agreement, and suggests some documentary and other considerations parties to a services agreement should be aware of where one or more of the parties is based in the eurozone.

Unless otherwise stated, we assume in this chapter that the relevant services agreement is governed by English law. If that is not the case, the parties are likely to need to consider similar points, by applying the relevant governing law.

30.2   Background: what form could a eurozone fragmentation take?

30.2.1   Possible outcomes: who exits?

Eurozone fragmentation in its simplest form means a Member State within the current eurozone (an Exiting State) adopting a new currency in place of the euro (an Exit Event). The hypothetical example most commonly used by commentators is Greece replacing euros with "new drachmas".

But a eurozone fragmentation could take many forms, for example:

(a)   Exits by a number of the Member States from the weaker economies in the eurozone.
(b)   Exits by one or more of the Member States from the stronger economies in the eurozone (e.g. Germany).

(c)   A complete collapse of the euro, with all current eurozone members returning to their own national currencies (a Full Break-up Event).

For simplicity, in the examples below we assume there is a single Exiting State, other than where alternatives are expressly mentioned.

30.2.2   Possible outcomes: exit process

The EU treaties do not make provisions for a Member State leaving the euro. They do include a mechanism to enable a country to leave the EU altogether, and it is implicit within the treaties that only Member States can participate in the euro. However, under the stated mechanisms an EU exit could potentially take two or more years to conclude: this protracted timetable would be unlikely to be practical for a country leaving the EU in order to change its currency.

So it is likely that the method of achieving an Exit Event would be determined on an ad hoc, practical basis, rather than by a prescribed procedure. This in turn makes it difficult to predict the legal and commercial effects of an Exit Event: for example, the attitude of the courts of other jurisdictions to changes in monetary and other law in an Exiting State may well depend on whether the Exit Event occurs unilaterally or on a consensual basis.

30.2.3   Likelihood of law change

Any legal analysis of the likely affects of an Exit Event must be based primarily on the current law. But an Exit Event may bring a wide range of law changes with it, at national and international level, far beyond the specific change to the monetary law of the Exiting State. If an Exit Event were to occur, the parties to a services agreement would need to consider its effect in light of any accompanying changes in law.

30.3   How could an Exit Event affect a services agreement?

The most likely ways in which an Exit Event could affect the performance of a services agreement are as follows:

(a)   Redenomination of charges/payment obligations.

(b)   Unenforceability of payment obligations.

(c)   Changes to counterparty risk.

Each of these is considered below.

30.4 Currency of payment obligations

If a services agreement states that the customer must pay the supplier in euros, what effect would an Exit Event have on that payment obligation?

This is particularly important for two reasons:

(a) If the customer's payment obligations were redenominated into the new currency of the Exiting State at the official exchange rate provided for in the Exiting State's new monetary law, the provider might well suffer a shortfall in practice even if it receives full settlement. The value of the replacement currency against the euro is likely to fall below the official exchange rate (although of course this would depend on the identity of the Exiting State).

(b) If the customer's payment obligations were redenominated into the new currency on an Exit Event, the customer could satisfy its payment obligations by making payments in that currency. This could be relevant in determining whether a non-payment event of default has occurred.

In the absence of a Full Break-up Event, if neither party has any connection to the Exiting State, an Exit Event will have no direct impact. So for example, an obligation on a Spanish customer to pay a German supplier in Euros would ordinarily be unaffected by a Greek Exit Event.

Redenomination is most likely where the customer is based in, or is otherwise making payments from, the Exiting State. If the agreement clearly defines "euro" as either (i) the single currency of the eurozone or (ii) the currency from time to time of the Exiting State, an English court will give effect to that designation. So in the case of (ii), it would redenominate the payment obligation into the new currency of the Exiting State at the official exchange rate. If it is unclear which of those interpretations of "euro" the parties intended to apply, the court will look at the "setting of the transaction" as a whole and its general and financial environment. In particular, the English courts will look at where the amounts due are payable.

If the contract envisages that all payments will be made by the customer into an account in the Exiting State, the English courts are likely to redenominate the payment obligation into the new currency of the Exiting State unless the agreement otherwise clearly links that obligation with another jurisdiction. If payments must be made outside the Exiting State (e.g. to a local bank account of the supplier), the court is likely to interpret "euro" as the single currency of the eurozone and will not redenominate the payment obligation following an Exit Event.

30.4.1   What about a Full Break-up Event?

If a Full Break-up Event occurred, the English courts would have to redenominate the payment obligation into another currency. If the agreement expressly defines the euro as the currency from time to time of the jurisdiction in which the customer is incorporated, or euro is not defined but payments are made by the customer in its own jurisdiction, the English courts are likely to redenominate euro payment obligations into the new currency of the Exiting State.

If there is no such link between the currency and/or payment with a particular state, the position is likely to be unclear. For example, if the agreement did not define "euro" and provided for payments in London, it seems unlikely the courts would redenominate the obligations into the currency of the place of payment (sterling), as this was clearly not the parties' intention.

It seems inconceivable that new, co-ordinated legislation would not be passed across the (former) eurozone and beyond, setting out how existing euro-denominated debts and payment obligations would be redenominated. That legislation might also address how such redenominated debts could be settled (only under the new currency or also by payment in euros during a transitional period?).

30.5   Exchange controls

30.5.1   What are exchange controls?

Exchange controls can take a variety of forms, but their usual basic purpose is to regulate the outflow of foreign exchange (i.e. foreign currency). Capital controls describe measures that restrict international capital movements (whether inward or outward across jurisdictions). The objective of imposing such exchange and capital controls could be to preserve foreign exchange and to stabilize the exchange rate. The EU Treaties generally prohibit restrictions on the movement of capital between Member States and between Member States and third countries.[1] However, there are exceptions under which the imposition of capital controls are justified under the EU Treaties; e.g. for prudential supervision of financial institutions and on the grounds of public policy and public security.

It is likely that an Exiting State would attempt to impose exchange/capital controls to preserve foreign exchange and to bolster the exchange rate between its new currency and other currencies.

---

[1]   See Article 63 of the Treaty on the Functioning of the European Union (being Article 56 of the former Treaty on the Functioning of the European Community).

30.5.2   Why might they matter?

If the customer is based in an Exiting State that imposes exchange or capital controls, this may restrict or prevent the making of international payments by the customer under the services agreement. This is most likely to be the case if, under the terms of the agreement, the customer is still required to make payments in Euros (on which see section 30.4 above) rather than in the Exiting State's new currency.

A payment obligation under an English law services agreement will not necessarily be unenforceable as a matter of English law because it would breach an Exiting State's exchange controls. Under the IMF rules, IMF members (which includes all EU members) agree that they will not enforce "exchange contracts" that would breach IMF-approved exchange controls. However, it is not clear whether this would apply to payments under a services agreement: in the past, the English courts have interpreted these IMF provisions narrowly, so that they only apply to currency exchange contracts. However, courts in other jurisdictions have taken the view that they have a wider application.

In any event, if a supplier were to attempt to take legal action in the Exiting State against the customer to enforce an obligation that would breach the Exiting State's exchange controls, the chances of success would be slim.

30.6   Credit risk

How will an Exit Event affect the businesses of the parties to the agreement generally? If an Exit Event creates a mismatch between the currency in which a party generates income and the currency of its payment obligations, this may affect its financial health.

Changes in credit risk can be direct as well as indirect. Companies not based in an Exiting State but with significant exposures to businesses in the Exiting State will also be affected.

The supplier may be concerned that the customer will be able to continue to pay it for its services. Equally, the customer may have concerns that the supplier will be unable to continue to run a profitable business.

30.7   Documentary and commercial changes to consider

In an attempt to address the risks summarised above, the parties to a services agreement involving one or more parties in an Exiting State may wish to consider the following before concluding the agreement:

(a) **Including express currency definitions**. Where the agreement provides for payments by the customer in euros, the supplier may wish to include a definition of "euro" that makes clear this refers to the "single currency", rather than the local currency of the customer or supplier from time to time. The customer may prefer the opposite. (This does of course depend on whether the potentially relevant "Exit Event" would be of one of the economically weaker EU Member States.)

(b) **Including express force majeure/material adverse change clauses**. Either party might consider including force majeure or material adverse change clauses to enable it to exit or renegotiate the agreement in the event of an Exit Event.

(c) **Credit support from outside Exiting State**. Either party may wish to receive a guarantee of the other party's obligations to address the increased risk of distress or insolvency that an Exit Event may bring. More specifically, a financial guarantee in favour of a supplier from a company based outside a potential Exit Event may reduce the risk of exchange controls preventing it receiving payment for its services under the services agreement.

(d) **Changing other commercial terms**. Companies entering into service contracts with counterparties in at-risk countries may insist on certain changes to the terms they would normally agree, with a view to reducing their exposure to an Exit Event. They might for example insist on receiving payments up-front and only sign up to relatively short term contracts.

(e) **Avoiding at-risk countries**. When a company is considering entering into a services agreement either as a customer or a supplier, if a potential counterparty is based in the eurozone, and in particular a potential Exiting State, the company should include the potential complications of an Exit Event (as described above) among the factors it considers in deciding whether to proceed with the contract.

Chapter 31

People Issues

31.1 Outline

Chapters 26 to 29 deal with termination-related matters, including the grounds for termination, the termination decision and assistance, and the effect that the insolvency of either party has upon these.

This chapter deals with people-related matters, whether on termination of the services arrangement or on its commencement.

It describes the impact of the application of the Acquired Rights Directive (properly known as Council Directive 2001/23/EC regarding the safeguarding of employees' rights in the event of transfers of undertakings) (ARD) to services arrangements.

It also assesses how employees of both the customer and the supplier can be affected by the services arrangements and it offers practical hints and tips on how each party can attempt to inject some control over the process and minimise its exposure to liability.

This chapter deals with legal and business issues. Where it deals with legal issues, it sets out the position under English law. Where a services agreement involves employees outside the UK, it is essential that the parties take advice on local employment law. Part 12 of this Guide deals with employment law issues in other key EU jurisdictions and Chapters 48 and 49 deal with the employment issues in India and China.

31.2 Mandatory provisions in ARD

The purpose of ARD is to "provide for the protection of employees in the event of a change of employer, to ensure that their rights are safeguarded".

Under ARD, there are a number of provisions which Member States must adopt in order to give effect to the Directive. Although some of the details may be subject to national law, the principles in Table 41 apply throughout the EU.

Table 41 Mandatory provisions in ARD

Application

ARD applies to any transfer of an undertaking, business or part of an undertaking or business to another employer as a result of a legal transfer or merger.

A transfer occurs where there is a transfer of an economic entity which retains its identity; an economic entity is an organised grouping of resources which has the object of pursuing an economic activity, whether that is central or ancillary, public or private, or profit-making or not.

Transfer of rights and obligations

ARD operates to transfer rights and obligations under the contract of employment from the transferor to the transferee.

Collective agreements

After a transfer, the transferee must honour the terms of any collective agreement.

Dismissal

The transfer of an undertaking must not itself constitute grounds for dismissal unless the dismissal is for an economic, technical or organisational reason entailing changes in the workforce; any termination of employment due to a substantial change in working conditions to the detriment of the employee shall be regarded as a dismissal by the employer.

Consultation

Any employees who are affected by a transfer are entitled to have representatives and the representatives must be given certain information about the transfer in good time before the transfer takes place and before the employees' conditions of work and employment are affected by the transfer; if measures are envisaged, the representatives must also be consulted in relation to the measures with a view to reaching an agreement.

If there are no employee representatives, the employees must be given the information directly.

31.3 Optional provisions in ARD

Under ARD, a number of provisions are either optional for Member States to adopt or can be limited to comply with national laws. Some examples of these provisions are described in Table 42.

Table 42 Optional provisions in ARD

Definitions

The definitions of "employee", "employee representatives" and "employment relationship" are matters for national law.

Joint and several liability

Member States can provide for joint and several liability (the UK has done this only in relation to liability for failure to inform and consult).

Transfer of information

Member States may adopt measures to provide for the transfer of information from the transferor to the transferee in relation to the employees.

Collective agreements

Collective agreements must transfer, but Member States can limit this to a year after the transfer.

Dismissal

Member States can limit the categories of employees who are protected from dismissal by virtue of the transfer.

Consultation

Member States may limit the information and consultation obligations to undertakings with a minimum number of employees.

31.4 Application of ARD and TUPE to contracting out

31.4.1 *Background*

ARD was originally implemented in the UK by the Transfer of Undertakings (Protection of Employment) Regulations 1981 (SI 1981/1794) (TUPE Regulations). The impact of the TUPE Regulations was not felt immediately, but grew over time.

Through a series of cases in the UK courts and the European Court of Justice (ECJ), the importance of the TUPE Regulations gradually increased as decisions held that the scope of the TUPE Regulations extended, for example, to non-commercial undertakings and to intra-group transfers.

In addition, a substantial body of case law developed in the late 1980s and 1990s on the issue of whether the contracting out of services and the change of contractors fell within the TUPE Regulations, with the courts taking a "multi-factorial" approach, looking at a series of relevant factors in each case and reaching a finding based on those facts. This resulted in courts drawing a distinction between asset-intensive undertakings and labour-intensive undertakings.

31.4.2 *New TUPE Regulations*

In April 2006 new TUPE Regulations (TUPE 2006) came into force in the UK which repealed and replaced the TUPE Regulations. TUPE 2006 expressly applies where there is a service provision change, and was intended to widen the scope so that it would be more likely to catch a contracting out scenario. Since 2006 there have been numerous cases which have provided useful guidance on how to assess where a service provision change has occurred. Recent cases have taken a more forensic approach than previously to whether a service provision change has occurred. Each element of the test has been carefully analysed. The government has also been considering TUPE as part of its ongoing employment law reform programme. In November 2011, the Department for Business Innovation and Skills published a call for evidence on the effectiveness of TUPE and the response to that consultation was published on 14 September 2012. Responses to the call for evidence indicated concern amongst business that the inclusion of service provision changes within TUPE, "gold-plated" the ARD obligations and was unwelcome. The government will now embark on a period of policy development and stakeholder engagement, following which it will issue its proposals for amending TUPE. The scope for change will be limited by the ARD obligations, but it is likely that some amendments to TUPE, and in particular service provision changes, will be proposed in the future.

31.4.3   Effect of TUPE 2006

TUPE 2006 provides for two alternative applications of TUPE (which are not mutually exclusive)—where there is a transfer of an economic entity and where there is a change in the provision of a service.

This is an extremely complex subject and this section is intended to provide a short summary of some of the key relevant factors. Customers and suppliers must take expert advice on this area before entering into any services agreement.

31.4.3.1   Identifiable economic entity

This is the "standard" TUPE scenario, and TUPE applies where there is an identifiable economic entity which retains its identity before and after the transfer, for example the catering function at a factory. Economic entity is defined as

> "an organised grouping of resources which has the objective of pursuing an economic activity, whether or not that activity is central or ancillary".

TUPE will not apply if there is no identifiable entity, so if, for example, the cleaning in an office is done on an ad hoc basis by all of the office staff in addition to their other duties, the cleaning function will not be an economic entity and the appointment of a cleaning contractor to take over this function will not be a TUPE transfer.

31.4.3.2   Service provision change

Under TUPE 2006, there is express reference to the application of TUPE to contracting out, contracting in and re-tendering, where there is an organised grouping of employees dedicated to meeting one client's needs. It does not apply to a single specific event or task of short-term duration, nor does it apply to contracts for the supply of goods.

TUPE will therefore apply in service provision situations, including:

(a)   the initial appointment of a supplier to provide services;
(b)   where the services are taken in-house by the customer from the supplier; or
(c)   where an existing services agreement with a supplier is terminated and the contract is granted to a new supplier.

31.4.3.3   *The sale of shares*

TUPE will not apply where the transaction is the sale of shares in a company (e.g. a subsidiary company of the customer which provides the service to the customer which is being contracted out to the supplier). If the supplier purchases the company, TUPE will not apply, but the people employed by that company will continue to be employed by that company. If they are to be dismissed, the normal unfair dismissal rules will apply.

31.4.3.4   *Changes in application of TUPE*

Sections 31.4.3.1 to 31.4.3.3 show that TUPE applies extremely widely, so that it will apply in many service provision arrangements. Parties should be aware, however, that the interpretation of TUPE can change as case law develops and if further amendments are made to the Regulations themselves. Therefore, specialist legal advice must be taken at the relevant time with regard to the individual services arrangement.

31.5   Legal effect of TUPE applying

There are various implications of TUPE applying to an individual services arrangement. Sections 31.2 and 31.3 explain the implications in outline. This section describes the specific implications for services transactions.

31.5.1   *Transfer of contracts of employment*

TUPE is designed to preserve employees' terms and conditions of employment when a business or undertaking, or part of one, is transferred to a new employer. Therefore, if TUPE applies, it will operate to transfer the contracts of employment of those employees engaged in the undertaking from the customer to the new supplier.

31.5.2   *Transfer rights, powers, duties and liabilities*

TUPE will also transfer to the new supplier all rights, powers, duties and liabilities under those contracts of employment, including accrued liabilities (but excluding certain rights under occupational pension schemes (see Chapter 32). This has the practical effect of putting the new supplier into the shoes of the customer (or the old supplier, if the transfer involves a change of supplier). This means that the new employer takes over all liabilities, including, for example, arrears of pay or liability for unlawful acts of discrimination, unless the parties agree to apportion the liability differently by way of indemnities[1] (see section 31.7 below).

31.5.3   Employees can object

Under TUPE, employees who are unhappy about the transfer can object to it, in which event their existing employment comes to an end at the point of transfer and does not transfer to the new supplier. In this situation, the individual generally has no remedy against either party.

If, however, the employee objects because they will suffer a fundamental breach to their employment contract, or a substantial change to their material detriment, then the employee is treated as having been dismissed, and can claim compensation.

31.5.4   Dismissals automatically unfair

Any dismissals by reason of a transfer are automatically unfair as are any dismissals in connection with a TUPE transfer unless they are for an "economic, technical or organisational reason entailing a change in the workforce" ("ETO reason") (reg.7(2)of TUPE).

The ETO reason must relate to the employer which carries out the dismissals, which means a customer cannot dismiss in anticipation of the services agreement and rely on the supplier's ETO reason.

Redundancy qualifies as an ETO reason, so any redundancies following a transfer will be fair, provided the procedure required for any redundancy dismissal is followed (the normal unfair dismissal rules will be used to assess the fairness of the dismissal). In the context of a transfer, it is particularly important that any selection is fair and it is not assumed that the existing employees of the supplier will have preference over those employees who have transferred from the customer.

Provided that he has the necessary period of continuous service, any employee (who works in the part of the business or undertaking being transferred) who is dismissed either before or after the transfer for a reason connected with the transfer, will be able to claim unfair dismissal. From 6 April 2012, the necessary length of qualifying service will increase from one year to two years. But this will only apply to those joining on or after 6 April 2012.

---

[1]   For a description of the legal effect of indemnities, see section 32.12.

In order to determine which party bears liability for TUPE-related dismissals, it is necessary to establish the nature and timing of the relevant dismissal:

(a) if an employee is dismissed by the customer or existing supplier before the change and that dismissal is by reason of or is connected with the change of supplier (but not for an ETO reason), liability will transfer to the new supplier; or

(b) if an employee is dismissed by the customer or existing supplier before the change, for an ETO reason, but the dismissal was procedurally unfair, liability will remain with the customer or existing supplier; or

(c) if an employee is dismissed by the customer or existing supplier before the change and that dismissal is for a reason unconnected with the change of supplier (e.g. if the dismissal is conduct related) liability will remain with that customer or supplier and will not transfer to the new supplier.

In practice, however, it is often difficult to establish whether such a dismissal is or is not connected with the transfer. Therefore, properly drafted indemnities are essential. Indemnities are considered in greater detail in section 31.7 below.

31.5.5 *Constructive dismissal*

Surprisingly, where an employee resigns from the customer or existing supplier and claims constructive dismissal on the grounds of an anticipated breach of contract by the new supplier after the transfer, for example if the new supplier proposes a variation to working conditions, liability remains with the old employer. Employees can also object (reg.4(9)) to a substantial change in their working conditions to their material detriment. If they do so pre-transfer, it is not clear whether the customer / existing supplier, or the new supplier, will be responsible.

31.5.6 *Union recognition agreements transfer*

TUPE also deals with collective rights and provides that collective agreements and union recognition agreements transfer automatically.

There is currently uncertainty about whether the transfer of collective agreements means that the collective bargaining machinery transfers over so that employees benefit from pay rises agreed after the transfer, even though the new supplier is not party to the collective agreement. This "dynamic" interpretation of collective agreements has been upheld in some cases. Others, however, support a "static" approach whereby the new supplier is bound by the terms of a collective agreement in force at the date of transfer, but not by subsequent agreements to which it was not a party. The UK Supreme Court has referred the issue to the ECJ.

31.6 Duty to inform, consult and supply information

There is also an obligation to inform, and in certain circumstances to consult, on a collective basis with the trade union, if one is recognised, or elected employee representatives. Note that the obligation to consult under TUPE may be in addition to other general consultation obligations that the employer may be subject to. There is also an obligation to supply certain information. The employer must inform the appropriate representatives of:

(a) the fact of the transfer, the proposed date when it is to take place and the reasons for it;

(b) the legal, economic and social implications of the transfer for the affected employees; and

(c) the measures which will be taken in connection with the transfer (or if there are no measures, that fact).

The existing employer must also provide information about any measures that the new employer envisages.

If measures are envisaged that trigger the obligation to carry out a formal consultation with the employee representatives.

31.6.1 *Obligations of existing employer*

As well as the obligation to inform and consult, under TUPE 2006, the existing employer is placed under a duty to provide "Employee Liability Information", which is:

(a) information regarding the identity of the employees transferring and their ages;
(b) information contained in their Employment Rights Act 1996 s.1 statement of particulars of employment;
(c) information relating to any relevant collective agreements;
(d) details of any disciplinary action taken or grievances raised within the previous two years; and
(e) details of any legal action within the previous two years or any potential legal action in relation to any of the transferring employees.

The information must be given at least 14 days before the transfer and be in writing or in a readily accessible format and must be updated if it changes after being given to the transferee.

If the existing employer fails to provide the information, a tribunal can award compensation to the new employer of at least £500 per employee in most cases.

31.6.2   Obligations of new employer

The new supplier (or the customer if the service is being taken in-house) is placed under a corresponding duty to provide the existing employer with information about any "measures" which it intends to take in respect of the employees after the purported transfer. These measures include, for example, any proposal to make redundancies or relocate the workforce.

31.6.3   Timing

Consultation must be carried out properly with a view to seeking agreement to the measures and so information must be made available long enough before the transfer actually occurs to enable meaningful consultation to take place.

31.6.4   Remedies

If information giving or consultation does not take place, or is carried out improperly or late, the employee representatives (or employees if no representatives have been appointed) are entitled to complain to an employment tribunal. The tribunal can award up to 13 weeks' gross pay for each employee depending on what a tribunal considers is just and equitable in the circumstances. Failing to make any effort to inform and consult is likely to result in the maximum award.

TUPE 2006 provides that the transferor and transferee are jointly and severally liable for any compensation awarded, but a tribunal cannot apportion liability between them.

31.7   Transfer of staff from customer to supplier

Sections 31.5 and 31.6 show that one of the effects of TUPE is to make one party responsible for the acts and failures of the other. For example, on commencement of the services arrangement, it makes the supplier responsible for the acts of the customer. It may be difficult for the supplier, without the cooperation of the customer, to defend a claim which arose before the transfer and which relates to the customer's actions.

On the basis that employees are not entitled to contract out of their rights under TUPE, there is no way for customers or suppliers to ensure that TUPE will not, as a matter of law, apply.

Therefore, customers and suppliers are always advised to include warranties and indemnities or other provisions to protect them.

31.7.1   Details of employees

A prudent supplier should ensure that the customer provides full warranties in relation to the due diligence information provided in respect of a specified list of transferring employees. A supplier may also ask the customer for warranties in relation to the Employee Liability Information, but the customer may resist this on the grounds that breach of this obligation carries its own remedy under TUPE.

31.7.2   Indemnity for pre-commencement liabilities

The supplier should request full indemnity protection against liabilities connected to the transferring employees which arise from acts or omissions of the customer prior to the commencement of the services agreement and which will transfer to the supplier pursuant to TUPE (including liability for failure to comply with the information and consultation requirements). The customer may specify that the indemnity is subject to it having conduct of any litigation by transferring employees.

31.7.3   Indemnity for employees not listed

The supplier should also request full indemnity protection against claims by any employees of the customer (other than the listed employees) that they transfer to the supplier under TUPE as a result of the services arrangement. This can include a provision allowing the supplier a window of time to dismiss the individual and claim under the indemnity. After that period, the employee becomes the supplier's responsibility. If the parties consider that TUPE will not apply, the customer would, in effect, be providing the supplier with full indemnity protection in relation to a claim by any person that he transfers to the supplier under TUPE as a result of the services arrangement.

31.7.4 Indemnities for constructive dismissal

The customer should request full indemnity protection against claims for constructive dismissal where the employee is relying on the anticipated breach of contract by the supplier.

31.7.5 Failure to consult

Each party will want an indemnity from the other against failure to comply with their obligations to inform and consult with the employees.

31.7.6 Mutual indemnities

In some cases, TUPE will effectively transfer staff from the customer to the supplier on the commencement, and from the supplier to the customer on termination of the services arrangement, so that the parties will be incentivised to agree broadly similar "mirror" provisions on commencement and termination.

31.7.7 Indemnities in favour of new supplier

In other cases, however, if the services are not brought back in-house on termination, TUPE will have the effect of transferring the employees and liabilities relating to them to the new supplier. Therefore, the customer will want any indemnities on termination to benefit the new supplier. Otherwise, if the indemnity is in the customer's favour only, it will not cover losses incurred by the new supplier, who will endeavour to pass these losses on to the customer in its charges. Section 31.8 below examines this situation in greater detail.

31.8 Second Generation TUPE

31.8.1 Effect of TUPE applying

If the services are to be provided by a new supplier rather than being contracted out for the first time, in the absence of any contractual provisions between the customer and the previous supplier dealing with this situation, TUPE will operate as follows:

(a) It will operate to transfer the relevant staff from the previous supplier to the new supplier. They will transfer on their existing terms and conditions, as explained above. As TUPE only catches those employees working on the contract immediately before the transfer, in the absence of agreement to the contrary, the previous supplier can "cherry pick" the best staff and move them away prior to the transfer date, and deploy their weakest staff so that they are the employees who transfer at the transfer date. This practice, which is sometimes referred to as "dumping", can render the new supplier unable to perform the services properly on commencement of the new services arrangement.

(b)   Liabilities under the contracts of employment also transfer. This means the new supplier inherits the workforce with all attendant liabilities, and has no means of controlling this. Not only does the new supplier inherit all liabilities, the previous supplier can effectively control what liabilities its competitor will have to pick up. The previous supplier can fail to pay wages or can increase the salaries and benefits of the transferring staff so that the new supplier is burdened with the extra costs.

(c)   There is an obligation on the previous supplier to consult or inform staff about the transfer, but the new supplier can suffer from failing to do this, as the liability is joint and several.

31.8.2   *Protections on termination*

To avoid the problems mentioned in section 31.8.1 above, during the last six months of the agreement or after notice of early termination has been given:

(a)   The customer may want to prevent the previous supplier from cherry picking the best staff and therefore may restrict the previous supplier from moving staff into or out of the undertaking, unless the customer has consented to the move. The supplier may see this as an unwarranted interference with its control of how it provides the services and may suggest that consent is only required if the move would adversely affect the provision of the services.

(b)   The customer may want to restrict the supplier from changing the employees' employment contracts unless the change is being made throughout the supplier's organisation, in the ordinary course of business.

(c)   The customer may also be concerned that staff will be demotivated during the final stages of the agreement and may seek the supplier's cooperation in ensuring that staff remain with the supplier and transfer to the customer or new supplier.

31.8.3   *Indemnities*

If the services are to be provided by a new supplier rather than being contracted out for the first time, the new supplier will also need indemnities similar to those required on commencement (see section 31.7 above) as described below.

31.8.4   Details of employees

The supplier will need the previous supplier to provide it with full details about the employees providing the service. Under TUPE 2006, there is the obligation to provide Employee Liability Information (see section 31.7 above).

From a practical perspective, this type of information is invaluable to a new supplier. It renders negotiations in relation to the retendering far less problematic: the new supplier will have access to at least some due diligence in relation to those employees who will transfer under TUPE and can, therefore, assess costs and contingent liabilities more accurately. However, one drawback is that TUPE only requires the information to be given 14 days before the transfer, which may be too late for the purposes of some negotiations. The parties can of course agree to provide the information at any earlier date.

The previous supplier should also be required to warrant the accuracy of due diligence information provided in respect of a specified list of transferring employees.

31.8.5   Indemnity for pre-commencement liabilities

The supplier will need indemnities relating to liabilities connected to the transferring employees which arise from acts or omissions of the previous supplier (or sub-contractor—see below) prior to the commencement of the services agreement and which will transfer to the new supplier pursuant to TUPE (including liability for failure to comply with the information and consultation requirements).

31.8.6   Indemnity for employees not listed

It will need indemnities relating to claims by any employees (other than the listed transferring employees) that they transfer under TUPE to the new supplier as a result of the services arrangement. This can include a provision by which the new supplier has a window of time to dismiss the individual and claim under the indemnity, after which the employee becomes the new supplier's responsibility.

31.8.7   Transfer from subcontractors

The new supplier will need the information and indemnities relating to employees whether they transfer from the previous supplier or from its subcontractors.

31.8.8   Failure to consult

Each party will want an indemnity from the other against failure to comply with their obligations to consult with the employees.

31.8.9   Grant of the indemnities

The supplier needs the indemnities listed in sections 31.8.4 to 31.8.8 above. The question arises as to how it will ensure that it is granted them:

(a)   If the customer has agreed that the previous supplier will grant indemnities in favour of the new supplier, as mentioned in section 31.7.7 above, then the new supplier will be able to benefit from these.

(b)   Can the new supplier agree indemnities directly with the previous supplier? In most situations, the transfer is taking place because the previous supplier has lost the customer's business and therefore may be uncooperative with the customer and with the new supplier, particularly where the new supplier is a direct competitor. However, if the customer has other ongoing commercial interests with the previous supplier or the previous supplier has assets that it wants to sell to the new supplier, there may be some scope for agreement. Also, the previous supplier may be willing to take a more pragmatic approach and provide some indemnities if it thinks that in the future it may win business from other customers of the new supplier and hence that staff may transfer from the new supplier to it.

If the supplier cannot agree indemnities with the incumbent supplier, then it will have to agree with the customer who will take the risks associated with TUPE applying. If the customer wants the supplier to accept the risks, then the supplier will usually increase its charges so that they include a risk premium.

31.9   "Soft" effects of TUPE

From a human perspective, the effect of TUPE can be extremely severe. Staff who have accepted employment with one company and in some cases worked loyally for that company for many years, find themselves being made redundant or working for another company. In the latter case, in some circumstances there may be significant differences between the culture in the customer and supplier organisations. For example, the customer may be a public sector body and the supplier may be a private sector body. For this reason, transferring staff may be worried and disturbed by the contracting out process.

It is extremely important that these concerns are dealt with properly, as the transferring staff are key to the success of the service provision arrangement in several ways:

(a) The transferring staff will usually have information about the services previously being provided to the customer and how those services will need to change to reflect the business objectives of the customer. Chapter 2 stresses the criticality of this information and Chapter 7 highlights the importance of ensuring that the customer has a clear and detailed description of the services that it requires. The transferring staff may be unwilling to cooperate or they may feel a conflict of interest in advising the customer on suitable service-level regimes if they are ultimately going to be working for the supplier.

(b) The standard of the services provided by the supplier will depend in part upon the motivation of the staff employed to provide the services. Most suppliers realise this and are extremely adept at dealing sensitively with the concerns of any transferring staff.

31.10   Secondment

Because of the concerns that staff will not be happy about transferring from the customer to the supplier, in particular where the customer is in the public sector and the supplier is in the private sector, in some cases the parties agree that the staff previously employed in providing the services will be seconded to work for the supplier rather than transferred. This approach has been adopted by many NHS Trusts, in particular those who use the "Retention of Employment Model" (ROE). In a recent case, the Employment Appeal Tribunal held that an employee who objected to the transfer but had worked for the transferee for a period on secondment had in fact transferred. This casts doubt on the effectiveness of this model. Concern has also been expressed by the Department of Health. In January 2009 it highlighted these concerns in a letter to all NHS chief executives. This led to the implementation of the National Health Service Pension Scheme (Amendment) Regulations 2009 (SI 2009/1298). These regulations provide that in respect of staff employed under ROE arrangements made after 13 January 2009, only those who have been specifically sanctioned by the Secretary of State can access the NHS Pension Scheme. This usually means higher sourcing costs for the NHS Trusts, which in turn has curtailed the use of ROE in the public sector.

Recent commentary has also suggested that ROE is out of place in the current economic times as it leaves costs and liabilities, particularly for pensions, with the public sector, thus reducing the opportunity for cost savings. The advantages and disadvantages of this approach are described in Table 43.

Table 43 Secondment of staff

Advantages
The staff remain employed in the public sector.
The staff are less likely to be hostile to the sourcing arrangement if they perceive that they have been protected.
Disadvantages
The supplier may feel that it has less control over the staff and hence less control over the provision of the services.
There may be practical issues relating to day-to-day management and disciplinary control over the staff.
The supplier may have less control over the activities carried out by the employees. For example, the employees may be seconded to the supplier so that it may provide the services, in which case the supplier will not be able to employ the staff in providing services to other customers.

Supplies of staff (including secondments) will normally be standard-rated supplies for VAT purposes, which may create a VAT cost where the supplier to whom the staff are seconded makes exempt supplies and therefore cannot recover the VAT chargeable on the supply.

Where staff are seconded to a person who belongs outside the UK, the supply of staff will be outside the scope of UK VAT. Where staff are seconded from a person who belongs outside the UK to a person who belongs inside the UK, the recipient of the seconded staff will generally have to account for VAT on the supply of staff under the reverse charge procedure.

There are certain limited concessions in relation to VAT on supplies of seconded staff which mean that in certain circumstances where the secondee comes under the exclusive control over the supplier to whom they are seconded and the supplier is responsible for paying the secondee's remuneration and/or discharging employer's obligations to pay PAYE, national insurance contributions, pension contributions and similar payments, then the value of these payments may be disregarded from the value of the supply of staff for VAT purposes.

31.11   Competence of transferring staff

As part of its due diligence exercise (see Chapter 6), the supplier will need to reassure itself that it will be able to provide the services. Therefore, the due diligence exercise may involve the supplier effectively interviewing the staff to ensure that they are appropriately experienced and skilled for the jobs that they will need to carry out. Most suppliers are aware of the sensitivity required to handle this procedure well, and gain the cooperation of the relevant staff.

Any decision to enter into a services arrangement must be made taking into account the effects of TUPE. Thus, one effect of TUPE is to hinder the customer from improving the quality of its services simply by changing supplier. If a customer is dissatisfied with the quality of staff carrying out the work for the supplier, the customer should bear in mind that, if it appoints a new supplier, that supplier may end up with the same employees. However, in some circumstances the new supplier may be able to retrain the employees or redeploy them.

31.12   Adequacy of transferring staff

There are various reasons why staff who have previously provided the services to the customer may not transfer to the supplier:

(a)   If there is no TUPE transfer, there will be no automatic transfer of employees.

(b)   Even where there is a TUPE transfer, the staff of the customer who are not engaged in that part of the undertaking do not transfer. This would apply to staff who provide support to many aspects of the customer's business including the part transferring but who are not actually "assigned" to that part.

(c)   Under TUPE, employees who are unhappy about the transfer can object to it, in which event their existing employment comes to an end at the point of transfer and their employment does not transfer to the new supplier. In this situation, the individual generally has no remedy against either party. But if a change to terms and conditions has caused the unhappiness, then the individual may have claims against either the transferee or transferor.

Where the staff who have previously provided the services do not transfer, the supplier will have to provide the services using its own resources. The supplier may be concerned if it is dependent upon the knowledge and skills of certain staff in order to provide the services and these staff do not transfer. The supplier will need to investigate this issue carefully when it carries out its due diligence (see Chapter 6). In appropriate circumstances, it may need to agree with the customer what will happen if the staff (or key staff) will not transfer. For example, the parties may decide that the supplier will have a transition period to carry out a skills transfer.

31.13   Managing transferring staff

Once the staff have transferred to the supplier, the supplier will be anxious to ensure that it can provide the services to the customer in the most efficient manner. However, the effect of TUPE is that the staff will transfer to the supplier on the same terms and conditions as those that they previously enjoyed. It also provides that any attempt to contract out of TUPE is void.

31.13.1   Varying terms and conditions on transfer

An agreement to vary terms and conditions on transfer for a transfer-connected reason is void and the employees do not have legal capacity to consent to a change unless the change is for an ETO reason (see section 31.5.4 above). This means that even consensual changes will be ineffective if they are transfer-connected and there is no ETO reason.

The main problem with the definition of an ETO reason is the requirement that the reason "entails a change in the workforce". This means that a change (even if consensual), such as a variation to benefits, which does not result in changes to employee numbers or functions will not qualify as an ETO reason.

There are less stringent provisions which apply in certain insolvency situations which allow changes to terms and conditions in order to safeguard employment opportunities by ensuring the survival of the undertaking.

31.13.2   Varying changes unrelated to transfer

The other way changes to terms can be introduced effectively with the consent of the employees is if it can be established that such changes do not relate to the transfer itself.

What is needed, essentially, is an event that can be said to break the link between the transfer and the change or the passage of time. A lengthy gap between the transfer and the change will increase the possibility of the changes being seen as not relating to the transfer itself, but instead to the changing circumstances of the business. The employment tribunal will carry out a factual assessment of the circumstances surrounding the change.

However, the new supplier will almost certainly be in a stronger position to enforce changes to terms and conditions of employment if it can demonstrate effectively that they have been introduced:

(a)   in respect of the entire workforce (and not specifically in relation to the staff who have transferred);
(b)   as part of a wider restructuring of the business as a whole; and

(c)   at a time distant from the date of the transfer.

31.13.3   *Dismissal of employees who refuse to agree changes*

If consent to the changes cannot be obtained and the new supplier dismisses an employee who refuses to accept the changes, there is a strong argument that the dismissal was for a reason connected with the transfer and there will, therefore, be the possibility of a claim for automatic unfair dismissal.

31.13.4   *Unilateral variation of the changes*

Alternatively, if the supplier pursues a strategy of unilaterally enforcing the changes on the staff after the transfer, not only is the variation unlikely to be legally binding, but also the affected individuals may claim that the new supplier has fundamentally breached the terms of the original contract of employment and as a result they have been constructively dismissed (i.e. dismissed by virtue of the employer's conduct rather than expressly dismissed). In the event that this is successfully established, the employees will have a claim for wrongful dismissal and unfair dismissal.

31.13.5   *"Two-tier" workforce*

Previously, when public services were contracted out, suppliers had to take note of the "two-tier" code. This was in fact two codes of practice on workforce matters which applied to central government and local government service agreements. The codes required contractors of services agreements from central government or local government to employ new recruits on "no less favourable" terms than staff who transferred under TUPE. The central government code was withdrawn in December 2010, and the local government code was withdrawn, in March 2011. Contracts entered into before these dates will have had to comply with the codes. And furthermore, certain authorities are still contractually requiring contractors to comply with the spirit of the codes, even though they have now been withdrawn.

31.14   Termination of the services agreement

On termination, the process described on commencement is reversed. Staff of the supplier or its subcontractors may transfer to the customer, the successor supplier or the successor supplier's subcontractors.

31.14.1   *Transfer to the customer*

In the first example, staff who are transferring back to the customer may include some of those who transferred from the customer to the supplier on the commencement of the services arrangement. These staff may have been persuaded by the supplier that their career prospects would improve after they moved to the supplier. Therefore, it may be difficult for them to come to terms with the fact that they are transferring back to the customer. They may even feel that the customer betrayed them by transferring them to the supplier.

31.14.2   *Transfer to incoming supplier*

Staff who transfer to other suppliers may feel ambivalent about a situation in which they are now working for competitors of their previous employer. Whether staff transfer to the customer or to an incoming supplier, the party to whom the employees are transferring will need to deal sensitively with their concerns.

31.14.3   *Indemnities*

In addition, the new supplier will need to ensure that it has indemnities similar to those described in section 31.7 above.

31.14.4   *Effect of the economic climate on termination*

Customers should bear in mind that the impact of TUPE depends upon the economic climate or financial position of the supplier when the agreement is terminated. Thus the application of TUPE depends on how the services are provided, a factor that will usually be within the control of the supplier depending, for example, upon whether dedicated staff are used on the contract or if the services are provided by a pool of employees who also work on other contracts. When there is a skills shortage, the supplier may be anxious to retain skilled staff. In contrast, if there is a recession and work is scarce, then the supplier may be anxious to reduce its head count. In a recession, staff who previously worked on services provided to several customers may find that they are working for only one customer if the supplier has lost the contracts for the other customers.

31.14.5   Changes in the law of TUPE

Parties should also be aware that the interpretation of TUPE could change as case law develops and if amendments are made to the Regulations themselves. Therefore, the effect of TUPE at the time of termination may be different from that anticipated when the agreement was drafted.

31.15   Redundancies

If the employer's requirement for employees of a particular kind in the place where they are engaged ceases or diminishes (or is expected to do so), there will be a redundancy situation.

31.15.1   When redundancies may occur

Redundancies can occur in the following situations:

(a)   In some cases the customer and the supplier may decide that staff who would otherwise have transferred to the supplier will be made redundant if the service provision project goes ahead.
(b)   The customer may have to make redundancies where the services are discontinued altogether. For example, a business may decide to stop offering a canteen service to its staff, so the employees providing the catering services will be redundant unless they can be redeployed by the supplier on another contract.
(c)   The customer may have to make redundancies among staff who do not transfer if, for example, their workload reduces as a result of the service provision. This might include central support staff, part of whose function was to support the business function being contracted out.

31.15.2   Legal background on redundancies

Redundancy is a potentially fair reason for dismissal, but the employer must follow a fair procedure in order to avoid liability for unfair dismissal. This involves consultation with the employee, fair selection and consideration for alternative employment as well as compliance with statutory dismissal procedures. Employees with more than two years' service will be entitled to a statutory redundancy payment if dismissed as a result of redundancy.

31.15.3   Redundancy costs

Where the parties anticipate that redundancies may occur, they can cater for the redundancy costs, whether within the charging framework or by use of a retention fund, out of which the redundancy costs, if any, are paid. If the parties do not expressly deal with the redundancy costs, then the supplier may include them in its charges irrespective of whether redundancies are actually made. The parties may also deal with the costs of redundancy when the contract terminates, although in the absence of any agreement, it will be the liability of the supplier (unless the dismissal is in connection with a TUPE transfer and is not for an ETO reason, in which case the liability will transfer to the customer or new supplier).

Chapter 32

Pensions Issues

32.1 Outline

32.1.1 *What this chapter deals with*

Chapter 31 describes the effect of the application of TUPE to services agreements. This chapter deals with a specific but related issue, the subject of the pension rights of employees transferring from the customer to the supplier (or a first-generation supplier to a second-generation supplier) under TUPE. This can be a particularly tricky issue and one which customers and suppliers ignore at their peril. It is not unheard of for services agreements to be primarily motivated by a desire to reduce the customer's headcount and resulting pensions' liabilities. Pensions issues will vary substantially from country to country, depending upon the types of pensions which are popular and any relevant local legislation. This chapter describes the situation in the UK.

32.1.2 *Pensions outside of the UK—a case-by-case approach*

Not only can occupational pension schemes in the UK be individual to a specific employer or a group of employers but, throughout Europe and the rest of the world, pension arrangements that predominate in one jurisdiction can vary significantly to those that are the norm in another.

Therefore, as far as Europe is concerned, it is hardly surprising that the original Acquired Rights Directive (ARD)[1] in 1977 and the later two directives[2] have fairly wide exclusions from the automatic transfer provisions for occupational pension rights.

The original 1977 directive carved out employees' rights to old age, invalidity and survivors' benefits under occupational pension schemes that are

---

[1] Council Directive 77/187/EEC.
[2] Council Directive 98/50/EC and Council Directive 2001/23/EC.

outside of the statutory social security scheme in the Member State from automatically transferring on the transfer of an undertaking.

Each Member State can decide on the level of pension protection and how it is to be achieved. They can implement their own approach under their own national legislation including, if they choose to, providing that benefits do transfer.

Consequently since, first, pension provisions differ throughout Europe; and, second, Member States can implement their own version of pension protection on the transfer of an undertaking, the result is that there is no "one fits all" approach.

Pension provisions on a multi-jurisdictional services arrangement (whether in Europe or elsewhere) must therefore be approached on a case-by-case basis.

32.2   Transfer of pension rights under TUPE

32.2.1   *No automatic transfer—occupational pension schemes*

There is an important exception to the provision in TUPE that automatically transfers employment contract rights and liabilities. That exception applies to occupational pension schemes. Specifically, the automatic transfer provisions do not apply to an employment contract, and the liabilities under that contract, to the extent to which they relate to old age, invalidity and survivors' benefits under an occupational pension scheme. Trust based company final salary and money purchase pension schemes (also known as defined benefit and defined contribution schemes) are occupational pension schemes.

32.2.2   *Automatic transfer—personal and stakeholder pension schemes*

Personal pension schemes and almost all stakeholder pension schemes[3] are not occupational pension schemes and therefore do not fall within the pensions carve-out in TUPE. Thus, obligations on the part of an employer under employment contracts or collective agreements to contribute to personal or stakeholder pension schemes of the transferring employees (including obligations under a group personal pension scheme) do automatically

---

[3]   The requirement to provide a stakeholder pension was deleted with effect from 1 October 2012.

transfer. The effect of this is that the receiving employer will be liable for future employer contributions at the requisite rate and for any arrears of employer contributions accrued to the point of transfer.

32.3 The Pensions Act 2004 and the Transfer of Employment (Pension Protection) Regulations 2005

32.3.1 *Implications of the legislation*

The Pensions Act 2004 and the Transfer of Employment (Pension Protection) Regulations 2005 (SI 2005/649) ("2005 Regulations") do not amend the situation described above (i.e. that rights under occupational pension schemes do not automatically transfer under TUPE). However, they do require the new employer, following a TUPE transfer, to offer pension arrangements meeting minimum standards ("Minimum Pension Protection"), if the transferring employees had access to an occupational pension scheme with their old employer.

32.3.2 *Description of Minimum Pension Protection*

The new employer must offer:

(a) a defined contribution (DC) arrangement in which the employer matches employees' contributions to a maximum of 6 per cent of basic pay (i.e. excluding bonus, overtime etc.); the arrangement has to be an occupational DC scheme or a stakeholder scheme and cannot be a group personal pension scheme—presumably so that transferring employees avoid the higher charges often found in group personal pensions; or

(b) a defined benefit scheme that meets the requirements of the so-called "reference scheme test" (the minimum standard required by law to allow a scheme to contract out of the State Second Pension); or

(c) a scheme providing benefits with a value equal to members' contributions plus 6 per cent of pensionable pay (however defined in the scheme rules); for example a "cash balance" plan (one in which the employer takes the investment risk by promising a defined pot of money at retirement—leaving the individual member to buy the pension and take the annuity cost/longevity risk).

32.3.3   *Changing Minimum Pension Protection arrangements*

The Pensions Act 2004 expressly allows the new employer and the transferring employees to agree, at any time after the transfer, to contract out of the effect of these new provisions.

32.4   Beckmann/Martin liabilities

Following two decisions of the European Court of Justice (ECJ), there is uncertainty about whether early retirement benefits (other than ill-health early retirement benefits) under an occupational pension scheme are covered by the exception in TUPE for old age benefits. This uncertainty has been clarified by *Procter & Gamble Co v Svenska Cellulosa Aktiebolaget SCA* [2012] EWHC 1257 (Ch); [2012] I.R.L.R. 733 as explained below.

32.4.1   *The Beckmann case*

Under the *Beckmann* case,[4] a former NHS employee whose employment was transferred to Dynamco under TUPE was subsequently dismissed on redundancy grounds. She claimed entitlement to an early retirement pension and other benefits on the basis that she had an entitlement to these under the terms of her employment contract (by virtue of a Collective Agreement), which had transferred to Dynamco under the ARD. The ECJ decided that only benefits paid from the time when an employee reaches the end of his normal working life as laid down by the general structure of the pension scheme can be classified as old age benefits. As a result, the right to an early retirement pension on redundancy was held to transfer.

32.4.2   *The Martin case*

In the *Martin* case,[5] Martin and others transferred into a different pension arrangement following the transfer of their employment from the NHS to South Bank University. The claimants subsequently opted to take early retirement on leaving the service in circumstances which the Employment Tribunal found to be "in the interests of efficiency of the service". They claimed that they were entitled to an early retirement redundancy pension payable with the agreement of their employers. It was held that the rights

---

[4]   *Beckmann v Dynamco Wicheloe Macfarlane Ltd* (C-164/000) [2002] I.R.L.R. 578.
[5]   *Martin v South Bank University* (C-4/01) [2004] I.R.L.R. 74.

that transfer under TUPE include those rights contingent upon either dismissal or early retirement by agreement with the employer.

32.4.3 Implications of Beckmann/Martin cases

It seems clear, therefore, that a contractual right to benefits payable on dismissal in the interests of efficiency of the service or redundancy will transfer under TUPE, limited under the Procter and Gamble decision to the benefits falling due before normal retirement age (NRA) (see below). However, it is arguable that similar benefits payable before normal retirement date under an occupational pension scheme, such as a simple early retirement pension (particularly if it is not actuarially reduced to take account of early receipt), may also transfer.

The problem with the *Beckmann/Martin* cases was that the exact scope of the ECJ's judgment was not known. Contractual benefits payable under an occupational pension scheme on dismissal in the interests of efficiency of the service or redundancy will transfer under TUPE. However, it was debatable whether other early retirement benefits will also transfer if they are contained only in the terms of the pension scheme and not specifically in the employment contract.

The decision in the *Procter and Gamble* case provided some clarification of this point, although at the date of publication, the decision is subject to appeal. In *Procter and Gamble*, the High Court decided that a flexible and pragmatic approach is needed when dealing with potential Beckmann rights. In particular, in respect of *Beckmann* rights TUPE should be interpreted and applied to ensure transferring employees are entitled to benefits from their new employer which are equivalent to those provided by their former employer, and which take into account any benefits retained by the employees under their former scheme so as to avoid granting the member a windfall benefit.

The Court's decision also helped to set out what did, and did not transfer under TUPE. Liability to benefits on and after a scheme's NRA does not transfer as this liability is satisfied by the deferred pension payable from NRA under the transferring employer's scheme and the transferring employer will remain liable to fund this benefit. This fits in with the existing scheme funding legislation which would otherwise have required a number of amendments to reflect this transfer of liability.

However, rights to benefits before and up to NRA which are not satisfied by the deferred pension will transfer under TUPE. This is the case even if the right is only that the person's employer will consider agreeing to provide enhanced early retirement benefits. The fact that a benefit is a discretionary one or may be terminated or varied by an employer will not prevent the right transferring. Any discretion will transfer to the employee's new employer.

To the extent that these types of benefits transfer under TUPE, the supplier will have to provide a defined benefit early retirement pension (or appropriate compensation for such). The supplier may only have intended and budgeted to provide simple money purchase benefits.

Accordingly, on an services transaction involving a TUPE transfer, it is important for the supplier to examine the pension terms which are currently offered by the customer and, in particular, to identify any special pension terms which apply on redundancy or in similar situations. The cost to the supplier of replicating these benefits may be substantial.

32.4.4   Hidden Beckmann/Martin liabilities

There is also the possibility of a "hidden" *Beckmann/Martin* liability in the following circumstances. If transferring employees have previously been transferred to the customer pursuant to a TUPE transfer, then it is possible that *Beckmann* rights may also have transferred. If they transferred to the customer, then they will similarly transfer on to the supplier. The customer may have no information about previous pension benefits of transferring employees whom it currently employs as a result of a series of TUPE transfers.

32.4.5   Risk of Beckmann/Martin liabilities

Where the customer's pension scheme is a money purchase occupational pension scheme and there are no "hidden" *Beckmann/Martin* liabilities, the treatment of pension benefits is unlikely to be problematic. *Beckmann/Martin* type benefits are almost exclusively found in defined benefit arrangements.

Beckmann/Martin liabilities can be a consideration even when pension benefits are provided on a defined benefit basis both pre and post transfer. However, they are most likely to create a greater degree of commercial exposure when pension provision changes from a generous defined benefit pension scheme pre transfer to a substantially less generous DC pension scheme post transfer.

32.4.6   Ill-health retirement benefits

Ill-health early retirement benefits will not transfer automatically under TUPE and do not need to be replicated. They continue to fall under the exception in TUPE for invalidity benefits.

32.5   Commercial service agreements—contractual agreement to continue to provide DC benefits post transfer

When the customer's existing pension arrangements are DC, the customer and the supplier may agree to continue to provide the same type of benefits with the same level of contributions post transfer despite the fact that this is more than the supplier has to do to provide Minimum Pension Protection.

This seldom gives rise to any significant issues. There is certainty around the cost of providing these benefits. This makes contractual agreement easier to achieve.

32.6   Commercial service agreements—contractual agreement to continue to provide defined benefits post transfer

In some commercial services contracts, when the customer has a defined benefit pension scheme, the customer and the supplier may agree that the supplier will continue to provide a defined benefit pension scheme post transfer. The commercial agreement will usually (but not always) be that the supplier's pension scheme provides defined benefits that are broadly comparable to the benefits provided by the customer's pension scheme.

32.6.1   Agreement regarding future benefits for service

The agreement might only relate to future benefits for service with the supplier. Transferring employees will retain their deferred benefits for service with the customer in the customer's pension scheme. The cost of providing defined benefits for future service with the supplier throughout the contract term is more difficult to price for than for money purchase benefits, but less difficult to price than when past service benefits are also involved.

32.6.2 *Agreement regarding past and future benefits for service*

When the supplier undertakes contractually to provide a defined benefit pension scheme for both past and future service, the transferring employees will usually be given an option to transfer the value of the benefits they have already accrued in the customer's pension scheme ("Transfer Value") from the customer's pension scheme to the supplier's pension scheme.

Depending on the commercial agreement, the supplier might undertake to procure that, in return for the Transfer Value, its scheme provides either:

(a) a service credit based on the amount of the Transfer Value; or
(b) a day-for-day service credit (or actuarially equivalent)

In both cases (and in particular when a day-for-day service credit (or equivalent) is being provided) pricing for past and future pension benefits is complex. The Transfer Value that comes across from the customer's pension scheme to fund the assumed liabilities in the supplier's scheme is crucial. Unless there are very few transferring employees and potential exposure is not material in the overall context of the transaction, this whole process requires actuarial input.

32.7 Commercial services agreements—contractual agreement to change pension benefits from defined benefit to DC

When the commercial agreement is to change from a defined benefit pension scheme to a DC pension scheme, post transfer, that agreement may go beyond what is required for Minimum Pension Protection.

That in itself is seldom an issue, since the money purchase benefits that the supplier undertakes to provide can be accurately priced for. However, *Beckmann/Martin* liabilities (and the costs associated with them) can potentially add to cost/risk.

In order to manage *Beckmann/Martin*-type liabilities there are a number of strategies that can be deployed. These include some or all of the following depending on the nature of the risk:

(a) effective due diligence to properly identify (and in some cases eliminate) risk;

(b) actuarial due diligence to determine the financial cost associated with risk; and

(c)   commercial agreement as to who bears what level/cost of risk.

32.8   The unintended charge

It may appear to employers that new pension legislation is usually designed to impose more onerous and prescriptive obligations on them. However, recent changes to The Occupational Pension Schemes (Employer Debt) Regulations 2005 (SI 2005/678) (the "Employer Debt Regulations") might actually be helpful to employers who are engaged in outsourcing.

32.8.1   Section 75 debt

An ever-present pensions exposure in services agreements is what is sometimes referred to as the "unintended charge". If the customer is one of a number of participating employers in a defined benefit occupational pension scheme ("Group Scheme") and both the customer and other participating employers employ active scheme members, Section 75 of the Pensions Act 1995 will trigger a debt which the customer will be liable for if it ceases to employ an active Group Scheme member ("Section 75 debt"). This can happen if all of the customer's active Group Scheme members transfer to the supplier under TUPE. The customer may not intend to trigger the debt. It can be unaware that it has done so until after the event.

The Section 75 debt can be substantial. It is calculated on a buyout basis (which is more expensive than ongoing funding). It is not solely based on the customer's liabilities. It may include "orphan liabilities". These are liabilities that relate to the Group Scheme's employers that are no longer around/not liable/cannot pay them. Alternatively it is possible for a scheme to be a "last man standing scheme" where the last active employer in the Scheme can find itself on the hook for all the liabilities of the other employers in the event that they become insolvent. All of this means that the customer can be faced with having to make a large capital payment to the Group Scheme.

This can cause difficulties at the beginning and end of the services agreement and during the term of the agreement.

32.8.2   Problems at the beginning of the agreement

At the beginning of the agreement, it can create a problem for the customer if the Group Scheme ceases to have an active Group Scheme member because all of the customer's active Group Scheme members transfer to the incoming supplier under TUPE.

32.8.3   Problems at the end of the agreement

At the end of the services agreement, the outgoing supplier could face the Section 75 debt if it has undertaken to continue to provide a defined benefit pension scheme and its pension fund ceases to have an active member because all of the customer's active members transfer to the customer or the successor supplier under TUPE.

32.8.4   Problems during the term

It is a natural process for transferred staff to leave employment with the supplier and be replaced by new employees during the agreement term. New employees are not necessarily given the same pension benefits in the same pension scheme. Over time, the last transferred active scheme member can simply leave employment with the supplier or retire. At that point a Section 75 debt can be triggered.

32.8.5   Options offered by Employer Debt Regulations

The Employer Debt Regulations offer a number of different possibilities for managing the Section 75 debt, even after it has been triggered. The changes that are likely to be the most helpful in sourcing situations are discussed below. They refer throughout to the customer, but could equally apply to the supplier.

32.8.5.1   Period of grace

This applies when the customer's last active member is leaving/has left the service but the customer intends to employ at least one active member within 36 months of that event. The customer may, by giving appropriate notice to the Group Scheme trustees, make use of the "period of grace" provision. If the customer does actually employ an active member within the 36 month period, effectively the Section 75 debt is deemed not to have been triggered. The customer will not have to pay the amount of the debt to the Group Scheme.

32.8.5.2   Scheme apportionment arrangement

This allows the customer not to pay any of, or to pay only part of, its Section 75 debt. The liability/remainder of the liability is apportioned to one or more of the other participating employers. The Group Scheme trustees must agree to the apportionment.

32.8.5.3   Withdrawal arrangement

This also allows the customer to pay less than its Section 75 debt (subject to a minimum level of payment). Here someone else (possibly but not necessarily one or more of the other participating employers) provides a guarantee in relation to the remainder of the Section 75 debt.

32.8.5.4   Approved withdrawal arrangement

This is similar to a withdrawal arrangement but here the customer proposes to pay less of the Section 75 debt than it would have to do under a withdrawal arrangement. This type of arrangement must be approved by the Pensions Regulator, who can impose additional conditions and can call in the guarantee early.

32.8.5.5   Flexible apportionment arrangement

A flexible apportionment arrangement allows the customer's total liabilities under the Group Scheme to be apportioned to one or more of the other Group Scheme employers. If a flexible apportionment arrangement becomes effective, no Section 75 debt arises. The arrangement involves the customer, the Group Scheme trustees and the affected Group Scheme employers but does not require approval of the Pensions Regulator. Nevertheless a flexible apportionment arrangement is a notifiable event. Consequently the Group Scheme trustees must notify the Pensions Regulator of their decision to take any action which will or is intended to result in such an arrangement taking effect.

32.8.5.6   Summary

All of the above options have been described only very briefly and very generally. Many detailed conditions are attached to them. Legal and actuarial advice is needed in order to consider using any of these in practice.

32.9   The situation in the public sector

Although TUPE applies in the same way to services agreements in both private and public sector outsourcing, additional protections are afforded to public sector employees' pension benefits when services are being outsourced from a public authority to a private sector supplier.

Public sector employers operate under guidelines which require them to procure pension protection for public sector employees who are transferring to a private sector supplier.

The protections and guidelines applicable to public sector outsourcing are subject to a number of proposed changes which are set out at the end of this section.

The provisions set out below describe the current situation under TUPE and the existing government guidance prior to the implementation of the proposed changes set out above.

Currently different public sector bodies can use different pension models to achieve the pension protection required for their transferring employees. Pension models that are commonly used in public sector services agreements are discussed below.

32.10 The guidelines for pension protection in the public sector

32.10.1 Fair Deal

For public sector service agreements that were entered into for the first time from 1999 onwards (with the possible exception of contracts that were in the process of being negotiated at that time), guidelines have existed which in practice require suppliers to provide broadly comparable pension benefits post transfer for transferring public sector employees on both first generation and second generation transfers. The guidelines are known as "Fair Deal".

32.10.2 The additional considerations

In addition to Fair Deal, there are further considerations when best-value authorities (BVAs) are concerned. BVAs include local authorities, the police authority, the fire authority and various other bodies. These are discussed below.

32.10.3 First generation and second generation transfers

First generation transfers occur when public sector employees transfer their employment to a private sector supplier for the first time. Second (and subsequent) generation transfers occur when the same ex-public sector employees subsequently transfer their employment from the outgoing contractor to the incoming contractor on a contract re-let.

32.10.4 *The pension models that are used to deliver the pension protection*

In order to deliver the required level of pension protection, three different pension models are commonly used in public sector service agreements. Which one applies in a particular contract depends on:

(a)   which public sector pension scheme is involved;
(b)   the supplier's choice; and
(c)   the basis on which the public sector body in question decides to contract.

The three commonly used pension arrangements are:

(a)   **A GAD-approved Scheme**: the supplier provides pension benefits for both past and future service through a pension scheme that the government actuary's department (GAD) has judged to be broadly comparable to the public sector pension scheme in question. This can be achieved by GAD providing a passport for the supplier's scheme or by GAD providing a certificate of broad comparability. GAD certificates relate specifically to one particular transfer. GAD passports are used by private sector suppliers who are engaged in a lot of service agreements. They apply for a fixed period (usually two years) which means the public sector supplier's scheme can be used for a number of outsources without having to revert to GAD each time there is a transfer.

(b)   **Admission Body**: when the transferring public sector or ex-public sector employees are members of the Local Government Pension Scheme (LGPS) the supplier can participate in the LGPS by becoming an Admission Body. To become an Admission Body, the supplier has to enter into an Admission Agreement with the relevant LGPS Fund. The terms of the Admission Agreement must provide for certain prescribed[6] matters but otherwise may differ for each locally administered LGPS Fund.

The Admission Agreement will specify which employees of the supplier are eligible to participate in the LGPS Fund and can be written on either an open or closed basis. A closed Admission Agreement will restrict participation to a defined group of the supplier's employees employed in the services, usually those who transferred to the supplier with the services. An open Admission Agreement allows all employees of the supplier, who are or become employed in the services, to participate for so long as they remain so employed. The choice of which employees are to be eligible is a matter for the supplier[7] but will be

---

6   The Local Government Pension Scheme (Administration) Regulations 2008 (SI 2008/239) reg.6(9), Sch.3.
7   The Local Government Pension Scheme (Administration) Regulations 2008 (SI 2008/239) regs 6(11) and (12).

determined ultimately by the level of pension costs for which the outsourcing authority agrees to be liable under the contract.

If the supplier is "a 2(a) transferee admission body",[8] the Admission Agreement must require an actuarial assessment of the risk of the supplier prematurely terminating the provision of the services through its insolvency, winding up or being liquidated. Where the level of risk identified by the assessment is such as to require it, the Admission Agreement will oblige the supplier to provide a bond or indemnity to meet the level of risk identified.

(c) **Retention of Employment**: in some sourcing arrangements from the NHS, a retention of employment model is used to retain employees in NHS employment. This allows them to continue to be members of the NHS Pension Scheme. The retained NHS employees are then seconded to the supplier for the period of the contract.

32.11 What is Fair Deal all about?

32.11.1 *The "Fair Deal" ethos and where it comes from*

For central government outsourcing, the Cabinet Office issued a Statement of Practice *Staff Transfers in the Public Sector* (COSOP) in 2000. This has appended to it a document issued by HM Treasury called *Staff Transfers from Central Government: A Fair Deal for Staff Pensions* ("Fair Deal 1999"). A revised edition of Fair Deal was issued in 2004 ("Fair Deal 2004") (together "Fair Deal"). Fair Deal 2004 sought to remedy some of the problems that had emerged in practice since Fair Deal 1999.

32.11.2 *Application of Fair Deal*

Fair Deal is essentially guidance for central government departments. It does not directly apply to local government outsourcing. The Local Government Act 1999 requires BVAs to follow directions issued by the government. In 2003 and again in 2007, the government issued directions to BVAs that relate to the treatment of pension benefits in public sector outsourcing ("2003 Direction" and "2007 Direction"). The 2003 Direction required BVAs to follow Fair Deal. The 2007 Direction builds on the 2003 Direction. Therefore, in practice, Fair Deal will apply to both central government and BVA outsourcing, with additional requirements in the 2007 Direction applying only to BVA outsourcing.

---

[8] The Local Government Pension Scheme (Administration) Regulations 2008 (SI 2008/239) reg.6(2)(a).

Fair Deal is not directly binding on suppliers. However, because central and local government departments must operate within its guidelines, the pension protection that Fair Deal seeks to achieve is imposed as obligations on the supplier in the services contract.

32.11.3   Description of Fair Deal

The thrust of Fair Deal is to ensure that public sector employees or ex-public sector employees who transfer their employment to a supplier when the services they perform are outsourced are provided with (at least) broadly comparable pension benefits for future service.

In addition, if they choose to transfer the value of their pension benefits from their public sector pension scheme to the supplier's pension scheme, they must also be provided with broadly comparable pension benefits for past service on a continuous service basis (or actuarial equivalent). This is the case on first generation and second generation transfers.

Fair Deal 2004 recognised that, on second generation transfers, Fair Deal 1999 required the new supplier to provide broadly comparable pension benefits only for employees' future service with the new supplier. It did not require the outgoing supplier to offer or the new supplier to accept a Transfer Value in respect of employees' accrued pensions in the outgoing supplier's scheme. The outgoing supplier is not a party to the re-let contract. Consequently, the public sector contracting authority had no direct control over the Transfer Value that the outgoing supplier's pension scheme might offer. More often than not, the Transfer Value was insufficient to fund broadly comparable past service benefits on a continuous service basis. The effect of this was that the incoming supplier was often at a commercial disadvantage as compared with the incumbent supplier when bidding on a contract re-let.

Fair Deal 2004 attempted to tackle this by requiring exit provisions to be put into services agreements. Consequently, most public sector contracts will now require the outgoing supplier to procure that, if the trustees of its pension scheme accepted a transfer payment in respect of public sector employees or ex-public sector employees at the start of the supplier's contract, they must provide a Transfer Value at the end of it calculated on a basis no less generous than that which applied to the transfer payment they received.

Despite the application of Fair Deal 2004, agreeing transfer values from outgoing suppliers to incoming suppliers continues to be problematic in public sector service agreements.

Fair Deal is not retrospective. It does not apply to ex-public sector employees who were the subject of a first generation transfer before 1999.

Fair Deal is kept under periodic review by the UK government and has already been revised in 2004.

In its most recent review the government proposed to make a number of fundamental changes to Fair Deal. These proposals follow an independent review of public sector outsourcing by Lord Hutton in 2010 which identified Fair Deal as being a barrier to private sector providers offering outsourcing services. Following this report, the government published a consultation on the future of 'Fair Deal' in March 2011, and the Treasury issued a ministerial announcement setting out the government's proposed approach to public sector pension provision on outsourcing on 4 July 2012.

In the announcement the government stated that it intended to bring forward legislation to allow staff in the public sector who transfer out of the public sector to the private sector to retain membership of their existing public sector pension scheme. The announcement also indicated that the existing option for private sector employers to provide a GAD approved scheme would be removed.

Suppliers and contracting authorities therefore need to check if Fair Deal still applies to their intended contract and, if so, the terms on which it applies.

32.11.4 Description of the 2007 Direction[9]

In BVA outsourcing, the 2007 Direction applies to outsourcing contracts entered into since 1 October 2007. It builds on Fair Deal. It has three significant effects:

(a) it provides a statutory framework for pension protection;

(b) it requires contracting BVAs to ensure that their contract with the supplier gives employees transferring from the BVA a right to enforce the pension protection directly against the supplier. For these employees pension protection means rights to pension benefits the same as, broadly comparable to or better than those the employee had as an employee of the BVA. Pension protection relates only to future service with the new supplier. There is no requirement to protect employees' past service pensions with the BVA; and

(c) it provides pension protection to ex-public sector transferring employees, even if they were not covered by Fair Deal on their first generation transfer, who are now the subject of a second (or subsequent) generation transfer. For these employees pension protection means rights to pension benefits the same as, broadly comparable to or better than those the employee had under the outgoing supplier's pension scheme. Pension protection relates only to future service with the new supplier.

---

[9] The Best Value Authorities Staff Transfers (Pensions) Direction 2007.

There is no requirement to protect employees' past service pensions with the outgoing supplier or any previous employer.

32.12   Beckmann/Martin liabilities in the public sector

Public sector defined benefit pension schemes generally have generous benefit structures. *Beckmann/Martin*-type benefits often form part of the benefit structure in public sector pension schemes and/or ancillary redundancy compensation schemes or regulations (e.g. the Civil Service Compensation Scheme or The Local Government (Early Termination of Employment) (Discretionary Compensation) (England and Wales) Regulations 2006 (SI 2006/2914)).

Public sector pension schemes can be funded or unfunded arrangements. However, even when the public sector scheme is a funded scheme, enhanced pension benefits on redundancy are not usually funded within the scheme on an ongoing basis. When they arise, the employer in question makes a capital payment to the scheme to fund the additional cost of providing the benefits.

Other early retirement benefits may be funded on an ongoing basis, but, because the funding is based on assumptions that may not match experience, there can be a funding shortfall.

Transfer values from public sector schemes will not normally be calculated on a basis that includes any element of funding for enhanced pension benefits on redundancy. They will be based on assumptions as to early retirement. It is therefore as important to assess the impact of Beckmann/Martin-type considerations in public sector services agreements as it is in private sector services agreements since they can give rise to a significant funding requirement.

32.13   The Two-Tier Workforce Code

32.13.1   *Two Tier Workforce Code withdrawn*

The standard of employment terms to be offered by suppliers to new employees recruited to work alongside employees transferred from the public sector are set out in:

(a)   The *Code of Practice on Workforce Matters in Local Authority Service Contracts* (issued in 2003 by the Office of the Deputy Prime Minister in relation to local authority services agreements); and

(b)   The *Code of Practice on Workforce Matters in Public Sector Service Contracts* (issued in 2005 by the government in relation to services agreements with central government).

Although they are two separate documents, their terms are popularly referred to simply as the Two Tier Workforce Code. The aim of the Two Tier Workforce Code (as its name suggests) is to prevent contractors from employing new recruits on terms less generous that those of former public sector employees, resulting in a "two-tier" workforce.

The government withdrew its Two Tier Workforce Code with immediate effect on 13 December 2010. The Department for Communities and Local Government withdrew the local authority Two Tier Workforce Code with immediate effect on 23 March 2011.

32.13.2   Effect of withdrawal

In an information note on the withdrawal of its Code the government confirmed:

(a)   if the parties to an existing contract subject to the Two Tier Workforce Code agree to extend the contract term, the Code continues to apply, unless the parties agree to remove it;

(b)   if the parties to an existing contract subject to the Two Tier Workforce Code agree to remove the Code, the changes will apply only to future new employees; and

(c)   if a contract previously subject to the Two Tier Workforce Code is retendered and replaced by a new contract, the Code will not apply.

The Department for Communities and Local Government has also confirmed withdrawal of the local authority Code is not retrospective and that existing contracts will continue to be subject to it.

32.13.3   Voluntary application

The Two Tier Workforce Code is a policy document; it does not have the force of law. It can only have effect if public authorities impose it on their suppliers as obligations in the services agreement. Public authorities, in theory at least, were free to ignore it. Similarly, public authorities could still seek to apply the Two Tier Workforce Code to new service agreements, notwithstanding its withdrawal.

One of the reasons given by the government for withdrawing the Two Tier Workforce Code is that it was driving up the costs of public sector service agreements. As the customer authority is likely ultimately to pick up the cost of applying the Code through the pricing mechanism in the agreement, applying the Code voluntarily would need to be justified.

32.14   Code requirements as to pensions

So far as pensions are concerned, the Two Tier Workforce Code requires that the supplier must give new employees one of the following:

(a)   (under the local authority Two Tier Workforce Code) membership of the Local Government Pension Scheme;

(b)   membership of:

    (i)   a good quality defined benefit occupational pension scheme; or

    (ii)   a good quality DC occupational pension scheme with matching employer/employee contributions of up to 6 per cent); or

(c)   membership of a stakeholder scheme (with matching employer/ employee contributions of up to 6 per cent).

Thus, the supplier can provide pension benefits considerably less valuable than those to which the former public sector employees were entitled and still satisfy the Code. Given that the other terms and conditions to be offered must be fair, reasonable and overall no less favourable than those of the former public sector employees, the pensions obligations of the Code are not unduly onerous.

32.15   Principles of Good Employment Practice

32.15.1   *Replacement of Two Tier Workforce Code*

The government has replaced its Two Tier Workforce Code with a *Statement of Principles of Good Employment Practice*. The Statement was issued by the Cabinet Office in December 2010 and sets out six principles the government sees as reflecting good employment practice.

The Statement confirms the principles set out with the formal procurement decision making process and that adherence to them is voluntary.

The government's aim is:

(a)   employers of all sizes and from all sectors to have the freedom and flexibility to motivate and reward their workforce, to meet business needs;

(b)   public, private, voluntary and community organisations to learn from each other and share best practice in the spirit of continuous improvement; and

(c)   employers to be aware of the best practice that fosters employee engagement, access to skills and development whilst securing quality outcomes in the provision of public services.

32.15.2   *Government as a good client*

Through its commissioning, procurement standards and processes, central government should encourage contracting authorities and contractors to promote good workforce practices in the delivery of public services. Government will ensure that the workforce practices of the contractor are considered throughout the procurement process, where appropriate.

32.15.3   *Training and skills*

The procurement process should recognise the importance of basic skills such as literacy, numeracy and spoken English, where relevant. Suppliers will be able to demonstrate that staff have:

(a)   appropriate training and qualifications;
(b)   access to continuing professional development as befits their role; and
(c)   support to develop their skills and grow their experience.

Where there is a recognised trade union, suppliers will consult on workforce training and development issues.

32.15.4   *A commitment to fair and reasonable terms and conditions*

The pay and terms and conditions for new employees working alongside former public sector workers should be fair and reasonable. Suppliers should consult with recognised trade unions on the terms and conditions for new employees.

32.15.5   *Equality*

Suppliers should be able to demonstrate their policies and processes are entirely consistent with the requirements of the Equality Act 2010. Suppliers will be expected to demonstrate how working practices support their responsibilities as good employers.

32.15.6   Dispute resolution

All suppliers delivering public services should have regard to good industrial relations practice on dispute resolution. This includes treating employees fairly and ensuring compliance with the law on trade union membership.

Suppliers will ensure employees are aware of and have access to clear processes for dispute resolution. Suppliers should consider using the services of ACAS when internal dispute resolution processes fail to resolve disputes.

Where an employee has a right to trade union representation, suppliers will work with the employee and recognised trade union representatives in resolving disputes.

32.15.7   Employee engagement

Leadership, the design and delivery of service improvements, communications and a framework for staff engagement are vital components in ensuring and enhancing employee engagement. Suppliers should develop effective staff engagement strategies that enable people to be the best they can be at work.

32.16   Special protections

Some pension scheme members benefit from specific statutory protections for their pension benefits. Commonly these occur in industry sectors that were previously nationalised industries with the protections being linked to denationalisation. Examples include the Electricity Supply Pension Scheme and the Railways Pension Scheme, but there are others.

The degree of protection varies depending on the legislation that it is derived from. These need to be considered on a case-by-case basis. They can impact significantly on the treatment of pension benefits.

32.17   Auto-enrolment and TUPE

From 1 October 2012, the government has begun to phase in requirements for employers in the UK to provide access to, and pay contributions into, a pension scheme on behalf of their workers (a term that includes employees, and some other members of staff such as workers with a contract of service). The basic requirements, following completion of the phase-in in October

2018 will be that employers will be required to auto-enrol staff who are between 22 and state pension age, and who earn more than the equivalent of £8,105 per annum or more in a pay period into a qualifying pension scheme, and pay a total of 8 per cent contributions (4 per cent employee contributions, 3 per cent employer contributions and 1 per cent tax relief) into that scheme on earnings between £8,105 and £42, 475 per annum.[10] This obligation is ongoing and requires re-enrolment for any staff member who is not in a qualifying scheme approximately every three years by the employer.

Two points arise from this in the context of TUPE, first a purchaser will want to confirm whether the phased auto-enrolment requirements apply to the staff in question and their relevant auto-enrolment dates, and second in terms of the level of contributions that need to be made for the staff, there is a disconnect between the TUPE pension protection requirements, and those that apply for auto-enrolment. The DWP has confirmed that it is looking at this issue and will clarify the overlap between TUPE pension protection and the auto-enrolment requirements by October 2013, but until then it will be important to bear these issues in mind when transferring staff

---

[10] All figures for 2012/2013 tax year.

Chapter 33

Competition Issues

33.1 Outline

Services, partnering and outsourcing arrangements can raise competition law issues.

First, in certain circumstances, a services, partnering or outsourcing arrangement can amount to a merger and, if so, it may require notification to the relevant competition authorities.

Second, if the arrangement does not amount to a merger (and most will not), any restrictions such as exclusivity or non-compete provisions could infringe the rules which prohibit anti-competitive agreements (set out in Article 101 of the Treaty on the Functioning of the European Union (TFEU) and/or Chapter I of the Competition Act 1998) if they have an appreciable anti-competitive effect on the relevant market and do not qualify for an exemption.

Third, the exchange of confidential information inherent in the transaction could also raise competition law concerns if the parties can be regarded as competitors.

This chapter considers these issues and provides some practical guidance on how to approach potential competition law concerns in the context of services, partnering and outsourcing arrangements.

33.2 Merger control

If a services, partnering or outsourcing arrangement amounts to a merger, it could be subject to the EU or UK merger control regimes and/or the merger control regimes of other jurisdictions, depending on where sales are made and or services are supplied. In many jurisdictions, clearance from the relevant competition authorities must obtained before the merger can be put into effect if the merger meets certain national turnover or market share thresholds (regardless of whether the transaction may adversely affect competition).

33.2.1   EU merger control

A transaction which is subject to the EU Merger Regulation (EUMR) (known as a concentration) and which meets the turnover thresholds must be notified to the European Commission and the parties cannot complete the transaction before EU merger clearance has been obtained, regardless of whether the merger raises any substantive competition concerns.[1] Such transactions will not require notification to the UK authorities or those of any other individual EU Member State.

However, a merger which meets the EUMR thresholds may be considered by the national competition authorities if its effects are confined to that particular territory and are likely to have a significant impact on competition in that territory. In these circumstances, the relevant national authority (or the parties themselves) can request that the merger be referred back to the national authority for consideration under the national merger rules.[2]

Under the EUMR, the European Commission must consider whether a merger notified to it "significantly impedes effective competition in the Common Market or in a substantial part thereof, in particular as a result of the creation or strengthening of a dominant position". If the European Commission does consider that the transaction significantly impedes effective competition, it may make clearance conditional on certain conditions, such as divesting a particular business, or it may even prohibit the transaction.

Failure to notify a merger which meets the EUMR thresholds can result in fines of up to 10 per cent of the parties' worldwide turnover. It is therefore important to establish from the outset whether a proposed arrangement is (a) likely to amount to a concentration and, if so, (b) whether the concentration has a "Community dimension"—i.e. whether the EUMR turnover thresholds are met.

Completion of a proposed concentration which meets the thresholds for notification must be conditional on clearance from the European Commission.

33.2.1.1   Does the arrangement amount to a concentration under the EUMR?

33.2.1.1.1   Change of control over an undertaking

Under the EUMR, a concentration arises where a change of control on a lasting basis results from the merger between previously independent undertak-

---

[1]   Regulation 139/2004 on the control of concentrations between undertakings OJ L24, 29.1.2004
[2]   Articles 4 and 9 of Regulation 139/2004.

ings or parts of undertakings;[3] the acquisition of control of the whole or parts of one or more undertakings (whether by purchasing securities or assets, by contract or by any other means)[4] or through the creation of a full-function joint venture.[5] [6]

The Commission's Consolidated Jurisdictional Notice (the "Jurisdictional Notice") provides guidance on the circumstances in which a transfer of services can amount to a concentration under the EUMR.[7]

If a supplier, in addition to taking over a previously internal activity, acquires associated assets which "constitute a business with a market presence, to which a market turnover can be clearly attributed", the arrangement will constitute a concentration.[8] The question is therefore whether a deal involves the transfer of a discrete section of a business, which, before the transfer, had provided services from which sales to third parties were generated.[9] In some circumstances, the transfer of a client base or an exclusive licence for intangible assets can constitute a "concentration" if this in itself generates turnover (i.e. sales revenue).[10]

The level of control necessary to establish a concentration may arise contractually, but the contract must confer control of the administration and assets, comparable with that arising from an acquisition of assets or shares conferring control.[11] The contract must be of "a very long duration" to result in a structural change, and must generally be without the possibility of early termination for the party granting the contractual rights—presumably the customer. Some commentators have suggested that this probably means the contract must be for a minimum of 8–10 years. It is not clear whether, or how typical, break clauses in such contracts would affect the Commission's view of control, especially as termination is not always realistic in practice.[12]

The assets transferred have to include at least those core elements that would allow the buyer to establish an independent market presence in order for there to be a concentration. Any assets previously dedicated to the in-house activities of the customer must be available for the buyer to provide services not only to the customer, but also to third parties, either immediately or "within a short period after the transfer" (normally not exceeding three years, but this will depend on the specific conditions of the market in

---

[3]   Article 3(1)(a) of Regulation 139/2004.

[4]   Article 3(1)(b) of Regulation 139/2004.

[5]   Article 3(4) of Regulation 139/2004.

[6]   Article 2 of Regulation 139/2004 OJ L24, 29.1.2004, p1.

[7]   Commission Consolidated Jurisdictional Notice under Regulation 139/2004 on the control of concentrations between undertakings, OJ 2008 C95/1, 16 April 2008 at *http://eurlex.europa.eu/LexUriServ/ LexUriServ.do?uri=OJ:C:2008:095:0001:0048:EN:PDF* [Accessed 20 September 2012]

[8]   Commission Consolidated Jurisdictional Notice, at para.24. See also Case M.3867—*Vattenhall/Elsam and Energi E2 assets.*

[9]   See Case M.3571 *IBM/Maerskdata/DMData* (2005/C28/02).

[10]   See COMP/M.4981 *AT&T/IBM*, 14 December 2007.

[11]   Commission's Consolidated Jurisdictional Notice, at para.18.

[12]   It is likely that normal contractual protections which permit termination on a material breach of the contract would not affect the Commission's conclusion.

question).[13] This will be the case if the assets being transferred are already being used to provide services to third parties. However, some services agreements prevent the service provider from using the transferred assets for third parties and such "sole use" restrictions would prevent the transaction from amounting to a concentration. Similarly, there will be no concentration if no assets or employees are transferred to the supplier, or if the supplier acquires only a right to direct the customer's assets and employees which will be used exclusively to service the customer.[14]

Where activities are transferred to a new subsidiary within the same corporate group, there is no "concentration" if the new subsidiary entity continues to be solely controlled by the ultimate parent of the group.

Many transfers of in-house facilities to a supplier will not amount to a concentration. In the case of manufacturing businesses, if third parties are not yet supplied, there will not be a concentration unless assets transferred contain production facilities, relevant know-how and the means for the purchaser to develop market access within a short period (e.g. including existing contracts or brands). In the case of services businesses, there will not be a concentration unless the assets transferred include the required know-how (e.g. relevant personnel and IP) and facilities which allow market access (e.g. marketing facilities).[15]

In order to qualify as a concentration, the target must be all or part of an undertaking. Some commentators argue that the transfer of the assets or personnel in a service agreement will only be so regarded if the transferred assets or personnel appreciably strengthen the market position of the supplier.[16] On this basis, a service agreement involving exclusively the transfer of employees and related office equipment previously engaged in in-house activities such as IT may not be a concentration. In those cases where the Commission has considered the requirements of a concentration to have been met, there was, in addition to the transfer of personnel, also the transfer of material assets allowing access to the market.[17]

33.2.1.1.2   Full-function joint ventures

The creation of a "full-function" joint venture on a "lasting basis" can also amount to a concentration under the EUMR. A full-function joint venture must operate independently on the market, its activities must go beyond

---

[13]   Commission's Consolidated Jurisdictional Notice, at paras 26, 97 and 100.
[14]   Commission Consolidated Jurisdictional Notice, at para.25.
[15]   Commission's Consolidated Jurisdictional Notice, at para.26.
[16]   See Jan Lohrberg and Matti Huhtamaki, "Outsourcing Transactions and Merger Control" (2008) *European Competition Law Review* 29(6), 349–55, at p.352. See also James Killick and Ashley Winton, "You can't outsource compliance: the relevance of competition law to outsourcing transactions" *Competition Law Insight* 7 April 2009.
[17]   See Case M.2629 *Flextronics/Xerox*; Case M.1841 *Celestica/IBM (EMS)*; Case M.1968*Solectron/Nortel*; Case M.1849 *Solectron/Ericsson*; Case M.286 *Zurich/MMI*.

one specific function for its parents, and it must not be reliant on its parents for sales and purchases.[18] To be a full function joint venture, the joint venture must be economically autonomous from an operational viewpoint,[19] dealing with the parent at arm's length on the basis of normal commercial conditions and supplying its goods or services to third parties in a revenue-maximising manner.[20] However, it may rely almost entirely on its parents during its start-up period, if it can build up sufficient market presence in a reasonable time.

However, a joint venture would not be full function, despite providing services to the customer and third parties if the transfer related to an internal business unit, without transferring associated assets or personnel, and/or if third-party revenues were likely to remain "ancillary" to the joint venture's main activities for the customer.[21]

There are a number of cases where the European Commission decided that a services arrangement was a full function joint venture and therefore a concentration for the purposes of the EUMR.[22]

33.2.1.2 *Does the concentration meet the EUMR turnover thresholds?*

A transfer of services arrangement which constitutes a concentration will require notification to the European Commission for clearance only if it has a "Community dimension", that is, if the turnover of the relevant parties satisfies certain turnover thresholds. There are two sets of alternative turnover thresholds which could be satisfied.

The first set of thresholds could be met if:

(a) the combined worldwide turnover of the relevant parties exceeds €5 billion; and

(b) each of at least two of the relevant parties has EU turnover exceeding €250 million.

The second set of thresholds could be met if:

---

[18] Article 3(4) of Regulation 139/2004, OJ L24, 29.1.2004, p.1 and para.100 of the Commission's Consolidated Jurisdictional Notice.

[19] *Cementbouw Handel & Industrie BV v Commission of the European Communities* (T-282/02) [2006] E.C.R. II-319.

[20] Case M.556 *Zeneca/Vanderhave*, 9 April 1996.

[21] Commission's Consolidated Jurisdictional Notice, at para.100. See also paras 25–27.

[22] For example, in *British Gas Trading/Group 4 Utilities* two parties assumed joint control of a venture providing meter-reading services to the gas industry. Case M.791 *British Gas Trading/Group 4 Utility Services* [1996] 5 C.M.L.R. 526; Case M.2122 *BAT/CAP Gemini*/Ciberion, 11 September 2000. Other examples include Case M.560 *EDS/Lufthansa*, 11 May 1995 and Case M.2478 *IBM Italia/Business Solutions/JV*, 29/6/2001 (2001/C/278/05), described below.

(a) the combined worldwide turnover of the relevant parties exceeds €2.5 billion; and

(b) each of at least two of the relevant parties has EU turnover exceeding €100 million; and

(c) in each of at least three EU Member States, the combined turnover of the relevant parties exceeds €100 million and, in the same three EU Member States, at least two of the relevant parties each has turnover over €25 million.

However, neither set of thresholds can be met if all the relevant parties generate more than two-thirds of their EU turnover in one and the same EU Member State.

In relation to business partnering, turnover of the "relevant parties" means the turnover in the preceding financial year of the whole of the supplier's group and the part of the customer's business that is being transferred.

Turnover is usually calculated from the most recent financial year's audited accounts. However, the Jurisdictional Notice states that where an outsourcing transaction involves a business unit which only had internal revenues in the past,

> "the turnover should normally be calculated on the basis of the previously internal turnover or of publicly quoted prices, where such prices exist".

Where this does not appear to correspond to a market valuation or the expected future turnover, "the forecast revenues to be received on the basis of an agreement with the former parent may be a suitable proxy".[23]

33.2.1.3   EU merger decisions

There have been only a few EU merger control decisions regarding transfer of services agreements, and these decisions are specific to their facts.[24] However, several of these merger decisions concern (and include useful guidance on) market definition in IT service markets, a major outsourcing market.[25] To date, no transfer of services transaction has been blocked by

---

[23] Commission's Consolidated Jurisdictional Notice, at para.163.

[24] A number of these cases also contain useful guidance on how the relevant product and geographic markets are defined in the IT service sector: Case M.4981—*AT&T/IBM*, 14 December 2007; Case M.3867—*Vattenhall/Elsam and Energi E2 assets*, 22 December 2005; Case M.3571 *IBM/Maerskdata/DMData* (2005/ C28/02); Case M.3583 *Flextronics/Nortel*, 28 October 2004; Case M.3171 *Computer Sciences Corporation/ Royal Mail Business Systems* (2003/C187/09); Case M.2478 *IBM Italia/Business Solutions/JV*, 29/6/2001 (2001/C/278/05); Case M.2122 *BAT/CAP Gemini/* Ciberion, 11 September 2000; Case M.1968 *Solectron/ Nortel*, 31 May 2000; Case M.1849 *Solectron/Ericsson*, 29 February 2000; Case M.1841 *Celestica/IBM (EMS)*,25 February 2000; Case M.791 *British Gas Trading/Group 4 Utility Services* [1996] 5 C.M.L.R. 526; Case M.560 *EDS/Lufthansa*, 11 May 1995; Case M.286 *Zurich/MMI*, 2 April 1993.

[25] See, for example, Commission decisions M.3555 *Hewlett Packard/Synstar*, September 9, 2004; and M.2478 *IBM Italia/Business Solutions/JV*, 29 June 2001.

the European Commission and, indeed, none have raised substantive competition concerns.

In *Computer Sciences Corporation (CSC)/Royal Mail Business Systems (RMBS)*, the European Commission decided that the provision of services by CSC to Royal Mail was a notifiable concentration, despite the lack of any market presence before the transfer.[26] The deal involved the acquisition of all the shares in a wholly owned subsidiary of Royal Mail, so was more clearly a "merger" than many transfers of service. However, this decision suggests (contrary to the guidance in the Jurisdictional Notice) that the transfer of an entity previously operating entirely in a captive market, with no wider market presence, may amount to a concentration under the EUMR.

The European Commission also concluded that the acquisition by Flextronics of control of parts of Nortel amounted to a "concentration" in its *Flextronics/Nortel* decision in October 2004.[27] Flextronics International Ltd provided electronics manufacturing services to original equipment manufacturers in the telecommunications, networking, consumer electronics, computer and medical device industries. These services involved the manufacturing of various types of electronic products on an outsourced procurement basis. Nortel Networks Limited was a supplier of products and services that supported the internet and other public and private data, voice and multimedia communication networks. As part of the arrangement, Flextronics acquired some of Nortel's manufacturing assets, employees and related supply chain activities and the Commission decided that this amounted to a transfer of control sufficient to amount to a concentration under the EUMR.

The *IBM/Fiat* case is a useful example of where a joint venture transfer agreement was considered to amount to a concentration under the EUMR.[28] In this case, Fiat combined two business units that had provided in-house IT services to the Fiat group with five IBM businesses which had previously been active in the wider market. The joint venture was intended to sell IT services not only to its founding companies (which would result in cost savings for Fiat) but also to third parties—around 50 to 70 per cent of the revenues of the joint venture would come from sales to third parties. This was an important factor in determining whether the joint venture was full-function in nature.

33.2.2 UK merger control

A transaction which does not require notification to the European Commission under the EUMR will fall to be considered under the national merger control rules of EU Member States. A merger may also require notification

---

[26] Case M.3171 *Computer Sciences Corporation/Royal Mail Business Systems* (2003/C187/09).
[27] Case M.3583 *Flextronics/Nortel*, 28 October 2004.
[28] Case M.2478 *IBM Italia/Business Solutions/JV*, 29/6/2001 (2001/C/278/05).

outside the EU (whether or not an EUMR filing is required) depending on where the supplier and customer generate turnover.

The UK merger control rules apply to transfer of services agreements which result in a "relevant merger situation".[29] If certain jurisdictional tests are met, the Office of Fair Trading (OFT) can investigate a merger and, if it considers that the merger has resulted (or may be expected to result) in a "substantial lessening of competition within any market(s) for goods or services in the UK", it has a duty to refer the merger to the Competition Commission (CC) for an in-depth investigation.[30] Ultimately, the CC can block a merger, clear it or clear it subject to conditions, for example, divestment.

Notification to the OFT is not compulsory if a merger meets the jurisdictional tests. However, if a merger meets the jurisdictional tests and could raise substantive competition concerns, a purchaser which does not apply for pre-completion clearance from the OFT takes the risk of being required by the authorities at a later stage to sell all or part of the business acquired. The authorities may also impose severe restrictions on the buyer's ability to deal with the acquired business while a competition investigation is carried out. In a transfer of services , the authorities could prevent the transfer of relevant people and assets to the supplier and frustrate both parties' commercial objectives by preventing the supplier from performing its obligations to the customer.

33.2.2.1   Does the transaction amount to a UK merger?

A transfer arrangement could amount to a merger for the purposes of UK merger control if it results in two or more "enterprises" which "cease to be distinct".[31]

An "enterprise" means "the activities or part of the activities of a business" including, typically, the assets and records needed to carry on the business, together with the benefit of existing contracts and/or goodwill. The OFT will consider in particular whether the arrangement involves the transfer of customer records or the application of the Transfer of Undertakings (Protection of Employment) Regulations 2006 and the OFT would normally (although not inevitably) expect to see the transfer of some payment for goodwill obtained by the purchaser.[32]

In its publication (dated June 2009) *Mergers - Jurisdictional and Procedural Guidance* the OFT states that:

---

[29]   Enterprise Act 2002 s.23.
[30]   Enterprise Act 2002 ss.22 and 33.
[31]   Enterprise Act 2002 s.23(1)(a).
[32]   OFT, *Mergers - jurisdictional and procedural guidance* (2009), para.3–10.

"Outsourcing arrangements involving ongoing supply arrangements will not generally result in enterprises ceasing to be distinct, but may do so where they involve the permanent (or long-term) transfer of assets, rights and/or employees to the outsourcing service supplier and where those may be used to supply services other than to the original owner/employer."[33]

33.2.2.2 Does the OFT have jurisdiction to investigate?

The OFT has jurisdiction over a merger if one of two tests is satisfied:

The first is a "turnover test". This would be satisfied, in the context of a transfer arrangement, if the UK turnover of the part of the customer's business being outsourced exceeds £70 million.

The second is a "share of supply test". This is satisfied in relation to transfer arrangements if, as a result of the transaction, the supplier and the part of the customer's business that is being transferred together account for 25 per cent or more of all the goods or services of a particular description supplied in the UK or in a substantial part of it. The share of supply test is not a market share test—it does not depend on the economic definition of the relevant product/service and geographic market(s)—it applies to the supply of any particular good or service and can, therefore, be relatively easy to satisfy.

33.2.2.3 UK merger decisions

There have been relatively few UK merger decisions relating to transfer arrangements and the cases which have been considered by the authorities have not raised substantive competition concerns on any particular market.[34] This may change over time if relevant markets become more concentrated.

In the *Exel/NHS Logistics Authority/NHS Purchasing and Supply Agency* case, the OFT concluded that the transaction did involve "enterprises ceasing to be distinct" which meant that the merger control rules applied.[35] In this case, Exel agreed to take over the provision of certain procurement and logistics services for consumable products to the Department of Health. The services had previously been provided (respectively) by the NHS Purchasing and Supply Agency and NHS Logistics who provided the services as in-house "shared services" centres. The arrangement involved the transfer from the NHS to Exel of up to 1,600 employees and certain assets (including information technology and office equipment) and the grant to Exel of the right to use certain NHS intellectual property rights. The agreement also

---

[33] OFT, *Mergers - jurisdictional and procedural guidance* (2009), para.3–13.

[34] See OFT decision *Nuclear Management Partners Limited/Sellafield Limited* (October 2008); OFT decision *University College London Hospitals NHS Foundation Trust/HCA International Limited* (October 2006); OFT decision *Exel/NHS Logistics Authority/NHS Purchasing and Supply Agency* (July 2006); OFT decision *Vertex/Marlborough Sterling* (May 2005); and OFT decision *Northgate/Systems Solutions* (May 2005).

[35] OFT decision *Exel/NHS Logistics Authority/NHS Purchasing and Supply Agency* (July 2006).

included the transfer of outsourcing agreements entered into by the shared services centres with the Department of Health and third parties (although the agreements with third parties were low value). The OFT considered that, because the contracts and assets had an "open market value" (of over £70 million), they could be considered as "enterprises" for the purposes of the merger rules.

In a later case concerning the *award of a management contract at University College London Hospital NHS Foundation Trust (UCLH) to HCA International Limited (HCA)*, the OFT took a different approach.[36] UCLH had leased (previously vacant) premises to HCA for five years for use as a private patient unit, including the use of certain equipment (a broken linear accelerator and MRI scanner), facilities (including two bunkers and a scanner room) and support services (relating to the operation and administration of a private patient unit e.g. pathology, facilities management, information technology and telecommunication services), and the secondment of some personnel. The OFT concluded that there was no relevant merger situation on the basis that there was no current business activity being carried on in the premises being transferred, no physical assets were passing ownership, and no UCLH employees, customer details or contracts (i.e. goodwill) were being transferred.

More recently, the OFT considered the potential contract award to Nuclear Management Partners Limited of the decommissioning of the Sellafield nuclear site.[37] In order to carry out this service, NMPL acquired the entire issued share capital of Sellafield. However, the OFT concluded that Sellafield was not an "enterprise" for the purposes of the merger control rules because NMPL's role would be limited to ensuring the effective decommissioning of the site and, in any event, Sellafield does not own the site—all relevant assets are the property of the Nuclear Decommissioning Authority which are used by Sellafield under licence. The NMPL will not own or control a market facing business as a result of this acquisition because it will not have the right to take certain key business decisions (for example using Sellafield's assets, entering into new contracts, appointing or removing directors, changing the nature of the business etc).

The *Odeon/BFI*[38] case is a useful example involving a management agreement under which Odeon became the manager and operator of a cinema business and supporting retail presence for an initial period of three years arrangements with employees transferring to Odeon. The OFT applied its guidance.[39] It did not consider that the period of the transfer was sufficiently long to amount to a merger which is a permanent and long-term transfer of a business and also relied on the control the transferor kept over the

---

[36] OFT decision *University College London Hospitals NHS Foundation Trust/HCA International Limited* (October 2006).
[37] OFT decision *Nuclear Management Partners Limited/Sellafield Limited* (October 2008).
[38] OFT decision *Odeon Cinema Holdings Limited/BFI IMAX Cinema*, 16 July 2012 ME/5483-12
[39] OFT *Mergers - jurisdictional and procedural guidance* (2009)

transferred operations (for example through performance monitoring of the level of service provided by the transferee against agreed indicators) as a reason why the transaction should not be regarded as a merger. It also noted that, at the end of the arrangement, assets and employees would transfer back to the transferor (so this too could not be regarded as permanent).

33.3   Anti-competitive agreements

The application of the EU and UK competition rules must be considered if a services agreement contains exclusivity or non-compete clauses or could involve the exchange of confidential information.

Article 101(1) of the Treaty on the Functioning of the European Union (TFEU) and Chapter I of the Competition Act 1998 prohibit agreements that have the object or effect of preventing, restricting or distorting competition and which may affect trade between EU Member States or within the UK. Agreements which infringe these prohibitions are punishable with heavy fines (up to 10 per cent of group turnover, although for enforcement at the UK level, a fine will amount to no more than 30 per cent of the undertaking's relevant turnover), the agreements themselves are unenforceable and the parties to them may be sued for damages. Under the Enterprise Act 2002, it is a criminal offence for individuals to be involved in the most serious anti-competitive ("cartel") agreements involving price fixing, market sharing or bid-rigging. Such individuals may be disqualified as directors for up to 15 years or subject to unlimited fines and up to five years' imprisonment.

However, there are a number of exclusions and exemptions which may apply:

(a)   First, a restriction which is "ancillary" to a merger/concentration is unlikely to infringe the rules;

(b)   Second, restrictions infringe the rules only if they have as their object the restriction of competition or they have an "appreciable" effect on competition. Some agreements may therefore by be considered as "de minimis" and not capable of infringing the rules;

(c)   Third, the agreement may be able to benefit from one of the "block exemptions" from Article 101/Chapter 1, even if it is capable of having an appreciable effect on competition, if the necessary conditions are met; and

(d)   Fourth, if the agreement does not fall within the scope of one of the block exemptions, it may qualify for individual exemption from Article 101/Chapter 1 if it meets certain exemption criteria.

The UK common law restraint of trade doctrine may also apply to an exclusivity or non-compete restriction in a services agreement. Under the restraint of trade doctrine, restrictions which go beyond what is necessary to protect the legitimate interests of the parties or are contrary to the public interest are unenforceable.[40] Any restrictions should therefore be limited in duration and in scope to what is reasonably necessary, i.e. limited to the products/services provided under the agreement and to the geographic scope of the agreement. However, a restriction which is valid and enforceable under Article 101(1) (and Chapter I of the Competition Act 1998) (because it benefits from an exemption, for example) is unlikely to be unenforceable under the UK restraint of trade doctrine.[41]

The above exclusions and exemptions are described in the following sections.

33.3.1   Ancillary restraints

A transfer of services agreement which amounts to a merger/concentration cannot in itself infringe Article101 of the TFEU or Chapter I of the Competition Act 1998 as its impact on competition is considered under the relevant merger control rules).[42] A restriction will also avoid infringing the rules if it is "ancillary" to a merger/concentration, i.e. if it is directly related and necessary to the implementation of the merger/concentration.

The European Commission has published a Notice ("the Ancillary Restraints Notice") on the circumstances in which a restriction is likely to be ancillary (or not) to a merger.[43]

The Ancillary Restraints Notice specifies that a clearance decision under the EUMR will cover any restrictions which are ancillary to the merger. If the merger does not meet the thresholds for notification under the EUMR, the merger will fall to be considered under the national merger rules of Member States (and countries outside the EU where relevant). These national (EU) competition authorities are likely to follow a similar approach to the

---

[40]   See, for example, *Esso Petroleum Co Ltd v Harper's Garage (Stourport) Ltd* [1967] 2 W.L.R. 871; *Panayiotou v Sony Music Entertainment (UK) Ltd* [1994] E.M.L.R. 229.

[41]   See *Days Medical Aids Ltd v Pihsiang Machinery Manufacturing Co Ltd* [2004] EWHC 44 (Comm); [2004] 1 All E.R. (Comm) 991, where the Judge applied Article 3 of EC Regulation 1/2003, which states that: "The application of national competition law may not lead to the prohibition of agreements...which do not restrict competition within the meaning of Article 81(1) of the Treaty, or which fulfil the conditions of Article 81(3) of the Treaty or which are covered by a Regulation for the application of Article 81(3) of the Treaty."

[42]   The circumstances in which an outsourcing agreement is likely to amount to a merger or "concentration" are discussed at the beginning of this chapter. Concentrations which fall within the scope of the EUMR must be appraised in accordance with the criteria set out in the EUMR (Article 2 EUMR) which means that Article101(1) does not apply. And mergers are explicitly excluded from the application of Chapter I Competition Act 1998 under Sch.1 of the Act.

[43]   European Commission Notice on restrictions directly related and necessary to concentrations, 2005/C56/03, OJ C56, 5.3.2005, p.24.

consideration of ancillary restrictions as the European Commission (and, indeed, are likely to apply the Commission's Notice on Ancillary Restraints). In the UK, the OFT has confirmed that it will follow the approach set out in the Ancillary Restraints Notice (whether or not the merger is notified to the OFT).[44]

Any restriction which is not considered to be ancillary to a transfer arrangement which amounts to a merger/concentration, would fall to be considered separately under Article 101(1) of the TFEU and/or Chapter I of the Competition Act 1998.

33.3.1.1   *Non-compete restrictions*

In the context of a services agreement (which amounts to a merger) any restrictions on the customer from providing the services in-house are likely to be considered (by the relevant competition authorities) as ancillary provided that, in accordance with the Ancillary Restraints Notice, they are limited in scope—to the products concerned and to the geographic areas where the business operates—and in duration to what is "necessary" to protect the value of the business being transferred.

According to the Ancillary Restraints Notice, when the transfer of a business includes both goodwill and know-how, a non-compete restriction on the seller is considered to be ancillary for a period of up to three years. When only goodwill is included in the transfer (i.e. without any know-how), a non-compete restriction on the seller can be justified for up to two years. However, non-compete restrictions between the parents and a full function joint venture are considered to be ancillary for the lifetime of the joint venture.

If the transfer is limited to physical assets (e.g. land, buildings or machinery) or to exclusive intellectual property rights, a non-compete restriction on the seller is not considered to be ancillary to the transfer.

33.3.1.2   *Licence agreements*

The seller of a business may remain the owner of certain intellectual property rights or know-how but, in order for the buyer to be able to properly exploit the business, it may be necessary for licensing agreements to be put in place. Similarly, intellectual property rights may be transferred with the business but the seller may need a licence back in order to continue with other business activities. Licences of patents, know-how or similar rights in these circumstances are, in accordance with the Ancillary Restraints Notice, considered to be ancillary to the transfer. These licences may be

---

[44] OFT guidance *Mergers: Substantive Assessment Guidance* (2003), para.11–13. The Ancillary Restraints Notice is considered to be a statement of the European Commission to which the OFT is bound to have regard under s.60 of the Competition Act 1998.

simple, exclusive, limited in time or perpetual and limited to the fields of use which correspond to the transfer. However, if they are more restrictive than this (for example, limiting the territories in which the buyer/seller can exploit the licence) they should be considered in accordance with the rules on non-competes (see above) and they may not be considered as ancillary to the arrangement.

33.3.1.3   Purchase or supply obligations (and service agreements)

According to the Ancillary Restraints Notice, any on-going purchase or supply obligations between the seller and the buyer, which are aimed at guaranteeing the quantities previously supplied, can be justified as ancillary to the transfer of a business for a period of up to five years. Obligations providing for fixed quantities, possibly with a variation clause, are considered as ancillary, but obligations providing for unlimited quantities, exclusivity or conferring preferred-supplier or preferred-purchaser status are not considered as ancillary – these would, therefore, have to be considered separately to the merger/concentration.

33.3.2   Agreements of minor importance

Restrictions in agreements are prohibited under Article101(1) of the TFEU and Chapter I of the Competition Act 1998 only if they have an "appreciable" impact on competition in the relevant market. The European Commission's Notice on agreements of minor importance (the "De Minimis Notice") provides that agreements will generally not appreciably restrict competition if:

(a)   the parties' aggregate market share on any relevant "affected market" does not exceed 10 per cent in the case of actual or potential competitors, or 15 per cent in the case of non-competitors; and

(b)   the agreement does not contain any "hardcore" restrictions (e.g. price-fixing or market-sharing arrangements, or those allocating markets or customers).[45]

Whether the market share thresholds are met, or not, will depend on the definition of the relevant market in each case. Market definition is complex, based on an economic assessment of demand- and supply-side substitutability. And it is possible for the parties to an agreement to have surprisingly high market shares in a narrowly-defined, niche market.

Where the parties' market shares are too high for the De Minimis Notice to apply, exclusive arrangements which have a duration of over five years may

---

[45]   In determining whether an agreement has an appreciable effect on competition, the OFT will have regard to the European Commission's approach as set out in the Notice on Agreements of Minor Importance. See OFT Guidance *Agreements and concerted practice* (2004), para.2–18.

be prohibited under Article 101(1) of the TFEU and/or Chapter I of the Competition Act 1998, particularly if the duration is "manifestly excessive" by comparison to the average duration of contracts concluded in the relevant market.[46] An excessive period of exclusivity might also be unenforceable under the UK common law principle of restraint of trade rules but, as discussed above, this is unlikely if the agreement is valid and enforceable under the Article 101(1) of the TFEU because, for example, it qualifies for exemption (see below).

33.3.3 *Exemption under Article 101(3) of the TFEU*

Arrangements that are not covered by the De Minimis Notice, but contain restrictions on competition, may qualify for an exemption from the application of Article 101(1) of the TFEU and Chapter I of the Competition Act 1998.

To benefit from an exemption, an arrangement must satisfy several conditions set out in Article 101(3) of the TFEU and s.9 of the Competition Act 1998, which are designed to ensure that the economic benefits provided by the arrangement outweigh its negative effects on competition. These conditions are that the agreement:

(a) must contribute to improving production or distribution, or to promoting technical or economic progress, while allowing consumers a fair share of the resulting benefit; and
(b) must not impose restrictions which are "not indispensable" to the attainment of those objectives, or give the parties the possibility of eliminating competition in respect of a substantial part of the products or services in question.

Some agreements are of their nature more likely to fulfil the conditions in Article 101(3) of the TFEU and the Commission has therefore issued block exemptions for certain types of agreement. An agreement which qualifies for an exemption under a Commission block exemption is automatically exempt from the application of Chapter I of the Competition Act 1998.[47]

33.3.3.1 *Vertical Agreements Block Exemption*

The Vertical Agreements Block Exemption (VABE) automatically exempts agreements concerning the purchase and/or sale of goods or services between parties operating at different levels of the manufacture/supply chain (for the purposes of the agreement) provided that the supplier and the

---

[46] See, for example, Case C-234/89 *Delimitis/Henninger Bräu*, Judgment of 28/02/1991, (Rec.1991, pI-935), at [26]; Case C-214/99 *Neste*, Judgment of 07/12/2000, (Rec.2000,p. I-11121) at [27] and [32]; and Commission Decision IV/29.021 *BP Kemi*, OJ L 286, 14/11/1979, at [68].
[47] Competition Act 1998 s.10.

buyer each have a market share under 30 per cent and the agreement does not contain certain specified "hardcore restrictions".[48]

The VABE will not apply to a services agreement between competitors unless the agreement is non-reciprocal and the buyer does not provide services competing with those it purchases from the supplier - for example because the buyer has outsourced all of those services to the supplier.

For the purposes of the VABE, a non-compete obligation in a transfer of services means any obligation on the customer not to compete with the contract services, or any obligation on the customer to purchase from the supplier more than 80 per cent of the customer's total purchases of the contract services (or substitutes for them). An obligation on the customer to buy specified services only from the supplier—that is, an exclusive purchasing obligation—is therefore treated as a "non-compete" provision. A non-compete provision can benefit from the VABE only if its duration does not exceed five years. An indefinite obligation—such as one which is renewed automatically after five years—will not benefit from the VABE and whether or not it can benefit from an exemption will depend on an assessment of whether it fulfils the criteria in Article 101(3).

33.3.3.2 *Specialisation Block Exemption*

A services agreement between competitors may be able to benefit from the European Commission's Specialisation Block Exemption (SBE). The SBE can apply to "unilateral specialisation agreements", when two competitors agree that one will stop producing (or not produce) certain products or services and will buy them from the other.[49] It can also apply to "reciprocal specialisation agreements", when two competitors agree that each will stop producing (or not produce) different products or services and will buy them from one another. And it also applies to "joint production agreements" where two or more parties agree to produce certain products jointly.

The SBE applies only if the parties' combined market share does not exceed 20 per cent and the arrangement does not contain any hardcore restrictions on competition (i.e. price fixing, agreeing output or sales limits or market sharing).

The SBE covers specialisation agreements which include exclusive purchasing and/or supply obligations and such obligations do not need to be limited in time (unlike non-compete obligations under the VABE which lose the benefit of the exemption if they exceed 5 years).

---

[48] Commission Regulation on the application of Article 101(3) of the Treaty on the Functioning of the European union to categories of vertical agreements and concerted practices (330/2010/EU).
[49] Commission Regulation on the application of Article 101(3) of the Treaty to categories of specialisation agreements (1217/2010/EU).

33.3.4   Outside the scope of a block exemption

If a services agreement contains restrictions on the parties (for example non-competes or exclusivity obligations) and the market shares of the parties are such that the agreement does not fall within the scope of the De Minimis Notice or a block exemption, this does not necessarily mean that it will infringe Article 101(1) of the TFEU or Chapter I of the Competition Act 1998. The restrictions may fall outside the scope of the rules altogether or they may qualify for an individual exemption if the conditions in Article 101(3) are met. The Commission has issued a number of notices which provide guidance on how to assess the risk of certain arrangements infringing the rules.

33.3.4.1   Notice on subcontracting agreements

The European Commission's Notice on subcontracting agreements provides that Article 101(1) of the TFEU (and Chapter I of the Competition Act 1998) will not apply where a contractor (customer) entrusts a sub-contractor (supplier) with the supply of services, manufacture of goods, or performance of work under the contractor's instructions, to be provided to the contractor.[50] This will be relevant where the supplier needs to use the customer's technology or equipment to provide services to that customer. Article 101(1) will not apply to clauses in these agreements which provide that the technology or equipment provided by the contractor may not be used except for the purposes of the subcontracting agreement, or may not be made available to third parties, or that services resulting from the use of that equipment or technology may be supplied only to the contractor. In each case, this applies only where the technology or equipment is necessary to enable the subcontractor to supply the services, not when the subcontractor already has them at its disposal or could obtain access to them under reasonable conditions. However, many suppliers will be selected precisely because of their technology or equipment.

33.3.4.2   Notice on Horizontal Cooperation Agreements

The Commission's Notice on Horizontal Cooperation Agreements (the "Horizontals Notice") provides guidance on how to assess the competition risks of services agreements between competitors and, in particular, whether the agreement may fulfil the criteria for individual exemption under Article 101(3).[51]

The Horizontals Notice makes it clear that the parties to a production (or specialisation) agreement are entitled to agree on the "output directly

---

[50]   Commission Notice of 18 December 1978 concerning its assessment of certain subcontracting agreements (79/C1/01) (OJ C1, 3.1.1979, p.2).
[51]   Commission Notice - Guidelines on the applicability of Article 101 of the Treaty to horizontal cooperation agreements (Horizontal Notice) (2010).

concerned by the production agreement" (such as the agreed amount of transferred products).[52]

The main competition concerns in the context of a services agreement are likely to be the coordination of the parties' competitive behaviour, i.e. collusion, leading to higher prices or reduced output, particularly if the arrangement involves an exchange of commercially sensitive information.[53] This would be a particular concern if the parties have relatively high market shares (or are each other's closest competitor) and/or the market is relatively concentrated. The guidelines state that a collusive outcome can result in particular (but not only) from a commonality of costs or an exchange of information. If prior to the agreement the parties already have a high proportion of variable costs in common, the additional incremental can tip the balance towards collusion. So, where the transferred element represents only a small proportion of the parties' variable costs of the final product, it is unlikely to lead to co-ordination of their competitive behaviour downstream.[54]

33.3.4.3 *Information Exchange*

Competition law requires businesses to act independently and not to coordinate their behaviour with their competitors. Exchanges of information between actual or potential competitors may therefore infringe Article 101(1) of the TFEU or Chapter I of the Competition Act 1998 where the object or effect of the information exchange is to influence competitors' competitive conduct, or to disclose a competitor's plans or intentions, thereby making the market artificially transparent. An exchange of information is more likely to infringe the rules if the data exchanged is strategic (relating to future conduct on the market) and therefore more likely to lead to collusion between competitors in terms of pricing or terms offered to customers.[55] And collusion is more likely if the parties have relatively high market shares (or are each other's closest competitor) and/or the market is relatively concentrated.

This will be particularly relevant where a customer enters into a services agreement with a competitor, or on a transfer of services from a supplier to a competing successor supplier. In the former case, the customer and its prospective supplier or suppliers will be discussing many details of the customer's business, including its required services, service levels and costs, which would not normally be disclosed by one competitor to another. In the latter case, negotiations leading to the transfer of services from the incumbent supplier to the successor supplier (who are likely to be competitors), will involve a degree of information exchange (perhaps via the customer) concerning the transferred business, although clearly the incumbent sup-

---

[52] Horizontals Notice, para.160.
[53] Horizontals Notice, paras 150–193, relating to production agreements.
[54] Horizontals Notice, paras 174–181.
[55] Horizontals Notice, paras 55–110.

plier will be anxious in these circumstances to ensure that it is not obliged to disclose any proprietary information to its competitor.

It is not always easy to distinguish legitimate from prohibited exchanges of information. The analysis should be carried out on a case-by-case basis, taking into account the nature and type of the information exchanged, the level and aggregation of the information, the period to which the information relates and the structural characteristics of the market on which the exchange takes place.

In general, however:

(a) commercially sensitive information that may influence the competitive conduct of actual or potential competitors (such as information regarding pricing policies, investment plans or capacity), or that discloses a competitor's unpublished competitive intentions, should not be exchanged; while
(b) information which is historical, anonymous, aggregated, independently compiled and publicly available may be exchanged.[56]

33.4   Abuse of a dominant position

Article 102 of the TFEU and Chapter II of the Competition Act 1998 prohibit the abuse of a dominant position in the relevant market. If one of the parties to a services agreement has a high market share (over 40 per cent), its competitors lag some way behind and there are significant barriers to new entry, it may be considered as dominant in the relevant market, in which case there are constraints on how it can behave in the market.

Dominant companies can abuse their position and infringe the competition law rules by taking unilateral decisions (for example, refusing to supply a product/service or charging excessive, discriminatory or predatory prices) which, ultimately, foreclose competitors from the market and harm consumers. There are no exemptions or exclusions from the prohibition on abuse.

In practice, any competition concerns in the context of a services arrangement are likely to be considered under Article 101(1) of the TFEU and Chapter I of the Competition Act 1998.

---

[56]   Horizontals Notice, paras 86–94.

33.5   Practical guidance on competition law in transfer of services agreements

Table 44 provides some practical guidance for dealing with competition law issues when transferring services to a business partner.

Table 44 Practical guidance for dealing with competition law issues in transferring services

Consider the structure of the arrangement and whether it would constitute a "concentration" or merger.
Consider whether the arrangement meets the relevant thresholds for mandatory notification to the European Commission or any other regulatory authority, in which case completion of the transaction must be conditional on merger clearance. If the EUMR does not apply, consider whether the arrangement merits voluntary notification to the OFT.
If merger control is relevant, allow time to resolve jurisdictional issues, gather market information and for pre-notification contacts with the competition authorities.
Agreements by the customer not to compete with a business transferred to the supplier are justifiable for up to three years if know-how is transferred, or two years if goodwill alone is transferred, if the transfer amounts to a "concentration" or merger.
Check the competition law implications of any non-compete, exclusivity obligation or any other restriction. Note that competition concerns are most likely if: (i) the arrangement is between actual or potential competitors; or (ii) the parties have relatively high market shares.
Information exchanged between competitors should be kept to the minimum required to negotiate, conclude or give effect to the relevant transaction, with appropriate information barriers established to restrict information to those who need to know it for those purposes.
Where information has to be exchanged to enable a successor supplier to take over from an incumbent supplier, ensure that the exchange of information is confined to what is necessary to serve that customer.
Exclusive purchasing obligations on the customer may benefit from the Vertical Agreements Block Exemption if they do not last for more than five years, provided that the parties each have a market share under 30 per cent.
Exclusive purchasing and supply obligations may be imposed for more than five years under the SBE if the parties' combined market share is not over 20 per cent. If market shares are higher and the duration is excessive compared with the market average, exclusivity may infringe competition law.

Part 9

Liability

Chapter 34

Liability and Risk

34.1 Outline

This chapter considers issues relating to the legal liability of the parties. These may sound like dry legal issues best left to the lawyers, but in fact they are crucial commercial issues that require careful consideration. There is no standard way of dealing with these issues and the choice of approach will affect the profitability of the deal from the supplier's perspective and the cost savings made by the customer.

34.1.1 *Different approaches to legal liability*

The various different ways of dealing with legal liability under a services agreement include:

(a) the supplier is liable for breach of contract except where its failure is due to a force majeure event (commercial contracts);

(b) the supplier is liable for breach of contract subject to provisions on relief events and force majeure (PFI regime in the public sector);

(c) the supplier is liable for breach of contract subject to provisions on compensation events (construction industry and facilities management agreements); or

(d) the supplier is liable for negligence only (custody and fund administration agreements in the financial services sector).

These different approaches are described below.

34.1.2 *Customer retains business risk*

Before describing the approaches to legal liability, it is necessary to emphasise that any discussion of liability must recognise the fact that the customer cannot transfer to the supplier the risk of the customer's brand being affected, or the customer being unable to operate its business, if the supplier is unable to provide the services. The customer may be entitled to terminate the agreement and claim damages from the supplier up to the agreed limitation of liability. However, this may not fully compensate the customer in circumstances where, for example, the customer's business has become insolvent as a result of the supplier's failure. Therefore, it is crucial that the customer considers at an operational level how it will deal with a failure by the supplier. This will involve the customer ensuring that it has satisfactory business contingency arrangements, supported by business interruption insurance cover where appropriate.

34.2 Liability of supplier for failure—force majeure

Chapter 7 explains how the agreement must specify the services to be provided by the supplier. Chapter 12 mentions the importance of documenting the steps which the customer must take to enable the supplier to provide the services.

The parties must also agree the circumstances in which the supplier will not be responsible for failure to comply with its obligations. In commercial contracts, the supplier will not be responsible for failure to the extent it is caused by an event of "force majeure". This approach has been adopted in many IT and services agreements.

Negotiation of a force majeure provision is about the allocation of risk. It is based on an assumption that, if risks are allocated to the party who has the most control over them, then they will be incentivised to take action to reduce that risk to both parties' benefit.[1]

34.3 Definition of force majeure

Force majeure does not have a strict meaning in English law and so must be defined by the parties. It may be defined in different ways. There are two approaches that can be taken in defining force majeure, both based upon the principle that the supplier should not be responsible for events outside its control.

34.3.1 Specific definition

The first approach involves listing (as exhaustively as possible) the events treated as outside the supplier's control, for example terrorist attack or floods. The advantage of this approach is that the definition is clear.

---

[1]   The principle of force majeure is different from the common law doctrine of frustration, which applies only in very narrow circumstances and brings a contract to an end where performance has become impossible.

The disadvantage of this approach, from the supplier's perspective, is that the list may, by omission, fail to cover a comparable event which is also outside the supplier's control. This approach puts the onus upon the supplier to predict all events from which it wants relief, which could be inappropriate if it is difficult for the supplier to predict such events.

34.3.2   *General definition*

The second approach, favoured by suppliers, is to define force majeure in general terms as any event beyond the control of the supplier. The definition may include a non-exhaustive list of possible events with a statement at the end that it will also include any other event beyond the control of the supplier.

Suppliers sometimes want to list circumstances in which they will not be responsible for failure to meet the service levels. It is usually better for the supplier to include these circumstances in the list of force majeure events. Drafted this way it protects the supplier more generally.

34.4   Conditions that the supplier must satisfy

The supplier will usually have to satisfy certain conditions before a force majeure provision will provide relief. Examples of possible conditions are listed in Table 45.

Table 45 Examples of conditions which the supplier must satisfy

Service continuity
It must have taken all reasonable steps to prevent and avoid the force majeure event.
It must carry out its duties to the best level reasonably achievable in the circumstances of the force majeure event.
It must take all reasonable steps to overcome and mitigate the effects of the force majeure event.
It must comply with an agreed disaster recovery or service continuity plan (where relevant).
Notification requirements
It must notify the customer of the force majeure event, usually within a specific time period.
It must provide reasonable evidence of the force majeure event.
It must notify the customer when the event of force majeure has stopped.

The customer may want the supplier's right to rely upon the force majeure event to be conditional upon the supplier satisfying all of the specified conditions. The supplier will prefer the notification requirements to be procedural requirements and it will not want to lose its substantive right to rely upon force majeure as a result of a failure to comply with the notification requirements. The supplier may also want to ensure that it has a reasonable period to satisfy the notice requirements. This will take into account the fact that the supplier may feel that its first priority should be to concentrate on seeking to deal with the force majeure event itself.

The customer may need notification of the force majeure event so that it can take steps to ensure that its business does not suffer as a consequence. Therefore, it may see the notification requirements as essential and not as a mere bureaucratic requirement. Much will depend upon the individual nature of the services.

34.5   Effect upon the charges

The parties will need to decide if the supplier will be paid if it is unable to provide the services as a result of a force majeure event. There are various possible approaches.

34.5.1   No payment

The customer may argue that it should not be obliged to pay for a service that it is not receiving. This approach involves a sharing of risk resulting from the occurrence of a force majeure event. The supplier will not have to pay the customer damages for failure to provide the services. Equally, the supplier will not receive the charges.

34.5.2   Payment of all of the charges

The supplier may argue that, as it has not been at fault, it should be paid all of its charges. It may argue that it will in fact be incurring additional costs in dealing with the force majeure event. Despite the fact that the service is not being provided, the supplier will still be incurring costs, for example the salaries of the employees engaged to provide the services and equipment lease costs. The supplier may stress that, if the services were still being provided in-house, the customer would have had to pay these costs despite the fact that the services could not be provided.

34.5.3   Part payment

If the supplier will incur fewer costs if it is not providing the services, then the parties may agree a compromise whereby the customer pays a specified percentage of the charges, perhaps reflecting the supplier's fixed costs.

34.5.4   *Payment or non-payment depending upon the force majeure event*

The parties may also decide that whether the customer pays the supplier will depend upon the nature of the force majeure event, for example whether it affects the customer's site or the supplier's site. The logic behind this is that the customer should bear a greater responsibility if its site is affected than if the supplier's site is affected. This is similar to liability for compensation events (see section 34.10).

34.6   Termination rights

The parties will also need to decide whether either party will have the right to terminate the agreement as a result of a force majeure event.

34.6.1   *Customer's right to terminate*

The customer may want the right to terminate the agreement if a force majeure event prevents the supplier from providing the services for a specific period of time. Normally, force majeure clauses do not distinguish between the types of force majeure events that entitle the customer to terminate the agreement. The supplier may want to ensure that it receives adequate compensation on termination to cover the investment it has made in the services (see section 20.11 and Chapter 28 for a discussion of termination charges).

34.6.2   *Supplier's right to terminate*

If the supplier is being paid in full, despite the fact that it has been prevented by an event of force majeure from providing the services, then it may not need a right to terminate the agreement in this situation. Otherwise it may require such a right.

34.7   Force majeure and service continuity

34.7.1   *Importance of service continuity*

The discussion of liability for events of force majeure should also tie in with the customer's risk assessment process described in Chapter 2. This process may highlight the risks that could affect the services, their likelihood and what actions should be taken by the customer and the supplier to manage the risks. The process will usually result in the supplier accepting obliga-tions to provide disaster recovery or service continuity arrangements. The obligations will be specific to the individual contract and will reflect the level of disaster recovery or service continuity which it is cost effective for the supplier to provide and which the customer wishes to pay for in the particular circumstances. The following paragraphs describe the different types of disaster recovery services.

34.7.2   Exclusive disaster recovery services

The disaster recovery service may be an exclusive service, in which facilities are developed exclusively for the customer and the customer bears the entire cost.

34.7.3   Shared disaster recovery services

Alternatively, the disaster recovery services may be a shared service in which facilities are shared between several customers and made available on a "first come first served" basis. In the shared service, the costs of the disaster recovery service will be shared between the various customers. In this situation, the customer may want to find out (or control) how many sites belonging to the various customers share the disaster recovery facilities and whether they are likely to be affected by incidents also affecting the customer (e.g. if they are all financial institutions near each other in the City of London).

34.7.4   Reliance upon force majeure

As stated in Table 45, if the services include a disaster recovery service, the supplier should not be able to rely upon force majeure unless an event of force majeure affects both the main site and the disaster recovery site, or the supplier is otherwise unable to provide the disaster recovery service (for example, because the service is a shared service and another customer has invoked it first).

34.8   Liability for sub-contractors and third-party suppliers

Whichever approach to force majeure is adopted, the parties should ensure that the supplier's liability is clear. A common area of confusion concerns the supplier's responsibility for sub-contractors and third-party suppliers.

34.8.1   Supplier's third-party suppliers

The customer will usually want the supplier to be responsible for third-party suppliers that the supplier selects and with whom it enters into subcontracts.

34.8.2   Customer's third-party suppliers—before novation to the supplier

But what about third-party contracts entered into by the customer which are to be novated to the supplier? Who will be responsible for the actions of the third-party supplier before the contract is novated? The supplier may be unwilling to accept responsibility for the actions of the third-party supplier until it has a contractual relationship with the third-party supplier. If the supplier is responsible for managing the third-party supplier in the interim, then it will usually accept responsibility for its failure to manage the third party.

34.8.3   Customer's third-party suppliers—after novation to the supplier

Should the supplier be responsible for the actions of the third-party supplier once the contract has been novated to it? If the supplier has not managed to carry out adequate due diligence in respect of the third-party supplier's performance, or if the customer has selected the third-party supplier, the supplier may want a honeymoon period during which it will not be responsible for the actions of the third-party supplier. The honeymoon period should ideally (from the supplier's perspective) give the supplier sufficient time to carry out due diligence on the third-party supplier and (if necessary) arrange for a replacement third-party supplier. This should take into account the period of time needed to give notice terminating the agreement with the third-party supplier.

If the customer wants the supplier to accept responsibility for the quality of the service before the supplier has had time to terminate the agreement with the unsatisfactory third-party supplier, then the supplier may have to arrange for another third-party supplier to provide the services, whilst still paying the unsatisfactory third-party supplier. In this situation, the customer will pay twice for the third-party service, until the agreement with the unsatisfactory third-party supplier can be brought to an end.

34.9 Liability of supplier for failure—PFI approach

34.9.1 *Principle behind PFI contracts*

The approach taken in limiting the liability of the supplier for events of force majeure is based upon the principle that the supplier should not be responsible for events outside its control. The logic behind the principle is that the overall risk under the contract will be reduced if each party is responsible for factors within its control.

A different approach is taken in PFI contracts, where one of the purposes of the contract is to transfer to the supplier risks that are more appropriately managed by the private sector. This may mean the supplier accepting risks that it cannot control but which the parties agree are best managed by the supplier. The supplier will usually add a risk premium to its charges to cover the additional risks that it is accepting.

The PFI approach to liability is described in sections 34.9.2 to 34.9.4 below. PFI contracts have fallen out of favour in the UK, although they are popular in other parts of the world. See Chapter 44 for a general explanation of PFI contracts. This is an extremely complex subject and this Guide only provides a short summary of some of the key issues.

34.9.2 *Definition of force majeure*

PFI contracts adopt the first approach described in section 34.3.1 above, where there are specific definitions of events. Confusingly for those used to commercial, non-PFI contracts, there are two separate definitions, one called "relief events" and one "force majeure".

(a) Relief events include some types of events that would be defined as force majeure events in a non-PFI contract. For example, they include natural events (such as fire, lightning, storm, tempest and flood); riots and civil commotion; failure by a public body or utility to carry out works or to provide services; accidental damage; failure or shortage of power, fuel or transport; blockades or embargoes or strikes generally affecting the supplier's industry, unless these have been caused by a wilful act or omission of the supplier.[2]

(b) Force majeure events are very narrowly defined and include, for example, war, terrorism, and nuclear and chemical contamination. These are generally viewed as catastrophic events which are unlikely

---

[2]   The premise is that relief events should cover events that are outside either party's control, but where the supplier is better placed to manage the impact.

to occur. Some of the risks may be uninsurable.[3] The intention is that force majeure events should cover events which are outside the control of either party and neither party is in a better position than the other to manage the risk.

34.9.3   Conditions that the supplier must satisfy

34.9.3.1   Relief event

The supplier cannot claim relief on the occurrence of a relief event unless it can demonstrate that it could not have avoided the event, or mitigated its effect, without incurring material expenditure. It must also demonstrate that it is using reasonable endeavours to perform its obligations under the contract. The supplier must also satisfy specific procedural requirements before it can claim relief.

34.9.3.2   Force majeure event

In the event of a force majeure event, both parties must use reasonable endeavours to prevent and mitigate the effects of any delay and the supplier must take all steps in accordance with good industry practice to overcome or minimise the consequences of the event, and to agree appropriate terms upon which the services can continue to be supplied to the customer.

34.9.4   Implications of relief and force majeure events

34.9.4.1   Relief events

The supplier bears all of the financial consequences of relief events. If the relief event results in poor or no service being supplied, the customer will be entitled to make appropriate deductions from the charges payable to the supplier on an indefinite basis. This is similar to the "no payment" option referred to in section 34.5.1. The supplier is expected to take out loss of profit or business interruption insurance against relief events, where available. The only "relief" which the supplier is in fact entitled to is relief against termination for failure to provide the full service.

34.9.4.2   Force majeure event

Similarly, if a force majeure event results in a limited service being supplied, the customer will be entitled to make appropriate deductions. However, the supplier does not bear all of the financial consequences of a force majeure event on an indefinite basis, since (given the severity of the definition of

---

[3]   There are conventional property insurance exclusions for nuclear, chemical, biological and radiation (NCBR) risks. Those and war risks are generally uninsurable. Terrorism risk is generally insurable with regard to business interruption risks affecting commercial property under the UK government backed Pool Re arrangements.

force majeure events) the effects are likely to last for a long time. Therefore, if the force majeure event continues to prevent full performance for a specified period, either the supplier or the customer may be entitled to terminate the agreement.

34.9.5   Termination rights

34.9.5.1   Relief event

Neither party will be entitled to terminate the agreement as a result of poor performance or failure to achieve milestones if the poor performance or failure is a result of a relief event, provided that the supplier is attempting to mitigate the effect of such event and satisfying the other related technical requirements. The customer will continue indefinitely to receive less than full services, and the supplier will continue indefinitely to receive less than full payment. This is seen as appropriate since, in practice, relief events are less severe than force majeure events and, in all probability, the supplier will be able to respond in an appropriate manner so as to resume full service.

34.9.5.2   Force majeure event

In the event of a force majeure event, which prevents full performance for a protracted period (often six months), if the parties cannot agree a suitable course of action whereby the contract can be preserved by amending the terms in some way, either party will be entitled to serve notice to terminate the agreement. If the notice is served by the supplier, the customer will be entitled to prevent termination of the agreement by electing to pay the supplier in full, as if the performance failure arising from the force majeure event was not continuing. Otherwise, the agreement will terminate, and the supplier will be paid a substantial compensation payment.[4]

34.10   Liability of supplier for failure—facilities management approach

In the construction industry, as in the PFI industry which grew out of it, it is common for liability to be apportioned to the party best able to manage and insure against risks. Some facilities management agreements adopt this approach by stating that the supplier will be responsible for the services except where it is prevented from providing the services by a "compensation event".

---

[4]   The compensation payment will not put the supplier in the same position as it would have been in if the contract had continued until its natural expiry, as would be the case if the contract terminated for customer default. The supplier will bear some of the pain, by agreeing to a reduced payment.

34.10.1   *Definition of compensation event*

A compensation event is defined as including breach of agreement by the customer, changes required by the customer as well as external events such as the following, provided that they affect the premises the subject of the facilities management services:

(a)   a third party carrying out unanticipated work on the premises;
(b)   unexpected defects in the physical condition of the premises; and
(c)   loss of or damage to any part of the premises due to war, civil war, rebellion, revolution, insurrection, military or usurped power, strikes, riots and civil commotion not confined to the supplier's employees, radioactive contamination, fire, lightning, explosion, storm, flood, escape of water from any water tank, apparatus or pipes, earthquake, aircraft and other aerial devices or articles dropped from them.

The definition thus catches external events which affect the customer's premises, which the customer can insure against.

The types of events which comprise compensation events could theoretically be drafted in general or specific terms (as for force majeure events). In practice, however, they tend to be specifically listed. The customer will need to ensure that they do not apply in circumstances where the supplier is responsible, as part of the facilities management services, for preventing the relevant event. For example, in the case of a flood caused by a boiler which has not been maintained when the supplier is responsible for maintaining it.

34.10.2   *Conditions that the supplier must satisfy*

The supplier will usually have to satisfy certain conditions relating to the compensation event before it can claim relief. The customer should consider whether the conditions listed in Table 45 are appropriate.

34.10.3   *Effect upon the charges*

In facilities management agreements that rely upon the compensation event concept, the customer bears the full financial consequences of the event.

34.10.4   *Termination rights*

Neither party is granted the right to terminate as a result of the occurrence of a compensation event.

34.10.5 *Application of the concept outside facilities management*

Customers may like to consider whether it is helpful in their services arrangements to deal with force majeure issues in the context of which risks are best managed by each party. For example, in a call-centre service where part of the services are provided on site (e.g. attending to the public) and part are provided from the supplier's premises (e.g. dealing with telephone queries) the customer may decide to take responsibility for fire or flood affecting its premises and the supplier may take responsibility for fire or flood affecting its premises. This will incentivise the supplier to provide (and charge for) a very high level of disaster recovery and service continuity support.

34.11 Liability of supplier for failure—custody and fund administration approach

34.11.1 *Liability in custody agreements*

All of the above approaches to liability are based on the supplier being responsible for breach of contract. Custody agreements in the financial services sector take a radically different approach. In these contracts the custodian sees itself as the directed agent of the customer. The custodian's fundamental obligation is to take reasonable care of the customer's assets and it is not unusual for the parties to feel that they do not need to document the custodian's obligations in a service description. Accordingly, the custodian excludes all liability for breach of contract and accepts liability only if it is negligent. In return, it accepts unlimited liability for the value of the assets in its custody. The customer usually has the ability to terminate the custody agreement on short notice (usually 30 days) at any time, so that the customer can terminate if it is dissatisfied with the services provided by the custodian. Custody services are commodity services and so moving the services to another custodian is not as substantial a task as in some outsourcing agreements, so termination may provide an effective remedy for the customer.[5]

---

[5] Note that this allocation of liability for custody is likely to change once the Alternative Investment Fund Managers Directive (AIFMD) is implemented. Whether matching changes would be made to the UCITS Directives, to bring them in line with the AIFMD's requirements on depositories remains unclear. Each alternative investment fund manager caught by the AIFMD will have to ensure that it enters into a written contract with a depository or custodian for each fund it manages. The depository will be liable to the relevant fund or its investors for losses of financial instruments held in custody (whether it is responsible for the loss or not) except if the loss has arisen as a result of an external event beyond its reasonable control, as well as for losses as a result of negligently or intentionally failing to perform its duties in the AIFMD. The provisions on depositaries are intended to protect investors but would, if implemented, place a greater burden on custodians to oversee tasks usually performed by fund managers. Furthermore, the custodian will be liable for any act of sub-custodians. It will only be able to escape such liability if the depositary enters into a written agreement with the third party sub-custodian that "explicitly transfers

34.11.2   *Liability in fund administration agreements*

Over the last few years, some custodians have endeavoured to extend their service offerings to include other services, including fund administration or management services. In this situation, they assume that liability will be based on a negligence basis, partly because that is what they are accustomed to seeing in custody agreements.

There are various problems with this approach, and the result is that the negotiation of the liability clauses is often the most difficult part of the negotiation of such agreements.

The first problem is that fund administration agreements are not commodity agreements like custody agreements, and cannot usually be terminated on short notice, and transferring the services on termination may involve substantial risk and expense.

The second problem is a cultural one as on the one hand, customers who negotiate fund administration agreements are often used to negotiating other commercial IT or sourcing agreements and hence are entirely unfamiliar with the idea of contracting on the basis of negligence. They see the restriction of liability to negligence as undermining the supplier's liability under the agreement and in particular the usefulness of the detailed service descriptions and service level agreements they negotiate with the supplier.

The supplier on the other hand, may be unfamiliar with accepting liability on a breach-of-contract basis and see the customer's approach as an attempt to force it to accept potentially greater liability than it has been used to or is comfortable with accepting. The supplier may not have negotiated the service level agreement with a view to accepting liability for breach. The supplier's concerns can be addressed to a certain extent by agreeing service levels which the supplier can achieve in practice, and thus making it clear that the supplier is not expected to meet all of the service levels 100 per cent of the time.

The problem of liability in fund administration agreements is a serious one. In the end, the problem is usually determined by the party with the most powerful bargaining power prevailing.

---

the liability of the depository to that third party." This can only be done if the depositary has also entered into a written agreement with the AIF, or the AIFM on the AIF's behalf, which complies with the AIFMD's requirements and permits the depositary to do so. See Chapter 38, for an explanation of which financial services Directives and rules apply to different sectors of the financial market.

34.12   Liability of the customer for failure

So far, this chapter has considered the circumstances in which the supplier should be responsible for failure to provide the services. Section 34.2 explained that one approach taken is for the *supplier* to be granted relief from failures arising as a result of force majeure events. The question arises as to whether the *customer* should also be protected in the event of force majeure events.

34.12.1   *Relief from delaying payment*

Suppliers may want to make it clear that the force majeure clause does not apply to the customer's obligation to pay the charges. In the past, customers may have agreed to this arrangement on the basis that a force majeure event was unlikely to prevent them paying the charges. As a result of the terrorist incidents on 11 September 2001, the credit crunch and recent instability in the euro, some customers have been more reluctant to agree to this clause. It is not inconceivable that a customer will be prevented from paying the charges as a result of a banking failure caused by a terrorist attack or otherwise.

34.12.2   *Customer's other obligations*

The issue is more complicated in respect of customer's obligations that do not relate to payment, for example the customer's obligation to make certain facilities available. The supplier will not expect to be liable for failure to provide the services as a result of the customer failing to comply with its obligations, whether the customer's failure has been caused by a force majeure event or not. Equally, the customer will not expect to be in breach of the agreement if it fails to comply with its obligations as a result of a force majeure event.

34.12.3   *Payment of compensation by customer*

If the supplier incurs additional expenditure as a result of the customer failing to comply with its obligations, then the supplier will usually expect to be compensated for this (see Chapter 12).

Should the customer have to pay compensation if it fails to comply with its obligations as a result of a force majeure event? If the approach is taken that parties should not be responsible for events outside their control, then it may be argued that the financial consequences of the services not being provided in these circumstances should be the same as if the services are not provided as a result of a force majeure event affecting the supplier, namely the consequences described in section 34.5 above.

An alternative approach is to argue that the customer is in the best position to manage risks affecting its actions and that therefore the financial consequences of the customer failing to comply with its obligations should be the same whatever the reason for the failure—namely that the customer will pay compensation, as described in Chapter 12. Note that in a PFI agreement the customer will not receive relief if it is unable to fulfil its obligations as a result of a "relief event". It will only be able to claim relief for events of "force majeure". (See section 34.9.2 above for a definition of relief events and force majeure in PFI contracts.)

34.13   Supplier's liability for damages

If the supplier fails to comply with its obligations and is unable to claim protection under force majeure provisions, then it may be liable to the customer for damages. Sections 34.13.1–34.13.6 describe the supplier's potential liability for damages. This is an extremely complex subject and this chapter provides a short summary of the key issues only. The paragraphs are only intended to summarise the law of damages.

34.13.1   *Measure of loss*

The aim of an award of damages is to compensate the innocent party for the loss it has suffered as a result of the other party's breach of contract. The innocent party will be expected to take reasonable steps to minimise its loss to the extent that this is possible.

34.13.2   *Expectation damages*

The general rule is that the compensation paid by the party in breach should, as far as possible, restore the innocent party to the position it would have been in had the contract been fully performed. This is referred to as the expectation measure of damages (the contract creates an expectation of performance). For example, in *Pegler Ltd v Wang (UK) Ltd*[6] Wang contracted with Pegler, a manufacturer of taps and valves, to provide computer hardware, software and related services designed to improve Pegler's business efficiency. The total price agreed was £1,198,130 plus £235,000 annually for three years for maintenance. Wang's performance was poor and it ultimately abandoned the contract. Pegler served formal notice of breach

---

[6]   *Pegler Ltd v Wang (UK) Ltd (No.1)* [2000] B.L.R. 218.

and required Wang to remedy its various breaches. Wang took no steps to comply. Pegler treated Wang's failure as a repudiation of the contract which it relied on to bring the contract to an end. In tandem, it also exercised a contractual right of termination. Pegler used third parties to provide the services it needed and issued proceedings against Wang claiming damages of nearly £23 million.

Wang eventually admitted liability and at trial the claim was principally concerned with the quantum of damages. Pegler was ultimately awarded £9 million, far in excess of the original contract price. Heads of loss included the following:

(a)   lost sales;
(b)   lost opportunity to increase margins;
(c)   lost opportunity to make staff cost savings;
(d)   cost of replacement systems and consultancy services;
(e)   lost opportunity to reduce finished stock held;
(f)   lost ability to negotiate improved purchasing terms; and
(g)   wasted management time.

This case demonstrates that, in addition to looking at damages that have already been incurred, this approach to assessment involves looking into the future to assess the value of benefits that should have been delivered.

The general rule that such losses should be valued at the date of the breach of contract. In certain circumstances the court will take into account matters which have (in fact) occurred since the breach and which impact upon the question how valuable the contractual rights lost or broken would have proved to be. If parties do not agree on the appropriate level of compensation then a court will make an assessment, usually on the basis of expert evidence, of the losses that are recoverable.

34.13.3   *Reliance damages*

There is an alternative basis of assessment to expectation damages, sometimes considered following early termination for breach, which an innocent party may elect to adopt in appropriate cases. This is referred to as reliance damages. The intention here is to put the innocent party into the position it would have been in if it had not entered into the contract at all. Broadly, this comprises the wasted expenditure incurred in reliance on the contract. This is not limited to expenditure incurred after the agreement. The innocent party can also claim expenditure incurred before the contract was signed provided it was within the reasonable contemplation of the parties that it would be likely to be wasted as a result of the other party's breach.[7]

---

[7]   *Anglia Television Ltd v Reed* [1972] 1 Q.B. 60; [1971] 3 W.L.R. 528 is an example of such a case. In this case, an actor failed to honour his contract with a TV company to appear in a film with the result that the film

This type of claim was made in the case of *Salvage Association v CAP Financial Services Ltd.*[8] The case concerned a contract for the development of new accounting software. When it became clear that the supplier would fail to resolve serious problems with the system before an extended deadline for completion of the project, the customer exercised a right of termination and engaged another company to design a replacement system from scratch. At first instance, the customer was awarded damages comprising (amongst other things):

(a)   the sum paid under the two (development and implementation) contracts entered into with the supplier; and
(b)   £231,866 wasted expenditure (including payments made to a bureau facility, on which the system was installed, for use of terminal time), wasted computer stationery, and payments to consultants and to an independent third party in connection with testing.

During a major services project, reliance expenditure may be substantial. However, it is important to note that certain costs will not be entirely wasted (for example, costs that have provided some value or relate to steps that will not need to be undertaken again if the contract is put out to tender a second time).

34.13.4   Which measure of loss to claim

Naturally enough, the innocent party will usually only be interested in pursuing the "reliance" measure of loss where it exceeds "expectation" damages. It may also prefer this measure if there are practical difficulties in proving what the expectation losses would have been.[9]

---

was not made. The TV company could not say what its profits on the project would have been and made a wasted-expenditure claim. The court found that the TV company was entitled to recover wasted expenditure on fees paid to the director, designer and stage manager both before and after the contract with the actor had been entered into.

[8]   *Salvage Association v CAP Financial Services Ltd* [1995] F.S.R. 654 (which was subsequently overturned, in part, by the Court of Appeal but not on this point). See also *South West Water Services Ltd v International Computers Ltd* [1999] B.L.R. 420 ; [1999] I.T.C.L.R. 439 in which the Judge permitted recovery (on the basis of a claim in restitution) of money paid for a package of hardware and software because SWW had received nothing of value. Although ICL had delivered compliant hardware this could not be used without appropriate bespoke software that ICL (in breach of contract) was unable to supply.

[9]   For example, in *McRae v Commonwealth Disposals Commission* [1951] 84 C.L.R. 377 one party contracted to sell to the other the wreck of a tanker said to contain oil and lying on the Jourmand Reef. The claimant embarked on an expedition to salvage the wreck which was found not to exist. Loss recovered included losses assessed by reference to its expenses incurred in connection with the expedition to locate the wreck and its prepayment to the other party. (See also *Anglia Television v Reed* [1972] 1 Q.B. 60; [1971] 3 W.L.R. 528).

34.13.5 *Limitations of recovery—remoteness of loss*

Loss that is too remote cannot be recovered. The thinking underlying this restriction on recovery is that it would be unfair to expect the defaulting party to be liable to cover all losses however unusual or unforeseeable. The general test is broken down into two parts to reflect the seminal decision in *Hadley v Baxendale*[10]. To recover a particular loss it must be either:

(a) a loss that occurs "naturally in the usual course of events" following a breach of contract; or

(b) the loss must have been within the reasonable contemplation of the parties at the time the contract was made (sometimes called "special loss").

One way to ensure that the loss is within the contemplation of the other party is to notify that party of any special loss that might be suffered as a result of breach.

The case of *Victoria Laundry (Windsor) v Newman Industries*[11] is one of the classic cases on special loss. In that case the defendant, an engineering company, had agreed to the immediate delivery of a boiler to the claimant, a laundry business. The boiler was delivered five months late and the claimant sued for loss of profits. The court found that the claimant was entitled to compensation for loss of normal profits (it being an entirely natural consequence of late delivery that the claimant's business should suffer). However, the claimant was not entitled to recover losses under especially lucrative contracts with the government. The defendant did not know about these lucrative contracts and so this loss was not within the reasonable contemplation of the parties.

34.13.6 *Liability for damages in PFI contracts*

An important point to note about PFI contracts is that the supplier in such a contract is not generally liable for damages. The extent of its liability for failure to provide the services will be deductions that the customer is entitled to make from the charges it pays. In the case of breaches leading to termination, the extent of liability will be the agreed basis upon which the termination payments to be made by the customer will be calculated. The parties may want to consider whether the certainty afforded by this approach is one that they would like to adopt in their services arrangement.

---

[10] *Hadley v Baxendale* (1854) 9 Ex. 341.

[11] *Victoria Laundry (Winsor) v Newman Industries* [1949] 2 K.B. 528; [1949] 1 All E.R. 997.

34.14 Liability under indemnities

34.14.1 *Legal effect of indemnities*

The supplier's liability will be different from that described in 34.13 above if it has accepted obligations to indemnify the customer for its own breach. An indemnity is an express primary contractual obligation to reimburse the other party for defined loss or damage, provided that the particular conditions set out in the indemnity are satisfied.[12] As a result:

(a) the company benefiting from the indemnity will not need to establish an independent cause of action;

(b) if the indemnity claim can be properly characterised as an action for debt (rather than an action for damages) then there is no duty to mitigate one's losses;[13] and

(c) it is possible that an indemnity may sidestep the test for remoteness by providing a guaranteed remedy in circumstances which may not necessarily give rise to a claim in damages. The question of whether this is the case will often turn on the wording of the indemnity itself.

Suppliers should therefore ensure all indemnities are narrowly drafted, for example referring to "direct losses" rather than "all losses" and are subject to appropriate controls.[14]

Indemnities are often used in services agreements to cover situations in which one of the parties agrees to compensate the other party against liability it incurs to a third party, as these claims may go beyond what the party could recover for breach of contract.

The limit of a supplier's liability under any indemnity must be dealt with clearly in the services agreement.

34.14.2 *IPR indemnity from the supplier*

The customer may want to be indemnified against any liability it incurs as a result of being in breach of third-party intellectual property rights (IPR).

---

[12] The conditions may include, for example, requirements that: (i) the customer notify the supplier promptly in writing of any claim of which it is aware; (ii) it will permit the supplier, at the supplier's expense, to conduct any litigation and negotiations for a settlement of the claim; (iii) it will, at the supplier's expense, give the supplier reasonable assistance; and (iv) it will not make any admission or take any other action which might be prejudicial without the express consent of the supplier.

[13] See *Royscott Commercial Leasing Ltd v Ismail* The Independent 17 May 1993.

[14] Staughton L.J., sitting in the Court of Appeal, stated in *Total Transport Corp v Arcadia Petroleum Ltd* [1998] C.L.C. 90 that an indemnity covers *"all loss suffered which is attributable to a specified cause, whether or not it was in the reasonable contemplation of the parties"*. However, he tempered this wide interpretation by confirming that there was no authority for the proposition that remoteness is always irrelevant to an indemnity obligation.

The supplier will usually provide an IPR indemnity for such liability arising out of the use of assets it has made available for the provision of the services. This may involve the supplier accepting liability, as prime contractor, for software it has licensed from third-party licensors, even if the licensors of the software are unwilling to grant the supplier IPR indemnities on similar terms. An extreme example of this arises if the supplier is using open source software. If the customer has requested solutions using open source software, then the supplier may be unwilling to take the risk that the open source software breaches third-party IPR.

34.14.3   *IPR indemnity from the customer*

The supplier will not want to provide an IPR indemnity for assets provided by the customer and may want the customer to indemnify the supplier for these assets. The customer may be willing to grant an IPR indemnity either mirroring that given by the supplier or reflecting that granted to it by its third-party suppliers.

34.14.4   *Other indemnities*

There may be circumstances in which the supplier may want an indemnity from the customer covering claims by other companies or individuals. For example, if a customer outsources its call-centre services, which provide advice to members of the public. In this situation, the supplier will usually deal with queries from the public in accordance with scripts written by the customer. If the scripts are incorrect, members of the public may seek to claim in negligence against the supplier. The supplier may want an indemnity from the customer covering this liability.

34.15   Liability to third parties

Some complex services arrangements may involve third parties and the customer may want the supplier to accept that it has potential liability to such parties.

34.15.1   *Members of the customer's group*

The customer may be contracting on behalf of other members of its group. The customer may want to be able to claim on behalf of other members of the group for losses suffered by them or may want all members of the group to have the ability to claim against the supplier.

In this situation, the supplier may want the customer to accept liability for compliance by other members of its group with relevant provisions in the services arrangement (e.g. confidentiality and licensing terms). The customer may need to enter into back-to-back agreements with the other members of its group.

34.15.2   Incoming contractor

Chapter 31 has already explained the importance of any incoming contractor being able to enforce TUPE indemnities on termination of the original services agreement (or the customer being able to claim for losses suffered by the incoming contractor).

34.15.3   Employees

In some circumstances, the customer may agree enhanced protections for transferring employees (for example, a commitment that the supplier will not make any of the transferring employees redundant within a specified timeframe). The customer may want the transferring employees to be able to rely upon these promises by the supplier.

34.15.4   Customer's clients

If the service being contracted out is key to the provision by the customer of services to its clients, the customer may want the supplier to accept responsibility for any claims made by those clients. Whether this is acceptable to the supplier will depend upon the particular circumstances and whether the supplier can evaluate and control this liability.

34.15.5   Contracts (Rights of Third Parties) Act 1999

The Contracts (Rights of Third Parties) Act 1999 allows a person who is not a party to a contract to enforce that contract in certain circumstances. If there is an intention to rely on this Act then the parties should state this clearly in the agreement. The third party who is intended to have a right to enforce the contract must be expressly identified either by name or generically. It is possible to exclude the application of this Act.

Chapter 35

Limitations of Liability

35.1   Outline

Chapter 34 explains the supplier's liability under the services agreement. This chapter describes how the supplier's liability may be limited and the extent to which such limitations of liability are enforceable. It also discusses whether the customer's liability should be limited.

35.2   Financial caps

The supplier will usually want to limit its liability for damages by agreeing a financial cap. This will usually be acceptable to the customer save in certain sectors where it is industry practice not to limit liability. For example, caps are not industry practice in some types of defence contracts or in some types of business process service agreements in the financial services sector.

35.3   Relevant factors in deciding the cap

From the customer's perspective, the limits of the supplier's liability should be negotiated taking into account the types of breaches that are likely to occur, the likelihood of the breaches occurring and the type and level of damage that the customer will suffer if breaches occur. The customer will need to consider its ability to bear loss in excess of any cap.

From the supplier's perspective, its exposure, and hence the limit of its liability, should reflect the benefit that it is receiving under the agreement, namely the total charges. The supplier may not want the limitation of liability to take into account capital expenditure it is making to be able to provide the services.

The limit of liability should always be agreed in the light of the insurance coverage the parties can arrange and whether it is easier for one party rather than the other to take out insurance. The courts often take this factor into account in assessing the reasonableness of any cap.

35.4   Structure of the cap

There are various ways in which the supplier's liability may be limited. These are considered below. Chapter 21 has already mentioned that the supplier will look to cap its exposure to service credits.

35.4.1   One limit

The supplier's liability may be limited to one overall figure or one annual figure.

35.4.2   Several limits

The limitation of liability clause may distinguish between different types of liability:

(a)   The supplier may fix a limit for damages caused by loss of or damage to physical property. As these losses will usually be covered by insurance, the supplier may be willing to accept a higher cap for them. The limitation will be determined in the light of the supplier's insurance cover but will not necessarily reflect the full extent of the insurance cover as the insurance policy will usually be required to cover other risks of the supplier's business.

(b)   The parties may agree to fix a separate, lower cap for specific types of liability, for example loss of profits (if it is not excluded).

(c)   The supplier may fix a separate liability limit for "other losses" (which may not be covered by insurance[1]). The limit may be a fixed amount or a percentage of the charges payable under the agreement. The customer may want to fix the limitation by reference to the greater of a fixed amount and a specified percentage of the charges so that the limitation increases as the amount of the charges increases (for example, because the customer orders additional services from the supplier). In circumstances where it may want to terminate the agreement early and has paid little for the services, the customer should avoid fixing the limitation of liability solely as a percentage of the charges paid.

There are benefits to the supplier in drafting the cap in "layers". If a court strikes out a provision on the grounds that the provision seeks to exclude liability which it is not reasonable to exclude, the courts will not re-write the provision so that it only covers liabilities which it is reasonable to exclude. Therefore, drafting the cap as a number of sub-clauses makes it more likely that the elements which are reasonable will stand. It is also helpful to include

---

[1]   It is more difficult to procure insurance cover for pure economic loss. Many policies contain exclusions for penalties or liquidated damages clauses.

a "severability" clause allowing part of a provision to be severed without affecting the remaining text.

35.4.3 *Unlimited*

As a matter of law, parties cannot limit their liability when it arises from:

(a) death or injury to persons resulting from their negligence;[2]
(b) fraud;
(c) breach of the implied obligations as to title;[3] or
(d) breach of the implied term as to quiet possession.[4]

The customer may want to extend the supplier's unlimited liability to cover other obligations, including, for example, the supplier's intellectual property rights indemnity or the confidentiality obligation (or to agree a higher cap for these types of liability).

There are various other circumstances in which the customer may want the supplier to accept unlimited liability. For example, the customer may want to avoid a situation where the supplier abandons or repudiates the contract because it realises that the customer has already suffered losses equal to the supplier's cap and hence the supplier is not concerned about the customer suffering further losses. Even without such an exception, the supplier may be advised not to abandon the contract once it believes that the customer has already suffered losses equal to the supplier's limitation of liability, because of the risk that the limitation of liability provision will be unenforceable for the reasons outlined in section 35.5 below.[5]

Suppliers are usually reluctant to accept unlimited liability except where the law prevents them limiting their liability. Ultimately, the details of any limitation of liability will be agreed by the parties and will depend upon the bargaining power of the supplier and customer.

---

[2] Unfair Contract Terms Act 1977 s.2.
[3] Sale of Goods Act 1979 s.12.
[4] Sale of Goods Act 1979 s.25.
[5] See also the controversial case of *Internet Broadcasting Corporation Ltd (t/a NETTV) v MAR LLC (t/a MARHedge)* [2009] EWHC 844 (Ch). In that case, the High Court held that there is a rebuttable presumption that an exclusion clause should not apply to a deliberate personal repudiatory breach of contract. Another High Court judge has subsequently declined to follow this decision (see *AstraZeneca UK Ltd v Albemarle International Corp* [2011] EWHC 1574 (Comm)). At the time of writing, the Court of Appeal is expected to consider this conflict of authority in the case of *Shared Network Services Ltd v Nextiraone UK Ltd* [2012] EWCA Civ 1171.

35.4.4 PFI approach

A different approach is taken in a PFI contract. Here the supplier's liability for most breaches of contract will be the amount that the payment mechanism permits the customer to deduct from the charges payable to the supplier and, ultimately, the deductions which the customer is entitled to make from termination payments to reflect the impact of the breach. The customer will waive its rights to claim damages from the supplier, other than for breaches of contract which are not covered by the payment mechanism.

35.5 Enforceability of caps

The supplier's limitation of liability is fundamental to an assessment of the risk it accepts in entering into the services arrangement and so the supplier will be anxious to ensure that its limitation of liability is enforceable at law. The following paragraphs describe the factors affecting the enforceability of the supplier's limitation of liability under English law.

35.5.1 UCTA 1977

The Unfair Contract Terms Act 1977 (UCTA 1977)[6] provides that a contractual term must be reasonable if it limits liability:

(a) for negligence causing loss (other than death or personal injury);
(b) for breach of the implied conditions of conformity; or
(c) for breach of contract when a party is *dealing* on the other party's *standard* written terms.

There are a number of key phrases wrapped up in this provision.

35.5.1.1 "Deals"

The requirement to deal on standard terms does not mean that there may be no negotiations on the terms, provided the terms ultimately agreed are in fact standard terms.[7]

35.5.1.2 "Standard"

To determine what constitutes standard terms, the courts take a clause-by-clause (as opposed to a whole contract) approach. This means that if the li-

---

[6] S.3(2)(a).
[7] See the judgment of Nourse LJ in the Court of Appeal in *St Albans v International Computers Limited* [1996] 4 All ER 481 at 490.

ability provisions are not materially amended, they will be standard terms covered by the UCTA 1977, even if there are many other changes to the contract.[8] It may not be easy to persuade a court that an exclusion/limitation clause is not a standard term, so if an agreement has been heavily negotiated it is advisable to keep the drafts.

35.5.1.3 *"Reasonable"*

The UCTA 1977 s.11(1) provides the following definition of reasonableness

> "in relation to a contract term, the requirement of reasonableness … is that the term shall have been a fair and reasonable one to have been included having regard to the circumstances which were, or ought reasonably to have been known to or in the contemplation of the parties when the contract was made."

It is for the party relying on the exclusion or limitation clause to show that it is reasonable.[9] Reasonableness is to be assessed at the date of the contract, not the date of breach. Generally speaking, the courts are more likely to give effect to a clause limiting liability than one excluding it.

In practice, reasonableness is assessed against the list of factors set out in Sch.2 of the UCTA 1977. The Sch.2 factors are:

(a) strength of bargaining position of the parties;[10]
(b) whether the customer received an inducement to agree to the term, or could have entered into a similar contract with someone else without the term;
(c) whether the customer knew or ought reasonably to have known about the term;
(d) where the term excludes or restricts liability if a condition is not complied with, whether it was reasonable to expect compliance with that condition; and
(e) whether the contract goods were provided to the special order of the customer.

A further (important) factor that the courts will take into account in assessing reasonableness is the availability of insurance. Where a party seeks to limit its liability to a financial cap the court must have regard to:

---

[8] In the case of *Pegler v Wang* [2000] B.L.R. 218 (see above), the contract included some of Pegler's standard terms and some of Wang's standard terms. The court held that Pegler had been dealing with Wang on Wang's standard terms: Wang had insisted on using its standard exclusion clauses which, apart from one small and inconsequential exception, were not negotiated.

[9] UCTA 1977 s.11(5).

[10] See *Watford Electronics Ltd v Sanderson CFL Ltd* [2001] EWCA Civ 317; [2001] 1 All E.R. (Comm) 696. This concerned a contract for supply of a bespoke integrated software system which included an exclusion of liability clause covering indirect and consequential loss. The court found that the parties were of equal bargaining power and well understood the allocation of risk reflected in the exclusion clause.

(a)   the resources available to that party to meet the liability, should it arise; and
(b)   how far it was open to that party to cover itself by insurance.[11]

It is the *availability* of insurance which is the key factor, not the actual cover. The position in respect of insurance—one of the most commonly overlooked aspects in drafting such clauses—should always be considered.

The following paragraphs explain how courts have applied the above principles in specific cases.

35.5.2   *St Albans City and District Council v International Computers Limited*[12]

ICL entered into a contract with St Albans council to supply a computer system to be used by the council in administering its collection of the community charge. Due to an error in the system, the population figure against which the community charge was calculated was overstated. The result was that the council set the community charge too low and its total receipts were £484,000 less than they ought to have been. It addition, it was obliged to make additional precept payments of £685,000 to the county council.

The council sued ICL for damages for breach of contract claiming these losses. The court (having established that the council had dealt on ICL's standard terms of business for the purposes of s.3(1) of the UCTA 1977) held that a limitation of liability clause in the contract, capping damages recoverable by the council to £100,000, was unreasonable in the circumstances of the case. Two of the principal factors taken into account were that:

(a)   ICL had very substantial resources and insurance cover; and
(b)   ICL was one of a small number of companies who were able to supply what the council had been looking for. Because of this, and the tight timescale to which the council was working, ICL had been in a better bargaining position than the council.

---

[11]   UCTA 1977 s.11(4).
[12]   *St Albans City and DC v International Computers Ltd* [1995] F.S.R. 686. This decision was reversed, in part, on appeal (see *St Albans City and DC v International Computers Ltd* [1996] 4 All E.R. 481), but not on this point.

35.5.3   *Watford Electronics v Sanderson*[13]

In this case, the court held that an exclusion of consequential loss and cap on contractual liability linked to the price paid were reasonable. The Court of Appeal explained:

> "Where experienced businessmen representing substantial companies of equal bargaining power negotiate an agreement, they may be taken to have had regard to the matters known to them. They should, in my view be taken to be the best judge of the commercial fairness of the agreement which they have; including the fairness of each of the terms in that agreement. They should be taken to be the best judge on the question whether the terms of the agreement are reasonable. The court should not assume that either is likely to commit his company to an agreement which he thinks is unfair, or which he thinks includes unreasonable terms. *Unless satisfied that one party has, in effect taken unfair advantage of the other—or that a term is so unreasonable that it cannot properly have been understood or considered—the court should not interfere.*"

35.5.4   *Horace Holman Group Limited v Sherwood International Group Limited*[14]

In this case, the court held that an exclusion of statutory implied terms, an exclusion of "anticipated savings and other benefits" and a cap on contractual liability to reflect the price paid were all unreasonable.

The evidence of the availability of insurance was a key factor in the decision. The court found that it would have been easier and cheaper for the supplier to insure against its software not performing, than for the customer to insure against its losses if the software did not perform.

35.5.5   *SAM Business Systems Ltd v Hedley & Co*[15]

The dispute arose in connection with the supply of a computer system by SAM to Hedley. It was accepted that the licence and maintenance contracts entered into by the parties were both on SAM's standard terms. Immediately after the system went live, Hedley experienced serious problems with it. SAM sued Hedley for non-payment. Hedley counterclaimed for damages in connection with delivery of a defective system.

The licence agreement contained an exclusion of liability provision. The

---

[13]   *Watford Electronics Ltd v Sanderson CFL Ltd* [2001] EWCA Civ 317.
[14]   This issue was determined as a preliminary issue (decision of the TCC dated April 12, 2000 (unreported)).
[15]   *SAM Business Systems Ltd v Hedley & Co* [2002] EWHC 2733 (TCC); [2003] 1 All E.R. (Comm) 465.

provision fell within the UCTA 1977 and the Judge therefore had to consider whether the clause was reasonable. In finding that it was reasonable, the Judge took into account the acceptance criteria procedure in the contract. Under this procedure, Hedley had the right to terminate the agreement and claim back all sums paid to SAM in the event a defective system was delivered by SAM and not remedied within the prescribed time. This provision reflected representations made by SAM that it offered a money back guarantee. Against this background the exclusion provisions were considered reasonable.

35.5.6   Frans Maas (UK) Ltd v Samsung Electronics (UK) Ltd [16]

In this case, the parties had contracted for the carriage of goods on the British International Freight Association (BIFA) standard terms. Mobile telephones belonging to Samsung worth over £2 million were stolen whilst under the control of Frans Maas. In determining that clause 27(A) of the BIFA standard terms (which provided the mechanism for a cap of £25,000) was reasonable, the court considered the following factors:

(a)   the parties were of equal bargaining power;
(b)   the limit in clause 27(A) was calculated in terms of weight, not value of the goods;
(c)   Samsung could have contracted under clause 27(D) of the BIFA terms "by special arrangement" for a higher limit had it wished to do so;
(d)   clauses such as clause 27(A) are commonly used by freight forwarders; and
(e)   Samsung could have obtained insurance cover in respect of the goods.

On UCTA 1977, the court relied on the remarks of the Court of Appeal in *Granville Oil & Chemical LtdvDavis Turner & Co Ltd*[17]:

> "The 1977 Act obviously plays a very important role in protecting vulnerable consumers from the effect of draconian contract terms. But I am less enthusiastic about its intrusion into contracts between commercial parties of equal bargaining strength, who should generally be considered capable of being able to make contracts of their choosing and expect to be bound by their terms."

---

[16]   *Frans Maas (UK) Ltd v Samsung Electronics (UK) Ltd* [2004] EWHC 1502 (Comm); [2005] 2 All E.R. (Comm) 783.
[17]   *Granville Oil & Chemicals Ltd v Davies Turner & Co Ltd* [2003] 1 All E.R. (Comm) 819.

35.5.7   *Regus (UK) Ltd v Epcot Solutions Ltd*[18]

The significance of the availability of insurance was also highlighted in this case, which concerned the provision of serviced office accommodation by Regus to Epcot.

The contract between the parties excluded any liability on the part of Regus for heads of loss including loss of business and loss of profits. Following a forced transfer to alternative accommodation, Epcot made a claim for relocation expenses. Having found that there was no inequality of bargaining power between the parties, the Judge found that it was entirely reasonable for Regus to restrict damages under these heads. He found that Regus had advised its customers to protect themselves by insurance for business losses and that it was generally more economical for the person by whom the loss would be sustained to take out insurance. In these circumstances the clause was found to meet the requirements of reasonableness.

35.5.8   *Changes in the law*

It is worth noting that changes are expected to this important area of law. In February 2005, the Law Commission published a final report and draft Bill dealing with the reform of the law on unfair contract terms. Whilst these recommendations were accepted by the then government, their implementation was put on hold pending the European Commission's proposal for a new Consumer Rights Directive. The UK government has since announced that it intends to implement a new Consumer Rights Bill to give effect to this Directive. The Law Commission was recently asked to review and update its 2005 report.

35.5.9   *Documenting discussion of the limitation of liability*

The supplier is advised to keep documentary evidence that will help it demonstrate that its limitation of liability is reasonable. This might include evidence that the customer had reasonable bargaining power and that the customer negotiated the agreement extensively. The supplier may also want to include a short preamble or recital at the beginning of a limitation of liability clause in order to explain the reasons for, or background to, its inclusion.

---

[18]   *Regus (UK) v Epcot Solutions Ltd* [2008] EWCA Civ 361; [2009] 1 All E.R. (Comm) 586.

35.6 Exclusion by the supplier of specified losses

35.6.1 *Exclusion of certain types of loss*

In addition to agreeing a financial cap on its liability under the agreement, the supplier may want to exclude certain types of loss in its entirety. In particular, the supplier will usually want to exclude liability for consequential and other specified losses. A number of recent cases have established (or confirmed) that, in this context, "consequential loss" equates to the special loss referred to in section 35.13.5 above.[19] These the losses falling within the second limb of the test for remoteness laid down in *Hadley v Baxendale*.

It is important to understand that consequential or special loss is does not equate to loss of profit. Certain loss of profit falls squarely within the first limb of *Hadley v Baxendale* and will be recoverable unless expressly excluded. To avoid this, and related problems, the agreement should specify precisely what categories of loss are being excluded as explained in section 35.6.2 below.

The difficulty of a supplier being able to rely on an exclusion of special losses was illustrated in the recent preliminary decision in *GB Gas Holdings Ltd v Accenture (UK) Ltd*.[20] In that case, the supplier enjoyed an exclusion of "indirect or consequential losses" (which was taken as meaning the same as special losses). However, that did not stop the supplier being potentially liable for a number of heads of loss including *ex gracia* compensation paid by British Gas to its own customers to compensate them for customer service failings that they had suffered.

The supplier will often also want to ensure that the exclusion clause protects in the event of its own negligence or deliberate breach. As stated above, such exclusions are not effective in the case of fraud and there is a risk of they will be struck out in their entirety if they do purport to exclude liability for fraud. It was because such exclusions cannot limit liability for fraud that Sky successfully claimed damages in excess of £300 million from HP (formally EDS) despite the fact that the contract capped liability at £30 million.[21] In that case, Sky were able to demonstrate that they had relied on a fraudulent misrepresentation made by EDS.

---

[19]   In the case of *Ferryways NV v Associated British Ports (The Humber Way)* [2008] EWHC 225 (Comm) the court reviewed a number of cases in which the meaning of this phrase had been judicially considered and concluded that it was now well-recognised as meaning losses that do not arise directly and naturally from the breach. It was argued that as the contract contained a definition of "indirect and consequential" that was wider than the recognised meaning, that definition excluding a particular kind of loss (liability to third parties) that would otherwise have been included. The court found that such loss was not excluded by the particular wording used, suggesting that the parties could not have intended to exclude such loss under the umbrella of "indirect or consequential loss" however widely defined.

[20]   *GB Gas Holdings Ltd v Accenture (UK) Ltd* [2010] EWCA Civ 912

[21]   *BSkyB Ltd and another v HP Enterprise Services UK Ltd (formerly t/a Electronic Data Systems Ltd)* [2010] EWHC 86 (TCC).

35.6.2   Definition of excluded loss

The supplier may want to define in greater detail losses for which it will not be responsible, for example:

(a)   indirect or consequential loss;
(b)   loss of profits or indirect loss of profits;
(c)   loss of business or loss of revenue;
(d)   loss of goodwill;
(e)   loss of data; and
(f)   loss of anticipated savings arising out of or in connection with the agreement.

35.6.3   Clarification of losses claimable

On the other hand, the customer is likely to want to clarify that certain losses (including the losses it is most likely to suffer) will not be excluded by an otherwise wide exclusion of liability. The customer will have to identify these losses in the light of the specific services it has outsourced and the specific damage it might suffer. It will also need to ensure that the exclusion of liability, and any carve outs from that exclusion, reflect the risk that the parties have agreed will be transferred to the supplier. For example, if the parties have agreed that the supplier will accept business outcome-related risks for the achievement by the customer of a certain level of improvement in its profits, the customer should ensure that the agreement does not incorporate standard liability clauses which exclude liability for loss of profits.

Table 46 provides some examples of losses which the customer may consider carving out from any exclusion of liability.

Table 46 Examples of carve outs from exclusion of liability

Costs of selecting and negotiating with a contractor or contractors to replace the supplier.
The difference in cost between what the customer would have paid to the supplier for the services that the supplier should have delivered under the agreement and what the customer reasonably contracts to pay a replacement contractor to provide services that are materially similar to the services.
The cost of taking emergency measures, including changing over to other computer systems.
Wasted management time.
Costs of internal and external staff including costs of staff providing, or re-providing, the services which should have been provided by the supplier.
The cost of idle time of staff, goods and facilities of the customer and any third parties engaged by the customer.
Costs associated with reconstruction of lost or corrupted data. (This will be particularly contentious from the supplier perspective.)
Any fines or payments imposed by a regulatory authority as a result of the supplier's failure to provide the services.

Losses suffered by other parts of the customer's group or its customers.
Losses resulting from breach of third-party intellectual property rights.
Losses covered by liquidated damages provisions.
Direct loss of profit.

35.7   Limitation of liability by the customer

The customer should consider whether it should limit its liability under the agreement, for example to protect itself if one of its employees causes damage when carrying out an audit inspection. The customer may also consider if it would be easier to agree a reasonable limitation of the supplier's liability if the clause is mutual.

The customer may suggest that the supplier's exclusion of liability for loss of profit should be mutual. In this situation, the supplier should be particularly careful about this suggestion, bearing in mind the importance of this claim to the supplier.

35.8   Insurance

The customer may want the supplier to take out certain insurance to cover its liability under the agreement. The parties should also ensure that it is clear who is responsible for insuring the assets and premises used to provide the services. The customer may also want the supplier to take out public/ product liability insurance and professional indemnity insurance. In certain cases, where the services give the supplier's employees an opportunity to commit fraud, the customer may want the supplier to take out fidelity insurance (including computer crime risks).

The customer will usually want to see evidence that the supplier has taken out the requisite insurance policies and may reserve the right to take out insurance at the supplier's cost if the supplier fails to take out such insurance itself.

Most suppliers will want to take out general group-wide insurance policies and the customer should bear in mind that, if it requests the supplier to take out additional insurance for the specific project, there will be a cost implication.

Chapter 36

Data Protection Law

36.1 Outline

Privacy, data security and confidentiality are high profile risks and have a particular resonance in services and outsourcing arrangements which usually involve a customer allowing a supplier to hold data (including personal data) on its behalf. There are a number of reasons for data protection having become a "top table" issue. First, there is the (almost daily) feed of news stories on data breaches. A significant data leak is likely to negatively impact your share price, so data protection and data security constitute reputational risk. Second, we are seeing a substantial strengthening of global data privacy laws. This includes prescriptive new legislation in the EU as well as a doubling in the number of jurisdictions worldwide that have adopted national data protection laws. So, the legal requirements are getting stricter and now impact many more jurisdictions than used to be the case. Many of these jurisdictions have chosen to follow the EU rules as their benchmark for privacy. This is also particularly pertinent in the context of cloud computing business models which involve the transfer of huge volumes of personal data across multiple jurisdictions, which each operate their own national data protection laws.

This chapter and the next chapter deal with the specific data protection and security risks that are likely to arise in services and outsourcing arrangements and how to manage them. This chapter describes data protection law and the next chapter describes provisions that customers and suppliers may want to include in their services agreements.

36.2 Background to the Data Protection Directive (95/46/EC)

The privacy and protection of personal data in the EU is currently governed by the Data Protection Directive (95/46/EC) (the "Data Protection Directive").[1] The Data Protection Directive has a new legal basis in what is now Article 8 of the Charter of Fundamental Rights which says that

---

[1]   In addition to the Data Protection Directive, there is also the Privacy and Electronic Communications Directive (2002/58/EC) but this applies, primarily, to telecoms companies, ISPs and other communica-

everyone has the right to protection for their personal data. This new legal basis for data protection demonstrates the increasing importance of data protection in the EU legal framework. Data protection law is also based on principles set out in the European Convention on Human Rights.

Each EU Member State, and those in the EEA[2] are required to implement the Data Protection Directive nationally in their jurisdictions. So each EEA Member State has its own national data protection law or equivalent. The primary obligation on the customer is to comply with that national data protection law.

36.3   Key data protection concepts

36.3.1   Personal data

The Data Protection Directive applies to "personal data" which is any information relating to an identified or identifiable individual (a "data subject"). Identification, in this context, may be direct or indirect, in particular by reference to an identification number or to one or more factors specific to an individual such as physical, physiological, mental, economic, cultural or social identity.

In practical terms, this includes customer data and HR data. Both are often the subject of services and outsourcing arrangements and both will trigger data protection obligations. The scope of "personal data" is also very broad. It can include customer contact details, online identifiers, customer purchase histories and sector-specific data such as smart metering usage, bank and credit card records, insurance claims files as well as HR and talent management data. Personal data can also include information about individual contacts at, or representatives of, corporate entities. This is much broader than, for example, the US law concept of "personally identifiable information" which generally covers names, social security numbers and biographical data.

36.3.2   Processing

The Data Protection Directive covers the "processing" of personal data. This is defined very broadly and covers all electronic processing of personal data. It also covers the holding of records in structured manual filing systems.

---

tion service providers and contains special rules about traffic, billing and location data. The Privacy and Electronic Communications Directive also includes rules relating to the use of customer data for direct marketing, the requirement to obtain consent for the use of cookies and the data breach notification rule for telecoms companies and ISPs.

[2] The European Economic Area comprises the 27 Member States of the European Union plus Norway, Iceland and Liechtenstein.

In practice, if the supplier holds, uses or has some degree of access to personal data, this will constitute "processing" which will trigger data protection law.

36.3.3 *Controller and processor*

The current way in which data protection law works is to impose obligations on the controller (but see section 36.8 for a description of future changes in the law). The controller means the person or entity who determines both the purposes (for which the personal data is used) and the means (by which it is processed). This means that the customer will be the controller and therefore bound to comply with applicable data protection law.

In addition, the Data Protection Directive also contains the concept of a "processor". This is the person or organisation who processes personal data on behalf of the controller. In this context, the supplier will be a processor.

The Data Protection Directive imposes obligations on the controller to ensure that its staff and any processors acting on its behalf comply with certain data protection requirements. Therefore the customer, as controller, must ensure that the supplier (i.e. the processor) is only appointed subject to a thorough data protection and data security due diligence and that the services agreement imposes on the supplier appropriate obligations to comply with certain data protection requirements and includes indemnities in the customer's favour.

36.4 Whose data protection law applies?

The customer (as controller) will be obliged to comply with the national data protection law of each EEA Member State in which it is established (in relation to personal data processed in the context of each such establishment).

Even if the customer is not established in any EEA Member State, it must, nevertheless, comply with the national data protection law of any Member State in which it uses equipment to process personal data (e.g. use of local servers, hosting facilities or any other IT equipment can trigger an obligation to comply).

As the processor's obligations are a function of the services agreement (rather than statutory law), the processor should, in the case of the customer outsourcing from multiple jurisdictions, accept a flow-down of the data privacy risk from each of those jurisdictions. While each national data protection law is intended to be harmonised, there are significant differences between individual EU Member States so the position should be validated by local counsel.

36.5 Key requirements of the EU Data Protection Directive

The core requirements of the Data Protection Directive impose obligations on the EU Member States to implement laws containing a number of key requirements as set out below.

Table 47 Key data protection provisions

Principles relating to data quality: Personal data must be processed fairly, lawfully and must be collected for specified, explicit and legitimate purposes. Personal data must be adequate, relevant and not excessive, accurate and, where necessary, kept up-to-date. Personal data should not be retained for longer than necessary and for the relevant purposes. These are, in effect, a "code of good information handling".

Criteria for legitimate processing: Personal data may only be processed if the controller complies with one of the criteria listed in the Directive. These include that the data subject has unambiguously given consent and that the processing is necessary for the purposes of the controller's legitimate interests or those of third parties to whom the data are disclosed.

Special categories of processing: Personal data revealing racial or ethnic origin, political opinions, religious or philosophical beliefs, trade union membership and the processing of data concerning health or sex life must comply with one of the additional conditions for processing. This usually requires the collection of explicit consent of the data subject.

Transparency: The controller (or his representative) must provide the data subject with information as to the controller's identity, the purposes of processing and certain further information to ensure transparency. This further information may include the recipients or categories of recipients to whom the data may be disclosed, whether the data subject's replies to questions are obligatory or voluntary as well as the possible consequences of failure to reply and the existence of the data subject's right of access to his/her data.

Data subject's rights: The data subject has a right of access to his/her personal data. The data subject can also object to certain processing of personal data (e.g. where data is processed on the basis of the controller's legitimate interests) and can opt out of direct marketing. Data subjects also have rights in connection with automated individual decisions where decisions are solely based on automated processing of data intended to evaluate certain personal aspects relating to the data subject such as performance at work, creditworthiness, reliability and conduct. Broadly speaking, such decisions are permitted provided the data subject has requested this in relation to the entering into or performance of a contract or suitable measures are taken to protect data subject's legitimate interests (for example, a right to make representations).

Data security: Personal data must be held securely. Security measures must be appropriate having regard to the state of the art and the cost of their implementation so that they ensure a level of security appropriate to the risks represented by the processing and nature of the data to be protected. Where a controller hires a processor (such as an outsourcing service provider) to store or process personal data on its behalf, it must ensure that a contract is entered into with the processor containing certain prescribed terms as to data security (these are set out in section 36.5.1 below).

Notification: Member States are required to implement a form of notification regime under which controllers are required to register with the national supervisory authority (i.e. the body responsible for data protection enforcement in the relevant jurisdiction). In practice, notification is operated on country-specific rules and vary significantly from one Member State to another.

Prior checking: Member States are to determine the processing operations likely to present specific risks to data subjects and check that processing operations are examined prior to commencement. It is the controller's obligation to notify the relevant supervisory authority according to national law. The prior checking regime has not been implemented in certain jurisdictions such as the UK.

> **Transfer of personal data to third countries**: Personal data may only be transferred to jurisdictions outside the EEA where steps are taken to ensure that it is protected adequately. This is further explained in section 36.5.2.

Please note that the above is a summary of the provisions of the Data Protection Directive and that actual legislative provisions will depend on the terms of the relevant national law.

36.5.1 Data security

The Data Protection Directive says that controllers must implement appropriate technical and organisational measures to protect personal data against accidental or unlawful destruction or accidental loss, alteration, unauthorised disclosure or access, in particular where the processing involves the transmission of data over a network, and against all other unlawful forms of processing. The controller must ensure that the measures provide an appropriate level of security to the risks represented by the processing and the nature of the data to be protected having regard to the state of the art and the cost of implementation. The controller must therefore assess the context and ensure that the technical and organisational measures to be adopted guarantee an appropriate level of security.

Special rules apply where a controller hires a processor to process personal data on its behalf. This is particularly relevant to services or outsourcing where the service provider will process personal data on behalf of the customer. In this case, the controller must choose a processor that provides sufficient guarantees in respect of the technical security measures and organisational measures and must ensure compliance with those measures. The controller must ensure that a contract is entered into with the processor that requires the processor to act only on instructions from the controller and imposes an obligation on the processor to hold the data securely. Table 48 summarises the key data security requirements.

Table 48 Key data security provisions

> **Security of processing**: The controller must implement appropriate technical and organisational security measures to protect personal data against accidental or unlawful destruction or accidental loss, alteration, unauthorised disclosure or access and against all other unlawful forms of processing.
>
> **Risk to be imposed on supplier**: The controller must obtain "sufficient guarantees" from the supplier in relation to the technical and organisational security measures.
>
> **Audit rights**: The customer must ensure that the supplier complies with the required technical and organisational security measures. This should be available to the customer on its election and, in particular, following a data breach or other security incident.
>
> **Written agreement**: The customer must ensure that there is a written agreement or other binding instrument in place with the supplier that stipulates that the supplier will only act on the controller's instructions in relation to processing personal data and will comply with the equivalent of the data security obligations imposed on the customer by data protection legislation.

36.5.2   *International Data Transfers*

The Data Protection Directive says that the international transfer of personal data to a country outside the EEA may only take place if arrangements are put in place to ensure that the data is protected on an equivalent basis to that applicable under the Data Protection Directive and local applicable implementing law.

"International transfers of personal data", for these purposes, include any arrangement whereby the data is made available or accessible to the supplier outside the EEA. This does not require the physical transfer of tangible media or hosting arrangements outside the EEA (although these are examples of international data transfers). Even if the supplier can simply access data hosted on the customer's UK or other local servers (including for IT maintenance and support purposes) this would constitute a data transfer. The only exception is where the data happens to be "in transit" through a country as this is an inherent part of the way the public internet works. The international data transfer issue is therefore likely to arise on any international services agreement involving a non-EEA component.

There are a number of ways in which to deal with this in services agreements. The following paragraphs describe the various options and associated pros and cons.

36.5.2.1   *White List*

The European Commission has approved certain non-EEA jurisdictions as being "adequate" for data protection and therefore on a "white list" for data transfers. These jurisdictions are listed in Table 49.

Table 49 White listed jurisdictions

Andorra
Argentina
Australia
Canada
Faeroe Islands
Guernsey
Israel
Isle of Man
Jersey
Uruguay
Switzerland

The list is short and therefore has limited application unless the international component of the services agreement relates exclusively to one or more of the white listed countries.

36.5.2.2   *Model Clauses*

The customer can legitimise the international transfer of personal data by putting in place model contractual clauses with the supplier. The clauses are in a prescribed form (which must be followed to the letter). They can form part of a discrete data transfer agreement or be appended to the services agreement.

The model clauses operate on the basis that the supplier (as data importer) agrees to comply with the data protection law applicable to the customer (as data exporter). The clauses contain a number of warranties to be given by the supplier including as to implementation of security measures, agreeing to audit rights for the customer in relation to its data-processing facilities and to manage the appointment of any sub-processors on equivalent terms. The model clauses also include an appendix which the parties need to complete to define the data subjects, categories of data, sensitive personal data and processing operations together with a summary of the supplier's security measures to protect the data.

The advantage of using the model clauses is that the approach is legally watertight and a relatively quick way to legitimise data transfers for service agreements involving one or a small number of EU jurisdictions.

The disadvantages of the model clauses are that:

(a) they are, inevitably, a "snap shot" of data processing at the relevant time, and so may require ongoing maintenance to update them;

(b) some jurisdictions require the agreements to be lodged and/or approved by local data protection regulators before they become effective which can add time and cost to the exercise; and

(c) separate contractual arrangements may be required for each country from which the customer is exporting data.

36.5.2.3 Binding Corporate Rules

The third way in which the customer can legitimise the export of personal data from the EEA is to adopt binding corporate rules (BCRs). These are an internal set of rules and policies drafted by the customer to provide adequate protection for personal data on a legally enforceable basis. BCRs comprise the implementation of privacy principles across the customer group and a mechanism to ensure that they are legally binding on the group companies (such as by using an intra group agreement).

Traditionally, BCRs have only been available for controllers (such as customers) in respect of intra-group data transfers. However, they are currently being extended so that data processors (such as services and outsourcing suppliers) can implement their own BCRs in order to operate as a "safe harbor" for the receipt of personal data from customers. We expect many outsourcing and services suppliers to adopt BCRs over the next few years so it is worth checking whether a supplier has BCRs in place. In this context, BCRs are, essentially, a "badge of privacy compliance". A cloud computing supplier, for example, will be able to adopt BCRs once the rules are extended so that customers do not have to put additional arrangements in place to legitimise the transfer of personal data to the cloud computing supplier.

The procedure for adopting BCRs is as follows:

(a) The entity seeking BCR approval selects a lead authority (i.e. the most appropriate data protection regulator; usually the regulator of the jurisdiction in which it has its main establishment).

(b) The entity must then complete an application form, draft privacy principles and sign an intra-group agreement (or another appropriate mechanism to ensure that the privacy principles are legally binding across the group). There are some ancillary documents that need to be produced.

(c) The lead authority will review the BCR application at each stage and provide comments and feedback. This will also involve review by two other authorities.

(d) Once approved by the lead authority, there is a mutual recognition procedure which, at the time of writing, includes 21 EU Member States. Those EU countries within the "mutual recognition area" will give approval once the application has been approved by the lead authority. Other Member States must be consulted.

(e) The BCRs may require national approval by supervisory authorities in each Member State as well.

The advantages of adopting BCRs is that they are the platinum standard in privacy compliance. They are a flexible solution and will expand and contract with the business. The disadvantage of adopting BCRs is that they are still being developed and may require national authorisation by the relevant data protection regulators in addition to approval by the lead authority. This is likely to become more streamlined under the new EU Data Protection Regulation.

36.5.2.4   US Safe Harbor

The fourth solution to legitimise international transfers of data from Europe is to rely upon the US Safe Harbor. This is essentially a self-certification regime under which US-based companies can publically declare that they will comply with the Safe Harbor Framework Privacy Principles. Provided a company has self-certified (and maintains its certification) an EU-based customer will be entitled to transfer personal data to it. This is subject to the self-certification covering the actual types of data required to be transferred and that there is a US regulator that has agreed to enforce the US company's compliance. Usually this is the Federal Trade Commission.

If the customer is relying upon the US Safe Harbor, it will need to ensure that the supplier agrees to self-certify and maintain its certification. The customer should also require the supplier to notify it if, in any case, the certification ceases to be effective, or in the event of enforcement or similar action, by the relevant US regulator.

The advantage of relying upon the US Safe Harbor is that it is a straightforward procedure and one which can be undertaken fairly quickly.

The disadvantage is that the US Safe Harbor only covers data transfers to the US. If data is to be transferred (or onward transferred) to other jurisdictions as well, the Safe Harbor will only provide a partial solution. Certain jurisdictions (such as Germany) also require separate data processing contracts to be put in place with a supplier even where the supplier is signed-up to the US Safe Harbor. Such data processing contracts are required to specify the data security measures implemented to protect the personal data. In addition, the US Safe Harbor is not available for financial services data (one of the biggest data exports from Europe to the US).

36.5.2.5   *Consent of the data subject*

The Data Protection Directive provides that a data controller (such as a customer) can transfer personal data outside the EEA where the relevant data subjects have given unambiguous consent for the proposed transfer. In order to be effective, the consents given must be specific, freely given and informed. This would require the customer to specify the country to which the data is to be exported and the purposes for which it will be processed in that country. Any specific risks should also be identified to the data subjects. In practice, this can be difficult to implement and carries the risk that some data subjects may choose not to give consent and others may give consent but later withdraw it. There is, therefore, an inherent non-compliance risk by relying on consent.

36.5.2.6   *Other derogations*

There are a number of other derogations available such as where the transfer is necessary for the performance of a contract between the data subject and the controller. However, these derogations tend to be interpreted narrowly. So for example, it would be necessary for a travel agent to send a hotel reservation to the relevant hotel in New York in order to perform the relevant customer contract but it would not be necessary for the same travel agent to transfer the reservation data to India simply because the travel agent has chosen to locate its call centre or data processing operation in that jurisdiction.

36.6   Implementation of the Data Protection Directive in the EU

Each Member State has enacted its own data protection legislation to implement the Data Protection Directive into its national law. In services agreements, it is important to consider the detail of each relevant jurisdiction's implementing legislation. This is particularly important as local implementing legislation can vary from country to country.

36.7   Implementation of the Data Protection Directive in the UK

In the UK, the Data Protection Directive has been implemented by the Data Protection Act 1998 ("the DPA 1998"). Data controllers who are either established in the UK (or who use equipment in the UK to process personal data) must ensure that they comply with the obligations set out in the DPA 1998.

Under the DPA 1998, the data controller must notify (i.e. register with) the Information Commissioner's Office (ICO) and comply with the eight Data Protection Principles listed in Table 50.

Table 50 Data protection principles—The Data Protection Act 1998

1   Personal data shall be processed fairly and lawfully and shall not be processed unless one of the conditions set out in Sch.2 to the DPA 1998 or, for sensitive personal data, Sch.3 to the DPA 1998, is also met.
2   Personal data shall be obtained only for one or more specified and lawful purposes, and shall not be further processed in any manner incompatible with that purpose or those purposes.
3   Personal data shall be adequate, relevant and not excessive in relation to the purpose or purposes for which it is processed.
4   Personal data shall be accurate and, where necessary, kept up to date.
5   Personal data processed for any purpose or purposes shall not be kept for longer than is necessary for that purpose or those purposes.
6   Personal data shall be processed in accordance with the rights of data subjects under the DPA.
7   Personal data shall be kept secure and appropriate technical and organisational measures shall be taken against unauthorised or unlawful processing of personal data and against accidental loss or destruction of, or damage to, personal data.
8   Personal data shall not be transferred to a country or territory outside the European Economic Area unless that country or territory ensures an adequate level of protection for the rights and freedoms of data subjects in relation to the processing of personal data.

36.7.1   The Information Commissioner's Office

The Data Protection Directive requires each EU Member State to provide one or more public authorities who will be responsible for monitoring and enforcing the local data protection law. In the UK, the regulator is the ICO. The ICO is an independent body set up to up-hold information rights, promote openness by public bodies and data privacy for individuals.

The ICO also issues guidance on the practical implementation of data protection rules, for example, on the notification of data security breaches to the ICO and the required practical steps in hiring a supplier. Specifically, the guidance is to help in selecting a reputable supplier and ensuring that the supplier has adopted appropriate data security measures. The guidance reminds businesses that, in the context of services and outsourcing arrangements, it is the customer who retains liability under the DPA 1998 for data protection compliance and, in particular, data security risk.

36.7.2   ICO Enforcement Powers

The data protection regulator in each of the EU Member States has its own set of enforcement powers. In the UK, the ICO can serve enforcement notices requiring a controller (e.g. a customer) to do (or cease doing) certain data processing. He can serve information notices requiring disclosure of information relating to processing. The ICO can also issues undertakings which effectively "name and shame" the offending controller.

Since 6 April 2010, the ICO has new powers to impose fines of up to £500,000 per breach. These have, to date, been used exclusively in relation to data breaches. The ICO must, in order to impose a fine, satisfy itself that there is a serious breach of the Data Protection Principles in relation to personal data and that the breach is likely to cause substantial damage or substantial distress and that the breach is deliberate or that the data controller knew, or ought to have known, that there was a risk of the breach and failed to take reasonable preventative steps (i.e. the data controller was negligent). The ICO does not, as yet, have the power to impose compulsory audits on controllers (although this has been conceded by the UK government in relation to central government departments). The new General Data Protection Regulation will introduce compulsory audit powers (see section 36.11 below).

36.8   The proposals for a new EU Data Protection Regulation

On 25 January 2012, the European Commission published a proposal for a new Data Protection Regulation. It is expected to be finalised early in 2014 and become effective in 2016. There will be no transitional relief so the interim period is, effectively, the period for customers and suppliers to plan for compliance. This will be a significant issue for services and outsourcing arrangements as the proposed new Regulation imposes a much more prescriptive regime for controllers and, for the first time, direct responsibility for processors (i.e. service providers). Some of the key proposed changes are set out in Table 51.

Table 51 Key changes under the proposed EU Data Protection Regulation

New legal framework: The Data Protection Directive will be replaced by a new EU Data Protection Regulation. The Regulation will apply to all Member States (i.e. it will not need to be implemented by national law). However, there are, at the time of writing, many areas where the European Commission will be entitled to add additional requirements to provide further detail on the proposed new rules. These will be contained in "delegated acts" and "implementing acts". These have not yet been published. In addition, Member States will be given rights to impose their own country-specific data protection rules in relation to HR data.

Scope and extra-territorial effect: The new rules will apply to both controllers and processors who are established in the EU. So EU service providers will, for the first time, be regulated directly by data protection law. In addition, controllers who are not established in the EU but who are offering goods or services to EU residents or monitoring their behaviour from outside the EU will also be caught.

Fines: Organisations that violate certain provisions of the new rules may be fined up to €1 million or 2 per cent of their global annual turnover. This is a substantial change from the current fragmented position where different regulators apply different penalties in the various countries.

Supra-national regulation: Data controllers and processors will be regulated by the data protection regulator in the EU country where they have their "main establishment". The aim is for this to become a "one stop shop" for enforcement for each controller or processor.

Data security breach notification: Organisations will be required, for the first time, to notify the national data protection regulator in the event of any data breach. The notification must be given without undue delay and, where feasible, within 24 hours of becoming aware of the breach. Service providers will also be required to notify their customers of data breaches immediately. Organisations who are public authorities or large private companies ("large" means a company with 250 staff or more) will be required to appoint a data protection officer to ensure compliance.

New "accountability" regime: Data controllers must adopt policies and procedures to ensure, and be able to demonstrate, compliance with the new rules. This is a new principle of "accountability" and requires a much more prescriptive "control framework" to be in place to ensure data protection compliance. Customers will want to impose contractual obligations on suppliers to comply with the relevant policies and procedures.

Increased responsibility for data processors: Data processors (e.g. service providers) will be subject to a substantial number of new rules including rules to ensure data security (and notify the relevant customer of any breach) as well as duties to keep detailed records and documentation relating to personal data to be processed under the services or outsourcing agreement. In addition, suppliers will be liable to third parties (corporates or individuals) for compensation arising as a result of unlawful processing. Customers and suppliers will be jointly and severally liable for such liability. This is likely to drive a greater focus on the contractual warranties and indemnities contained in the services agreement from both the customer's and supplier's perspective.

International data transfers: The current options available to permit international data transfers will be bolstered by the explicit incorporation of Binding Corporate Rules (the EU "data passport") to legitimise the international transfer of data across a corporate group. In

> addition, Processor BCRs will also be available so suppliers can certify themselves as "safe processors" to receive customer data under services agreements.

36.9   Cloud Computing

Cloud computing describes an IT Infrastructure which is either dedicated to an individual organisation (known as the "private cloud") or an infrastructure which is owned by a provider but which is made available to multiple users, businesses and organisations (the "public cloud"). There are also intermediate and hybrid versions of these alternatives. Cloud computing can bring some significant benefits: access to top class technology and improvements in security, increased "speed to market" and attractive "pay as you use" pricing models.

36.9.1   Cloud computing: Data protection issues

However, cloud computing (and, in particular, use of the "public cloud") raises significant data protection issues. Please see Table 52 for a summary of these issues. The issues need to be addressed early and as part of the procurement process to ensure compliance.

Table 52 Cloud Computing Data Protection Issues

Data security: The customer must apply the general data protection rules to any cloud computing service provider which requires the customer to undertake due diligence of the supplier and to ensure that the services contract includes the following: (a) "sufficient guarantees" in relation to data security; (b) audit rights; (c) obligations to ensure that personal data will be kept secure and appropriate technical and organisational measures shall be taken against unauthorised or unlawful processing of personal data and against accidental loss or destruction of, or damage to, personal data (d) obligation to act only on the instructions of the customer in relation to processing personal data. These can create particular challenges where the cloud computing provider offers a "one size fits all" global solution for cloud computing not drafted for EU data privacy compliances, in particular, where the solution involves the "public cloud". Therefore, this point needs to be addressed at the outset as part of the procurement process.
International data transfers: The customer must ensure compliance with Principle 8 of the DPA 1998 – i.e. that personal data shall not be transferred to a country or territory outside the EEA unless that country or territory ensures an adequate level of protection for the rights and freedoms of data subjects in relation to the processing of personal data. While cloud computing could involve storage of data within European data centres only, many cloud computing business models involve the transfer of personal data across multiple data centres and many jurisdictions worldwide. If this involves the export of personal data from the EEA, the customer is obliged to ensure that the cloud computing supplier complies with one of the international data transfer solutions described above. In practical terms, this is likely to require the cloud computing supplier to sign up to the model clauses or restrict data processing to the US and self-certify under the US Safe Harbor. There is likely to be significant change in this area in the foreseeable future as cloud computing suppliers will be eligible to imple-

ment their own binding corporate rules which are likely to provide the most robust and flexible solution for customers.

Transparency: The customer must ensure that the relevant data subjects (e.g. employees or customers) are informed that their data may be transferred to a country outside the EEA which may have lower levels of data protection than those applicable in the EEA.

Conditions for processing: The customer must ensure that the use of cloud computing complies with the relevant conditions for processing set out in Schs 2 and 3 of the DPA 1998. This requires the customer to ensure that the use of cloud computing is necessary for the customer's legitimate interests[3] and does not prejudice the rights and freedoms or legitimate interests of the data subjects. This can be harder to achieve in relation to sensitive personal data.[4]

Disclosures to law enforcement bodies: One of the particular challenges with the use of cloud computing solutions is the concern that the data may be disclosed to law enforcement or other government bodies, in foreign jurisdictions perhaps without the customer being notified.[5] For example, US cloud computing suppliers could be asked to disclose information pursuant to the US Patriot Act. However, the Patriot Act is, itself, subject to court procedures and legal safeguards and specifically addresses criminal and anti-terrorist investigations. Indeed, most other jurisdictions will have law enforcement bodies with powers to require access to data for similar purposes. In any event, this is something to be addressed by the customer at the outset.

Sector Regulatory Requirements: Customers will also need to comply with sector-specific regulatory requirements which may limit the extent to which they can legitimately use cloud computing solutions. For example, financial services regulation currently presents particular challenges in use of cloud computing solutions.[6]

36.9.2   Cloud computing: The Future

At the time of writing, the Article 29 Working Party[7] has published an Opinion (05/2012) on Cloud Computing. While the Opinion does not iron out all the data protection issues on cloud computing, it is a useful indication as to the "direction of travel" for privacy regulation in the cloud. The Opinion accepts, for example, that cloud computing can bring benefits. The Opinion sets out a number of observations on data protection compliance on cloud computing including as follows:

(a)   **Primary obligations**: a controller (i.e. the customer) bears the regulatory risk and so is incentivised to ensure compliance. However, under the draft Data Protection Regulation, compliance risk will be extended to processors as well, such as cloud service providers.

---

[3]   The "legitimate interests" condition is contained in Sch.2(6) of the DPA 1998 and applies to processing which "is necessary for the purposes of legitimate interests pursued by the data controller or by the third party or parties to whom the data are disclosed, except where the processing is unwarranted in any particular case by reason of prejudice to the rights and freedoms or legitimate interests of the data subject".

[4]   Sensitive personal data refers to information relating to the data subject's racial or ethnic origin, political opinions, religious beliefs or beliefs of a similar nature, trade union membership, physical or mental health or condition, sexual life, or the commission or alleged commission of any offence or the proceedings relating to such offence.

[5]   This was a particular concern in connection with SWIFT (the global bank inter-bank messaging service) which, it transpired in 2008 had disclosed certain information to US government and law enforcement bodies without the knowledge of the banks whose customer data have been supplied to SWIFT.

[6]   See Chapters 38 to 42 for a description of financial services regulation.

[7]   The Article 29 Working Party is a committee made up of representatives of the data protection regulators across the EU which publishes non-binding but persuasive guidance on key data protection issues.

(b) **Key risks**: the two main data protection risks in connection with cloud computing are data security and international data transfers.

(c) **Risk analysis**: the customer should conduct a comprehensive and thorough risk analysis at the outset and select a cloud service provider that guarantees compliance with data privacy rules.

(d) **Contractual links**: there should be a contractual link between the customer and the cloud service provider and, separately, between the cloud service provider and any relevant sub-contractors. The Opinion says that the customer should be able to terminate the contract if the provider changes sub-contractors and the customer does not agree.

(e) **Transparency**: the customer should be informed about sub-contractors, locations of processing and "meaningful information" as to security measures; data subjects should also be informed of sub-contractors and locations of processing.

(f) **Safeguards**: the contract should provide "sufficient guarantees" as to security and specify the customer's instructions and service levels.

(g) **Independent certification**: the Opinion backs the use of third party certifications as a means for cloud providers to demonstrate compliance; we have yet to see this area develop but it is a sign of things to come.

(h) **Disclosures to law enforcement bodies**: the Opinion wants to reinstate the original proposal in the draft Regulation that you can only disclose data to another country's law enforcement bodies pursuant to an international agreement or mutual legal assistance treaty. More work is needed here to develop a workable solution.

(i) **European cloud**: the Opinion supports the European Cloud Partnership and the idea of promoting European clouds "sovereignty governed by European data protection law".

The Opinion also emphasises the importance of transparency, confidentiality and compliance with the rules on international data transfers. Clear and consistent guidance will be required across Europe in order to provide clarity for business as to the way in which they can use cloud computing services in a data protection compliant manner.

Chapter 37

Data Protection, Data Security and Confidentiality Obligations

37.1 Outline

The previous chapter described data protection law. This chapter describes the steps that the customer and supplier must take to comply with data protection law and to deal with data security and confidentiality issues.

37.2 Supplier obligations

Data protection, data security and confidentiality issues should be considered by the appropriate IT/technical and legal experts at each stage of the procurement.

37.2.1 During the procurement stage

Chapter 3 explains the importance of the customer considering its confidentiality and data security concerns and the supplier considering its potential security obligations during the procurement stage.

37.2.1.1 Due diligence

The customer, as controller, is obliged to ensure that it undertakes sufficient due diligence of each prospective supplier to validate that the supplier will have appropriate technical and organisational security measures in place at all times to protect all relevant personal data. The security measures should ensure a level of security appropriate to (a) the risks represented by the processing and (b) the nature of the data to be protected while having regard to the state of the data. In practice, this means that the controller must undertake an assessment of the personal data to be processed by the supplier, the risks arising and the appropriate security measures that are required. In practical terms, more is expected of larger organisations.

37.2.1.2   Key data protection provisions

The services agreement will need to include the customer's specific data protection, confidentiality and security requirements.

In order to comply with UK data protection law, the customer **must** include the provisions in Table 53 in its services agreement.

Table 53 Key data protection provisions

Appropriate technical and organisational security measures: The controller must implement appropriate technical and organisational security measures to protect personal data against accidental or unlawful destruction or accidental loss, alteration, unauthorised disclosure or access and against all other unlawful forms of processing.
The supplier must ensure that the technical and organisational security measures are implemented and maintained at all times during the agreement.
Note - This includes IT/technical measures (e.g. encryption) and organisational measures (e.g. building security and authorisation controls). The measures must ensure a level of security, having regard to the state of technological development and the cost of implementing any measures, to ensure a level of security appropriate to the harm that may result from a breach and the nature of the data to be protected.

Sufficient guarantees: The controller must choose a data processor providing sufficient guarantees in respect of the technical and organisational security measures. In practice, this means that the services agreement must include appropriate data protection/security warranties.

Audit rights: The customer must have audit rights enabling it to ensure that the supplier has implemented and maintains the required security measures. This should be available to the customer on its election and, in particular, following a data breach or other security incident. [1]

Act on instructions: The supplier must only act on the customer's instructions in relation to processing personal data. This must be set out in a written contract.

Comply with data protection legislation: The supplier must comply with the equivalent of the data security obligations imposed on the customer by data protection legislation. This must be set out in a written contract.

Staff assurance: The data controller must take reasonable steps to ensure the reliability of any employees who have access to the personal data.
Note - This is not a specific requirement of the Data Protection Directive but is set out in the Data Protection Act 1998.
The customer should, therefore, require warranties as to staff qualifications, experience and training. Staff vetting may also be appropriate (e.g. undertaking Criminal Records Bureau checks) and requiring rights to remove employees from the service provision where appropriate.

37.2.1.3   Optional data protection provisions

There are also a number of additional protections that the customer could seek. Although these are optional, they increasingly reflect best practice in

---

[1]   See section 10.14 for a detailed discussion of audit rights.

services agreements. Please see Table 54 for a description of these optional protections.

Table 54 Data Security—Optional Protections

Scope of protected data: The Data Protection Directive applies to personal data. This should be defined in the services agreement to include any personal information which is provided, generated or output by the supplier in providing the services. However, the customer may want to extend the data security and other data-related warranties to all information (whether personal or not) which is provided to, generated or output by the supplier. This helps ensure seamless protection for the customers' "information assets" and avoids legal debate as to whether particular records constitute personal data or not.

Customer's security IT requirements and policies: The customer could require the supplier to comply with specific IT and other security requirements in providing the services to the customer. The exact data security requirements are likely to vary from one services agreement to another, depending upon the nature of the data being processed, the harm that may result from unauthorised or unlawful processing and the balance between the state of the art of technology development and the cost of implementing the relevant security measures. In some cases, sector-specific guidance or regulation may apply. One of the best ways of documenting security requirements is for the customer to rely upon the structure provided by ISO27000 to document its requirements, going into greater detail than ISO27000 where relevant.

If the security requirements are stated in the form of a security policy, the customer should ensure that the supplier agrees to comply with the policy as a term of the agreement. The customer could also require the supplier to comply with the security policy as updated from time to time to ensure that security measures implemented by the supplier continue to reflect good practice as this evolves. The supplier may want to impose some limits on the changes the customer can introduce to its security policies so they do not exceed, for example, good practice in the industry.

Subject access requests: It is becoming increasingly common for the customer to require the supplier to assist it in responding to subject access requests and to inform the customer if an access request is received by the supplier. A subject access request is a request by an individual data subject for access to all personal data relating to that individual. It is for the customer (as controller) to respond to such requests but requests could be received by the supplier and, in any event, the customer may need the supplier's help in collating the relevant personal data to respond to a request.

International data transfers: The customer should prohibit the supplier from transferring customer data from the customer's home jurisdiction or, at least, the jurisdictions in the EEA. Where the supplier is certified under the US Safe Harbor Framework, the customer should require the supplier to warrant that it is so certified and that it will maintain the certification and notify the customer if the certification ceases for any reason or if any enforcement action is taken or investigation launched in respect of it.

Loss or corruption of data: If the customer's data is lost, it will need to be restored to a fully operational state. Usually, the customer should require the supplier to restore the data from backups or disaster recovery systems if the supplier is best placed to do this. The supplier should restore the data regardless of the cause and with all possible speed. The supplier will usually expect the customer to pay the reasonable costs of doing this if it is the result of the default or wilful act of the customer (or one of its group companies). In other cases, the customer should expect the supplier to pay for this.

Disposal of data: The customer should prohibit the supplier from disposing, reassigning or reusing any equipment or any electronic, magnetic or other medium which has been used to store customer data without ensuring that such data has been entirely removed or otherwise obliterated. This is an inherent security risk and one which, when things go wrong, can result in significant breach and enforcement risk.

Regulatory enquiries: The customer should require the supplier to inform it of any enquiry, complaint, notice or any communication received from a data protection regulator such as the ICO and assist it in responding.

Data breach: The customer should require the supplier to specifically notify it in the event of a data breach and provide all reasonable assistance including co-operating with data protection regulators and co-ordinating, if required, in relation to public relations.

Indemnity: It is increasingly common for the customer to require the supplier to indemnify it for any breach of the data privacy warranties or, as a minimum, those relating to data security. The limits of liability in respect of such indemnities are usually agreed at a higher level than the general limit of liability or the liability is agreed to be unlimited. Indemnity protection will help insure the customer against certain costs of a data breach (e.g. the costs of re-carding or ID theft in relation to a bank or credit card data breach) but it may be difficult to quantify the management time or loss of profits flowing from a data breach which can make these (potentially significant) losses difficult to claim. In addition, the customer should ensure that the indemnity also covers the risk of administrative penalties and fines although it will be for the relevant courts to decide the extent to which the indemnity can be enforced in respect of fines and penalties.

Sub-contractors: The customer should also require the supplier to ensure compliance with equivalent data security requirements by any approved sub-contractors and that it will put in place appropriate back-to-back arrangements to flow these requirements down to all sub-contractors.

37.2.1.4 *Confidentiality requirements*

The confidentiality requirements may include for example (in addition to the normal confidentiality undertaking) the following specific supplier obligations:

(a) Keeping a register of confidential information identified by the customer.
(b) Taking specified measures to ensure that the information is protected.
(c) Restricting the taking of certain documents off site.
(d) Restricting the printing of certain documents.
(e) Ensuring printed documents with confidential or sensitive data are disposed of securely in accordance with an agreed policy.
(f) Providing guidance on the destruction of confidential or sensitive data including specific guidance for staff travelling or working at home.

37.2.2   *During the term*

During the term of the services agreement, the customer will need to monitor the supplier's compliance with its data protection, data security and confidentiality obligations.[2]

In addition, the parties must review the security requirements on an ongoing basis (particularly given the speed with which technology has been evolving) and agree appropriate changes, where required to reflect good practice.

37.2.3   *On Termination*

On termination, the supplier should be obliged to hand back and/or destroy (at the election of the customer) all relevant customer data. The data should be supplied in a form and format that is either requested by the customer or reflects industry standards.[3]

37.3   Customer obligations

37.3.1   *During the procurement stage*

Chapter 3 discusses the supplier's confidentiality concerns during the procurement stage.

37.3.2   *During the term*

The supplier will want to document what information it regards as its confidential information and include in the contract an obligation for the customer to keep this information confidential. This should not be a contentious issue.

In the public sector, the supplier may want the customer to agree a list of commercially sensitive information which the supplier does not wish the customer to disclose under the Freedom of Information Act 2000. The customer may want to negotiate the list and confirm that the agreement of any list is without prejudice to its obligation to comply with the Freedom of Information Act 2000 itself.

---

[2]   See Chapter 10 for a detailed description of the governance of services arrangements.
[3]   See Chapter 27 for a detailed description of the termination process.

The situation is slightly more complicated if the supplier wishes the customer to take responsibility for the actions of third parties. In local authority situations, the customer will have to disclose details relating to the proposed arrangement to its elected members but will not want to take responsibility for the actions of the elected members, as it has no control over them.

All public sector bodies will have to ensure that confidentiality provisions enable them to disclose information to their auditors and to other regulators who may investigate them. Suppliers who work for public sector customers need to understand and co-operate with public sector audit requirements.

The supplier may also want the customer to commit to maintaining specified security measures to protect the supplier's assets and data.

37.3.3 On termination

Confidentiality issues are more likely to be contentious on termination. The customer will be anxious to make sure that it will have access to the information that it requires to ensure that the services can be provided by the customer itself or by a successor supplier. However, the supplier will want to ensure that its proprietary procedures and information, which it regards as giving it a competitive advantage over other suppliers, will not be disclosed. Usually, these issues are resolved in the context of the specific circumstances of the services agreement, before the agreement is signed.[4]

37.4 Publicity

In private sector services agreements, it is common for the customer and supplier to agree that neither party will publicise the agreement or arrangement without the approval of the other side. Suppliers may want to be able to refer to the agreement in their marketing material but be particularly anxious to ensure that customers do not publicise security breaches by the supplier.

In the public sector, the situation is more complex, in that a public sector body may want to reserve the right to publicise the agreement in accordance with any legal obligation and to comment on issues relating to the contract when it is deemed appropriate politically. However, the supplier may be extremely reluctant to allow the customer a right to comment on the services arrangement in circumstances where the supplier has no right to respond.

---

[4] See Chapter 27 for a detailed description of the termination process.

37.5 Security and data protection issues in the financial services sector and the public sector

This chapter and the previous one have described general data protection and security regulations and issues. Firms in the financial services sector are subject to additional regulation in the form of EU directives and FSA regulations, some of which relate to security issues. They are also subject to the supervision of the FSA, which has enforcement powers in excess of those of the Information Commissioner. These aspects of FSA regulation and others are described in the following chapters.

Part 10

Regulations

Chapter 38

Financial Services Sector: General Regulatory Principles

38.1 Outline

38.1.1 Scope

Chapters 38 to 46 describe requirements that will be relevant for specific sectors (the financial services sector, the public sector and the utilities sector), highlighting in addition any lessons that organisations which are not subject to such requirements can learn from the approach taken in the regulations.

Chapters 38 to 42 deal with the growing amount of regulation of the financial services sector. This chapter outlines the general principles of regulation affecting all firms in the financial services sector including general international guidance. Chapters 39 to 41 cover, respectively, specific regulation affecting banks and investment firms, insurance companies and investment funds and managers. Chapter 42 covers UK financial regulatory expectations relating to data security.

38.1.2 Application to the UK and other EU countries

The EU Directives and the international standards referred to in Chapters 38 to 42 will be relevant throughout the EU, although the chapters focus on how the relevant Directives have been implemented within the UK, mainly through the rules of the Financial Services Authority (FSA). The other FSA requirements mentioned in the chapters will apply to the UK only.

38.1.3 Key themes

Although this guide covers services and outsourcing contracts, the regulations mainly focus on outsourcing. It should be borne in mind that the regulations and guidance affecting outsourcing arrangements are several hundred pages in length. Chapters 38 to 41 summarise the key issues covered by the relevant regulations. They cannot be comprehensive. In particular, they focus on the following key themes in the regulations:

(a) outsourcing policies;
(b) processes and systems;
(c) notifications to the FSA;
(d) due diligence;
(e) written agreement between service provider and firm;
(f) control over service provider's employees and sub-contractors;
(g) service management;
(h) change management;
(i) disclosure and audit;
(j) confidential information, intellectual property rights (IPR) and security;
(k) business continuity;
(l) rights of termination;
(m) termination assistance; and
(n) offshore outsourcing.

They do not deal with specific issues such as those relating to the outsourcing of a controlled function, outsourcing of a firm's internal audit function, use of third-party processors in home finance and insurance or use of a rating system or data.

The FSA's rules are part of its *Handbook of Rules and Guidance*, which can be found on the FSA's website (*http://www.fsa.gov.uk/pages/handbook* [Accessed 24 September 2012]). The rules particularly relevant to outsourcing agreements are in the *Senior Management Arrangements, Systems and Controls* part of the Handbook (SYSC).

38.1.4 Consistency

Chapters 38 to 42 demonstrate that the outsourcing provisions of the Markets in Financial Instruments Directive (MiFID)[1] which deal with the investment activities of credit institutions and investment firms (and which also includes specific principles relating to portfolio management outsourcing), the Alternative Investment Fund Managers Directive (AIFMD),[2] which deals with managers of non-UCITS investment funds, the UCITS Consolidation Directive,[3] Solvency II,[4] which deals with insurers, SYSC 8, SYSC 13, the Principles of the Joint Forum of the Basel Committee on Banking Supervision and the International Organisation of Securities Commissions (IOSCO), the IOSCO principles and the Guidelines of the then Committee of

---

[1] Directive 2004/39/EC
[2] Directive 2011/61/EU
[3] Directive 2009/65/EU
[4] Directive 2009/138/EC

European Banking Supervisors (CEBS), now the European Banking Authority (EBA) are broadly consistent.

38.1.5   *Best practice*

The FSA's view is that its rules reflect best practice in outsourcing and this is no doubt correct in many cases.

38.1.6   *Contentious*

Some rules or recommendations are particularly contentious with service providers, in particular the audit provisions, the provisions regarding control over the service provider's employees and sub-contractors and the termination provisions.

Both service providers and firms have raised issues with the provisions relating to concentration risk, the issue being that the firm has a duty to use service providers with the appropriate expertise. A service provider with the appropriate expertise is likely to be used by other firms and this increases the concentration risk.

38.1.7   *Not exhaustive*

It should be stressed that, as the regulatory requirements include a non-exhaustive list of issues mainly concerned with controlling operational risk, there are numerous other key issues which firms will need to consider to ensure that their outsourcing arrangements are successful, for example issues of liability, limitations of liability, TUPE, preparation of the service description, charging and service credit issues and protections against service provider insolvency.

38.2   FSA's interest in outsourcing

The FSA's interest in how firms use outsourcing remains keen. It has reminded firms of the risks associated with outsourcing in several contexts:

(a)   In the context of its integrated approach to stress testing,[5] stating that:

---

[5]   FSA's emphasis on the importance of stress testing has been driven by Europe, in particular the CEBS (now European Banking Authority (EBA) stress testing of banks EU-wide, of which there have now been two rounds, with the latest results published in July 2011. It introduced new rules on stress testing generally at the end of 2009, but no new rule applies specifically to outsourcing.

"Outsourcing presents specific issues for firms regardless of their size, both in normal circumstances and more so when a firm encounters the effects of a stressed environment. A firm's dependence on an external provider may result in the firm being susceptible to risk factors above and beyond those that directly affect it and over which it might be able to exert some influence and control. Firms retain responsibility for identifying and managing risks that exist in their outsourced operations and should recognise this in their stress testing exercises – firms cannot transfer responsibility to the providers of outsourced services to anticipate potential threats to outsourced services, but should engage fully with the providers to comprehensively assess any risks that might arise in stressed circumstances."

(b) In the context of transaction reporting,[6] stating that:

"If a firm outsources critical or important operational functions or any relevant services and activities, it remains fully responsible for discharging all of its obligations under the regulatory system. See Chapter 8 of the Senior Management Arrangements, Systems and Controls (SYSC) sourcebook (SYSC 8.1.6R). Outsourcing may present risks to transaction reporting because the party providing the outsourcing services may not have robust governance arrangements and internal control mechanisms that a transaction reporting firm may have in place to control the accuracy and completeness of its reporting.

For transaction reporting purposes, reporting firms may outsource the submission of their transaction reports to a third party (also known as the submitting firm). Where a firm outsources the submission of its transactions to a third party who is not party to the transaction and only serves as a channel to submit the reports to the FSA, the reporting firm has the ultimate obligation of ensuring the transaction reports we receive are accurate and complete. To meet this obligation, we expect the reporting firm to ensure that it has effective procedures for checking the accuracy and completeness of its reports; this may extend to checking the service provided by the submitting firm."

Firms in the financial services sector who enter into services agreements should note that FSA's enforcement attitude is becoming increasingly harsh. Focusing on a theme of "credible deterrence", it levies large fines and, at worst, bans, on firms and relevant approved individuals who have breached its rules—sometimes regardless of whether the breach has resulted in actual harm to customers. When the FSA is replaced by the Prudential Regulation Authority and Financial Conduct Authority (which is expected to happen in 2013), there is every indication that the current attitude to enforcement will remain. So it is in the interests of all senior individuals involved with the firm's systems and controls and specifically with its services agreements to ensure all relevant regulatory standards are met.

---

[6] Market Watch Newsletter No. 38

The FSA has also been granted financial stability information-gathering powers under the Financial Services Act 2010. The regulator was concerned that over time a large number of firms may increasingly come to rely on a single service provider for critical services. The FSA has noted that its information-gathering power could enable it to assess concentration risk in terms of the number of firms using the same provider or geographical location, which may impact financial stability.

38.3   Definition of outsourcing

In the FSA Handbook, outsourcing is defined (except in SYSC 8, FSA's Personal Account dealing rules in COBS and its definition of a "relevant person") as:

> "the use of a person to provide customised services to a firm other than:
>
> (a)   a member of the firm's governing body acting in his capacity as such; or
>
> (b)   an individual employed by a firm under a contract of service."

In the MiFID Implementing Directive,[7] from which FSA's definition stems and which is further discussed in Chapter 39, outsourcing is defined as

> "an arrangement of any form between a firm and a service provider by which that service provider performs a process, a service or an activity which would otherwise be taken by the firm itself."[8]

38.4   High level Principle 3—organisation of affairs and risk management

FSA's Principle 3 of its Principles for Businesses sets out the high level principle which requires a firm to take reasonable care to organise and control its affairs responsibly and effectively, with adequate risk management systems. In practice, breach of the other guidance on outsourcing in the FSA Handbook will be seen as breach of Principle 3.

---

[7]   Commission Directive No. 2006/73/EC Implementing Directive 2004/39/EC of the European Parliament and of the Council as regards organisational requirements and operating conditions for investment firms and defined terms for the purposes of that Directive ("MiFID Implementing Directive").

[8]   Article 2(6) of the MiFID Implementing Directive.

38.5   Reputational risk

The prudential sourcebooks outline risks specific to particular types of business or firm that firms should consider. The *Prudential Sourcebook for Banks, Building Societies and Investment Firms (BIPRU)* para.2.2.62G requires an asset management firm, when assessing reputational risk to consider issues such as how poor customer services can affect its financial position. For example, a firm which has outsourced the management of customer accounts may want to consider the impact on its own reputation of the service provider failing to deliver the service.

38.6   Systems and controls

SYSC (primarily in Chapter 3 for insurers and Chapters 4 to 7 for common platform firms (those covered by MiFID and the CRD) requires a firm to take reasonable care to establish and maintain appropriate systems and controls. In an outsourcing context, this means that a firm must obtain sufficient information from the service providers to assess the impact of outsourcing on its systems and controls.[9]

38.7   Internal controls

SYSC requires all firms to have in place robust internal controls. These are discussed in Chapter 39 for non-insurers and Chapter 40 for insurers.

38.8   Responsibility for regulatory obligations

The FSA is particularly concerned that firms which outsource their activities may suffer some loss of control over them.

A firm cannot contract out of its regulatory obligations. So, for example, under Principle 3, a firm should take reasonable care to supervise the discharge of outsourced functions by its service provider.

38.9   Business continuity

A firm should have in place appropriate arrangements, having regard to the nature, scale and complexity of its business, to ensure that it can continue to function and meet its regulatory obligations in the event of an unforeseen

---

[9]   FSA CP142/02 discussed the actions a firm should consider.

interruption. These arrangements should be regularly updated and tested to ensure their effectiveness. (See SYSC 3 for insurers and SYSC paras 4.1.6 and 4.1.7 for common platform firms).

38.10   Record keeping

38.10.1   *Records to be retained*

FSA's rules generally require a firm to take reasonable care to make and retain adequate records. (SYSC 9 sets out general record-keeping requirements for all common platform firms).

The FSA Handbook includes various detailed record-keeping requirements, which are summarised in Sch.1 to each module of the Handbook.

38.10.2   *Retention periods*

A firm should have appropriate systems and controls in place to fulfil the firm's regulatory and statutory obligations with respect to adequacy, access, periods of retention and security of records. The general principle is that records should be retained for as long as is relevant for the purposes for which they are made. (See SYSC 3 for insurers and SYSC para.9.1 for common platform firms.)

The FSA Handbook contains extensive provisions relating to the retention and treatment of records, each being linked to the type of record or transaction. These general provisions are not covered in this guide.

38.11   Notification

Principle 11 requires a firm to deal with its regulators in an open and co-operative way and to disclose to the FSA appropriately anything relating to the firm of which the FSA would reasonably expect notice.

SUP para.15.3.8G clarifies that compliance with Principle 11 includes, but is not limited to, giving the FSA notice of any proposed restructuring, reorganisation or business expansion which could have a significant impact on the firm's risk profile or resources, including, but not limited to entering into, or significantly changing, a material outsourcing arrangement.

A material outsourcing arrangement is defined as

"outsourcing services of such importance that weakness, or failure, of the services would cast serious doubt upon a firm's continuing satisfaction of the threshold conditions or compliance with the Principles".

38.12   Audit arrangements

The FSA imposes upon firms that enter into material outsourcing agreements an obligation to take reasonable steps to ensure that the service provider:

(a)   provides access, with or without notice, during reasonable business hours to any of its business premises (SUP para.2.3.5R);

(b)   deals in an open and co-operative way with the FSA (SUP para.2.3.7R);

(c)   makes itself readily available for meetings with the FSA if reasonably requested (SUP para.2.3.3G);

(d)   gives the FSA reasonable access to any records, files, tapes or computer systems, which are within the service provider's possession or control, and provides any facilities which the FSA reasonably requests (SUP para.2.3.3G);

(e)   produces to the FSA specified documents, files, tapes, computer data or other material in the service provider's possession or control as reasonably requested (SUP para.2.3.3G);

(f)   prints information in the service provider's possession or control which is held on computer or on microfilm or otherwise converts it into a readily legible document or any other record which the FSA reasonably requests (SUP para.2.3.3G);

(g)   permits the FSA to copy documents or other material on the premises of the service provider and to remove copies and hold them elsewhere, or provides any copies, as reasonably requested (SUP para.2.3.3G); and

(h)   answers truthfully, fully and promptly all questions which are reasonably put to it by representatives or appointees of the FSA (SUP para.2.3.3G).

The FSA Handbook acknowledges that, in some circumstances, a firm may find it beneficial to use externally validated reports commissioned by the service provider, to seek comfort as to the adequacy and effectiveness of its systems and controls. However, it is stressed that the use of such reports does not absolve the firm of responsibility to maintain any other oversight. In addition, the firm should not normally have to forfeit the right for it or its agents to gain access to the service provider's premises. (See SYSC para.13.9.7G in relation to insurers)

38.13 Outsourcing of a controlled function

If the outsourcing services involve the provision of a controlled function, then the outsourcing arrangement falls within the "approved persons" regime. This means that the regulated firm will need to obtain approval from the FSA for any person who performs the controlled function. It is outside the scope of this guide to describe the approved person's regime in greater detail.

38.14 Segregation of duties

38.14.1 *Common platform firm*

A common platform firm must ensure that the performance of multiple functions by its relevant persons does not and is not likely to prevent those persons from discharging any particular functions soundly, honestly and professionally.[10] (SYSC para.5.1.6R)

The senior personnel of a common platform firm must define arrangements concerning the segregation of duties within the firm and the prevention of conflicts of interest.[11] (SYSC para.5.1.7R)

38.14.2 *Insurers*

When determining the adequacy of its internal controls, a firm should consider both the potential risks that might hinder the achievement of the objectives listed in SYSC para.14.1.28G, and the extent to which it needs to control these risks. More specifically, this should normally include consideration of the need for adequate segregation of duties (see SYSC para.3.2.5G and SYSC para.14.1.30G–SYSC 14.1.33G). (SYSC para.14.1.29G)

---

[10] Article 5(1)g of the MiFID Implementing Directive.
[11] Annex 1 para.V of the Banking Consolidation Directive.

38.15   International guidance

38.15.1   Outline

38.15.1.1   International guidance

Outsourcing has attracted considerable international regulatory interest in recent years. In addition to the EU regulations described above:

(a)   The Joint Forum established a set of high level, voluntary principles designed to provide a minimum standard against which firms in the banking, securities and insurance sectors can evaluate their approach to outsourcing. It also sets out broad guidance for regulators in dealing with outsourcing. The Joint Forum has also released a paper on High Level Principles of Business Continuity.[12] The Joint Forum was established in 1996 under the aegis of the Basel Committee on Banking Supervision, IOSCO and the IAIS to deal with issues common to the banking, securities and insurance sectors. The UK representative is the FSA.

(b)   IOSCO, an international association of securities regulators, produced a set of principles on outsourcing, aimed at securities companies, which are designed to be complementary to the Joint Forum's set of principles. The member agencies currently assembled together in the International Organisation of Securities Commissions have resolved, through its permanent structures to co-operate to promote high standards of regulation in order to maintain just, efficient and sound markets, to exchange information on their respective experiences in order to promote the development of domestic markets, to unite their efforts to establish standards and an effective surveillance of international securities transactions and to provide mutual assistance to promote the integrity of the markets by a rigorous application of the standards and by effective enforcement against offences. The UK member is the FSA. The US member is the Securities and Exchange Commission (SEC).

38.15.1.2   Sector-specific guidance

Sector-specific guidance on outsourcing includes the following:

(a)   On 14 December 2006, the then CEBS published Guidelines on Outsourcing aimed at credit institutions' business activities. The Guidelines take into account international initiatives, such as the work by the Joint Forum, and EU initiatives, such as MiFID. CEBS also issued a "mapping" document to ensure the standards are compatible with MiFID.

(b)   In January 2008 the Hedge Funds Working Group (HFWG) published its Final Report intended to assist hedge fund managers by setting out

---

[12]   See *http://www.iosco.org/library/pubdocs/pdf/IOSCOPD224.pdf* [Accessed 25 September 2012].

revised best practice standards (the "Standards") based on the results of consultation it carried out in October 2007.

38.15.1.3   *Relationship between the different guidance*

There is considerable overlap and cross-fertilisation between the various regulatory groups. For example, the FSA participates as a member or as a technical adviser in CESR, Bank of International Settlements—Basel Committee, EBA, IOSCO and the Joint Forum.

Regulators and central banks from other jurisdictions participate in a similar way. These organisations either have direct influence upon developing legislation, for example as members of the (now) European Securities and Markets Authority (ESMA) ((formerly the Committee of European Securities Regulators (CESR)) has the mandate under MiFID on level 2 technical advice, or can influence industry standard (e.g. the Basel Committee).

38.15.2   *Joint Forum principles*

A summary of the Joint Forum principles is set out in Table 55.

Table 55 Joint Forum principles

Outsourcing policy

I.   A regulated entity seeking to outsource activities should have in place a comprehensive policy to guide the assessment of whether and how those activities can be appropriately outsourced. The board of directors or equivalent body retains responsibility for the outsourcing policy and related overall responsibility for activities undertaken under that policy.

Risk management

II.   The regulated entity should establish a comprehensive outsourcing risk management programme to address the outsourced activities and the relationship with the service provider.

Obligations and supervision

III.   The regulated entity should ensure that outsourcing arrangements neither diminish its ability to fulfil its obligations to customers and regulators, nor impede effective supervision by regulators.

Due diligence

IV.   The regulated entity should conduct appropriate due diligence in selecting third-party service providers.

Written contracts

V.   Outsourcing relationships should be governed by written contracts that clearly describe all material aspects of the outsourcing arrangement, including the rights, responsibilities and expectations of all parties.

Business continuity

VI.   The regulated entity and its service providers should establish and maintain contingency plans, including a plan for disaster recovery and periodic testing of backup facilities.

Confidentiality

VII.   The regulated entity should take appropriate steps to require that service providers protect confidential information of both the regulated entity and its clients from intentional or inadvertent disclosure to unauthorised persons.

> **Regulatory supervision**
> VIII.   Regulators should take into account outsourcing activities as an integral part of their ongoing assessment of the regulated entity. Regulators should assure themselves by appropriate means that any outsourcing arrangements do not hamper the ability of a regulated entity to meet its regulatory requirements.
> **Risks of outsourcing**
> IX.   Regulators should be aware of the potential risks posed where the outsourced activities of multiple regulated entities are concentrated within a limited number of service providers.

The Basel Committee, in its June 2011 paper on Principles for the Sound Management of Operational Risk,[13] built on some of the 2005 Principles. It stresses that outsourcing policies and risk management activities should encompass:

(a)   procedures for determining whether and how activities can be outsourced;

(b)   processes for conducting due diligence in the selection of potential service providers;

(c)   sound structuring of the outsourcing arrangement, including ownership and confidentiality of data, as well as termination rights;

(d)   programmes for managing and monitoring the risks associated with the outsourcing arrangement, including the financial condition of the service provider;

(e)   establishment of an effective control environment at the bank and the service provider;

(f)   development of viable contingency plans; and

(g)   execution of comprehensive contracts and/or service level agreements with a clear allocation of responsibilities between the outsourcing provider and the bank.

38.15.3   IOSCO principles

The key IOSCO principles are set out in Table 56.[14]

Table 56 IOSCO principles

> **Topic 1: Due diligence in selection and monitoring of service provider and service provider's performance**
> Principle: An outsourcing firm should conduct suitable due diligence processes in selecting an appropriate third-party service provider and in monitoring its ongoing performance.
> **Topic 2: The contract with a service provider**

---

[13]   See *http://www.bis.org/publ/bcbs195.pdf* [Accessed 25 September 2012]

[14]   IOSCO also published a paper looking at the practices of funds of hedge funds, including in relation to outsourcing. The paper is at *http://www.iosco.org/library/pubdocs/pdf/IOSCOPD276.pdf* [Accessed 25 September 2012]

Principle: There should be a legally binding written contract between the outsourcing firm and each third-party service provider, the nature and detail of which should be appropriate to the materiality of the outsourced activity to the ongoing business of the outsourcing firm.

Topic 3: Information technology security and business continuity at the outsourcing firm

Principle: The outsourcing firm should take appropriate measures to determine that procedures are in place to protect the outsourcing firm's proprietary and customer-related information and software; and its service providers establish and maintain emergency procedures and a plan for disaster recovery, with periodic testing of backup facilities.

Topic 4: Client confidentiality issues

Principle: The outsourcing firm should take appropriate steps to require that service providers protect confidential information regarding the outsourcing firm's proprietary and other information, as well as the outsourcing firm's clients, from intentional or inadvertent disclosure to unauthorised individuals.

Topic 5: Concentration of outsourcing functions

Principle: Regulators should be cognisant of the risks posed where one service provider provides outsourcing services to multiple regulated entities. See comments in Table 59 about concentration risk.

Topic 6: Termination procedures

Principle: Outsourcing with third-party service providers should include contractual provisions relating to termination of the contract and appropriate exit strategies.

Topic 7: Regulator's and intermediary's access to books and records, including rights of inspection

Principle: The regulator, the firm, and its auditors should have access to the books and records of service providers relating to the outsourced activities and the regulator should be able to obtain promptly, upon request, information concerning activities that are relevant to regulatory oversight.

38.15.4   CEBS/EBA Guidelines

The CEBS/EBA guidelines are set out in Table 57. The Guidelines on Outsourcing can be found at *http://www.eba.europa.eu* [Accessed 25 September 2012].

Table 57 Committee of European Banking Supervisors Guidelines

Guideline 2—responsibility

The ultimate responsibility for the proper management of the risks associated with outsourcing or the outsourced activities lies with an outsourcing institution's senior management.

Guideline 3—no delegation

Outsourcing arrangements can never result in the delegation of senior management's responsibility.

Guideline 4—restrictions on outsourcing

4.1   An authorised entity may not outsource services and activities concerning the acceptance of deposits or to lending requiring a licence from the supervisory authority according to the applicable national banking law unless the service provider either: (i) has an authorisation that is equivalent to the authorisation of the outsourcing institution; or (ii) is otherwise allowed to carry out those activities in accordance with the relevant national legal framework.

4.2   Any area of activity of an outsourcing institution other than those identified in Guidelines 2 and 3 may be outsourced provided that such outsourcing does not impair:

(a)   the orderliness of the conduct of the outsourcing institution's business or of the financial services provided;

(b)   the senior management's ability to manage and monitor the authorised entity's business and its authorised activities;

(c)   the ability of other internal governance bodies, such as the board of directors or the audit committee, to fulfil their oversight tasks in relation to the senior management; and

(d)   the supervisory authority's ability to fulfil its supervisory tasks.

4.3   An outsourcing institution should take particular care when outsourcing material activities. The outsourcing institution should adequately inform its supervisory authority about this type of outsourcing.

Guideline 5—no other restrictions on non-material outsourcing

There should be no restrictions on the outsourcing of non-material activities of an outsourcing institution.

Guideline 6—outsourcing policy

6.1   The outsourcing institution should have a policy on its approach to outsourcing, including contingency plans and exit strategies.

6.2   An outsourcing institution should conduct its business in a controlled and sound manner at all times.

Guideline 7—risk management

An outsourcing institution should manage the risks associated with its outsourcing arrangements.

Guideline 8—written contract

All outsourcing arrangements should be subject to a formal and comprehensive contract. The outsourcing contract should oblige the service provider to protect confidential information.

Guideline 9—service management

In managing its relationship with an outsourcing service provider an outsourcing institution should ensure that a written agreement is put in place. This should include definitions of the responsibilities of the parties and quality descriptions. The agreement should contain a mixture of quantitative and qualitative performance targets.

Guideline 10—chain outsourcing

10.1   The outsourcing institution should take account of the risks associated with "chain" outsourcing.

10.2   The outsourcing institution should agree to chain outsourcing only if the subcontractor will also fully comply with the obligations existing between the outsourcing institution and the service provider, including obligations incurred in favour of the supervisory authority.

10.3   The outsourcing institution should take appropriate steps to address the risk of any weakness or failure in the provision of the subcontracted activities having a significant effect on the service provider's ability to meet its responsibilities under the outsourcing agreement and SLA.

Part 3: Guidelines on outsourcing addressed to supervisory authorities

Guideline 11—audit

Supervisory authorities should require that the outsourcing institution has established supervisory authority access to relevant data held by the service provider and, where provided for by the national law, the right for the supervisory authority to conduct onsite inspections at a service provider's premises.

Guideline 12—concentration risk

Supervisory authorities should take account of concentration risk.

38.15.5   *Hedge Funds Working Group*

Standards 19 and 20 of the HFWG Final Report are summarised in Table 58.

Table 58 Hedge Fund Standards 19 and 20

Governance Standards Guidance (19)

A hedge fund manager should ensure that careful due diligence on third-party service providers is conducted before recommending them to the fund governing body.

This could include using Due Diligence Questionnaires or evaluating "reports on controls" from an independent reporting accountant issued by the respective third-party service provider.

A hedge fund manager should do what it reasonably can to enable and encourage the fund governing body to review third-party service providers properly and regularly.

Valuation and administration

A hedge fund manager should, where appropriate, do what it reasonably can to enable and encourage the fund to put a service level agreement (SLA) in place with relevant service providers (commonly, this will be attached as a schedule to the agreement between the fund and the relevant service provider).

An SLA would normally be expected to:

– set out in precise detail the services to be provided by the relevant service provider along with deadlines for completion of the services;

– make clear accountability and responsibility for the orderly operation of all administration or other functions performed by the relevant service provider on behalf of investors; and

– include "Key Performance Indicators" to provide hedge fund managers and fund governing bodies with a means of measuring whether the objectives set out in the SLA are met by the relevant service provider.

Further examples of the contents of SLAs are provided in Appendix J of the Hedge Funds Standards: Final Report. (Examples of functions often covered by service level agreements).

A hedge fund manager should do what it reasonably can to enable and encourage the fund governing body to review the services provided by the relevant service provider against contractual or other agreed standards.

Prime brokers

A hedge fund manager of a large hedge fund should carefully consider whether it is appropriate for the hedge fund to appoint more than one prime broker (taking into account in particular the potential advantages of diversification of funding and other services) and do what it reasonably can to enable and encourage the fund governing body to act accordingly.

HFSB is aware that there is a spectrum of criteria to consider when choosing a prime broker, including efficiency and operational risk considerations.

In carrying out due diligence on a prime broker, a hedge fund manager should consider the potential prime broker's credit rating, policy on re-hypothecation and general ability to fulfil all process functions accurately and efficiently.

Auditors

A hedge fund manager should do what it reasonably can to enable and encourage the fund governing body to appoint reputable auditors.

In addition to the Standards set out in this report, AIMA provides further guidance in its Guide to Sound Practices for European Hedge Fund Managers, (2007) (Chapter 3.8).

Disclosure Standards and Guidance (20)

A hedge fund manager should disclose the names of its principal third-party service providers in its due diligence documents or upon request.

A hedge fund manager should, to the extent it is able or permitted to do so, provide information on the fund's committed funding or financing arrangements with prime brokers/lenders to investors in its due diligence documents or upon request.

A hedge fund manager should disclose the nature of any special commercial terms with its third-party service providers which result in potential conflicts of interest (e.g. in-house brokerage or rebates).

A hedge fund manager to the extent applicable should disclose the monitoring procedures in relation to its third-party service providers in its due diligence documents or upon request.

> *In addition to the Standards set out in this report, AIMA provides further guidance in its Guide to Sound Practices for European Hedge Fund Managers, (2007) (Chapter 3.8).*

38.16   Lessons for customers not regulated by the FSA

Can customers who are not regulated by the FSA learn any lessons from the guidance? The FSA guidance is interesting because of its emphasis upon the need for flexibility as a result of the great variety of outsourcing arrangements. This is a point which this Guide has also taken care to stress. However, the concern to ensure flexibility has meant that much of the FSA guidance is extremely high level.

There are a few instances of specific advice. In particular, customers outside the financial services sector may like to take into account the suggestions that, if they outsource business continuity services, they should evaluate the likelihood and impact of multiple calls on shared resources.

The FSA's approach of analysing the effect of the outsourcing agreement upon the customer's operational risk is also an interesting approach, which may be helpful for other sectors.

Lastly, the FSA's insistence that firms may need to retain certain controls over the supplier supports the argument raised in Chapter 7 that there may be circumstances when the customer will need control over the manner in which the services are provided.

38.17   Shari'ah compliant outsourcing

Where the outsourcing agreement is carried out with regard to customers offering Shari'ah compliant products, specific concerns will arise, including those relating to the payment of interest, liquidated damages, service credits, additional governance regimes and specific approval of the agreement.

Chapter 39

Specific regulation affecting Banks and Investment Firms

39.1 Outline

This chapter describes specific EU directives that affect banks and investment firms, namely MiFID and CRD, and discussed their application to FSA-regulated firms. Banks and investment firms are referred to in SYSC as "common platform firms" as they are subject to both MiFID and the CRD. Many of the SYSC "common platform" requirements, however, apply equally to other regulated firms (such as investment managers).

SYSC para.4.1.1R states a common platform firm must have robust governance arrangements, which include a clear organisational structure. The structure should:

(a) be well defined with transparent and consistent lines of responsibility;

(b) have effective processes to identify, manage, monitor and report the risks it is or might be exposed to; and

(c) contain internal control mechanisms, including sound administrative and accounting procedures and effective control and safeguard arrangements for information processing systems.

The arrangements must address specific risks described in SYSC, including risk management procedures and business continuity arrangements. BIPRU firms must also ensure that their internal control mechanisms and administrative and accounting procedures permit the verification of compliance with rules adopted in accordance with the Capital Adequacy Directive at all times. (SYSC para.4.1.3R)

This chapter also describes the "living wills" regulations and their implication for outsourcing.

39.2   MiFID

39.2.1   Background to MiFID

MiFID replaced the Investment Services Directive of 1993. It is part of the EU's Financial Services Action Plan, which was intended to create an integrated market for financial services throughout the EU, in which investors are effectively protected and the efficiency and integrity of the overall market are safeguarded.

MiFID is currently under review, and in October 2011 the European Commission published a proposal to amend it. One of the major effects would be to bring more businesses and activities within its scope. While the proposals published to date contain little specific changes to outsourcing requirements, the reach of regulation will be wider, catching more outsourcing arrangements within its scope. The MiFID Review forms part of the plans for overhaul of financial regulation, and the EU is committed to adopting the changes as soon as possible. It stated a hope for political agreement on the changes by the end of 2011, but there was a delay. Final legislation by the end of 2012 is still the goal.

39.2.2   Application

39.2.2.1   Application to firms

Outsourcing by retail banks, investment banks, venture capital firms, stockbrokers, investment managers, proprietary trading firms, corporate finance firms, wholesale market brokers and the providers of custody services that provide investment services or which undertake investment activities will be governed by MiFID. Where the firms that provide the services are "investment firms" under MiFID or are "credit institutions" prudential regulation will come from the Banking Consolidation Directive.

39.2.2.2   Definition of investment services and activities

Investment services are covered by MiFID. Investment services and activities include (Annex 1 Section A of MiFID):

(a)   reception and transmission of orders in relation to one or more financial instruments;
(b)   execution of orders on behalf of clients;
(c)   dealing on own account;
(d)   portfolio management;
(e)   investment advice;

(f)   underwriting of financial instruments and/or placing of financial instruments on a firm commitment basis;

(g)   placing of financial instruments without a firm commitment basis; and

(h)   operation of multilateral trading facilities.

39.2.2.3   *Ancillary services*

MiFID also includes a range of ancillary services. Where ancillary services are covered by MiFID, an investment firm can apply for passporting[1] rights that include ancillary services, but only if these are carried on together with one or more investment services and activities.

Ancillary services include (Annex 1 Section B of MiFID):

(a)   safekeeping and administration of financial instruments for the account of clients, including custodianship and related services such as cash/collateral management;

(b)   granting credits or loans to an investor to allow them to carry out a transaction in one or more financial instruments, where the firm granting the credit or loan is involved in the transaction;

(c)   advice to undertakings on capital structure, industrial strategy and related matters and advice and services relating to mergers and the purchase of undertakings;

(d)   foreign exchange services where these are connected to the provision of investment services;

(e)   investment research and financial analysis or other forms of general recommendation relating to transactions in financial instruments;

(f)   services related to underwriting; and

(g)   investment services and activities as well as ancillary services related to the underlying of certain derivatives and connected to the provision of investment or ancillary services.

39.2.3   *Exemptions*

There are various exemptions from the application of MiFID, for example:

(a)   Article 2 of MiFID contains various exemptions relevant to a wide range of persons, services and activities including insurers, group treasurers, members of professions providing incidental investment services, professional investors who invest only for themselves, company pension schemes, collective investment undertakings and their operators, commodity producers, commodity traders and locals; and

---

[1]   Passporting permits a firm which has the right to perform a particular function in one EU country to perform the same function in another EU country (a "third country").

(b) Article 3 of MiFID creates an optional exemption for certain receivers, transmitters and advisers who do not hold client money or securities and comply with other prescribed conditions.

Where investment funds are concerned, a key point to note here is that the fund itself will not be covered by MiFID. MiFID catches those who manage or advise funds insofar as those advisers are investment firms. It does not matter where the fund is situated. Only the investment firm itself is caught by MiFID to the extent that its critical functions are outsourced. Under the proposals to revise MiFID, some of the Article 2 exemptions will be removed entirely or will apply more narrowly, which would have the effect of bringing more businesses within the scope of both MiFID and the FSA's rules.

39.2.4 *Levels of legislation*

MiFID is a so-called "Lamfalussy Directive". This is a type of legislation that follows a process to allow the Council of Ministers and Parliament to focus on key political decisions. The technical implementing details are worked through afterwards. This is why the Directive is split into two levels.

The Level 1 Directive is intended to set out broad, general "framework" principles.

The Level 2 Directive contains "technical implementing measures". The intention is that Level 2 implementing measures should be used more frequently, to ensure that the technical provisions can be kept up to date with market and supervisory developments. Regulators are expected to issue interpretative guidance on provisions in the Level 2 Directive to clarify the practical application of the requirements in the Directive. The Commission and the European Securities and Markets Authority (ESMA) (formerly the Committee of European Securities Regulators (CESR)) may also issue guidance on the Directive, and there is an increasing move towards ESMA issuing standards in its own name. CESR had the mandate under MiFID to provide level 2 technical advice. Its advice will be transcribed into legislation and from there it will flow into the implementation procedures adopted by the regulator in each EU Member State. Following a change to the European Supervisory Architecture from the beginning of 2011, ESMA will in future, and in relation to MiFID 2, have more intrusive and direct powers.

MiFID and its Level 2 measures had to be implemented by November 2007.

The remainder of this section addresses the provisions of the current MiFID Level 1 and 2 Directives, with reference to the FSA's implementing rules.

39.2.5   Key elements of the Level 1 Directive relating to outsourcing

Table 59 summarises some of the key elements of the Level 1 legislation.

Table 59 MiFID Level 1 Directive

Article 13(5)—Critical outsourcing—obligation to avoid undue additional operational risk
A firm must take reasonable steps to avoid undue additional operational risk arising from the outsourcing of critical operational functions.
Critical operational functions are defined as those operational functions which are critical for the provision of continuous and satisfactory service to clients and the performance of investment activities on a continuous and satisfactory basis.
A firm must ensure that outsourcing of "important" operational functions is not carried out in a way which materially impairs the quality of a firm's internal controls or the regulator's ability to monitor the firm's compliance with its obligations.
Article 13(2)—Outsourcing of investment services—obligation to have adequate policies and procedures
The firm must establish adequate policies and procedures sufficient to ensure compliance of the firm including its managers and employees and tied agents with its obligations under the Directive, as well as appropriate rules governing personal transactions by such persons

39.2.6   Other relevant requirements

The Directive contains other general organisational requirements which are of general application but which will also be relevant to a firm considering an outsourcing project. These are described in Table 60.

Table 60 Other relevant requirements

Business continuity
The firm must take reasonable steps to ensure continuity and regularity in the performance of investment services and activities (Article 13(4)).
General requirements
The firm must have sound administrative and accounting procedures, internal control mechanisms, effective procedures for risk assessment and effective control and safeguard arrangements for information processing systems (Article 13(5)).

39.2.7   Key elements of the Level 2 Directive

The following paragraphs summarise some of the key provisions in the Level 2 Directive.

39.2.7.1   When outsourcing is permitted

The MiFID Implementing Directive specifies that regulators should not make the authorisation to provide investment services or activities subject to a general prohibition on the outsourcing of one or more critical or important functions or investment services or activities. Investment firms should be allowed to outsource such activities if the outsourcing arrangements established by the firm comply with certain conditions

However, if the outsourcing of critical or important operational functions or investment services or activities would lead to a delegation of functions to such an extent that the firm becomes a "letter-box entity" then this should be considered to undermine the firm's authorisation conditions. (Article 5 MiFID, and see below for the detail of Article 14 of the Level 2 Directive.)

39.2.7.2   Notification

The outsourcing of investment services or activities of critical and important functions is capable of constituting a material change of the conditions for the authorisation of the investment firm, as referred to in Article 16(2) of the Level 1 Directive. If such outsourcing arrangements are to be put in place after the firm has obtained an authorisation, the outsourcing arrangements should be notified to the competent authority where required by Article 16(2) of the Level 1 Directive.

39.2.7.3   Risk management policy

The preamble to the MiFID Implementing Directive makes it clear that outsourcing is of such concern that it is necessary to "specify concrete organisational requirements and procedures for investment firms involved in outsourcing".

This takes the form of a requirement for a firm to establish, implement and maintain an adequate risk management policy that should cover risks associated with the outsourcing of critical or important functions or of investment services or activities. Such risks should include those associated with the firm's relationship with the service provider and the potential risks posed where the outsourced activities of multiple investment firms or other regulated entities are concentrated within a limited number of suppliers.

39.2.7.4   Meaning of critical and important operational functions

An operational function shall be regarded as critical or important if a defect or failure in its performance would materially impair the continuing compliance of an investment firm with the conditions and obligations of its authorisation or its other obligations under the Level 1 Directive, or its financial performance, or the soundness or the continuity of its investment services and activities.

The following functions shall not be considered as critical or important (Article 13, implemented in SYSC para.8.1.5R):

(a)   the provision to the firm of advisory services, and other services which do not form part of the investment business of the firm, including the provision of legal advice to the firm, the training of personnel of the firm, billing services and the security of the firm's premises and personnel; and

(b) the purchase of standardised services, including market information services and the provision of price feeds.

39.2.7.5   Role of the firm

The firm must remain fully responsible for discharging all of its regulatory obligations and comply, in particular, with the following conditions:

(a) the outsourcing must not result in the delegation by senior management of its responsibility;

(b) the relationship and obligations of the firm towards its clients under the terms of MiFID must not be altered;

(c) the conditions with which the firm must comply in order to be authorised in accordance with Article 5 of MIFID, and to remain so, must not be undermined; and

(d) none of the other conditions subject to which the firm's authorisation was granted must be removed or modified. (Article 14)

39.2.7.6   Managing the outsourcing relationship under MiFID

Firms must exercise due skill, care and diligence when entering into, managing or terminating any arrangement for the outsourcing to a service provider of critical or important operational functions or of any investment services or activities (SYSC para.8.1.7). The firm must retain the necessary expertise to supervise the outsourced functions effectively and manage the risks associated with the outsourcing and must supervise those functions and manage those risks.

In particular, the firm must comply with the management requirements in Table 61.

Table 61 Managing the outsourcing arrangement under MiFID

Due diligence
The firm must ensure the service provider has the ability, capacity and any authorisation required by law to perform the outsourced functions, services or activities reliably and professionally. (Article 14.2(a), implemented in SYSC para.8.1.8R(1))
Service management—standard of performance
The service provider must carry out the outsourced services effectively, and, to this end, the firm must establish methods for assessing the standard of performance of the service provider. (Article 14.2(b), implemented in SYSC para.8.1.8R(2))
Service management—supervision

The firm must properly supervise the carrying out of the outsourced functions, and adequately manage the risks associated with the outsourcing and must retain the necessary expertise to supervise the outsourced functions effectively and to manage the risks associated with it. (Article 14.2(c) and (e), implemented in SYSC paras 8.1.8R(3) and (5))

Service management—appropriate action

In managing the outsourcing arrangement, the firm should take the appropriate action if it appears that the service provider may not be carrying out the functions effectively and in compliance with applicable laws and regulatory requirements. (Article 14.2(d), implemented in SYSC para.8.1.8R(4))

Disclosure

The service provider must disclose to the investment firm any development that may have a material impact on its ability to carry out the outsourced functions effectively and in compliance with applicable laws and regulatory requirements. (Article 14.2(f), implemented in SYSC para.8.1.8R(6))

Audit

The service provider must co-operate with the competent authorities of the investment firm in connection with the outsourced activities. (Article 14.2(h), implemented in SYSC para.8.1.8R(8))

The investment firm, its auditors and the relevant competent authorities must have effective access to data related to the outsourced activities, as well as to the business premises of the service provider, and the competent authorities must be able to exercise those rights of access. (Article 14.2(i), implemented in SYSC para.8.1.8R(9))

The service provider must make available on request to the regulator all information necessary to enable the authority to supervise the compliance of the performance of the outsourced activities with the requirements of the MiFID Implementing Directive. (Article 14.5, implemented in SYSC para.8.1.11R)

Maintenance of records of personal transactions

The investment firm must ensure that the firm to which an activity is outsourced maintains a record of personal transactions entered into by any relevant person and provides that information to the investment firm promptly on request (Article 12(2), implemented in COBS para.11.7.4R(2)B)

Confidential information

The service provider must protect any confidential information relating to the investment firm and its clients. (Article 14.2(j), implemented in SYSC para.8.1.8R(10))

Business continuity

The investment firm and the service provider must establish, implement and maintain a contingency plan for disaster recovery and periodic testing of backup facilities, where that is necessary having regard to the function, service or activity that has been outsourced. (Article 14.2(k), implemented in SYSC para.8.1.8R(11))

Termination

The firm must be able to terminate the arrangement for outsourcing where necessary without detriment to the continuity and quality of its provision of services to clients. (Article 14.2(g), implemented in SYSC para.8.1.8R(7))

Written agreement

> The respective rights and obligations of the investment firms and of the service provider must be clearly allocated and set out in a written agreement. (Article 14.3, implemented in SYSC para.8.1.9R)

39.2.7.7   Intra-group outsourcing

MiFID applies to intra-group outsourcing arrangements. However, if the investment firm and the service provider are members of the same group, the investment firm may take into account the extent to which the firm controls the service provider or has the ability to influence its actions when considering the application of the conditions to the outsourcing arrangements. (Article 14.4, implemented in SYSC para.8.1.10R)

39.2.7.8   Retail client portfolio management

When an investment firm outsources the investment service of portfolio management provided to retail clients to a service provider located in a third country (that is, a country outside the EEA), that investment firm must ensure that the following conditions are satisfied (Article 15(1), implemented in SYSC para.8.2.1R):

(a)   the service provider must be authorised or registered in its home country to provide that service and must be subject to prudential supervision; and
(b)   there must be an appropriate co-operation agreement between the competent authority of the investment firm and the supervisory authority of the service provider.

If these conditions are not satisfied, a firm must give prior notification to its regulator about the outsourcing arrangement. The notification must include:

(a)   details about which of the conditions is not met;
(b)   if applicable, details and evidence of the supplier's authorisation or regulation, including the regulator's contact details;
(c)   the firm's proposals for meeting its obligations under SYSC on an ongoing basis;
(d)   why the firm wishes to outsource to the supplier;
(e)   a draft of the outsourcing agreement between the supplier and the firm;
(f)   the proposed start date of the outsourcing arrangement; and
(g)   confirmation that the firm has had regard to the guidance in Table 62 below, or if it has not, why not.

Table 62 Retail client portfolio management—FSA guidance

Sub-contracting

If the outsourcing allows the supplier to sub-contract any of the services to be provided under the outsourcing, any such sub-contracting shall not affect the supplier's responsibilities under the outsourcing agreement. (SYSC para.8.3.4G)

Termination

The firm should be entitled to terminate the outsourcing if the supplier undergoes a change of control or becomes insolvent, goes into liquidation or receivership (or equivalent in its home state) or is in persistent material default under the agreement. (SYSC para.8.3.5G)

The following should be taken into account where the supplier is not authorised or registered in its home country and/or not subject to prudential supervision.

Voluntary regulation

The firm should examine, and be able to demonstrate, to what extent the supplier may be subject to any form of voluntary regulation, including self-regulation in its home state. (SYSC para.8.3.6(1)G)

Sufficient, competent resources

The supplier must be obliged to devote sufficient, competent resources to providing the service. (SYSC para.8.3.6(2)G)

Disclosure

In addition to the requirement to ensure that a supplier discloses any developments that may have a material impact on its ability to carry out the outsourcing (SYSC para.8.1.8R(6)), where the conditions are not met, the developments to be disclosed should include, without limitation (SYSC para.8.3.6(3)G):

(a)   any adverse effect that any laws or regulations introduced in the supplier's home country may have on its carrying on the outsourced activity; and

(b)   any changes to its capital reserve levels or its prudential risks.

Ability to meet liabilities

The firm should satisfy itself that the supplier is able to meet its liabilities as they fall due and that it has positive net assets.

Annual reports and accounts

The firm should require that the supplier prepares annual reports and accounts which (SYSC para.8.3.6G(5)):

(a)   are in accordance with the supplier's national law which, in all material respects, is the same as or equivalent to the international accounting standards; and

(b)   have been independently audited and reported on in accordance with the supplier's national law which is the same as or equivalent to international auditing standards.

Audited annual report and accounts

The firm should receive copies of each set of the audited annual report and accounts of the supplier. If the supplier expects or knows its auditor will qualify his report on the audited report and accounts, or add an explanatory paragraph, the supplier should be required to notify the firm without delay. (SYSC para.8.3.6(6)G)

Confidential information

The firm should satisfy itself, and be able to demonstrate, that it has in place appropriate procedures to ensure that it is fully aware of the supplier's controls for protecting confidential information. (SYSC para.8.3.6(7)G)

In addition to the requirement at SYSC para.8.1.8R(10) that the supplier must protect any confidential information relating to the firm or its clients, the outsourcing agreement should require the supplier to notify the firm immediately if there is a breach of confidentiality. (SYSC para.8.3.6(8)G)

Governing law

> The outsourcing agreement should be governed by the law and subject to the jurisdiction of an EEA state. (SYSC para.8.3.6(9)G)
>
> *The following should be taken into account by a firm where there is no co-operation agreement between the FSA and the supervisory authority of the supplier or there is no supervisory authority of the supplier.*
>
> **Provision of Information**
>
> The outsourcing agreement should ensure the firm can provide the FSA with any information relating to the outsourced activity that the FSA may require in order to carry out effective supervision. The firm should therefore assess the extent to which the supplier's regulator and/or local laws and regulations may restrict access to information about the outsourced activity. Any such restriction should be described in the notification to be sent to the FSA. (SYSC para.8.3.7(1)G)
>
> The outsourcing agreement should require the supplier to provide the firm's offices in the UK with all requested information required to meet the firm's regulatory obligations. The FSA should be given an enforceable right to obtain such information from the firm and to require the supplier to provide the information directly. (SYSC para.8.3.7(1)G)

The guidance applies whether a firm outsources portfolio management directly or indirectly via a third party. The firm must only notify the FSA of the arrangement once it has carried out due diligence regarding the supplier and has taken into account the FSA guidance in Table 62.

If a firm can demonstrate that it has taken the guidance in Table 62 into account and has satisfactorily concluded that it would be able to continue to satisfy the common platform outsourcing rules and provide adequate protection for consumers despite not satisfying the conditions, the FSA is unlikely to object to the outsourcing arrangement. (SYSC para.8.3.3G)

The regulator is not expected to authorise or otherwise approve any such arrangement or its terms. The purpose of the notification, rather, is to ensure that the competent authority has reasonable time to intervene in appropriate cases. It is the responsibility of the investment firm to negotiate the terms of any outsourcing arrangement, and to ensure that those terms are consistent with the obligations of the firm, without the formal intervention of the competent authority.

The firm's notice must include adequate details of the outsourcing arrangement. The FSA may seek further information about the outsourcing proposal.

The firm may enter into the outsourcing arrangement if it has not received notice of objection or a request for further information from the FSA within one month. (SYSC para.8.2.4G)

Where the FSA has not objected to the outsourcing agreement, the firm should notify the FSA of any matters which could affect the firm's ability to provide adequate services to its customers or could result in serious detriment to its customers or where there has been material change in the information previously provided to the FSA in relation to the outsourcing. (SYSC para.8.2.9G)

39.2.7.9   Other relevant requirements

The Level 2 Directive contains other organisational requirements which are of general application, but which will also be relevant to outsourcing arrangements. These are described in Table 63.

Table 63 Level 2 Directive—other relevant requirements

General organisational requirements
Taking into account the nature, scale and complexity of the business of the firm, and the nature and range of the investment services and activities undertaken in the course of that business, a firm must (Article 5(1) final paragraph, implemented in SYSC para.4.1.4R):
(a) establish, implement and maintain decision-making procedures and an organisational structure which clearly and in a documented manner specifies reporting lines and allocates functions and responsibilities;
(b) establish, implement and maintain adequate internal control mechanisms designed to secure compliance with decisions and procedures at all levels of the firm (Article 5(1)(c)); and
(c) establish, implement and maintain effective internal reporting and communication of information at all relevant levels of the firm (Article 5(1)(e)).
Business continuity
A firm must establish, implement and maintain an adequate contingency and business continuity policy aimed at ensuring, in the case of an interruption to its systems and procedures, the preservation of essential data and functions, and the maintenance of investment services and activities, or, where that is not possible, the timely recovery of such data and functions and the timely resumption of its investment services and activities. (Article 5(3), implemented in SYSC para.4.1.7R)
Regular monitoring
A firm must monitor and, on a regular basis, evaluate the adequacy and effectiveness of its systems, internal control mechanisms and arrangements established and take appropriate measures to address any deficiencies. (Article 5(5), implemented in SYSC para.4.1.10R)
General
The systems, internal control mechanisms and arrangements established by a firm must take into account the nature, scale and complexity of its business and the nature and range of investment services and activities undertaken in the course of that business. (Article 5(1) final paragraph, implemented in SYSC para.5.1.13R)
A firm must monitor and, on a regular basis, evaluate the adequacy and effectiveness of its systems, internal control mechanisms and arrangements established in accordance with this chapter, and take appropriate measures to address any deficiencies. (Article 5(5), implemented in SYSC para.5.1.14R)

39.3   Capital Requirements Directive (CRD)

39.3.1   *Introduction to the CRD*

The CRD consists of the recast Capital Adequacy Directive ("recast CAD") and the recast Banking Consolidation Directive ("recast BCD"). The CRD is also under review, and changes are expected to be adopted alongside the changes to MiFID.

39.3.2   *Application*

Broadly, the CRD applies to credit institutions and investment firms to which MiFID applies. Most banks and fund managers will therefore need to comply with the CRD, unless an exemption applies.

Exemptions and special arrangements apply to firms with a business profile that limits their risks. For example, broadly speaking, a UCITS management firm will be regarded as a limited licence firm and will therefore be exempt from the requirement to hold capital to cover operational risk.

39.3.3   *Robust governance arrangements*

Article 22 of the recast BCD requires that credit institutions have robust governance arrangements with a clear organisational structure, well-defined, transparent and consistent lines of responsibility and adequate internal control mechanisms.

These requirements also apply to all outsourcing arrangements, including non-MiFID business whether of critical or important functions or not.

39.3.4   *Business continuity*

BCD Annex V, para.13 states that a firm must have a contingency and business continuity policy in place aimed at ensuring its ability to operate on an ongoing basis and limiting losses in the event of severe business disruption.

39.3.5   *Outsourcing fees as part of the relevant indicator*

The full implications of CRD are not discussed in this Guide. However, it is important for reporting requirements to note that the fee relating to outsourcing can be deducted from the relevant indicator when the outsourcing is to a third party which is:

(a)   a parent or subsidiary of the firm whose process, service or activity is being outsourced, or a subsidiary of the parent which is also the parent of the firm; or

(b)   subject to supervision under, or equivalent to, the CRD.

Otherwise, fees paid for outsourcing shall be included in operating expenses (and so not deducted from the relevant indicator).

If a firm falls within the scope of the CRD, this represents an opportunity for firms to reduce their regulatory capital as a result of the outsourcing of services, provided the services are either outsourced to a group company or a service provider that is subject to supervision under the CRD or equivalent prudential capital regulation. For service providers to firms, the FSA is obviously concerned that there is no outflow of regulatory capital from banking and financial services systems and so service providers that are subject to the CRD (or equivalent) will need to calculate their indicator, taking into account the services they are providing, in the usual way.

It is assumed that, in determining whether a service provider is subject to supervision under, or equivalent to, the CRD, this means that the service provider must be subject to supervision in respect of the activities outsourced. This may be problematic, for example, where functions such as transfer agency are outsourced to jurisdictions such as the US.

39.3.6   Timetable

From 1 January 2007, CRD firms had to comply with the CRD provisions for systems and controls (SYSC Chapter 3) and continue to apply the existing SYSC provisions until they moved to the common platform. The common platform provisions applied to all CRD firms from 1 November 2007 but firms had the option to adopt them earlier in 2007 if they wished to do so for practical reasons.

39.4   Implementation of MiFID in the UK

39.4.1   Impact of MiFID

From an outsourcing perspective, MiFID did not introduce a substantially different position, as insurers, banks and building societies had previously been regulated by the outsourcing provisions in the Interim Prudential Sourcebook for Insurers, Interim Prudential Sourcebook for Banks and the Interim Prudential Sourcebook for Building Societies (respectively). Investment services had not previously been regulated but many fund managers had in practice implemented similar protections as they regarded that the regulations represented good practice.

39.4.2   General approach—no super-equivalence

The FSA's general approach to implementing CRD and MiFID was that rules were based on copied-out Directive text, to avoid the FSA placing any unintended additional obligations on firms. For this reason, Table 61, which describes the MiFID Directives, also lists the sections in the FSA Handbook in which the relevant provisions in the Directives were implemented.

39.4.3   Exception to no super-equivalence—common platform

Despite its intention to limit "super-equivalence", the FSA chose to create a unified set of requirements applying to common platform firms[2] implementing MiFID and CRD as:

(a)   both MiFID and CRD cover management oversight, internal governance and systems and controls requirements;
(b)   although both MiFID and CRD have independently set requirements for management oversight, internal governance and systems and controls, they share a common approach and their requirements are broadly compatible, even if they are formulated differently;
(c)   most firms which are subject to CRD will also be subject to MiFID; and
(d)   a unified set of requirements will be simpler and more cohesive.

39.4.4   Exception to no super-equivalence—extension to non-insurers

From 1 April 2009, the FSA decided to apply most of its rules drafted for "common platform" firms under MiFID and the CRD to other firms. As a result, SYSC 4 and 8 apply to all firms except insurers, Lloyd's managing agents and the Society of Lloyd's itself. However, they apply largely as guidance rather than absolute rules.

---

[2]   Broadly speaking, the following will be subject to the common platform:
    (a)   investment firms to which MiFID applies;
    (b)   banks and building societies.
    An investment firm for MiFID purposes is any legal person whose regular occupation or business is:
    (a)   the provision of one or more investment services to third parties; and/or
    (b)   the performance of one or more investment activities on a professional basis.

39.4.5 *Exception to no super-equivalence—extension to insurers*

See Chapter 40.

39.4.6 *Exception to no super-equivalence—application of guidance*

The FSA decided that the unified standard for outsourcing would apply to common platform firms' outsourcing of critical or important functions relating to:

(a) a firm's MiFID business;
(b) non-MiFID regulated activities;
(c) listed activities under the BCD; and
(d) ancillary services under MiFID.

This goes beyond the MiFID minimum standards, which is limited to regulating outsourcing of critical or important operational functions related to a firm's MiFID business but is only super-equivalent to the extent that it goes beyond CRD requirements.

39.4.7 *Exception to no super-equivalence—extension to non-material outsourcing*

The FSA decided that compliance with the general principle in the recast BCD Article 22 (that a firm has robust governance arrangements and adequate internal control mechanisms for example) should cover all outsourcing arrangements (both material and non-material) in relation to the whole of a firm's business. Failure by a firm to have adequate arrangements regarding its outsourcing would be a failure to have robust governance arrangements or internal control mechanisms under Article 22.

The FSA has stated that firms should take the other material outsourcing rules into account, as appropriate and proportionate, for its non-material outsourcing (SYSC para.8.1.3).

39.5 MiFID Connect guidelines on outsourcing (May 2007)

39.5.1 *MiFID Connect*

MiFID Connect is a joint project set up by 11 trade associations to support their members in implementing the Directive. MiFID Connect has published guidelines on implementing MiFID and, in particular, guidelines on applying MiFID to particular circumstances, as described below.

39.5.2 *Which activities constitute outsourcing?*

The MiFID Connect guidelines suggest that firms should consider the following in deciding whether an activity constitutes outsourcing:

(a) If the firm provides investment services part of which are contracted to a third party, does the client have a direct contract with the third party? If the answer is yes, this should fall outside the definition of outsourcing.
(b) If the firm provides investment services part of which are contracted to a third party, does the client have a direct contract with the third party? If the answer is no, this may fall within the definition of outsourcing.
(c) Is the service by a third party the provision of a particular process, service or activity that is not within the service offered by the firm? If yes, this is not likely to be outsourcing.

The guidelines give the example of a global custodian putting in place a sub-custodian arrangement. This would not be outsourcing. However, if a global custodian delegates its central custody functions by appointing a global custodian, then this would be outsourcing.

39.5.3 *Which functions are critical and important?*

The MiFID Connect guidelines stress that what is critical or important will be a subjective test and will depend upon the nature and circumstances of a particular firm. However, the guidelines classify the following as likely to be outsourcing and likely to be critical and important:

(a) provision of regular or constant compliance, internal audit, accounting or risk management support;
(b) provision of credit risk control and credit risk analysis;
(c) portfolio administration or portfolio management by a third party;
(d) provision of data storage (physical and electronic);
(e) provision of ongoing, day-to-day systems maintenance/support; and

(f)   provision of ongoing, day-to-day software/systems management (e.g. where third party carries out day-to-day functionality and/or runs software or processes on its own systems).

The guidelines classify the following as unlikely to be outsourcing or, if they are outsourcing, unlikely to be critical and important functions:

(a)   appointment of sub-custodians;
(b)   participation in securities settlement systems and payment systems;
(c)   provision of one-off, expert assistance with compliance, internal audit, accounting or risk management issues;
(d)   provision of logistical support, for example cleaning, catering and procurement of basic services/products;
(e)   provision of human resources support, for example sourcing of temporary employees and processing of payroll;
(f)   buying standard software "off the shelf" or engaging a software designer to develop bespoke software; and
(g)   reliance on software providers for ad hoc operational assistance in relation to off-the-shelf systems.

39.5.4   Sub-contracting

The MiFID Connect guidelines suggest that sub-contracting by an outsourcing service provider should require the prior consent of the firm to the possibility and circumstances of any sub-outsourcing and that the firm should ensure that any terms agreed between the service provider and any third party do not contradict the terms of the agreement between the firm and the service provider. SYSC para.8.1.9R is used as the basis for this interpretation.

39.5.5   Supervision of services

The MiFID Connect guidelines suggest that a firm can use a number of tools to assess the standard of services including:

(a)   agreeing and documenting quantitative and qualitative service level standards/performance targets for the performance of the outsourced functions so as to ensure that the outsourced functions meet the performance and quality standard that would apply if the firm were to perform the relevant activities itself;
(b)   putting in place procedures to continuously monitor and assess the performance of the service provider (e.g. scheduling regular update meetings with the service provider, assessing the appropriate frequency and carrying out on-site inspections);
(c)   adopting measures to identify and report instances of unsatisfactory

performance or non-compliance, such as service delivery reports, self-certification or independent review by auditors; and

(d) imposing regular reporting obligations on the service provider and scheduling update meetings with the service provider to monitor compliance with obligations.

39.5.6 Actions to be taken if services are not provided to an adequate standard

Whether a particular action is "appropriate" will depend on the nature of the breach and the terms of the agreement between the parties. The MiFID Connect guidelines suggest that steps that firms might take in complying with this requirement include:

(a) implementing a service credit regime for non-compliance with performance targets in order to address minor breaches; and

(b) warning the service provider, activating step-in rights or terminating the agreement where a significant or persistent breach is identified.

The requirement for "step-in" rights is frequently referred to as a regulatory obligation. This is not the case—step in is not expressly mentioned in the FSA Handbook. However, the requirement to ensure business continuity may mean that firms need the step-in right in appropriate cases, if it is a practical remedy in practice.

39.5.7 Status of guidance

The MiFID Connect guidelines are not mandatory and are not FSA guidance. In May 2007, however, the FSA confirmed that its supervision of outsourcing by firms will in future take account of the guidance which has been issued by MiFID Connect. This was the first industry-developed guidance recognised by the FSA since publishing its Discussion Paper *FSA confirmation of Industry Guidance* in November 2006. The FSA treats confirmed industry guidance in a similar way to its own guidance and will not take disciplinary action against firms who have acted in compliance with appropriate current guidance. However, on 16 May 2010, the MiFID Connect guidance on outsourcing expired so as at 31 August 2010 it no longer has FSA confirmed status. The FSA has not made any announcements about the expiry of the guidance.

39.6 Recovery and Resolution Plans (living wills)

Both the FSA and EU regulators are consulting on introducing requirements on significant financial firms to produce plans addressing how they could recover from a serious crisis or, where recovery is not possible, to wind business down in an orderly way, with minimum effects on the markets and customers.

39.6.1 FSA proposals

The FSA consulted in August 2011[3] on detailed proposals that would apply to all UK incorporated deposit-takers and significant UK investment firms with assets exceeding £15 billion. It would require each firm to have:

(a) **A recovery plan**: under these rules, firms must identify options to achieve recovery, to be implemented when a crisis occurs. The plans must be developed and maintained by the firm, in co-ordination with the FSA, but should have certain common features, including enough credible options for dealing with a range of scenarios, including disposal of all or part of the business;

(b) **A resolution pack**: the FSA would develop this, on the basis of data the firm would provide. Resolution packs will assist the authorities to wind-down a firm if it fails for whatever reason. The resolution data and analysis to be provided by firms is intended to identify significant barriers to resolution, to facilitate the effective use of the powers under the Special Resolution Regimes that apply in relation to the insolvency of banks and investment firms and so reduce the risk that taxpayers' funds will be required to support the resolution of the firm.

39.6.2 EU plans

In May 2012, the European Commission published plans for an EU wide recovery and resolution framework.[4] The plans are similar to the FSA's but there are differences, including that the EU plans would cover all investment firms subject to the CRD (without the monetary threshold the FSA proposes).

---

[3] Consultation Paper 11/16: *http://www.fsa.gov.uk/library/policy/cp/2011/11__16.shtml* [Accessed 22 November 2012].

[4] European Commission Proposal for a Directive on the Recovery and Resolution of Credit Institutions and Investment Firms *http://ec.europa.eu/internal__market/bank/docs/crisis-management/2012__eu__framework/COM__2012__280__en.pdf* [Accessed 22 November 2012].

As a result of the EU plans, the FSA postponed its final rules, but stated[5] that the development and submission of recovery plans and resolution packs would continue as planned. Notwithstanding the lack of rules, the FSA expects large firms involved in its pilot exercise to submit recovery plans and resolution packs and other large firms to provide sufficient information to their supervisors to meet the timetable set by the Financial Stability Board (FSB).[6]

39.6.3 *Implications for outsourcing*

Firms affected, or likely to be affected, by the regime should take its requirements into account when entering into outsourcing or other relevant service contracts, including ensuring that relevant contracts are severable, if necessary to deal with the possible disposal of all or part of the business.

---

[5]   FSA Recovery and Resolution Plan Update *http://www.fsa.gov.uk/library/communication/pr/2012/052.shtml* [Accessed 22 November 2012].
[6]   Financial Stability Board Key Attributes for Effective Resolution Regimes *http://www.financialstabilityboard.org/publications/r__111104cc.pdf* [Accessed 22 November 2012].

Chapter 40

Specific regulation affecting Insurance Companies

40.1 Outline

This chapter describes specific regulations applying to insurance companies. It looks at the current regime under SYSC, specifically SYSC 13 and at the changes Solvency II and the proposed SOLPRU rules will bring. Insurance companies should also comply with the general regulatory requirements set out in Chapter 38.

40.1.1 SYSC General Principles

SYSC para.3.2 provides guidance on issues which a firm is expected to consider in complying with SYSC para.3.1.1R. It includes various guidance on delegation within the firm, which it states is also relevant to external delegation or outsourcing. This guidance includes the following:

> "SYSC 3.2.3G
>
> A firm's governing body is likely to delegate many functions and tasks for the purpose of carrying out its business. When functions or tasks are delegated, either to employees or to appointed representatives, appropriate safeguards should be put in place.
>
> When there is delegation, a firm should assess whether the recipient is suitable to carry out the delegated function or task, taking into account the degree of responsibility involved.
>
> The extent and limits of any delegation should be made clear to those concerned.
>
> There should be arrangements to supervise delegation, and to monitor the discharge of delegates' functions or tasks.
>
> If cause for concern arises through supervision and monitoring or otherwise, there should be appropriate follow-up action at an appropriate level of seniority within the firm."

SYSC para.3.2.4G specifically refers to outsourcing, stating that guidance for delegation within firms is also relevant to external delegation. It reminds firms they cannot contract out of their regulatory obligations so must take reasonable care to supervise the discharge of outsourced functions by contractors. This will entail getting sufficient information from a contractor to enable a firm to assess the impact of outsourcing on its systems and controls.

SYSC para.3.2.6R states that a firm must take reasonable care to establish and maintain effective systems and controls for compliance with applicable requirements and standards under the regulatory system. This includes prevention of financial crime and money laundering.

40.1.2   Internal controls

SYSC para.14.1.27R states that a firm must take reasonable steps to establish and maintain adequate internal controls. The outsourcing of control functions to third parties creates a particular risk and firms should consider the consequences of such actions especially if it would compromise the objectives as set out in SYSC para.14.1.28G of:

(a)   safeguarding both the assets of the firm and its customers, as well as identifying and managing liabilities;

(b)   maintaining the efficiency and effectiveness of its operations;

(c)   ensuring the reliability and completeness of all accounting, financial and management information; and

(d)   ensuring compliance with its internal policies and procedures as well as all applicable laws and regulations.

40.2   FSA's focus on outsourcing by insurers

The FSA's interest in how insurance companies use outsourcing remains keen. In the context of Solvency II,[1] it has reminded firms of the risks associated with outsourcing, stating that:

> "Outsourcing involves you delegating a process, service or activity to a service provider. This provider may be a regulated entity, an entity in the same group or otherwise. Any outsourcing undertaken must not:
>
> • materially impair the quality of your system of governance;
>
> • unduly increase your operational risk; or
>
> • impair the supervisor's ability to monitor your compliance with your obligations.

---

[1]   Directive 2009/138/EC. See below for further detail.

You must notify the supervisor before any outsourcing of a critical or important function or activity, as well as upon any subsequent material developments with respect to those functions or activities.

You must establish an outsourcing policy if you outsource or propose to outsource any functions or insurance or reinsurance activity. The factors that you must consider under this include the impact of outsourcing on your business, and the reporting and monitoring arrangements that you will implement for the outsourcing relationship.

When selecting a service provider for any critical or important operational function or activity, you must ensure that certain conditions are met, including:

- the potential service provider has the ability, capacity and any authorisation required by law to deliver the required functions or activities satisfactorily, and that no law – in particular regarding rules on data protection – will be breached as a result of the outsourcing; and

- it has adopted all means to ensure that no explicit or potential conflicts of interest arise between you and the provider."

40.3   SYSC 13

40.3.1   *Application*

Outsourcing of services by insurance companies in the UK is currently subject to guidance in SYSC 13.

40.3.2   *Background*

40.3.2.1   *Application*

SYSC 13 covers all outsourcing, including:

(a)   non-material outsourcing (although particular care should be taken to manage material outsourcing agreements); and
(b)   intra-group outsourcing.

It will be relevant to some extent to other forms of third-party "dependencies" (SYSC para.13.9.1G).

SYSC 13 applies to new arrangements and retrospectively to existing contracts (which may have to be renegotiated if they do not satisfy the Policy Statement).

40.3.2.2   *Guidance*

Operational risk can have a different application for different firms. Therefore, SYSC 13 is drafted in the form of guidance. A firm must assess the appropriateness of the guidance in the light of the scale, nature and complexity of its activities. (SYSC para.13.2.2G)

However, the status of a service provider as either a regulated firm or intra-group should not, in itself, necessarily imply a reduced operational risk. (SYSC para.13.9.3G)

Table 64 summarises some of the key elements of SYSC 13.

Table 64 Key elements of SYSC 13

Business strategy

The FSA states that, before it enters into an outsourcing contract, the firm should consider the extent to which the outsourcing arrangements support its business strategy. The FSA also adds that the firm should continue to check its business strategy on an ongoing basis throughout the term of the agreement. (SYSC para.13.9.4G(1))

Processes and systems

SYSC para.13.7.1G states that a firm should ensure that its service provider establishes and maintains appropriate systems and controls for the management of operational risks that can arise from inadequacies or failures in processes and systems. This process might include, but is not limited to, consideration of:

(a)   the importance and complexity of the processes and systems used in the end-to-end operating cycle for a firm's products and activities (e.g. whether systems are sufficiently integrated, in particular, for high-volume business);

(b)   the controls that will help a firm to prevent system and process failures or identify them to permit prompt rectification (e.g. pre-approval or reconciliation processes);

(c)   whether the design and use of a firm's processes and systems allow it to comply adequately with regulatory and other requirements;

(d)   a firm's arrangements for the continuity of its operations in the event that a significant process or system becomes unavailable or is destroyed; and

(e)   the importance of monitoring indicators of process or system risk (such as reconciliation exceptions, compensation payments, and documentation errors) and experience of operational losses and exposures.

Notification

The FSA reminds firms of their obligations under SUP para.15.3.8G(1)(e) to notify the FSA when it intends to enter into a material outsourcing arrangement.

Due diligence of service provider

The FSA highlights the need for firms to carry out appropriate due diligence relating to the service provider's financial stability and expertise. (SYSC para.13.9.4G(3))

Risk management

The FSA stresses the importance of firms analysing, before entering into the outsourcing agreement and on an ongoing basis, how the proposed outsourcing will affect their overall risk profile and their ability to meet their regulatory obligations. (SYSC para.13.9.4G(1))

The FSA suggests that firms consider whether the arrangements will allow them to monitor and control their exposure to operational risks from outsourcing. (SYSC para.13.9.4G(2))

Firms should also consider whether any concentration risks may arise. The FSA gives the example of business continuity risks where several firms use one service provider (SYSC para.13.9.4G(5))

Transition

The FSA states that firms must consider how they will ensure a smooth transition of their operations from their current arrangements to a new or changed outsourcing arrangement. (SYSC para.13.9.4G(4))

Service management—control over the outsourced service providers

The FSA reminds firms that, under SYSC para.3.2.4G, they cannot contract out of their regulatory obligations and must take reasonable care to supervise the discharge of outsourced functions by the service provider.

In SYSC para.13.6.2G, the FSA suggests that firms, in establishing appropriate systems and controls for managing operational risk from their own employees, consider the following. The guidance adds that, to the extent that it is necessary, a firm should review and consider the adequacy of the staffing arrangements and policies of a service provider. (SYSC para.13.6.2G(7)):

(a)   the service provider's operational risk culture and variations in risk culture and HR management practices across its operations;

(b)   whether the way the service provider's employees are remunerated exposes the firm to the risk that it will not be able to meet its regulatory obligations;

(c)   (if the outsourcing involves client-facing processes) the extent to which inadequate or appropriate training exposes clients to the risk of loss or unfair treatment, including by not enabling effective communication with the firm;

(d)   compliance with applicable regulatory and statutory requirements relating to the welfare and conduct of the service provider's employees;

(e)   the service provider's arrangements for the continuity of operations in the event of unavailability or loss of its employees; and

(f)   the relationship between indicators of people loss (such as sickness and turnover rates) and exposure to operational losses.

Service management

The FSA states that firms should consider the inclusion of reporting and notification requirements, in particular so that the firm can monitor and control its exposure to operational risks. (SYSC para.13.9.5G(1))

It states that, in implementing a relationship framework and drafting service level agreements, a firm should consider the need for (SYSC para.13.9.6G):

(a)   the identification of qualitative and quantitative performance targets to assess the adequacy of service performance;

(b)   the evaluation of the service provider's performance through service delivery reports, periodic self-certification or independent review by internal or external auditors; and

(c)   remedial action and escalation processes for dealing with inadequate performance.

Service provider's resources

The FSA suggests that firms consider the extent to which exclusivity arrangements are needed to protect access to the service provider's resources, and the extent to which the service provider should provide business continuity for the outsourced services. (SYSC para.13.9.5G(6))

Change management

The FSA suggests that the firm consider the processes for making changes to the outsourcing arrangement including changes in processing volumes, activities and other contractual terms. (SYSC para.13.9.5G(8))

The FSA suggests that the firm consider the conditions under which the firm or service provider can choose to change the outsourcing arrangement, such as:

(a)   a change of ownership or control of the service provider or firm;

(b)   insolvency or receivership of the service provider or firm, significant change in the business operations of the service provider or firm (including subcontracting); and

(c)   inadequate provision of the services may lead to the firm being unable to meet its regulatory obligation. (SYSC para.13.9.5G(8))

Audit

The FSA suggests that the firm should consider whether sufficient access to the firm's "books, accounts and vouchers" will be made available to internal auditors, external auditors, actuaries and the FSA under s.341of the FSMA 2000.

In particular, the FSA reminds firms of their obligations under SUP para.2.3.5R (access to premises) and SUP para.2.3.7R (service providers under material outsourcing arrangements). (SYSC para.13.9.5G(2))

The FSA points out that, in certain circumstances, it may be of benefit to seek comfort as to the adequacy and effectiveness of systems and controls in place at the service provider, through the use of externally validated reports commissioned by the service provider itself. However, the use of these reports should not imply that a firm is absolved of the responsibility to maintain any other oversight. In addition, the firm should not normally have to forfeit the right for itself or its agents to gain access to the premises of the service provider. (SYSC para.13.9.7G)

Confidentiality and IPR

The FSA suggests that firms consider the need for information ownership rights, confidentiality agreements and Chinese walls to protect client and other information (including on termination). (SYSC para.13.9.5G(3))

Security

The FSA points out that failures in the processing of information or the security of the systems on which it is maintained can lead to significant operational exposure, with not only financial but also regulatory, legal and reputational implications. (SYSC para.13.7.7G)

The FSA stresses that a firm should establish and maintain appropriate systems and controls for the management of its information security risks. This might include, but is not limited to, consideration of:

(a)   confidentiality: ensuring that information is accessible only to an authorised person or system (this may require firewalls within a system, as well as entry restrictions);

(b)   integrity: safeguarding the accuracy and completeness of the information and its processing;

(c)   availability: ensuring that an authorised person or system has access to the information when required;

(d)   authentication: ensuring that the identity of the person or system processing the information is verified; and

(e)   non-repudiation and accountability: ensuring that the person or system that processed the information cannot deny their action. (SYSC para.13.7.7G)

The FSA recommends that a firm should consider the adequacy of the systems and controls used to protect the processing and security of its information and may wish to have regard to established security standards such as ISO 17799 (Information Security Management). (SYSC para.13.7.8G)

Firm's policies and procedures

The FSA suggests that firms consider the extent to which the service provider must comply with the firm's policies and procedures (e.g. information security). (SYSC para.13.9.5G(5))

Business continuity

In SYSC para.13.8, which again applies generally, not just to outsourcing arrangements, the FSA clarifies that the high-level requirement in SYSC para.3.1.1R for appropriate systems and controls applies at all times, including following the invocation of a business continuity plan (although GEN para.1.3 (Emergency) sets out conditions for relief from complying with this rule). (SYSC para.13.8.4G)

The FSA stresses that a firm should implement appropriate arrangements to maintain the continuity of its operations. This might include, but is not limited to, the use of:

(a)   activities to reduce the likelihood of a disruption, such as succession planning, systems resilience and dual processing; and

(b)   activities to reduce the impact of a disruption, such as contingency arrangements and insurance. (SYSC para.13.8.6G)

The FSA highlights the need for firms to document appropriate business continuity arrangements. (SYSC para.13.8.7G)

In particular, it stresses the need for the firm to ensure that it has appropriate contingency arrangements to allow business continuity in the event of a significant loss of services from the service provider, such as:

(a)   a significant loss of resources at the service provider;

(b)   financial failure of the service provider; and

(c)   unexpected termination of the outsourcing arrangement. (SYSC para.13.9.8G)

It points out that firms should consider the extent to which the service provider will provide business continuity for outsourced operations. (SYSC para.13.9.5G(6))

It includes a useful suggestion (often overlooked by firms) that where firms are outsourcing the business continuity services themselves, as part of a shared disaster recovery service, they should evaluate the likelihood and impact of multiple calls on shared resources. (SYSC para.13.8.8G)

The guidance also points out that firms should consider the concentration risk implications of using a particular service provider, such as the business continuity implications where a single service provider is used by several firms. (SYSC para.13.9.4G(5)) Some firms feel that this conflicts with the requirement that firms use experienced service providers, as the most experienced firms are likely to have a higher proportion of the market. In addition, leading service providers may be concerned that this comment could discourage firms from using them.

Lastly, the guidance stresses the need to ensure continued availability of software. (SYSC para.13.9.5G(7))

Rights of termination

471

The FSA reminds firms to consider including in their outsourcing agreements the usual rights for either party to terminate the agreement for insolvency or receivership. (SYSC para.13.9.5G(8)(a))

The FSA suggests that firms consider other termination issues, including whether they should have a specific right to terminate the agreement if the inadequate provision of services might lead to the firm being unable to meet its regulatory obligations. (SYSC para.13.9.5G(8)(c))

Comment—It is assumed that this is intended to be in addition to the right of the firm to terminate for breach.

The guidance also suggests that firms consider a right of termination for change of ownership or control. (SYSC para.13.9.5G(8)(a))

Comment—Although this is not an unusual requirement, it is a contentious issue with service providers as it undermines the value of their business.

Lastly, it suggests that firms consider a right to terminate if there are significant changes in the business operations of the service provider including subcontracting. (SYSC para.13.9.5G(8)(b))

Comment—This is also likely to be an extremely contentious issue with service providers.

The FSA also suggests that firms consider whether service providers should have the right to terminate the agreement if there is a change of control or significant change in the business operations at the firm. (SYSC para.13.9.5G(8))

Comment—The FSA has included these provisions to cover the situation where the service provider is also an authorised firm or is subject to further regulatory controls for example under competition law. In other situations, it may not be in the customer's interests to include this provision, as any termination of the outsourcing arrangement by the service provider is likely to increase the customer's operational risk.

Comment—Before taking action to terminate under any of the above rights to terminate, the firm will clearly need to consider whether it will be able to ensure a smooth transition on termination.

Termination assistance

The FSA states that firms must consider how they will ensure a smooth transition of their operations on termination of an outsourcing arrangement. The FSA reminds firms that this needs to be considered before entering into the outsourcing arrangement—it is too late to consider termination assistance issues when the agreement is about to expire or be terminated. The guidance stresses the importance of firms reconsidering termination assistance requirements whenever they are about to change the outsourcing arrangements significantly—a point which is often overlooked. (SYSC para.13.9.4G(4))

Guarantees and indemnities

The FSA suggests that firms consider the adequacy of any guarantees or indemnities. (SYSC para.13.9.5G(4))

Comment—The FSA does not suggest what types of guarantees or indemnities might be regarded as adequate.

Offshore outsourcing

The FSA has specific guidance for offshore outsourcing projects (SYSC para.13.7.9G) and reminds firms that they should consider:

(a)   the business operating environment of each country, for example the likelihood and impact of political disruptions or cultural differences;

(b)   relevant local regulatory and other requirements regarding data protection and transfer;

> (c) the extent to which local legal and regulatory requirements may restrict a firm's ability to meet its regulatory requirements in the UK; and
>
> (d) the timeliness of information flows to and from its headquarters and the levels of delegated authority and risk management structures.

40.4 Solvency II

40.4.1 *Description of Solvency II*

Solvency II will involve a number of changes to the way in which insurance firms calculate their regulatory capital and demonstrate operation of their risk management activities, as well as change the way in which they are supervised.

The Level 1 Solvency II Directive was published in the Official Journal of the European Communities in December 2009. The FSA published its first major consultation on its implementation of Solvency II into UK law in November 2011. The consultation sets out the proposed structure of a new Sourcebook, the Prudential Sourcebook for Solvency II Insurers (SOLPRU).

Solvency II envisages outsourcing of various functions by insurers covered by the Directive. It applies similar criteria as those described in Chapter 39 in relation to MiFID. Table 65 sets out the relevant provisions of Solvency II.

Table 65 Solvency II provisions on outsourcing

Powers of supervisors to oversee outsourcing

Recital 37 states: "In order to ensure effective supervision of outsourced functions or activities, it is essential that the supervisory authorities of the outsourcing insurance or reinsurance undertaking have access to all relevant data held by the outsourcing service provider, regardless of whether the latter is a regulated or unregulated entity, as well as the right to conduct on-site inspections. In order to take account of market developments and to ensure that the conditions for outsourcing continue to be complied with, the supervisory authorities should be informed prior to the outsourcing of critical or important functions or activities. Those requirements should take into account the work of the Joint Forum[2] and are consistent with the current rules and practices in the banking sector and Directive 2004/39/EC and its application to credit institutions."

Supervisory Requirements for Outsourcing

Article 38 of Solvency II provides that Member States shall ensure that insurance and reinsurance undertakings which outsource a function or an insurance or reinsurance activity take the necessary steps to ensure that the following conditions are satisfied:

Co-operation with supervisors

(a) the service provider must co-operate with the supervisory authorities of the insurance and reinsurance undertaking in connection with the outsourced function or activity;

Access to data

---

[2] See Chapter 38

(b) the insurance and reinsurance undertakings, their auditors and the supervisory authorities must have effective access to data related to the outsourced functions or activities;

Access to service provider premises

(c) the supervisory authorities must have effective access to the business premises of the service provider and must be able to exercise those rights of access.

On-site inspection rights

2. The Member State where the service provider is located shall permit the supervisory authorities of the insurance or reinsurance undertaking to carry out themselves, or through the intermediary of persons they appoint for that purpose, on-site inspections at the premises of the service provider. The supervisory authority of the insurance or reinsurance undertaking shall inform the appropriate authority of the Member State of the service provider prior to conducting the on-site inspection. In the case of a non-supervised entity the appropriate authority shall be the supervisory authority.

Delegation of inspection rights

The supervisory authorities of the Member State of the insurance or reinsurance undertaking may delegate such on-site inspections to the supervisory authorities of the Member State where the service provider is located.

Conditions for Outsourcing

Responsibility stays with Insurer

Article 49 states that:

1. Member States shall ensure that insurance and reinsurance undertakings remain fully responsible for discharging all of their obligations under this Directive when they outsource functions or any insurance or reinsurance activities.

Restrictions on Outsourcing

2. Outsourcing of critical or important operational functions or activities shall not be undertaken in such a way as to lead to any of the following:
(a) materially impairing the quality of the system of governance of the undertaking concerned;
(b) unduly increasing the operational risk;
(c) impairing the ability of the supervisory authorities to monitor the compliance of the undertaking with its obligations;
(d) undermining continuous and satisfactory service to policy holders.

Notification to Supervisor

3. Insurance and reinsurance undertakings shall, in a timely manner, notify the supervisory authorities prior to the outsourcing of critical or important functions or activities as well as of any subsequent material developments with respect to those functions or activities.

40.4.2   Implications of Solvency II for outsourcing

The draft SOLPRU includes, in Chapter 9.7, draft text on Outsourcing. The FSA intends to apply SOLPRU only to firms covered by Solvency II, so the existing rules on insurance outsourcing will in principle continue to apply to non-Directive insurers. This means SOLPRU will cover all but the smallest insurers. It will cover all Lloyd's business.

Table 66 sets out the FSA's suggestion for SOLPRU provisions.

Table 66 FSA's suggestion for SOLPRU provisions (SOLPRU 9.7)

Firm retains responsibility

SOLPRU para.9.7.1 R states that if a firm outsources a function or any insurance or reinsurance activity, it remains fully responsible for discharging all of its obligations under the rules and other laws, regulations and administrative provisions adopted in accordance with Solvency II.

Outsourcing of critical or important operational functions

SOLPRU para.9.7.2 R says a firm must not outsource a critical or important operational function or activity in such a way as to lead to any of the following:

(1) materially impairing the quality of the firm's system of governance;

(2) unduly increasing the operational risk;

(3) impairing the ability of the supervisory authorities to monitor the firm's compliance with its obligations;

(4) undermining continuous and satisfactory service to policyholders.

Notification to the FSA

SOLPRU para.9.7.3 R states that a firm must, in a timely manner, notify the FSA prior to the outsourcing of critical or important functions or activities as well as of any subsequent material developments with respect to those functions or activities.

Co-operation with the FSA

SOLPRU para.9.7.4 R states that without prejudice to SOLPRU para.9.7.1R to SOLPRU 9.7.3R, a firm outsourcing a function or an insurance or reinsurance activity must take the necessary steps to ensure that the following conditions are satisfied:

(1) the service provider must co-operate with the FSA and, where relevant, any other supervisory authority of the firm in connection with the outsourcing of the function or activity;

(2) the firm, its auditors, the FSA and, where relevant, any other supervisory authority of the firm must have effective access to data related to the outsourcing of the functions or activities; and

(3) the FSA and, where relevant, any other supervisory authority of the firm must have effective access to the business premises of the service provider and must be able to exercise those rights of access.

40.5   Extension of the common platform in SYSC 8

In 2009, the FSA said it wishes to extend the common platform in SYSC 8 (as described in Chapter 39) to insurers, with SYSC 8 replacing SYSC 13. However, these proposals have not progressed and the SOLPRU provisions so far proposed merely "copy-out" the Solvency II Level 1 text.

Chapter 41

Specific regulation affecting Investment Funds and Managers

41.1 Outline

This chapter describes specific regulatory requirements that apply to investment funds and managers. Many investment managers will be subject to MiFID, if they carry on, for example, portfolio management activities for individual discretionary portfolios or other MiFID investment services and activities described in Chapter 39. Those managers should refer also to Chapter 39.

All firms covered by this chapter should also refer to Chapter 38 and the FSA's General and SYSC requirements.

41.2 UCITS IV

The UCITS IV Directive was implemented into UK law in July 2011. It places requirements on regulated investment funds and their managers. Many of the managers would in any event be regulated in the UK. However, UCITS IV and its implementing Directive set out specific expectations relating to what it describes as "delegation to third parties". Table 67 sets out the relevant provisions.

Table 67 UCITS IV Article 13

1. If the law of the management company's home Member State allows management companies to delegate to third parties for the purpose of a more efficient conduct of the companies' business, to carry out on their behalf one or more of their own functions, all of the following preconditions shall be complied with:
Notification of Delegation
(a) the management company must inform the competent authorities of its home Member State in an appropriate manner; the competent authorities of the management company's home Member State must, without delay, transmit the information to the competent authorities of the UCITS home Member State;
Continuing Effective Supervision

(b) the mandate must not prevent the effectiveness of supervision over the management company, and, in particular, must not prevent the management company from acting, or the UCITS from being managed, in the best interests of its investors;

Restriction on Permitted Delegates

(c) when the delegation concerns the investment management, the mandate must be given only to undertakings which are authorised or registered for the purpose of asset management and subject to prudential supervision; the delegation must be in accordance with investment-allocation criteria periodically laid down by the management companies;

Cross-Border Delegation

(d) where the mandate concerns the investment management and is given to a third-country undertaking, co-operation between the supervisory authorities concerned must be ensured;

Conflicts of Interest

(e) a mandate with regard to the core function of investment management must not be given to the depositary or to any other undertaking whose interests may conflict with those of the management company or the unit-holders;

Effective Monitoring

(f) measures must exist which enable the persons who conduct the business of the management company to monitor effectively at any time the activity of the undertaking to which the mandate is given;

Power of Management Company

(g) the mandate must not prevent the persons who conduct the business of the management company from giving further instructions to the undertaking to which functions are delegated at any time or from withdrawing the mandate with immediate effect when this is in the interest of investors;

Qualifications of Delegate

(h) having regard to the nature of the functions to be delegated, the undertaking to which functions will be delegated must be qualified and capable of undertaking the functions in question; and

Disclosure of Delegated Functions

(i) the UCITS' prospectuses must list the functions which the management company has been allowed to delegate in accordance with this Article.

Liability of Management Company

2. The liability of the management company or the depositary shall not be affected by delegation by the management company of any functions to third parties. The management company shall not delegate its functions to the extent that it becomes a letter-box entity.

Duties of Management Company(UCITS IV Implementing Directive Recital 4)

As far as allowed by national law, management companies should be able to make arrangements for third parties to carry out some of their activities. The implementing rules should be read accordingly. The management company should in particular perform due diligence in order to determine whether, having regard to the nature of the functions to be carried out by third parties, the undertaking performing those activities can be considered as qualified and capable of undertaking the functions in question. The third party should therefore fulfil all the organisational and conflicts of interest requirements in relation to the activity to be carried out. It also follows that the management company should verify that the third party has taken the appropriate measures in order to comply with the said requirements and should monitor effectively the compliance by the third party with these requirements. Where the delegatee is responsible for applying the rules governing the delegated activities, equivalent organisational and conflict of interests requirements should apply to the activity of monitoring the delegated activities. The management company should be able to take into account in the due diligence process the fact that the third party to whom activities are delegated will often be subject to Directive 2004/39/EC.

Managers who manage portfolios for retail clients should refer also to Chapter 39 of this Guide, which sets out the MiFID requirements for outsourcing in this specific sector.

41.3   AIFMD

41.3.1   Outline of AIFMD

The AIFMD was adopted in July 2011 and will be implemented in 2013. The Level 2 implementing measures and UK implementing measures are not yet final (as at September 2012). However, the Level 1 Directive contains specific requirements relating to delegation of functions, which will place further requirements on alternative investment funds covered by the AIFMD and their managers, when outsourcing specific functions or activities. Table 68 shows the relevant provisions.

Table 68 AIFMD Article 20: Delegation

Notification of Delegation
1. AIFMs which intend to delegate to third parties the task of carrying out functions on their behalf shall notify the competent authorities of their home Member State before the delegation arrangements become effective. The following conditions shall be met:
Justification for Delegation
(a) the AIFM must be able to justify its entire delegation structure on objective reasons;
Resources of Delegate
(b) the delegate must dispose of sufficient resources to perform the respective tasks and the persons who effectively conduct the business of the delegate must be of sufficiently good repute and sufficiently experienced;
Restrictions where Portfolio or Risk Management Outsourced
(c) where the delegation concerns portfolio management or risk management, it must be conferred only on undertakings which are authorised or registered for the purpose of asset management and subject to supervision or, where that condition cannot be met, only subject to prior approval by the competent authorities of the home Member State of the AIFM;
Cross-border Delegation of Portfolio or Risk Management
(d) where the delegation concerns portfolio management or risk management and is conferred on a third-country undertaking, in addition to the requirements in point (c), co-operation between the competent authorities of the home Member State of the AIFM and the supervisory authority of the undertaking must be ensured;
Continuing Effective Supervision of AIFM
(e) the delegation must not prevent the effectiveness of supervision of the AIFM, and, in particular, must not prevent the AIFM from acting, or the AIF from being managed, in the best interests of its investors;
Qualifications of Delegate
(f) the AIFM must be able to demonstrate that the delegate is qualified and capable of undertaking the functions in question, that it was selected with all due care and that the AIFM is in a position to monitor effectively at any time the delegated activity, to give at any time further instructions to the delegate and to withdraw the delegation with immediate effect when this is in the interest of investors.
Review of Services
The AIFM shall review the services provided by each delegate on an ongoing basis.

Restrictions on Delegation of Portfolio or Risk Management

2. No delegation of portfolio management or risk management shall be conferred on:

(a) the depositary or a delegate of the depositary; or

(b) any other entity whose interests may conflict with those of the AIFM or the investors of the AIF, unless such entity has functionally and hierarchically separated the performance of its portfolio management or risk management tasks from its other potentially conflicting tasks, and the potential conflicts of interest are properly identified, managed, monitored and disclosed to the investors of the AIF.

Liability of Manager

3. The AIFM's liability towards the AIF and its investors shall not be affected by the fact that the AIFM has delegated functions to a third party, or by any further sub-delegation, nor shall the AIFM delegate its functions to the extent that, in essence, it can no longer be considered to be the manager of the AIF and to the extent that it becomes a letter-box entity.

Sub-Delegation

4. The third party may sub-delegate any of the functions delegated to it provided that the following conditions are met:

(a) the AIFM consented prior to the sub-delegation;

(b) the AIFM notified the competent authorities of its home Member State before the sub-delegation arrangements become effective;

(c) the conditions set out in para.1, on the understanding that all references to the "delegate" are read as references to the "sub-delegate".

Restrictions on Sub-Delegation

5. No sub-delegation of portfolio management or risk management shall be conferred on:

(a) the depositary or a delegate of the depositary; or

(b) any other entity whose interests may conflict with those of the AIFM or the investors of the AIF, unless such entity has functionally and hierarchically separated the performance of its portfolio management or risk management tasks from its other potentially conflicting tasks, and the potential conflicts of interest are properly identified, managed, monitored and disclosed to the investors of the AIF.

The relevant delegate shall review the services provided by each sub-delegate on an ongoing basis.

Conditions for Further Sub-Delegation

6. Where the sub-delegate further delegates any of the functions delegated to it, the conditions set out in para.4 shall apply mutatis mutandis.

Further Requirements to be Set by European Commission

7. The Commission shall adopt, by means of delegated acts in accordance with Article 56 and subject to the conditions of Articles 57 and 58, measures specifying:

(a) the conditions for fulfilling the requirements set out in paras 1, 2, 4 and 5;

(b) the conditions under which the AIFM shall be deemed to have delegated its functions to the extent that it becomes a letter-box entity and can no longer be considered to be the manager of the AIF as set out in para.3.

41.3.2   *Implications of AIFMD for Custodians*

The allocation of liability for custody is likely to change once the AIFMD is implemented. Each AIFM caught by the AIFMD will have to have a written contract with a depository or custodian for each fund it manages. The Commission will set minimum contents for this contract.

41.3.3 Liability of custodians for loss of financial instruments

The depository will be liable to the relevant fund or its investors for the loss of financial instruments held in custody (whether it is responsible for the loss or not) except if such loss has arisen as a result of an external event beyond its reasonable control. It will also be liable for all other losses arising from negligently or intentionally failing to perform its AIFMD duties, including ensuring subscriptions, redemptions and value calculations comply with both the relevant fund's constitution and applicable national law.

The provisions on depositaries will place a greater burden on custodians to oversee tasks usually performed by fund managers. They are also likely to have a broader impact, as sub-delegation will only be possible where the sub-delegate satisfies certain conditions, including how the sub-delegate holds the assets and how it is regulated. However, in some jurisdictions, local law requires that certain financial instruments are held in custody by a local entity. If no local entity in such a jurisdiction satisfies the delegation conditions, the depositary can only discharge itself of its liability if it meets certain conditions in the AIFMD, including that the fund's rules allow for such a discharge and that investors have been notified prior to investing.

41.3.4 Liability of custodians for sub-custodians

The custodian will be liable for any act of the sub-custodians. It can only escape liability if the depositary enters into a written agreement with the third party sub-custodian that explicitly transfers the liability of the depository to that third party. This is possible only where the depositary has also entered into a written agreement with the AIF, or the AIF manager on the AIF's behalf, which complies with AIFMD requirements and permits the depositary to do so. The same requirement for a chain of contracts transferring liability also applies in the case of delegation by the sub-custodian. These provisions of the AIFMD, along with others affecting depositories, were extremely controversial during the negotiation of the AIFMD as they impose additional liability, and the get-out is not practicable.

41.3.5 Extension of AIFMD approach to cover UCITS funds

A major focus of the criticism was that the AIFMD standards exceed those currently applicable to UCITS funds, which is inconsistent with the philosophy of imposing more stringent obligations where funds are targeted at retail customers. However, it is likely changes will be made to bring the UCITS Directives in line with AIFMD requirements on depositories. It seems that the AIFMD requirements are to be a benchmark but not necessarily a ceiling.

Chapter 42

FSA Data Security Guidance

42.1 Outline

This chapter covers specific FSA guidance on data security.

42.2 Application of general FSA provisions to data security

42.2.1 Background to FSA report

Confidentiality and security are both extremely topical issues at the moment.[1] The FSA has taken a particular interest in this topic. In April 2008, it published a report on *Data Security in Financial Services* following an FSA review of current data security standards. It also fined several firms for failings in data security.

The report concluded that poor data security was a serious, widespread and high-impact risk to the FSA's objective to reduce financial crime. Recent incidents of data loss have brought many firms to consider data security for the first time. Some progress has been made, in that firms are beginning to understand more about this risk and are becoming more assertive in their efforts to contain it. However, there exists a very wide variation between the good practice demonstrated by firms committed to ensuring data security, and the weaknesses seen in firms that are not taking adequate steps to treat fairly the customers whose data they hold. Overall, the report found that data security in financial services firms needs to be improved significantly. Many firms, particularly small firms, still need to make substantial progress to protect their customers from the risk of identity fraud and other financial crime. As a result of the FSA's findings, one firm was referred to the FSA's enforcement division.

More recently, on 24 August 2010, the FSA fined Zurich Insurance £2,275,000 for its failure to have adequate systems and controls in place to prevent the loss of customers' confidential information. The loss was a result of

---

[1] See Chapters 36 and 37 for a description of general data protection and security issues.

inadequate risk management and reporting in relation to its outsourcing arrangements for the data processing of its general insurance customer data. The fine is the highest levied to date on a single firm for data security failings.

FSA has now included the recommendations of its report in its *Financial Crime Guide*, which it finalised at the end of 2011.

42.2.2   Contents of report

The report:

(a)   stresses the importance of implementing adequate security measures to ensure compliance with relevant FSA and data protection regulation; and

(b)   identifies good practice to share with the industry and highlights areas where improvement is required.

The FSA said that if firms failed to take account of the report and continue to demonstrate poor data security practice, the FSA may refer them to enforcement. The FSA has also declared that it will issue further guidance to supervisors to ensure that data security is reviewed as part of normal supervision. By enshrining the principles from the report in its *Financial Crime Guide*, the FSA has made its intentions clear.

Although the report is not directed specifically at outsourcing, clearly data security is an extremely important issue in outsourcing agreements[2] and so the following paragraphs summarise the key points made in the report.

42.2.3   FSA requirements on customer data

The report stresses the importance of safekeeping customer data to ensure compliance by the firm with the regulatory obligations described below.

42.2.3.1   FSA Principles for Businesses

The FSA "Principles for Businesses", Principle 2 requires that "a firm must conduct its business with due skill, care and diligence" and Principle 3 states that "a firm must take reasonable care to organise and control its affairs responsibly and effectively, with adequate risk management systems".

---

[2]   See in particular the speech published by Philip Robinson, FSA Director Financial Crime & Intelligence Division, on 26 November 2008, on financial crime, in which he said "Increasing numbers of data loss incidents involve outsourcing".

42.2.3.2   *FSA Rule SYSC 3.2.6R*

FSA Rule SYSC para.3.2.6R states that:

> "a firm must take reasonable care to establish and maintain effective systems and controls for compliance with applicable requirements and standards under the regulatory system and for countering the risk that the firm might be used to further financial crime".

42.2.3.3   *FSA Rule SYSC para.3.2.6A*

Firms have a responsibility to assess the risks of data loss and take reasonable steps to prevent that risk occurring. SYSC para.3.2.6A states that firms' relevant systems and controls must be "comprehensive and proportionate to the nature, scale and complexity of their operations". In essence, firms should put in place systems and controls to minimise the risk that their operations and information assets may be exploited by thieves and fraudsters.

42.2.3.4   *"Treating Customers Fairly"*

The report highlights that the secure handling of customer data is also part of the "Treating Customers Fairly" standard that all firms must adhere to. Financial services firms, particularly banks, are often the first to be told when a customer becomes the victim of fraud. Indeed, the principal response to financial fraud in the UK is action by firms, mainly through anti-fraud systems and controls that must constantly evolve to counter the threat.

It is good practice for firms to have procedures in place to investigate fraud and help the customer where appropriate. For example, firms can place blocks or anti-fraud flags on an account, change details and passwords and provide advice to the consumer on how they can protect themselves from further fraud.

42.2.3.5   *Legal Responsibilities under the Data Protection Act 1998*

The Data Protection Act 1998 (DPA 1998) gives legal rights to individuals in respect of personal data processed about them by others. The legal responsibilities of firms in relation to these rights are referred to in Chapters 36 and 37. Firms should note that the FSA supports the Information Commissioner's position that it is not appropriate for customer data to be taken off site on laptops or other portable devices which are not encrypted. The FSA may take enforcement action if firms fail to encrypt customer data taken off site.

42.2.4 Examples of Good and Poor Data Security Practice

The report identified examples of good and poor practice to share with the industry. These examples, which are included in the Financial Crime Guide, are listed in Table 69.

Table 69 Examples of good and poor practice from the FSA Report Data Security in Financial Services (April 2008)

Governance

Good practice

Identification of data security as a key specific risk, subject to its own governance, policies and procedures, and risk assessment.

A senior manager with overall responsibility for data security, specifically mandated to manage data security risk assessment and communication between the key stakeholders within the firm such as: senior management, information security, human resources, financial crime, security, IT, compliance and internal audit.

A specific committee with representation from relevant business areas to assess, monitor and control data security risk, which reports to the firm's board. As well as ensuring co-ordinated risk management, this structure sends a clear message to all staff about the importance of data security.

Written data security policies and procedures that are proportionate, accurate and relevant to staff's day-to-day work.

An open and honest culture of communication with predetermined reporting mechanisms which make it easy for all staff and third parties to report data security concerns and data loss without fear of blame or recrimination.

Firms seeking external assistance if they feel they do not have the necessary expertise to complete a data security risk assessment themselves.

Firms liaising with peers and others to increase their awareness of data security risk and the implementation of good systems and controls.

Detailed plans for reacting to a data loss including when and how to communicate with affected customers.

Firms writing to affected customers promptly after a data loss, telling them what has been lost and how it was lost.

Firms offering advice on protective measures against identity fraud to consumers affected by data loss and, where appropriate, paying for such services to be put in place.

Poor practice

Treating data security as an IT issue and failing to involve other key staff from across the business in the risk assessment process.

No written policies and procedures on data security.

Firms do not understand the need for knowledge sharing on data security.

Failing to take opportunities to share information with, and learn from, peers and others about data security risk and not recognising the need to do so.

A "blame culture" that discourages staff from reporting data security concerns and data losses.

Failure to notify customers affected by data loss in case the details are picked up by the media.

Training and awareness

Good practice

Innovative training and awareness campaigns that focus on the financial crime risks arising from poor data security, as well as the legal and regulatory requirements to protect customer data.

Clear understanding among staff about why data security is relevant to their work and what they must do to comply with relevant policies and procedures.

Simple, memorable and easily digestible guidance for staff on good data security practice.

Testing of staff understanding of data security policies on induction and once a year after that.

Competitions, posters, screensavers and group discussion to raise interest in the subject.

Poor practice

No training to communicate policies and procedures.

Managers assuming that employees understand data security risk without any training.

Data security policies which are very lengthy, complicated and difficult to read.

Reliance on staff signing an annual declaration stating that they have read policy documents without any further testing.

Staff being given no incentive to learn about data security.

Staff recruitment and vetting

Good practice

Vetting staff on a risk-based approach, taking into account data security and other fraud risk.

Enhanced vetting—including checks of credit records, criminal records, financial sanctions lists and the CIFAS Staff Fraud Database—for staff in roles with access to large amounts of customer data.

Liaising between HR and financial crime to ensure that financial crime risk indicators are considered during the vetting process.

A good understanding of vetting conducted by employment agencies for temporary and contract staff.

Formalised procedures to assess regularly whether staff in higher-risk positions are becoming vulnerable to committing fraud or being coerced by criminals.

Poor practice

Allowing new recruits to access customer data before vetting has been completed.

Temporary staff receiving less-rigorous vetting than permanently employed colleagues carrying out similar roles.

Failing to consider continually whether staff in higher-risk positions are becoming vulnerable to committing fraud or being coerced by criminals.

Controls—access rights

Good practice

Specific IT access profiles for each role in the firm, which set out exactly what level of IT access is required for an individual to do their job.

If a staff member changes roles or responsibilities, all IT access rights are deleted from the system and the user is set up using the same process as if they were a new joiner at the firm. The complexity of this process is significantly reduced if role-based IT access profiles are in place—the old one can simply be replaced with the new.

A clearly defined process to notify IT of forthcoming staff departures in order that IT accesses can be permanently disabled or deleted on a timely and accurate basis.

A regular reconciliation of HR and IT user records to act as a failsafe in the event of a failure in the firm's leavers process.

Regular reviews of staff IT access rights to ensure that there are no anomalies.

Least privilege access to call recordings and copies of scanned documents obtained for "know your customer" purposes.

Authentication of customers' identities using, for example, touch-tone telephone before a conversation with a call centre adviser takes place. This limits the amount of personal information and/or passwords contained in call recordings.

Masking credit card, bank account details and other sensitive data like customer passwords where this would not affect employees' ability to do their job.

Poor practice

Staff having access to customer data that they do not require to do their job.

User access rights set up on a case-by-case basis with no independent check that they are appropriate.

Redundant access rights being allowed to remain in force when a member of staff changes roles.

User accounts being left "live" or only suspended (i.e. not permanently disabled) when a staff member leaves.

A lack of independent checking of changes effected at any stage in the joiners, movers and leavers process.

Controls—passwords and user accounts

Good practice

Individual user accounts—requiring passwords—in place for all systems containing customer data.

Password standards at least equivalent to those recommended by Get Safe Online—a government-backed campaign group. At present, their recommended standard for passwords is a combination of letters, numbers and keyboard symbols at least seven characters in length and changed regularly.

Measures to ensure passwords are robust. These might include controls to ensure that passwords can only be set in accordance with policy and the use of password-cracking software on a risk-based approach.

"Straight-through processing", but only if complemented by accurate role-based access profiles and strong passwords.

Poor practice

The same user account and password used by multiple users to access particular systems.

Names and dictionary words used as passwords.

Systems that allow passwords to be set which do not comply with password policy.

Password sharing of any kind.

Controls—monitoring access to customer data

Good practice

Risk-based, proactive monitoring of staff's access to customer data to ensure it is being accessed and/or updated for a genuine business reason.

The use of software designed to spot suspicious activity by employees with access to customer data. Such software may not be useful in its "off-the-shelf" format so it is good practice for firms to ensure that it is tailored to their business profile.

Strict controls over super-users' access to customer data and independent checks of their work to ensure they have not accessed, manipulated or extracted data that was not required for a particular task.

Poor practice

Assuming that vetted staff with appropriate access rights will always act appropriately. Staff can breach procedures, for example by looking at account information relating to celebrities, be tempted to commit fraud themselves or be bribed or threatened to give customer data to criminals.

Failure to make regular use of management information about access to customer data.

Failing to monitor super-users or other employees with access to large amounts of customer data.

Controls—data backup

Good practice

Firms conducting a proper risk assessment of threats to data security arising from the data backup process—from the point that backup tapes are produced, through the transit process to the ultimate place of storage.

Firms encrypting backed up data that is held off site, including while in transit.

Regular reviews of the level of encryption to ensure it remains appropriate to the current risk environment.

Backup data being transferred by secure internet links.

Due diligence on third parties that handle backed-up customer data so the firm has a good understanding of how it is secured, exactly who has access to it and how staff with access to it are vetted.

Staff with responsibility for holding backed-up data off site being given assistance to do so securely. For example, firms could offer to pay for a safe to be installed at the staff member's home.

Firms conducting spot checks to ensure that data held off site is done so in accordance with accepted policies and procedures.

Poor practice

Firms failing to consider data security risks arising from the backing up of customer data.

A lack of clear and consistent procedures for backing up data, resulting in data being backed up in several different ways at different times. This makes it difficult for firms to keep track of copies of their data.

Unrestricted access to backup tapes for large numbers of staff at third-party firms.

Backup tapes being held insecurely by firms' employees; for example, being left in their cars or at home on the kitchen table.

Controls—access to the internet and email

Good practice

Giving internet and email access only to staff with a genuine business need.

Considering the risk of data compromise when monitoring external email traffic, for example by looking for strings of numbers that might be credit card details.

Where proportionate, using specialist IT software to detect data leakage via email.

Completely blocking access to all internet content which allows web-based communication. This content includes web-based email, messaging facilities on social networking sites, external instant messaging and peer-to-peer file-sharing software.

Firms that provide cyber cafés for staff to use during breaks ensuring that web-based communications are blocked or that data cannot be transferred into the cyber café, either in electronic or paper format.

Poor practice

Allowing staff who handle customer data to have access to the internet and email if there is no business reason for this.

Allowing access to web-based communication internet sites. This content includes web-based email, messaging facilities on social networking sites, external instant messaging and peer-to-peer file-sharing software.

Controls—key-logging devices

Good practice

Regular sweeping for key-logging devices in parts of the firm where employees have access to large amounts of, or sensitive, customer data. (Firms will also wish to conduct sweeps in other sensitive areas, for example, where money can be transferred.)

Use of software to determine whether unusual or prohibited types of hardware have been attached to employees' computers.

Awareness raising of the risk of key-logging devices. The vigilance of staff is a useful method of defence.

Anti-spyware software and firewalls etc. in place and kept up to date.

Controls—laptops

Good practice

The encryption of laptops and other portable devices containing customer data.

Controls that mitigate the risk of employees failing to follow policies and procedures.

Maintaining an accurate register of laptops issued to staff.

Regular audits of the contents of laptops to ensure that only staff who are authorised to hold customer data on their laptops are doing so and that this is for genuine business reasons.

The wiping of shared laptops' hard drives between uses.

Poor practice

Unencrypted customer data on laptops.

A poor understanding of which employees have been issued or are using laptops to hold customer data.

Shared laptops used by staff without being signed out or wiped between uses.

Controls—portable media including USB devices and CDs

Good practice

Ensuring that only staff with a genuine business need can download customer data to portable media such as USB devices and CDs.

Ensuring that staff authorised to hold customer data on portable media can only do so if it is encrypted.

Maintaining an accurate register of staff allowed to use USB devices and staff who have been issued with USB devices.

The use of software to prevent and/or detect individuals using personal USB devices.

Firms reviewing regularly and on a risk-based approach the copying of customer data to portable media to ensure there is a genuine business reason for it.

The automatic encryption of portable media attached to firms' computers.

Providing lockers for higher-risk staff such as call centre staff and super-users and restricting them from taking personal effects to their desks.

Poor practice

Allowing staff with access to bulk customer data—for example, super-users—to download to unencrypted portable media.

Failing to review regularly threats posed by increasingly sophisticated and quickly evolving personal technology such as mobile phones.

Physical security

Good practice

Appropriately restricted access to areas where large amounts of customer data is accessible, such as server rooms, call centres and filing areas.

Using robust intruder deterrents such as keypad entry doors, alarm systems, grilles or barred windows, and closed circuit television (CCTV).

Robust procedures for logging visitors and ensuring adequate supervision of them while on site.

Training and awareness programmes for staff to ensure they are fully aware of more-basic risks to customer data arising from poor physical security.

Employing security guards, cleaners etc. directly to ensure an appropriate level of vetting and reduce risks that can arise through third-party suppliers accessing customer data.

Using electronic swipe card records to spot unusual behaviour or access to high-risk areas.

Keeping filing cabinets locked during the day and leaving the key with a trusted member of staff.

An enforced clear-desk policy.

Poor practice

Allowing staff or other persons with no genuine business need to access areas where customer data is held.

Failure to check electronic records showing who has accessed sensitive areas of the office.

Failure to lock away customer records and files when the office is left unattended.

Disposal of customer data

Good practice

Procedures that result in the production of as little paper-based customer data as possible.

Treating all paper as "confidential waste" to eliminate confusion among employees about which type of bin to use.

All customer data disposed of by employees securely, for example by using shredders (preferably cross-cut rather than straight-line shredders) or confidential waste bins. Checking general waste bins for the accidental disposal of customer data.

Using a third-party supplier, preferably one with BSIA accreditation which provides a certificate of secure destruction, to shred or incinerate paper-based customer data. It is important for firms to have a good understanding of the supplier's process for destroying customer data and their employee vetting standards.

Providing guidance for travelling or home-based staff on the secure disposal of customer data.

Computer hard drives and portable media being properly wiped (using specialist software) or destroyed as soon as they become obsolete.

Poor practice

Poor awareness among staff about how to dispose of customer data securely.

Slack procedures that present opportunities for fraudsters, for instance when confidential waste is left unguarded on the premises before it is destroyed.

Staff working remotely failing to dispose of customer data securely.

Firms failing to provide guidance or assistance to remote workers who need to dispose of an obsolete home computer.

Firms stockpiling obsolete computers and other portable media for too long and not in secure environments.

Firms relying on others to erase or destroy their hard drives and other portable media securely without evidence that this has been done competently.

Managing third-party suppliers

Good practice

Conducting due diligence of data security standards at third-party suppliers before contracts are agreed.

Regular reviews of third-party suppliers' data security systems and controls, with the frequency of review dependent on data security risks identified.

Ensuring third-party suppliers' vetting standards are adequate by testing the checks performed on a sample of staff with access to customer data.

Only allowing third-party IT suppliers access to customer databases for specific tasks on a case-by-case basis.

Third party suppliers being subject to procedures for reporting data security breaches within an agreed timeframe.

The use of secure Internet links to transfer data to third parties.

Poor practice

Allowing third-party suppliers to access customer data when no due diligence of data security arrangements has been performed.

Firms not knowing exactly which third-party staff have access to their customer data.

Firms not knowing how third-party suppliers' staff have been vetted.

Allowing third-party staff unsupervised access to areas where customer data is held when they have not been vetted to the same standards as employees.

Allowing IT suppliers unrestricted or unmonitored access to customer data.

A lack of awareness of when/how third-party suppliers can access customer data and failure to monitor such access. Unencrypted customer data being sent to third parties using unregistered post.

Internal audit and compliance monitoring

Good practice

Firms seeking external assistance where they do not have the necessary in-house expertise or resources.

Compliance and internal audit conducting specific reviews of data security which cover all relevant areas of the business including IT, security, HR, training and awareness, governance and third-party suppliers.

Firms using expertise from across the business to help with the more technical aspects of data security audits and compliance monitoring.

Poor practice

Compliance focusing only on compliance with data protection legislation and failing to consider adherence to data security policies and procedures.

Compliance consultants adopting a "one size fits all" approach to different clients' businesses.

Chapter 43

Public Procurement

43.1 Outline

Chapters 38 to 42 deal with outsourcing and services agreements entered into by financial services firms regulated by the FSA. This chapter concerns regulation in the public sector. It includes a short description of the directives affecting public sector procurement.

43.2 Public Procurement Directives

Public procurement within the EU is governed by EU legislation in the form of separate directives covering the procurement of services, works and supplies by the public sector and procurement of the same by utilities.[1] The directives are designed to regulate the award of public contracts above specified financial thresholds by providing transparent award procedures and promoting the equality of treatment of all undertakings in Member States of the EU.

The World Trade Organization (WTO) agreement on government procurement (GPA) governs public procurement relations between EU Member States and a number of non-EU states that have chosen to accede to that agreement. The GPA governs the procurement of works, services and supplies and supersedes the old General Agreement on Tariffs and Trade (GATT), as well as a number of other related WTO agreements.

43.2.1 *Application of the directives—countries*

(a)   The GPA is an optional agreement for WTO members and only undertakings in those states that have acceded to the GPA can benefit from it. The EU has acceded to the GPA on behalf of all of its Member States and some of the non-EU states that have acceded to the GPA are as follows: US, Canada, Japan, Switzerland, Israel, Korea, Norway,

---

[1]   This chapter focuses on the directive applicable to public sector procurement (as opposed to utilities sector procurement which is dealt with in Chapter 46).

Liechtenstein and Iceland. Public bodies in states that have acceded to the GPA must comply with its requirements when conducting procurements over specified thresholds. The provisions are similar to the procurement directives, and, in the EU, compliance with the procurement directives constitutes compliance with the GPA.

(b) India is not a signatory to the GPA and so Indian suppliers are not protected by the procurement directives. China's long running application for membership is yet to be finalised, although Chinese Taipei (Taiwan) joined in 2009.

See Chapter 47 for a discussion of offshore outsourcing.

43.2.2 *Main changes in the directive*

The Consolidated Public Procurement Directive (referred to in this chapter as the "Public Procurement Directive")[2] consolidated three pre-existing directives relating to public works contracts, public services contracts and public supplies contracts. It also updated the legislation to reflect more recent case law, sought to clarify certain points over which questions were raised in the previous directives and introduced a number of innovations.

The Public Procurement Directive provided a legislative basis for the use of framework agreements, which have become increasingly popular, created a new procurement procedure known as the competitive dialogue and facilitated the use of electronic procurement systems.

43.3 When does the Public Procurement Directive apply?

For a proposed services agreement to be subject to the Public Procurement Directive, a number of requirements must first be met. These requirements are as follows:

(a) the entity putting the contract out to tender must be a "contracting authority";

(b) the contract in question must be a "public service contract", "public works contract" or "public supply contract";

(c) the estimated value of the contract must equal or exceed the relevant financial threshold; and

---

[2] Directive 2004/18/EC.

(d) the contract must not fall within one of the exemptions contained in the Public Procurement Directive.

These issues are described in Table 70. All four of the requirements in Table 70 must be met in order for the Public Procurement Directive to apply. Therefore, even if only one of these requirements is not met, the Public Procurement Directive will not apply. If the Public Procurement Directive does not apply, the entity in question may establish its own rules of competition, following private sector tender principles.

However, it should be noted that "contracting authorities" are bound not only by the Public Procurement Directive but also by the general principles derived from the Treaty of the Functioning of the European Union ("Treaty") of equal treatment, non-discrimination, transparency and proportionality. As a result, even if the Public Procurement Directive itself does not apply or does not apply in full, the general Treaty principles may still apply. This is relevant in two particular instances:

(a) for a particular type of "public service contract" known as an "Annex II B" service contract; and

(b) for contracts with an estimated value that falls below the relevant financial threshold.

These two particular instances (Annex II B service contracts and below threshold contracts) are also discussed in Table 70 and an explanation of the impact of the general Treaty principles in these instances is also provided.

Table 70 When does the Public Procurement Directive apply

Contracting authorities

The concept of a "contracting authority" is defined in Article 1.9 of the Public Procurement Directive. The definition is broad and covers essentially public sector bodies, including the state, regional and local authorities, bodies governed by public law, and associations formed by regional or local authorities. It is generally clear whether an entity is a public sector body falling within the definition of a "contracting authority", although this determination can be more complicated in the case of mixed public/private partnerships or companies.

Public contracts

"Public service contracts", "public works contracts" and "public supply contracts" are defined in Article 1.2 of the Public Procurement Directive. Most services contracts are likely to fall within the definition of "public service contracts": "contracts for pecuniary interest concluded in writing between one or more economic operators and one or more contracting authorities having as their object the provision of services ..."

Annex II A and Annex II B services

Annex II to the Public Procurement Directive classifies services as either "Annex II A" or "Annex II B" and this classification determines the level of regulation that will apply to the procurement of a service.

Annex II A services

Annex II A services are subject to the full application of the Public Procurement Directive. Annex II A services include, for example, maintenance and repair, certain financial and insurance services, computer and related services, architectural services and refuse collection.

Annex II B services

Annex II B services include educational services, health services and legal services. These services are only partially covered by the Public Procurement Directive. In the case of Annex II B services, contracting authorities:

(a)   must comply with the requirements as to technical specifications; and

(b)   must publish a contract award notice in the Official Journal of the European Union.

There is therefore no obligation under the Public Procurement Directive to advertise Annex II B service contracts at an EU level. Nevertheless, case law has established that Annex II B service contracts are subject to the general Treaty principles (highlighted above). This means that, where an Annex II B contract may be of certain cross-border interest (e.g. due to its nature or value), the obligation of transparency will require some form of advertisement and open competition. Therefore, the letter of the Public Procurement Directive need not be followed, although the Directive may serve as a guide. In many cases, advertisement on the contracting authority's web portal or buyer profile[3] may suffice for an Annex II B service contract, although this should be assessed on a case-by-case basis. In any event, it is always open to a contracting authority to advertise an Annex II B contract free of charge at EU level in the Official Journal of the European Union.

Financial thresholds

The Public Procurement Directive will only apply to contracts worth more than a specified threshold. The thresholds were most recently revised on 1 January 2012 and are €130,000 in relation to public services contracts (* With the exception of certain services, which have a threshold of €200,000. These include Annex II B (residual) services, Research & Development Services (Category 8), certain types of telecommunications services in Category 5 (including CPC 7524—Television and radio broadcast services, CPC 7525—Interconnection services, CPC 7526—Integrated telecommunications services) and subsidised services contracts under Article 8 of the Public Procurement Directive.) for central government bodies and €200,000 for other public sector bodies.
* The thresholds are revised every two years, so the next time they are due to be revised is 1 January 2014.

In the case of below threshold contracts, the application of the general EC Treaty principles must still be considered. Their application is broadly the same as set out above in respect of Annex II B service contracts, meaning that generally some form of advertisement and open competition will be necessitated. Advertisement and competition may not be required, however, if the contract value is very modest (i.e. significantly below the relevant financial threshold), such that it is unlikely to generate cross-border interest. For very small contracts, therefore, it may be possible for a contracting authority to make a direct award of contract (although this is subject to any other national laws or policies that may be relevant).

Exemptions to the Public Procurement Directive

Article 16 of the Public Procurement Directive contains various specific exemptions covering, for example, contracts for the acquisition of land and buildings and contracts for certain R&D services.[4] Exempted contracts fall fully outside the scope of the Public Procurement Directive and, as such, may be entered into directly by a contracting authority and its preferred provider, although authorities may still need to consider whether they need to comply with the Treaty principles.

---

[3]   The buyer profile is one of the new innovations introduced by the latest Public Procurement Directive. It is effectively a page on an authority's website which displays, for the benefit of interested providers, information on the authority's past, ongoing and future tender processes, as well as general information on and contact details for the authority.

[4]   The exemption covers R&D services for the general public's benefit, as well as R&D services for the sole benefit of the authority where those services are partly or wholly funded by the private sector.

43.4 The award procedures

If a proposed services arrangement is subject to the Public Procurement Directive, the contracting authority has to decide which award procedures it will use.

43.4.1 *Open procedure*

Under the open award procedure all interested parties may tender for a contract. There is no scope for negotiation pre or post submission of tenders. Post tender submission, any discussions between the contracting authority and bidders must be limited to clarifications. A contracting authority is bound to make its choice solely on the basis of the written tender, subject to such clarifications. There is also no opportunity for the contracting authority to limit the number of tenders it has to consider.

As a result, this procedure is not used for the procurement of complex contracts. It is most applicable for the procurement of goods, where there is a clear and comprehensive specification, and price is likely to be the key determinant.

43.4.2 *Restricted procedure*

In the restricted procedure, the contracting authority invites expressions of interest and only those organisations short-listed by the contracting authority may submit tenders. The contracting authority must invite a minimum of five bidders to tender, provided there are five suitably qualified candidates.

Similarly to the open procedure, there is no scope for negotiation pre or post submission of tenders (post tender discussions are limited to clarifications on the information provided or the content of the tenders) and the contracting authority is bound to make its choice solely on the basis of the written tenders, subject to these clarifications. Again, this procedure is seen as inappropriate for complex projects.

If the proposed services project is not complex, however, the restricted procedure is a relatively quick and straightforward procedure to use. Where, for reasons of urgency, the standard timescales for the restricted procedure are impractical, a streamlined process may be operated. In practical terms, this "accelerated" restricted procedure permits a contract to be awarded within one month, compared to the three-month timescale under the normal restricted procedure. Public authorities must justify their use of the accelerated restricted procedure; the automatic "economic climate" justification which was available to public authorities between 2009 and 2011 was withdrawn in 2012.

43.4.3 Competitive dialogue procedure

The competitive dialogue procedure may only be used for the procurement of "particularly complex contracts". A contract will satisfy this requirement where it is not objectively possible for the contracting authority to define the technical means capable of satisfying its needs or to specify either the legal or financial make-up of a project.

Under the competitive dialogue procedure, contracting authorities may select a shortlist of bidders with whom to conduct a dialogue. The shortlist must contain a minimum of three bidders, provided there are three suitably qualified bidders.

The dialogue may cover all elements of the contract and the aim should be to identify the means best suited to satisfying the contacting authority's needs. Once the contracting authority is able to identify this, it must invite all of the bidders to submit final tenders and select the winning bidder using its pre-stated award criteria (which must go to determining the most economically advantageous tender, rather than the lowest-priced tender).

Discussions post tender are confined to clarification, specification and fine tuning (the scope of such discussions is essentially limited in the same way as post tender discussions under the open or restricted procedures). Once the preferred bidder is appointed, the contracting authority may ask it to clarify aspects of its tender or confirm commitments, provided this does not have the effect of altering substantial aspects of the tender (e.g. risk, price) or call for competition and does not lead to a distortion of competition or cause discrimination. Changes to the preferred bidder's tender may be accommodated where they are necessitated by external circumstances that could have affected the preferred bidder, regardless of the preferred bidder's identity. Changes should not in any event affect the status of the preferred bidder as the most economically advantageous tender.

The governments *Procurement Policy Note—Material for Supporting Growth*[5] builds further on Francis Maude's announcement[6] that government departments (and their agencies) must work on the presumption against the use of competitive dialogue. The government's position is that competitive dialogue is suitable for complex contracts and that procurers have incorrectly used competitive dialogue as a way of engaging in dialogue with suppliers.

Guidance is provided for procurers (including, for example, that procurers should engage with suppliers through pre-market engagement and that most procurements should be completed within 120 working days). The note adds that the presumption against competitive dialogue should not result in the increased use of the negotiated procedure. Therefore govern-

---

[5]   Action Note 04/12 9 May
[6]   21 November – Presumption against Competitive Dialogue

mental departments are encouraged to use the restricted procedure and the open procedure. The government target is that by 2014 it will be 40 per cent faster to do business with public bodies.

Competitive dialogue might still be suitable for large complex procurements that will not complete within 120 working days. Complex projects could include those:

(a)   requiring iterative design;
(b)   with an element of private finance;
(c)   that require planning permission; and
(d)   where complex commercial arrangements apply.

43.4.4   Negotiated procedure

The negotiated procedure may only be used in exceptional circumstances where the conditions required for its use are fulfilled. Under the negotiated procedure, the contracting authority consults suppliers of its choice and negotiates the terms of the contract with one or more of them.

There are two types of negotiated procedure: a competitive version which is pre-advertised in the Official Journal of the European Union and a non-competitive version which does not have to be advertised.

43.4.5   Competitive negotiated procedure[7]

The competitive negotiated procedure can only be used exceptionally, for example when the nature of the services to be provided, or the risks involved, do not allow prior overall pricing, or where, because of the nature of the services, the specifications cannot be established with sufficient precision to permit a contract award using the open or restricted procedures.

43.4.6   Non-competitive negotiated procedure[8]

The use of the non-competitive negotiated procedure is very exceptional and can only be used under certain conditions which have been construed narrowly by the courts, and the burden of proving that these conditions have been met rests with the contracting authority. The conditions include, for example:

---

[7]   Article 30 of the Public Procurement Directive.
[8]   Article 31 of the Public Procurement Directive.

(a) where a restricted or open procedure has failed (e.g. all bids were unacceptable, being irrelevant to or totally incapable of meeting the contracting authority's requirements);

(b) where there is only one possible provider (where due to technical or artistic reasons or reasons connected with the protection of exclusive rights[9] the services can be provided by only one provider); or

(c) where additional services are required from an existing provider and the services were unforeseen at the time of the original advertisement, provided that there are technical or economic reasons why the new services could not be separated from those already provided without great inconvenience to the authority; or the new services are strictly necessary for the completion of the contract. The additional services must be worth less than 50 per cent of the original contract value.

43.5   The procurement process

Once it has been established that a proposed services project is subject to the Public Procurement Directive and the contracting authority has chosen an appropriate award procedure, the next step is to embark upon the actual procurement process.

43.5.1   *Advertising the project—the OJEU notice*

The choice of award procedure will determine the advertising obligations that a contracting authority will be subject to. The OJEU notice (also referred to as the contract notice) is basically a short advert for the contract prepared by the contracting authority, using an OJEU notice template, which must be published in the Official Journal of the European Union; hence the name OJEU.

The OJEU notice is an essential document for the tender process and great care must be taken in drafting the notice as it sets the parameters for the entire project. If the contract notice is incomplete or poorly drafted it may be open for interested parties to claim subsequently that all or part of the project has not been advertised properly. There is a prescribed form of OJEU notice that must be used[10] and if the correct information is not included it can become necessary to re-advertise the award procedure.

The Public Procurement Directive sets out various time limits for the dispatch of the OJEU notice and time limits for interested parties to respond

---

[9]   Exclusive rights does not extend, however, to situations where the exclusive right is licensed or can be reasonably obtained on licence.
[10]   Standard form OJEU notices are available on the SIMAP website: *http://www.simap.europa.eu* [Accessed 26 September 2012]

to the contract notice. These periods normally begin to run from the date on which the notice is sent to the OJEU.

43.5.2 *Pre-qualification*

Pre-qualification is essentially the initial shortlisting of the respondents to the OJEU notice. The Public Procurement Directive sets out prescriptive rules for this shortlisting,[11] including eligibility, financial and economic standing and technical or professional ability. The rules include mandatory requirement to exclude economic operators in certain circumstances where, for example, directors or other decision-makers in a company have been convicted of criminal offences, including corruption and money laundering or bribery.

43.5.3 *Tender stage*

The tender stage follows pre-qualification. Here the pre-qualified bidders will be issued with the tender documents which they will use to prepare their tenders.

Article 53 of the Public Procurement Directive provides that a contract must be awarded on the basis of either the most economically advantageous tender (MEAT) or the lowest price.[12]

The contracting authority is required to specify clearly in advance, in either the OJEU notice or the invitation to tender, the criteria by which it will select its preferred bidder. The contracting authority must, if possible, state the weighting which it gives to each of the criteria chosen.

Once bids have been evaluated in accordance with the evaluation criteria the contract will be awarded.

43.5.4 *Framework agreements*

The Public Procurement Directive provides a statutory basis for the use of framework agreements for the procurement of works, services and supplies in the public sector, although they had been used in various form prior to the implementation of the Public Procurement Directive.

---

[11] Articles 45 to 52 of the Public Procurement Directive.
[12] Most outsourcing contracts would be awarded on the basis of the most economically advantageous tender, as otherwise the customer is prevented from assessing tenders on a qualitative basis.

Framework agreements are agreements between one or more contracting authorities and one or more economic operators establishing the terms under which future contracts may be awarded.

The procedures relating to the award of a framework agreement are identical to those for all other public sector contracts.

Where multiple economic operators are appointed under a framework agreement, it may be necessary to hold a mini-competition prior to awarding any contract under the framework agreement. Where only a single economic operator is appointed under a framework agreement, contracts may be awarded directly to that economic operator without further competition.

The existence of a framework agreement can limit competition in relation to the award of future contracts. Accordingly, they are generally only permitted to last a maximum of four years. A contracting authority may set up a framework agreement for longer than four years if it can justify that there are exceptional circumstances for doing so. One such exceptional circumstance might be where the framework agreement must be longer, for example six years, to allow the supplier appointed under it to recoup its investment and make a reasonable profit too. However, the contracts that are awarded under the framework agreement may last for more than four years.

43.5.5   *Electronic procurement*

The Public Procurement Directive provides for the use of email and electronic procurement systems. The rules allow the use of an e-auction phase under the open, restricted or negotiated procedures, as well as when competition is re-opened among parties to a framework agreement. Only those elements of tenders that are quantifiable may be subject to an e-auction as these systems are not suitable for subjective evaluation.

43.5.6   *Mandatory standstill periods*

The standstill period between the decision on contract award and the contract being entered into emerged originally from judgments of the European Court of Justice, including the *Alcatel* case. The standstill period, now part of the Remedies Directive, is intended to avoid any "race to signature" that might deprive unsuccessful bidders of effective remedies, including a review of the contract award decision.

The Remedies Directive[13] required all Member States to implement specific rules on the application of the standstill period. The standstill period should, if properly applied, mean that effective pre-contractual remedies are available in the majority of circumstances, and also serve to allow aggrieved parties to challenge award decisions before contracts are let. The Directive requires the standstill period to be a minimum of 10 calendar days (if bidders are notified of the start of this period by email or fax) or 15 calendar days (if notification is by post). When contracting authorities notify bidders of the start of the standstill period, they must provide bidders with a summary of the reasons why they have been unsuccessful, as well as a summary of the characteristics and relative advantages of the successful tender, together with the name of the successful tenderer. Contracting authorities must not enter into the contract (or conclude the framework agreement) before the end of the standstill period.

43.5.7   Contract award

Following contract award, Article 35.4 of the Public Procurement Directive requires a contracting authority to send a contract award notice to the OJEU within 48 days. This notice must be prepared using a specific template.[14]

43.6   Remedies for breach of Public Procurement Directive

43.6.1   Current remedies regime

The Public Sector Remedies Directive[15] establishes a system of safeguards to protect bidders' rights when tendering for public contracts. It provides that unsuccessful bidders may apply to the relevant national court or body[16] for remedies in certain circumstances if they consider that the contracting authority has breached the Public Procurement Directive.

Remedies available in the UK include:

(a)   automatic standstill, where a claim is filed in Court during the 10 or 15 day standstill period (authorities are prevented from awarding a contract until they have obtained an order from the Court allowing them to proceed);

---

[13]   Directive 2007/66/EC
[14]   Also available on the SIMAP website, referred to in Footnote 12 above.
[15]   Directive 89/665/EC.
[16]   In England, Wales and Northern Ireland, the relevant forum for public procurement actions is the High Court. In Scotland, actions should be brought in the Sheriff Court or Court of Session.

(b)   final set aside of a contracting authority's decision or a requirement to amend discriminatory aspects of tender documents;
(c)   damages; and
(d)   prospective contractual ineffectiveness.

Following the implementation of the Remedies Directive by Member States in December 2009, the remedy of "ineffectiveness" became available to bidders in addition to the remedies that were available under the original regime. This provides for the possibility of concluded contracts to be set aside. The precise meaning of "ineffectiveness" (and the associated consequences) will be for each Member State to determine. The Directive provides that "ineffectiveness" may mean retroactive cancellation of all contractual obligations or cancellation of only future contractual obligations, yet to be performed. The Directive allows Member States to leave the decision of which type of "ineffectiveness" to apply in each case to the discretion of the national court or review body. The UK, for example, where ineffectiveness is a new legal concept, implemented the Directive so as to apply ineffectiveness only to prospective obligations under the contract. Should the national court or review body consider that there are overriding reasons concerning the general interest why a particular contract should not be set aside, the court or body will retain the discretion to award alternative penalties (e.g. imposition of fines or shortening of contracts).

Certain limits are placed on the availability of this remedy of ineffectiveness. First, it is available to bidders only in respect of fundamental breaches of the Public Procurement Directive. This includes where the contracting authority has failed to advertise a contract that should have been advertised. It also includes where the contracting authority has not complied with the standstill period, thus depriving an unsuccessful bidder of the opportunity of bringing an action that it would otherwise have been brought for interim or final measures (i.e. pre-contract) in respect of a breach of the Public Procurement Directive. Second, its availability is limited in time. Special time limits apply to those seeking a declaration of ineffectiveness. Where a contract award notice has been published then the claimant has 30 days to start proceedings (beginning the day after the date of the contract award notice or the day after the date on which the claimant was informed of the conclusion and given reasons). Where no contract award notice was published, proceedings must be started within six months of the day after the date on which the contract is entered into.

It is in the interests of both the public authority and the successful bidder to ensure that the tender process leading up to contract award has been in line with the public procurement rules. A contract could stand to be rendered "ineffective" whether or not the successful service provider is aware of the alleged breach. It is possible to seek to "pre-agree" what would happen in the event of retrospective or prospective ineffectiveness being applied in a separate collateral contract, but any clause in such an agreement which attempted to circumvent the ineffectiveness remedy would be void.

43.6.2   Conditions for claiming remedies

In any case, before a bidder can secure any remedies in the UK the bidder must fulfil certain requirements:

(a) it must have the necessary standing to bring the action (e.g. having bid for the contract or it would have bid for the contract had it been put out to tender or by being able to satisfy the court that there are good reasons for granting the party standing); and

(b) it must bring the action within the relevant national timescale for doing so (if one is provided for). In the UK, following the *Uniplex*case[17] the Public Procurement (Miscellaneous Amendments) Regulations 2011[18] changed the time limits for bringing claims where the claimant first knew or ought to have known the grounds for starting proceedings on or after 1 October 2011. Proceedings must be started within 30 days beginning with the date when the claimant first knew or ought to have known the grounds for starting proceedings. The court may extend this time limit where it considers that there is a good reason for doing so, but must not exercise this power so as to permit proceedings to be started more than three months after the date on which the claimant first knew or ought to have known the grounds for starting proceedings.

43.6.3   Complaints to the EC

While a remedies regime is provided for in the Remedies Directive, bidders may decide, as an alternative, to make a complaint to the European Commission. This is a less direct course of action for a bidder—the complaint is made against the Member State, not the contracting authority in question and the bidder itself is not entitled to any remedies. The Commission, if they choose to take up the case, will seek to negotiate a solution with the Member State and, if necessary, take action before the Court of Justice of the European Union. There is also no time limit on such a complaint.

There are pros and cons to both remedies routes; a bidder will have to decide on a case-by-case basis which one is most suited to its particular situation and priorities.

---

[17]   *Uniplex (UK) Limited v NHS Business Services Authority* (C-406/08)
[18]   Public Procurement (Miscellaneous Amendments) Regulations 2011 (SI 2011/2053)

43.7 Procurement implications of change control procedures

Public authorities and utilities should be aware that the public and utilities procurement directives are still relevant even after a contract has been entered into. They cannot rely on a widely drafted variation clause to bring about endless changes to a contract that was originally tendered in accordance with these directives. Instead, public authorities and utilities alike must take care that variations to an existing contract are not "material", giving rise in effect to a new contract. This is an important consideration—if a new contract arises, this will require the advertisement of a new contract (or OJEU) notice. If this is not done, the essential requirement for the EU-wide advertisement of contracts will not have been met in respect of the new contract.

There are three alternative tests for how a "material" change might arise:[19]

(a) Is the change such that, had it been incorporated in the original contract (or OJEU) notice and tender documents, the outcome of the pre-qualification or bid evaluation process would have been different?

(b) Does the change considerably expand the scope of the original contract?

(c) Does the change swing the economic balance of the contract in favour of the contractor?

If one of these tests is satisfied, the change may constitute a "material" one. At this stage, a public authority or utility has a number of options:

(a) do not proceed with the change for fear of breaching the directives;

(b) scale back the change so it is not "material"; or

(c) proceed with the "material" change having first weighed up the potential risk of challenge to the public authority or utility sector for doing so.

One way to minimise the possibility of this issue arising in the first instance is for the public authority or utility to anticipate as many of the potential changes as possible up front in its tender documents and accompanying draft contract. In this way, the potential changes may be said to form part of the original tender process and not to give rise to a new contract.

---

[19] These alternative tests are derived from the European Court of Justice case of *Pressetext* (C-454/06).

43.8   Public procurement in the UK

The UK implemented the Public Procurement Directive in the UK through the Public Contracts Regulations 2006 (SI 2006/5). These Regulations came into force in the UK on 31 January 2006 and apply to all contracts awarded on or after that date.

The Public Contracts Regulations 2006 give effect to all of the provisions of the Public Procurement Directive described above, including framework agreements, competitive dialogue and electronic auctions and have been amended to take account of the changes to the Remedies Regime.

Much guidance has been published by the Cabinet Office's Efficiency and Reform Group and its predecessor organisation the Office of Government Commerce since the Regulations took effect and covers a range of areas, such as framework agreements, competitive dialogue, mandatory exclusion of tenderers and the standstill period.

43.9   The future of public procurement

At the time of writing the European Commission is in the process of preparing three new directives—replacements for the Consolidated Public Sector Directive and the Utilities Directive and a new directive regulating the award of public services concession contracts.

The new Commission's proposals in respect of the consolidated directives introduce a greater degree of flexibility in relation to issues such as the choice of procedure. The Commission has also taken the opportunity to codify many judgments from the Court of Justice meaning the law should be clearer from the face of the directives.

The Commission proposes that a new directive regulating public services concession will also be introduced. This will apply to contracts where the risk of undertaking the activity, together with the right to collect revenue generated, is transferred to a private sector partner. Such contracts are not currently regulated under the Public Procurement Directive.

Chapter 44

Private Finance Initiative

44.1   Outline

The last chapter described the Public Procurement Directives. This chapter continues the public sector theme by describing a particular form of outsourcing, the Private Finance Initiative (PFI).

44.2   Introduction to PFI

44.2.1   History

PFI is a procurement method which uses the private sector to deliver public infrastructure projects, allocating risk to the party best able to manage it and hence achieve better value for money for the public sector. The emphasis is to look at the whole-life cost of a project being the construction or provision of the asset and its ongoing upkeep including renewal or replacement. Typically the private sector will raise the finance to design, build and operate a project, recouping money from the public sector over the life of the project.

PFI schemes were introduced by the Conservative government in the 1990s and expanded under Labour from 1997. They were seen to be a cheaper and more efficient way of delivering public infrastructure and services. Currently there are 712 projects in construction or operation, with an estimated capital value of around £20 billion[1]. Since 2008, with credit markets drying up, public sector spending cuts and private finance becoming more expensive, the future of PFI remains uncertain (the number of PFI projects agreed in the first four months of 2012 fell by 85 per cent compared with the same period in 2011[2]). In November 2011, HM Treasury (the **Treasury**) launched a review into the future of PFI, the results of which are due to be issued at the beginning of December 2012 as part of the government's Autumn Statement 2012. Contrary to earlier arguments, it has been more recently contested that PFI in its current form in the current economic climate no

---

[1]   *http://www.hm-treasury.gov.uk/d/pfi__signed__projects__list__november__2011.xls* [Accessed 26 September 2012]

[2]   "PFI review leads to slump in new deals", *Financial Times* 11 May 2012.

longer represents value for money. It has also been criticised for its perceived lack of transparency. As part of its wide ranging review, the Treasury will be looking into alternative models of financing, streamlining lengthy procurement processes and the balance of risk between the private and public sector. The Treasury review is discussed further at section 44.15.4.

Whilst the government has yet to detail what the new reformed PFI model will look like, it is likely that the government will continue to seek input from the private sector. Furthermore, the PFI model continues to be exported overseas being applied in countries including, Australia, Canada, the Czech Republic, Finland, France, Greece, India, Ireland, Israel, Japan, Malaysia, the Netherlands, Portugal, Singapore, Spain and the United States. For the purposes of this book, PFI therefore remains a relevant form of procurement.

44.2.2   Guidance

The development of PFI has been assisted by guidance and best practice notes being issued by the public sector. The first edition of the standardisation of PFI contracts was published in July 1999. This has been updated on a number of occasions and the current edition of the standardisation of PFI contracts is version 4 issued in April 2007 (with 2008, 2009 and 2012 updates) and commonly referred to as "SoPC4". Standard contracts have also been published for transactions in a variety of sectors including health, schools and street lighting.

44.3   Contract structure

Typically in a PFI contract, the supplier will incorporate a special purpose vehicle (SPV) which is a limited company with the major sub-contractors and any third-party equity providers being the shareholders. The SPV enters into the project agreement or concession with the customer, whilst at the same time entering into back-to-back arrangements with construction and operation and maintenance subcontractors and financing documentation in order for the SPV to fund the capital costs of providing the assets.[3]

The customer will be required to enter into a direct agreement with the funders, primarily to enable the funders to exercise rights of step in (that is, the takeover of the supplier's rights and obligations under the project agreement) if the supplier defaults. The customer will have the benefit of direct warranties from the subcontractors, although these will only be enforceable in very limited circumstances.

Figure 1 sets out a typical structure.

---

[3]   The structure is, in effect, a particular type of prime contractor relationship—see section 17.2 above.

Figure 1 Typical contract structure

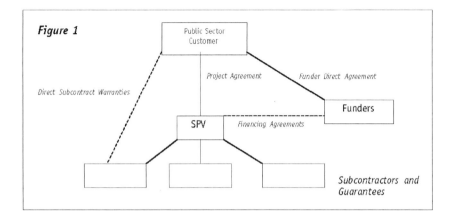

44.4   Finance

PFI transactions are financed with a mixture of debt and equity. The debt and equity ratio varies from project to project. The typical ratio for UK projects pre credit crisis was approximately 90 per cent senior debt to 10 per cent equity. Post credit-crisis, the equity ratio is more in the region of 20 per cent.[4] Project finance techniques are used to finance PFI transactions with the senior debt being raised either through bank financing or via the capital markets, most usually by way of wrapped index-linked or fixed bonds. However due to a more expensive credit market, consideration is being given to accessing a wider range of financing sources, including encouraging a stronger role to be played by pension fund investments. The financing depends largely on the customer being a public sector body, and therefore having an extremely strong covenant. Accordingly, there are tight controls (e.g. limited assignment rights) to ensure the public sector status is preserved for the life of the project.

44.5   Service description

As with many services agreements, the public sector customer under a PFI contract specifies its requirement in terms of outputs. The outputs are intended to describe what the customer requires the supplier to supply and

---

[4]   For example the Norfolk Waste PFI which closed February 2012, has £150 million financing package with £40 million equity.

the standards of performance required.[5] The supplier is afforded the flexibility to determine how the specified outputs are to be met. The customer must resist being prescriptive as to the methodology for service delivery as, by doing so, design or performance risk may be retained rather than being passed to the supplier.

44.6   Commencement of payment

A fundamental part of PFI contracts is that the customer pays for a service rather than for the construction or procurement of an asset. The doctrine is "no service—no fee". Accordingly, no payments are made until service provision commences. By way of example, in a PFI contract for the provision of accommodation services, the customer makes no payments to the supplier until the construction of the building required to provide the services is complete and it can move into the accommodation. The supplier therefore takes the risk of cost overruns or delays.

44.7   Financial deductions

Once service provision has commenced, the customer pays a unitary payment or service fee for the services it receives, subject to those services being provided to the standards specified in the contract. If the services are not provided to the required standards, the customer is entitled to operate the payment mechanism so as to make financial deductions for poor performance.[6]

The primary remedy in a PFI contract for poor performance is the application of the payment mechanism deduction regime. This is often expressed as a "sole remedy", thereby preventing the customer from suing the supplier for breach of contract for failure to deliver the required services. However, the customer will also typically reserve to itself other contractual remedies if service delivery is below standard, including rights of self-help and the right to require the supplier to change its sub-contractor.

44.8   Relief events and compensation events

Whilst the supplier accepts the risk of non-payment where services are not delivered even in no-fault situations, for example insured events, the supplier is given an element of relief against certain no-fault events, known as

---

[5]   PFI contracts will generally be either "business outcome" or "service output" based—see section 1.7 above.
[6]   This type of payment arrangement is discussed more fully in section 18.4 above.

"relief events" or "force majeure events". These are described in greater detail in section 34.9 above.

44.9 Adjustments to the charges

Typically, the unitary payment is indexed annually by reference to the RPI or other indexes. The supplier is generally not able to adjust its prices during the term of the project unless the customer changes the services required, in which case a prescribed change procedure will be followed (see Chapter 25). The project agreement may also provide for the adjustment of the unitary payment by the application of benchmarking or market testing of the services.

44.10 Term

Chapter 26 deals in detail with issues relating to the term of a services agreement and the basis for termination, although a few issues need to be considered in the context of PFI transactions. Generally, PFI contracts have a longer term than pure services agreements. This is particularly the case where significant capital expenditure has to be made by the supplier; the ability to cover this expenditure over, typically, 20 to 30 years assists the customer with affordability issues.

The length of the contract will cover any construction or procurement phase as well as the operational phase, during which the assets are made available to the customer. The duration is generally fixed, and a delay in service commencement will not entitle the supplier to an extended contract term. This further underpins the transfer of risk to the supplier.

44.11 Termination

The grounds for termination referred to in Chapter 26 apply to PFI agreements, although specific provisions apply in relation to force majeure and relief events (see section 34.5 above).

44.12 Termination compensation

On termination of a PFI contract (other than for supplier default) the customer pays compensation to the supplier. SoPC4 sets out how that compensation should be calculated in a typical PFI. It ranges from extensive compensation for the supplier, its subcontractors and funders if the authority defaults or voluntarily terminates, to a requirement to compensate only senior funders fully, with more limited compensation to the supplier and its subcontractors on a termination following force majeure.

On termination or expiry, usually the asset transfers or reverts to the customer. Exceptionally, where the supplier accepts the residual value risk of the asset, the customer "walks away" leaving the asset with the supplier.

44.13   Change in law

The approach to changes in law relating to services agreements is covered in Chapter 25.

44.14   Insurance

Historically, the public sector has not taken out commercial insurance, but has, in effect, self-insured. Under PFI contracts, the private sector supplier mitigates the impact of risks it has accepted by a matrix of insurances. For instance, if a building operated under a PFI agreement is damaged by a fire and the customer is unable to occupy it, the customer will not be required to make any service payment to the supplier. Therefore, the supplier will look to insurance cover to meet not only the cost of reinstating the building, but also its loss of income. Insurance arrangements (including which party should provide insurance) are one of the areas under consideration in the Treasury review.

44.15   PFI Developments

As described in the following paragraphs, a number of reports have been issued by the Treasury setting out and justifying the role of PFI in future projects. With the onset of the credit crisis and the squeeze on government spending, the Treasury have most recently launched a review into reforming PFI to improve its cost effectiveness and transparency. The results of this review are due to be issued at the beginning of December 2012 as part of the government's Autumn Statement 2012

44.15.1   *PFI: Meeting the Investment Challenge*

The report *PFI: Meeting the Investment Challenge* was issued by the Treasury in May 2003. It covers PFI projects only and not other PPPs and relates to

England. It does not apply in Scotland, Wales and Northern Ireland as policy on PFI is devolved in these regions.

The report stated that the government would only use PFI where it is appropriate and where it would deliver value for money. The report concluded that PFI is appropriate where:

(a)   there are major and complex capital projects with significant ongoing maintenance requirements;

(b)   the structure of the services allows the public sector to define its needs appropriately as service outputs; and

(c)   the nature of the assets to be procured allows them to benefit significantly from whole-of-life costing.

It concluded the PFI is appropriate for projects such as the provision of schools and hospitals. The report concluded that PFI was no longer appropriate for IT projects for the following reasons:

(a)   Fast pace of change:

the fast pace of change in the sector and the close links with the organisations' operational needs makes it difficult for the public sector to establish requirements in the long term. The service requirement in an IT project is likely to change frequently during the course of the contract.

(b)   Integration:

higher levels of integration with public sector business systems make it difficult to clearly delineate areas of responsibility to the client and the supplier and so make an appropriate sharing of risk more difficult to discern and enforce. IT projects are intricate and may involve the integration of proprietary technologies so that it is sometimes impossible to substitute in a timely manner a second IT service provider if the supplier fails to meet its obligations under the contract. This means that, if an adequate service is not delivered, the authority is often at a disadvantage in negotiating with its existing supplier.

(c)   Third-party finance:

there is little or no market for third-party finance. This imposes constraints on the ability of the supplier to finance long, upfront development costs and often requires these costs to be met from corporate borrowing. This has limited the number of suppliers bidding for PFI projects and weakened competition. It also removes a valuable source of due diligence which could ensure appropriate and effective risk allocation in a project.

(d)   Duration:

the duration and phasing of investment, where IT projects have a short life and include significant asset refresh, makes defining and enforcing long-term service needs more problematic.

(e) Capital investment:

the fact that the costs of IT projects are dominated not by large up-front investment but by running costs.

44.15.2 *PFI: strengthening long-term partnerships*

The report *PFI: strengthening long-term partnerships* was issued by the Treasury in March 2006. The report confirmed that PFI would continue to play a small but important role in the government's overall objective of delivering modernised public services. It stated that PFI has and is expected to continue to make up 10–15 per cent of public sector investment.

It stated that value for money would continue to be the predominant determinant as to whether to use PFI, but that there would be an increasing emphasis on employees' terms and conditions.

44.15.3 *Infrastructure procurement: delivering long-term value*

The report *Infrastructure procurement: delivering long-term value* was issued by the Treasury in March 2008. It set out the government's policy for securing value for money in its procurement of significant assets, infrastructure and long-term service provision and builds, to a significant extent, on its experience of PFI. It stated that the government expected procuring authorities and the private sector to consider the lessons from PFI.

The report reaffirmed the government's support of the benefits that PFI can bring to the public sector and that PFI would continue to play a "small but important" part in its investment plans, repeating its statements in *PFI: strengthening long-term partnerships*. It also stated that the government would seek to embed these benefits within other approaches.

It confirmed that it would continue to use SoPC4 as the standard form of contract. It also highlighted a number of areas where further government guidance is being made available including use of the competitive dialogue procedure, project maturity, joint ventures and a range of specific PFI financing issues.

The report reaffirmed that value for money should continue to be the test to determine whether to use conventional procurement, PFI or an alternative PPP approach. Value for money can be defined as being the optimum combination of whole-life cost and fitness for purpose to meet the user's requirement. The report also set out the key principles driving value for money in procurements, building on the guidance developed for PFI. These included asking procuring authorities to:

(a) be clear in their objectives;
(b) focus on whole-life costs;
(c) use an output specification approach;
(d) optimise the allocation of risks;
(e) ensure there is a competitive market;
(f) structure the procurement process appropriately;
(g) leave sufficient flexibility;
(h) ensure there are sufficient incentives; and
(i) allow for robust competition.

One key aspect of the report was its emphasis on a risk-based approach to project structures, with risk being borne by the party best able to manage it, and also to project scrutiny. It stressed that appropriate risk allocation and associated contractual incentives are essential for cost-effective delivery.

44.15.4 Reform of the Private Finance Initiative

This forms the latest paper of the Treasury review into the future of PFI. The review is intended to create a reformed PFI model which:

(a) is less expensive and that uses private sector innovation to deliver services more cost effectively;
(b) can access a wider range of financing sources, including encouraging a stronger role to be played by pension fund investment;
(c) strikes a better balance between risk and reward to the private sector;
(d) has greater flexibility to accommodate changing public service needs over time;
(e) maintains the incentive on the private sector to deliver capital projects to time and to budget, and to take performance risk on the delivery of services;
(f) delivers an accelerated and cheaper procurement process; and
(g) gives greater financial transparency at all levels of the project, so that the public sector is confident that it is getting what it paid for, and that the taxpayer is sure it is getting a fair deal now and over the longer term.

The consultation period for the review closed in February 2012 and the outcome of the review is due to be issued in the government's Autumn State-ment 2012. It therefore remains uncertain what the reformed PFI model will look like. However the paper does reaffirm the government's belief in private sector skills and innovation in delivering public sector assets and services but with the need to do so at a lower cost to the taxpayer.

Chapter 45

Relevant Government policy

45.1   Outline

Chapter 43 described the EU Public Procurement Directives and Chapter 44 described PFI projects. This chapter describes relevant UK government policy and guidance on public sector projects which are not PFI projects, including:

(a)   government ICT strategy;

(b)   policy on agile software development approaches;

(c)   government policy on making government business more accessible to SMEs; and

(d)   other laws and guidance.

45.2   Guidance for ICT Procurement

In March 2011, the government published a new ICT strategy.[1] The ICT strategy is split into four parts:

(a)   Part 1 - Reducing waste and project failure, and stimulating economic growth;

(b)   Part 2 - Creating a common ICT infrastructure;

(c)   Part 3 - Using ICT to enable and deliver change; and

(d)   Part 4 - Strengthening governance.

---

[1]   Cabinet Office, *Government ICT Strategy* (2011) *http://www.cabinetoffice.gov.uk/content/government-ict-strategy* [Accessed 26 September 2012]

45.2.1 Reducing waste and project failure, and stimulating economic growth

The government aims to streamline the procurement process that prevents SMEs from bidding for government ICT contracts. This will be achieved by the government promoting the use of smaller sized projects and moving away from large expensive projects that are slow to implement and pose a greater risk of failure. In particular, the government will cap ICT project value at £100 million (when possible).

The government proposes to apply the "agile" methodologies that will allow projects to respond to changing requirements to reduce the risk of project failure.[2] Where appropriate, government will procure open source solutions.

45.2.2 Creating a common ICT infrastructure

The 2011 ICT strategy notes that government departments have often worked independently, relying on large scale infrastructure components. This has resulted in expensive fragmented ICT infrastructures with duplicate solutions often found across government departments. The government's 2011 ICT strategy aims to create a common and secure ICT infrastructure across government. This will be achieved through open common standards and greater use of cloud solutions. The use of common standards will allow for reuse and sharing across government.

45.2.3 Using ICT to enable and deliver change

The 2011 ICT strategy highlights how a flexible ICT infrastructure will assist in the delivery of open, responsive and diverse public services. By opening up the market, the government hopes that costs will decrease and innovation will increase. The government aims to be more responsive to the public; one way the government will achieve this is through greater use of social media.

45.2.4 Strengthening governance

As part of the ICT strategy, the government developed a new governance structure for ICT projects. This will include a new ministerial committee

---

[2] Chapter 24 defined agile software development and describes the implications of employing such a methodology.

(the Public Expenditure Committee (Efficiency and Reform), a CIO Delivery Board and the CIO Council.

45.2.5 *Periodic reviews*

To assess the success of the government's ICT Strategy, the National Audit Office will carry out periodic reviews on its implementation. In May 2012 the first one year report was published.[3] The report concluded that good progress had been made.

45.3 Agile Methodology

In addition to *The Government ICT Strategy 2011* and *The Government ICT Strategy – Implementation Plan 2011* (which both set out objectives for agile delivery in ICT projects) the National Audit Office, in July 2012, published a review on governance for agile[4] delivery.[5]

The report states that the government is interested in the use of agile methodologies to combat waste and reduce the risk of project failure. The government aims to use agile methodologies in half of all major ICT-enabled programmes by April 2013 and to reduce delivery times in these programmes by 20 per cent by 2014.

This National Audit Office report aims to provide support to publicly funded bodies who are using, or considering, using agile methodologies in business change programmes.

45.3.1 *Guidance on ICT Contracts less than £100 million*

The Cabinet Office published a Procurement Policy Note[6] (the PPN) providing that from 1 April 2012, all future ICT projects or contracts (involving central government departments, their agencies and non-departmental bodies) will be designed on the basis they will have a total lifetime cost of less than £100 million, unless an exception applies, e.g. that doing so would

---

3 Cabinet Office, *One Year On: Implementing the Government ICT Strategy* (2012) *http:// www.cabinetoffice.gov.uk/resource-library/one-year-on-implementing-government-ict-strategy* [Accessed 26 September 2012]
4 Chapter 24 defined agile software development and describes the implications of employing such a methodology.
5 National Audit Office: *Governance for Agile delivery* (2012) *http://www.nao.org.uk/publications/1213/ governance_for_agile_delivery.aspx* [Accessed 26 September 2012]
6 Cabinet Office, *Procurement Policy Note - Guidance on ICT Contracts less than £100m* (2012) *http:// www.cabinetoffice.gov.uk/resource-library/procurement-policy-note-0212-ict-contracts-less-100m* [Accessed 26 September 2012]

increase the overall cost to the taxpayer. The PPN suggests that future projects will need to be structured to be flexible, with a greater link between core business needs and requirements.

The PPN aims to:

(a)   reduce the risk of paralysis on projects, due to single supplier failure;
(b)   increase competition between suppliers and increase the number of qualifying bidders;
(c)   increase individual company contracts and share contracts amongst companies;
(d)   encourage standardisation and improve costs;
(e)   reduce over complicating project structures; and
(f)   procure contracts to provide maximum benefits to the maximum number of parties.

45.3.2   *Small and Medium Sized Enterprises*

In February 2011, the government set an objective that, by the end of current Parliament, 25 per cent of central government procurement spending should go to small and medium sized enterprises (SMEs). The government announced a series of measures to achieve this aim including:

(a)   launching Contracts Finder[7] (a website enabling contractors to search live opportunities, tender and contract documents and tender results);
(b)   abolishing pre-qualification questionnaires, for procurements below £100,000;
(c)   publishing recommendations to streamline the procurement process; and
(d)   facilitating the challenges that face SMEs.

According to a report[8] by the Cabinet Office, progress has been made, government procurement has become streamlined and transparent. The Cabinet Office recommended further measures that should be taken to enable the government to reach its objective. These measures include:

(a)   obtaining commitments from nine large private sector companies that they will publish their government sub-contracting opportunities on Contracts Finder;
(b)   providing flexible government IT contracts suitable for SMEs. The government will achieve this by including breakpoints in contracts and ensuring future contracts are flexible and cheaper;

---

[7]   *http://www.contractsfinder.businesslink.gov.uk/* [Accessed 26 September 2012]
[8]   Cabinet Office, *Making Government business more accessible to SMEs – One Year On Progress report on enabling more SMEs to tender for government procurements* (2012) *https://update.cabinetoffice.gov.uk/resource-library/making-government-business-more-accessible-smes-one-year* [Accessed 26 September 2012]

(c)   ensuring that the tendering processes is transparent;

(d)   ensuring that SMEs will have the opportunity to rate government departments and investigating complaints regarding unfair practice; and

(e)   ensuring SMEs receive payment quicker.

45.3.3   *Other laws and guidance*

There are numerous other laws and guidance relating to public sector outsourcing, including:

(a)   Human Rights Act 1998;

(b)   Freedom of Information Act 2000;

(c)   guidance on Crown copyright;[9]

(d)   guidance on shared services;[10]

(e)   guidance on offshoring by government;[11]

(f)   various guidance on open source software;[12]

(g)   various guidance on greening government;[13] and

(h)   various guidance on speeding up government procurement.[14]

---

[9]   See, for example, The National Archives, *Crown copyright – An overview for government departments* at *http://www.nationalarchives.gov.uk/documents/information-management/crown-copyright-an-overview-for-government-departments.pdf* [Accessed 26 September 2012]

[10]   See the report by the National Audit Office, *Efficiency and reform in government corporate functions through shared service centres* 7 March 2012 *http://www.nao.org.uk/publications/1012/shared__service__centres.aspx* [Accessed 26 September 2012]

[11]   See the report by the Cabinet Office on *Government ICT Offshoring (International Sourcing) Guidance* July 2011 *http://www.cabinetoffice.gov.uk/resource-library/government-ict-offshoring-international-sourcing-guidance* [Accessed 26 September 2012]

[12]   See, for example, Cabinet Office, *All about Open Source: An Introduction to Open Source Software for Government IT http://www.cabinetoffice.gov.uk/sites/default/files/resources/All__About__Open__Source__v2__0.pdf* [Accessed 26 September 2012]

[13]   See, for example, Cabinet Office, *Greening Government: ICT Strategy*(2011) *http://www.cabinetoffice.gov.uk/resource-library/uk-government-ict-strategy-resources* [Accessed 26 September 2012]

[14]   See, for example, Cabinet Office, *Accelerating Government Procurement* (2011). *http://www.cabinetoffice.gov.uk/sites/default/files/resources/lean-study-accelerating-government-procurement.pdf* [Accessed 26 September 2012]

Chapter 46

Utilities Sector

46.1   Outline

Chapter 43 deals with the procurement of services by public sector bodies. This chapter concerns regulation in utilities including procurement directives, which are in some ways similar to the public procurement directives.

46.2   Introduction

The Utilities Directive[1] is designed to regulate the award by utility bodies of works, services and supplies contracts above specified financial thresholds by providing transparent award procedures and promoting the equality of treatment of all suppliers.

46.3   When does the Utilities Directive apply?

In deciding whether the Utilities Directive will govern a proposed services arrangement, a utility must consider the issues described in Table 71.

Table 71—When does the Utilities Directive apply?

Contracts for works, supplies or services
For a proposed services arrangement to be subject to the Utilities Directive, the contract must come within the definition of "service contracts", "works contracts" or "supply contracts" as set out in Article 1 of the Utilities Directive. Most services contracts are likely to fall within the definition of "service contracts": "contracts for pecuniary interest concluded in writing between one or more [of the] contracting entities … and one or more contractors, suppliers, or service providers".
Utilities
The Utilities Directive applies to a utility that seeks offers in relation to a proposed supply contract, works contract or service contract. The Utilities Directive refers to utilities as "contracting entities". Contracting entities are defined in Article 2(2) of the Utilities Directive and include public bodies, public undertakings and private undertakings, provided those private undertakings operate on the basis of "special or exclusive rights" (see further below).

---

[1]   Directive 2004/17/EC which replaces the previous Utilities Directive 93/38/EEC.

Moreover, each of these bodies and undertakings must undertake one of the relevant utility activities referred to in Articles 3 to 7 of the Directive in order to fall within the definition of a "contracting entity". (For ease of reference, this chapter will continue to refer to "contracting entities" as "utilities".) The relevant utility activities are activities in the gas, electricity, water, transport and postal sectors (e.g. operation of a fixed electricity network or supply of electricity into that network).

Special or exclusive rights

The Utilities Directive only applies to private sector undertakings where they carry out one of the relevant utility activities, where the contract is awarded in pursuit of that activity and they carry on that activity on the basis of special or exclusive rights.

Financial thresholds

The Utilities Directive will only apply to contracts worth more than a specified threshold. The thresholds were most revised on 1 January 2012; the threshold is €400,000 in respect of services contracts.[2]

Annex XVII A and Annex XVII B services

Annex XVII of the Utilities Directive classifies services as either "Annex XVII A" or "Annex XVII B" and this classification determines the level of regulation that will apply to the procurement of a service.

Annex XVII A services are subject to the full application of the Utilities Directive and include, for example maintenance and repair services, financial services, insurance services, computer and related services, architectural services and refuse collection.

In relation to Annex XVII B services, utilities are required to ensure a certain degree of transparency in relation to their procurement process insofar as they must comply with the requirements concerning technical specifications and publish a contract award notice in the Official Journal of the European Union. It is not absolutely clear at present whether the implications of the case law for Annex II B public services contracts (i.e. the requirement to advertise these contracts and hold a fair competition where such contracts may be of certain cross-border interest) applies to Annex XVII B utilities services contracts. This will depend on the status of the utility in question. For example, if a utility is wholly or majority state owned, the case law is more likely to be relevant.

Exemptions to the Utilities Directive

Articles 19–26 of the Utilities Directive contain various specific exemptions covering, for example, contracts for the acquisition of land and buildings and certain contracts for research and development services.

However, the key exemption for many utilities is the "affiliated undertaking" exemption contained in Article 23 of the Utilities Directive. This exemption permits utilities to award contracts (for works, services or supplies) directly to "affiliated undertakings" as defined in the Directive (i.e. subsidiaries or fellow subsidiaries) provided the essence of the affiliated undertaking is to provide such works, services or supplies to the utility or other undertakings within the group of companies. A test is laid down in the Directive to determine whether that in fact is the case. Should a utility wish to rely on this exemption, it must consider in each case whether the affiliated undertaking acquired at least 80 per cent of its average turnover from the provision of such works, services or supplies to the utility or other undertaking with the group of companies. If this cannot be said to be the case, the exemption will not be available to the utility. In the case of start-up businesses, business projections may be used to establish the credibility of this test being met in the future.

In a similar vein, there is an exemption for the award of contracts between members of a joint venture established exclusively by utilities.

Special exemption mechanism

---

2   The thresholds are revised every two years, so the next time they are due to be revised is 1 January 2014.

The current Utilities Directive introduced a special exemption mechanism whereby Member States or utilities themselves can apply to the European Commission to have certain sectors exempted from the scope of the Utilities Directive. An exemption will be granted only if evidence can be adduced to show that the utility activity in question is directly exposed to competition and access to the market is not restricted (e.g. because steps have been taken in line with relevant Community law to liberalise the market). Examples of some sectors excluded on this basis include electricity and/or gas supply in England, Scotland and Wales,[3] the supply of certain courier and parcel services in Denmark,[4] the supply of certain postal services in Finland[5] and the production and sale of electricity in Sweden.[6]

46.4 The award procedures

If a proposed services arrangement is subject to the Utilities Directive, the utility may freely decide which award procedure it will use. The procedures it may choose from are set out below. It is worth noting that the competitive dialogue procedure which is available under the Public Procurement Directive is not provided for in the Utilities Directive.

46.4.1 Open procedure

Under the open procedure, all interested parties may tender for a contract. There is no scope for negotiation pre or post submission of tenders. Post tender, discussions between the utility and bidders must be limited to clarifications. A utility is bound to make its choice solely on the basis of the written tender, subject to clarifications. There is also no opportunity for the utility to limit the number of tenders it has to consider—tenders from all suitably qualified candidates must be evaluated.

As a result, this procedure is not used for the procurement of complex contracts. It is most applicable for the procurement of goods, where there is a clear and comprehensive specification, and price is likely to be the key determinant.

46.4.2 Restricted procedure

In the restricted procedure, the utility invites expressions of interest and only those organisations shortlisted by the utility may submit tenders. The number of organisations shortlisted must be sufficient to ensure genuine competition. At least three organisations would generally ensure sufficient competition, although this should be assessed on a case-by-case basis.

---

[3] Commission decision 2007/141/EC of 26 February 2007.
[4] Commission decision 2007/169/EC of 16 March 2007.
[5] Commission decision 2007/564/EC of 6 August 2007.
[6] Commission decision 2007/706/EC of 29 October 2007.

Similarly to the open procedure, there is no scope for negotiation pre or post submission of tenders (post-tender discussions are limited to clarifications on the information provided or the content of the tenders) and the utility is bound to make its choice solely on the basis of the written tenders, subject to those clarifications. Again, this procedure is seen as inappropriate for complex projects.

46.4.3 *Negotiated procedure*

Under the negotiated procedure, the utility consults suppliers of its choice and negotiates the terms of the contract with one or more of them.

There are two types of negotiated procedure: a competitive version which is pre-advertised in the Official Journal of the European Union and a non-competitive version which does not have to be advertised.

46.4.4 *Competitive negotiated procedure*

Under the competitive negotiated procedure, the utility negotiates the terms of the contract with one or more organisations shortlisted by it. Like the restricted procedure, the number of organisations shortlisted must be sufficient to ensure genuine competition (i.e. at least three).

46.4.5 *Non-competitive negotiated procedure*

The use of the non-competitive negotiated procedure is very exceptional and can only be used under certain conditions which have been construed narrowly by the courts, and the burden of proving if these conditions have been met rests with the utility. The conditions include, for example:

(a) where a previous procedure has failed (e.g. no bids were received or the bids received do not address the utility's requirements);
(b) where there is only one possible provider (where due to technical or artistic reasons or reasons connected with the protection of exclusive rights[7] the services can be provided by only one provider); or
(c) where additional services are required from an existing provider and the services were unforeseen at the time of the original advertisement, provided: (i) there are technical and economic reasons why the additional services could not be separated from those already provided without great inconvenience to the utility; or (ii) the additional services are strictly necessary for the completion of the contract. In contrast to

---

[7] However, exclusive rights does not extend to situations where the exclusive right is licensed or can be reasonably obtained on licence.

the Public Procurement Directive, there is no threshold on the value of the additional services. However, it may be prudent to apply some form of threshold and the 50 per cent threshold in the Public Procurement Directive may be a suitable guide.

46.5   The procurement process

Once it has been established that a proposed services arrangement is subject to the Utilities Directive and the utility has chosen an appropriate award procedure, the next step is to embark upon the actual procurement process.

46.5.1   *Advertising the project*

Where a utility is undertaking a competitive award procedure it must advertise the project. It can do this in one of three ways:

(a)   place a contract (or "OJEU") notice in the Official Journal of the European Union;
(b)   place a periodic indicative notice (or "PIN") in the Official Journal; or
(c)   place a notice on the existence of a qualification system in the Official Journal.

These notices, which are essentially standard forms, are available on the SIMAP website.[8] Utilities commonly use qualification systems, as they are convenient. Qualification systems enable utilities to establish a list of qualified suppliers from which it can select suppliers to tender for a particular contract without having to go back out to the market each time. Moreover, a qualification system can be set up to run for up to three years without any further or refresher notice having to be published. A qualification system may be used in conjunction with the restricted or negotiated procedures only. (See also section 46.5.4 below.)

With all of these notices, it is important to take great care when drafting them as they set the parameters for the entire project or projects. If the notice is incomplete or poorly drafted it may be open for interested parties to claim subsequently that all or part of the project has not been advertised properly.

The Utilities Directive set out various time limits for the dispatch of the various notices and time limits for interested parties to respond to the notices. These periods normally begin to run from the date on which the notice is sent to the OJEU.

---

8   See SIMAP website at: *http://www.simap.europa.eu* [Accessed 26 September 2012].

46.5.2   Pre-qualification

Pre-qualification is essentially the initial shortlisting of the respondents to the notice. The Utilities Directive require utilities to use objective criteria for shortlisting. This may include financial and technical capacity, although the Utilities Directive is not as prescriptive on this point as the Public Procurement Directive. There are also now grounds on which public sector utilities must exclude certain economic operators, such as those convicted of corruption or money laundering. Private sector utilities may exclude economic operators on this basis, but they do not have to.

46.5.3   Tender stage

The tender stage follows pre-qualification. Here the pre-qualified bidders will be issued with the tender documents which they will use to prepare their tenders.

Article 55(1) of the Utilities Directive provides that a contract must be awarded on the basis of either the most economically advantageous tender (MEAT) or the lowest price.[9]

The utility is required to specify clearly in advance, in either the OJEU notice or the contract documents, the criteria by which it will select its preferred bidder. The utility must, if possible, state the weighting which it gives to each of the criteria chosen.

Once bids have been evaluated in accordance with the evaluation criteria the contract will be awarded.

46.5.4   Framework agreements and qualification systems

The Utilities Directive provides for the use of framework agreements and qualification systems.

The requirements for awarding a framework agreement are the same as for other contracts covered by the Utilities Directive. Where a utility awards a framework agreement in accordance with the Utilities Directive, it may call off contracts under that framework agreement without being required to advertise the contract by way of a separate notice. It is worth noting that the rules on framework agreements are more flexible for utilities than for contracting authorities under the Public Procurement Directive. For example, utilities are not subject to a specified time limit on such agree-

---

[9]   Most outsourcing contracts would be awarded on the basis of the most economically advantageous tender, as otherwise the customer is prevented from assessing tenders on a qualitative basis.

ments, whereas framework agreements in the public sector cannot usually exceed four years. The Utilities Directive requires, nevertheless, that framework agreements must not be used to hinder, limit or distort competition. This means that, for example, framework agreements should not be so long that they prevent new organisations from entering the marketplace.

Qualification systems are akin in certain ways to framework agreements. As noted above, they enable utilities to establish a list of qualified suppliers. However, the key difference with qualification systems is that they are an open list of qualified suppliers; a utility must allow economic operators to apply for qualification at any time during its operation. Framework agreements are closed lists; a supplier that fails to apply to qualify by the stated time limit may not be allowed to join the framework agreement at a later date.

46.5.5   Electronic procurement

The Utilities Directive provides for the use of email and electronic procurement systems for the first time. It allows the use of an e-auction phase under the open, restricted or negotiated procedures. Only those elements of tenders that are quantifiable may be subject to an e-auction as these systems are not suitable for subjective evaluation.

46.5.6   Mandatory standstill period

The Remedies Directive (see section 43.5.6) also apply to utilities contracts and imposes a standstill period between the decision on contract award and the contract being entered into, codifying the requirement of the *Alcatel* judgment. The Remedies Directive (the provisions of which were implemented in all Member States by 20 December 2009) states that the standstill period must last at least 10 calendar days (if all bidders are notified of the utility's decision at the beginning of this period by email or fax) or 15 days (if notification is by post). Utilities must notify bidders with a summary of the reasons as to why they have been unsuccessful, the name of the successful tenderer and the reasons why that tenderer was successful.

46.5.7   Contract award

Following contract award, Article 43 of the Utilities Directive requires a utility to send a contract award notice to the OJEU within two months. This notice must be prepared using a specific template.

46.6   Remedies for breach of the Utilities Directive

There is a specific Utilities Remedies Directive[10] which sets out the remedies available to bidders participating in tender processes run by utilities under the Utilities Directive. The remedies and the requirements for obtaining them before the relevant national court or review body are the same as set out in the Public Sector Remedies Directive (see section 43.6 above). In the same way as the Public Sector Remedies Directive, the Utilities Remedies Directive was revised and implemented into national law on 20 December 2009 (again, see section 43.6 above).

In addition to the remedies set out in the Utilities Remedies Directive, an unsuccessful supplier also has a right to make a complaint to the European Commission where it suspects the Utilities Directive has been breached. However, this may be a less fruitful route if the utility is not in some way controlled or influenced by the State. In practice, most complaints to the Commission are in relation to public sector bodies.

46.7   Implementation of the Utilities Directive in the UK

The Utilities Procurement Directive has been implemented in the UK by the Utilities Contracts Regulations 2006 (SI 2006/6) ("Utilities Regulations"). These Regulations came into force in the UK on 31 January 2006 and apply to all contracts awarded on or after that date. They reflect the new utilities regime brought about by the Utilities Remedies Directive which was implemented in the UK by the Utilities Contracts (Amendment) Regulations 2009.[11]

---

[10]   Directive 92/13/EEC as amended by Directive 2007/66/EC.
[11]   Utilities Contracts (Amendment) Regulations 2009 (SI 2009/3100).

Part 11

Offshore Outsourcing

Chapter 47

Offshore and Near-shore Outsourcing

47.1   Outline

Chapters 38 to 46 deal with issues affecting different sectors. This chapter covers the general commercial and legal issues relating to offshore and near-shore outsourcing, including: the additional due diligence which must be carried out; additional factors relating to structuring the offshore and near-shore outsourcing or services arrangement; special tips for preparing service descriptions, service levels and charging regimes for offshore and near-shore arrangements; termination grounds; the FSA guidance on offshore and near-shore arrangements; data protection issues and the relevance of TUPE.

Chapters 48, 49, 53 and 57 deal with specific issues relating to outsourcing to India, China, Spain and Ireland.

47.2   Services offshored and offshore destinations

47.2.1   Services offshored

Services commonly outsourced to offshore locations include software development and some types of business process services. There is a growing trend in the UK for customers to opt to retain their customer-facing operations in the UK and offshore only back-office processes.

47.2.2   Offshore destinations

Services are outsourced to various different countries, depending upon the country from which the services are being outsourced and hence the language spoken by the customer. In Germany, the most common offshore outsourcing destinations are Africa and Eastern Europe (in particular Poland and the Czech Republic). In France they are North Africa, and in

Spain they are South and Central America.[1] In the UK, the most common offshore outsourcing destination has been India.

47.3   Political implications of offshore service arrangements

Offshore sourcing arrangements are often highly political, high profile and extremely unpopular.

Offshoring became a political issue in the US during the last decade, particularly beginning with the US presidential election of 2004. As a result, several legislative initiatives have been introduced at the federal level from time to time to "reign in" offshoring through proposed changes in tax policy, proposed strengthening of privacy controls or restricting offshoring of certain government contracts. But such initiatives have not generally been successful.

A few of the states have been more successful in implementing legislation or regulations that disfavour offshoring in state government procurement initiatives (by providing preferences for on-shore solutions), but the introduction of new initiatives has declined. As a result, there are no significant impediments at the federal or state level to outsourcing or offshoring that affect a large segment of the market.

In the UK, the Prime Minister, David Cameron has spoken out in favour of free trade.

47.4   Preparation by the customer

Chapters 2 and 4 emphasise the importance of the customer carrying out sufficient due diligence to ensure that its business objectives will be satisfied by the services arrangement. Customers considering offshore outsourcing arrangements will need to consider all of the issues raised in those chapters. They will also need to consider additional factors such as those mentioned in Table 72.[2]

---

[1]   See Part 12 of this Guide for further information about outsourcing in key EU countries.
[2]   In September 2005, PwC examined experiences and best practice in offshoring by financial institutions, following a survey of 156 senior executives in financial institutions. In the resulting report *Offshoring in the financial services industry: risks and rewards*, PwC stated that many firms felt that they would have benefited from investing more in planning and shaping the deal.

Table 72 Additional factors to be considered in due diligence

Customer's business objective

Will offshore outsourcing arrangements satisfy the customer's short-term business objectives?

Will it continue to satisfy future business objectives (e.g. if the economy changes and the customer's business objective changes from cutting costs to expansion)?

Knowledge of the customer's business

How important is it that the staff providing the services understand the customer's business, operating practices and culture?

Will the staff of an offshore supplier have the necessary understanding?

How will any lack of understanding of such factors affect the services provided by the supplier?

How can any lack of understanding be addressed?

Time difference

What is the time difference between the customer's location and the supplier's location?

Is this an advantage (e.g. by enabling the development of software or the provision of call-centre services 24 hours a day, seven days a week)?

Is it a disadvantage (e.g. by making communication between the parties difficult)?

Will the customer need to select a supplier with a presence within the UK to liaise with the offshore service delivery unit?

Will the customer need to amend other services arrangement it has? For example, If the customer has previously outsourced its IT and now outsources its business processes, will it need to amend its agreement with its IT supplier to extend the services hours during which IT systems are available?

Termination

How would the customer bring the services back in house or transfer them to another supplier on termination of the offshore agreement? Should the customer adopt a multi-sourcing approach to ensure continuity on termination?

Will offshoring result in a loss of technical expertise or business knowledge? How will the customer ensure that it will have the information to transfer the services to another supplier or to bring the services back in house on termination?

Stability and security issues

How stable is the business and political climate?

What is the risk of natural disasters affecting the location from which the services will be provided?

Is the offshore country involved in a political conflict that may affect the safety and security of the location from which the services will be provided?

Are there any problems with data security and corruption?

Reputation

If the offshore element is unpopular, how will this affect the customer's brand or sales of the customer's products?

Government and laws

How supportive to offshore outsourcing arrangements is the government in the offshore location?

What is the legal system in the offshore location?

Are there any regulatory obligations which must be satisfied in the UK (e.g. FSA requirements) or in the offshore location?[3]

How difficult would it be to enforce a judgment against the supplier in the foreign court?

---

3   For a description of data protection issues, see Chapters 46 and 47.

Should the customer deal with any enforcement difficulties by agreeing that disputes will be resolved by alternative dispute resolution procedures or by requiring the supplier to provide a performance bond?

What protection is provided in the offshore legal system for the customer's IPR, for example is the offshore location a signatory of the WTO's TRIPS agreement and/or other international instruments?[4]

Is confidential information protected by the relevant legal system?

Are there any exchange controls?

If the arrangement will involve a transfer of technology, will export controls apply?

Are there any restrictions on the customer owning companies in the offshore jurisdiction?

Are there any restrictions on software exports?

Will the relevant foreign court enforce a clause stating that the agreement will be governed by English law and that the English courts will have the exclusive jurisdiction to determine disputes?

Does the local law imply any provisions into the outsourcing agreement?

Are there any relevant employment laws which will affect the provision of the services?

Will the law in the offshore location limit the enforceability of certain provisions in the outsourcing agreement, for example limitations of liability, termination rights or dispute resolution provisions?

Costs and charges

How much cheaper will the services be if they are provided offshore?

For how long are the services likely to remain at this price? For how long will the supplier guarantee the same prices?

How will fluctuations in exchange rates affect costs and who will bear the risk of these?

Are there any hidden costs of offshore outsourcing arrangements?

What increased costs will be incurred in the training of and knowledge transfer to offshore staff before they can provide the services being outsourced?

What increased costs will be incurred in training onshore staff?

What increased costs will be incurred in managing the transition to the offshore supplier?

Will the customer need to amend its existing software licences to ensure that they cover a supplier in the offshore location and, if so, how much will this cost?

What increased costs will be incurred in managing the services after transition?

What increased costs will be incurred during the term of the arrangement?

What travel costs will be incurred in travelling to the offshore location?

Will there be additional telecommunications costs? Who will be responsible for these?

Will outsourcing the service result in a reduction in revenue for the customer (e.g. if the services comprise the provision of a call centre taking orders for the customer's products)?

Taxation

Will the offshoring be regarded as a permanent establishment for taxation purposes?

Are there any transfer pricing issues?

Will withholding tax apply?

Are there any taxation incentives or lower tax rates? When will the taxation incentives expire?

Labour pool characteristics

What is the quality of the staff who will provide the services?

---

[4] TRIPS stands for Trade-Related Aspects of Intellectual Property Rights, which is part of the World Trade Organization (WTO) agreement on international trade. Signatories to TRIPS are obliged to provide certain minimal standards of intellectual property protection. Customers entering into agreements with Indian suppliers must take specialist advice on IPR issues. The customer may want the supplier to hold seminars for its employees explaining about the protection of IPR.

Are there independent standards which can be used to assess the quality of the services to be provided by the staff?

Are the staff graduates?

What is the turnover rate for staff in the offshore location and how does it compare with the turnover rate at the customer's business?

Is the turnover rate likely to change over time?

What are the language skills of the staff who will provide the services?

Do they need to be improved, for example by accent training?

What is the work ethic of the staff?

Geographical location

How far away is the supplier?

Where is the nearest airport and how difficult is it to get to the supplier's premises for the purpose of service management or audit visits?

Infrastructure

What is the quality of the communications, power and utility infrastructure at the offshore location?

How reliable is the internet bandwidth (where relevant)?

How reliable is the electricity network?

How reliable is the telecommunications network?

Culture and training

How different is the supplier's culture from that of the customer (and where relevant, the customer's users or the customer's clients)?

What training will be required to ensure that the supplier can provide the services?

Customer's skills

Does the customer have the skills necessary to run the procurement and then manage the service?

If not, what external advice or training would be necessary?

47.5 Structuring the arrangement

If the customer comes to the conclusion that there is a business case for transferring a service or business function to an offshore location, there are various ways in which it can do this, as described in Table 73.

Table 73 Types of offshore structures

Offshore insourcing

As an alternative to outsourcing services, the customer may decide to set up its own subsidiary (or "captive") in an offshore location and not to outsource the services or function.

Offshore/onshore supplier

The customer may contract with a local subsidiary of the offshore supplier, which has been established to market the services of the offshore company or to assist in managing the arrangement with the customer, on a day-to-day basis.

Onshore/offshore supplier

The customer can contract with an established UK supplier with an offshore subsidiary.

Offshore supplier

The customer may enter into an agreement with an offshore supplier.

Joint venture

The customer may enter into a joint venture with an offshore supplier. See Chapter 19 for a discussion of the implications of the parties entering into a joint venture arrangement. As most offshore outsourcing arrangements are motivated by the customer's desire to achieve cost savings, joint ventures may be inappropriate, unless there are particular taxation incentives. If the customer does decide upon this approach, as well as the additional costs described in Chapter 19, it may have to relocate staff to the offshore location.

BOT (build, operate and transfer) deals

A variation on the joint venture approach is a BOT arrangement. This involves the customer entering into an agreement with an offshore supplier whereby the supplier builds and operates the offshore facilities for the customer for a fixed period of time. At the end of this period, the customer has the option of purchasing the offshore entity or terminating the arrangement and leaving the supplier with the offshore facilities, which the supplier can then use to provide services to other customers.

The factors to be taken into account by the customer in deciding between the various structures described in Table 73 are listed in Table 74.

Table 74 Relevant factors

Control

Clearly the customer will have more control over the quality of the offshore operation if it sets up a captive.

Dependence

If the customer sets up a captive, it will avoid becoming dependent upon a third-party supplier.

Cost

Entering into an agreement with a third supplier (whether an established UK company or an offshore company) may avoid some of the set up costs of creating a captive, although once the captive has been established, all of the cost efficiencies will be passed on to the customer.

Adopting a BOT approach may reduce the costs involved if the customer decides against setting up a captive after an initial trial period.

Entering into an agreement with an established UK company with an offshore subsidiary will usually be more expensive than entering into an agreement with an offshore company, as the UK company will charge for providing service management services.

Before the customer selects an appropriate offshore approach, it must take specialist taxation advice and consider the taxation implications of the different options, in particular if the offshore facility is going to be income generating, for example an offshore call centre taking orders for the customer's products.

Management

Contracting with a supplier with an onshore presence:

(a)   may improve the management of the services, if the onshore supplier acts as a link between the customer and the offshore supplier, ensuring that the offshore supplier understands the customer's requirements and culture;

(b)   may undermine the quality of the services if it means that there is a distance between the customer and the offshore supplier who is actually providing the services to the customer; and

(c)   may mean that the customer does not gain a real understanding of the risks and benefits of offshore outsourcing, if it is isolated from the offshore provider.

Financial standing

If the customer enters into an agreement with an established UK company then it will enjoy the benefit of entering into an agreement with a substantial company.

If it enters into an agreement with the onshore subsidiary of an offshore company, it should check the financial standing of the onshore company. Chapters 4 and 29 stress the importance of the customer investigating the financial standing of the supplier and ensuring that it has sufficient financial guarantees. If the onshore subsidiary is merely a marketing company then the customer may want to consider obtaining a parent company guarantee from the offshore company, entering into an agreement directly with the offshore company and ensuring that the onshore company takes out all appropriate insurance covering its liabilities under the agreement.

Enforcement

If the onshore company has substantial assets, enforcing a judgment against it will be easier than having to enforce a judgment against an offshore company.

Political implications

Contracting with an established UK supplier may make it less apparent that the customer has entered into an offshore outsourcing arrangement, particularly if the services being outsourcing are not front-line services such as call centres.

In practice, the first phase of offshoring involved customers setting up their own captive or entering into agreements with established UK suppliers with an offshore subsidiary. In early 2006, a second phase of offshoring took off, in which customers, having become more confident about offshoring, entered into agreements directly with offshore suppliers. Some customers found that their smaller captives were expensive to run and that it was difficult to recruit staff for them. The Great Recession has seen some financial services institutions selling off their captive to reduce costs.

47.6   The services

Chapter 7 describes how the customer should prepare its service description, to communicate to the supplier what its exact requirements are. Everything that has been explained in Chapter 7 applies equally to offshore outsourcing arrangements. In fact, in offshore arrangements, the customer usually finds that it needs to describe the services in greater detail, first, because the differences of culture and experience mean that the supplier will not have the same shared assumptions as the customer and second, because the staff previously providing the services will not usually transfer to the supplier. The issue of describing the services and ensuring an adequate knowledge transfer relating to the performance of the processes being outsourcing may be particularly key in business process outsourcing arrangements, where essential information relating to the processes may be lost when the current staff cease to provide the services. This information will be vital to the customer on termination of the offshoring arrangement.

In some cases, the service documentation may need to be translated into the language of the offshore supplier.

47.7   How the services are provided

Chapter 8 describes ways in which the customer should control the manner in which the services are provided. This chapter is equally appropriate for offshore arrangements. However, in offshore arrangements, the customer often expects to have substantially more control over how the services are provided than would be usual in other outsourcing arrangements, in particular the staff used to provide the services, because the services are being provided from a site remote from the customer.

47.7.1   *Staff used to provide the services*

In offshore outsourcing arrangements, the staff who previously provided the services (whether they transfer to the supplier under the Acquired Rights Directive by law or not) will not usually be employed to provide the services. Therefore, the customer will usually want to specify in detail the qualifications which the relevant staff must have and the training they must complete.

In the past some customers were concerned that offshore suppliers would find it difficult to find suitably qualified staff to provide the services, as the popularity of offshore outsourcing increased. Staff attrition was a serious problem in India for call centre staff. It was less likely to be a problem for more skilled jobs such as those involved in knowledge process outsourcing. Staff attrition has become less of a problem during the current Great Recession although it may be a problem in the future.

The customer may want to agree a level of "buffer" staff who will have been suitably trained and will be available to provide the services to deal with problems of attrition.

The customer may also want to monitor the staff turnover rate at the supplier and have additional remedies if the staff turnover rate at the supplier increases. The parties need to consider how staff attrition will be measured, whether in total, by country, by location or by type of work. The supplier may want to exclude staff attrition relating to, for example:

(a)   staff who leave within six months of joining the supplier;
(b)   staff who are dismissed by the supplier for performance-related failings; or
(c)   staff who are promoted within the supplier by agreement between the parties.

In addition, offshore outsourcing arrangements are often "resource-based" rather than "service-based" agreements. As a result, some customers include clauses which penalise the supplier if key management or other positions remain vacant.

Lastly, the customer may want the supplier to notify it of any changes which might have an adverse effect upon the supplier's performance.

47.7.2   *Premises used to provide the services*

Some customers feel the need to control not only the location from which the services will be provided but also the facilities which will be made available to staff providing services for them at that location. This may include a floor plan with details of the desks and other equipment to be made available to staff. The customer may also want to consider the branding of the location.

47.8   Service levels and service credits

Chapters 9 and 21 describe how the customer should draft suitable service levels and service credits. Once again, everything that has been explained in these chapters applies equally to offshore outsourcing arrangements. Indeed, if it is more difficult to enforce an outsourcing arrangement, service levels and service credits may be particularly important in explaining to the supplier the priorities between the different service elements and encouraging the supplier to meet the customer's requirements, although the customer should obtain local advice on whether the service credits will be enforceable or not.

47.9   Service management

Chapter 10 describes the service management issues that the customer and supplier will need to consider. These are as relevant for offshore arrangements as for onshore arrangements, although the transition may be more complex than for an onshore arrangement. In the transition phase, the question arises as to who should bear the cost if the parties move the services to the offshore location, the supplier is unable to provide them and they need to be moved back to the onshore location and the transition is undertaken for a second time.

Also, it may be more difficult for the customer to manage the relationship with a supplier who is geographically remote from it. If the supplier does not have a presence in the UK, the customer may need to establish a local presence in the offshore location, send out inspectors to the offshore location or appoint a local manager who will monitor the performance of the supplier on an ongoing basis. The customer may also want the supplier to demonstrate that it can carry out self-audits.

Lastly, some customers are concerned that problems with staff attrition and the shortage of staff in key offshore countries will undermine the supplier's ability to manage the services it provides and hence insist upon service levels and service credits applying to the failure to comply with key service management obligations such as the provision of key staff and the production of reports.

47.10   Charges

Chapter 20 describes various charging regimes appropriate for services arrangements. Everything described in Chapter 20 is applicable to offshore outsourcing arrangements, although resource-based charging structures are more common in offshore arrangements (e.g. based on the number of full-time equivalent staff (FTEs) used to provide the services) than onshore outsourcing arrangements.

In addition, the customer may find that there are cultural differences which impact upon the charging arrangements. For example, the Indian culture does not favour the granting of credit and so the customer may find it more difficult to agree arrangements whereby payments are delayed or amortised over the term of the agreement.

If the customer is entering into an arrangement with a UK supplier with an offshore subsidiary, where only part of the work is being provided by the offshore company, the parties will need to clarify what work will benefit from the lower charges applicable to the offshore services. In addition, some customers, because they are nervous of offshore outsourcing arrangements, initially enter into short-term contracts. The customer should consider whether it can negotiate an option to extend the agreement at an agreed price. This could protect the customer if the popularity of the offshore services results in salary increases.

The parties will need to ensure that they document and agree any charging assumptions, for example who pays for telephone calls or video conferencing facilities. They will also need to document clearly who takes the risk of taxation changes which impact on the customer or supplier.

In addition, the customer may want to consider incorporating mechanisms whereby it shares in any future efficiency gains achieved by the supplier. The gainshare can be expressed as a sharing of any actual reductions in FTEs engaged in providing the services or as a reduced price per headcount which comes into effect at a certain point. In the latter case, both parties need to ensure that this point is defined clearly and is fair. If, for example, it is defined by reference to the end of the transition period, are there events which can delay the formal end of the transition period so that the customer is not technically entitled to the reduced rates?

Lastly, the parties will have to decide in what currency the services will be paid for and hence who will bear the risk of currency fluctuations.

47.11   Termination

In an offshore outsourcing arrangement, the customer will usually want the right to terminate the agreement in the general circumstances described in Chapter 26. The customer may want to consider whether it needs the right to terminate the agreement in specific circumstances relevant to the particular transaction, for example if the supplier is guilty of some form of corruption.

It may also need to amend the force majeure clause to allow a right to terminate if the supplier is affected by a natural disaster, whether or not the force majeure has continued for a specific period of time.

If the customer wants the right to terminate for insolvency related grounds, it will need to take local advice on how insolvency is dealt with by local law.

47.12   FSA regulations

Firms regulated by the FSA will have to comply with the FSA's guidance on outsourcing. Chapters 38 to 42 describe the general FSA guidance. The FSA Handbook also includes specific guidance on offshore outsourcing for insurance companies in SYSC 13—see Chapter 40.

The customer should also bear in mind the FSA's specific reminder to implement and document appropriate business continuity arrangements. The guidance also points out that firms should consider the concentration risk implications of using a particular supplier, such as the business continuity implications where a single supplier is used by several firms.

Lastly, firms should ensure that they include adequate FSA audit provisions in offshore outsourcing agreements (as described in Chapters 38 to 42) and should not assume that the FSA will not want to audit offshore locations.

47.13   Data protection

The data protection issues described in Chapters 36 and 37, particularly those relating to transfers of data within or outside the EU, are particularly relevant for offshore outsourcing agreements.

47.14   TUPE

Customers often assume that if they enter into an offshore outsourcing arrangement TUPE will not apply. However, this is incorrect. As long as the legal requirements for its application are satisfied, namely that there is a transfer of an undertaking situated in the UK immediately before the transfer, then TUPE will apply. Chapter 31 explains the application and effect of TUPE. The important point for the offshore outsourcing supplier to note is that, if TUPE applies:

(a) the customer will have an obligation to inform or consult with the trade union or elected employees' representatives; and

(b) it will operate to transfer to the outsourcing supplier the contracts of employment and the liabilities of the employer (which may include liability for failure to consult) under those contracts.

Therefore, it is imperative for any offshore outsourcing supplier to obtain specialist legal advice on the application of TUPE to the particular facts of the case and to seek full TUPE indemnities from the customer.

The situation on termination is that TUPE will not apply as the transferor will not be situated in the UK immediately before the transfer.

47.15   Publicity

As a result of the unpopularity of offshore outsourcing in some sections of the press, the customer may want to restrict the supplier from publicising the outsourcing transaction. The supplier will usually be eager to publicise its success in procuring the new business.

Chapter 48

India

Sajai Singh, Partner

J. Sagar Associates

48.1   Outline

This chapter describes the specific considerations that need to be taken into account when outsourcing to India, including regulatory, contract, data protection, employee, IP and jurisdiction issues.

48.2   Background

48.2.1   Government support for outsourcing

The Indian government is aware of the importance and impact of the outsourcing industry on the economy and as a result has declared IT one of its five priorities. The government has also instituted a wide range of measures to support the outsourcing sector in order to ensure its growth.

In particular, the government has set up establishments and institutions to attract foreign investors who might be willing to outsource to Indian companies. These include "software technology parks" (STPs) and "special economic zones" (SEZs). The Indian government has also granted tax holidays to increase the attractiveness of India to potential foreign investors.

Another measure taken has been to ensure that the Foreign Investment Implementation Authority (FIIA) facilitates quick delivery of foreign direct investment (FDI) approvals by helping foreign investors to access the necessary paperwork, sort out operational issues and find solutions to their routine and unique problems. The FIIA, with the help of the Fast Track Committee (FTC), operates in about 30 government ministries, monitoring and solving problems that affect sector-specific projects.

48.2.2   NASSCOM

Another institution, the National Association of Software and Service Companies (NASSCOM),[1] has created platforms for the dissemination of knowledge and research in the industry through the medium of surveys and conferences. NASSCOM acts as an adviser, consultant and co-ordinating body for the process outsourcing and IT industries and liaises between the federal and state governments and industry.

48.2.3   *Types of services outsourced to India*

Services commonly outsourced to India include customer care, call centres, medical transcription, billing services, database marketing, web sales and marketing, accounting, tax processing, transaction document management, telesales and telemarketing, engineering services, financial services, creative services, web analysis services, healthcare services, digital image editing services, software services, research and analysis services.

48.2.4   *Anticipated growth*

In spite of the impending economic growth and security concerns, one of NASSCOM's recent studies (Indian IT-BPO Industry Factsheet), estimates that the aggregate revenue generated in the Financial Year 2012 by India's IT-BPO is set to reach a significant milestone, crossing $100 billion. The aggregate IT software and services revenue (excluding hardware) is estimated at $88 billion. This forecast is strengthened by the fact that India's business process outsourcing industry demonstrated an increase in its market share of the global sourcing industry from 51 per cent in 2009, to 58 per cent in 2011.

48.3   Legal system

48.3.1   *India's constitution*

India has one of the oldest legal systems in the world and the country's commitment to the rule of law is enshrined in its Constitution. India's diversity in terms of religions, cultures, habits, nationalities, languages and written scripts is recognised within the Indian legal system. This can be explained to some degree by the sheer size of the country (in terms of

---

[1]   *http://www.nasscom.org* [Accessed 26 September 2012].

geographic size India is the seventh-largest country in the world and the second largest in terms of population).

India is governed by a federal system, with a central federal Parliament, state governments, an independent judiciary, guaranteed fundamental rights and the Directive of Principles of State Policy, which contains the governing principles of the nation. Both the central and state governments are granted power to legislate by the Constitution.

48.3.2 India's judicial system

A special feature of the Indian Constitution is its judicial system. There is a single integrated network of courts that administers federal as well as state laws. The highest body in the judicial system is the Supreme Court based in New Delhi. Beneath the Supreme Court are the State High Courts and then a hierarchy of subordinate courts. Unlike the decisions of the Supreme Court, which are binding on all other Indian courts, the decisions of a High Court are binding only on courts within the same state. However, High Court decisions can be used persuasively to lend support in similar cases in other states.

The highest judicial role in the country is the position of the Chief Justice of India. The President of India appoints the Chief Justice and all the other judges in the Supreme Court. The scope of the Supreme Court's functions includes providing original and appellate hearings and advisory services. The jurisdiction of the Supreme Court encompasses the enforcement of fundamental rights and dealing with any legal dispute between the states *inter se* and between the states and the Government of India.

Arbitration is recognised by the government and by Indian businesses as being an alternative mechanism for dispute resolution. India's Arbitration and Conciliation Act 1996 is based on the UNCITRAL model. Mediation is slowly gaining popularity in some courts as a dispute resolution mechanism. Conciliation and negotiation, prior to any legal process, are often adopted by courts and businesses, as methods of alternate dispute resolution, by court reference or under contract.

48.4   People issues

48.4.1   Sources of employment law

Indian employment law is comprehensive and well developed. Traditionally, an employer has been considered to be in a stronger leveraged position in comparison to its employee, and therefore employment laws tend to strengthen employees' rights.

Based on federal and state regulations, employees in India are granted rights and benefits such as: the right to a minimum wage, a limit on working hours, a minimum number of days off, compensation in the event of redundancy and statutory benefits in the shape of gratuity, provident fund etc.

The following paragraphs cover federal and state employment legislation which may be relevant to outsourcing arrangements.

48.4.2   Shops and Establishments Act 1953

The Shops and Establishments Act 1953 is state-made legislation and each state has framed its own Act and Rules based on it. The aim of the Act, as applicable in a state, is to regulate employment conditions and provide statutory obligations and rights to employees and employers in the unorganized sector of employment, that is, shops and other establishments. The term "establishment" as defined means a shop or a commercial establishment. This definition includes within its purview businesses carrying out outsourcing activities.[2] The main provisions of the Act cover working hours, rest intervals, overtime, holidays, leave, termination of service and the maintenance of shops and establishments.

48.4.3   Employees' Provident Fund and Miscellaneous Provisions Act 1952

This Act provides for the compulsory institution of contributory provident funds, pension funds and deposit-linked insurance funds for employees. It endeavours to secure the future of employees after retirement. Under the Act and the related schemes, both, the employer and the employee contribute towards the employee's provident fund on a monthly basis. The statutory rate for the contribution is currently set at 12 per cent of an employee's basic pay.

48.4.4   Equal Remuneration Act 1976

This is a gender anti-discrimination law. It guarantees equal pay for men and women performing the same or similar work. It prohibits discrimination against women during the recruitment or promotion processes, as well as during training or on any transfer. The provisions of the Act apply regardless of whether the employer has sufficient money to pay the male and female employees equally.

---

[2]   The term "establishment" will hereinafter, for ease of reference, be referred to as "business", with specific emphasis to outsourcing businesses.

48.4.5 Payment of Gratuity Act 1972

The Act applies to every business that has 10 or more employees. Owners of such businesses are obliged to pay a lump sum to an employee on retirement or on any other occasion when an employee's job is terminated, except on grounds of misconduct. To be entitled to receive the payment, an employee must have worked at the business for at least five consecutive years, except where a gratuity is payable on the death or disablement of the employee. The level of payment is calculated at the rate of 15 days' wages multiplied by the number of completed years of service or part thereof in excess of six months. The current maximum amount payable is INR 10,00,000. In order to ensure that an employer is capable of paying the sum due, it is compulsory for all employers, to whom the Act is applicable, to obtain insurance to cover the potential liabilities.

48.4.6 The Payment of Bonus Act 1965

The aim of this Act is to allow the payment of bonuses which are linked to the profit of the organisation or productivity of the workforce. The Act dictates a minimum bonus of 8.33 per cent of the salary earned by an employee during a financial year or a lump sum of INR 100, whichever is higher, whether or not the employer has any allocable surplus in that year. The Act also prescribes a maximum bonus to be paid by an employer to its employees at a rate of 20 per cent of the salary earned in that year, when the allocable surplus in that year exceeds the amount of the minimum bonus payable. However, the statute only applies to employees earning up to INR 10,000 per month. Employees earning more than this would only be eligible to earn a bonus if their employment agreement provides for one. The Act applies to every factory and to every business where 20 or more workers are employed on any given day during an accounting year.

48.4.7 Payment of Wages Act 1936

This Act regulates the payment of wages, imposition of fines, deductions from wages and the elimination of all malpractice by setting out wage periods and the timing and means for paying wages. The Act fixes an interval for the payment of wages, which must not exceed a month. It is the duty of every employer to ensure that wages are paid to employees without unauthorised deductions and that the necessary registers are maintained and the required notices are displayed at the premises. This Act is not applicable to people whose wages exceed INR 6,500 per month.

48.4.8   The Employees' State Insurance Act 1948

This Act and the related Scheme covers non-seasonal factories employing 10 or more persons. It has been extended to shops, hotels, restaurants, cinemas including preview theatres, road-motor transport undertakings, newspaper establishments and private medical and educational institutions employing 20 or more persons. It provides for employees and their families to be given comprehensive medical care as well as cash benefits during sickness and maternity leave with monthly payments in the event of death or disablement. The benefits provided under the Act apply to employees who earn up to INR 15,000 per month. Where an employee is covered under an Employee State Insurance Scheme, no compensation may be claimed from an employer under the Employees' Compensation Act 1923 in respect of any injury sustained by the employee in the course of their employment.

48.4.9   The Employees' Compensation Act 1923

This Act requires the payment of compensation to a worker or his family in the event of accidents arising out of employment, or in the course of employment, that cause either death or permanent or temporary, partial or non-partial, disablement. This Act is applicable to certain sectors of employment as specified in Schedule II to the Act. The amount of compensation payable depends on the age of the worker, the degree of injury suffered and the average monthly wage paid to that individual. There are fixed limits to the minimum amount of compensation payable to the employees or their dependants in case of various kinds of injuries suffered (e.g. INR 1,20,000 if the accident results in death).

48.4.10   The Employment Exchanges (Compulsory Notification of Vacancies) Act 1959

This Act requires both public and private enterprises to publicise any vacancies before filling them, other than vacancies for unskilled jobs, vacancies of a temporary duration and vacancies proposed to be filled through promotion. Further, employers are also required to provide to the employment exchanges, at regular intervals, reports on the number of staff employed.

48.4.11   The Trade Unions Act 1926

This Act provides for the registration of trade unions in order to enable collective bargaining by workers. Under the Act, seven or more people may form a union and apply to have the union registered. Indian trade unions are given the same status as companies so that they enjoy perpetual succession and have a common seal. Like companies, they can also sue and be sued in their name.

48.4.12   The Maternity Benefit Act 1961

The aim of this Act is to protect the health and life of any pregnant employee and her baby, especially in the six weeks before and after delivery. This Act applies to all factories, mines and plantations, as well as to all other establishments employing at least 10 persons. It covers all female employees who have worked for at least 80 days in the 12 months immediately preceding the date of actual delivery. The Act states that, within this timeframe, a woman is entitled to be absent from work while claiming maternity benefit for up to a maximum of 12 weeks. The 12-week window includes a period of six weeks immediately following the day of her delivery, miscarriage or medical termination of pregnancy. The Act forbids employers from employing the female employee during such period. If a woman does not avail herself of the six-week leave prior to the expected delivery date, that woman may not be required to do any arduous work or work which involves long hours of standing or which is likely to interfere with her health and her pregnancy. The employee is further entitled to a maternity benefit payable at the rate of the average daily wage for the actual period of her absence.

48.4.13   Child Labour (Prohibition and Regulation) Act 1986

This Act has five main goals:

(a)   to ban the employment of children under the age of 14 years in specified occupations and processes;
(b)   to lay down a procedure for modifying to the schedule of banned occupations and processes;
(c)   to regulate the working conditions of children in jobs where they are not prohibited from working;
(d)   to lay down enhanced penalties for the employment of children in violation of the provisions of this Act and other related statutes; and
(e)   to obtain uniformity in the definition of "a child" in related laws.

The Act applies, with a few exceptions, to all businesses and workshops where any industrial process is carried on.

48.4.14 *Foreign workers*

India has several restrictions and requirements relating to the employment of foreigners in India. The most important thing a foreigner needs to do when he is planning to work in India is to apply for an Indian work permit or Employment visa (E-Visa) at the Indian Embassy or High Commission in his country of residence. Alternatively, the employer offering the position may initiate the visa application process in India on behalf of the prospective employee. Applicants seeking an E-Visa are required to submit proof of employment by the relevant company or organisation in India.

Applicants who are nationals of certain countries (such as Sri Lanka and the Philippines) need to produce a letter from their employer justifying the appointment of a foreigner for that position.

Further, the Ministry of Labour and Employment has recently introduced guidelines under which a foreign national may be employed in India only if he is a highly skilled or qualified professional engaged in work for which qualified Indians are not available, and if he is drawing a minimum annual salary of $25,000. This annual limit on income does not apply to ethnic cooks, language teachers/translators (other than English language teachers/translators), and staff working for the relevant embassy/high commission in India.

The E-Visa is a multiple entry visa which can be granted for a maximum duration of five years. However, there may be certain categories of E-Visas which can be granted for a period of three years only. Where the visa is valid for a period of more than 180 days, there must be a clear stipulation stating this. Further foreign employees, including those of Indian origin, must register with the Foreigners Registration Office (FRO) or Foreigners Regional Registration Office (FRRO) within 14 days of arrival in India.

Under the "Foreign Exchange Management (Foreign Currency Accounts by a Person Resident in India) Regulations", foreign nationals resident in India have been permitted to open and maintain foreign currency accounts with a bank outside India. This facility is available to foreign nationals who are employees of a foreign company, and are on seconded to the office/branch/subsidiary/joint venture, in India, of the foreign company. The salary payable to the employee for his services in India can be credited directly to the foreign currency account, provided that the amount to be credited to the account does not exceed 75 per cent of the salary accrued to the person from the foreign company. The remaining salary is required to be paid in India, in Indian rupees. For the purposes of India's double-taxation agreements, employee salaries that a foreign company (and not its permanent establishment in India) pays for services rendered in India are taxable in India if the employee works for more than 182 days during any tax year.

48.5   Data protection

With the growth of the outsourcing sector in India, a number of data protection offences involving employees of BPO suppliers have come to light. The following paragraphs describe data protection regulations in India.

48.5.1   *Legislative safeguards*

48.5.1.1   *Constitution of India*

Article 21 of the Constitution contains various relevant fundamental rights, including the right to life and personal liberty and the right to freedom of speech and expression, which includes the right to impart and receive information. The Supreme Court has recognised the right to privacy as being part of this right to life and personal liberty.

48.5.1.2   *Information Technology Act 2000 ("IT Act 2000")*

The IT Act was enacted in 2000 with a view to providing legal recognition to transactions carried out electronically and to facilitate the emergence of electronic commerce in India. With the rapid increase in the use of computer systems and the internet in India, the government found itself unable to effectively deal with cyber crimes and issues of data protection. Therefore, the Act was amended in 2008 to deal with these issues.

The IT Act 2000, as amended in 2008, complies with all the mandatory regulations of the Model Law on Electronic Signatures as adopted by UNCITRAL.

48.5.1.2.1   Definition of Data

"Data", under the IT Act 2000, means a representation of information, knowledge, facts, concepts or instructions which are being prepared or have been prepared in a formalised manner, and is intended to be processed, is being processed or has been processed in a computer system or computer network, and may be in any form (including computer printouts, magnetic or optical storage media, punched cards and punched tapes) or stored internally in the memory of the computer. Due to the fact that the definition was drafted in the widest possible terms, it covers all types of data in electronic form.

The main purpose of the IT Act 2000 is to address privacy issues relating to computer systems. In addition to this, the Act contains provisions which provide protection for stored data, which are described below.

555

48.5.1.2.2   Prohibition on causing damage to computer, data and computer systems

Sections 43 and 66 of the IT Act state that if a person accesses, downloads or copies any data, introduces viruses, causes denial of access or destroys or alters any information stored on a computer without the permission of the person in charge of that computer system then, on proof that they acted dishonestly or fraudulently, they will be punishable either with imprisonment for up to three years or with a fine up to INR 500,000 or both.

Section 43(i) of the IT Act also makes any person who steals, conceals, destroys or alters any computer source code liable to the punishments prescribed above.

Section 43A of the IT Act provides that if any body corporate which owns, operates or handles sensitive personal data or information in a computer resource is found to have been negligent in implementing and maintaining reasonable security practices and procedures, it will be liable to pay damages by way of compensation. The compensation will be calculated taking into account the amount of gain or unfair advantage where quantifiable, the amount of loss caused to the person as a result of the default and the repetitive nature of the default. However, the compensation will not exceed INR 25,000. Reasonable security includes such security practices and procedures, as appropriate to the nature of the information, to protect that information from unauthorised access, damage, use, modification, disclosure or impairment as specified either by agreement between the parties or as may be prescribed by the government, in consultation with the self-regulatory bodies of the industry. The measures haves been further elucidated in the Information Technology (Reasonable Security Practices and Procedures and Sensitive Personal Data or Information) Rules 2011 ("Privacy Rules"), as discussed below.

48.5.1.2.3   Protected systems

Under s.70, of the IT Act, if the federal or state government decides that the incapacitation or destruction of a computer system will have a debilitating impact on national security, the economy, public health or safety then the appropriate government may declare such computer resource to be a protected system affecting the facility of "Critical Information Infrastructure" and only permit authorised persons to access the system. Any person who secures access, or attempts to secure access to a protected system, in contravention of s.70 would be liable to imprisonment of up to 10 years and fine.

48.5.1.2.4   Disclosure of information

Section 72 of the IT Act addresses issues regarding disclosure of information by any person who has gained access to such information in pursuance of a power granted under the IT Act 2000 (including the controller and every person authorised through him). If a person who has secured access to any electronic record, book, register, correspondence, information, document or other material discloses any of these to any other person, he will be punished with imprisonment for a term of up to two years, or with a fine of up to INR 100,000 or both. Section 72A punishes any person who, while providing services under contract, discloses any material containing the personal information about another person without his consent or in breach of a lawful contract with imprisonment for a term that may extend to three years or with fine up to INR 500,000, or both.

48.5.1.2.5   Privacy Rules and Sensitive Personal Information

The Privacy Rules govern, regulate and protect the collection, storage, use, disclosure and transfer of sensitive personal information through electronic means. "Sensitive personal data or information" (SPDI) has been defined as personal information which consists of information relating to passwords, financial information such as bank account or credit or debit cards or other payment instrument details, physical, physiological and mental health conditions, sexual orientation, medical records and history, biometric information, any detail relating to the aforementioned information, with the exception of information that is available or accessible freely in the public domain, or may be furnished under the Right to Information Act 2005 or any other law in force in India.

The Privacy Rules include a mandatory requirement of obtaining the written consent of the information provider prior to collection of any SDPI. Further, the information provider must be notified prior to obtaining consent, of the purpose for collecting the information as well as the intended recipients of the information. The information provider should also be given an option to not provide the SDPI that is sought to be collected. Further, the SDPI that is collected by a body corporate should only be used for the specified purpose, and should be retained only so long as it is required for the purpose for which it has been collected.

The Privacy Rules also require a body corporate to obtain the prior consent of the information provider before disclosing the SDPI to a third party, except where the disclosure has been agreed to in a lawful contract or where the information is required to be disclosed under any applicable law, court judgment, or governmental direction, etc.

All bodies corporate that store, collect or transfer SDPI are required to maintain reasonable security practices and procedures, in order to prevent any unauthorized access to the same. The Privacy Rules provide that bodies corporate may either follow the International Standard IS/ISO/IEC 27001 on "Information Technology – Security Techniques – Information Security Management System – Requirements", or they may develop their own codes of best practices, which must be duly approved and notified by the central government, for effective implementation. Any third party transferee of SDPI is also required to maintain the same standards as the transferor under these Privacy Rules.

48.5.1.2.6   Enforcement

The provisions of the IT Act 2000 are enforced through an adjudicating officer and the form of the enquiry follows the framework laid down by the government. The decisions of the adjudicator are open to appeal to the Cyber Appellate Tribunal and the findings of the Cyber Appellate Tribunal may, in turn, be appealed to the High Court of the relevant state.

Enforcement is also undertaken by the Cyber Crime Investigation Cell (CCIC), set up by the Central Bureau of Investigation (CBI) with a mandate to investigate offences under the IT Act 2000 and all other high-technology crimes. The CCIC operates by establishing cells across India based on need, and the organisation is a member of the Interpol Working Party on Information Technology Crime for South East Asia and Australia.

48.5.2   *Other legislation*

In addition to the above legislation, some of the general legislation mentioned in section 48.8 below may be relevant to data protection.

48.5.3   *Possible reform of data protection law*

Despite there being a comprehensive data protection law regarding the storage, collection, usage and transfer of personal data or information through electronic means, India does not have a comprehensive data protection law that governs all forms of data, either electronic, physical, etc. Currently, scholars in India are debating the practical necessity of comprehensive data protection legislation in India.

48.5.4   Non-legislative safeguards

48.5.4.1   Guidelines

In addition to the cluster of laws which may be used to some extent for data protection, non-governmental organisations co-operate with the outsourcing industry in an attempt to create alternatives to meet customers' data protection concerns. For instance, NASSCOM has issued guidelines on privacy and confidentiality, but these guidelines are not binding.

48.5.4.2   Contractual provisions

In order to better address the issue of data protection, many suppliers unilaterally make efforts to meet customers' data protection expectations by agreeing to specific data protection provisions in contracts with their customers. Contracts customarily contain clauses covering confidentiality, privacy and related compliance processes and obligations.

When defining data protection terms, suppliers often find it useful to commit to meeting international data protection standards. Commonly used standards include the ISO Certificate or the BS 7799, a global standard that covers all security domains. In order to support these efforts, the Ministry of Information Technology has set up the Standardization, Testing and Quality Certification (STQC) Directorate. The STQC functions as an independent third-party certification scheme as per BS 7799 Part 2 and provides services such as testing hardware and software products and product certification, and it also trains personnel in quality and security standards and processes.

Another measure taken by Indian suppliers aiming to convince their customers of their data protection capability is to allow their customers to conduct periodic inspections of their facilities, processes and compliance levels.

48.6   Intellectual property protection

Protecting intellectual property (IP) is a major concern for customers outsourcing services. As a consequence, India has established IP laws to ensure adequate protection is available.

IP protection in India takes two forms. On the one hand, there is IP protection based on statutes, such as the Copyright Act 1957 or the Patents Act 1970. On the other, there is protection based on international agreements, including the agreement on Trade Related Aspects of Intellectual Property Rights (TRIPS).

48.6.1   *Copyright*

The Copyright Act 1957 ("Copyright Act"), as amended in 1999, contains provisions stating that the Act applies to works first published outside India. The Act is also TRIPS compliant.

An author owns any copyright in the first instance. However, where the copyright arises out of work done by an employee in the course of his employment, an employer owns the copyright if there is no specific agreement to the contrary. The same general rule applies between an outsourcing customer and a supplier, so it is important to have provisions dealing with the ownership rights to any new IP that is developed in the course of a relationship. Although the "work for hire" concept does exist in India, it may still be advisable to specify clear terms of transfer in the contractual agreement as well. Under the Copyright Act, it has been clearly stipulated that in the case of work made in the course of the author's employment under a contract of service or apprenticeship, the employer will, in the absence of any agreement to the contrary, be the first owner of the copyright therein. However, in the specific context of outsourcing agreements, the "work for hire" rule as per the Copyright Act would apply to the employees of the outsourcing organisation, which would be the first owner of the copyright. Hence, specific clause should be included in the outsourcing agreement, mandating the assignment and transfer of the entire copyright in the work, to the customer.

The author, publisher, owner or any other person with an interest in the copyright of a work may make an application to the Registrar for the particulars of that work to be recorded in the Register of Copyrights.

Copyright subsists in any literary, dramatic, musical or artistic work (other than a photograph) published within the lifetime of an author and lasts for 60 years beginning with the calendar year following that in which the author died.

The owner of the copyright in an existing work or the prospective owner of the copyright in a future work may assign the copyright, either wholly or partially, either generally or subject to limitations, and either for the whole term of the copyright or any part thereof to any person.

Copyright is deemed to be infringed:

(a)   when any person, without a licence granted by the owner of the copyright or the Registrar of Copyrights under the Act or in contravention of the conditions of a licence so granted or of any conditions imposed by a competent authority under the Act:

   (i)   does anything, the exclusive right to do which is conferred upon the owner of the copyright by the Act; or

    (ii)   permits any place to be used for the communication of the work to the public for profit where such a communication constitutes an infringement of the copyright in the work, unless he was not aware and had no reasonable ground for believing that such a communication to the public would be an infringement of the copyright; or

(b) when any person:

    (i)   makes for sale or hire, or sells or lets for hire, or by way of trade displays or offers for sale or hire;

    (ii)   distributes either for the purposes of trade or to such an extent as to prejudicially affect the owner of the copyright;

    (iii) by way of trade exhibits in public; or

    (iv) imports into India, any infringing copies of the work; or

(c) where any offence under this Act has been committed by a company, every person who at the time the offence was committed, was in charge of, or was responsible for the conduct of the business of the company, is deemed to be guilty of an offence and is liable to face prosecution.

48.6.2   *Patents rights*

The Patent Act 1970 has been amended three times so that it reflects changing economic conditions. Since 2005, the Act has complied to all the mandatory regulations of the TRIPS Agreement.

Some key provisions of the Act are as follows:

(a)   The creator is the first owner of the patent, and not the company he works for.
(b)   An application for a patent may be made to any of the Patent Offices located in Kolkata (Head office), Delhi, Chennai or Mumbai.
(c)   Patent protection lasts for 20 years from the date of filing of the application for the patent.
(d)   The burden of proof is on the accused to show there has not been an infringement.

The Act protects biodiversity and provides safeguards and measures for protecting traditional knowledge. The right to apply for a patent should be made the subject of an agreement between an employer and employee or a customer and a supplier, as, in the first instance the creator is the owner. A common practice is for an employer to include a general assignment in the employment documentation, with a commitment to execute future documents to perfect the assignment and transfer of title as necessary. When a patentable work is identifiable, a specific assignment is executed between the employer and employee assigning the rights to the employer.

48.6.3   Trademarks

Under the Trademarks Act 1999, a trademark is defined as:

> "a mark capable of being represented graphically and which is capable of distinguishing the goods or services of one person from those of others and may include the shape of goods, their packaging and a combination of colours".

Some key provisions of the Act are as follows:

(a)   Trademarks may be registered in the Trademark Register with detailed information such as the name of the owner. The Register classifies goods and services in accordance with international classification standards for the registration of trademarks.
(b)   Registration may be refused if registration of the trademark would create confusion among a part of the public.
(c)   Opposition to registration of a trademark must be made within four months.
(d)   Registration lasts for 10 years and may be renewed.
(e)   It is an infringement of a trademark owner's rights:

    (i)   for an unregistered trademark which is identical or similar to a registered trademark to be used in the course of business,

    (ii)   for an unregistered trademark to be used in relation to goods or services which are not comparable to those for which an identical or similar trademark is registered; and

    (iii)   for any unauthorised use of a registered trademark.
(f)   Infringement is punishable with imprisonment or fine, or both.

The Trademarks (Amendment) Act 2010 mandates a trademark to be registered by the Registrar, within 18 months from the filing of the application, (thus aligning the Trademarks Act 1999 with the provisions of the Madrid Protocol). Efforts are also currently being made to simplify the law relating to the transfer of ownership of trademarks.

48.7   Protection of confidentiality

There is no specific law on confidentiality in India and so there are limited civil remedies to protect confidentiality. The recently formulated Privacy Rules, as discussed earlier, regulate and govern the protection of SDPI in India. These Rules mandate the requirement of prior consent of the information provider while collecting, using, storing, transferring or disclosing SDPI available with a body corporate. However, a Clarification issued by the Ministry of Communications and Information Technology, dated August 24, 2011, specifies that any body corporate that is providing services relating to the collection, storage, dealing or handling of SDPI under a contractual obligation with any legal entity located within or outside India, is not subject to the requirement of prior consent as provided under Rules 5 and 6 of the Privacy Rules. It is therefore, unclear whether an outsourcing supplier in India would be liable to follow the precautionary procedures of obtaining prior consent of the information providers while dealing with SDPI regarding the individual clients of the customer, made available to them under the outsourcing agreement with the customer. Hence, in outsourcing agreements, it is essential that the supplier and the customer include appropriate provisions relating to the confidentiality of data processed and collected during the performance of the services by the supplier. Such provisions usually stipulate the consequences in the event of a failure by the supplier to ensure the security of confidential information. Thus protection is achieved by contractual means until there is adequate legislation on the point.

48.8   Other relevant legislation

The following legislation may also be relevant for outsourcing arrangements in India.

48.8.1   *Indian Contract Act 1872*

If the parties agreed that the outsourcing agreement will be governed by Indian Law, then the Indian Contract Act 1872 will be the substantive law governing the contract. Care needs to be taken while drafting certain provisions as the Contract Act 1872 discourages agreements in restraint of trade and agreements in restraint of legal proceedings. The Indian Contract Act 1872 will not, in general, permit a contractual provision that imposes a post employment restraint on an employee to carry on employment and such a restraint will be considered to be void. Similarly, an agreement in restraint of initiation of legal proceedings by either of the parties is void. However, this provision is subject to provisions in agreements, under which the parties have agreed to arbitration as a dispute resolution mechanism.

48.8.2   *Specific Relief Act 1963*

The Specific Relief Act 1963 is complementary to the provisions of the Indian Contract Act 1872 and states that a party, in the event of breach, can, apart from claiming damages, also sue for specific performance of the Contract.

48.8.3   The Indian Penal Code

The Indian Penal Code punishes, amongst other things, fraud, misrepresentation, forgery and the making of false documents.

48.8.4   The Department of Telecommunication (DOT) Regulations

In accordance with the New Telecom Policy (NTP) 1999, other service providers (OSPs) are allowed to operate by using infrastructure provided by various access providers for non-telecom services. In May 1999, the Telecom Commission accorded in principle approval for registration of call centres, both international and domestic, in the country under the above category. In accordance with the notification issued on 2 November 2005, the BPOs have been included under OSPs and the provisions applicable to such OSPs are also applicable to call centres.

A call centre is allowed to use internet telephony to the extent it is permitted by the ISPs. The call centre operator may or may not use internet telephony depending on their business model.

48.8.5   Reserve Bank of India Act 1934

A BPO company undertaking support of banking and financial services overseas will need to ensure that its operations in India are not considered to be a non-banking financial institution under the RBI Act 1934. If so deemed, it would have to fulfil obligations cast upon it by the RBI Act.

48.8.6   Indian Evidence Act 1872

By virtue of the Information Technology Act 2000 computer-generated documents are admitted as evidence under the provisions of the Indian Evidence Act 1872. There are three types of computer-generated documentary evidence:

(a)   computer-generated calculations and analyses obtained through software operations and information received;
(b)   computer-generated documents and records that are copies of information obtained from humans; and
(c)   a combination of both computer-generated calculations and analyses and computer-generated documents based on information from human beings.

48.8.7   Tort law

The law of tort in India is derived from the English law of tort and has evolved from English common law principles. However, Indian courts depart from common law rules if they are unsuitable for Indian conditions. The Code of Civil Procedure, which enables the civil courts to try all suits of a civil nature, impliedly confers jurisdiction on such courts to apply the law of torts as principles of justice, equity and good conscience. These include principles of negligence and vicarious liability.

48.8.8   Securities Exchange Board of India (SEBI)

Outsourcing service providers need to take care that they are not construed as "brokers" while providing security market analysis and inputs on performance of scripts.

48.9   Enforceability of jurisdiction clauses

Indian companies often incorporate the laws of foreign jurisdictions into contracts, either in whole or in part. Such terms are generally accepted by the courts provided both the contracting parties are in agreement. Where there are no governing law provisions within the contract, the jurisdiction most appropriate to the transaction will be applied.

If a contract is valid under the law of its governing jurisdiction clause but its enforcement by the Indian courts would be contrary to public policy or law in India, then the contract may not be enforced by an Indian court.

In any event, issues regarding the transfer of IP, real estate, criminal acts, labour law or the enforcement of a foreign judgment or award will usually be subject to Indian law and not to the law which was agreed to within the terms of the contract.

48.10   Enforcement of judgments

India's approach to the enforcement of judgments made by foreign courts, is to adapt the judgments in terms of the "res judicata". This approach has been expressed by a jurist to mean that:

> "We (India) are not so provincial as to say that every solution to a problem is wrong because we deal with it otherwise at home and we shall not brush aside foreign judicial process unless doing so would violate some fundamental principle of justice, some prevalent concep-

tion of good morals, some deep-rooted tradition of the common wealth."

In practice, this approach leads to two categories of judgments, as described below.

48.10.1   *Judgments from courts of reciprocating countries*

Any judgment of a court of a reciprocating country can be directly enforced by filing an execution petition before an Indian court. The definition of a reciprocating country is shown in s.44A of the Code of Civil Procedure 1908; a reciprocating country is a country or territory outside India which the central government has declared as such. Examples include the UK, Australia, Singapore or Hong Kong, but the US is not a reciprocating country for Indian purposes. India and USA are yet to sign a treaty in this regard.

48.10.2   *Judgments from courts of non-reciprocating countries*

The judgment of a court in a non-reciprocating country may be enforced by filing an application for a judgment in an Indian court based on the foreign award. The suit must be filed within three years of the date of the foreign judgment.

Regardless of how enforcement is pursued, a foreign judgment will not be considered as conclusive if the judgment:

(a)   has been given by a court lacking competent jurisdiction;
(b)   has not been given based on the merits of the case;
(c)   is not founded on a correct view of international law;
(d)   follows proceedings in breach of the principles of natural justice;
(e)   has been obtained by fraud; or
(f)   breaches any law in force in India.

48.10.3   *Enforcement of national and international arbitration awards*

UNCITRAL Model Law based Indian Arbitration and Conciliation Act 1996 states that an arbitration settlement shall be binding on all the claimants. Section 36 of the Act states that if after three months from the date of the award no application has been made to set aside the award or if such an application has been made and rejected, then the settlement will be enforceable as a decree of the court.

The following agreements will apply to any settlement regardless of whether it was awarded inside or outside India:

(a) the Geneva Protocol on Arbitration Clauses 1923;
(b) the Geneva Convention on the Execution of Foreign Arbitral Awards 1927; and
(c) the New York Convention 1958 on the Recognition and Enforcement of Foreign Arbitral Awards.

Arbitration clauses are commonly used in most outsourcing agreements. As mentioned above, India is a signatory to the New York Convention so awards made in other signatory countries are enforceable in India.

48.11   Enforceability of other clauses

48.11.1   Non-compete provisions

Non-compete provisions are included in some outsourcing agreements. Sometimes these apply to service providers and sometimes they apply to an individual working on a particularly sensitive assignment. Whether they are enforceable or not in India depends upon the application of s.27 of the Indian Contract Act 1872. Section 27 states that no person may be restricted from carrying on a lawful profession, trade or business unless the purpose of such a restriction on an individual is to ensure the reasonable protection of a party's proprietary or commercial interest following the acquisition of a business with goodwill. A restriction will be reasonable if it is limited in duration, geographical scope or in some other way. Generally, the courts will enforce restrictive covenants that operate "during terms of employment or service" and not those that operate "after terms of employment", unless adequate consideration has passed and the restriction is deemed reasonable and necessary to protect the confidentiality, trade secrets and/or goodwill of the party proposing to impose to such a restriction.

48.11.2   Provisions limiting liability

Parties to a contract are generally liable for all damages stemming from any breach unless that damage is remote or indirect. When assessing liability for breach, the courts tend to use the two basic principles of mitigation and restitution. The principle of mitigation requires a party suffering a loss as a result of a breach of contract to try to mitigate that loss. The principle of restitution seeks to put the party suffering a loss in the same position it would have been in had the breach not occurred. If the parties have agreed to liquidated damages the courts will generally accept those figures, after weighing them on the parameters of reasonableness and remoteness.

The courts are likely to accept the validity of outsourcing agreements which include terms limiting the liabilities of the contracting parties, provided the terms are reasonable. Notwithstanding this approach, terms limiting the liability of the parties in the event of death, personal injury, fraud or gross negligence are unenforceable under Indian law.

48.11.3   Termination provisions

The Indian Contract Act 1872 gives contracting parties the freedom to agree to termination clauses. However, the courts may look at the overall fairness of a contract when enforcing terms and it is not unusual to find damages being awarded in the event of termination of the contract.

48.12   Regulatory restrictions

48.12.1   Restrictions on software exports

There are limited restrictions on software exports, as explained below. Software exporters and exporters of specified services are required to register with the Electronics and Software Export Promotion Council.

48.12.2   Exchange regulation

Foreign exchange transactions are regulated by the Foreign Exchange Management Act 2000 ("FEMA 2000"). FEMA 2000 provides that capital and current account transactions are fully convertible for non-residents. Generally foreign currencies may be purchased for trade and account purposes at market value, except for certain specific transactions which might require prior approval of RBI.

There are no such restrictions for the outsourcing sector. A customer who may be considering starting a business in India has multiple options, including the following.

48.12.2.1   Subsidiary company

The customer may set up a subsidiary company which must be incorporated in compliance with the requirements of the Indian Companies Act 1956. It may be funded via equity, debt and internal accruals. The company will be treated as a domestic company for tax purposes. This option allows maximum flexibility for conducting business in India.

48.12.2.2   Branch offices

Instead of establishing a subsidiary company in India, the customer may set up a branch office. This will require specific approval from the RBI, which will limit the scope of activities undertaken in India by the branch office. The branch office will then be treated as an extension of the foreign company for tax purposes. In pure administrative terms, it is simpler to operate and close branch offices as opposed to setting up a subsidiary company in India.

48.12.2.3   Liaison offices

Alternatively, the customer could establish a liaison office. This will also require specific approval from the RBI, which will limit the activities that the office may undertake in India. It will not be able to undertake any business or revenue-generating activity in India.

48.12.2.4   Project offices

Lastly, the customer has an option to set up a project office. Permission for a project office is linked to execution of a project in India. The foreign company must report to the relevant regional RBI office. For tax purposes, the project office will be treated as an extension of the foreign company in India.

48.12.3   Export regulation

In general, goods and services may be exported unconditionally, although there are regulations covering certain items listed on the Special Chemicals, Organisms, Materials, Equipment and Technologies list (SCOMET). The Foreign Trade (Development and Regulation) Act 1992 read with the Foreign Trade Policy formulated by the government from time to time, govern and regulate the export and import of products and services in India.

Appendix 3 to Sch.2 of ITC(HS) Classification of Export and Import Items details those items which are included in the SCOMET list. Export of SCOMET items is only permitted where an export licence has been issued and a licence may be denied if certain criteria are not met. Technological products on the SCOMET list include:

(a)   Category 0 (nuclear materials, nuclear-related materials, equipment and technology);
(b)   Category 3 (materials, material processing equipment and related technologies);
(c)   Category 4 (nuclear-related equipment and technology not controlled under Category 0);
(d)   Category 5 (aerospace systems and equipment, including production and test equipment, and related technology);

(e) Category 6 (defence products as listed in Annex VI to Appendix D of the Defence Procurement Policy of 2008); and

(f) Category 7 (electronics, computers and information technology including information security).

In order to export any of these items, an export licence must be secured from the Directorate-General of Foreign Trade (DGFT).

48.13 General taxation issues

India's tax legislation has two branches. Direct taxes like personal income tax or corporate taxes and indirect taxes like central sales tax and service tax are levied by the federal government. Professional and similar taxes and state sales taxes are levied by the state governments.

The Indian fiscal year starts on 1 April and ends on 31 March the following year. Every company which has any Indian taxable income needs to register with the correct authority and file its annual tax return by 31 October.

To attract investors, the Indian government has created a number of incentives, including duty-free import of capital goods and a system of tax holidays which benefit much of the outsourcing industry. Free Trade Zones (FTZs), Electronic Hardware Technology Parks (EHTPs) and Software Technology Parks (STPs) have additional tax benefits for companies located there, such as 100 per cent tax exemption for the first five business years followed by five years of 50 per cent tax exemption.

India has entered into tax treaties with a number of countries including the UK, Germany, Mauritius and the US in order to avoid double taxation.

48.14 Other considerations

48.14.1 *Specific call-centre regulation*

In order to set up a call centre there is a requirement for the centre to be registered under the category "other service provider" with the Department of Telecommunications. Depending on the kind of services the centre will provide, it may also have to obtain other specific approvals.

48.14.2 *Environmental regulations*

Apart from the Constitution in which India's commitment to a clean environment is mandated, the Environmental (Protection) Act 1986 is the source of India's environmental legislation. The Act authorises the federal government to protect and improve environmental quality and to control and reduce pollution from all sources and to prohibit or restrict the setting-up and/or operation of any industrial facility on environmental grounds. Under the Forest Conservation Act 1980 an approval is required for every project which it is proposed will take place in forestland.

48.14.3 Other local laws

In addition to complying with the legislation and regulations above, suppliers have to ensure they comply with local laws. The applicability of a specific local state or municipality's laws will be decided based upon the location of the company's facilities as well as the location of the principal customer company of the supplier.

Chapter 49

China

Anthony Chan and Lawrence Cheng

Dentons / Brandt Chan & Partners

49.1   Introduction

This chapter deals with legal considerations when entering into outsourcing deals in China including specific considerations that customers need to take into account when outsourcing in the People's Republic of China ("China") which for this purpose means mainland China (excluding the jurisdictions of Hong Kong, Macau and Taiwan). Specifically, this chapter looks into the following issues:

(a)   legal systems in China;

(b)   human resources issues;

(c)   data protection, confidentiality and intellectual property rights;

(d)   enforcement of contract terms including dispute resolution issues;

(e)   enforcement of judgments and arbitral awards;

(f)   government support and regulatory restrictions; and

(g)   taxation issues.

49.2   Background

49.2.1   Recent Developments

China as a centre for outsourcing has grown rapidly in the last decade. Low labour costs and government support have been important contributors to the industry's success. Indeed, China together with India is often regarded as the destination of choice for companies looking to outsource all or parts of their operations.

To date China has predominantly been involved in providing IT and business process outsourcing services. IT outsourcing services account for 65 per cent of total outsourcing revenue in China, while business process outsourcing has nearly tripled since 2007, growing from RMB 1.2 billion to RMB 3.5 billion in 2010.[1] It is forecast that China's business process outsourcing market may reach RMB 10 billion by 2015. China is now considered a relatively mature market for offshore outsourcing services and it will remain a viable option for international IT companies seeking to cut labour costs, despite competition from Southeast Asian and South Asian countries.

China's outsourcing market is spread throughout the country with centres such as Beijing, Shanghai and Guangzhou, which can provide good product research and development, and supported by second-tier cities such as Nanjing, Xi'an, Wuhan, Dalian and southern Chinese cities and towns (such as Shenzhen).

The Chinese government has made significant policy changes to encourage the provision of outsourcing services, such as offering businesses financial support, subsidies, and tax relief. These will be explored in further detail in this chapter.

49.2.2   *Education and Expertise*

With its education system focusing on economic modernisation and internationalisation, China is increasing the number of undergraduates and doctoral degree holders, and fast improving the population's literacy. The official language in China is Mandarin, which is widely used in the country. Whilst English proficiency varies from location to location, with its huge populace, locating adequately qualified staff even though challenging is viable.

In relation to the outsourcing industry, the central government proposed a project entitled "Thousand-Hundred-Ten Projects" in its "Eleventh Five-Year" plan, aimed at training 300,000–430,000 personnel needed by the service outsourcing industry within five years time. The industry is also expected to employ some 200,000–300,000 college students to solve labour shortages.

---

[1]   Everest Group, *Everest Group: China's global services market projected to grow 20-25 percent CAGR by 2015,* Press Release, November 2011.

49.3   Legal system

49.3.1   *Civil Law System*

China adopts a civil law system with codes and regulations which the judiciary is bound to follow when determining cases. Unlike common law jurisdictions such as the United Kingdom and Australia, there is no concept of case precedent. Each case, in theory, stands on its own and does not bind the court trying another similar case. In practice, however, judges in a lower people's court often attempt to follow the interpretation of the law determined by a higher court.[2]

49.3.2   *Sources of law*

The 1982 Constitution is the highest source of law in China. It established the framework of the Chinese government as well as codified the general principles of society and listed the fundamental rights and duties of its citizens. The next level are the national laws enacted by the National People's Congress, which is the highest organ of state power. The Standing Committee of the National People's Congress can also enact regulations, decisions and resolutions. At the next level, laws and regulations may also be enacted by the State Council, which is the executive arm of the Chinese government. The most common measures enacted by the State Council are administrative regulations. At the local level, the people's congress at provincial level can enact local regulations and the local people's governments can make local administrative rules.

Although there is no concept of case precedent, the judiciary in China does make law. The Supreme People's Court issues judicial interpretations or opinions, from time to time, over different matters to clarify points of law and these are given weight in reaching decisions.

49.3.3   *Hierarchy of Courts*

The court hierarchy in China is as follows: the highest court is the Supreme People's Court, followed by the Higher People's Courts, the Intermediate People's Courts and lastly the Basic People's Courts. There are about 430 Intermediate People's Courts and 30 Higher People's Courts located in different provinces. The Basic People's Courts comprise of more than 3,000 courts at county level.[3]

---

[2]   Ronald C. Brown, *Understanding Chinese Courts and Legal Process: Law with Chinese Characteristics*, (Kluwer Law International, 1997), p.82.
[3]   Albert HY Chen, *An Introduction to the Legal System of the People's Republic of China*, (Lexis Law Publishing, 1998), pp.107–108

The Basic People's Courts mainly adjudicate civil and criminal cases, at first instance, but they do not have jurisdiction over certain foreign related civil and criminal cases carrying the penalty of death or life imprisonment. Foreign related cases are mainly dealt with in the Intermediate People's Court—for instance, a request for the enforcement of a foreign judgment or foreign arbitral award—see section 49.10.1 Enforcement of Foreign Judgments and section 49.10.3 Enforcement of Foreign Arbitral Awards for details.

The Higher People's Court mainly hears cases and appeals transferred from lower courts as well as major criminal cases which may have an impact on the entire province. The Supreme People's Court deals with appeals or protests from the Higher People's Court. In addition, it also issues judicial interpretations or opinions, from time to time, to clarify points of law and for effective implementation.

49.4 Human Resources Issues

49.4.1 *General*

Employment in China is predominantly covered by the Labour Contract Law and the Labour Law. The Labour Contract Law, updated in 2008, focuses on the legal protection of employees' rights and combats potential exploitation amidst China's fast economic development. The Labour Contract Law deals with, amongst other things, probationary periods, redundancy, liquidated damages, severance payments, non-compete covenants and labour dispatching. The State Council further published the Labour Contract Law Implementation Rules to provide additional details and clarification for the interpretation and execution of the Labour Contract Law.

As expected, the Labour Contract Law is of significance for both the service provider and customer as it provides provisions which limit the termination of employment with employees, those employed on a contractual basis, seconded workers as well as non-compete covenants. This is especially important for an outsourcing business involving the transfer of employees.

The amendments to the Labour Contract Law in 2008 caused tremendous consternation amongst employers and there continues to be much debate as to the economic viability of the changes.

49.4.2   *Termination of Employment*

Under the Labour Contract Law, there is a list of categories of employees who cannot be terminated even if the employment contract has expired. These employees include:

(a)   pregnant women;[4]
(b)   any employee who has worked for the employer for at least 15 years continuously and is within five years of legal retirement age;[5] and
(c)   any employee engaged in occupational disease-prone work who has not had a medical examination to determine he is free from work related disease, or is in any diagnostic or observation period pending such determination.[6]

Where an employer and an employee have already entered into a fixed term labour contract twice successively and the parties intend to renew such contract upon its expiry, an indefinite term must be made in the labour contract with the employee.

If an employer terminates the employment in breach of the Labour Contract Law, the employee can request specific performance. Alternatively, the employee may seek payment from the employer in the amount of twice the usual severance payment.

49.4.3   *Transfer of Employees*

In an outsourcing services context, employees may commonly be transferred from the customer to the services provider because a particular employee possesses certain skills or knowledge which is essential for the provision of services. Employees can be transferred either by secondment, or by entering into a new employment contract with the services provider, in which case the employment contract with the customer should be terminated. In this regard, customers should pay attention to the restrictions on termination of contract stated in section 49.4.2.

Additionally, in respect of the secondment of staff, the services provider and the customer should take precautions to structure the arrangement such that it does not fall within the definition of providing "labour dispatch services", these are services that only registered labour services agencies can provide.[7] In order to avoid being treated as providing labour dispatch services as opposed to secondment arrangements, the service provider and customer must satisfy the following rules:

---

[4]   Article 42(4) of the China Labour Contract Law.
[5]   Article 42(5) of the China Labour Contract Law.
[6]   Article 42(1) of the China Labour Contract Law. The grounds listed here are non-exhaustive.
[7]   Articles 57–67 of the China Labour Contract Law.

(a) the secondment of employees cannot be the main business of the service provider;
(b) the number of secondees should be kept to a minimum;
(c) the length of the secondment arrangement should be kept to a minimum; and
(d) no fees should be charged for the secondment arrangement.

Whether by way of secondment or entering into a new contract with the service provider, the employee's prior consent should be obtained before the transfer. In addition, the customer should discuss the proposed outsourcing arrangement with the employees' representative if the outsourcing would materially affect the employees' welfare.

49.4.4 Non-competition

Another relevant employment issue is the treatment of a non-compete covenant under the Labour Contract Law. The law provides that upon the termination of the employment contract, there will be a two-year limitation period on the employee during which time he cannot engage in the provision of services or production of products of the same category or industry as his employer.[8]

Within the labour contract or a confidentiality agreement, an employer may stipulate the extent of non-competition with the employee. The employer may also stipulate compensation to be given to the employee within the period of the non-compete. If the employee is in violation of the non-complete clause, he is liable to a penalty for breach of contract.[9] Thus in China, a non-compete provision made by an employee in favour of his employer is specifically enforceable.

49.5   Data Protection

49.5.1   Current Position

At present, China does not have a comprehensive legal framework on data protection, and the relevant rules and regulations are piecemeal. These laws and regulations include the Contract Law, the Protection of the Safety of Computer Data Systems Regulations and the Tentative Provisions of Administration of Basic Personal Credit Information Database.

---

[8]   Article 24 of the China Labour Contract Law.
[9]   Article 23 of the China Labour Contract Law.

The regulation which is most relevant for data protection for the outsourcing industry is the Several Provisions for the Protection of Information in Undertaking International Service Outsourcing by Domestic Enterprises ("Information Provisions") enacted by the Ministry of Commerce (MOFCOM). The Information Provisions require the service provider to set up an Information Protection Agency or designate a full-time member of staff responsible for developing the service provider's information protection rules and regulations to take reasonable, specific and effective security measures, including:

(a)   restrictions on access to confidential information to certain personnel;
(b)   well-protected data carrier and storage sites to avoid leakage of information;
(c)   restrictions on visitor access to confidential information in the factory, workshop, office and other relevant places; and
(d)   the establishment of an effective network management and data protection measures to build a strict authentication and access authorization system, using complete system backup and recovery tools, regular security patches and virus database upgrades for computers with confidential information.[10]

49.5.2   New Guidelines

In 2011, the General Administration for Quality Supervision, Inspection and Quarantine and the Commission for the Administration of Standardization published draft guidelines entitled *Information Security Technology—Guide to Personal Information Protection* ("Draft Information Guidelines"). The Draft Information Guidelines comprise three main parts namely, (1) principles for handling personal data; (2) rights enjoyed by the owner of personal data; and (3) concrete requirements for the protection of personal data.

49.5.2.1   Principles for handling personal data

These general principles state that the purpose and use of collecting personal data must be clear and reasonable. The holder of the personal data should notify the individual data owner of the purpose of collecting the personal data, the period during which the data is preserved, the policies in place for data protection and the rights of the individual, and so forth. The holder of personal data should also adhere to the principle of keeping the data safe, processing the data reasonably, ensuring the data is accurate and complete and not handling the data without the consent of the individual data owner.

---

[10]   Article 5 of the Several Provisions for the Protection of Information in Undertaking International Service Outsourcing by Domestic Enterprises promulgated by MOFCOM, 1 February 2010.

49.5.2.2   Rights enjoyed by the owner of personal data

The Draft Information Guidelines confer the followings rights on the owner of personal data:[11]

(a)   Right to confidentiality: the owner can request the holder to preserve the confidentiality of the personal data collected;
(b)   Right to knowledge: the owner can request the holder to disclose the content of his personal data, the source of that data and the scope of disclosure made to third parties (if any);
(c)   Right to choose: the owner can choose to accept or refuse to provide personal data;
(d)   Right to amend: the owner can request the holder to amend any wrongful personal data; and
(e)   Right to delete data: the owner can request the holder to stop processing the data or to delete the data in its entirety.

49.5.2.3   Concrete requirements for the protection of personal data

The Draft Information Guidelines impose several requirements to protect personal data. For instance, they expressly prohibit the collection of personal data from individuals under the age of 16 unless with the guardian's consent.[12] The Draft Information Guidelines also prohibit the collection of data which is not directly connected to the stated purpose, especially information relating to ethnicity, religious belief, genetic information, fingerprints, health status and sexual orientation. In relation to the transfer of personal data, the Draft Information Guidelines generally prohibit any transfer, unless with the owner's consent. Article 5.3.5 expressly prohibits the transfer of data to a foreign data administrator except with the consent of the customer's senior management, which may pose challenges to the service provider.

Though the Draft Information Guidelines are yet to be enacted, they provide valuable guidance as to what protections or restrictions are necessary or desirable for the transfer and receipt of data.

---

[11]   Article 4 of the Several Provisions for the Protection of Information in Undertaking International Service Outsourcing by Domestic Enterprises promulgated by MOFCOM, 1 February 2010.
[12]   Article 5.1.4 of the Several Provisions for the Protection of Information in Undertaking International Service Outsourcing by Domestic Enterprises promulgated by MOFCOM, 1 February 2010.

49.6 Protection of Intellectual Property Rights

49.6.1 *General*

China's promulgated intellectual property laws generally adhere to international standards. In 2001, China became a signatory of the Agreement on Trade-Related Aspects of Intellectual Property Rights promulgated by the World Trade Organization. China then passed the Regulations on the Customs Protection of Intellectual Property Rights in 2004. Therefore in theory, China has effective and appropriate means for the enforcement of trade-related intellectual property rights.

Intellectual property rights in China are protected in different ways:

(a) For copyrights: copyright owners may register their work with the National Copyright Administration, since registration provides a public record and serves as useful evidence in court.
(b) For patents: owners of patents should file applications with the State Intellectual Property Office for both their core and fringe technologies and ensure their patents are properly translated.
(c) For trademarks: owners of trademarks should register their brand names (both Chinese and English) with the Trademark Office of the State Administration for Industry and Commerce (SAIC). They should carefully select the product categories and sub-categories and check the sub-categories for similar trademarks filed by competitors and infringers.

49.6.2 *Enforcement*

Where there is a breach of intellectual property rights, several types of remedial actions are possible:

(a) Administrative action: this is suitable for clear infringement or pure counterfeiting and straightforward contravention of IP rights. Aggrieved parties should apply to SAIC, which may impose monetary penalties on the infringers.
(b) Civil claim: civil claims are suitable for more complex infringement claims where administrative bodies are not able to make a determination. Cases should be filed at the respective provincial Peoples' Court. However, infringers may halt a claim for patent infringement by filing an administrative challenge to the patent with the State Intellectual Property Office.
(c) Criminal prosecution: cases involving blatant and serious infringement may be investigated by the Public Security Bureau.

49.6.3   *Protection of IP rights and Outsourcing*

The Labour Contract Law specifies that employers and employees may stipulate issues, such as protection on misuse of intellectual property rights by the employee, in the labour contract.[13]

Nevertheless, adequate protection of IP rights is crucial when outsourcing certain services in China, especially in relation to the pharmaceutical, IT and biotech industries, or other industries in which inventions and technology transfers are involved. The concern largely stems from issues involving copyright infringements, theft of trade secrets and counterfeiting where local enforcement authorities appear to be lacking the effective ability to police and enforce IPR contravention. When establishing outsourced activities in China, it is essential to carry out due diligence on the locality where such activities are to take place to ensure that the local IP rights are respected and enforced.

Contracts for outsourcing in China should include all standard intellectual property protection, data protection and confidential information provisions. After entering into an outsourcing contract with the service provider, the customer should, as a habitual matter, check distribution networks at all levels for possible leakage and weak links. "Guanxi" (good relations) with local officials especially the local patent bureau and IP enforcement bodies are tremendously important in China.

49.7   Protection of confidentiality

49.7.1   *General*

There is no comprehensive legal framework in China for the protection of confidential information. The only relevant provision relating to confidentiality specific for outsourcing business is the Several Provisions for the Protection of Information in Undertaking International Service Outsourcing by Domestic Enterprises ("Information Provisions"). As the name implies, the Information Provisions provide that service providers should take effective measures to ensure the protection and confidentiality of certain types of data provided in connection with outsourcing.

49.7.2   *Contractual Protection of Confidentiality*

One of the most valuable intangible assets of a customer or service provider is typically know-how and trade secrets. However, due to the lack of

---

[13]   Article 23 of the China Labour Contract Law.

national-wide applicable confidential information protection law, such assets cannot be effectively protected by just relying on the Information Provisions. As such, know-how and trade secrets should be protected by written agreement. In China, it is commonly understood that contractual protection plays a key role to maintain confidentiality. The Contract Law imposes confidentiality obligations on contracting parties in relation to trade secrets and allows a customer or service provider to contractually protect these intangible assets by the inclusion of provisions addressing non-competition and confidentiality issues.[14]

The Contract Law imposes confidentiality obligations on the transferee for the protection of secrets received under contract.[15] It further states that the liability for the breach of such obligations would include liquidated damages.[16] Nonetheless, it is essential for the service provider and customer to have a comprehensive contract with adequate confidentiality provisions and provisions dealing with breaches and their consequences.

A customer may consider including specific data protection safeguards into its contract with the service provider, including allowing the customer to set up effective mechanisms to monitor the service provider's performance of its confidentiality and other obligations, as well as requiring the service provider to implement contingency plans to deal with unauthorised disclosures.

The Labour Contract Law specifies that employers and employees may stipulate such issues as keeping confidential the business secrets of the employer in the labour contract,[17] and that these provisions will be enforceable.

49.8 Enforceability of Jurisdiction Clauses

49.8.1 *General*

Whilst parties to an outsourcing arrangement may prefer to choose another jurisdiction such as English law or Hong Kong law as the governing law in the outsourcing contracts, the governing law in these contracts may not always be recognised by a Chinese court due to restrictions imposed by Chinese law. There are two main principles which prohibit the application of a foreign governing law:

(a) if the relevant choice of foreign law is an attempt by the parties seeking to avoid the mandatory laws or administrative measures or regulations

---

[14] Article 60, Articles 347–352 of the China Contract Law.
[15] Article 350 of the China Contract Law.
[16] Article 352 of the China Contract Law.
[17] Article 23 of the China Labour Contract Law.

imposed by Chinese law, then the foreign law will not be applicable and such contracts shall be governed by the Chinese law;[18] or

(b) if the application of any foreign laws or international practice violates the public interest in China, then the relevant laws or practice will not be applicable and Chinese law shall apply.[19]

49.8.2 *Exclusive Jurisdiction*

The Opinions of the Supreme People's Court on Several Issues concerning the Implementation of the General Principles of the Civil Law[20] further provide that for cases where the Chinese court has exclusive jurisdiction, it is not open for the parties to choose a jurisdiction other than Chinese law as the governing law in the relevant written agreement. In this connection, Chinese courts have exclusive jurisdiction on and over the following matters:

(a) contracts for Chinese-foreign equity joint ventures, Chinese-foreign contractual joint ventures, or Chinese-foreign co-operative exploration and development of natural resources;[21]

(b) contracts transferring shares in Chinese-foreign equity ventures, Chinese-foreign contractual joint ventures and wholly foreign owned enterprises (WFOEs);[22]

(c) contracts for the management by a foreign party of Chinese-foreign equity or Chinese-foreign contractual joint ventures established in China;[23]

(d) contracts for the purchase of shares in non-foreign invested enterprises located in China by a foreign party;[24]

(e) contracts for the subscription to increase capital in a non-foreign invested enterprises located in China by a foreign party;[25]

(f) contracts for the purchase of assets from non-foreign invested enterprises located in China by a foreign party;[26]

(g) proceedings brought for real estate and harbour operations, which shall be under the jurisdiction of the people's court located in the place where the real estate and the harbour is located respectively;[27] and

(h) proceedings concerning an inheritance, which shall be under the jurisdiction of the people's court located in the place where the

---

[18] Article 6 of the Provisions of the Supreme People's Court on Certain Issues Concerning the Proper Law When Trying Cases regarding Dispute about Civil and Commercial Contracts Involving Foreign Elements, 11 June 2007 ("2007 Provisions").

[19] Article 7 of the 2007 Provisions and Article 150 of the General Principles of Civil Law.

[20] Article 305 of the Opinions of the SPC on Several Issues concerning the Implementation of the General Principles of the Civil Law of the China promulgated 14 July 1992.

[21] Article 244 of the Civil Procedure Law and Article 8(1)–(3) of the 2007 Provisions.

[22] Article 8(4) of the 2007 Provisions.

[23] Article 8(5) of the 2007 Provisions.

[24] Article 8(6) of the 2007 Provisions.

[25] Article 8(7) of the 2007 Provisions.

[26] Article 8(8) of the 2007 Provisions.

[27] Article 34 of the Civil Procedure Law.

deceased had his domicile upon his death, or where the principal portion of his estate is located.[28]

In addition, if the parties agree that an outsourcing contract is to be governed by foreign law, the party seeking to rely on that foreign law bears the burden to demonstrate to the Chinese court the applicable substantive foreign law should the court request.[29] If the parties fail to provide the court with the relevant law, the court can declare that the contracts should be governed by Chinese law.

Parties should therefore be aware that a choice of a foreign law that contravenes any of the above restrictions will be regarded as invalid whereupon Chinese law may apply to the contract.

49.9 Enforceability of Other Clauses

49.9.1 *Limitation of Liability*

One of the problems that parties to an outsourcing contract may encounter is the enforceability and effectiveness of a standard clause seeking to limit a party's liability. It is common for a service provider, in an outsourcing arrangement, to include a limitation or exemption clause purporting to exempt or limit its liability owed to the customer during the course of providing outsourcing services. The Contract Law provides that the party supplying the standard terms should, in a reasonable manner, draw the other party's attention to the provisions whereby such party's liabilities are excluded or limited and explain such provisions upon request by the other party.[30]

The Supreme People's Court has further explained that the party supplying the standard terms should draw the other party's attention to such clauses by using special marking for such clauses in the contract, such as using different text, punctuation and typeface. That party also bears the burden of proof to the court to demonstrate that it has used reasonable efforts to highlight such clauses to the other party.

In the event that such party does not take such action or fails to satisfy the court that it has exerted reasonable efforts, the court may declare such clauses to be void and inoperative.[31]

---

[28] Article 34 of the China Civil Procedure Law.
[29] Article 9 of the Provisions of the Supreme People's Court on Certain Issues Concerning the Proper Law When Trying Cases regarding Dispute about Civil and Commercial Contracts Involving Foreign Elements, 11 June 2007.
[30] Article 39 of the China Contract Law.
[31] Articles 9 and 10 of the SPC's Second Interpretation of Several Issues Concerning the Application of the Contract Law.

49.9.2 Arbitration

Another issue parties may encounter is the enforceability and effectiveness of arbitration clauses. According to Chinese law, an agreement to have disputes arising under a contract resolved through arbitration may be void on the following grounds:[32]

(a) the scope of arbitration is beyond what is permitted by applicable law;[33]
(b) the contract permits the disputes to be resolved by both arbitration and litigation;
(c) only one party to the dispute has the right to commence arbitration; and
(d) the contract provides for domestic disputes to be resolved by a foreign arbitration institution.

In respect of ground d above, Chinese law draws a distinction between domestic disputes and foreign-related disputes. A foreign-related dispute refers to a dispute in which (i) at least one of the parties is a foreigner, or (ii) the subject matter of the contract is located in a foreign country, or (iii) the act creating, modifying or extinguishing rights and obligations under the contract occurs in a foreign country.[34] For a domestic dispute, the parties to the dispute can only choose an arbitration institution registered in China, and the seat of the arbitration must also be in China.

If both parties to the outsourcing contract are Chinese and the relevant dispute involves no "foreign" element, as explained above, the parties cannot submit such dispute to a foreign arbitration institution (such as the International Chamber of Commerce (ICC)) for arbitration. Rather, the parties must settle the dispute through a Chinese arbitration institution, for instance, China International Economic and Trade Arbitration Commission (CIETAC). China has many domestic arbitration bodies.

49.10   Enforcement of Judgments and Arbitral Awards

49.10.1   Enforcement of Foreign Judgments

The basis for enforcing judgments granted by a foreign court in China is found in the Civil Procedure Law.[35] A party enforcing a judgment, and the foreign court which made the judgment, can apply for recognition and

---

[32] Article 20 of the SPC's Several Regulations on Dealing with Foreign Related Arbitration and Foreign Arbitration Cases for Lower courts (Draft Version) issued on 12 December 2003. The grounds set out here are non-exhaustive.
[33] Please refer to Article 3 of the China Arbitration Law which sets out the permitted scope of arbitration.
[34] Article 304 of the Opinions of the SPC on Several Issues concerning the Implementation of the General Principles of the Civil Law of the China promulgated on 14 July 1992.
[35] Article 265 of the China Civil Procedure Law.

enforcement of the judgment. The application should be made to the intermediate people's court who would consider the application and determine whether the conditions for recognition and enforcement are met. These key conditions are set out below:[36]

(a) the foreign judgment or ruling granted by the foreign court must have already been legally effective;
(b) the recognition and enforcement must be made in accordance with the provisions of international treaties concluded or acceded to by China or based on the principle of reciprocity. As a result, the foreign state and China must have concluded a bilateral treaty or have both acceded to a multilateral treaty relating to mutual recognition and enforcement of court judgments, or have a reciprocal relationship of recognition and enforcement of court judgments; or
(c) the foreign judgment or ruling does not contradict the basic principles of Chinese law and does not violate the national, social, and public interest of China.

In relation to condition (b) above, China has concluded bilateral treaties on reciprocal judgment recognition and enforcement with various countries including France, Italy, Vietnam and Brazil. It should be noted that China has not yet concluded any such bilateral treaty with many of its usual trading partners including the United States and the United Kingdom. Moreover, the Convention on the Recognition and Enforcement of Foreign Judgments in Civil and Commercial Matters obliges signatories to recognize and enforce foreign judgments in accordance with the Convention. Unfortunately, China is not yet a signatory. In the absence of such treaty or reciprocal relationship, the Chinese court is likely to refuse to recognise and enforce a foreign judgment and the applicant will need to re-litigate in China.

49.10.2 *Enforcement of Hong Kong, Macau and Taiwan Judgments in China*

The enforcement of judgments obtained in Hong Kong, Macau and Taiwan is relatively easier in China. The Hong Kong government and the Chinese government signed the Arrangement on Reciprocal Recognition and Enforcement of Judgments in Civil and Commercial Matters by the Courts of the Mainland and of the Hong Kong Special Administrative Region Pursuant to Choice of Court Agreements between Parties Concerned ("Hong Kong Arrangement"), which came into force in 2007. Under the Hong Kong Arrangement, final and conclusive money judgment of commercial cases given by specified courts of Hong Kong made pursuant to a valid exclusive choice of court agreement in writing can be recognized and enforced in China.

---

[36] Article 266 of the China Civil Procedure Law.

However, the Hong Kong Arrangement also provides for grounds which the court may refuse enforcement of the judgments, including that (1) the choice of court agreement is invalid; (2) the court of the place of enforcement has exclusive jurisdiction over the dispute; or (3) the people's court considers the enforcement of the Hong Kong judgment is contrary to social and public interest in China.

Similarly, the Arrangement between Mainland and the Macau Special Administrative Region on Reciprocal Recognition and Enforcement of Civil and Commercial Judgments and the Regulation on the Recognition of People's Courts' of Civil Judgments by Taiwan Courts was implemented respectively in 2006 and 1998 which provide easier means for enforcing Macau and Taiwan judgments in China respectively.[37]

49.10.3   *Enforcement of Foreign Arbitral Awards*

An alternative means by which the parties to an outsourcing contract can resolve disputes is through arbitration, and the enforcement of a foreign arbitral award is relatively easier than enforcing a foreign judgment in China. The basis for enforcing arbitral awards granted by a foreign arbitration institution is found in the Civil Procedure Law.[38] A party to the arbitration can apply for recognition and enforcement of the judgment to the intermediate people's court.

The court will then deal with the matter according to the relevant provisions of the international treaties concluded or acceded to by China. To this end, China is a party to the Convention on the Recognition and Enforcement of Foreign Arbitral Awards ("New York Convention"), a treaty governing international recognition and enforcement of foreign arbitral awards.

According to the New York Convention, member states are required to recognise foreign arbitral awards unless such awards are not enforceable by any of the reasons stated in Article V of the Convention, such as the invalidity of the arbitration agreement or procedural irregularities. Also noteworthy is that in China, the Supreme People's Court has a system whereby a local court's decision not to enforce an arbitral award must first be reviewed by it.[39]

---

[37] Article 9 of the Arrangement on Reciprocal Recognition and Enforcement of Judgments in Civil and Commercial Matters by the Courts of the Mainland and of the Hong Kong Special Administrative Region Pursuant to Choice of Court Agreements between Parties Concerned.

[38] Article 267 of the China Civil Procedure Law.

[39] Circular of the Supreme People's Court on Issues in the People's Courts' Handling of Foreign-related Arbitrations and Foreign Arbitrations, Fa Fa [1995] No. 18.

49.10.4 Enforcement of Hong Kong, Macau and Taiwan Arbitral Awards in China

As with the enforcement of foreign judgments, the enforcement of arbitral awards obtained in Hong Kong, Macau and Taiwan are separately dealt with. The Arrangement concerning Mutual Enforcement of Arbitral Awards between Mainland China and HKSAR, signed in 1999 provides for reciprocal recognition and enforcement of arbitral awards between China and Hong Kong. A similar arrangement, the Arrangement on Mutual Recognition and Enforcement of Arbitral Awards Made in the Mainland and Macau SAR came into force 2008, which provides for the reciprocal enforcement of arbitral awards between China and Macau. As for arbitral awards in Taiwan, the Supreme People's Court promulgated the Regulations Concerning Recognition by People's Courts of Civil Judgments of Taiwan Courts which provide for recognition and enforcement of civil judgments and arbitral awards rendered by Taiwan courts.

49.10.5 Mediation

Mediation is now becoming increasingly popular as a means of dispute resolution. Mediation does not and should not have the formality associated with litigation and arbitration, yet it is particularly appropriate in China in that it is consistent with the approach of Chinese courts to pressure litigants to find a settlement between themselves.

Mediation in China is mainly governed by the People's Mediation Law enacted in 2011. Parties to a dispute may apply to a people's mediation commission recognized by law for mediation. However, both parties must agree to resolve their dispute through mediation. No application for mediation can be made if one party expressly refuses to settle the dispute by mediation.[40]

A written mediation agreement can be made once an agreement is reached and such an agreement is binding on the parties. An oral agreement can be made if the parties believe that it is unnecessary to make a written mediation agreement, in which case the people's mediators shall note down the contents of the oral agreement.[41] Within 30 days after the mediation agreement becomes effective, where necessary, the parties can jointly apply to the people's court for judicial confirmation. The people's court will examine the agreement and confirm it is effective and it will then become enforceable. If one of the parties refuses to perform or fails to fully perform its obligations

---

[40] Article 17 of the People's Mediation Law
[41] Article 28 of the People's Mediation Law

under the mediation agreement, the other party may apply to the people's court for enforcement.[42]

49.11 Government Support and Regulatory Restrictions

49.11.1 *Government Support*

49.11.1.1 *The "Thousand-Hundred-Ten Project"*

The Chinese government has been supportive towards the development of its outsourcing industry in the past decade. In the "Eleventh Five-Year Plan" for National Economic and Social Development announced in 2005, the government promoted the "Thousand-Hundred-Ten Project" which is aimed at developing service outsourcing and preparing for the transfer of the international service industry.[43]

In particular, efforts are being made to develop 10 base cities for service outsourcing with international competitiveness, to promote 100 well-known transnational corporations to transfer their service outsourcing businesses to China and to cultivate 1,000 large and medium-sized service outsourcing enterprises with international qualification. Such supportive policies have continued to be reflected in the recent "Twelfth Five-Year Plan" announced in 2011 to develop the outsourcing industry on a large scale.

49.11.1.2 *Human Resources and Training*

The Chinese government has also dedicated special funds for public training for outsourcing services and for college graduates to enhance expertise and techniques of service outsourcing. The government has also been encouraging service outsourcing enterprises to conduct training programmes oriented towards adding new jobs, with new graduates, graduating students and newcomers in service outsourcing enterprises. The outsourcing industry expects to train 300,000–430,000 talents needed for service outsourcing businesses and is looking to create job opportunities for 200,000–300,000 college graduates. It is hoped that this will effectively solve the problem of a talent shortage in the service outsourcing industry.

---

[42] Article 33 of the People's Mediation Law
[43] Circular of MOFCOM on Implementing the "Thousand-Hundred-Ten Project" of Service Outsourcing, Shang Zi Fa [2006] No.556.

49.11.1.3   Base Cities for Service Outsourcing

The Chinese government has selected a series of central cities with the potential for service outsourcing. The government is facilitating their development from various aspects, such as macro-policy, plan and design, personnel training, investment invitation and comprehensive co-ordination. Currently, the approved service outsourcing base cities include Dalian, Shanghai, Xi'an, Chengdu, Shenzhen, Beijing, Tianjin, Jinan, Wuhan, Nanjing and Zhengzhou. Each base city has its own distinct advantages in providing outsourcing services.

Dalian and Zhengzhou, are two lead examples of how government support has resulted in extensive growth of the outsourcing industry:

(a)   Dalian has been developed into a software outsourcing centre with governmental support. In Dalian, companies wanting to hire software engineers can save up to 43 per cent more if they hire locals.
(b)   In Zhengzhou, a string of measures were adopted to boost its outsourcing industry. Zhengzhou set up a special fund to bring in outsourcing talent, to provide subsidies to outsourcing companies, and to build advanced outsourcing bases. It has also made substantial efforts to protect intellectual property rights. Some 30 outsourcing companies have been established in Zhengzhou and several multinational companies are planning to transfer part of their businesses there, with others to follow.

49.11.1.4   Incentives for Software Exports

Software exports are the subject of government support in the Circular Concerning Questions about Software Exports ("Software Circular") issued by the Ministry of Foreign Trade and Economic Co-operation, or MOFTEC, the predecessor of MOFCOM.[44] The Software Circular applies to any export of licence software technology, computer software, information system or built-in software as well as services relating to information data including time sequence and data processing of data development, storage and internet connection. In short, software exporters may:

(a)   apply to MOFCOM for small to medium-sized enterprise funds for international market development;
(b)   apply to MOFCOM for financial aid for those exporters that need to go through certain authentication of Quality Assurance System and Capacity Maturity Model;

---

[44]   Circular of the Ministry of Foreign Trade and Economic Co-operation, the Ministry of Information Industry, the State Administration of Taxation, the General Administration of Customs, the State Administration of Foreign Exchange and the National Bureau of Statistics Concerning Relevant Questions about Software Export, JiFa [2002] No. 680 of MOFTEC.

(c)   enjoy preferential interest rates from the Export-Import Bank of China; and

(d)   enjoy certain taxation and foreign exchange relief.

49.11.2   *Regulatory Restrictions*

49.11.2.1   *Transfer of Technology*

The import and export of technology is restricted in China. The Administrative Regulations of Technology Import and Export ("Technology Regulation") applies to any act which involves the transfer of technology into or out of the territory of China by way of trade, investment, economic or technical co-operation. These acts include:

(a)   assignment of the patent right or patent application right;
(b)   contract for licence or transfer of exclusively-owned technology;
(c)   contract for licensed use of computer software;
(d)   contract for co-operative technology services, design or research;
(e)   assignment of technical secrets and technical services; and
(f)   any transfer of technology by other means.[45]

The Technology Regulation classifies imported and exported technology into three categories, namely prohibited, restricted and unrestricted. Any prohibited technology should not be imported or exported. As for technologies which are restricted, the importer / exporter should file an application to MOFCOM and obtain a proposed licence before signing the contract with the transferor. A formal licence will be issued after the parties signed the relevant outsourcing contracts involving the transfer of technology.[46]

As for unrestricted technology, although non-registration will not affect the validity of the relevant outsourcing contracts, parties may not be able to go through foreign exchange, banking, taxation and custom formalities without obtaining the certificate of registration.[47] Therefore, registration should still be made with MOFCOM.[48] The registration of import and export contracts are regulated by the Administrative Procedures of Technology Import and Export Contracts Registration. These Procedures set out the content requirements of such contracts, which should include the basis of the contract, terms of payment and other contractual terms.[49]

---

[45]   Article 2 of the Administrative Regulations on Technology Import and Export promulgated by MOFCOM on 1 January 2002 ("Technology Regulation")
[46]   See Chapter 2 and Chapter 3 of the Technology Regulation.
[47]   Articles 17 and 20 of the Technology Regulation.
[48]   Articles 18 and 40 of the Technology Regulation
[49]   Article 10 of the Administrative Procedures of Technology Import and Export Contracts Registration, promulgated by MOFCOM, Decree [2009] No. 3.

The classification of restricted and prohibited technology can be found in the catalogues of prohibited or restricted technology published by the relevant foreign trade department. More than 100 or so types of technology are banned or restricted from being imported. These cover 19 sectors including agriculture, food manufacturing, textiles, raw chemical materials, pharmaceuticals, metal smelting, and other areas which are likely to endanger national security, affect public moral and public interests, or cause harm to the health of human beings.

49.11.2.2 Software Exports

For outsourcing businesses involving software development, the service provider and customer should pay attention to the Software Circular. This applies to any export of licence of software technology, computer software, information system or built-in software on equipment as well as service trade related to information data including time sequence and data processing of data development, storage and internet connection. The software exporters need to register the relevant export contracts with MOFCOM, both at the time of and after entering into the export contracts.[50]

49.11.2.3 Foreign Exchange Controls

Complying with China's foreign exchange rules remains a key concern for outsourcing businesses in China and for foreign customers with service providers in China. Matters relating to foreign exchange controls are regulated by the State Administration of Foreign Exchange (SAFE) and its local bureaux. In light of the proliferating number of cross-border transactions, the government promulgated the revised Administrative Regulations of the People's Republic of China on Foreign Exchange in 2008 ("2008 Foreign Exchange Rules") to replace the old 1996 rules.[51] For current account transactions, one of the previous concerns for service providers and customers was that revenues in foreign exchange were required to be converted into RMB and that monies retained overseas had to be remitted back to China. Such requirements were abolished under the 2008 Foreign Exchange Rules. Revenues in foreign currencies can be retained or sold to financial institutions in exchange for RMB. Moreover, domestic entities are allowed to retain their foreign exchange revenues outside China.[52]

As for the administration of foreign exchange in respect of capital account transactions, direct offshore investment will need only to be registered with SAFE but will not require SAFE approval.[53] In addition, revenues in foreign currency under capital account transactions may be retained in foreign

---

[50]   Article 2(1) and (2) of the Software Circular.
[51]   Regulations of the People's Republic of China on Foreign Exchange Administration, Decree [2008] No. 532 ("2008 Foreign Exchange Rules").
[52]   Article 5 of the 2008 Foreign Exchange Rules.
[53]   Article 16 of the 2008 Foreign Exchange Rules.

exchange or be settled in RMB upon approval by SAFE.[54] For the use of foreign capital remitted into China, the 2008 Foreign Exchange Rules require that the use of such capital should be for purposes approved by the relevant government authority.[55]

49.12   Taxation Issues

49.12.1   *General Taxation*

In general, a domestic service provider is subject to 25 per cent corporate income tax (CIT) for any taxable income it gains from the provision of outsourcing services. However, as part of the Chinese government's efforts to boost the outsourcing services industry, outsourcing service providers can qualify as an advanced technology service enterprise if registered in one of the named 21 cities in China are entitled to a reduced tax rate of 15 per cent, effective from 1 January 2009 to 31 December 2013.[56]

If the outsourcing arrangement involves the transfer of assets to the service provider, then assuming the customer is a Chinese resident business entity, it is subject to a 25 per cent rate of income tax rate, gained as a result of the asset transfer, as well as a 5.5 per cent business tax. However, income received by enterprises registered in one of the named 21 pilot cities mentioned below are exempt from business tax from 1 July 2010 to 31 December 2013.[57]

In addition, if there are goods sold or imported, or certain services (such as processing, repair and replacement) are provided by a services provider, those goods or services are subject to VAT at a rate of 13 per cent to 17 per cent. The service provider may also be subject to stamp duty at a rate of 0.003 per cent to 1 per cent depending on the type of services provided in the outsourcing transaction.

49.12.2   *New Tax Incentives for Outsourcing Businesses*

The Chinese government continues to promote the outsourcing industry by providing tax incentives. In 2009, the government formulated a tax incen-

---

[54] Article 21 of the 2008 Foreign Exchange Rules.
[55] Article 23 of the 2008 Foreign Exchange Rules.
[56] Circular on Tax Policies Concerning Advanced Technology Service Enterprises, Caishui [2009] No.63, is-sued by the Ministry of Finance (MOF), the State Development and Reform Commission (SDRC), the State Administration of Taxation (SAT), the Ministry of Science and Technology (MST) and the Ministry of Commerce (MOFCOM) on 24 April 2009 ("Circular No. 63"); Notice on the Business Tax Exemption on the Offshore Outsourcing Business in Pilot Cities, Caishui [2010] No. 64 (Circular 64) and Caishui [2010] No. 65 issued by the MOF, SDRC and MOFCOM ("Circular 65")
[57] Circular 63 and Circular 65.

tive scheme for advanced technology service enterprises engaged in the outsourcing industry. These tax incentives provide that enterprises engaged in service outsourcing and registered in one of the named 21 pilot cities are entitled to the following favourable tax treatment:

(a) preferential CIT rate of 15 per cent;
(b) CIT deduction of actually-incurred staff education charges, up to a limit of 8 per cent of the total payroll; and
(c) business tax exemption for offshore outsourcing service income.

The 21 pilot cities mentioned above include Beijing, Tianjin, Dalian, Harbin, Daqing, Shanghai, Nanjing, Suzhou, Wuhan, Changsha, Guangzhou, Shenzhen, Chongqing, Chengdu and Xian. Advanced technology service enterprises providing (1) IT outsourcing services, (2) business process outsourcing services; and (3) knowledge process outsourcing services are qualified to benefit from the scheme.

49.13   Summary

Outsourcing business in China continues to blossom. With the shift of the world economy to Asia, it is expected that China will take an even more important role as an outsourcing engine in the coming years. Coupled with government efforts to promote its outsourcing industry, we will see changing landscapes for service providers and customers alike active in this industry.

The speed with which the outsourcing industry continues to expand and develop is matched somewhat by improvements in China's legal system. Despite such improvements, there remains plenty of room in advancing legislation as well as practical and effective procedures and processes that would provide protection for foreign owners and customers outsourcing their processes to China. Much improvement is still needed in the practical application of the law and the ability to smoothly enforce IP rights and remedy theft of business and industrial secrets and counterfeiting. Adding to these factors is the difficulty of enforcing foreign judgments in China.

Despite problems associated with a fast-developing economy and a populace hungry for knowledge, China remains a preferential jurisdiction for outsourcing businesses. After all, outsourcing when distilled to its basic essence is a "peoples' business" involving a continuing development of a relationship and Chinese "guanxi" fits very well with this concept. Whilst this chapter has focused on legal issues, customers will have inevitably considered a whole spectrum of costs, business and cultural issues before deciding to place outsourced services in China. As seen from this chapter, the Chinese government sees the development of outsourcing industry as one of the major goals of the country. It has provided various incentives such as financial and tax relief to attract customers and further incentives are anticipated.

Chapter 50

United States

John Funk

Partner, Dentons, Dallas, US

50.1 Outline

Parts 1 to 11 of this book describe the key business issues relevant for outsourcing and other services agreements. They also describe the key legal issues under English law. This chapter describes the specific legal and business issues which affect services and outsourcing arrangements in the United States.

50.2 People issues

The Acquired Rights Directive does not apply in the United States.

In most outsourcing transactions, the customer must consider each of its employees whose position or job description will be affected by an outsourcing of a process or a function to a supplier. The customer may chose to (1) keep such employee, either in a "retained" position overseeing or interacting with the supplier on an ongoing basis or transfer such employee to another position; (2) agree with the supplier that the supplier will offer employment to such employee; or (3) terminate the employment relationship with the employee.

In the early decades of outsourcing in the United States, suppliers frequently committed to offer to hire a significant number of the customer's affected employees. Affected employees frequently delivered services from space leased or licensed by the customer to the supplier in customer-owned facilities. Suppliers hired the customer's employees because they required qualified staff to grow their businesses, and they opened or sublet property in or near the customer's facilities in order to retain the affected employees. More recently, suppliers have reduced the number of customer employees to whom they offer employment as they seek to further leverage their existing work force, limit staff to employees trained in the suppliers methodologies, and move work to supplier facilities remote from the customer's premises, either located elsewhere in the United States or in offshore locations. As a result, hiring of the customer's employees to the supplier has become less frequent. Where certain services must be delivered at the customer's location on an ongoing basis, and the supplier doesn't have trained staff in those geographic areas, the supplier may want to offer employment to some or all of the customer's affected employees already providing such services. In addition, some employees of the customer may have particular or special knowledge of the process or function being outsourced and both customer and supplier believe it helpful and in some circumstances essential that such employees continue performing their functions as employees of the supplier after the customer transitions the process or function to the supplier.

The Worker Adjustment and Retraining Notification Act of 1988[1] (WARN Act) requires most employers with 100 or more employees to provide notification 60 calendar days in advance of plant closings and mass layoffs. If the customer is covered by the WARN Act and as few as 50 employees (depending on the size of the total workforce) of the customer will be terminated as a result of the outsourcing, the customer must give notice to the employees. The 60 day notice period must be taken into account by the customer and the supplier in planning for the transition of the services and any employees to be offered employment by the supplier. If an employer fails to give 60 days notice, each affected employee is entitled to 60 days of back pay and benefits from the employer, less wages paid by the employer during the 60 day period.

While initial considerations concerning a potential outsourcing are usually closely restricted within a company, rumours frequently arise. It is not unusual for employees who think they may be affected by a rumoured or confirmed outsourcing arrangement to immediately begin the search for new employment. Because the most competent and valuable employees find suitable opportunities more quickly, the customer risks the loss of the employees on whom it depends to maintain ongoing operations (including those who the supplier would like to hire) or who the customer wants to retain. It is critical that the customer has a plan to communicate with its employees who will be affected by an outsourcing transaction quickly, openly and as frequently as practicable consistent with the decision-making process and the status of the negotiations between the customer and the supplier. The supplier may have an important role in the communication plan, particularly with respect to the employees to be offered employment by the supplier, and should be included in the planning and, if appropriate, the communication process.

If the supplier is not going to offer employment to the customer's key employees, it may be important for the customer to develop and implement a retention program designed to retain key employees through the transi-

---

[1]   Worker Adjustment and Retraining Notification Act, 29 U.S.C. (2006) ss.2101–2109.

tion of services to the supplier. The retention program may include a combination of incentive compensation for working through the transition, accelerated or enhanced retirement benefits for those approaching retirement, additional outplacement services following transition, or a commitment to assign key employees to other positions at the customer. It may also be important for the supplier to offer incentives for key affected employees to accept employment with the supplier in order to retain specialised or critical knowledge of the customer's requirements, procedures, processes, methodologies, or systems.

The terms pursuant to which the supplier offers employment to employees of the customer are subject to negotiation by the customer and the supplier. Many customers desire to negotiate protections for their employees who are hired by the supplier, such as comparable salary and benefits, accelerated vesting in benefits plans, credit for deductibles paid under health care plans, and a protected period of employment with the supplier. Customers who seek to provide such protection for their former employees must recognise that such protections may increase the supplier's cost of providing services and result in higher charges for those services. Working with its legal and human resources departments, the customer should consider the following matters:

(a) hiring requirements, if any;

(b) the process by which employees may be hired by the supplier, including identification of the customer's employees eligible for hire by the supplier, along with relevant employment information, identification of any hiring requirements of the supplier (such as drug testing and background checks), and the process of making and accepting offers of employment;

(c) any requirement by the customer for a protected period of employment for some or all of the transferring employees;

(d) any requirements by the customer about the positions to be offered (including location), work days and work schedules, holiday schedules, and terms of the current employment agreement that should be honoured by the supplier;

(e) any requirements by the customer about comparable compensation, including base salary, bonuses and other employee incentive compensation arrangements;

(f) a detailed comparison of benefits offered by the customer versus benefits offered by the supplier;

(g) any requirements by the customer about employee benefits for the transferring employees, including eligibility for participation in the supplier's benefit plans and recognition by the supplier of employees' years of service with the customer;

(h) any compensation for the loss of benefits offered by the customer that are not offered by the supplier; and

(i) whether the customer will have the right to solicit such employees upon expiration or termination of the outsourcing contract.

50.3 Pensions issues

Since the Acquired Rights Directive does not apply in the United States, there is no "automatic transfer" of any rights under pension schemes when an employee of the customer becomes an employee of the supplier in connection with an outsourcing. Typically, as discussed in section 50.2, transitioned employees are eligible to participate in the pension plans of the supplier, subject to the rules applicable to these plans. The parties may agree, as discussed in section 50.2, that an employee's years of service with the customer be recognised for certain purposes under the supplier's pension plans.

50.4 Contract law

50.4.1 *Contract law in the United States*

Before addressing the specific topics in this and subsequent sections, it is important to have a fundamental understanding of the sources of contract law in the United States. The legal system in the United States has several different layers:

(a) federal law that applies to all fifty states and US territories;
(b) state law that applies within that particular state; and
(c) "local" laws that apply within a smaller unit of government, such as a county or a city.

As a general rule, the law governing contracts, including outsourcing and other services contracts, is found at the state level. Almost without exception, contract law at a state level in the United States has at its roots the same common law principles inherited by the initial states from England and as a result the general principles of contract law at a high level are common throughout the fifty states. However, the details of contract law may vary from state to state. Generally speaking state contract law recognises the "right to contract" on agreed terms and will enforce the terms of a contract between commercial parties.

There have been attempts through recent decades to bring some uniformity to contract law across the fifty states through the adoption of "uniform acts". An act governing a range of commercial activities known as the Uniform Commercial Code (or UCC) is the most successful of such efforts and has been adopted, with some revisions, by all of the states except Louisiana. Article 2 of the UCC applies to the sale of goods. There has been a split of opinion in the case law about whether Article 2 applies to the licensing of software and some courts have applied Article 2 to "mixed" contracts that include both the sale of goods (or the licensing of software) and the provision of services. Outsourcing and other technology contracts include the sale of goods or the licensing of software and may be subject to Article 2 concepts. As a result, many of the concepts embodied by Article 2 of the UCC have been applied by courts to outsourcing contracts. In addition, common law applicable to sale of services frequently follows the principles of Article 2 applicable to the sale of goods.

50.4.2 Choice of governing law

Because state law largely governs the interpretation and enforceability of contracts, the parties to outsourcing and other commercial contracts usually agree in the contract upon the "governing law" that will apply to the contract. The choice of law may not be simple because many customers have operations in a number of states or countries that will be impacted by the contract and the supplier may be providing solutions from yet other states or countries. The customer will usually want the contract to be governed by the law of the state in which it is incorporated or headquartered. The supplier will similarly want the contract to be governed by the law of the state in which it is incorporated or headquartered. Both customer and supplier try to standardise the choice of governing law in its contracts as much as possible in order to simplify contract interpretation and legal support (lawyers are generally licensed to practice law in a particular state). Alternatively, the parties may agree that the law of a third state will apply. Since the State of New York is usually considered as having a well-developed body of contract law, because of the number of commercial contract cases brought and decided by New York courts, New York law is a frequent choice for a "neutral" state law in complex commercial contracts. When selecting the law of a particular jurisdiction, it is important for the customer to understand key provisions of applicable law that may make one jurisdiction favourable to others.

Another uniform act, the Uniform Computer Information Transactions Act or UCITA, was proposed by the National Conference of Commissions of Uniform State Laws (NCCUSL) in 1999, with revisions in 2000 and 2002. UCITA provides a comprehensive set of rules for licensing computer information, whether computer software or other clearly identified forms of computer information. Only two states, Maryland and Virginia, have adopted UCITA. The NCCUSL states that UCITA does not provide any rules governing mixed transactions, in which computer information is part of a transaction also involving goods or services, which would include many if not most outsourcing agreements and many services agreements dealing with computer or information technology. Regardless, the governing law provision of many outsourcing and other services contracts involving computer information technology will disclaim the application of UCITA. In addition, many such provisions also disclaim the applicability of the United Nations Convention on Contracts for the International Sale of Goods 1980, and all international and domestic legislation implementing such Convention.

50.4.3   *Different approaches to legal liability*

Of the approaches identified in Chapter 35 dealing with legal liability under outsourcing and other services contracts, only two are generally applicable in the United States:

(a)   the supplier is liable for breach of contract except where its failure is due to a force majeure event (commercial contracts) and

(b)   the supplier is liable for damages that result from its negligence.

There is no concept in the United States generally corresponding to the Private Finance Initiative (PFI) in the UK.

50.4.4   *Liability of supplier for failure—force majeure*

One of the general principles of contract law, regardless of which state law applies, is the concept of force majeure. The issues discussed in sections 34.2 to 34.7 are generally addressed in outsourcing and services contracts in the United States with largely similar approaches as those discussed in those sections.

50.4.5   *Liability under indemnities*

Like the UK, agreements to indemnify are generally enforced under contract law in the United States. Like other contract concepts, the law of each state may differ in some aspects of the construction and enforcement of indemnity provisions. While a survey of contract law in the fifty states is beyond the scope of this chapter, there are potential traps under state law that might derail the parties' intent. For example, under Texas law, if a party seeks indemnification from the other for its own negligence, there must be fair notice, including complying with what is called the "express negligence" rule and conspicuousness. Under the "express negligence" rule, the contract must explicitly state that the "Party A" is indemnifying "Party B" for "Party B's" own negligence. If it is not explicit and conspicuous, it is not enforceable. Prior to selecting governing law, the parties may desire to check that state's law on indemnification.

Indemnities in US services and outsourcing contracts are usually, but not always, limited to third party claims (that is, situations in which one of the parties agrees to defend and compensate the other party against and for liability such other party incurs to a third party). In some situations, the customer may also want the supplier to agree to compensate the customer for its own losses, and these "direct claim" indemnities are usually vigorously resisted by the supplier.

One driving concern is whether or not the indemnities will be subject to the limitations of liability. The parties will generally negotiate which of the indemnities are subject to some or all of the limitations of liability and which are not. If an indemnity is not subject to the limitations of liability, then the party giving the indemnity will want the indemnity to be drafted as narrowly as possible. The supplier may view a "direct claim" indemnity as a devise to avoid the limitations of liability that would otherwise apply to such claim. As a result, many services and outsourcing contracts now approach liability for such direct claims as an exception to the limitations of liability, rather than as indemnities. Outsourcing and services contracts frequently include a waiver of all but direct damages (e.g., a waiver of incidental, indirect, consequential, exemplary and punitive damages). Where a contract provides for the indemnification of third party claims, and includes a waiver of all but direct damages, it may be important for the customer to clarify that all third party claims will be considered direct damages (since the customer must pay the third party), even if the underlying claim of the third party includes damages that may not be classified as direct.

50.4.6   Liability to third parties

As discussed in section 34.15, the supplier's potential liability to third parties is a matter of some concern to the supplier. Specific allocation of any potential third party liability should be negotiated as part of the contract. While there is no parallel in the United States to the Contract (Rights of Third Parties) Act 1999, the parties will generally provide in the contract that they do not intend that the contract will benefit or create any right of action in any person or entity other than the parties to the contract. Potential exceptions, such as those identified in section 34.15, are specified in some detail in the contract, based upon the agreed allocation of risk between the parties. Some of those exceptions may also be contained in the indemnities that deal with third party claims for which one party may indemnify the other party under the contract.

50.5   Limitations of liability

Services and outsourcing contracts in the United States generally include the same considerations of limitations of liability as discussed in Chapter 35. As previously mentioned in this chapter, state contract law upholds the "right to contract" and will usually enforce the terms of a contract between commercial parties, including limitations of liability. In many states parties may not limit their liability for gross negligence or wilful misconduct and many outsourcing or services contracts contain express provisions to that effect. It is important for customers to recognize that in some states, including New York, the wrongful abandonment of a contract is considered an economic breach and does not constitute wilful misconduct.

50.5.1   *Financial caps*

It is customary in the United States for a services or outsourcing contract to include a cap or caps, typically mutual, on a party's liability under the contract. The structure and the amount of the cap may vary, depending upon the type of services, the customer's industry, the relative bargaining position of the parties, and other factors.

50.5.2   *Unlimited*

Under the laws of most states, a party cannot limit its liability for damages related to death or personal injury arising from its negligence or for fraud. Unlike the UK where a party cannot limit its liability arising from breach of the implied obligation as to title, most US services contracts contain a disclaimer of implied warranties, such as title, and such disclaimers are generally recognized under contract law.

50.5.3   *Enforceability of caps*

Financial caps and other limitations of liability are generally enforceable under state contract law unless they are unconscionable or violate public policy.

50.5.3.1   *UCC and unconscionability*

As mentioned previously in this chapter, all of the states except Louisiana have adopted a version of the Uniform Commercial Code. Although Article 2 of the UCC, which covers the sale of goods, does not expressly apply to contracts for services, courts have borrowed concepts from Article 2 in construing contracts for services. One such borrowed concept is the limitation of remedies. Section 2-719 of the UCC provides that

> "[c]onsequential damages may be limited or excluded unless the limitation or exclusion is unconscionable. Limitation of consequential damages for injury to the person in the case of consumer goods is prima facie unconscionable but limitation of damages where the loss is commercial is not."

Section 2-302(i) of the UCC further states that

> "[i]f the court as a matter of law finds the contract or any clause of the contract to have been unconscionable at the time it was made the court may refuse to enforce the contract, or it may enforce the remainder of the contract without the unconscionable clause, or it may so limit the application of any unconscionable clause as to avoid any unconscionable result."

It is unusual for a court to find that a commercial contract negotiated at arms length between two commercial entities is unconscionable. But unconscionability should caution a supplier from being too aggressive in its limitations of liability.

50.5.4 *Exclusions from limitations of liability*

One additional carve-out from the financial caps and the consequential loss exclusion commonly requested by US customers in a services or outsourcing contract beyond those described in sections 35.4.3 and 35.6.3 is for gross negligence and wilful misconduct. Depending on the supplier, this carve out may be particularly contentious. Some suppliers may accept both, others wilful misconduct but not gross negligence and still others may refuse to accept either. One of the concerns typically raised by the supplier is that the concepts of gross negligence, a tort concept under many state laws, and wilful misconduct are not well defined in the case law for contractual relationships. Some states have case law defining gross negligence in a contract context, but many do not. Some suppliers, having faced this argument many times, offer instead a contractual definition of "gross negligence" or "wilful misconduct" or both that if met will be considered a carve-out from some or all of the limitations of liability or to which a higher financial cap will apply.

An example of wilful misconduct, included in the discussion of unlimited liability in section 35.4.3, is abandonment or repudiation of the contract by the supplier. Sometimes the customer and the supplier will treat abandonment separately, by agreeing upon a contractual definition of "Abandonment" that if met will be subject to unlimited liability or a higher financial cap and may include some measure of consequential loss despite the consequential loss exclusion.

50.5.5 *Limitation of liability by the customer*

It is generally customary for well-advised customers in outsourcing and other complex service contracts to insist that the limitations of liability be reciprocal, subject to a carve-out for failure to pay.

50.6   Data protection

The Data Protection Directive does not apply in the United States. The European Commission determined in 1999 that the United States was one of those countries outside of the European Union that does not ensure an adequate level of protection of personal data of EU citizens by reason of its domestic law or its international commitments. In response, the US Department of Commerce and the European Commission worked out a "safe harbor" framework. Under the safe harbor, a supplier operating in the United States can join the safe harbor by agreeing to comply with the safe harbor principles. As a result, transfers of personal data of EU citizens to that supplier in the United States will satisfy the adequate level of protection required. A number of suppliers have joined the safe harbor and a list of these suppliers may be found at *https://safeharbor.export.gov/list.aspx* [Accessed 26 September 2012]. See Chapter 36 for details of relevant EU data protection law.

Unlike the UK, there is no uniform legislative regime for data protection, usually referred to in the US as privacy protection, applicable across the United States. There are privacy laws at both the federal and state level that impact outsourcing and other services contracts and that need to be considered when structuring the transaction.

50.6.1   *Federal Privacy Legislation*

At the federal level, there are over two dozen separate legislative acts covering privacy of various segments of the United States population. However, in most commercial outsourcing or services transactions, two significant federal laws applying to a large portion of the population may apply depending on the circumstances—the Gramm-Leach-Bliley Act[2] (GLB) and the Health Insurance Portability and Accountability Act of 1996[3] (HIPAA).

---

[2] Graham-Leach-Bliley Act, 15 U.S.C. (2006) ss.6801-6809.
[3] Health Insurance Portability and Accountability Act of 1996, Pub. L. No 104-191 (1996).

50.6.1.1 Gramm-Leach-Bliley

Gramm-Leach-Bliley, enacted in 1999, requires financial institutions to safeguard sensitive data of their customers and to explain their information-sharing practices to their customers. Sensitive data includes names, addresses and phone numbers; bank and credit card account numbers; income and credit histories; and Social Security numbers. Financial institutions are broadly defined as companies that offer consumers financial products or services like loans, financial or investment advice, or insurance. In addition to banks and insurance companies, companies subject to GLB include check-cashing businesses, data processors, mortgage brokers, nonbank lenders, personal property or real estate appraisers, and retailers that issue credit cards to consumers. The United States Federal Trade Commission has published a rule implementing GLB called the Safeguards Rule.[4] The Safeguards Rule establishes standards relating to administrative, technical and physical information safeguards for financial institutions subject to the FTC's jurisdiction. Five federal regulators of financial institutions in the United States also promulgated guidelines for the financial institutions they regulate on standards for safeguarding customer information.[5]

Outsourcing of an IT function or a business process to a supplier does not relieve a financial institution of its obligation to comply with GLB. As a result, any financial institution covered by Gramm-Leach-Bliley will need to make sure that its outsourcing contract addresses the supplier's obligations with respect to GLB if the supplier will have access to sensitive customer data covered by GLB. In fact, the Safeguards Rule requires the customer to

> "oversee [its] service providers, by: (1) [t]aking reasonable steps to select and retain service providers that are capable of maintaining appropriate safeguards for the customer information at issue; and (2) [r]equiring [its] service providers by contract to implement and maintain such safeguards."[6]

While the customer would like the supplier to assume responsibility in broad terms in the contract for violations of Gramm-Leach-Bliley and the Safeguards Rule, the supplier tries to narrow its liability since in many areas the customer must decide how it interprets, and how it will meet, its obligations under GLB and the Safeguards Rule.

50.6.1.2 HIPAA

The Health Insurance Portability and Accountability Act enacted in 1996, among other things, directed the US Department of Health and Human Services (HHS) to adopt uniform, national standards for the protection of

---

[4] Standards for Safeguarding Customer Information, 16 C.F.R. Part 314 (2011).
[5] Interagency Guidelines Establishing Standards for Safeguarding Customer Information, 12 C.F.R. Parts 30, 208, 211, 225, 263, 308, 364, 568 and 570 (2011).
[6] 16 C.F.R. s.314.4(d) (2011).

privacy and security of personal health information (PHI) for physicians, hospitals, health plans and others if Congress did not enact such standards by August, 1999. Since the deadline passed without congressional action, HHS adopted standards for the protection of privacy of PHI in the first Privacy Rule in 2000 and a modified Final Privacy Rule in 2002.[7] In 2003, standards for the security of electronic PHI (e-PHI) were adopted in the Security Rule.[8]

50.6.1.2.1   Covered Entities

The Privacy Rule and the Security Rule apply to "Covered Entities." Covered Entities include health care providers, health plans, and health care clearinghouses, all of which are defined. Obviously, if a health care provider, such as a hospital system, enters into an outsourcing agreement or other services agreement under which PHI will be disclosed to the supplier, the Privacy Rule and the Security Rule apply. Customers in the health care industry deal with the Privacy Rule and the Security Rule on a daily basis and are sensitive to the impact of outsourcing on their obligations. However, some aspects of these rules may apply to companies that do not think of themselves as Covered Entities. For example, the definition of "health plans" includes self-insured employee welfare benefit plans. Many customers in industries other than the health care industry self-insure one or more of their employee welfare benefit plans and as a result are a Covered Entity that has to comply with the Privacy Rule and the Security Rule. Any customer contemplating entering into an outsourcing or other services agreement must determine if it is a Covered Entity (if it has not already done so) and if it is must consider the Privacy Rule and the Security Rule in connection with the outsourcing.

50.6.1.2.2   The Privacy Rule

Broadly speaking, the Privacy Rule establishes national standards to protect individuals' medical records and other personal health information. The Rule requires appropriate safeguards to protect the privacy of personal health information, and sets limits and conditions on the uses and disclosures that may be made of such information without patient authorisation. If a Covered Entity discloses PHI to any entity or person for purposes of such person or entity performing or assisting in performing a function on behalf of the Covered Entity, that entity or person is a "Business Associate." In the case of outsourcing or other services agreement involving the disclosure of PHI, the supplier will be a Business Associate of the Covered Entity. A Covered Entity is required to enter into a Business Associate agree-

---

[7]   67 Fed. Reg. 53182 (August 14, 2002); codified at 53 C.F.R. ss.160, 164 (2011).
[8]   68 Fed. Reg. 8334 (February 20, 2003); codified at 53 C.F.R. ss.160, 164 (2011).

ment with a Business Associate that obligates the supplier to comply with certain requirements of the Privacy Rule. If for example a manufacturer with a self-insured benefit plan enters into an IT outsourcing agreement with a supplier and the supplier manages the servers on which PHI of the employees of the manufacturer resides, then the customer and the supplier are required to enter into a Business Associates agreement.

50.6.1.2.3   The Security Rule

The Security Rule includes three categories of safeguards that a Covered Entity must take to secure e-PHI: administrative safeguards, physical safeguards and technical safeguards. While all three of these categories may be implicated by an information technology outsourcing agreement, it is likely that the supplier will, as a part of the services, assume some management or operational responsibility for the technical and perhaps physical safeguards. As a result the parties should contemplate the application of and compliance with the Security Rule when developing the applicable solution, and compliance should be included in the charges for the services. Other types of outsourcing or services agreements with Covered Entities may implicate these safeguards and should be analysed with them in mind.

50.6.1.2.4   The HITECH Act

The American Recovery and Reinvestment Act of 2009[9] is included as Title XIII the Health Information Technology for Economic and Clinical Health Act (HITECH Act). The HITECH Act contains the most significant changes to the HIPAA Privacy and Security Rules since 2003. The HITECH Act imposed new obligations with respect to the privacy and security of PHI and imposed upon Covered Entities and certain others breach notification obligations. As a result of the HITECH Act, the Security Rule now applies directly to a Business Associate, such as the supplier under an outsourcing or other services agreement with a Covered Entity, and the Business Associate has a direct obligation to comply with the breach notification requirements promulgated as a result of the HITECH Act. In other words, prior to the HITECH Act, if the supplier violated its Business Associate agreement with the customer, the supplier's potential liability was a breach of contract claim by the customer. After the HITECH Act, the supplier is now also subject to the same civil and criminal penalties for violation of its Business Associate agreement as is the customer that is a Covered Entity that violated the rule.

This scope of this chapter provides only very high-level overview of HIPAA, the HITECH Act and associated regulations. HIPAA, the HITECH Act, the

---

[9]   Pub. L. No. 111-5 (2009).

Privacy Rule, the Security Rule and the breach notification rules promulgated as a result of the HITECH Act are a very technical and detailed areas of US law. The customer who is a Covered Entity contemplating entering into an outsourcing or other services agreement should consult with appropriate subject matter experts within the customer organisation and potentially outside counsel in order to comply with the various requirements imposed by these laws and regulations.

50.6.2 State Privacy Legislation

The fifty states have a varied and diverse patchwork of legislation dealing with privacy. It is beyond the scope of this chapter to survey privacy laws in each state.[10] The customer in an outsourcing or other services agreement must consider each of the state privacy laws to which it is subject and identify its obligations in the context of the contemplated outsourcing or services arrangement. The customer should not assume that the supplier understands the state privacy legislation that applies to the customer's business.

State privacy legislation covers a broad range of activity, including online privacy protection, identity theft, electronic eavesdropping and unsolicited telephone marketing. Potential areas of state privacy law that might impact an outsourcing or services arrangement include state financial privacy statues, privacy of insurance-related information and statutes governing the use of Social Security numbers. One type of state privacy legislation, commonly called security breach legislation, requires consumer notification when there is a security breach involving private information. Provisions in an outsourcing or services agreement dealing specifically with the responsibilities of the customer and the supplier in the event of a security breach involving consumer private information have become much more common and contentious in the past few years.

One example will suffice to show the breadth of the potential application of state privacy legislation. Massachusetts law[11] requires persons or entities that "own or license" personal information of Massachusetts residents to take specific measures to protect such personal information. Personal information means the name of the employee in combination with confidential numbers (such as a Social Security number, driver's license number, bank account number or credit card number). Among those with such personal information are employers of any Massachusetts resident. As a result, among other things, employers of Massachusetts residents must create and update on an annual basis a written information security plan addressing the privacy concerns and that plan must be approved by the employer's top management or a designated committee. Computer security

---

[10] For a comprehensive survey of state privacy law, see, e.g., Kristen J. Mathews (ed), *Proskauer on Privacy: A Guide to Privacy and Data Security Law in the Information Age*, (Practicing Law Institute, 2012), Chapter 5.
[11] Mass. Gen. Laws ch 93H (2008) and implementing regulations

protections are required, including the use of encryption for all personal information stored on a laptop or other portable device or transmitted across public networks in electronic form. The Massachusetts law requires employers to supervise all third party service providers possessing personal information of Massachusetts residents. Employers must only engage providers capable of complying with applicable privacy laws and must also ensure by contract that the provider will implement and maintain appropriate security measures required by the Massachusetts law and implementing regulations. For example, a contract between any employer (whether or not headquartered in Massachusetts) with Massachusetts employees and a supplier of payroll processing services will involve the possession of such personal information and the customer and the supplier must comply with the Massachusetts law and regulations.

50.7 Insolvency issues

50.7.1 *US bankruptcy law*

In the United States, bankruptcy legislation has been enacted at the federal level and, under the doctrine of pre-emption, with the notable exception of insurance company debtors, any bankruptcy legislation (that is, legislation that discharges debtors from previously-incurred obligations) by the states is not enforceable. The Bankruptcy Code, Title 11 of the United States Code, recognises a number of proceedings, but the most common are Chapter 7 liquidations and Chapter 11 reorganisations. Bankruptcy law in the United States is a highly specialised practice and beyond the limited scope of this chapter. However, parties to an outsourcing or other complex services agreement should be familiar with a few key concepts.

50.7.1.1 *The automatic stay*

Upon the proper filing of a voluntary or involuntary bankruptcy case, the Bankruptcy Code provides for an "automatic stay"—an automatic injunction that halts actions by creditors, with certain exceptions, to collect debts from the debtor in the bankruptcy case. The automatic stay is seen as a fundamental debtor protection, protecting the assets of the debtor pending the bankruptcy proceedings. Similarly, the automatic stay is also intended to protect the creditors by facilitating equality of distribution among creditors. The result of the automatic stay is that the party to an outsourcing or other services agreement cannot bring an action against the party in bankruptcy to enforce its rights under the contract. Any termination provision in the agreement giving one party the right to terminate the contract upon the bankruptcy of the other party cannot be exercised once the bankruptcy action has been filed.

50.7.1.2 *Assumption or rejection of executory contracts*

Another key concept of US bankruptcy law of particular interest to parties to an outsourcing or other complex services agreements is the "executory contract". An executory contract is a contract between the debtor in bankruptcy and another party under which both parties still have important performance remaining. Although not defined by the Bankruptcy Code, most courts consider a contract an "executory contract" if the failure of either party to complete performance would constitute a material breach excusing the performance of the other. Of course, by its nature, an outsourcing or other complex services agreement is an executory contract until it has been fully performed by the parties.

In bankruptcy, the debtor (or the trustee appointed over the debtor's estate) has the right to "assume" (that is, agree to perform) or "reject" (refuse to perform and be subject to a damages claim) executory contracts. The other party to the executory contract doesn't have such a right and, subject to some exceptions, is required to continue to perform its obligations under the executory contract unless and until it is rejected by the debtor.

50.7.1.3 *Intellectual property*

Most outsourcing agreements and other complex service contracts contain provisions concerning intellectual property of both the customer and the supplier. The supplier is often granted a right or license to use the intellectual property of the customer in providing the services and the customer is often granted a right or license to use the intellectual property of the supplier during the term of the contract and sometimes after the term.

The treatment of intellectual property rights in bankruptcy is a complex matter. In general, intellectual property rights like trademarks, patents and copyrights which are held by non-exclusive licenses of the debtor in bankruptcy generally cannot be assigned without the consent of the licensor. In fact, there is a split among the federal circuits whether or not the debtor can even assume such intellectual property without the consent of the licensor.

With the proliferation of the use of computer technology in business, the treatment in bankruptcy of licenses to intellectual property, such as software licenses, was of paramount concern to licensees of intellectual property. A software license, for example, may be critical to the business of the licensee, but a software license is probably an executory contract. What was the effect of the bankruptcy of the licensor on the software licensee? Could the license be rejected by the licensor in bankruptcy?

To protect the licensee from such a potentially disastrous result, s.365(n) was added to the Bankruptcy Code in 1988. Section 365(n) provides that if the debtor or the trustee rejects an executory contract under which the debtor is the licensor of intellectual property (as defined by the Bankruptcy Code), the licensee may elect to treat the contract as terminated or the licensee may elect to retain its rights (as they existed before the bankruptcy was filed) for the remainder of the term of the licenses and for any additional period for which the licensee could extend it under applicable non-bankruptcy law.

Many US outsourcing or services agreements include a provision that the parties agree that the rights and licenses granted by the supplier to the customer under the agreement are, for purposes of s.365(n), licenses to rights to "intellectual property" as defined under the Bankruptcy Code and that the customer, as licensee of such rights under the contract, will retain and may fully exercise all of its rights and remedies available to it under the Bankruptcy Code, including s.365(n).

50.7.1.4   The customer's bankruptcy

If the customer is the debtor in a bankruptcy proceeding, the supplier cannot terminate or bring an action against the customer for unpaid amounts under the contract. The supplier may assert its claims for unpaid amounts and other damages in the bankruptcy court. However, many services provided by the supplier under an outsourcing or services agreement may be considered administrative expenses of the bankruptcy proceeding and, with the bankruptcy court's approval, the supplier is entitled to be paid for ongoing services provided after the bankruptcy filing as an administrative expense. However, as discussed in section 50.7.1.3, the customer in bankruptcy may not assign intellectual property rights like trademarks, patents and copyrights which are held by non-exclusive licenses granted in the contract without the consent of the supplier and there is a split among the federal circuits whether or not the customer as a debtor can even assume such intellectual property without the consent of the supplier as the licensor of such rights.

50.7.1.5   The supplier's bankruptcy

If the supplier is the debtor in a bankruptcy proceeding, the customer cannot terminate or bring an action against the supplier for breach of the contract. In a Chapter 7 liquidation, the supplier will cease operations, including the provision of the services, and any damages suffered by the customer must be pursued in the bankruptcy court. In a Chapter 11 reorganisation, the supplier will continue to provide the services throughout the proceedings, unless and until the contract is rejected by the supplier. If the contract includes licenses to intellectual property by the supplier to the customer, if the supplier rejects the contract, the customer may elect to retain its rights as a licensee in accordance with s.365(n).

50.7.2   State insolvency laws

Although the Bankruptcy Code pre-empts state law discharging debtors from previous-incurred debts, various state law concepts remain that deal with other aspects of insolvency, including the insolvency of insurance companies. Another example of a common state law insolvency concept is making an assignment for the benefit of creditors. Some outsourcing and other service contracts may include termination rights based on an insolvency event of the other party, such as making an assignment for the benefit of creditors, becoming subject to the control of a receiver or trustee or committing an act of insolvency, including the failure to pay obligations as they become due. However, almost all insolvency situations with the notable exception of insurance company debtors result in a voluntary or involuntary filing under the Bankruptcy Code and, because of the automatic stay, state insolvency concepts are seldom independently invoked.

50.8   Financial services regulation

Regulation and oversight of the financial services sector in the United State is a complex and evolving topic, particularly in light of the effects of the financial crisis that began in 2008 and the enactment in 2010 of The Dodd-Frank Wall Street Reform and Consumer Protection Act (Dodd-Frank). There are a number of federal regulators with jurisdiction over certain institutions within the financial services sector. Almost all have been active in publishing guidance on outsourcing transactions.

50.8.1   Bank Service Company Act of 1962[12]

Under the Bank Service Company Act, third party suppliers providing outsourcing services to FDIC-insured banks are subject to examination and oversight by the Federal Reserve regulators.[13] A provision giving similar oversight authority over suppliers providing outsourced services to thrifts is found in the Home Owners' Loan Act.[14]

---

[12]   12 U.S.C. ss.1861-1867 (2006).
[13]   Section 7(c)(2) of the Bank Service Company Act states "…whenever a bank that is regularly examined by an appropriate Federal banking agency, or any subsidiary or affiliate of such a bank that is subject to examination by that agency, causes to be performed for itself, by contract or otherwise, any services authorized under this chapter, whether on or off its premises – (1) such performance shall be subject to regulation and examination by such agency to the same extent as if such services were being performed by the bank itself on its own premises…" (12 U.S.C. s.1867(c) (2006)).
[14]   12 U.S.C. s.1464(d)(7) (2006).

50.8.2 *Regulatory guidance on outsourcing before Dodd-Frank*

Prior to Dodd-Frank, there were five federal regulators with jurisdiction over the US banking system: the Board of Governors of the Federal Reserve, the Federal Deposit Insurance Corporation (FDIC), the Office of the Comptroller of the Currency (OCC), the Office of Thrift Supervision (OTS) and the National Credit Union Administration (NCUA). These agencies were the five members of the Federal Financial Institutions Examination Council (FFIEC). Various regulators and the FFIEC published guidance for outsourcing transactions generally, including:

(a) Federal Financial Institutions Examination Council (FFIEC) *Statement on Risk Management of Outsourced Technology Services* (November 28, 2000);
(b) Federal Deposit Insurance Corporation (FDIC) *FIL-50-2001, Bank Technology Bulletin on Outsourcing* (June 4, 2001);
(c) Office of the Comptroller of the Currency (OCC) *Bulletin 2001-47: ThirdParty Relationships* (November 1, 2001); and
(d) Federal Reserve Board Bank Holding Company Supervision Manual (July, 2008), *Section 2060.05: Policy Statement on the Internal Audit Function and its Outsourcing (Management Information Systems)*.

Generally, these regulations impose responsibility on the board of directors and the management of a financial institution to:

(a) understand the risks associated with outsourcing arrangements and put in place effective risk management practices;
(b) conduct adequate due diligence in selecting a supplier;
(c) make sure that the contract is clearly written and sufficiently detailed and reviewed by legal counsel; and
(d) implement effective ongoing oversight of the supplier's controls, condition and performance.

50.8.3 *Regulatory guidance on offshoring before Dodd-Frank*

With the advent of offshoring in the late 1990's and its rapid growth in the first decade of the twenty-first century, these regulators issued additional guidance specifically for offshoring transactions, including:

(a) Federal Reserve Board SR 00-4 (SUP), *Outsourcing of Information and Transaction Processing* (February 29, 2000) (see "International Considerations" section);
(b) FFIEC *Information Technology Examination Handbook: Outsourcing*

> *Technology Services* (June, 2004) (see Appendix C: Foreign-Based Third-Party Service Providers);
>
> (c) OCC Bulletin 2002-16: *Bank Use of Foreign-Based Third-Party Service Providers* (May 15, 2002); and
>
> (d) OTS Thrift Bulletin 82a: *Third Party Arrangements* (September 1, 2004 (replaced by OCC Bulletin 2001-47: Third Party Relationships (November 1, 2001) on May 17, 2012)).

Recognising that offshoring raises country, compliance, contractual, reputation, operational and strategic issues in addition to those presented by use of a domestic supplier, this guidance generally requires financial institutions account for such issues and their implications as part of the risk assessment, due diligence, contracting and ongoing management and oversight of the supplier. The guidance also deals with issues of regulatory oversight of suppliers arising from foreign-based suppliers.

50.8.4 The Dodd-Frank Wall Street Reform and Consumer Protection Act

The Dodd-Frank Act, enacted in 2010 in the wake of the financial crisis that began in 2008, encompassed the widest-ranging regulatory reforms in the financial services sector since the Great Depression. While Dodd-Frank did not specifically address outsourcing, its focus on the mitigation of systemic risk in the US financial system portends the need for financial institutions to review and strengthen their approach to operational risk mitigation in outsourcing transactions. The broad legislative directives found in much of Dodd-Frank remains to be implemented by rule-making by many federal agencies and most of that rule-making has just begun in 2012.

Dodd-Frank affected the oversight and supervision of financial institutions. Among other things, it created a new independent bureau within the Federal Reserve, the Consumer Financial Protection Bureau (CFPB), to implement and enforce compliance with consumer financial laws. It also created a "governing board" to oversee financial institutions—the Financial Stability Oversight Council (FSOC). The oversight and regulatory responsibilities of the Office of Thrift Supervision (OTS) were moved to the Federal Reserve, the OCC and the FDIC.

50.8.5 Post Dodd-Frank regulatory guidance

On April 13, 2012, the new Consumer Financial Protection Bureau issued CFPB Bulletin 2012-03 on service providers. The bulletin emphasises that the CFPB "expects supervised banks and nonbanks to oversee their business relationships with services providers in a manner that ensures compliance with Federal consumer financial law, which is designed to protect the interests of consumers and avoid consumer harm."

The CFPB reminds supervised banks and nonbanks that Dodd-Frank gives the CFPB supervisory and enforcement authority over "supervised service providers," as defined in the Act, and sets out the CFPB's expectations of the steps that supervised banks and nonbanks should take to "ensure that their business arrangements with service providers do not present unwarranted risks to consumers."

50.8.6   Other regulatory considerations

50.8.6.1   Other federal laws

We have already discussed the Gramm-Leach-Bliley Act, which applies to financial institutions, in section 50.6.1.1. There are several other federal laws that impact outsourcing transactions in the financial services sector depending upon the scope and solution of the proposed outsourcing, including:

(a)   Sarbanes-Oxley[15] (see discussion at section 50.12.2);
(b)   USA PATRIOT Act[16] (anti-money laundering);
(c)   Regulations of the U.S. Treasury Office of Foreign Asset Controls (OFAC);
(d)   The Foreign Corrupt Practices Act of 1997;[17] and
(e)   US export control requirements.

50.8.6.2   US securities industry

The primary federal regulator of the securities industry in the US is the Securities and Exchange Commission (SEC), but the securities industry is also subject to the listing requirements of the various exchanges and self-regulatory organisations, such as The Financial Industry Regulatory Authority (FINRA), an independent regulator of securities firms and brokers doing business in the United States. Some of these self-regulatory organisations have issued rules and guidance to its member firms concerning outsourcing and other service contracts.

---

[15]   Pub. L. No. 107-204 (2002).
[16]   Uniting and Strengthening America by Providing Appropriate Tools Required to Intercept and Obstruct Terrorism (USA Patriot Act) Act of 2001, Pub. L. No. 107-56, 115 Stat. 272 (2001) (codified in scattered titles of U.S.C.).
[17]   15 U.S.C. ss.78dd-1, 78dd-2, 78dd-3 (2006).

In July, 2005, the National Association of Security Dealers (now part of FINRA) issued guidance in to its member firms concerning their responsibilities when outsourcing activities to third-party services providers.[18]

FINRA proposed FINRA Rule 3190 (Use of Third-Party Service Providers) in March, 2011, to clarify a member firm's obligation and supervisory responsibilities regarding outsourcing arrangements.

50.8.6.3 *State regulatory requirements*

While this chapter has focused on federal regulation, there are state laws and regulations applicable to various portions of the financial services sector that might impact upon an outsourcing transaction. For example, insurance companies are largely regulated at the state level and if an insurance company enters into an outsourcing arrangement with a supplier it must consider areas that should be addressed in the outsourcing agreement so that it can continue to comply with its regulatory requirements in the states in which it does business after the outsourcing.

50.9 Public Procurement Directives

The Public Procurement Directives do not apply in the United States.

A few of the states have been successful in implementing legislation or regulations that either disfavour offshoring in state government procurement initiatives (by providing preferences for on-shore solutions) or by restricting certain services from being provided offshore, but the introduction of new initiatives has declined in recent years.

50.10 Utilities Directive

The Utilities Directive does not apply in the United States.

50.11 Competition law

Competition law, as discussed in Chapter 33, is generally called antitrust law in the United States, but similar concepts as discussed in Chapter 33 are found in US antitrust law.

---

[18] NASD Notice to Members 05-48, *Members' Responsibilities When Outsourcing Activities to Third-Party Service Providers* (July, 2005).

50.11.1   *Antitrust reviews under Hart-Scott-Rodino*

The Hart-Scott-Rodino Antitrust Improvements Act of 1976 established the federal premerger notification program, which provides the US Federal Trade Commission (FTC) and the US Department of Justice (DOJ) with information about large mergers and acquisitions before they occur. The parties to certain proposed transactions must submit premerger notification to the FTC and DOJ. Premerger notification involves completing an HSR Form, also called a "Notification and Report Form for Certain Mergers and Acquisitions", with information about each company's business. The parties may not close their deal until the waiting period outlined in the HSR Act has passed, or the government has granted early termination of the waiting period.

Occasionally an outsourcing transaction will include the transfer of assets, such as information technology assets in an IT infrastructure outsourcing, from the customer to the supplier. If the value of the assets being transferred meets the thresholds for premerger notification and review, the transfer is subject to Hart-Scott-Rodino. In 2012, the threshold for antitrust review is $68.2 million. It is very unusual for current outsourcing transactions to include an asset transfer of such value and to trigger the notification requirement.

50.11.2   *Restraints of trade*

The Sherman Act of 1890 outlaws "every contract, combination, or conspiracy in restraint of trade," and any "monopolization, attempted monopolization, or conspiracy or combination to monopolize." The US Supreme Court decided decades ago that the Sherman Act does not prohibit every restraint of trade, only those that are unreasonable. However, certain acts are considered so harmful to competition that they are almost always illegal. These include arrangements among competing individuals or businesses to fix prices, divide markets, or rig bids. These acts are "per se" violations of the Sherman Act; in other words, no defence or justification is allowed.

The penalties for violating the Sherman Act can be severe. Although most enforcement actions are civil, the Sherman Act is also a criminal law, and individuals and businesses that violate it may be prosecuted by the US DOJ. Criminal prosecutions are typically limited to intentional and clear violations such as when competitors fix prices or rig bids. The Sherman Act imposes criminal penalties of up to $100 million for a corporation and $1 million for an individual, along with up to 10 years in prison. Under federal law, the maximum fine may be increased to twice the amount the conspirators gained from the illegal acts or twice the money lost by the victims of the crime, if either of those amounts is over $100 million.

While an outsourcing or services agreement may include provisions that arguably constitute a "restraint of trade," such as an exclusivity provision or non-compete provisions (for example, limitations on the assignment of the supplier's employees who provide services to the customer to the accounts of competitors of the customer for some period of time), such provisions are governed by the "rule of reason" (versus being a "per se" violation) and generally do not appear to have raised restraint of trade concerns under US antitrust law.

Of course, one area of concern is the exchange of information between the customer and the supplier when the two parties are competitors. In that instance, the exchange of certain information can raise concerns that the exchange may be in furtherance of an arrangement to fix prices or divide markets, which are "per se" violations of Sherman Act. In such a case, the customer and the supplier should each consult with its antitrust advisors before the information exchange begins.

In any event, it is advisable for both the customer and the supplier to keep antitrust considerations in mind while structuring a transaction. For example, in a recent procurement outsourcing, part of the supplier's offering was to leverage purchasing across multiple customers in order to provide more favourable pricing for all of those customers. The customer was concerned about joint purchasing (sometimes referred to a group purchasing organizations or buying groups), which under certain circumstances can raise a number of antitrust concerns. The customer's concern was solved by the supplier expressly assuming responsibility for compliance with laws relating to joint purchasing.

50.12   Other relevant laws and best practice

50.12.1   Service taxes

Chapter 20 includes a discussion about value added tax. The taxing regime in the United States does not currently include value added tax. However, similar issues as those discussed in Chapter 20 in respect of VAT arise under US tax regimes.

Like the US legal regime as discussed elsewhere in this chapter, the US taxing regime has several different layers – there are federal taxes, state taxes, and "local" taxes that apply within the jurisdictional geography of a smaller unit of government, such as a county or a city.

While there are federal taxes that apply to some services, particularly telecommunications services, most of the taxes that may apply to an outsourcing or other services contract are at the state level. States traditionally have imposed a tax on the sale of goods at the consumer level. Over the past decade or so, looking for new revenue streams, many states began taxing various services and some of these states have adopted various "services" taxes that apply to outsourcing, such as an information technology services tax.

When the customer is considering the financial value of outsourcing, the business case must contemplate any additional taxes that might be payable as a result of the outsourcing. Depending on the facts, service taxes of more than one state may be implicated depending on where the customer facilities are located and the locations from which the supplier provides the services. As most services taxes are taxed where the benefit of the services is received, a customer with operations in multiple states may receive the benefit of the services in more than one state and therefore be subject to the service taxes of more than one state. The allocation of state taxes among states is a very complicated issue and beyond the scope of this chapter. However, since the potential supplier deals with state tax issues on a regular basis, the customer's tax subject matter experts should work with the supplier's tax subject matter experts to develop the parties' best estimate of the applicability and impact of state taxes on the transaction.

Once the impact has been estimated, the parties then must allocate financial responsibility for the taxes. In recent years, it seems that more often than not the customer bears responsibility for payment of applicable service taxes (or, in other words, the supplier's charges do not include such taxes). However, in addition, the parties often allocate responsibility for incremental or "new" taxes that become applicable during the term of the contract, which may be a more difficult discussion as each party tries to preserve its business case by minimizing the impact of an incremental or new tax.

With the growth of offshoring, taxation issues at the supplier's location have become more contentious. From the customer's perspective, taxation issues at the supplier's offshore location is simply part of the supplier's cost of doing business and the customer, particularly if the customer does not otherwise have a presence in the offshore country, should not bear the risk of changes in the taxation regime. The supplier, however, trying to protect its business case, would like to allocate all or at least some of the risk of increased or new taxes to its customers. For example, many of the suppliers with service centres in India enjoy a particular tax holiday for services provided to its customers outside of India. When it appeared that the tax holiday would not be renewed, affecting the suppliers' after-tax margin, the suppliers tried to allocate the risk of non-renewal to its customers through a fee adjustment. Customers, of course, objected. Like incremental or new state service taxes, the allocation of risk between customer and supplier is largely a matter of leverage and bargaining position.

50.12.2 *Sarbanes-Oxley*

If the customer is a US public company, then it needs to consider the impact of the outsourcing or services agreement on its obligations to comply with the Sarbanes-Oxley Act of 2002 (SOX).[19] The customer's enquiry should focus on two distinct but related enquiries.

First, within the scope of the services being contracted out, what operational responsibilities will the supplier need to perform in order for the customer to be able to comply with the customer's reporting obligations? Second, what audit reports from the supplier and other audit rights are required in order for the customer to comply with its reporting obligations?

Congress enacted SOX after a wave of financial reporting abuses by major public companies. Section 404 of the Act requires management teams of U.S. public companies to include information in their annual filings about the adequacy and effectiveness of internal controls over financial reporting. In response to independent auditors' failure to uncover and report such abuses, the Act also established the Public Company Accounting Oversight Board (PCAOB) to provide independent oversight of and standards for public accounting firms that provide audit services. Some companies began to outsource certain accounting functions to help alleviate SOX requirements, and many companies had outsourced or would outsource functions directly related to financial reporting (such as operation of accounting systems), but outsourcing did not relieve management's obligations to evaluate controls – outsourced or not - over financial reporting. Therefore, public companies that outsourced functions related to financial reporting continued to grapple with ways to include and evaluate financial reporting and information technology controls their service providers perform. To help management evaluate controls within outsourced functions, the PCAOB eventually adopted the American Institute of Certified Public Accountants (AICPA) pre-existing Statement on Auditing Standard No. 70, or SAS70, as a vehicle to assist management comply with SOX requirements.

Over time, partly due to pressure from their customers, many US-based service providers, and some international service providers, began conducting annual SAS70 audits of relevant operations and locations as a matter of course. In the mid-2000s, well-advised publicly-held customers began to require service providers to conduct an annual SAS70 audit and provide the report to the customer in their outsourcing or services agreement. It also became more common for practitioners of public accounting to attest to matters in addition to financial reporting controls within SAS70 reports. Most commonly, practitioners would also attest to compliance with privacy laws, such as Gramm-Leach-Bliley and the Health Insurance Portability and Accountability Act. Coincidentally, customers became more concerned about their service providers' compliance in such areas.

---

[19] Pub. L. No. 107-204 (2002).

To help reconcile the market's demand for attestation beyond financial reporting and SAS70's scope limitations, the AICPA developed the Statement on Standards for Attestation Engagements 16 (SSAE16) and made it effective for reports on controls at service providers for periods ending on or after June 15, 2011. According to SSAE16, there are three kinds of "Service Organization Control" (SOC) examination reports: SOC 1, SOC 2, and SOC 3.

(a) A SOC 1 report covers the service provider's controls relevant to the customer's internal control over financial reporting. It provides information and the CPA's opinion about the customer's financials statement and SOX controls to the customer's auditor.

(b) A SOC 2 report covers the service provider's controls relevant to security, availability, processing integrity, confidentiality and privacy. It provides information and the CPA's opinion about such controls to the management of the service provider and to the management of its customers.

(c) A SOC 3 report covers the same ground as the SOC 2 report, but provides an interested party (that does not have the need for the level of detail provided in a SOC 2 report) with the CPA's opinion about the service provider's controls relevant to security, availability, processing integrity, confidentiality and privacy. As such, the service provider that undergoes a SOC 3 report can elect to have its name added to the AICPA's website, along with the SSAE16 SOC 3 seal, for interested parties to view.

Each SOC report is available as a Type 1 or a Type 2 report. If the service provider elects to undergo a Type 1, the service auditor will only give an opinion on the design of the service provider's controls as of a specific date. In a Type 1, the service auditor is essentially saying, "In our opinion, as of this date, the service provider has designed controls that will reduce its customer's risk to an acceptable level." By contrast, the Type 2 report will state the auditor's opinion on the design of the service provider's controls as well as an opinion on if those controls actually operated as described over a specified period. Usually, the Type 2 report will cover one fiscal year. Additionally, service provider management must assert to the performance of the controls in the SSAE16 report and specify the basis on which it can make its assertion.

The customer contemplating an outsourcing or services arrangement must work with its internal auditors and external auditor to determine if it needs a SOC 1, SOC 2, or a SOC 3, and which type of report (Type 1 or Type 2), taking into account the type of services being performed by the supplier, the customer's reporting requirements and the expanded scope of a SOC 2 or SOC 3 audit beyond financial reporting controls.

Many outsourcing or services contracts entered into over the past several years have a hard-coded requirement for an annual SAS 70 Type II audit, which is an outdated standard that is no longer available. Outsourcing customers should adjust these contracts to contemplate the new standard. There are few differences between SAS70 and SSAE16, but the differences are significant. SSAE16 places more emphasis on risk and management's oversight than its predecessor. How smoothly an organisation transitions to the new standard will likely depend on how well the organisation understands controls, monitoring, and frameworks. As such, a transition strategy will likely prove effective and beneficial.

Chapter 51

UNITED ARAB EMIRATES

Joby Beretta

Partner, Dentons UAE

51.1   Outline

Parts 1 to 11 of this book describe the key business issues relevant for outsourcing and other services agreements. They also describe the key legal issues under English law. This chapter describes the specific legal and business issues which affect services and outsourcing arrangements in the United Arab Emirates (UAE).

51.2   Background to the regulatory framework

51.2.3   *Regulatory Framework*

To understand the UAE regulatory framework affecting outsourcing, it is imperative to understand the Federal Constitution ("Constitution"). The UAE was formed in 1971 and comprises seven Emirates (Abu Dhabi, Ajman, Dubai, Fujairah, Ras al-Khaimah, Sharjah and Umm al-Quwain). The Constitution established the Supreme Council as the main federal authority in the UAE. A Sheikh, commonly known as the Ruler, rules each Emirate and has authority to pass its own laws on matters not assigned to the exclusive federal jurisdiction of the Supreme Council. In addition the UAE has a number of free-zones with their own laws and regulations. Regulation of the services sector in the UAE is therefore a patchwork of federal, Emirate specific and free zone specific laws, decrees, ministerial decisions and regulations.

51.3   People issues

Employment laws in the UAE are set at the federal level and apply to all Emirates and free zones apart from financial free zones such as the Dubai

International Financial Centre (DIFC). The main law is the Federal Law No. 8 of 1980 (as amended) (the "Labour Law"). The Labour Law sets out certain minimum employment benefits which cannot be contracted out of.

There are no applicable transfer regulations in the UAE similar to the ARD Regulations. In the absence of any contractual arrangements, a supplier would have no obligations to transfer any of the customer's existing workforce. The Labour Law provides little recourse to employees in the event of such termination unless the employee can prove it was made arbitrarily. The concept of redundancy is not recognised under the Labour Law and each case will be reviewed on its own merits. Dismissal of employees, unless for material reasons,[1] is generally subject to payment of the end of service benefit mentioned below.

Other aspects of the Labour Law relevant to services and outsourcing arrangements are: (a) specified maximum working hours; (b) reduced working hours during the month of Ramadan; (c) overtime payments; and (d) the fact that strikes and lock-outs are illegal in the UAE. It is also worth noting that the normal working week in the UAE is Sunday to Thursday but suppliers offer 24x7 service to customers where required.

The UAE relies heavily on a foreign workforce and across the UAE, the national population is now less than 10 per cent of the total. Although the Labour Law establishes a preference for hiring nationals, the Emiratisation policies have not been fully implemented or enforced. UAE law affords UAE nationals certain preferential treatment to foreign workers e.g. in relation to minimum wage, pensions and restricted rights of termination.

51.4 Pensions issues

Expatriate employees in the UAE are not entitled to a pension. Instead, the Labour Law[2] requires employers to pay a lump-sum to an employee upon termination of his or her employment in the UAE, provided that the employee has completed at least one year of continuance service ("Severance Pay"). Severance Pay is in addition to any other amounts that are payable, such as unutilised leave, repatriation expenses and any contractual termination benefits. Severance Pay is calculated depending on whether the employment contract is for a fixed or indefinite period. The amount of Severance Pay also depends on whether the employee resigns or is fired. In the event of employees transferring from the customer to supplier in an outsourcing arrangement, the accrued Severance Pay could either be paid out to the employee or transferred over to the supplier.

---

[1]   Article 120 of the Labour Law
[2]   Articles 132–139 of the Labour Law

Some larger multinational companies in the UAE do have pension schemes for foreign employees but this is normally offered in place of the Severance Pay entitlement. Although employees cannot contract out of Severance Pay entitlement all together, such alternative schemes can be offered provided that they are in excess of the statutory entitlement.

UAE and Gulf Cooperation Council (GCC) nationals are entitled to a monthly pension contribution by their employers in accordance with Federal Law No.7 of 1999 regulating pensions and social insurance ("Pensions Law"). The pension contributions are payable to the Public Authority of Pensions and Social Security and vary depending on the employee's nationality.

51.5 Contract law

51.5.1 *General*

The UAE operates under a civil legal system and the primary source of law that governs services and outsourcing contracts is the Civil Transactions Law[3] (the "Civil Code").

For major international services and outsourcing projects, the parties often elect to choose a foreign governing law such as English, which is permitted pursuant to Article 19 of the Civil Code. A UAE court may however refuse to give effect to a transaction which would be inconsistent with UAE public order or morals or Islamic Shari'ah principles.[4] In addition, there are certain mandatory UAE laws which cannot be excluded by contract e.g. the Labour Law and the Federal Law No. 8 of 1984 (the "Companies Law"). Even if the services or outsourcing agreement is subject to a foreign law, both customer and supplier will therefore need to be aware of some of the key provision of UAE law.

The Civil Code is interpreted and understood through the rules and principles of Islamic jurisprudence. As a consequence, contractual relations are subject to an obligation that the performance of contracts accord with "public order". Public order includes commercial concepts such as freedom of trade, the circulation of wealth and rules of private ownership. One practical example is that it would not be possible for an international betting or gambling company to outsource its activities to the UAE. Such activities are deemed to be contrary to Islamic Shari'ah principles and public order.[5]

---

[3] Federal Law No. 5 of 1985
[4] Article 27 of the Civil Law
[5] Furthermore, Article 1021 of the Civil Code provides that any contract involving gambling or in respect of a prohibited competition shall be void.

Should a contractual provision offend public order, a court may amend or remove the provision to the extent necessary. One practical effect of this is that if a provision in a contract is seen as unduly onerous or unfair on one party, that party may, on application to a court, have the provision determined as being null and void. This obviously creates an element of uncertainty especially where one party forces the other to use an overly onerous standard form agreement.

The remainder of this section now looks at some specific points that apply if the governing law of the services or outsourcing contract is UAE law.

51.5.2 Force Majeure and Hardship

As with most jurisdictions, under UAE law the customer cannot simply pass all contractual liability to the supplier. UAE law provides for force majeure events and for events of hardship, both of which may relieve a supplier of its obligations in certain circumstances.

The general force majeure provision is found in Article 273 of the Civil Code, which states:

> "(1) In contracts binding on both parties, if force majeure supervenes which makes the performance of the contract impossible, the corresponding obligation shall cease, and the contract shall be automatically cancelled.
>
> (2) In the case of partial impossibility, that part of the contract which is impossible shall be extinguished, and the same shall apply to temporary impossibility in continuing contracts, and in those two cases it shall be permissible for the obligee to cancel the contract provided that the obligor X is made aware."

As this is a rather narrow test of force majeure (i.e. linked to impossibility of performance[6]) most services and outsourcing agreements include a more detailed definition linked to events outside of the reasonable control of the parties.

The Civil Code also provides a statutory hardship provision to complement its general force majeure provision. The Civil Code allows a party to apply to the court for a variation of its obligations under a contract if unforeseen events cause a contractual obligation to become oppressive to the obligor.

Article 249 states:

---

[6] This is also reflected in the Civil Code in Article 472, which provides that if performance becomes impossible for extraneous cause, then the obligor's obligation is extinguished.

> "If exceptional events of a public nature which could not have been foreseen occur as a result of which the performance of the contractual obligation, even if not impossible, becomes onerous for the obligor so as to threaten him with grave loss, it shall be permissible for the judge, in accordance with the circumstances and after weighing up the interests of each party, to reduce the onerous obligation to a reasonable level if justice so requires, and any agreement to the contrary shall be void."

To be successful the claimant would generally have to prove that the threat of harm as a result of the supervening event is exorbitant in nature and not just an ordinary hardship. Again rather than relying on the statutory rights, most service and outsourcing agreements include a more detailed definition of force majeure.

51.5.3   Good faith

Another concept which is well established in civil law jurisdictions is the obligation of good faith which is implied into contracts under UAE law by virtue of Article 246 of the Civil Code. Recent UAE court judgments have held that a party may seek termination of an agreement if the other party acts contrary to good faith.

51.5.4   Damages

Under the UAE law, contractual liability can only be established in the presence of the following criteria:

(a)   non-performance or breach of a validly existing contract;
(b)   damages sustained by one of the parties; and
(c)   causation between the damages sustained and the breach of the contract.

Under the Civil Code, harm can be direct or consequential and Article 283(2) provides that

> "if the harm is direct, it must unconditionally be made good, and if it is consequential there must be a wrongful or deliberate element and the act must have led to damage."

Loss of profit and consequential loss therefore requires a "malicious" element, which has been interpreted by the Court of Cassation as requiring a stronger element than mere negligence.

The extent to which damage is direct or consequential is often a grey area but in general the courts will look to make awards for actual losses sustained so that, for instance, a court may make an award for loss of profit if the occurrence of the damage is fairly certain and not merely hypothetical or speculative. The same concept applies in respect of loss of opportunity.

If the supplier does not deal directly with caps on liability in the services or outsourcing contract the courts will decide the quantum of damages based on the forseeability of harm at the time the contract was entered into.

The courts have also recognised contractual damages claims for moral damages under the Civil Code,[7] which provides that

> "the right to have a damage made good shall include moral damage, and an infringement of the liberty, dignity, honour, reputation, social standing or financial condition of another shall be regarded as moral damage".

51.6   Limitations of Liability

51.6.1   *Contractual Limitations*

Similar to most jurisdictions, neither party may fully exclude its liability under contract. It is not, for example, possible to contract out of mandatory obligations imposed by statute e.g. the Labour Law. It is also not possible to exempt liability for tortious acts such as gross negligence. In addition, agreements which attempt to exclude all liability for compensation resulting from a wrongful act causing loss would be treated by the courts as void.[8]

It is however permissible for parties to contractually limit compensation to a certain amount or to a specified remedy provided it does not violate existing law, regulation or public order. For example, while a party may contractually limit its liability for categories of loss including property damage, personal injury, consequential loss and lost commercial opportunity, conditions which purport to limit liability for gross negligence, fraud or wilful conduct may be considered contrary to public order and consequently would be unenforceable.

Nevertheless, the courts have discretion to vary such limits so as to make the compensation equal to the loss and any agreement to the contrary shall be void.

---

[7]   Article 293(1) of the Civil Code
[8]   Article 296 of the Civil Code

51.6.2   Liquidated Damages

The Civil Code allows parties to agree fixed compensation to apply to certain breaches of contract.[9] It is however important to note that an application can be made by either contracting party to adjust these amounts. The court has a discretion to adjust the pre-agreed amount of compensation to ensure the damages are equal to the loss suffered and the parties cannot contract out of this term. This concept is markedly different from the position in common law jurisdictions—where courts generally uphold the terms of the contract which the parties have freely negotiated and are reluctant to interfere with the parties' intentions (save for exceptional circumstances, such as where the service credits would amount to a penalty).

Parties will need to take this into consideration when negotiating any service credits or liquidated damages and in particular, whether to agree to such payments being the exclusive remedy of the customer.

51.7   Data protection

51.7.1   General

There is no federal or Emirate data protection legislation in the UAE similar to the Data Protection Directive. That said, the principle of a right to privacy of personal information is enshrined in the Constitution and other UAE laws. In addition, some legislation does exist in some free zones (DIFC and Dubai Healthcare City) which is similar to the Data Protection Directive.

Other than those free zones, there are no clear legal guidelines determining how and when personal data may be collected, stored, transferred, used or otherwise processed in a services or outsourcing transaction. There are provisions set out in various laws which apply to the use/disclosure of data, however these laws generally focus on confidentiality of information rather than the processing and export of personal data.

51.7.2   Relevant Legislation

Customers will be protected against disclosure of certain confidential information under UAE laws. Certain provisions of the UAE Federal Penal Code ("Penal Code") and the Constitution guarantee the right to privacy. Article 31 of the Constitution states that "Freedom of communication by post, telegraph or other means of communication and the secrecy thereof shall be guaranteed in accordance with the law".

---

[9]   Article 390(2) of the Civil Code

The Penal Code protects individuals from the interception and subsequent disclosure or publication of their personal data. Article 378 of the Penal Code provides that the publication of an individual's private affairs is prohibited. Article 379 contains another offence of any individual who by reason of his profession, craft, situation or art is entrusted with a secret and who discloses it in cases other than those permitted by the law, who uses it for his own advantage or another person's advantage. Both offences carry risks of fines and imprisonment.

Suppliers in particular will need to be aware of these provisions when handling personal data as part of the outsourcing services.

51.7.3   Data Protection in Practice

Regardless of the lack of comprehensive data protection law in the UAE, many multinational businesses operating in the country follow their international data protection procedures/guidelines which have been developed according to best practices overseas. This reflects the reality that although personal data may be collected in the UAE, often such data will be processed overseas where such processing is subject to other laws. Many companies now have in place global binding corporate rules for data protection and privacy which are complied with by all entities globally including those in the UAE.

In terms of practical tips, customers often insert detailed data protection provisions in their services and outsourcing agreements to cater for the lack of local legislation and to provide the level of comfort they are used to in other jurisdictions.

51.8   Insolvency issues

The UAE insolvency regime is governed, primarily, by the Companies Law and Federal Law No. 18 of 1993 (the "Commercial Code"), although certain provisions of the Civil Code and Federal Law No. 11 of 1992 (the Civil Procedures Code) also apply.

The laws referred to above set out the procedure for the liquidation of a company and for dealing with a bankrupt entity. The latter procedure is primarily concerned with discharging a corporate entity from its debts and liabilities. The insolvency regime also allows a debtor to enter into a compromise with its creditors to avoid being declared bankrupt. The debtor corporation can do this voluntarily, or such an arrangement can be imposed by the courts as part of ongoing insolvency proceedings.

Under the Commercial Code, creditors are ranked in order of priority. First priority is given to the payment of wages and salaries due to employees of the trader for the 30-day period prior to the declaration of bankruptcy and payment of court fees. The next class of creditors in order of priority are known as "preferred creditors" and include secured creditors with rights over the trader's assets.

Unsecured creditors are at the lower end of the creditor rankings and will share the remainder of the trader's assets. Parties to a services or outsourcing agreement will fall into this category. Creditors are generally not allowed to pursue claims against the company after the declaration of bankruptcy with the exception of secured creditors. Secured creditors are permitted to enforce their security interests notwithstanding a declaration of bankruptcy.

The UAE insolvency regime remains untested (at least in terms of any major corporate failures), so there is uncertainty surrounding how the courts would apply the regime in practice.

51.9 Financial services regulation

51.9.1 General

Different financial services regulations apply depending on whether the outsourcing services are provided on-shore within the UAE or from within the DIFC free-zone.

51.9.2 Onshore Regulations

There is no federal legislation in the UAE similar to MiFID. UAE laws regulate the carrying on of various activities within the financial services sector, rather than individual financial products. Under the existing enacted laws, the Central Bank of the UAE (the "**Central Bank**") has jurisdiction over the UAE as a whole, except within the DIFC (see below).

Under Central Bank Resolution No. 164/8/94 (as amended), investment business or banking, financial and investment consultancy business may only be carried on within the UAE if the relevant individual or company has been duly licensed. As part of the licensing process, the investment, banking, financial and investment consultancy business must provide the Central Bank with details of any products or services which it intends to outsource to a third party.

51.9.3   DIFC/DFSA Regulations

The Dubai Financial Services Authority (the **DFSA**) (the regulatory authority for financial services within the DIFC) has various requirements in relation to outsourcing. First, in any applications for licences, the DFSA requires details such as the rationale for outsourcing, the functions to be outsourced, confirmation of whether outsourcing will be intra-group or externally, justification of choice of entity, any contingency plan, plans for monitoring and controlling performance.

In addition, the DFSA Rulebook[10] sets out the following requirements a regulated firm must follow when outsourcing:

(a)   undertaking due diligence in choosing the supplier;
(b)   effectively supervising outsourced functions or activities; and
(c)   dealing effectively with any actions or omissions of the supplier, which lead or may lead to breaches of legislations applicable in the DIFC by the third party provider.

Also any material outsourcing arrangements entered into by a regulated firm must contain particular terms such as allowing the DFSA access to their premises to view information on a firm and dealing in an open and co-operative way with the DFSA.[11]

Although not legally binding, a DFSA communication also recommends that outsourcing agreements should also consider best practice as outlined in international standards. Such standards include the guiding principles for outsourcing in financial services issued by the Joint Forum as covered in Chapter 36.

51.10   Public Procurement Directives

51.10.1   The Law

At federal level government procurement is dealt with under Law No. 16 of 1975, regulating all contracts of public, works, services, supplies and the public tender process (the "Public Tender Law"). The Public Tender Law acknowledges the importance of public expenditure and sets out a legal framework to channel the needs of the different public authorities.

At an Emirate level, Abu Dhabi and Dubai each have laws and regulations dealing with government procurement (the "Procurement Laws"). In Abu Dhabi Law No 6 of 2008 deals with procurement, tenders, bids and ware-

---

[10]   GEN Rules 5.3.21(3).
[11]   SUP Module, SUP Rule 2.4.1.

houses (the "Abu Dhabi Law"). In Dubai, Law No 6 of 1997 in respect of the contracts of Government Departments (the "Dubai Law"), is very similar to the Abu Dhabi Law.

It is worth noting that there is no federal legislation which applies to PPPs, with PPPs being relatively uncommon in the UAE. However examples of infrastructure being procured and maintained under long-term concession contracts do exist, particularly in Abu Dhabi. For instance the Abu Dhabi Water and Electricity Authority (ADWEA) maintains a programme of procurement of power and water facilities under PPP structures and there are similar initiatives in transport and other infrastructure sectors across the UAE. In addition in Dubai, certain laws expressly empower specific government departments, such as the Dubai Electricity and Water Authority (DEWA) and the Roads and Transportation Authority (RTA), to enter into PPP-type arrangements with private companies.

51.10.2   The Scope of the law

The Procurement Laws apply to procurement by government entities, including the purchase and import of goods, service contracts and contracts for all works. Procurement is thus given a broad meaning and the laws and regulations focus on the methods and mechanisms that are to be used in the procurement process. It is worth noting that the respective Procurement Laws are mandatory for any government department, agency or entity whose budget is part of or attached to the general budget of the Abu Dhabi or Dubai governments. In practice therefore there is some uncertainty surrounding quasi-government bodies, which may determine their own procedures, rather than following the applicable Procurement Laws.

51.10.3   The Tender process for the purchase of equipment and services

For government contracts, requests for tenders will be advertised in national media or selected bidders may be contacted directly. Tenders can be submitted by a local or foreign company. Foreign companies may be required to have a local service agent and usually, if successful in the tender process, foreign companies may be required to establish a local presence by the time the contract is ready to begin.

All tenders for government contracts must be accompanied by a bid bond, though if the contract value is less that AED 100,000 (approximately £17,000) this is not usually required, subject to the competent authority's approval. If successful in tendering for a government contract, the bidder will be required to provide a local-bank approved performance bond equal to 5-15 per cent of the contract value before proceeding to execution of the contract.

The tender process should be secured by signing a contract which will govern the relationship between the parties in connection with the provision of services, works or goods and to set out certain milestones to be adhered to by the parties throughout the contract. Failure to adhere to these milestones may result in punitive measures against the service provider, including termination of the contract and the loss of the performance bond.

The Procurement Laws span the entire life cycle of the procurement process and the delivery of the product/services. The law does not deal with all aspects of procurement but it does provide a consistent legal framework for the purchase of goods and services, with UAE government entities having an important role to play in the implementation of the law and the procurement process.

51.11   Utilities Directive

There are no specific regulations which govern the procurement of services by utilities companies. Utilities companies in the UAE are, generally, government owned and as such the Procurement Laws referred to above apply on a federal and Emirate level.

51.12   Competition law

There are no specific competition, anti-trust laws or merger control laws in the UAE. That said, provisions in relation to "monopoly practices" can be found in the Protection Law (Federal Law 24 of 2006) (the "Consumer Protection Law") and its implementing regulations of 2007 ("Regulations"). Article 4 of the Consumer Protection Law specifies that the Consumer Protection Department will have the responsibility to "promote fair competition and eradicate monopoly". This may need to be taken into consideration when drafting any exclusivity or non-compete provisions in any services or outsourcing agreements.

The Consumer Protection Law is focused primarily on matters in relation to the manipulation of prices of goods and services, quality of goods and services, packaging and labelling.

The Regulations however deal with anti-competitive and monopolistic conduct. Article 6 states that practices, agreements, or contracts—whether written or verbal, explicit or implicit—shall be prohibited if their purpose or effect gives rise to a "state of monopoly". Article 7 states that the Consumer Protection Department shall take

> "the necessary procedures and measures in accordance with the provisions of Law and this Regulation ... against any monopoly practices or dealings, which cause damage to the national economy or consumers"

The Consumer Protection Department therefore has fairly wide powers in relation to what actions it may take against entities it sees as involved in arrangements leading to a "state of monopoly".

The Commercial Transactions Law[12] also deals with "unlawful competition". However, once again such articles are more concerned with protecting consumers against fraudulent activity and counterfeit goods into the market rather than what is perceived in European jurisdictions as antitrust and competition law.

51.13   Other relevant laws and best practice

51.13.1   Dealing with Disputes

As the UAE courts are not obliged to consider previous decisions as precedent and as each judge may have his own view as to how Islamic jurisprudence should be utilised in interpreting the Civil Code, the outcome of legal proceedings can be fairly unpredictable. For this reason, and also because of the lengthy delays that are involved in UAE court proceedings, arbitration clauses are increasingly common in international services and outsourcing contracts in the UAE.

The UAE courts recognise arbitration clauses and a court will stay proceedings and refer the parties to arbitration if a valid arbitration clause exists and if the jurisdiction of the court is challenged by a party at the first hearing of the case. If the issue of jurisdiction is not raised at the first hearing, the court will assume the parties have waived their rights to refer the matter to arbitration in favour of submitting to the jurisdiction of the court.

There are generally no statutory restrictions on choice of arbitral institutions, arbitral rules or the seat of arbitration.[13] The DIFC-LCIA Arbitration Centre is reputable and the rules are all but identical to that of the LCIA in London. The main alternatives are the Dubai International Arbitration Centre (DIAC) and the Dubai Commercial Conciliation and Arbitration Centre (ADCCAC) which sometimes tend to be the preferred arbitral institutions of local and government owned companies.

In June 2006 the UAE ratified the New York Convention of 1958 on the Recognition and Enforcement of Foreign Awards. Since ratification there have been a number of reported cases in which the UAE courts have enforced a foreign arbitral award.

---

[12]   Volume 1, chapter 2, part 3 of Federal Law No. 18 of 1993
[13]   Please note however that Article 36 of the Government Contracts Law No. 6 of 1997 provides that if arbitration is selected as the method of dispute resolution, it must be in Dubai.

51.13.2   Property Aspects

In the UAE, foreign companies or individuals can only own freehold title in certain defined areas of the country. This may need to be taken into consideration if a UAE company holding freehold interests is looking to sell their current premises to the supplier as part of a services or outsourcing deal.

51.13.3   Different Supplier Models

If the supplier and the customer decided to enter into a joint venture on-shore in the UAE, any non-UAE entity will only be entitled to own up to 49 per cent of the joint venture company. More traditional 50/50 joint ventures are however possible in the free zones but are then restricted from carrying out business onshore in the UAE.

51.13.4   The Charging Regime

A few points to note in relation to the charging regime in the UAE include:

(a)   The currency in the UAE (the UAE Dirham "AED") is currently pegged to the US Dollar at a rate of $1 = 3.6725 AED;

(b)   Generally in commercial matters the UAE courts will uphold stipulations for contractual interest, and will award compensatory interest, subject to certain restrictions (for example, a bar on the compounding of interest); and

(c)   There is currently no VAT or equivalent of VAT in the UAE (apart from municipality charges and service charges levied on some industries such as food and drink in restaurants in Dubai).

51.13.5   Other Relevant Laws / practical points

51.13.5.1   Dual English / Arabic Contracts

Some UAE government entities still require contracts to be in dual English and Arabic with the Arabic text taking precedence in UAE court proceedings.

51.13.5.2   Commercial Agencies Law

In the event the services or outsourcing agreement is signed with a UAE national (or a company 100 per cent owned by UAE nationals) where the supplier represents a customer on an exclusive basis to "distribute, sell, offer, or provide goods or services within the UAE for a commission or profit" the UAE Federal Law No. 18 of 1981 or the Commercial Agencies Law (CAL) may apply. If the services or outsourcing agreement constitutes a commercial agency agreement and is registered by the supplier, the supplier will be entitled to the benefits of the CAL. These include compensation for unjust termination and the ability to claim commission allocated to the next appointed agent.

Part 12

Other Key EU Jurisdictions

Chapter 52

Germany

Prof. Dr. Peter Bräutigam / Dr. Thomas Thalhofer

52.1 Outline

Parts 1 to 11 of this book describe the key business issues relevant to services and outsourcing agreements. They also deal with the key legal issues under English law. This chapter deals with the specific legal and business issues which affect services or outsourcing arrangements in Germany.

52.2 People issues—ARD

52.2.1 *Implementation of ARD in Germany*

The Acquired Rights Directive (ARD) relating to the safeguarding of employees' rights in the event of transfers of undertakings, businesses or parts of businesses has been implemented in s.613a of the German Civil Code (Bürgerliches Gesetzbuch, BGB).

52.2.2 *Application of s.613a BGB to services and outsourcing*

It is necessary to precisely grasp the individual aspects of every specific services or outsourcing project in order to determine its legal requirements. Where projects contain aspects of a transfer of equipment, workforce, know-how and/or customer base s.613a BGB is of concern. In the simplest situation—whenever a business as a whole is transferred—s.613a BGB is always applicable. Section 613a BGB continues to apply in case of a partial business transfer if the transferred part is an economic and organisational subdivision that serves a specific purpose within the overall purpose of the business and if these properties are retained throughout the transfer.

Employment agreements, including all rights and obligations derived from them, automatically transfer from the transferor (customer) to the transferee (s.613a (1) BGB).

Section 613a (1) 1 BGB specifies that the transferee (supplier) enters into the rights and obligations of the employment relationship existing at the time of the transfer. In that regard, (the transferor) and the supplier are jointly and severally liable of any claims arising from the employees' rights and obligations (see s.613a (2) BGB). If these rights and obligations are subject to a collective labour or company agreement, they can generally not be altered for the duration of a year (see s.613a (1) 2 BGB). By way of exception, the supplier's different and corresponding working conditions apply when they are also regulated by a collective agreement or works agreement (see s.613a (1) 3 BGB). The transferred employees principally retain any contractual benefits arising from their original employment agreement, such as accrued overtime and holiday entitlements. However, the German Federal Labour Court has ruled that the new employers may impose disadvantageous regulations for employees if such are justified by objective causes.[1] An objective cause is for instance given, if the regulations are necessary to preserve jobs.[2]

According to s.613a (4) BGB, the termination of an employment relationship due to the transfer of a business or a part of a business is ineffective. The employer does however retain the right to terminate the employment relationship for other reasons. A dismissal based exclusively on operational reasons (betriebsbedingte Kündigung) may be valid.

With employment agreements being transferred as a matter of law under s.613a BGB, the parties cannot establish valid clauses that classify the transfer as a secondment. Furthermore, the transferor is not required to make redundancy payments, unless this was agreed upon in an existing collective bargaining agreement or social plan.[3]

According to s.613a (5) BGB, the previous employer or the new owner must notify employees affected by a transfer in text form prior to transfer. If the employer plans a mass dismissal he must additionally inform the Employment Agency, s.17 German Employment Protection Act, Kündigungsschutzgesetz, KSchG. A dismissal is classified as a mass dismissal when it involves either the dismissal of 5 employees in a workforce of 20–60; more than 25 employees or more than 10 per cent of all employees in a workforce of 60–499; or at least 30 employees in a workforce of at least 500, each within 30 days.

---

[1]   See German Federal Labour Law Court - "Bundesarbeitsgericht" (BAG), NZA 2006, 145.
[2]   See Meyer, *Arbeitsvertragsänderungen bei Betriebsübergang*, (NZA, 2002), pp.246 (250 et seq.).
[3]   Ascheid/Preis/Schmidt, Kündigungsrecht, 4. Auflage 2012, s.613a BGB Rn. 229 et seq.

52.3 People issues—other employment issues

The works council, as the employees' representative body, is one of the most important specifics of German labour law. According to ss.1, 7 and 8 of the Works Constitution Act (Betriebsverfassungsgesetz, BetrVG); the election of a works council is possible in every company with more than five employees over 18 years of age, provided that three of them have been employed for at least six months. Nevertheless—as it is ultimately up to the employees— many small companies do not have a works council. The following remarks thus focus exclusively on companies where works councils exist. The BetrVG grants such works councils an array of specific rights of participation. First of all, according to s.80 (2) BetrVG, the employer shall supply comprehensive information to the works council in a timely and thorough manner to enable it to discharge its duties under the BetrVG. Besides this general right of information the works council has some specific rights of co-determination. In matters in which such rights apply, the decision-making process is no longer the privilege of the employer.

According to s.111 BetrVG, in companies with an average number of over twenty employees, the employer shall inform the works council in full and in good time of any proposed alterations which may entail substantial disadvantages for the staff or a large part thereof and consult the works council on the proposed alterations. In conjunction with s.112 BetrVG, the employer and the works council shall reach an agreement to reconcile their interests in connection with the proposed alterations (so called "reconciliation of interests" (Interessenausgleich)).[4] If an internal agreement between employer and works council is not reached, either side may ask the board of the Federal Employment Agency for mediation (see s.112 (2) BetrVG). After all, there is no legally enforceable right of the works council to demand from the employer an agreement to the reconciliation of interests. By law the employer is only obliged use reasonable efforts to reach an agreement with the works council on whether, and in what manner, the management plans will be carried out.

Regardless of whether management has fulfilled its duties to inform the works council and has tried to reach a reconciliation of interests, the works council is always entitled to enforce a so called "social compensation plan" if a substantial number of employees are affected by the changes. A social compensation plan serves to offset or reduce the disadvantages and losses that the employees will experience as a result of planned restructuring. According to s.112 (4) BetrVG, if no agreement is reached on the social compensation plan, a conciliation committee makes a binding decision (see s.112 (4) BetrVG).

---

[4] To take but one example of such a reconciliation of interests (in the case of Siemens): see *http://www.siemens.com/press/en/pressrelease/?press=/en/pressrelease/2010/corporate__communication/axx20100889.htm* [Accessed 28 September 2012]

In 2007 the German Federal Labour Law Court ruled that the transferor's trade union is entitled to demand a collective agreement (so called Tarifsozialplan) and to call a strike in order to fix its terms.[5]

52.4 Pension issues

Pensioners and former employees do not have their pension rights passed on to the supplier as they are no longer active employees. These entitlements remain with the customer. If active personnel are affected, however, their vested benefits under the customer's pension plan are generally transferred by law to the supplier's pension plan. The parties cannot exclude this transition by contract.

52.5 Contract law

In the majority of cases, services and outsourcing contracts will include complex duties of the supplier (e.g. the supply of hardware and software, establishment of a network infrastructure, transition etc.). Since the BGB contains no specific provisions for outsourcing contracts, it is important to categorise every individual service as German civil law sets out different implied warranties and liability provisions depending on the basic type of contract. German courts ruled that if an individual service is not delivered on time or not performed as owed, the liability or warranties of that basic contract type apply which fits best to the individual service owed.[6]

52.5.1 *Classification of the services or outsourcing contract*

Due to the huge variety of the different services in services or outsourcing arrangements, there is no way of categorising such agreements in a general "one size fits all" manner. However, it is possible to assign some typical services to the basic types of contracts according to the BGB. The distinction that one has to make is mainly between sales contracts (Kaufvertrag, ss.433–453 BGB), lease agreements (Mietvertrag, ss.535–597 BGB), service contracts (Dienstvertrag, ss.611–630 BGB) and contracts to produce a work (Werkvertrag, ss.631–651 BGB).

---

[5]   BAG, *Urteil* vom 24.04.2007 - 1 AZR 252/06.
[6]   See Richardi/Fischinger, *Staudinger BGB*, (Neubearbeitung, 2011), Vorb. zu s.611 ff. Rn. 85.

52.5.1.1   Sales contract

The central provision for sales contracts under German law is s.433 BGB. Under this provision, a seller is obliged to hand over the sales object to the buyer and to transfer ownership (s.433 (1) BGB). The buyer is under the obligation to pay the seller the contract price and to take delivery of the sales object (s.433 (2) BGB). Sales agreements are typical in outsourcing-projects, when objects—especially hardware and software—are literally "sold". For instance, if the customer wants to transfer his former IT-operations to a supplier, the legal provisions of ss.433 et seq. BGB are applicable.

52.5.1.2   Lease contract

If objects—especially software or hardware—are not to be obtained permanently, a lease contract is the appropriate legal form. The provisions for lease contracts are regulated in ss.535 et seq. BGB. A lease contract provides the customer with a temporary right to use specific goods, although he does not obtain property. Whether a company should purchase or lease is determined by what is in a company's best interest, and this will be decided on the basis of economic considerations. An extension can be a hire-purchase agreement where the customer has the option to buy the goods after deducting the rent paid. In 2007 the German Federal Court of Justice[7] ruled that application service providing (ASP) agreements are qualified as lease contracts.

52.5.1.3   Service contract

Under the provision of a service contract, a person who promises to perform a service is obliged to perform such services promised, and the other party is obliged to grant the agreed remuneration (s.611 BGB). The service provider does not owe a specific success. Typical services in the meaning of s.611 BGB are consulting and general support services.

52.5.1.4   Contract to produce a work

Last but not least, most of the outsourcing agreements contain elements of contracts to produce a work (Werkverträge), where the contractor owes a certain success. Contracts to produce a work are regulated in s.631 (1) BGB. Section 640 (1) 1 BGB obliges the customer to accept a work which the supplier produced in conformity with the contract (Abnahme). Obtaining the acceptance is of utmost importance for the supplier, as this is decisive for the legal existence of a supplier's claim for remuneration. A typical part of outsourcing-projects classified as contracts to produce a work are the creation of customised software, the transition-agreement and—under certain circumstances—business process outsourcing.

---

[7]   Bundesgerichtshof (BGH), NZM 2007, 379.

52.5.2 *Warranty provisions*

For sale contracts (see s.437 BGB), lease contracts (see ss.536, 536a BGB) and contracts to produce a work (see s.634 BGB) specific warranties are implied by law. Contrary hereto, only the general provisions of ss.280 et seq. BGB are applicable to faulty service performances in the meaning of s.611 BGB.

In the case of delivery of a defective purchase item, according to s.437 BGB, the customer may demand a remedy under s.439 BGB; he may revoke the agreement under ss.440, 323 and 326 (5) BGB or reduce the purchase price under s.441 BGB and finally, under ss.440, 280, 281, 283 and 311a BGB, he may demand damages, or under s.284 BGB reimbursement of futile expenditure.

In the case of contracts to produce a work, the statutory warranties are regulated in a functionally comparable manner, although under s.637 BGB the customer may remedy the defect himself and demand reimbursement for his required expenses.

Section 536 BGB comprises, in the case of lease contracts, a statutory rent reduction, whereas s.536a BGB grants a compensation for damages and expenses caused by the defective lease object.

Since no specific statutory warranty regulations exist for service contracts in the meaning of s.611 BGB, it is advisable that rights and obligations are contractually regulated. Such agreements regarding customer protection typically include service level agreements stipulating the required qualities of service, monitoring of service performance (usually in combination with audit rights), reporting upon service performance in regular intervals and specified termination rules.

This comprehensive system of warranties and remedies in case of defective performance is one reason why warranties in services and outsourcing contracts are typically limited to a certain quality of service, often according to a defined "current state of the art". Additionally, indemnities are commonly given for third party claims due to violations of IP rights.

52.5.3 *Compensatory damages*

52.5.3.1 *Breach of Duty*

Sections 280–284 and 286 BGB constitute the core provisions for compensatory damages for the breach of a duty. In absence of a contractual liability provision, each party is liable for all damages caused by a negligent or intentional breach of a duty, without limitation as regards the amount of compensation. In principle, German civil law distinguishes between compensation instead of performance (ss.281–283 BGB) and compensation for delay (s.286 BGB). All remaining forms of damages suffered because of a breach of duty by the other party can result in compensation under s.280 I BGB.

52.5.3.1.1 Damages instead of performance

The customer may demand compensation instead of performance in the case of impossibility (s.283 BGB), in the case of the violation of certain ancillary duties (s.282 BGB) and, most important and most common, in the case of non-performance or failure to render performance as owed (s.281 BGB).

52.5.3.1.1.1 Impossibility

German civil law does not limit impossibility to those cases in which performance is not (or no longer) possible. The supplier may refuse performance if it requires expense and effort which, taking into account the subject matter of the obligation and the requirements of good faith, is grossly disproportionate to the interest in performance of the customer (s.275 (2) BGB). In addition, the supplier may refuse performance if he is to render the performance in person and, when the obstacle to the performance is weighed against the interest of the customer in performance, performance cannot be reasonably required of him (s.275 (3) BGB). Finally, s.311a BGB addresses cases in which performance had already become impossible (in the meaning of s.275) at the time when the contract was concluded.

Section 311a (1) BGB stipulates that a contract is not prevented from being effective by the fact that under s.275 (1) to (3) BGB the supplier does not need to perform and such obstacle to performance already exists when the contract is entered into. If the supplier is at fault for the impossibility, the requirements of ss.280 (3), 283 BGB will be met in most cases, and the customer can therefore demand compensatory damages instead of performance.

52.5.3.1.1.2 Violation of certain ancillary duties

If the supplier breaches an ancillary duty under s.241 (2) BGB, the customer may, if the requirements of s.280 (1) BGB are satisfied, demand damages instead of performance, if he can no longer reasonably be expected to accept performance by the supplier. However, such cases are very rare, especially in business to business relationships.

52.5.3.1.1.3 Damages for non-performance or failure to render performance as owed

Section 281 BGB is applicable in the case that the supplier does not render performance when it is due, or does not render performance as owed, and if the requirements of s.280 (1) BGB are met. In addition, the customer must have provided the supplier with a period for his performance, and such period must have expired without the supplier completing the performance owed. Setting a period for performance may be dispensed if the supplier seriously and definitively refuses performance or if there are special circumstances which, after the interests of both parties are weighed, justify the immediate assertion of a claim for damages (s.280 (2) BGB). The claim for performance is excluded as soon as the customer has demanded damages instead of performance (s.280 (4) BGB).

52.5.3.1.2 Compensation for delay

The customer can only claim damages for delay if the supplier is in default (Verzug). Section 286 (4) BGB stipulates that the supplier is not in default for as long as performance is not made as the result of a circumstance for which the supplier is not responsible. According to s.276 (1) BGB, the supplier is responsible for intentional breach or negligence, if a higher or lower degree of liability is neither laid down nor to be inferred from the other subject matter of the obligation, including but not limited to the giving of a guarantee or the assumption of a procurement risk. Additionally, the claim must be vested (wirksam), enforceable (durchsetzbar) and the supplier has to be put on notice about the delay (Mahnung). Under s.286 (2) BGB, the remedy for delay is available without prior notice under the following circumstances. There is no need for a warning notice if:

(a) a period of time according to the calendar has been specified for the performance;
(b) performance must be preceded by an event, and a reasonable period of time for performance has been specified in such a way that it can be calculated, starting from the event, according to the calendar;
(c) the obligor seriously and definitively refuses performance; or
(d) for special reasons, weighing the interests of both parties, the immediate commencement of default is justified.

52.5.3.1.3 Remaining cases of damages under section 280 (1) BGB

In all other cases the customer may demand damages if the supplier breaches a duty arising from the obligation and if the damages are caused thereby (s.280 (1) BGB). This does not apply if the supplier is not responsible for the breach of duty (s.280 (2) BGB).

52.5.3.2 Burden of proof

In the case of contractual damages according to s.280 (1) 2 BGB the supplier carries the burden of proof that it is not responsible for the breach of duty in the meaning of s.276 BGB (i.e. not having caused the breach negligently or intentionally). The customer on the other hand has to prove that the supplier has indeed breached its duty which resulted in damages. Additionally, the customer has to prove the causal connection between the breach of duty and the damages.

52.5.4 Pre-contractual liabilities

The liability for breach of protective duties (s.241 (2) BGB) during the negotiations preceding a contract (regardless of the final contract) is codified in ss.311(2), 241 (2) BGB. According to s.311 (2) BGB, an obligation with duties under s.241 (2) BGB also comes into existence by:

(a) the commencement of contract negotiations;
(b) the initiation of a contract where one party, with regard to a potential contractual relationship, gives the other party the possibility of affecting its rights, legal interests and other interests, or entrusts these to the other party; or
(c) similar business contacts.

52.5.5 Frustration of contract

Section 313 BGB regulates interference with the basis of the transaction (Störung der Geschäftsgrundlage), whereas s.314 BGB, which stipulates a statutory termination right for good cause, is only applicable for contracts containing a continuing obligation (e. g. service contracts). Codified in 2002, s.313 BGB regulates a well-established case law doctrine of contractual adaptation if circumstances which became the basis of a contract have significantly changed since the contract was entered into. In this case, the adaptation of the contract may be demanded to the extent that, taking account all the circumstances of the specific case, one of the parties cannot reasonably be expected to uphold the contract without alteration. If adaptation of the contract is not possible or one party cannot reasonably be expected to accept it, the disadvantaged party may revoke the contract (s.313 (3) BGB).

52.5.6 Revocation

Sections 323–326, 346 BGB specify the requirements for the revocation of contracts and its consequences. The main provision is s.323 BGB which regulates conditions under which one party may revoke the contract. For instance, under s.323 (1) BGB the customer may revoke a contract if the supplier does not render an act of performance which is due, or does not render it in conformity with the contract. Regularly, the customer has to specify, without result, an additional period for performance or cure. Section 325 BGB stipulates that the right to demand damages in the case of a reciprocal contract is not excluded by revocation, while s.326 BGB regulates the conditions under which the customer is released from consideration when the supplier is excluded from his duty of performance according to s.275 (1)–(3) BGB.

52.5.7 Responsibility of the supplier

52.5.7.1 Standard responsibility of the supplier

Section 276 (1) BGB stipulates the standard responsibility of the supplier, whereupon he is responsible for intention and negligence if a higher or lower degree of liability is neither laid down nor to be inferred from the other subject matter of the obligation, including but not limited to the giving of a guarantee or the assumption of a procurement risk. According to s.278 BGB, the supplier is equally responsible for fault on the part of his legal representative and of persons whom he uses to perform his obligation (in particular sub-contractors). This principle of fault-based liability applies for contractual (ss.280 et seq. BGB) as well as tortious liability (ss.823 et seq. BGB). Basically, liability is unlimited and there is no maximum liability limit by law. It is obvious, that this statutory basis is great for the customer and unsatisfactory for the supplier. Therefore, the supplier has a legitimate interest to agree on a reasonable limitation of the otherwise incalculable risk. This implicates the importance of a contractual limitation of liability (see section 52.7).

52.5.7.2 Product liability and liability for telecommunication providers

The situation is different if product liability law applies. The German Product Liability act (Produkthaftungsgesetz, ProdHaftG) stipulates both a strict responsibility and a maximum liability limit of €85 million for personal injuries (see s.10 ProdHaftG). Even if hardware components and software (if saved on a data carrier) are seen as products in the meaning of s.2 ProdHaftG, the legal responsibility in accordance with the ProdHaftG plays hardly any role in a business to business environment. This is due to the fact that according to s.1 (1) 2 ProdHaftG the producer is—in the case of property damage—only liable for damages on property for the personal use and consumption.

It should also be mentioned that there are particularities for telecommunication providers. According to s.7 (2) TKV, the liability for pecuniary damage is limited to €12,500 per client and €10 million per harmful event stated that the damage was not caused intentionally.

52.5.7.3 *Force majeure*

Thanks to the principle of fault-based liability in German civil law, the supplier is basically not liable for any damages in the event of force majeure, unless the supplier took over a performance guarantee.

52.6 Limitations of liability

As described above, the unlimited liability bears an unpredictable risk for the supplier. If the supplier causes, for example, an IT break down which leads to a stop of the production, this may result in a multi-million loss within a short period of time. It is obvious that no supplier can accept this statutory liability and that every supplier will therefore try to modify his legal position.

According to s.276 (3) BGB, any exclusion of liability is not possible if the offending party acts intentionally. In the field of product liability, s.14 ProdHaftG prohibits any contractual limitation. Section 1 (2) TKV stipulates that the maximum liability limits for the telecommunication providers are imperative. In all other cases the enforceability of the exclusion of liability or warranties differs whether the services or outsourcing terms constitute standard business terms in the meaning of s.305 BGB or individual agreements.

To emphasise this: The limitation of liability in standard business terms is not possible for:

(a) any exclusion or limitation of liability for damage from injury to life, body or health due to negligent breach of duty by the user or intentional or negligent breach of duty by a legal representative or a person used to perform an obligation of the user (s.309 no. 7a BGB);

(b) any exclusion or limitation of liability for other damage arising from a

> grossly negligent breach of duty by the user, or from an intentional or grossly negligent breach of duty by a legal representative of the user, or a person used to perform an obligation of the user (s.309 no. 7b BGB); or

(c)   any exclusion of liability for a breach of cardinal contractual obligation that sets the liability limit lower than the "typically foreseeable damage". Cardinal obligations are, in particular, the central performance duties under a contract.

That said, for standard business terms, it is essential under German law to establish the difference between simple (limited liability) and gross (unlimited liability) negligence. This problem is further aggravated as there is no legal definition of gross negligence. Hence, the German courts came up with a definition of gross negligence as

> "a failure to act or conduct that is so reckless that it demonstrates a substantial lack of concern for whether damage will result or not.[8]"

Additionally, pursuant to s.307 (1) BGB—which is also applicable in b2b-relationships—provisions in standard business terms are ineffective if, contrary to the requirement of good faith, they unreasonably disadvantage the other party to the contract with the user. Such an unreasonable disadvantage may also arise from the provision not being clear and comprehensible.

Where standard business terms infringe these statutory requirements they are void and replaced by the statutory scheme (see s.306 BGB). With this risk in mind, it is highly recommended for the supplier to negotiate such clauses (e.g. liability limitations going beyond what is described above) in detail with the customer to ensure that they are not construed as standard business terms, but as individual agreements to which the above restrictions do not apply.

In practice, liability is typically limited contractually by the parties agreeing on a maximum amount of damages. To calculate this amount, factors like the contract volume, the probability of damage and insurability are taken into account.

Liability regardless of negligence or fault and liability due to slight negligence will typically be limited to a yearly amount (e. g. €300,000). Liability due to gross negligence will be limited as well, albeit to a higher amount (e. g. €600,000). Liability due to intentional breach—as described above—cannot be limited.

Furthermore, the parties of a services or outsourcing agreement often incorporate a limitation of liability for consequential loss in their contract.

---

[8]   E.g. BGH, NJW 2003, 1118 (1119).

Difficulties can arise in this case however as German law does not clearly differentiate between direct and indirect loss.

52.7   Data protection

52.7.1   *Implementation of the Data Protection Directive in Germany*

The Data Protection Directive 95/46/EC was implemented into German law by an amendment of the Federal Data Protection Act (Bundesdatenschutzgesetz, "BDSG") from 18 May 2001 (Gesetz zur Änderung des Bundesdatenschutzgesetzes und anderer Gesetze).

52.7.2   *Data processing in Germany*

It is important to distinguish personal and non-personal data as the provisions of the BDSG are exclusively applicable to the former.

According to the BDSG any processing of personal data must either be justified by consent of the data subject or statutory law.

The requirements concerning data processing differ, depending on the type of services or outsourcing transaction. Basically, there are two different scenarios. The first option is commissioned data processing according to s.11 BDSG. The second option is the transfer of functions according to s.28 BSDG.

52.7.2.1   *Section 11 BDSG: Commissioned data processing*

Commissioned data processing means that other bodies collect, process or use personal data on behalf of the customer. Since the supplier just acts as a "technical assistant" being strictly bound to the customer's orders in this case, the customer remains in control of the data at all times. Therefore, the supplier is not considered a third party with regard to data privacy but part of the customer's business in the broadest sense. As the transfer of data between these two units is not seen as a transfer that has to be justified in terms of data protection, s.11 (2) BDSG provides that the supplier shall be chosen carefully, with special attention to the suitability of the technical and organisational measures applied by him.

It is exclusively the customer who is responsible for complying with any data protection regulations. He is therefore legally obliged to contractually establish control mechanisms that allow him to periodically inspect the supplier.

52.7.2.2   *Section 28 BDSG: Transfer of functions*

Section 28 BDSG applies if the transfer of data takes place as a transfer of functions. One example of this might be not just storing the data but analysing or grouping it. The primary criterion to distinguish between a commissioned data processing and a transfer of functions is the freedom of choice and action the supplier has in regard to the data transfer. In the case of a transfer of functions, the supplier is considered a third party and is thus responsible for complying with the relevant regulations.

52.7.3   **Data processing to other countries**

The transfer of data out of Germany is regulated in s.4b BDSG. If the data is transferred to Member States of the EU or the EEA, the transfer is regularly subject to the same statutes as a domestic German transfer would be.

If one side of the services or outsourcing contract resides outside the EU/ EEA, a transfer is not to take place if the data subject has a legitimate interest in this regard. Such an interest is usually assumed if an adequate level of data protection cannot be established in the country to which the data is transferred. To provide some legal certainty the European Commission has declared a number of states to provide adequate data protection. These include Argentina, Canada and Switzerland.

If the other country does not fall under any of these regulations, there are several options to ensure adequate data protection:

(a)   obtain the consent of the data subject;
(b)   use of EU standard clauses (model clauses approved by the European commission for data exports);
(c)   binding corporate rules; and
(d)   safe harbour principles (for export to the US only).

Please note that the German Data Protection authorities still require a data protection agreement (see above) to be concluded in addition to the above measures.[9] Even if such a data processing agreement is in place however, the customer has to refrain from transferring personal data if, in the individual case, prevailing interests of the data subjects affected exist (s.28 para.1 sentence 1 no. 2 BDSG).

---

[9]   Cf. *Orientierungshilfe – Cloud Computing der Arbeitskreise Technik und Medien der Konferenz der Datenschutz-beauftragten des Bundes und der Länder*, Version 1.0, 26 September 2011, p.11.

52.8   Insolvency issues

The insolvency of the supplier usually causes severe problems for the customer, which can hardly be compensated by "Backsourcing". It is important to differ between two main phases, the insolvency during transition ("build-phase") and the insolvency during operation ("run-phase").

52.8.1   *Insolvency during transition ("build-phase")*

At the beginning of the services or outsourcing process, during the so called "build-phase", the supplier is obliged to carry out the transition, which means he is obliged to transfer the IT-operations of the customer to his company. This is usually construed as a contract to produce a work in the meaning of s.631 BGB.

If the supplier goes into insolvency during this period, the opening of the insolvency proceedings (Eröffnung des Insolvenzverfahrens) results in an unenforceability of the contractual relationship. However, the insolvency administrator (Insolvenzverwalter) has a right of choice to demand fulfilment of the contract works according to s.103 InsO. If he chooses "non-fulfilment", the customer may claim damages for non-performance according to s.103 (2) 1 InsO. This claim constitutes as a simple insolvency claim in the meaning of s.38 InsO.

52.8.2   *Insolvency during operation ("run-phase")*

The situation is different if the supplier goes into insolvency after the IT-operations were transferred. As ss.103 et seq. BGB differ between the types of contract; it is essential to classify the affected contract. Section 108 InsO applies for service contracts in the meaning of s.611 BGB, and constitutes an exemption of the general right of choice of the insolvency administrator according to s.103 InsO on whether to fulfil a contract or not. In the case of s.108 InsO the insolvency has no impact on the effectiveness of the contract. Even after the opening of the insolvency proceedings both parties stay contractually obliged. The contract can then only be terminated if statutory or contractual rights of termination apply.

This differentiation between service contracts and contracts to produce a work is seen as unsatisfactory by a view in experts' literature. This view favours an analogy to s.103 InsO that results in a right of choice for the receiver of insolvency even for services contracts. The courts have not yet decided the case.

52.8.3   *Practical hint*

As shown, all services and outsourcing contracts have in common that they are threatened by termination in the case of insolvency. To prevent a break down of the IT-system it is essential to take precautions. One solution is to oblige the supplier to deposit the source code of any software necessary to provide the services in escrow.

52.9   Financial services regulation

The Markets in Financial Instruments Directive 2004/39/EC (MiFID) was introduced in Germany by law from 16 July 2007 (Gesetz zur Umsetzung der Richtlinie über Märkte für Finanzinstrumente und der Durchführungsrichtlinie der Kommission). This resulted in significant amandments of the Securities Trading Act (Wertpapierhandelsgesetz), the Stock Exchange Law (Börsengesetz) and the Banking Act (Kreditwesengesetz).

Especially relevant to outsourcing matters is s.25a (2) Kreditwesengesetz, (KWG), which provides that credit institutions must take the appropriate measures to avoid any excess risk relating to the outsourcing process. The outsourcing must not lead to a delegation of responsibility from the credit institution to the party performing outsourced services. The credit institutions rather remain responsible for complying with the legal requirements at all times.

In addition to the European directives, the German Financial Market Supervisory Authority BaFin regularly issues circulars regarding the regulation of financial services. The most recent circular *11/2010 (Outsourcing Circular/MaRisk)* issued on 15 December 2010 constitutes rules regarding the minimum standards for risk management during the outsourcing process. The BaFin circulars are informal acts and as such not legally binding. They are, however, universally accepted and regarded as guidelines for proper management. Failure to comply with the regulations of the circulars may even lead to supervisory measures.

52.10   Public Procurement and Utilities Directive

Germany was late in implementing the Public Procurement Directive 2004/18/EC as well as in implementing the Utilities Directive 2004/17/EC. Both directives should have been implemented into German Law by 31 January 2006. This was accomplished only partially and belatedly with effect from 1 November 2006 by the amendment of the Public Procurement Regulation (Vergabeverordnung VgV), the Construction Tendering and Contract Regulations (VOB/A 2006), the Procurement and Contract Procedures for

Supplies and Services (VOL/A 2006) and the Procurement Law for Supplies and Services of Freelancers (VOF 2006).

It was not until 24 April 2009 that the EU directives were fully implemented with the entry into force of the Act to modernise the public procurement law (Gesetz zur Modernisierung des Vergaberechts). Additionally, there were further amendments. Especially relevant to the procurement of IT services is VOL/A from 20 November 2009.

Section 2 Public Procurement Regulation stipulates that an invitation to tender according to ss.97 et seq. Law Against Restraints on Competition (Gesetz gegen Wettbewerbsbeschränkungen GWB) must be carried out if the estimated value of a contract procured by a public body exceeds a certain amount (e. g. €130,000 for supply and service contracts of the top or upper federal authorities, for all other service and supply contracts of €200,000, see s.2 VgV). The invitation to tender must generally be public and thus open to an unlimited number of companies (s.101 (7), (2) GWB).

If the estimated contract value does not reach the amount regulated in s.2 VgV, ss.30 Law on Budgetary Procedures (Haushaltsgrundsätzegesetz HGrG), 55 Federal Budget Code (Bundeshaushaltsordnung BHO) and 55 State Budget Code (Landeshaushaltsordnung LHO) are applicable. These provisions also stipulate a public invitation to tender. Unlike the VgV and GWB however, they are merely internal rules of conduct and thus not legally binding.

If the procurement has an international context, the WTO Government Procurement Agreement from 1994 (GPA) must be observed. Its main purpose is to prohibit discrimination of foreign suppliers.

52.11   Competition law

Competition law applies where services or outsourcing arrangements constitute a merger. In this case, EU merger control is applicable if companies from different Member States are involved (see Chapter 33 for details), whereas services or outsourcing arrangements that take place exclusively within Germany are regulated under German law (see ss.35 to 43 GWB). A merger is only relevant to the latter if:

(a)   the combined aggregate worldwide turnover of all the undertakings concerned is more than €500 million; and

(b)   the aggregate turnover in Germany of at least two of the undertakings concerned is more than €25 million; and

(c)   the aggregate turnover in Germany of another one of the undertakings concerned is more than €5 million.

Section 35 (2) GWB provides certain exceptions from the general control of mergers. If a merger is approved, it can still be subject to certain conditions and obligations according to s.40 (3) GWB.

Section 42 GWB contains the so called "ministerial approval". It entitles the Federal Minister of Economics and Technology to approve a merger that was previously rejected by the cartel office if the negative impacts of the restraints of competition are outweighed by macroeconomic advantages or if the merger is justified by an overwhelming public interest.

52.12   Main tax issues

52.12.1   Transfer of assets

In the case of a transfer of assets, the customer is basically obliged to pay income tax (corporate income tax, solidarity surcharge, trade tax), tax on the transfer of real estate and value added tax (VAT). Beyond that, withholding tax consequences may result if transfers are made below fair market value to a supplier that is related to the transferring customer.

In principle every transfer of assets to the supplier is seen as a supply of goods or services and therefore subject to German VAT. However, if the transfer is treated as a transfer of business as going concern this does neither account for nor charge VAT.

52.12.2   Value added tax (VAT)

The services supplied by a third party to the customer trigger a VAT charge. Therefore, the services or outsourcing arrangement may give rise to substantial VAT costs if the customer's turnovers are not fully subject to VAT (for example if the customer is an insurance, bank or healthcare company). Possibilities to avoid or minimise these VAT costs need to be taken into consideration. However if the customer's turnovers are subject to VAT, he is entitled to fully reclaim charged VAT.

For the purposes of VAT, any set-off of purchase price for assets transferred to the supplier against fees for services supplied by the supplier leads to VAT liability on the gross consideration of each supply (and not only on the net consideration paid). The price of each supply should therefore be specified in the relevant agreements.

52.12.3 Constructive dividends

"Dealing at Arms Length – Principle (Fremdvergleichsgrundsatz)" applies in Germany. Therefore if the supplier is not fully independent but related to the customer (e.g. as an affiliated enterprise), and the prices used for the services are below fair market value, the profit of the supplier may be increased followed by a constructive dividend, triggering withholding taxes.

52.12.4 Income taxes

In principle, service fees charged by the supplier are deductible expenses for the customer and therefore lower his income tax (corporate income tax, solidarity surcharge and trade tax). However, for trade tax purposes under the requirements of s.8 Trade Tax Act ("Gewerbesteuergesetz") some expenses (e. g. rent, leasing and licence expenses) have to be added back partially if they exceed the amount of €100,000.

Chapter 53

Spain

José Ramón Morales, Partner

Garrigues

53.1 Outline

Parts 1 to 11 of this book describe the key business issues relevant for
outsourcing and other services agreements. They also describe the key legal
issues under English law. This chapter describes the specific legal and business issues which affect services and outsourcing arrangements in Spain.

53.2 People issues—ARD

53.2.1 *The employment law framework governing services outsourcing arrangements in Spain*

Services and outsourcing arrangements will be covered by the general
regulations on business succession, in Article 44 of the Workers' Statute.
This provision derives from Council Directive 2001/23/EC, of 12 March
2001, on the approximation of the laws of the Member States relating to the
safeguarding of employees' rights in the event of transfers of undertakings,
businesses or parts of undertakings or businesses (ARD). Article 44 is
described in more detail in this section below.

Once a succession or transfer has taken place on the terms set forth in Article
44 of the Workers' Statute, the customer and supplier will enter into a
contract for services subject to the rules in Article 42 of the Workers' Statute,
which are described in section 53.3 below.

53.2.2 Business successions in the context of services or outsourcing contracts

53.2.2.1 Definition of a business succession

According to Article 44, a business succession will be considered to occur where the transfer affects an economic unit that retains its identity, as a set of resources organised so as to pursue an essential or ancillary economic activity. It will be necessary to analyse the structure of each services or outsourcing deal individually to assess whether it will be classified as a "business succession" on the terms of Article 44 of the Workers' Statute given that, if it is, the application of this regime is compulsory.

53.2.2.2 Requirement for a business succession

The Spanish Supreme Court (Supreme Court Judgment of 27 October 1986, among others) has held that two essential requirements must be met for a business succession to exist:

(a) *owner requirement*, consisting of a change of ownership: a direct transfer or a chain of title comprising any type of transfer; and

(b) *subject-matter requirement*, consisting of the actual delivery of all of the essential elements enabling the business to continue. In other words, the assets transferred must form a production unit that can be operated on an independent basis and is capable of supplying goods and services to the market.

Nevertheless, in light of the case law precedents handed down by the European Court of Justice,[1] this second requirement has generally been restrictively interpreted to mean that:

> "where the business activity essentially lies in the hands of the workforce, the identity may be retained following the transfer where the new employer does not restrict itself to continuing the activity in question, but rather also takes on an essential part, in terms of number and skills, of the personnel specifically assigned by its predecessor to that task".

With this in mind, the Spanish Supreme Court announced (with certain reservations) in judgments on 20 and 27 October 2004, that:

> "succession applies not only where there is a transfer of assets, but also in any other circumstances in which the transferee of an activity takes on, in significant qualitative and numerical terms, part of the personnel

---

[1] See Süzen, dated 11 March 1997; Hernández Vidal, dated 10 December 1998; Sánchez Hidalgo, dated 2 December 1999; Allen, dated 14 September 2000; Collino, dated 26 September 2000; Mayeur, dated 25 January 2001; Liikenn, dated 15 January 2002; Temco, dated 24 January 2002; and Sodexho, dated 20 November 2003.

of the transferor".

This has come to be referred to as "workforce succession".

53.2.2.3 *Employment law consequences of business succession*

53.2.2.3.1 Principle of continuity

The consequences of the occurrence of a business succession under Article 44 of the Workers' Statute are as follows:

  (a) the employment contracts of the employees assigned to the performance of the relevant tasks will be transferred to the supplier;
  (b) the employees at the customer company will become part of the workforce of the supplier of the service, without the need for employees' consent; and
  (c) the employees at the customer company will be able to claim in court for their status as workers at the supplier company.

Thus, the legislation on business succession imposes the principle of continuity of the employment relationships with the new supplier of the service.

53.2.2.3.2 Liability for employment obligations

Social security legislation notwithstanding, the customer and the new supplier will be jointly and severally liable for three years following the transfer in respect of any employment obligations that arose before the transfer and which have not been satisfied.

The customer and the supplier will also be jointly and severally liable in respect of any obligations that arise after the transfer, where the transfer is held to be in breach of the law or illegal (i.e. with the purpose of depriving employees of their rights).

53.2.2.3.3 Pensions

The comments made above also apply in relation to pensions: pursuant to Article 44 of the Workers' Statute, where the services or outsourcing process entails the transfer of employees as part of the transfer of an undertaking, of a workplace or of an independent production unit, the employment relationship is not extinguished, and the rights and obligations of the former business owner are transferred to the new business owner, including the pension obligations and, generally speaking, any and all supplementary welfare obligations that the former employer may have acquired.

53.2.2.3.4 Collective agreements

Unless agreed otherwise, after the succession, the employment relationships of the workers affected by the succession will continue to be governed by the collective employment agreement which, at the time of the transfer, was in force at the company, workplace or independent production unit transferred. This agreement will remain in force until the expiration date of the original collective employment agreement or until the entry into force of another new collective employment agreement that is applicable to the transferred business unit.

53.2.2.3.5 Workers' legal representatives

Where the transferred business, workplace or production unit preserves its independence, the change of business owner will not per se extinguish the mandate of the workers' legal representatives, who will continue to perform their functions on the same terms and subject to the same conditions as those previously in force.

53.2.2.3.6 Notification

The customer and the supplier must inform the legal representatives of the workers affected by the change of ownership of the following particulars:

   (a)   scheduled date for the transfer;
   (b)   grounds for the transfer;
   (c)   legal, economic and welfare consequences for the workers of the transfer; and
   (d)   planned measures with respect to the workers.

If the workers have no legal representatives, the customer and the supplier must supply the information mentioned above to the workers who may be affected by the transfer.

The customer will be required to provide the information mentioned above with sufficient notice before the transfer is performed. The supplier will be required to notify the workers of these details with sufficient notice and, in all cases, before the workers have their employment and working conditions affected by the transfer.

53.2.2.3.7   Consultation

Any customer or supplier who intends to adopt, by reason of the transfer, employment measures in relation to their workers, will be required to commence a consultation period with the workers' legal representatives on the planned measures and their consequences for the workers. This consultation period will have to be held with sufficient notice, before the measures are brought into effect. In the consultation period, the parties must negotiate in good faith, to secure an agreement. Where the planned measures consist of collective transfers or substantial modifications of working conditions on a collective basis, the procedure for the consultation period must conform to the provisions in the Workers' Statute for making such modifications to contracts.

The information and consultation obligations provided for in this chapter will be applied regardless of whether the decision relating to the transfer has been adopted by the customer or supplier business owners or by companies exerting control over them. Any justification by them based on the fact that the company that took the decision did not provide them with the necessary information is irrelevant.

53.3   People issues—other employment issues— outsourcing arrangements and subcontracts for services under Article 42 of the Workers' Statute

If the new supplier is not to take on the employees of the customer company (or the supplier is to take on part of those employees and therefore they must be considered on an individual basis), the applicable legislation is Article 42 of the Workers' Statute governing subcontracts for projects and services, as amended by Law 43/2006 of 29 December 2006.

The use by a company of contracts with external parties to decentralise the production process is considered to be a lawful procedure based on the constitutional principle of freedom of enterprise. However, a series of protection mechanisms has been established to avoid the fraudulent use of services or outsourcing contracts to disguise an unlawful supply of workers, which is prohibited in Article 43 of the Workers' Statute.

53.3.1   Definition of unlawful supply of workers

According to Article 43 of the Workers' Statute, an unlawful supply of workers occurs where either:

(a)   the subject matter of the services agreements between the companies is confined to the supply of the workers of the supplier company to the recipient company; or
(b)   the supplier company has no activity or does not have its own stable organisation, does not have the resources needed to perform its activity, or does not carry out the functions inherent to a business owner.

53.3.2   Implications of unlawful supply

The consequences of a breach of the above provisions are that the supplier and recipient will be liable jointly and severally for the salary and social security obligations relating to the workers. The workers supplied unlawfully will have the right to become part of the permanent staff, at either the supplier or recipient, at their choice; their rights and obligations will be the same as those of a worker of an equivalent category or position; and they will have the length of service they had when the unlawful supply commenced.

53.3.3   Exception—temporary employment agencies

The only exception to the above prohibition relates to temporary employment agencies which, through supply contracts, create a triangular relationship between the temporary employment agency, the worker and the user company.

53.3.4   Application to services and outsourcing arrangements

A contract for services will be lawful where the supplier meets the following requirements:

(a)   it carries out its own business activity and has stable assets, instruments and machinery and a stable organisation assigned to that activity;
(b)   it is allocated actual contractual obligations, it manages the performance of the contract for services and assumes the risk of non-performance of the services; and
(c)   it retains the right to control its workers and preserves with respect to

them the rights, obligations, risks and liabilities inherent to its status as employer.

53.3.5 *Recommendations to avoid an unlawful supply of workers*

The following are recommendations to avoid the consequences of having a contract for services between customer and supplier classed as an unlawful supply of workers:

(a) ensure that the powers of control and discipline of the supplier's staff are exerted directly by the supplier and not by the customer;

(b) ensure that the supplier's employees receive their instructions from the supplier's manager and that the supplier organises what work is to be carried out by which employee;

(c) avoid any type of participation by the customer's personnel in the selection of the personnel of the supplier;

(d) ensure that the working hours and shifts of the employees of the customer and supplier are different;[2]

(e) avoid charging for work performed by the hour, or by the person, but rather by the project or service;

(f) ensure that the supplier provides its own tools, work equipment and maintenance items for that equipment, and (where necessary) has, at the customer's facilities, areas used exclusively by its workers; and

(g) ensure that the employment regime for the supplier's workers is its own regime based on its applicable collective employment agreement.

53.3.6 *Implications of a contract for services*

The employment law effects of a contract for services are provided for in Article 42 of the Workers' Statute, which states as follows.

53.3.6.1 *Salary and social security obligations*

Any business owners who enter into contracts or sub-contracts with others to perform services relating to their own business activity must ascertain that the suppliers of those services are up to date with payment of their social security contributions. To do this, they must obtain in writing, specifying the name of the company concerned, a certificate verifying that the supplier pays the corresponding social security contributions. Social security

---

[2] Note that, as stated in section 53.2.1 above, in this case transfer legislation would not apply. Thus, outsourcing will fall under the scope of Article 42 of the Workers' Statute governing subcontracts for projects and services where the continuity of employment relationships (and related rights) does not apply.

authorities must issue the certificate within a non-extendable period of 30 days following the request and on the terms determined in the legislation. At the end of this period, the applicant company will be released from any liability vis-à-vis social security contributions.

Unless the 30-day period mentioned above has expired, for a year following the end of the services contract, the customer will be jointly and severally liable for the salaries of the supplier's (and sub-contractors') workers and for their social security contributions.

53.3.6.2   *Notification*

The workers of the supplier and sub-contractors must be informed in writing by the business owner of the name of the principal for which they will be performing work at any given time. This information must be supplied before the respective services start to be provided and must include the name or business name of the customer business owner, its registered office and taxpayer identification number. The supplier or sub-contractors must also notify the Spanish social security authorities of the name of the customer company on the terms determined in the legislation.

In addition to the information to be provided to the workers' representatives under the provisions on subcontracts in the Workers' Statute, where the company enters into an agreement for a project or service with a supplier or sub-contractor company, it must inform the legal representatives of its workers of the following:

(a) the name or business name, address and taxpayer identification number of the supplier or sub-contractor company;
(b) the subject matter and term of the services or outsourcing agreement;
(c) the place of performance of the agreement;
(d) if applicable, the number of workers that will be put to work by the supplier or sub-contractor at the customer's workplace; and
(e) the measures envisaged for the co-ordination of functions from the standpoint of the prevention of occupational risks.

Where the customer, supplier or sub-contractor share the same workplace on an ongoing basis, the customer must have a book in which it records the above information in relation to all of those companies. That book must be available to the workers' legal representatives.

The supplier or sub-contractor must also inform the workers' legal representatives before the contract for services starts to be performed of the particulars described in section 53.3.6.2 and points (b)–(e) above.

53.3.6.3 *Queries by workers*

Where the workers of the supplier or sub-contractor companies do not have legal representatives, they will be entitled to submit queries to the representatives of the workers of the customer on the conditions for the performance of their activity of employment while they share the workplace and have no representatives. This will not apply to any claims by the workers with respect to the company they are accountable to.

53.3.6.4 *Workers' representatives*

Where the workers' representatives at the customer and at the supplier or sub-contractor share a workplace on an ongoing basis, they may hold meetings to co-ordinate with each other in relation to the conditions of employment on the terms provided in the Workers' Statute.

The representative capacity and scope of the functions of the workers' representatives, and their paid time for union duties will be determined by the current legislation and by the applicable collective employment agreements, if any.

53.3.6.5 *Liability*

The liability regime applicable to contracts for services pursuant to Article 42 of the Workers' Statute is as follows:

(a) Salaries: the customer and supplier will be jointly and severally liable during the term of the services or outsourcing arrangement and up to one year later.

(b) Social security obligations:

   (i) obligations before the term of the contract for services: the customer will have secondary liability unless the customer does not apply for a certificate of no deficiency in payment to the social security authorities, or applies for a certificate but no certificate is granted, in which case it will have joint and several liability;

   (ii) obligations during the term of the services agreement and one year later: the customer and supplier will be jointly and severally liable;

   (iii) obligations after expiry of the contract for services: from the second to the fourth year following its termination date, liability is secondary.

(c) Occupational risk prevention: in addition to the liabilities acquired respectively by each business owner (principal contractor and supplier) in this respect, the supplier acquires the obligation to co-ordinate its occupation risk prevention activity with the customer company.

53.4 Contract law

53.4.1 Introduction

53.4.1.1 Principle of freedom of contract

As in other systems based on Civil Law, however, Spanish law is based on the principle of freedom of contract (Article 1,255 of the Civil Code), which gives the contracting parties the right to establish the covenants, clauses and conditions they see fit, except those against the law, morality and public policy. Obligations arising from services and outsourcing contracts between private parties will be enforceable (Articles 1,091 and 1,258 of the Civil Code). Where the two parties to a services and outsourcing contract are business owners, in principle they can include in the contract any conditions that they may freely agree upon, with some exceptions based on compulsory rules, some of which are mentioned in this section. Where the customer is a public authority, the specific provisions on public contracts must be taken into account (see sections 53.8 and 53.9 below).

53.4.1.2 Outsourcing agreements as service or project agreements

The acknowledgment of the outsourcing of services in Spanish case law is relatively recent. It has been discussed whether in Spanish law the outsourcing contract may be treated as a services agreement (and accordingly the supplier would perform its obligation by providing the resources, and it would be the customer who must prove the breach and also fault on the part of the supplier); or project work (which would compel the supplier to obtain a result, and accordingly if the result is not obtained, the supplier could only be released from blame by proving the existence of a fortuitous event or force majeure). There is a court judgment[3] that states that, although in simple projects a contract could be concluded in which the outsourcing arrangement could be formulated as project work, in which the result sought by the user is perfectly defined, for legal commentators outsourcing has more in common, in principle, with the concept of a services agreement. This is the case above all in large projects where it is difficult at the pre-contract stage to define the actual needs of the customer, specify the conditions on which the project must be delivered, or give an exact estimate of the total cost of the project and in which quality and efficiency in the work performed has priority over the cost of the work.

---

[3] Madrid Provincial Appellate Court judgment dated 7 June 2004.

53.4.1.3 Services and outsourcing agreements as adhesion agreements

There is also a judgment[4] that expressly states that the outsourcing contract could also be an adhesion contract, in which case it would be subject to the provisions in Law 7/1998 of 13 April 1998 on Standard Business Terms (Ley de Condiciones Generales de la Contratación) that refer to contracts between business owners. The main purpose of these provisions is to ensure that both parties have an adequate opportunity, before entering into the contract, to acknowledge and accept the contents of the standard business terms.

53.4.2 Contractual obligations

53.4.2.1 Basic obligation

The parties to a services or outsourcing contract are required to meet the agreed terms (Article 1,091 of the Civil Code). In particular, the supplier is required to perform its agreed obligations in accordance with the agreed terms and conditions (Article 1,098 of the Civil Code).

In addition, Article 1,258 of the Civil Code incorporates the duty to comply with any obligations that, in accordance with the type of contract, are implied by law, including implied obligations that result from usage and custom and from the obligation to act in good faith.

53.4.2.2 Practical hints

In the above circumstances, in view of the complexity of some services and outsourcing projects, when drafting the contract the customer is advised to:

(a) State clearly and categorically the obligations that the supplier is required to perform, stating in as much detail as possible the important features that define the obligation, including a description of the services, service levels and methods for measuring them, terms, duties of the supplier to co-operate with the customer, and any other significant obligations. What is advisable is to identify as far as possible the circumstances that would determine whether the supplier is complying with or breaching its obligations.

(b) Provide information in the contract that could help to identify the standard of care required of the supplier, including by referring to the standards of the industry in which it operates, the professional qualification of the supplier, the type of services to be provided, the specific risks associated with the customer's business activities, or other similar standards.

---

[4] Navarra Provincial Appellate Court judgment dated 1 October 2003.

(c) Determine what level of breach of the agreed obligations is considered sufficiently serious to entitle the customer to terminate the contract. Contractual mechanisms can be established to provide a solution to minor breaches (e.g. penalties for breach of certain level of service parameters).

53.4.3 Force majeure events

53.4.3.1 Statutory force majeure provisions

Under Spanish law, the supplier will not be required to provide compensation where the breach of its obligations was caused by events that could not be foreseen or, if they could be foreseen, were unavoidable (force majeure), unless the law or the contract provides that it must be liable in such cases (Article 1,105 of the Civil Code).

53.4.3.2 Contractual force majeure provisions

It is common practice for the parties to include express clauses in services and outsourcing contracts releasing the supplier from liability in force majeure events. Force majeure events are sometimes defined in the contract in general terms (e.g. events that could not be foreseen or, if they could be foreseen, were unavoidable, in line with Article 1,105 of the Civil Code) and sometimes they are defined in a list of specific events.

It must be borne in mind that the Spanish courts interpret force majeure clauses restrictively. In particular, the supplier cannot be released from liability for a breach if it has clearly acted with negligence, either in its supervision (culpa in vigilando), or in its choice of agents (culpa in eligendo).

53.4.3.3 Practical hints

In any event, in drafting the services or outsourcing contract, the customer is advised to:

(a) Ensure that the supplier is not entitled to rely upon the force majeure regime (Article 1,105 of the Civil Code) in the case of certain unforeseeable or unavoidable events that the parties have expressly agreed to cover (e.g. in respect of obligations relating to business continuity and contingency plans in the case of natural disasters).

(b) Expressly provide certain rules on the conduct of the parties in the case of force majeure events that prevent the supplier from providing the services, to ensure, as far as possible:

    (i) basic continuity of the services (e.g. a right for the customer to obtain the services from other suppliers on a transitional basis, with the supplier having a duty to co-operate with these suppliers);

(ii)   rapid resumption of the services (e.g. an obligation on the supplier to act with the greatest standard of care to recover them);

(iii)   a definitive change of supplier if the force majeure event continues beyond a certain length of time (e.g. a right for the customer or of any of the parties to request termination of the contract); and

(iv)   notification of the events so that the parties, in good faith, can do everything possible to fulfil their obligations.

53.4.4   Remedies for breach—performance or termination

In the event of a breach of contract by the supplier, Spanish law gives the customer the right to choose between two alternatives (Article 1,124 of the Civil Code):

(a)   Require performance of the obligation. To give effect to this right, the judge may order the supplier to carry out its obligation at its own cost (Article 1,098 of the Civil Code).
(b)   Require termination of the agreement.

53.4.5   Remedies for breach—damages

53.4.5.1   Liability for damages

In both of the cases mentioned in section 53.4.4 above, the customer will be entitled to claim compensation from the supplier for damage caused by the breach (Article 1,124 of the Civil Code) but only if there has been wilful misconduct or negligence by the supplier (Article 1,101 of the Civil Code). The supplier will not be required to pay compensation if it can be proved that the breach was due to an event of force majeure. In determining whether there has been negligence, the standard of care will be that required according to the nature of the obligation and, if no measure of the standard of care is mentioned, the standard of care of a good *pater familias* will be required (Article 1,104 of the Civil Code).

53.4.5.2   Quantum of damages

Spanish law establishes that the obligation to provide compensation is to cover not only the value of the loss that has taken place or *"damnum emergens"* but also the gains that the customer failed to make or "loss of profit" (Article 1,106 of the Civil Code). Compensable damage and losses are those that were foreseeable, or could have been foreseen, when the obligation was created and are a necessary result of the breach of that obligation.

However, where the breach is due to wilful misconduct, the debtor must be liable for all of the damage and losses that are known to result from a breach of the obligation (Article 1,107 of the Civil Code).

53.4.5.3   Limitations on liability

Under the principle of freedom of contract (Article 1,255 of the Civil Code) it is lawful for business owners[5] who are parties to a services oroutsourcing contract to agree in the contract to exclusions from, and limitations of, liability, subject to the conditions described below:

(a)   It is expressly prohibited to exempt from liability, or limit the liability of, any party who breaches an obligation as a result of wilful misconduct. This is a compulsory rule, and therefore a contractual clause of this type would be considered null and void as a matter of law (Article 1,102 of the Civil Code).
(b)   Nor is it allowed for the contract to contain an exclusion from, or limitation of, liability for breach if there is serious or very serious negligence, although in these cases the liability could be moderated by the courts (Article 1,103 of the Civil Code).

These legal limits on the ability of the parties to agree on exclusions from, or limitations of, liability will apply regardless of the contractual mechanisms that are agreed upon to de-limit liability (e.g. maximum amount of compensation, exclusion of certain types or compensable items).

53.5   Data protection

53.5.1   Relevant statutory provisions

In Spain, the right to personal data protection is included in the Constitution as a basic right (Article 18.4). The right to personal data protection as a fundamental right per se, distinct from the right to privacy regulated under Article 18.1 of the Constitution, was expressly recognised by the Constitutional Court under Judgment 292/2000 of 30 November 2000.

This right is also implemented in the law in Organic Law 15/1999, of 13 December 1999, on the protection of personal data (LOPD), which implemented in Spain the provisions of Directive 95/46/EC of the European

---

[5]   Where one of the parties is a consumer, the specific rules on the protection of consumers and users must be taken into account, which allows less room for freedom of contract to provide the appropriate protection for the weaker party in the contractual relationship.

Parliament and of the Council of 24 October 1995 on the protection of individuals with regard to the processing of personal data and on the free movement of such data. The LOPD provisions were implemented by Royal Decree 1720/2007, of 21 December 2007, approving the LOPD Regulations ("Royal Decree 1720/2007"), which entered into force on 20 April 2008.

53.5.2   Obligations of the data controller

The basic aim of the LOPD and of Royal Decree 1720/2007 is to secure and protect, as regards personal data, the public freedoms and basic rights of individuals, and in particular their rights to their honour, personal privacy and the privacy of their family. To do this, it sets out a series of obligations that must be performed by the data controllers for data files containing personal data.

The LOPD defines "data file" as "a structured set of personal data, regardless of the form or way in which it is created, stored, organised and accessed".

These obligations are described below.

53.5.3   Registration with the AEPD

The data controller has a formal duty to register the data files with the Registrar of the Spanish Data Protection Agency (AEPD) before they are created.

53.5.4   Quality of data and the duty of secrecy

The data controller is responsible for ensuring the quality of the data. This requirement is linked to the principle of proportion of the data, and requires data kept to be appropriate, relevant and not excessive in relation to the scope of and purposes for their collection. Moreover, the law obliges a data controller to ensure that personal data is accurate and up to date, so it gives a true reflection of the current situation of the data subject.

53.5.5   Duty to provide information

One of the main principles of the LOPD and its implementing legislation is that the data subject must be informed before his personal data is obtained. The minimum of information that must be conveyed to the interested party includes the name and address of the data controller, the purpose behind collecting the data and the interested party's option to exercise rights of access, rectification, cancellation and objection to the data processing.

53.5.6   *Consent for the processing and disclosure of data*

As a general rule, the inclusion of personal data in a data file will involve processing personal data, which will generally require the consent of the data subject. The LOPD provides for both express and implicit consent according to the type of data to be processed, and states that in all cases consent must be freely given, specific, informed, and unequivocal.

53.5.7   *International data transfers*

Under the LOPD, international data transfers made from Spain will generally require prior authorisation from the AEPD.

Article 34 of the LOPD provides certain exceptions to the principle of prior authorisation, notably the prior consent of the data subject, or where the transfer is to a Member State of the European Union, the European Economic Area, or a state which the European Commission has declared guarantees an appropriate level of protection (currently, Switzerland, Canada, Argentina, Guernsey, Isle of Man, Jersey, and the US but only in relation to those US companies that adhere to the Safe Harbour Principles developed by the Department of Commerce in co-ordination with the European Commission[6]).

The rules on authorisation or prior consent have a direct effect and are critical in relation to services or outsourcing contracts where the provision of services involves the supplier processing personal data and where the service is provided outside the EU, the EEA or countries that are held to have appropriate levels of protection.

53.5.8   *Allowing citizens to exercise their rights*

As a general rule, the data controller must comply with its duty to allow individuals to exercise their rights of access, rectification, cancellation and objection. If those rights are denied, the data subject can apply for the protection of the AEPD.

---

[6]   To obtain more information on the "Safe Harbour" framework, see *http://export.gov/safeharbor/eu/ eg_main_018476.asp* [Accessed 28 September 2012].

53.5.9 Implementation of security measures

Article 9 of the LOPD applies the principle of security to personal data and imposes on the data controller the obligation to adopt the technical and organisational measures needed to ensure the security of the personal data and to prevent data from being altered, lost, processed or accessed without authorisation. The obligation extends to cover both automated and hard-copy data files. These security measures were implemented by Royal Decree 1720/2007, which allocated security levels: basic, medium and high, according to the type and sensitivity of the data. The appropriate security level must be described in the relevant security document.

53.5.10 Inspection and enforcement activities of the AEPD

The AEPD is a public legal entity, with its own legal personality and full authority to act vis-à-vis citizens, companies, other private entities and public authorities. The main functions of the AEPD include:

(a) overseeing compliance with data protection legislation and controlling its application, particularly in relation to the rights of information, access, rectification, objection and cancellation regarding personal data;
(b) dealing with the claims and petitions of citizens;
(c) promoting public information initiatives on the LOPD and implementing legislation;
(d) issuing instructions and recommendations for bringing processing into line with the LOPD;
(e) securing the rights and protection of subscribers and users in the area of electronic communications, including the delivery of unsolicited commercial communications by email or equivalent electronic communications media; and
(f) exercising enforcement power.

In relation to the last activity on this list, the LOPD establishes penalties of up to €600,000 for each infringement relating to a data subject whose rights to personal data protection have been infringed. To date, the AEPD has been particularly active in its inspection and enforcement functions. It publishes the relevant decisions of its director on its website.

53.5.11 *Implications of the data protection legislation in relation to services and outsourcing contracts*

Under article 12 LOPD, any services that imply access by the supplier to personal data included in the data files controlled by the customer must be set forth in a contract that is required, inter alia, to provide for the following:

(a) Processing: obligations on the data processor (i.e. the supplier), to process data only according to the instructions it receives from the data controller (the customer) and not apply or use them for any purpose other than that stated in that contract.

(b) Disclosure: prohibition on the data processor (i.e. the supplier) from disclosing the data, not even for storage, to other persons.

(c) Security measures: description of the security measures that the data processor (i.e. the supplier) is required to implement, according to the type of processing and the type of personal data to which it will have access during the provision of the services.

(d) Destruction or return: it must state that, once the contractual obligation has been performed, the personal data (in addition to any media or documents containing any of the processed personal data) must be destroyed or returned to the data processor (i.e. the customer) or to any controller that the processor may have appointed. Royal Decree 1720/2007 clarifies this principle and establishes that:

  (i) the data will not have to be destroyed where there is a legal provision requiring it to be stored, in which case it must be returned and the controller must ensure that it is stored; and

  (ii) the data processor shall store the data, duly blocked, whilst any liability may arise from its relationship with the data controller.

(e) International data transfers: in the case of international data transfers, it is necessary:

  (i) to obtain the authorisation of the Director of the AEPD or the consent of the data subjects to the data transfer (these requirements are not necessary where the European Commission has held that the destination country for the international data transfer affords an appropriate level of protection); and

  (ii) that the data processor can comply at all times with the security measures that are applicable to the processed data.

These rules are particularly important in cases of offshore outsourcing, especially where the supplier is based and is going to provide its services from places that have not been acknowledged by the European Commission to be countries with appropriate levels of data protection. This means that the frequent cases where services are provided from India or from the US (in this latter case, except for the companies that have adhered to the special Safe Harbour system for the protection of data), among other locations, are required to comply with the *ad casum* authorisation regime.

With respect to the foregoing, mention should be made of the legal difficulties currently arising for companies when it comes to contracting outsourcing services provided as cloud-based services. The very nature of providing cloud-based services can at times (depending on how the cloud service is configured) make it hard to comply with the data protection legislation in relation to international transfers of data, the regime of which was summarised in section 53.5.7 above.

Such problems, currently the subject of a far-ranging review by the Article 29 Data Protection Working Party, took up a large part of the IV Annual Open Session hosted by the Spanish Data Protection Agency (AEPD) in Madrid on January 27, 2012.[7] Pending specification of a new European legislative data protection framework, with the approval in the medium-term of more clear-cut regulations in a bid to set in place clearer, more standardised and straightforward regulations in relation to international data transfers, the AEPD has put forward certain solutions aimed at overcoming some of the legal problems raised by cloud-based services, without neglecting the protection of data subjects' rights, as well as situations in which services are contracted out to a data processor. In this last case, the AEPD has provided for a new standard contract whereby it is the data processor who applies for the mandatory clearance in order to carry out international data transfers in favor of the sub-processor, for the benefit of its clients (data controllers) and without such controllers having any obligation to process such clearance with the Director of the AEPD.

53.6 Insolvency issues

In Spain, insolvency is regulated by the Insolvency Law ("Ley 22/2003, de 9 de julio, Concursal"), in force since 1 September 2004, which brought about a sweeping change to the legislation previously in force.

As a general rule, an insolvency order does not in itself interrupt the debtor's activity (controlled or replaced by insolvency managers), although it may have an effect on the debtor's power over his assets.

The aim of this section is to outline:

(a)   the general principles of Spanish insolvency law regarding the effects of the insolvency order in relation to creditors; and

(b)   the steps available under Spanish law, to protect the position of a creditor in the event of insolvency.

---

[7]   The documents and conclusions of the IV Annual AEPD Open Session can be accessed at *http:// www.agpd.es* [Accessed 28 September 2012]

53.6.1   General principles

The general principles in the Spanish insolvency law covering the effects of an insolvency order on any creditors are the following:

(a)   there is a ban on individual action by creditors against the debtor's property or enforcement of security interests (i.e. a mortgage);
(b)   there is a ban or prohibition on offsetting once the insolvency order has been made;
(c)   the accrual of interest stops;
(d)   contractual clauses that establish termination of a contract as the consequence of an insolvency order become null and void;
(e)   contracts do not mature automatically or early upon the insolvency order;
(f)   contracts with reciprocal obligations remain in effect, without prejudice to the right to terminate them in certain cases, either in the interests of the insolvency proceeding or due to a breach of the acquired obligations;
(g)   hire purchase contracts may be reinstated;
(h)   recovery action may be brought, that is, action may be brought to render invalid any acts that may be detrimental to the assets available to creditors carried out by the debtor within a two-year period prior to the insolvency order;
(i)   liability arises for the directors of a company subject to an insolvency order; and
(j)   Spanish insolvency law establishes a classification of the insolvency claims against the assets available to creditors.

53.6.2   Steps to be taken by creditors

Once a creditor becomes aware of an insolvency order on any of its debtors (assuming that this creditor had not initiated the insolvency proceeding), the first step it must take is to assert its rights to appear in the insolvency proceeding, and notify the insolvency managers of its claim.[8]

A claim regarding obligations which fell due before or after the insolvency order, in principle, will be recognised as an ordinary claim and will be paid according to the terms and conditions established in the creditors' agreement. If the insolvency order leads to liquidation, these claims will be paid after claims against assets available to creditors and preferred claims. If a claim is secured (with a mortgage or pledge, for example) it will be

---

[8]   The insolvency order must be published either in the Spanish Official Gazette (BOE) or in a widely read newspaper in the place where the debtor's domicile is located. Before this publication, the Commercial Courts inform of insolvency proceedings (if initiated) regarding debtors whose domicile is located in the area where the court has jurisdiction.

considered a special preferred claim and will be paid against the assigned assets, with preference over the debtor's other creditors.

If a creditor wishes to continue working with the debtor (or providing additional financing during the insolvency proceeding), the expenses arising for the debtor after the insolvency order from its normal business or from obligations acquired during the insolvency proceeding (by the insolvency managers or by the debtor with the approval of the managers) will be treated as claims against assets available to creditors and must be paid when they fall due.

53.6.3   Protecting the creditor

On the basis of the comments outlined above, the ways to protect the position of a creditor, prior to the insolvency order, and reduce risks in the event of a possible insolvency order affecting its debtors are described below.

Whenever a creditor suspects that any of its customers may be experiencing financial hardship which may lead to an insolvency order, the parties, by mutual consent, may renegotiate the terms of payment established in the contract in order to eliminate deferred payment or shorten the payment period.

Another solution to protect any creditor's position in the event of the risk of insolvency of its customers would be to request that the transaction be guaranteed by a third party (company shareholder, bank etc.) or by the debtor (with a mortgage or pledge of his assets). In all of these cases, in the following two years, the insolvency managers or other creditors can bring action to render these guarantees invalid if they are detrimental to the other creditors (recovery or claw-back actions).

In the case of refinancing, if the debtor is later held to be insolvent, the provider of the financing will be a creditor for the amount of the principal and interest, and any sums that accrued before the insolvency order will qualify as a subordinated claim. If financing is provided by a parent company, this claim will be classified as a subordinated claim. Under Spanish law, loan acceleration is valid if there is a default in payment by the debtor. However, the insolvency managers for the company may request the re-establishment of loans, credit facilities and other financing agreements, if any of those agreements were "accelerated and fell due" in the three months prior to the insolvency order, provided that the creditor did not initiate enforcement of its claim prior to the insolvency order, subject to certain conditions.

If a debtor breaches the contract, and the creditor has a commercial interest in the assets forming the subject matter of the contract, it is important to file an action to request enforcement of the contract or termination of the contract due to a breach, plus damages if appropriate.[9] After the insolvency order, only the creditor bound to the insolvent debtor by a contract with reciprocal obligations is able to request termination of the contract on the grounds of a breach of the contract carried out by the debtor after the insolvency order.

53.7 Financial services regulation

Spanish regulations implementing MiFID and the Capital Requirements Directive principles provide specific rules for outsourcing by certain financial firms. These regulations are in addition to the general rules described above relating to outsourcing agreements (e.g. employment law and data protection regulations).

53.7.1 *Outsourcing of the activities of credit institutions*

Outsourcing by banks and other credit institutions is regulated by Article 71 of Royal Decree 216/2008, dated 15 February 2008 ("RD 216/2008"), which was implemented in a Circular of the Bank of Spain (Circular number 3/2008), dated 22 May 2008, which covered the determination and control of own funds/equity ("Circular 3/2008"). Article 72 of RD 216/2008 states that any credit institution performing investment services will also be subject to article 70.ter.2.d of Law 24/1988 (Securities Market Law, Ley del Mercado de Valores), in accordance with the provisions of RD 216/2008.

These regulations have implemented most of the Joint Forum's high-level principles for outsourcing in financial entities (affecting the outsourcing of critical and non-critical functions), as well as the MiFID rules for the outsourcing of critical operational functions, in terms similar to those described in Chapters 38 to 42 of this Guide. Nevertheless, some of these principles and rules have been implemented by the Spanish regulations with a number of particular features:

(a) There are certain rules on the scope of the services that can be outsourced (the outsourcing arrangement must not leave the entity "devoid of content" in its general activity; and the outsourced services or functions cannot involve the delegation of any of the functions which are reserved to credit institutions, except for the delegation of certain tasks to an agent for credit institutions).

(b) The written contract for the formalisation of the delegation agreement

---

9   In the case of contracts in which a creditor makes instalment sales of moveable property with a retention of title clause executed pursuant to Law 28/1998 of 13 July 1998 on instalment sales of moveable property, if those assets are subject to or assigned to a business activity it would be advisable, in the event of default in payment of two instalments or the last instalment, to bring action immediately in order to recover the asset.

must contain certain provisions, among others, those intended to preserve the supervisory powers of the Bank of Spain and to give the Bank of Spain the right to confirm the suitability of all systems, tools and applications used to perform the outsourced services or functions.

(c) Due diligence duties of the credit institution when selecting the supplier and negotiating the agreement expressly refer to assessing the quality, experience and stability of the potential suppliers, the degree of dependence they may cause, and the level of control they may have over the agreement (the credit institution should have a right to terminate the agreement when considered appropriate, at a reasonable cost).

(d) As regards business continuity, credit institutions are required to ensure that the contingency plans they have in place include or make appropriate provision for the outsourced services or functions, in particular those considered critical functions.

(e) Outsourcing of critical functions (*servicios o funciones esenciales*): Spanish rules incorporate a definition of "critical functions"[10] and regulate the specific duties and conditions applicable to the outsourcing of such functions. These specific duties and conditions (which are additional to those generally applicable to the outsourcing of any kind of services) are in line with some of the Joint Forum's high-level principles: duty of the credit institution to establish a comprehensive policy for the management of its outsourcing of functions; retention of responsibility by the senior management of the credit institution; the outsourcing arrangement must not undermine the conditions with which the credit institution must comply in order to remain authorised to operate, alter the relationships and obligations of the credit institution towards its clients, or diminish internal control mechanisms.

Finally, it should be noted that the Bank of Spain retains the power to establish further limitations on the delegation of functions at each credit institution, by reference to the type and critical nature of the functions or their effects on the internal governance of the institution.

53.7.2   Outsourcing of investment firms' functions

The outsourcing of investment firms' critical operational functions is regulated in Article 70.ter.2.d of Law 24/1988 (Securities Market Law, Ley del Mercado de Valores), as implemented by Article 36 and Article 37 of Royal Decree 217/2008 dated 15 February 2008 (RD 217/2008). Article 38 of RD 217/2008 regulates the delegation of portfolio management services to outsourcing suppliers based in any third country.

---

[10] Critical functions are those in which any deficiency or anomaly in their performance may have a material effect on the capacity of the credit institution to fulfil on an ongoing basis the conditions and obligations resulting from its authorisation to operate as such and from its legal regime, or may have an effect on the financial performance or the soundness or continuity of its activity (Article 71.5 RD 216/2008).

In addition, as noted before, Article 72 of RD 216/2008 states that any credit institutions performing investment services will also be subject to Article 70.ter.2.d of Law 24/1988 but in accordance with the provisions of RD 216/2008.

The conditions established by the Spanish regulations for the outsourcing of critical services or functions of investment firms are those necessary to implement and develop key elements and other relevant requirements set forth in the MiFID regulations and in the Joint Forum's high-level principles, in terms similar to those described in Chapters 38 to 42 of this Guide, with a number of particular features that are detailed in Articles 36 and 37 of RD 217/2008.

The term "critical functions" has been defined, in the field of investment services (article 70 ter.2.d of Law 24/1988), consistently with the definition stated for credit institutions (see point (e) of section 53.7.1 above), although a non-exhaustive list of activities that shall not be considered critical functions has been added, namely advisory services outside the company's investment activities (including legal advice, employee training, invoicing services and surveillance and security services for the company's premises and personnel) and the purchase of standardised services (including information services regarding markets and prices).

53.8   Public Procurement Directives

53.8.1   *Regulations based on EU Directives*

Since Spain joined the European Community in 1986, the Public Procurement Directives have been implemented by Spanish public procurement legislation.

The first Spanish legislation to result from the implementation of European Community directives was Law 13/1995, dated 18 May 1995 on public authority contracts, which incorporated into Spanish law the provisions of Directives 92/50/EEC, 93/36/EEC and 93/37/EEC, among others. This legislation marked a turning point in Spanish public procurement provisions.

A new law on public procurement, which implemented Directive 2004/18/EC, has been in force since May 1, 2008: Law 30/2007, dated 30 October 2007, on public sector contracts (LCSP). Recently this rule was repealed by Royal Decree legislative 3/2011, of November 14, which approves the revised text of the Public Sector Contracts Law (TRLCSP). The TRLCSP came into force on 16 December 2011 and its purpose has been to adopt a single text covering all the changes to the LCSP since its adoption.

Spanish law requires compliance with all European Community public procurement principles: equal access to procurement processes, advertising and transparent procedures, non-discrimination and equal treatment for tendering parties. Spain has chosen to apply European law to the greatest extent on many occasions.

53.8.2 Reform of Spanish law

LCSP, and subsequently the TRLCSP, did not merely implement Directive 2004/18/EC, since the opportunity was also taken to reform the law applicable to public procurement contracts. Spanish public procurement legislation is one of the most extensive and complex that exists, especially when compared to the legislation of Spain's closest neighbours.

Broadly speaking, the TRLCS has a very complex systematic structure, it is difficult to read and gives rise to doubts as to its interpretation.

53.8.2.1 Application of the TRLCS

The Spanish regulation on public sector contracts and the above-mentioned principles are applicable to the procurement processes run by what the EC legislation calls "contracting authorities", and applies more widely than merely to those institutions which, according to the law, may be deemed to be public authorities.

53.8.2.2 Relevance for services and outsourcing arrangements

The TRLCS governs public authority contracts for works, public works concessions, management of public services, supplies, services and co-operation between the public and private sectors. Contracts for services, defined by the law as

"having in their subject matter affirmative covenants consisting of the performance of an activity or the achievement of a result other than a work or works project or a supply"

will be subject to the TRLCS. Contracts for the purchase or lease of equipment and communication systems or for the processing of data are not considered as "contracts for services" but "supply contracts" (except for those contracts for procurement of computer programs developed for the client), also subject to the TRLCS although with certain specificities.

The provisions on public authority contracts for services in Spain contain certain specific features that stem from traditional Spanish law rather than the EC Directives.

53.8.2.3   *Effect, performance and termination of contracts*

The TRLCS deals with the effect, performance and termination of the above-mentioned contracts for services. These specific features include:

(a)   a limit on their term to four years, with extensions up to a total term of six years (this limit would not be applied, for example, if the contract for services complements another for a longer term);
(b)   the supplier's liability, to third parties and the public authorities, for the technical quality of the services provided and for the consequences of the errors made in performing the contract; and
(c)   the wide powers of the public authorities when it comes to amending, interpreting and unilaterally terminating the contract.

53.8.2.4   *Exercising public authority*

In relation to contracts for services, it must be taken into account that, under Spanish law, public bodies cannot enter into agreements which imply that the supplier will be exercising the authority inherent to public powers.

53.8.2.5   *Waiver of rights*

As regards exclusions from and limitations to the supplier's liability, under the principles of public procurement and case law, public authorities cannot, by entering into agreements, waive the rights and powers conferred on them by the law, which include claiming liability from the contractors for the poor technical quality of their work or the errors made in performing the contract.

53.9   Utilities Directive

53.9.1   *Implementation of the EU Directive*

Directive 2004/17/EC of the European Parliament and of the Council dated 31 March 2004 co-ordinating the procurement procedures of entities operating in the water, energy, transport and postal services sectors ("Utilities Directive") was implemented in Spanish law in Law 31/2007, dated 30 October on procurement procedures in special sectors. This Law replaces the provisions in Law 48/1998 (with the exception of the provisions relating to the Spanish Public Airports and Aviation Agency), and came into force, generally, on 1 May 2008 (although for postal services the law came into force on 1 January 2009).

53.9.2   Application of the EU Directive

In principle, Law 31/2007 applies to contracting entities that are public law agencies or public companies, and contracting entities which, without being public law agencies or public companies, have special or exclusive rights, provided that they carry out any of the functions listed in Article 7–Article 12. The Law considers "entities with special or exclusive rights" to be those entities which, without being contracting authorities or public companies, carry on, among their functions, any of those envisaged in Article 7–Article 12 of the Law or more than one of those functions and have special or exclusive rights conferred by a competent body of a public authority, of a public law agency or of a business public company.

The Law will therefore apply to certain water, gas, heating, electricity, transport, postal, oil and coal companies.

53.9.3   Minimum threshold

Law 31/2007 will only be applicable to contracts for services, supplies and works that exceed the minimum thresholds for the various types of contract envisaged, in this case, in Article 16. That is:

(a)   €400,000 in contracts for supplies and services; and
(b)   €5,000,000 in works contracts.

53.9.4   Exceptions

Law 31/2007 will be applicable unless any of the exceptions provided in Article 18 of the Law applies, in line with the terms provided in the Utilities Directive. Special attention must be paid to the exceptions in sub-articles 4, 5 and 6 of the same Article 18, which state that the Law will not be applicable to:

(a)   contracts awarded by a contracting entity to an affiliate, meaning a company which, under Article 42 of the Commercial Code, files consolidated financial statements with the contracting entity; and
(b)   contracts awarded by a joint venture, set up exclusively by several contracting entities to carry out the functions envisaged in Article 7–Article 12, to an affiliate of one of the contracting entities.

These last two exceptions will be applied to contracts for services, where at least 80 per cent of the average volume of business that the affiliate has had in the past three years in relation to services comes from the provision of these services to affiliate companies.

Lastly, Article 18.6 states that the Law will not apply to contracts awarded:

(a) by a joint venture, set up exclusively by several contracting entities to carry out the functions envisaged in Article 7–Article 12, to any of those contracting entities; and

(b) by a contracting entity to a joint venture of which it is part, where the joint venture was set up to carry out the activity concerned for at least three years, and that the instrument in which the joint venture is created stipulates that the contracting entities that created it will be part of it at least in the same period.

53.9.5   Effect of application

As regards the principles of procurement, capacity and classification of the business operators, contract techniques and procedures for awarding contracts, Spanish law has substantially the same terms as the Utilities Directive.

53.10   Competition law

The implications of Spanish competition law on services and outsourcing arrangements are similar in most respects to those contained in Chapter 33 of this Guide: merger control, exchanges of information and the enforceability of exclusivity and non-compete provisions. The aim of this section is to address those specific rules in Spanish competition legislation that may affect services and outsourcing deals in the Spanish market.

53.10.1   EU merger control

The contents on "EU merger control" in Chapter 33 of this Guide apply in full to those services and outsourcing deals involving Spanish parties that can be classed as a "concentration" with a "Community dimension".

53.10.2   Spain merger control

Spanish merger control applies to services and outsourcing deals that constitute mergers on the conditions described below.

53.10.2.1 Legal framework

Under Spanish Competition Law 15/2007 dated 3 July 2007 (the "Competition Law"), concentrations above certain thresholds (as described in section 53.10.2.3 below) must be notified to the Spanish competition authorities (Comisión Nacional de la Competencia, or "CNC"). Notification in Spain is mandatory in such cases and the transaction cannot be carried out until it is cleared either expressly or implicitly by the CNC. The CNC has the power to impose fines for failure to notify (including daily penalties until notification is filed), for providing incorrect or misleading information, and/or for any failure to abide by the final decision.

Proceedings are governed by the Competition Law and by Royal Decree 261/2008, dated 22 February 2008 (the "Competition Provisions").

53.10.2.2 Services and outsourcing deals subject to merger control

Services and outsourcing arrangements may constitute a merger which is subject to Spanish merger control where they meet the requirements to qualify as a concentration.

Although there are no decisions from the Spanish authorities relating to IT or business process outsourcing transactions, there are specific cases involving the outsourcing of industrial activities in which the CNC held that the transaction was subject to Spanish merger control.[11]

53.10.2.3 Thresholds

Given that Article 7 of the Competition Law largely borrows the definition of concentration from the EU Merger Regulation, notification is compulsory in Spain where a transaction does not fall within the exclusive jurisdiction of the European Commission under the EU Merger Regulation and at least one of the two following circumstances occurs:

(a)   as a consequence of the concentration, a share equal to or greater than 30 per cent of the relevant product or service market at a national level or in a geographical market defined within that same market, is acquired or increased;the control procedure does not apply to concentrations in which, while fulfilling the terms in this paragraph a), the global turnover in Spain of the acquired company or of the assets acquired in the last fiscal year is not higher than €10 million, provided the parties do not have an individual or joint share equal to or higher than 50 per cent in any of the defined markets, in the national market or in a defined geographic market within that market.

---

[11]   Decision of the Council of the CNC dated 7 February 2008 in case C-0043/08, *Fuertes/Carrefour.*

(b) the combined aggregate turnover in Spain of the undertakings concerned in the last accounting year exceeds the amount of €240 million, providing that at least two of the undertakings concerned achieve an individual turnover in Spain exceeding €60 million.

53.10.2.4 *Proceedings*

53.10.2.4.1 Pre-notification phase

Prior to formal notification, the undertakings concerned may submit a draft of the notice to the CNC in order to clarify either issues of form or substance relating to the concentration.

53.10.2.4.2 Phase one

Following notification, and assuming that the transaction does not raise competition concerns, the concentration may be approved implicitly (i.e. without an express decision) if no objection is received within one month of notification. The Council of the CNC usually clears the transaction with a formal decision, issued within a month of notification, and includes the report from the Investigation Directorate of the CNC on the concentration.

If the Council of the CNC (usually following the recommendation contained in the Investigation Directorate's report) has doubts about the transaction, because it may hinder the maintenance of effective competition in the Spanish market, the Council may request that the parties propose commitments in return for clearing the transaction in phase one. In such a case, the term of phase one will be extended for a further 10 days.

Where there are serious doubts over a transaction, the CNC will decide to initiate phase two.

53.10.2.4.3 Phase two

If the concentration has not been cleared in phase one, the Investigation Directorate of the CNC will draft a statement of objections which will be given to the interested parties so that they can file any pleadings within 10 days. At the request of the notifying parties, a hearing will be held before the Council of the CNC. The Council of the CNC will have two months to adopt the final resolution.

When obstacles for the maintenance of effective competition may result from the concentration, the Council of the CNC may request that the parties propose commitments in return for clearing the transaction. In such a case, the term of phase two will be extended for a further 15 days.

Notice of the final decision will be given simultaneously to the interested parties and to the Minister of Economy and Finance. In cases where a concentration is prohibited or subject to commitments, the Minister of Economy and Finance may decide to refer the concentration to the Spanish government for reasons of general interest within 15 days. In such a case, the final decision on the concentration lies with the Spanish government who will have one month to decide whether to confirm the decision issued by the Council of the CNC or to authorise the concentration with or without conditions.

The parties may appeal decisions issued by the Council of the CNC to the Administrative Chamber of the National Appellate Court. The Spanish government's decision can be contested at the Spanish Supreme Court.

53.10.3 Prohibited anti-competitive agreements

In addition to the prohibition contained in Article 81(1) of the EC Treaty for anti-competitive agreements which may affect trade between EU Member States (see Chapter 33 of this Guide), Spanish Competition Law (Article 1) prohibits agreements that have the object or effect of preventing, restricting or distorting competition and which may affect trade within Spain (the "Prohibition"). Breaches of the Prohibition attract heavy fines (up to 10 per cent of turnover); infringing agreements are unenforceable and the parties to them may be sued for damages. In addition, when the offender is a legal entity, fines of up to €60,000 may be imposed on each of its legal representatives or on the persons on the managing bodies that have participated in the agreement or decision involving a breach of competition law.

53.10.3.1 Exclusivity and non-compete clauses

Exclusivity and non-compete provisions contained in services and outsourcing arrangements may restrict competition and must be considered in light of the Prohibition in article 1 of the Spanish Competition Law and Article 81(1) of the EC Treaty. For these reasons, the general considerations in section 33.3.1 of this Guide will apply.

53.10.3.2 Information exchange

Anti-competitive agreements that may arise from certain outsourcing agreements (where a customer outsources services to a competitor, or in a transfer of outsourced services from a supplier to a competitor) as a result of information exchanged between actual or potential competitors, should be analysed in the light of the general considerations in section 33.3.4.3 of this Guide.

53.11   Other relevant laws and best practice

53.11.1   *Best practice in the Spanish market*

Recently the AEC, an association of the main consultancy firms established in Spain, has published two important documents which attempt to describe best practice in the industry:

(a)   Código de la Actividad de Consultoría para las Administraciones Públicas[12] (Code of Conduct for Consultancy Services Provided to Public Authorities). This code contains the basic rules of conduct for consultants who are members of the AEC in projects for providing services to their customers, including public authorities. The rules are classified under the headings of Professional Conduct, Services Agreement, Mutual Trust, Objectivity and Impartiality, Incompatibility, Quality and Confidentiality.

(b)   White paper of good practices in the consultancy market.[13] The intention behind the paper, submitted in 2008, was to propose practices that could contribute to improving market relationships between customers and suppliers of consultancy services. It is the result of research performed by the AEC and leading companies in the industry, in which large organisations in the public and private sector, that use consultancy services, took part. It contains a catalogue of good practices classified according to each of the phases of a project: presale and needs identification; specifications; selection of suppliers; negotiation and the contract; provision of the service; continuity or close of the project

53.11.2   *Some tax implications of services and outsourcing*

53.11.2.1   *VAT on services*

Spanish law generally requires 18 per cent (21 per cent from 1 September 2012) VAT to be charged on the provision of services. This will in principle be neutral in financial terms, that is, it will not create a tax cost since the company receiving the services can deduct all of the input VAT it has paid with the charge for the services.

---

[12]   This document can be accessed in Spanish at:
http://consultoras.c2csoluciones.com/frontend/aec/LA-MODERNIZACION--DE-LOS-SERVICIOS-PUBLICOS--EN-LAS-ECONOMIAS-AVANZADAS-vn184-vst16 [Accessed September 28, 2012].

[13]   This document can be accessed in Spanish at:
http://consultoras.c2csoluciones.com/frontend/aec/La-AEC-Potencia-El-Esquema-%91ganador-ganador%92-En-Las-Relaciones-Entre-Clientes-Y-Proveedores-Con-La-C-vn7999-vst272 [Accessed September 28, 2012].

However, this neutrality will not be possible for customers (who are required therefore to bear the VAT charged on the services they receive) who perform VAT-exempt activities and therefore cannot deduct all of the input VAT paid (e.g. financial, educational, healthcare or welfare institutions). In these cases, the receipt of services developed by an external supplier may entail a higher tax cost than if the services had been performed internally by the company's own personnel (on which VAT would not be charged).

Services in the financial industry can be VAT exempt if their effect is to provide the essential and specific activities of an exempt financial service. Since 2008, a special regime for groups of companies for VAT purposes has been in force which allows this negative effect to be reduced or eliminated where the supplier belongs to the same group as the customer company.

53.11.2.2 *Potential liability for the customer in respect of certain of the supplier's tax debts*

Article 43.1f of the General Taxation Law 58/2003, dated 17 December 2003, includes a case of secondary liability for individuals or entities that enter into a contract or subcontract to perform projects or services relating to their main business activity. According to these provisions, the customer could be held secondarily liable for tax obligations relating to taxes that the supplier must charge or to tax that must be withheld from workers, professionals or other business owners, in the portion relating to the project or services under the contract or subcontract.

The liability would include VAT chargeable by the supplier, in addition to the corporate income tax, personal income tax or non-resident income tax that the supplier must withhold. However, the customer would have a right to be reimbursed by the supplier on the terms provided in civil law (Article 41.6 of the General Taxation Law).

The liability under Article 43.1f of Law 58/2003 cannot be claimed where the supplier provides a specific certificate issued by the tax authorities evidencing that it is up to date with its tax obligations. This certificate must be issued within 12 months before the payment of each invoice relating to the contract or subcontract. The tax authorities have to issue these certificates within three days of a request by the supplier or sub-contractor, and they must provide copies upon request.

In practice, in services and outsourcing contracts it is advisable:

(a) to include as a contractual obligation for the supplier the duty to evidence to the customer that the supplier is up to date with its payment and compliance with its tax obligations by delivering on a periodic basis valid certificates issued by the Spanish Tax Agency; and

(b) to establish an obligation for the supplier to protect the customer from and against potential claims from the tax authorities in respect of the supplier's debts, to avoid being forced to pay for these items (without prejudice to the right to be reimbursed, which is recognised in the law).

Chapter 54

Italy

Gabriele Capecchi, Partner

Legance

54.1 Outline

Parts 1 to 11 of this book describe the key business issues relevant for outsourcing and other services agreements. They also describe the key legal issues under English law. This chapter describes the specific legal and business issues which affect services and outsourcing arrangements in Italy.

54.2 People issues—ARD

54.2.1 Application of ARD/ICC

The Italian Supreme Court has described outsourcing as an ensemble of

> "various techniques, through which an enterprise terminates the direct management of one or more of its products or services activities, which are not part of its core business"

(decision no. 21287/2007). The court added that outsourcing projects can involve the parties entering into a services contract or the customer transferring a portion of its business to the supplier.

In the second scenario, the customer's employees will be transferred along with the business and the employees' consent is not required. The employees will be protected by the provisions of ARD, which Italy has implemented by means of Article 2112 of the Italian Civil Code (ICC).

The parties involved in the transfer of a business (or part thereof) have contractual freedom to determine which assets, liabilities, receivables and contracts will be transferred. However, a business (or part thereof) must exhibit some "functional autonomy" for the purposes of Italian labour laws (Article 2112, para.5). This measure restricts the parties from creating artificial parts of businesses, with the exclusive purpose of transferring employees without their consent.

54.2.2 Consequences of application of ARD/ICC

In the event of a business transfer, a number of safeguards exist for the benefit of the employees, which are described below.

54.2.2.1 Continuity of employment

Whenever a business transfer takes place, the same conditions of employment that applied to the personnel employed in the transferred business will bind the transferee by operation of law. The employees who are transferred will retain any rights deriving from the employment agreements that are in force when the transfer takes place.

54.2.2.2 Rights of the transferred employees

The transferor and the transferee will be jointly liable for the employees' accrued and existing rights at the date of the transfer. However, subject to certain procedures, the employees may exempt the transferor from the obligations deriving from the employment relationships.

54.2.2.3 Economic and legal treatment

The transferee will be required to apply the economic and legal treatment set forth in the national, territorial and company collective agreements in force at the time of the transfer, until their expiration or unless they are replaced by other collective agreements applicable to the transferee at the same level (i.e. national, territorial or company level).

54.2.2.4 Termination of employment relationships as a consequence of the transfer

The transfer of a business is not per se a valid reason for terminating an employment relationship. However, employees whose employment conditions are materially affected as a result of the transfer may resign stating this cause within three months from the transfer date. In this case the business transfer will be regarded as the cause of resignation and, as a consequence, the resigning employees will be entitled to receive statutory termination payments (i.e. severance payments, compensation in lieu of unused holidays etc.), as well as a payment in lieu of the notice period they would have been entitled to in the case of dismissal.

54.2.2.5   *Liability for salaries and social security payments*

If the transferor and the transferee enter into a services or outsourcing agreement after the completion of the transfer, they will be subject to the general joint liability regime in relation to the payment of salaries and social security payments to the suppliers' employees (see section 54.5 below).

54.3   People Issues - Information and consultation

54.3.1   *Recipients of the notice*

Pursuant to Article 47 of Law 428/90, whenever a business transfer is planned, and the business (or part thereof) to be transferred employs more than 15 employees, the transferor and the transferee will be required to give written notice of the transfer in advance, to:

(a)   the works councils ("Rappresentanze Sindacali Unitarie" or "Rappresentanze Sindacali Aziendali") at the locations concerned; and
(b)   the external unions that entered into the National Collective Agreement that applies to the companies concerned.

In the absence of a works council, the notice will only need to be sent to the external unions.

54.3.2   *Timing of notice*

The notice must be given at least 25 days prior to the earlier of:

(a)   the date on which the contract for the transfer is executed; or
(b)   the date on which the parties reach a binding agreement.

54.3.3   *Contents of notice*

The notice must contain the following information:

(a)   the date, or the proposed date, of the transfer;
(b)   the reasons for the transfer;
(c)   the legal, economic and social impact upon the employees; and
(d)   any proposed measures which will affect the employees (e.g. possible reorganisation of the transferee's activity entailing a reduction in headcount etc.).

54.3.4   Consultation

If a written request is submitted by any of the addressees within seven days of receipt of the notice, the transferor and the transferee will be required to start a joint consultation procedure with them within the following seven days. The consultation will be considered complete 10 days after the start date, regardless of whether or not an agreement is reached.

54.3.5   Result of non-compliance

Should the parties fail to comply with the information and consultation requirements, this will amount to "anti-union conduct" pursuant to Article 28 of Italian Law No. 300/70 and the trade unions may seek a court order against the employer in order to force it to comply with its information and consultation duties.

54.3.6   Application of information and consultation obligations

The information and consultation obligations in Article 47 will also apply when the decision regarding the transfer of business is made by a separate entity exercising control over the transferor or the transferee. Should the controlling entity fail to provide the necessary information, this will not justify the transferor's or the transferee's failure to comply with the obligations.

54.3.7   Application of Directive 2002/14/EC

In this context, it is worth noting that Italy has implemented Directive 2002/14/EC by means of Legislative Decree 25/2007. The Directive creates a harmonised framework for informing and consulting employees across the European Community. The new Decree applies to employers with at least 50 employees.

54.3.8   Consequences of application of Directive 2002/14/EC

The Directive creates various information and consultation obligations, concerning, inter alia, any decisions that are likely to cause material changes to the organisation of a business's work. It is anticipated that the provisions of the Decree will be implemented by collective bargaining agreements, although they appear to be directly applicable and enforceable. In particular, information and consultation obligations will be directly enforceable in relation to the following matters:

(a) possible future developments of the employer's activities and of the general employment conditions within the company, particularly when there is a threat to jobs; and

(b) any company's decision which is likely to lead to substantial changes in the organisation of a business's work.

The scope of the new law is broad enough to catch any corporate transactions (in theory, including significant services and outsourcing agreements), which may cause substantial changes to the organisation of a business's work.

54.3.9   *Remedies for breach of Directive 2002/14/EC*

Any breach of these information and consultation obligations will be punishable by an administrative penalty ranging from €3,000 to €18,000 and it may be considered anti-union conduct, for the reasons indicated above.

54.4   People issues—other employment issues

54.4.1   *Liability for salaries, social security and withholding tax*

It is worth noting that Italy has a joint liability regime that applies to customers, suppliers and sub-contractors in relation to the payment of salaries, social security and withholding tax to the employees of suppliers and sub-contractors:

(a) customers will be jointly liable with the supplier, as well as with any sub-contractor, for a period of two years after termination of the contract for payment of salaries and social security to the employees of the supplier (and of any sub-contractor) accrued during the period when the contract has been performed (Legislative Decree 276/2003);

(b) suppliers will be jointly liable with their sub-contractors for the payment of withholding tax, social security and mandatory charges to the employees of their sub-contractors. The two-year limitation period relevant to customers does not apply (Law Decree 223/2006); and

(c) according to Article 1676 ICC, employees of the suppliers and sub-contractors will be able to claim from the customer (or from the supplier when acting, in turn, as customer) payment of their salaries, to the extent that they are unpaid by their employer, up to an amount not exceeding the price still to be paid, at the time of the claim, by the customer to the supplier.

54.4.2   *Indemnities*

In the light of this regime, customers frequently insert specific indemnification clauses into their services and outsourcing agreements (and suppliers include them in their subcontracts). Under these clauses the supplier/sub-contractor agrees to keep the customer/supplier indemnified against any costs or expenses that it may incur as a consequence of any breach committed by the supplier/sub-contractors of any of the mandatory provisions relating to salaries, social and insurance payments, etc.

54.4.3   *Other co-operation*

The supplier/sub-contractor will also be asked to provide the customer/ supplier with detailed documentation from time to time, attesting to their regular compliance with the statutory obligations or to co-operate with the customer/supplier if there are labour disputes or investigations by the authorities. Although these clauses will not overcome the statutory joint liability regime, they will provide contractual protection for the customer/ supplier.

54.4.4   *Guarantees*

The customer/supplier may also request specific guarantees (e.g. bank or insurance guarantees) from the supplier/sub-contractor that can be enforced in the event of any breach of the supplier/sub-contractor's indemnity obligations.

54.4.5   *Health and safety liability*

If the supplier is expected to provide the services on-site at the customer's location, Decree 81/2008 ("Consolidated Code on protection of safety and health on workplaces") will:

(a)   impose the duty on the customer and the supplier to co-operate in order to mitigate the potential risk of them interfering in each other's operations (e.g. by separating, whenever possible, the working areas of their teams or by informing their employees of any potential risks that may result from the activities of the other team); and

(b) make the customer jointly liable with the supplier and its sub-contractors for all damages (excluding those relating to the specific risks characterising the activities of the supplier and its sub-contractors) suffered by the employees of the supplier or its sub-contractors, which are not indemnified by INAIL (the Italian agency for the insurance of injuries at work).

Therefore, the customer (and supplier) will usually seek indemnities and guarantees from the supplier (and sub-contractor respectively) to cover the above liabilities.

Services and outsourcing agreements which fall under the scope of Decree 81/2008 must:

(a) contain a technical attachment, which explains how the parties will deal with the risk of interference; and
(b) indicate the cost that has been allocated to address any risk of interference.

It is worth mentioning that breaches of safety rules are frequently also subject to criminal sanctions.

Some exemptions are provided for services or outsourcing agreements, which do not determine significant risk of interference (i.e., agreements which cover only intellectual services or mere supply of materials or equipment or which have a duration no longer than two days).

54.5   Pensions issues

An objective of the provisions of Article 2112 of the ICC, is that accrued public pension rights will not be jeopardised by the transfer of business. After the transfer, the employees will continue to belong to the public pension system, and the transferee, as the new employer, will be liable for the payment of the relevant social security charges.

In certain cases, transferred employees will also be able to participate in pension funds (supplementary to the public scheme), in accordance with the applicable national collective agreement, to which both the employer and the employees adhere. In this case, if the same national collective agreement is also applied by the transferee, any transferred employee will continue to take part in the same scheme (and the transferee will pay the relevant charges). However, if there is a change in the national collective agreement applicable to the employees as a consequence of the transfer, the contributions previously accrued will be transferred, in principle, to the new fund, if any, indicated by the different national collective agreement applied by the transferee (but the nature of the transfer may depend on the regulations of the relevant funds).

54.6   Contract law

Complex service agreements (*"appalti"*) will be governed by Article 1655 et seq. ICC, which is described below.

If the supplier is expected to provide its goods or services on an ongoing basis, the agreement will also be covered by the provisions that govern supply agreements (*"contratti di somministrazione"*) (Article 1559 et seq. ICC).

54.6.1   *Service agreement—statutory guarantee*

Article 1667 ICC states that a supplier will be liable for any defect in its work or products and that it will guarantee that its work or products will be free from any defect. This guarantee will not apply if the customer is aware that the supplier's work contains defects and it nevertheless accepts it, or if such defects could be easily detected (provided that the supplier does not intentionally hide them). In order to enforce the guarantee, the customer will have to report any defect within 60 days of the date on which it becomes aware of it. The guarantee will expire two years after the delivery of the work.

54.6.2   *Remedies for breach of statutory guarantee*

The statutory guarantee will entitle a customer to require the supplier to cure any defects at the supplier's expense or to receive a reduction in the price as well as compensation for damages, if the defects are the result of the supplier's gross negligence.

In the event of a material defect that results in the customer being unable to use the work in the manner anticipated, the customer will have the right to terminate the agreement. This means that the supplier will be obliged (in accordance with the general principles of contract law) to reimburse the customer for any fees paid or expenses incurred and to compensate the customer fully for any damages suffered.

54.6.3   *Agreements for specific projects, technical or technological know-how, models or prototypes*

If a supplier provides services relating to projects, technical or technological know-how, models or prototypes *which have been specifically provided by the customer*, then the agreement will also be governed by Law 192/1998. This law has been enacted to protect "captive" suppliers (or customers) against abuse by dominant customers (or suppliers). The main rules introduced by this law, which apply to the narrow range of services or outsourcing agreements which fall within its scope, are:

(a) the agreement must be in writing or it will be invalid;
(b) the technical specifications for the products or services, their prices and the terms of payment must be clearly set forth in the agreement (and, in principle, payment must be made within 60 days, subject to some exceptions);
(c) without the authorisation of the customer, the supplier must not subcontract more than 50 per cent of its work to third parties;
(d) the customer will retain any IP rights relating to the projects and the technical specifications contained in communications with the supplier and any communications must be treated as confidential by the supplier; and
(e) any dispute will be subject to mandatory mediation, and, in the event of the failure of the mediation process, to a mandatory fast-track arbitration procedure, to be completed, in principle, within 60 days.

54.6.4 *Agreements for specific projects, technical or technological know-how, models or prototypes*

In the case of those services and outsourcing agreements which fall within the scope of Law 192/1998, the supplier will be responsible for the proper performance and quality of those services that it has contracted to provide. The supplier will also be responsible for the assembling tasks delegated to the supplier, in accordance with the applicable contractual terms and best industry practice. However, the supplier will not be held liable for defects in the materials or equipment supplied by the customer, as long as the supplier gives prompt notice of these defects. Any provisions in a services or outsourcing agreement which contradict these principles will be null and void.

54.6.5 *Performance impossible*

According to the general principles of contract law, if a supervening event renders performance of the work impossible, the supplier will be released from liability (Article 1463 ICC). If performance is only partially possible, the customer may ask for a proportional reduction in the fee or may terminate the agreement if it no longer has a valuable interest in the performance of the contract.

According to well-established case law, the impossibility to perform must stem from events that were unforeseeable at the time of the agreement's execution and that result in an objective impossibility (not a mere obstacle) to perform.

54.7   Limitations of liability

It is possible to set out limitations to liability in services and outsourcing agreements which do not fall within the scope of Law 192/1998. However, a supplier cannot limit liability for wilful misconduct or gross negligence (Article 1229 ICC).

In relation to those agreements which fall within the scope of Law 192/1998, any limitation of the supplier's liability for the proper functioning or quality of those parts that it is responsible for and for the assembling tasks delegated to the supplier is null and void.

54.8   Data protection

54.8.1   *Implementation of the Directive into Italian law*

Italy was one of the first EU Member States to implement the Personal Data Protection Directive through Law 675/1996. The Italian public body responsible for monitoring the application of this law is the *"Garante per la protezione dei dati personali"*. Law 675/1996 has now been repealed by Legislative Decree 196/2003, the "Data Protection Code" (*"Codice in materia di protezione dei dati personali"*). The latter consolidates the provisions of Law 675/1996 and other pieces of legislation on the subject of data protection.

54.8.2   *Services supplier as data processor*

When looking at services and outsourcing agreements, the supplier may be defined as a "data processor" (*"responsabile del trattamento"*) depending upon the specific content of its duties. A data processor will be responsible, on behalf of the data controller, for data processing.

Appointing a data processor is not mandatory and is not a strict requirement of the Data Protection Directive. However, the *Garante* suggests that if the customer-data controller assigns any tasks relating to data processing to the supplier then it is advisable for the customer to appoint the supplier as a data processor.[1]

From a practical viewpoint, if a services and outsourcing agreement imposes upon the supplier the obligation to share with the customer any element of its data processing activities then that agreement should specify clearly whether or not the supplier is appointed as a data processor.

---

[1]   See the opinion on "Postel" or electronic mail services of 19 December 1998 and the resolution of 27 April 2007 regarding insurance services.

54.8.3 Implications of the supplier being a data processor

If the customer appoints the supplier as a data processor then:

(a) the customer must select the supplier on the basis of its experience, skills and reliability and its thorough compliance with the applicable provisions regarding data processing and security matters;

(b) the customer must check the procedures which the supplier intends to employ to deal with data subjects' information rights, confidentiality and security;[2]

(c) in general, the duties assigned to the data processor must be detailed in writing by the data controller;

(d) the data processor must abide by the instructions given by the data controller and the agreement should specify the specific instructions which the supplier must follow; and

(e) the data controller must supervise the data processor's activity (Article 29, Data Protection Code). In this situation, it is advisable that the agreement specifies clearly how the customer intends to monitor the data processing activities performed by the supplier, as well as the supplier's obligation to co-operate with the monitoring activities by the customer.

The same principles apply if the data controller is a public entity and entrusts external suppliers with the performance of tasks which fall under its remit.[3]

54.8.4 Notifying data subjects

With a few exceptions, the customer must inform any data subject whose data is to be processed under the terms of a services and outsourcing agreement and obtain his consent for the processing and supply the data subjects with details of the external supplier.

54.9 Insolvency issues

Generally, Decree 267/1942 governs Italian insolvency issues.

---

[2] See the resolution of 15 November 2007 concerning the outsourcing of customer care, post-sale, booking and phone banking services and the Guidelines for Data Processing within the Framework of Clinical Drug Trials of 14 July 2008.

[3] See the release of 15 October 2007.

54.9.1 *Right of the non-insolvent party to terminate*

54.9.1.1 *Right to terminate under contract*

In contrast to the law in jurisdictions which are more creditor-oriented than Italy, in the case of insolvency, pursuant to Article 72, para.6 of Decree 267/1942, termination rights exercisable by one party in the event of another party's insolvency will be rendered null and void. This means that, in case of the insolvency of one party, the non-insolvent party may terminate the agreement only if it is allowed to do so by the provisions of Decree 267/1942, notwithstanding any provision of the contract to the contrary.

54.9.1.2 *Right to terminate under law*

If the agreement can be classified as a "service agreement" and the insolvent party is the supplier, the customer will be able to terminate the agreement, if it can prove that it entered into the agreement strictly in reliance on the supplier's personal qualities (Article 81, para.2).

54.9.2 *Right of liquidator to disclaim*

As a rule, if one of the parties is insolvent, the liquidator appointed to liquidate the assets of that party, may decide, under certain circumstances, whether to keep the existing agreement in force or to disclaim it. Specific rules will apply, depending on the type of agreement (e.g. sale, lease, loan etc.). As noted above, if the agreement is classified as a "service agreements" ("*appalti*") under para.41.6, where they also cover the ongoing provision of services or supply of products, the provisions that apply to "supply agreements" ("*contratti di somministrazione*") will govern them. This means that:

(a) if, upon the insolvency of one of the parties, the agreement has not yet been performed, wholly or partly, by both parties, the liquidator may, with the approval of the creditors' committee, decide to keep it in force or to disclaim it (Article 72, para.1);

(b) if the agreement can be classified as a "service agreement", this option must be exercised within 60 days from the declaration of insolvency and if the liquidator decides to keep the agreement in force, adequate guarantees must be provided (Article 81, para.1); and

(c) if the agreement can be classified as a "supply agreement" and the liquidator decides to keep it in force, the liquidator must pay for the delivery of services that have already been performed (Article 74).

54.10 Financial services regulation

54.10.1 *Implementation of MiFID*

Italy has implemented the provisions of MiFID by means of Legislative Decree 164/2007, which contained a number of amendments to the Consolidated Financial Act (Legislative Decree 58/1998).

Most of the fundamental principles introduced by MiFID in relation to outsourcing agreements regarding the financial sector were already contained in existing Italian legislation, especially those which referred to the specific regulations issued by Consob (the public authority responsible for regulating and supervising the securities market) and the Bank of Italy.

However, in accordance with the provisions in MiFID, Legislative Decree 164/2007 required Consob and the Bank of Italy to implement joint regulation governing the procedures that customers who are financial intermediaries should follow upon outsourcing important or essential operational functions, among other matters.

This joint regulation was issued in October 2007 (Bank of Italy's and Consob's Joint Regulation under Article 6, para.2-bis of the Consolidated Financial Act, 29 October 2007).

54.10.2 *Definition of important or essential*

According to the regulation, a function is considered important or essential if failure to perform it:

(a) may seriously prejudice the customer's ability to fulfil the conditions and obligations necessary for authorisation to carry out its activity, as well as any other obligations concerning investment services; or
(b) may seriously prejudice the financial results, the soundness or the business continuity of the customer.

54.10.3 *Responsibilities of the customer*

The customer will remain fully responsible for the activities it outsources to the supplier. In particular, the customer must ensure that:

(a) the outsourcing does not imply the assignment of corporate responsibilities;
(b) relationships with, and duties towards clients will not be prejudiced; and

(c)   none of the conditions under which the customer received the necessary authorisation to carry out its activity will be changed or cancelled.

54.10.4   *Obligations of customers*

The customer must evaluate diligently and execute any outsourcing
agreement. In particular, it must ensure that:

(a)   the supplier has the professional skills, capacity and any necessary
authorisation to perform its services diligently and professionally;
(b)   the supplier performs the services efficiently. To ensure this, the
customer must follow adequate evaluation criteria;
(c)   the supplier monitors the performance of the services and the relevant
risks;
(d)   appropriate measures are adopted to address the risk of failure by the
supplier;
(e)   the customer has efficient internal systems to monitor the activities assigned to the supplier as well as to address the relevant risks;
(f)   the supplier informs the customer of any situation that might prejudice
its ability to duly perform the services;
(g)   the customer is able to terminate the outsourcing agreement, if necessary, without prejudicing the business continuity and the quality of the
services;
(h)   the supplier co-operates with the relevant authorities;
(i)   the customer, its auditors and the relevant authorities have access to
any information concerning the outsourced services, as well as to the
premises where the services are performed by the supplier;
(j)   the supplier guarantees confidentiality in the interests of the customer
and of its clients; and
(k)   the customer and the supplier implement a disaster recovery plan.

The outsourcing agreement must clearly define and specify the rights and
obligations listed above.

54.10.5   *Outsourcing outside the EU of retail asset*
management services

If the customer is outsourcing retail asset management services and the supplier is located within the territory of a non-EU country, the customer must
also ensure that:

(a)   the supplier is authorised to perform retail asset management services
in its own country and is subject to prudent supervision; and
(b)   a co-operation agreement is in force between the Italian authorities and
the authorities of the country where the supplier is based.

If these conditions are not met, the customer must inform the relevant Italian authorities and may only enter into the outsourcing agreement if the authorities do not raise any objection within 60 days of receiving notice.

54.11   Public Procurement and Utilities Directives

54.11.1   *Implementation of the Directives*

Legislative Decree 163/2006 (the "Public Procurement Code") governs public procurement and utilities.

In fact, the Public Procurement Code regulates contracts for public works, public supply contracts, public service contracts, and project financing for public works and also implements European Directives 2004/18/EC and 2004/17/EC which apply to the award of such contracts to entities operating in the water, energy, transport and postal service sectors.

The Public Procurement Code does not merely restate the Directives; it sets out all procedures governing award procedures regardless of their threshold.

Given that the provisions of the Directives are substantially in line with those of the Government Procurement Agreement (GPA), the Public Procurement Code ensures that the GPA will be complied with in Italy.

54.11.2   *Application of the Public Procurement Code to concession agreements*

The Public Procurement Code also applies to concession contracts awarded in relation to public works but not to service concessions (concessions contracts are similar to service agreements, the difference being that the supplier does not receive cash as valuable consideration, but is granted the right to manage the infrastructure for a period of time). However, the Public Procurement Code also applies the general principles of transparency, non-discrimination, equal treatment and proportionality to concession contracts.

54.11.3   *Project financing for public works*

In October 2008, the Public Procurement Code was amended and new provisions regarding project financing for public works were introduced. The previous provisions and regulations had been criticised for their complexity, which deterred many operators from entering this sector of the market.

The October 2008 reforms provided for two alternative procedures (a third one may be triggered if the awarding entity fails to tender for public works that are eligible for private financing and that have been included in the relevant annual list): a single-phase and a double-phase procedure.

The purpose of the single-phase procedure is to concentrate, in one sequence, the different phases which the contractor selection procedure consisted of under the previous regime.

The double-phase procedure is divided into two phases:

(a) in the first phase, the awarding administration carries out a competitive procedure, aimed at selecting a preliminary project to be financed. At the end of the procedure, the promoter, who presented the project selected by the awarding administration, is admitted to the next phase; and

(b) in the second phase, the awarding administration calls for a new tender procedure, on the basis of the promoter's approved preliminary project and the associated economic and contractual conditions. The promoter is entitled to exercise a pre-emption right within 48 days of being informed that a more favourable bid than its own has been received. The pre-emption right is conditional upon the promoter's agreement to bring the terms of its bid in line with those of the more favourable bid.

Finally, if a public administration fails to tender for public works that are eligible for private financing and that have been included in the relevant annual list, the prospective contractors, if any, may implement the third procedure (mentioned above), which is aimed at forcing the public entity to carry out an awards procedure.

54.12   Competition law

54.12.1   The antitrust law

The Italian antitrust regime was created by Law 287/1990. This Law introduced a full set of substantive and procedural rules regarding mergers and restrictive practices (i.e. agreements between undertakings and abuse of dominant positions). Law 287/1990 was expressly based on the acquis communautaire and, as a consequence, currently all of the principles (and guidelines) developed at EU level apply at domestic level, subject to EU law prevailing. In particular, only those mergers which do not meet the EU thresholds and which satisfy the conditions set forth in Law 287/90 have to be filed in Italy. Moreover, investigations of agreements between undertakings and abuses of dominant position are carried out in compliance with the provisions of EC Regulation no. 1 of 2003.

54.12.2   The competition authority

The *Autorità Garante della Concorrenza e del Mercato* is the Italian public authority responsible for monitoring the application of antitrust legislation.

54.12.3   Relevant breaches of competition law

With respect to services and outsourcing agreements, it is worth noting that Law 192/1998 (see section 54.6.4 above) introduced a specific type of abuse: pursuant to Article 9, a customer or a supplier is not allowed to abuse the economic dependence of a supplier or a customer, respectively. In this context, economic dependence is synonymous with economic "captivity": the supplier (or the customer) is so intensely dependent on the other party that it is unable to negotiate its contractual rights and obligations at arm's length.

Article 9 contains some examples of abuses: typically, an abuse may be the refusal to provide (or to acquire) services or products, the imposition of discriminatory or excessively severe contractual terms or the arbitrary inter-ruption of commercial relationships.

54.12.4   Implications of breach of competition law

Contractual undertakings which are tainted by abuse are null and void and the aggrieved party may seek interim protective measures from the Court as well as payment of compensation for damage. In the case of abuses which may be prejudicial to fair competition, the *Autorità Garante* may issue "cease-and-desist" orders and apply fines, in compliance with Law 287/1990.

54.13   Summary—key issues

54.13.1   Consultation

Customers and suppliers entering into services or outsourcing agreements which involve the transfer of a business or material changes to the organisa-tion of a business's work where employees affected by the arrangement include those in Italy will need to consider the specific consultation provi-sions described in section 54.4 above.

54.13.2   Indemnities for the salaries and social security payments of the supplier/sub-contractor

Customers entering into services or outsourcing agreements where the supplier is in Italy will need to ensure that they include in their agreements indemnities for any liability they have for the salaries and social security payments of the supplier's employees. Suppliers entering into subcontracts where the sub-contractor is in Italy will need to ensure that they include similar indemnities in their subcontracts.

54.13.3   On-site services

Where the supplier is to provide the customer with services on site at the customer's premises, in Italy, the parties will need to have regard to any health and safety liability they may have under Decree 81/2008 and may want to include suitable indemnities. If the sub-contractor is to provide the supplier with services on site at the supplier's premises in Italy, the parties will want to include similar terms in the subcontract.

54.13.4   Data protection

Under Italian law, the customer must decide whether or not to appoint the supplier as a data processor and the agreement must specify clearly whether or not the supplier is appointed as a data processor and set out other arrangements relating to how data protection issues will be dealt with.

54.13.5   Insolvency

Under Italian law, termination rights exercisable by one party in the event of another party's insolvency will be rendered null and void.

54.13.6   Public Procurement and Utilities Directives

The Public Procurement Code extends the Public Procurement and Utilities Directives so that they govern all award procedures regardless of their threshold.

Chapter 55

Sweden

Jörgen Axelsson, Partner

Setterwalls

55.1   Outline

This chapter describes the specific legal issues that will be relevant if the services, partnering or outsourcing agreement covers Sweden.

55.2   People issues

55.2.1   *Acquired Rights Directive*

First, the general point of view is that the Acquired Rights Directive (ARD) is applicable to outsourcing in Sweden. The Swedish regulations concerning the said Directive are generally applicable to both private and public businesses (and the Swedish regulations therefore cover a slightly wider range than the original Directive).

The ARD has been implemented in Sweden mainly through four paragraphs, two in the Employment Protection Act 1982 and two in the Co-Determination Act 1976. The regulations can be considered to contain three essential rules.

55.2.1.1   *Transfer of employment relationship*

Employment relationships will be transferred from the previous supplier to the new supplier as an effect of the outsourcing (see s.6b of the Employment Protection Act).

55.2.1.2   Not a just reason to terminate employment relationship

Second, the transfer is not considered a just reason to terminate an employment relationship (see s.7 of the Employment Protection Act). In Sweden, the employer has to show "just cause" for the termination of an employment relationship. Redundancy or misconduct/personal reasons may amount to just cause. A transfer of business is not just cause for dismissal by either the former supplier or the new supplier. There is essentially, therefore, a prohibition on dismissal of personnel from the transferred business.

55.2.1.3   Application of collective bargaining terms of conditions

Third, the new supplier is, during a transitional period of 12 months, required to apply the terms and conditions stated in any collective bargaining agreement that the transferred employees had agreed with the former employer (see s.28 of the Co-Determination Act). Further, the Directive has been implemented such that the acquirer is required not only to take over the employment of transferred employees and apply the terms in a collective bargaining agreement, but also to observe existing, accrued vacation benefits and flexi time etc.

55.2.2   Other employment issues

55.2.2.1   Collective bargaining agreements

Collective bargaining agreements, the terms and conditions of which a new supplier/employer is required to observe, are very common in Sweden. More or less all large Swedish companies are bound by collective bargaining agreements, either directly in relation to trade unions or by membership in the national Employers' Association. Collective bargaining agreements apply for all employees, except top managers who are not covered by the Employment Protection Act 1982.

Swedish collective bargaining agreements include terms and conditions regarding working hours, leave, overtime compensation, vacation, salary, notice period and additional benefits such as pension plans and certain insurances.

55.2.2.2   Duty to negotiate

In addition to regulating applicable terms of employment, entering into a collective bargaining agreement also means that an employer is required to co-operate and negotiate with trade unions on a regular basis in accordance with the Co-Determination Act 1976 (that mainly applies in relation to employers that are bound by such agreements).

The requirement to negotiate can be a significant issue in relation to outsourcing. The Co-Determination Act not only states that the employer is required to inform and negotiate with the union on a regular basis, but also that the employer has a primary obligation to negotiate in certain circumstances. For instance, before the employer makes a decision on the transfer of the business (or part of the business) the employer has to initiate negotiation with applicable trade union(s). If the employer is bound by a collective bargaining agreement, the employer has to initiate negotiation with the union party to the collective bargaining agreement. Where the employer is not bound by any collective bargaining agreements, the employer is still required to initiate negotiation before a decision to transfer a business is made. In that case, the employer has to initiate negotiation with every union of which any of the employees is a member. An employer that does not initiate negotiation risks liability to pay damages to the applicable unions.

55.3   Pensions issues

Collective bargaining agreements often contain terms and conditions regarding pension benefits. The liability for pension insurances agreed in collective bargaining agreements is transferred from the previous employer to the new employer. However, in relation to pensions there is an exception to the obligation of the new supplier/employer to observe the terms and conditions of collective bargaining agreements. Pension benefits set forth in the individual employment agreement are not automatically transferred to the new employer. However, the employer and the employee are not prohibited from reaching an express agreement to transfer such benefits.

55.4   Contract law

55.4.1   *General principles*

According to general contract law in Sweden, businesses on equal terms are free to enter into contracts and freely decide terms and conditions. A contract term may be modified under the Swedish Contracts Act should it be found to be unreasonable or to have arisen from a questionable situation. Aside from those exceptions, the main rule is that terms and conditions shall be upheld and respected by the parties in order to avoid breach of contract.

55.4.2   *Force majeure*

Should a party be found to be in breach of contract, the usual consequence is "liability payment". Liability can be avoided despite a breach of contract in some cases. For example, it is common to free a party to a services or outsourcing agreement of liability where the failure to comply is the result of a force majeure event.

There is no statutory definition of force majeure or its implications on the duty to comply with the agreed terms and conditions in the Contracts Act. However, it is an accepted term in legal literature and case law. Should the parties leave out a clause on force majeure altogether, it is plausible that a court would find that it is an implied clause. Although force majeure is an accepted concept, it ought to be defined by the parties to a contract in order to expressly state the width of events to be included.

Depending on whether force majeure is defined with an exhaustive list or an exemplifying list, it will be more or less preferable to the supplier and customer. Should the list be unreasonable, it can, as any unreasonable condition, be attacked under the Contracts Act. Furthermore, unpleasant or expensive consequences are more likely to be palatable when the parties recognise that risks and responsibilities were allocated fairly. The benefits of an exhaustive list include the certainty achieved and the incentive to avoid circumstances that are not within the definition. The common solution in Sweden is a general definition consisting of a non-exhaustive list and a list of conditions which the party asserting the force majeure must satisfy in order to avoid liability (such as a notification requirement or a requirement to avoid the event and/or to take reasonable steps to overcome the event).

The contract should also state the effect, other than in relation to liability, where it is not possible to provide the agreed services and whether or not the forfeited party shall have the right to terminate the agreement. Both parties may want to have the right to terminate in certain events, depending on the consequences inferred. If the supplier fails to perform services due to force majeure, although it may be free from liability, it may also miss out on expected payments and be forced to comply with a remedy plan. In such cases, termination may be seen as a more attractive option to the supplier.

55.5   Limitations of liability

As in many other countries, it is common for the supplier to require that its liability for breach of contract is limited to direct damages and to a maximum amount. It is common for the parties to insist on a higher liability limit for intellectual property rights infringement and breach of confidentiality clauses.

55.6 Data protection

55.6.1 *Implementation of Data Protection Directive*

The principal data protection legislation in Sweden is the Personal Data Act. This Act implements the Data Protection Directive adopted by the EU in 1995. Compliance with the Personal Data Act is supervised by the Swedish Data Inspection Board.

55.6.2 *Basic principles*

The basic starting point is that the responsibility for ensuring that personal data is conducted in a lawful manner rests with the person processing such data for his/her own purposes, i.e. the data controller. The data controller determines *how* and *why* the data is being processed and the data processor, performing the practical handling of the data, can be likened to a tool, solely acting on the controller's instructions.

The main function of the Personal Data Act is to protect against the violation of people's personal integrity by the processing of data. The Personal Data Act lists certain fundamental requirements concerning the processing of personal data.

55.6.3 *Requirement for consent*

One such requirement is that personal data may only be processed for specific, explicitly stated and justified purposes. Personal data may, with some exceptions, in principle only be processed if the registered person gives his consent. However, there are exceptions to this rule: if it is necessary in the exercise of official powers, when a work task of public importance is to be performed, in order to enable the controller of public data to fulfil a legal obligation or in order that a contract with the registered person may be performed.

55.6.4 *Exclusions from the Act*

The Act does not apply to the processing of personal data that forms part of a course of operation of a purely private nature, and does not contravene the constitutional provisions relating to freedom of press or freedom of expression or limit the principle of access to public information. Processing of personal data in unstructured material, for example running text, may take place as long as this processing does not entail a violation of the personal integrity of the persons whose data is registered. If another act or ordinance contains rules that deviate from the Personal Data Act, those other provisions apply instead.

55.6.5   Notification

The processing of personal data must be notified to the Data Inspection Board. However, this does not apply if the person who is responsible for the processing has appointed a personal data representative. A person who contravenes the Act may be liable to pay damages or be sentenced to a criminal penalty.

55.6.6   Sensitive personal data

Particularly stringent rules apply to the processing of personal data that is sensitive, for example concerning political views, sexual orientation or health. This also applies when data is transferred to other countries. The person whose personal data is processed must always be informed of the processing of data that concerns him.

55.6.7   Application to services and outsourcing

In a services or outsourcing relationship, the party responsible for processing will usually be the customer, as the supplier will be processing data solely as part of the services and in accordance with the instructions from the customer. That is, the customer will be controlling the data and making the decisions as to how and why the data is processed, but the supplier may be doing the actual processing and thus acting as processor. In such cases, the customer will be the controller.

55.6.8   Application to processing in Sweden

The Personal Data Act applies to controllers established in Sweden. The Act is also applicable when a controller from a country outside the EU and EEA uses equipment, such as terminals, situated in Sweden for the processing of personal data. In such cases, the controller must appoint an agent established in Sweden who will be treated as a controller for the purposes of the Act.

55.7   Financial services regulation

55.7.1   Implementation of MiFID

The Markets in Financial Instruments Directive 2004/39/ec (MiFID) has been implemented in Swedish legislation by the Securities Markets Act (2007:528), which replaced the Securities Operations Act (1991:1981) and the Securities Exchange and Clearing Operations Act (1992:543). The Implementation Regulation 1287/2006 is directly applicable in Sweden and the Implementing Directive 2006/73/EC has been implemented by the Swedish Financial Supervisory Authority (FSA) in two regulations:

(a)   Regulation regarding Securities Operations Business (fffs 2007:16); and
(b)   Regulation regarding Operations on the Securities Market (ec 2007:17).

Several regulations and general guidelines issued by the FSA have either been rescinded or amended as a result of the MiFID implementation. MiFID was fully implemented in Sweden on 1 November 2007.

The Swedish legislature chose to make the wording of the new legislation as similar as possible to the wording used in MiFID. Several new words and expressions not previously used in Swedish financial legislation have been introduced as a result. Subsequently, a number of other legal Acts have been amended to reflect the "new" MiFID terminology in Swedish legislation.

MiFID has now been applicable in Sweden for some time and yet it is still to be seen how the FSA and the Swedish courts will enforce and apply the new legislation.

55.7.2   The FSA and authorisation

The FSA is the supervisory authority of companies operating in financial markets in Sweden. All companies offering financial services in Sweden must obtain authorisation issued by the FSA. Such authorisations are provided for a number of different types of securities operations. The securities companies carrying authorisation to conduct securities operations under the rescinded Securities Operations Act were automatically granted new "MiFID authorisations". These covered the same operations as the former authorisations, with new MiFID-compliant wording, when the current Securities Markets Act came into force on 1 November 2007. In addition, two new authorisations were introduced as a result of the implementation of MiFID in Sweden:

(a)   investment advice to clients regarding financial instruments; and
(b)   operations of multilateral trading facilities (MTF).

Since the rescinded Securities Operations Act did not contain any equivalents to the above authorisations, companies providing investment advice or operating an MTF have been obliged to apply for such authorisations.

55.7.3   Classification of marketplaces

A partly new classification of marketplaces has also been introduced in Sweden as a consequence of the implementation of MiFID. Until the new Securities Markets Act came into force there were two different marketplaces in Sweden, an exchange marketplace and an authorised marketplace. The term "authorised marketplace" has no equivalent in the current Securities Markets Act. However, the term "exchange" still exists and refers to the legal entity operating a regulated market instead of, as previously, the marketplace itself. OMX and Nordic Growth Market (NGM) currently operate regulated markets in Sweden.

As indicated above, an MTF constitutes a new kind of marketplace in Sweden which requires authorisation. Previously, a financial institution could act as an intermediary between buyers and sellers of financial instruments in a way comparable to an MTF without a specific marketplace authorisation. Today, such institutions have to apply for authorisation if they intend to operate an MTF. However, if the operations in question are not regarded as operations of an MTF, the activity is still likely to be subject to authorisation. The rationale is that the business activity includes the receipt and forwarding of transaction orders with regard to financial instruments, something that the Securities Markets Act considers is an operation subject to authorisation.

55.8   Public Procurement Directives

55.8.1   Implementation of the EU Directives

Public procurement annually amounts to approximately SEK 500 billion (approximately €51 billion), which equates to about 20 per cent of the Swedish annual gross domestic product. Public procurement in Sweden is governed by the two Public Procurement Acts which came into force on 1 January 2008: the Swedish Public Procurement Act and the Swedish Procurement Act on procurement of water, energy, transportation and postal services. They are based on the EC Public Procurement Directives, the Classical Directive and the Utilities Directive.

The Swedish Competition Authority is responsible for information on and supervision of public procurement.

As a Member State, Sweden is automatically compliant with the World

Trade Organization's agreement on government procurement, after implementing the procurement directives.

55.8.2 Application

The Acts regulate almost all types of public procurement, meaning that contracting entities, such as local government agencies, county councils, government agencies as well as certain publicly-owned companies must comply with the Acts when they purchase, lease, rent or hire purchase supplies, services and public works. The contracting entity must choose which award procedure to apply. However, the rules are different for public procurement above and below a number of so-called threshold values, as is stated in the directives. It should be noted, however, that the telecommunications sector is not covered by the Swedish Procurement Acts.

55.8.3 Fundamental principles

The Swedish Acts on public procurement are based upon the following fundamental principles of EC and Swedish law.

55.8.3.1 Principle of non-discrimination

The principle of non-discrimination prohibits all discrimination based on nationality. No contracting entity may, for example, give preference to a local company simply because it is located in the municipality.

55.8.3.2 Principle of equal treatment

According to the principle of equal treatment, all suppliers must be treated equally. All suppliers involved in a procurement procedure must, for example, be given the same information at the same time.

55.8.3.3 Principle of transparency

According to the principle of transparency, the procurement process must be characterised by predictability and openness. In order to ensure equal conditions for tenderers, the contract document has to be clear and unambiguous and contain all of the requirements made of the items to be procured.

55.8.3.4 Principle of proportionality

The principle of proportionality states that qualification requirements and requirements regarding the subject matter of the contract must have a natural relation to the supplies, services or works which are being procured and not be disproportionate.

55.8.3.5   *Principle of mutual recognition*

The principle of mutual recognition means, among other things, that documents and certificates issued by the appropriate authorities in a Member State must be accepted in the other Member States.

55.8.4   *PFI/PPP*

There are very few PFI or PPP projects in Sweden, although these projects are believed to be coming. There are no special rules on the procurement of PFI or PPP projects. Instead, the contracting entity is obliged to apply the Swedish Public Procurement Act or the Swedish Procurement Act of water, energy, transportation and postal services.

55.9   Competition law

55.9.1   *Implementation of EU law*

The newly amended Swedish Competition Act (SFS 2008:579) ("2008 Competition Act") came into force on 1 November 2008, replacing the 1993 Competition Act (SFS 1993:20). The 2008 Competition Act is the most important Act regulating competition in Sweden. In addition to technical legal amendments, there were several different substantive changes to the 2008 Competition Act providing even further alignment with EC legislation. Overall, Sweden is highly influenced by EC legislation concerning national competition law. Almost all of the EC Block Exemption Regulations are implemented in Swedish legislation through different Acts referring to the EC Regulations. Swedish competition law is also influenced by EC legislation in other ways. When it comes to merger control for example, the notions and guidelines published by the European Commission are used to a large extent. Terms such as concentration and control do not differ from EC legislation and nor does the calculation of turnover.

55.9.2   *Specific points relevant to Sweden*

From a competition law point of view, there are no material differences in Swedish legislation compared to EC legislation which in the author's opinion would raise new issues in relation to services or outsourcing arrangements. However, there are some general points specific to Swedish competition law which may be worth highlighting.

According to the 2008 Competition Act, a mandatory notification of a concentration is required if:

(a) the combined aggregate turnover in Sweden of the undertakings concerned in the preceding financial year exceeds SEK 1 billion; and
(b) not less than two of the undertakings involved had a turnover in Sweden during the preceding financial year exceeding SEK 200 million for each of the undertakings.

Furthermore, the 2008 Competition Act provides that if criterion (a) above is fulfilled but the turnover does not exceed the threshold in criterion (b), the Competition Authority may, if special circumstances exist, order a party to a concentration to notify this. In this case, the parties may also hand in a voluntary notification.

Sanctions against infringements of prohibited anti-competitive agreements are administrative fines of up to 10 per cent of the undertaking's turnover in the preceding financial year. The 2008 Competition Act introduces the possibility of imposing a trade prohibition (disqualification order) on business leaders engaging in unlawful collusion in cartels.

Chapter 56

Switzerland

Michele Bernasconi, Nicola Bernardoni and Philippe Fuchs

Bär & Karrer AG

56.1   Outline

Parts 1 to 11 of this book describe the key business issues relevant for services and outsourcing agreements. They also describe the key legal issues under English law. This chapter describes the specific legal and business issues which affect services and outsourcing arrangements in Switzerland.

Switzerland is not part of the EU. However, it will be apparent that, in several areas, Switzerland has been influenced by legal developments within the EU and has introduced legislation which is similar to that in the EU.

56.2   Employment issues

56.2.1   Transfer of employees

56.2.1.1   Transfer of a business or a business unit

Under Swiss law, if an employer transfers a business or a part of a business (a business unit) to a third party,[1] the employment relationship is transferred to such third party, including all rights and obligations as of the date of the transfer, unless the employee declines the transfer (Article 333 of the Swiss Code of Obligation (CO)).[2]

Accordingly, in an outsourcing that involves the transfer of a business unit from the customer to the supplier, all employment relationships relating to

---

[1]   Article 333 CO applies to an outsourcing agreement if the business or business unit to be transferred is a kind of self-contained organisational business division, clearly separable from other parts of the business. In this respect it is of essence that the business unit to be outsourced maintains an independent and distinct economic identity (organisation, business purpose and individual character), regardless of whether or not this unit is economically autonomous.

[2]   RS 220 (RS: *Recueil systématique du droit fédéral*, i.e. Classified Compilation of Federal Legislation).

the business unit are automatically transferred from the customer to the supplier.[3]

However, the former employer (customer) remains jointly and severally liable with the new employer (supplier) for certain claims (Article 333 para.3 CO). This applies in particular to:

(a) claims of the employees that become due prior to the transfer; and
(b) claims that arise prior to expiry of the period of ordinary termination of the employment relationship (see section 56.2.2.1 below).

If the business activity to be outsourced does not qualify as a business or business unit, as defined in Article 333 CO, the transfer of the employment agreements from the customer to the supplier requires the consent of each employee unless the circumstances or the employment agreements provide for the contrary (Article 333 para.4 CO).

56.2.1.2 *Duty of information and consultation*

Prior to the transfer, the customer must inform the employees' representative body or, in the absence of such body, the employees (Article 333a para.1 CO) of:

(a) the reason for the transfer; and
(b) the legal, economic and social consequences of the transfer.

In addition, if the business transfer requires measures that have an effect on the employees, the employer has a duty to consult the employees' representative body or, in the absence of such body, the employees (Article 333a para.2 CO).[4]

56.2.2 *Redundancies: termination of employment agreements/mass dismissals*

56.2.2.1 *Termination of employment agreements*

In Switzerland, the termination of employment agreements depends on the type of agreement. A distinction is primarily made between:

---

[3] Without the consent of the employees, the customer cannot terminate the employment agreements in connection with an outsourcing which involves the transfer of a business or business unit to the supplier and, at the same time, offer through the supplier, new employment agreements with different terms and conditions. This would circumvent the employees' protection rights under Article 333 CO.

[4] The consultation must take place before the decision on transfer is made. However, the employer is not obliged to follow or implement the suggestions made by the employees. Further information and consultation duties may also arise if the outsourcing involves a mass redundancy (see section 56.2.2.2), or if provided by any separate agreement.

(a) employment agreements for a definite duration, which end at the expiration of the time limit (Article 334 CO); and

(b) employment agreements for an indefinite duration, which may be terminated by giving the contractual or, if there is none, the statutory notice period (Article 335 CO).

The notice period and the formalities of the notice[5] are often specified in the employment agreement.[6] However, the duration of the notice period must be the same for both the employer and the employee (Article 335a CO).[7]

Swiss employment law is quite liberal when it comes to terminating employment agreements. The reason for terminating the agreement does not have to be an "important reason".[8]

56.2.2.2 *Mass dismissal*

According to Article 335d CO, termination for reasons unrelated to the employees as people qualifies as a mass dismissal if the number of redundancies within a time period of 30 days is:

(a) at least 10 employees in an establishment with 20–100 employees; or

(b) at least 10 per cent of the employees in an establishment with 100–300 employees; or

(c) at least 30 per cent of the employees in an establishment with more than 300 employees.

If the employer plans a mass dismissal, before it takes a definitive decision it has to:

(a) consult with the employees' representative body or, if there is none, all of the employees;[9] and

(b) inform the employees in writing of:

---

[5] For evidence purposes notice of termination is usually given in writing.
[6] If the notice period is not specified in the agreement, the following applies:
  (a) during the trial period (which cannot exceed three months), seven days' notice is sufficient to terminate the agreement;
  (b) after the trial period, the agreement may be terminated at the end of a month:
  (i) with one month's notice during the first year of employment;
  (ii) with two months' notice from the second year through the ninth year; and
  (iii) with three months' notice after the ninth year.
[7] Usually agreements provide for a two or three-month notice period for regular employees and for a six-month notice period for executive employees.
[8] Upon request by the employee, the employer has to state in writing the reasons for terminating the agreement.
[9] The employer has to give the employees reasonable time to at least make suggestions on how to avoid the dismissals or to limit the number of dismissals and to alleviate the consequences. Contrary to the majority of countries in the EU, Switzerland has no rules imposing the duty to offer a social plan to the dismissed employees. The Collective Labour Agreements, if applicable, normally provide for additional compensations or benefits payable to employees in connection with mass dismissal or closing down of a business, but their financial significance is regularly far more limited than in other western European countries.

(i)   the reasons for the mass dismissal;

(ii)   the number of employees to be dismissed;

(iii) the number of persons usually employed; and

(iv) the time period within which the notification of the dismissal is to be given.[10]

However, there is no formal right of approval by the employees, the representative body or the Cantonal Labour Office.[11]

56.3   Pensions issues

Swiss law requires employers to set up or join a pension scheme for employees who meet certain minimum requirements. The pension scheme is independent from the employer's business.

Generally, when employees are transferred under Article 333 CO (see section 56.2.1.1 above), the employees' vested benefits under the transferor's pension scheme are transferred to the transferee's pension scheme. After the transfer, the employees' pension benefits are calculated according to the new scheme's regulations.

However, if the workforce that forms part of the transferor's pension scheme reduces substantially, the respective pension scheme must be partially liquidated. The employees will then have individual or collective claims to a portion of the non-committed funds (free reserves) in addition to their ordinary claims to the vested benefit.

56.4   Contract law

Swiss contract law does not contain specific provisions for outsourcing agreements. Outsourcing agreements belong to the numerous types of contracts that are developed in accordance with the principle of "freedom of contracts" and that are not regulated by statute (so-called "innominate contracts").

---

[10] A copy of the notification described above must also be sent to the Cantonal Labour Office.

[11] If the employer does not comply with the requirements to consult with the employees, the termination would be considered abusive, even though it remains valid. This entails a liability of the employer to grant to the dismissed employees an indemnity of up to two months' salary. In addition, the employer would have to compensate the dismissed employees for damages related to the fact that the consultation procedure has not taken place. Further, non-compliance with the requirement to notify the Cantonal Labour Offices may result in a delay of the effective date of termination and in administrative sanctions according to cantonal labour regulations.

However, outsourcing agreements often incorporate or display several elements of the various statutorily regulated contracts, such as:

(a)   the services contract (Article 394 et seq. CO);

(b)   the works contract (Article 363 et seq. CO);

(c)   the sales contract (Article 184 et seq. CO);

(d)   the simple partnership (Article 530 et seq. CO); and

(e)   rent (Article 253 et seq. CO).

As a consequence, in the case of a dispute, a Swiss court will have to determine which statutorily regulated contract type should best be applied, directly or by analogy, taking into consideration the intention of the parties, the most prominent contractual type and the general principles of law.

One of the key questions is whether the supplier will be liable in the event of failure to achieve a particular result (as per works law) or whether it should be liable for failure to perform its obligations without due care (as per services law). In other words, if the supplier promises the customer a certain result, works law will apply. Alternatively, where the supplier has only agreed to deliver certain services to the customer and not guaranteed the achievement of a particular result, services law will apply.

There is a general tendency for the courts to assume that the rules for works contracts will apply, particularly in cases where the parties have agreed certain service levels. Sales contract law usually applies to the transfer of assets from the customer to the supplier in cases where the parties agree on the transfer of title. If this is not the case, the courts would be inclined to apply the provision of the rent or the lease.

In order to reduce the legal uncertainty as to the rules that the courts will apply, outsourcing and services agreements are usually drafted with very detailed provisions aimed at providing a comprehensive set of rules that shall apply in case of dispute. In this case, the courts will apply the rules in the contract and not attempt to decide which statutory contract type could apply.

56.5   Exclusion and limitation of liability

Under Swiss contract law, the parties are generally free to exclude or limit their liability, subject to the following mandatory limitations:

(a)   the exclusion or limitation in advance of liability for unlawful intent or gross negligence is null and void (Article 100 para.1 CO); and

(b) the exclusion or limitation in advance of liability for death or personal injury is null and void.

In addition, a waiver of liability for simple negligence agreed in advance may be considered null and void at the discretion of the judge if the party making the waiver was employed by the other party at the time of the agreement, or if the liability arises out of the conduct of a business that is carried out under an official licence (e.g. banks, insurance companies).

In principle, liability for auxiliary persons (e.g. employees or other persons helping the principal in performing a contractual obligation) may be limited or excluded in advance (Article 101 para.2 CO). However, if the party making the waiver was employed by the other party at the time of the agreement, or if the liability arises out of the conduct of a business that is carried out under an official licence, a waiver in advance is only possible for simple negligence (Article 101 para.3).

It is also a fundamental principle of Swiss contract law that liability for the obligations that constitute the essence of the contract (e.g. the duty of care under services law) cannot be excluded in full. Here it is assumed that an exclusion of liability would create a contradictory situation. Such restrictions are therefore unlawful and unenforceable.

Subject to the above restrictions, the customer and the supplier are free to negotiate any exclusions or limitations of liability (including caps, liquidated damages, direct damages etc.).

Excessively high liquidated damages (and also, therefore, under certain circumstances, excessively high service-level penalties) can be reduced at the discretion of the judge (Article 163 para.3 CO).

56.6 Data protection

56.6.1 *Federal Act on Data Protection*

In Switzerland, data protection is primarily governed by the Federal Act on Data Protection of 19 June 1992 (FADP).[12] In contrast to most of the European countries, Swiss data protection law applies to the personal data of both natural persons and legal entities ("data subjects").

The processing of personal data must be done in good faith and must be proportionate. Data accuracy and data security must be ensured. Data subjects are protected from their personal data being processed in ways that

---

[12] RS 235.1. Outsourcing of personal data by banks, securities dealers and insurance companies is subject to stricter regulations (see section 56.8).

do not comply with the law or with the purposes intended at the time of collection, unless data subjects approve such data processing or another statutory justification applies.

Stronger legal protection is provided for sensitive personal data[13] and personality profiles.[14] The disclosure of such data to third parties[15] without lawful justification (e.g. consent of the data subjects) is prohibited.

56.6.2 Outsourcing of personal data processing within Switzerland

Data processing may be outsourced, within Switzerland, to a third-party supplier under an outsourcing agreement,[16] provided that the supplier processes data only to the same extent as the customer was authorised to do and that no legal or contractual confidentiality obligations prohibit the outsourcing. The customer must further ensure that the supplier will comply with the applicable data security standards.

Explicit consent[17] of the data subjects is required for the transfer of sensitive personal data or personality profiles.

56.6.3 Cross-border transfer of personal data

The transfer[18] of personal data out of Switzerland is subject to further restrictions.

56.6.3.1 Countries with an adequate level of data protection

In principle, personal data may not be transferred to countries which lack an adequate level of data protection. The website of the Federal Data Protection

---

[13] The FADP classifies personal data as "sensitive personal data" if it relates to:
  (a) religious, philosophical, political or trade union-related views or activities;
  (b) health, the intimate sphere of the person or racial origin;
  (c) social security files; or
  (d) criminal or administrative proceedings and penalties.
  Personal data within this definition will almost always relate to a natural person rather than a legal entity.
[14] Personality profile is defined in the FADP as a collection of data that permits an assessment of essential characteristics of the personality of a natural person.
[15] A third party is any entity other than the disclosing entity, irrespective of the existence of an economic link between the disclosing entity and the recipient entity. Companies within the same group (parent and sister companies or subsidiaries) are considered third parties and thus the sharing of personal data within a group is deemed to be a disclosure to third parties for the purposes of the FADP.
[16] For outsourcing of personal data by banks and securities dealers additional requirements must be complied with (see section 56.8.1.2).
[17] Implied consent is not sufficient.
[18] This includes allowing personal data to be accessed from abroad.

and Information Commissioner (FDPIC) contains a list of the countries with adequate data protection legislation.[19]

56.6.3.2 Countries without an adequate level of data protection

In the absence of legislation that guarantees adequate protection, personal data may exceptionally be disclosed abroad if, amongst other reasons:

(a) the data subject has consented in the specific case;
(b) sufficient safeguards, in particular contractual clauses,[20] ensure an adequate level of protection abroad; or
(c) disclosure is made within the same legal person or company or between legal persons or companies that are under the same management, provided those involved are subject to data protection rules that ensure an adequate level of protection.

The FDPIC must be informed[21] of the safeguards and the data protection rules referred to under points (b) and (c) above.

56.7   Insolvency issues

56.7.1   Outline

Swiss insolvency law is comprehensively regulated on a federal level by the Federal Act on Debt Enforcement and Bankruptcy (FADEB).[22]

When a court opens bankruptcy proceedings against a debtor, all of the bankrupt's assets form an estate which may no longer be disposed of by the debtor. All claims against the bankrupt estate become due and the estate is realised. The proceeds are then distributed among the creditors, some of

---

[19] The countries which have implemented the Directive 95/46/EC of the European Parliament and of the Council of 24 October 1995 on the protection of individuals with regard to the processing of personal data and on the free movement of such data (EU Directive) are considered to provide the required adequate level of data protection for personal data of individuals. However, the EU Directive, unlike the FADP, does not provide such protection for legal entities. Consequently EU countries which have not implemented protection for legal entities in their national data protection laws cannot be considered to provide an adequate level of data protection for the personal data of legal entities pursuant to the FADP. For non-EU countries, it is necessary to check on a case-by-case basis whether they provide an adequate level of data protection. Neither US federal law nor the laws of any US state are considered to provide an adequate level of data protection, even if the recipient has adhered to the safe-harbour rules of the US Department of Commerce. See FDPIC website at: *http://www.edoeb.admin.ch* [Accessed 28 September 2012].
[20] The EU model clauses are recognized by the FDPIC as providing for sufficient safeguards. Nevertheless, it is necessary to amend the EU model clauses so that, also, data of legal entities is protected.
[21] Information to the FDPIC must be provided before the first transfer of data is made or, if that is not possible, immediately after the disclosure has occurred.
[22] RS 281.1. Separate laws apply to enforcement actions against countries and cantons as well as bankruptcy and composition proceedings against financial institutions and bankruptcies of insurance companies.

which may be granted priority. Each creditor receives a certificate of shortfall for the unrecovered portion of its claim.

56.7.2 *Effects on debtor's assets*

Upon the opening of the bankruptcy proceedings by a competent court, all seizable assets of the debtor at that time, irrespective of where they are situated, constitute the "bankruptcy estate" destined for the satisfaction of the creditors.

Assets situated with the debtor but belonging to a third party do not fall within the bankruptcy estate. Such assets have to be singled out, either directly by the bankruptcy administrator or, if the ownership is unclear, by way of judicial proceedings in which the third party claims its proprietary interests.

56.7.3 *Effects on creditor's rights*

As regards claims based on a contractual relationship, the opening of the bankruptcy proceeding has the consequence that all obligations of a debtor become due vis-à-vis the bankruptcy estate.[23]

With the exception of certain types of contracts, the contractual relationship itself does not automatically terminate with the opening of bankruptcy proceedings. However, filings for bankruptcy or composition proceedings are often considered to be sufficiently serious to justify immediate termination of the contract by the other party.[24]

---

[23] Claims which do not have as their object a sum of money are converted into monetary claims of a corresponding value.

[24] If the agreement does not provide for an automatic termination in the event of the bankruptcy of a contractual party and there is no possibility of an immediate termination, the bankruptcy administration can choose whether to terminate the agreement or to insist on the performance of the contract. In the latter case, the creditor cannot rescind the agreement, but can only ask for a security in relation of the performance of his obligations, and the related claims will be regarded as a debt against the bankruptcy estate, which has the effect that such claims rank prior to those of the other creditors.

56.8 Financial services regulation

56.8.1 Banks and securities dealers

56.8.1.1 Banking secrecy

The Swiss banking secrecy law is set out in article 50 of the Federal Law on Banks and Savings Banks (FLBSB).[25] The banking secrecy law applies to all banking institutions in Switzerland and protects customer-related data from disclosures to any third party.[26] Any disclosure of non-encrypted data to a supplier would breach banking secrecy law if the bank's customer has not given his prior consent.

56.8.1.2 Circular letter on the outsourcing of the Swiss Financial Market Supervisory Authority

Outsourcing of business activities from banks and securities dealers organised in accordance with Swiss law, including Swiss branches of foreign banks and securities dealers, must comply with certain requirements. These requirements are set out in the "Outsourcing of Business Areas" Circular Letter no. 2008/7 (issued on 20 November 2008 and effective as from 1 January 2009) (the "Circular") of the Swiss Financial Market Supervisory Authority (FINMA).[27]

The purpose of the Circular is to set out the conditions and requirements for outsourcing arrangements in terms of the bank's duties as an appropriate organisation, banking secrecy and data protection. In principle, the outsourcing of every business area is possible without the approval of the FINMA, provided that the provisions of the FADP[28] and the requirements for secure outsourcing[29] are complied with and, in the case of offshore outsourcing, the required documentary support can be provided. If an enterprise cannot fulfil these requirements prior to the outsourcing agreement being signed, it

---

[25] RS 952.0.

[26] Entities belonging to the same group are—from a Swiss banking secrecy perspective—deemed to be a "third party" irrespective of existing corporate law and/or regulatory links.

[27] With the entering into force of the Federal Act on the Swiss Financial Market Supervisory Authority on 1 January 2009, three supervisory bodies—the Federal Office of Private Insurance (FOPI), the Swiss Federal Banking Commission (SFBC) and the Anti-Money Laundering Control Authority—merged into the Swiss Financial Market Supervisory Authority (FINMA). Even though circulars issued by the FINMA do not qualify as statutory law, they do have an enormous practical relevance as they lay down the principles and requirements imposed by the FINMA when exercising its supervisory powers. The Circular letter issued by the FINMA basically reflects the "old" Circular Letter no. 99/2 issued on 26 August 1999 by the Swiss Federal Banking Commission.

[28] Customer-related data must be protected against access by unauthorised persons through appropriate technical and organisational measures.

[29] The customer and the supplier shall develop and set out in the contract a security concept which will allow the customer to monitor compliance with the security requirements which the supplier has to fulfil and permit the continuation of the outsourced business area in case the supplier, for whatever reason, is not able to provide its services.

must submit an application and justification to the FINMA for an individual exemption.

The Circular specifically addresses "significant" outsourcings, that is, the outsourcing of services which can impact in particular on the identification, limitation and monitoring of market, credit, default, settlement, liquidity, image, operational and legal risks.[30]

According to the Circular, any activity, function or operation of a bank can be outsourced to a third-party supplier, provided that the bank does not outsource:

(a) the supervision, ultimate management and control by the board of directors as well as other central management tasks; and

(b) decisions concerning the commencement and discontinuation of business relationships.

The Circular lays down the following general principles to be followed to satisfy the requirement of secure outsourcing:

(a) the determination of the business area to be outsourced;[31]
(b) the customer's responsibility vis-à-vis the supervisory authority;[32]
(c) the relevant security measures which will be taken by the parties to protect the customer's business operations;[33]
(d) compliance with business and banking secrecy and data protection laws;[34]
(e) an obligation of the bank to inform its customers about the outsourcing;[35]
(f) the right of the supervisory body and the customer to enjoy unrestricted audit and supervision over the supplier;[36]
(g) additional requirements for offshore outsourcing;[37] and
(h) the requirement for a written contract.[38]

---

[30] Outsourcing examples that are applicable in the Circular and examples that are not applicable in the Circular are included in the appendix to the Circular.

[31] In accordance with the goals pursued with the outsourcing, the precise requirements for the provision of services are to be laid down and documented.

[32] The enterprise must carefully select, instruct and control the supplier.

[33] The proper conduct of business operations must be capable of being ensured at all times. The customer and the supplier must ensure the confidentiality, availability and accuracy of the data in order to guarantee the appropriate protection of data.

[34] The Swiss supplier shall be subject to business secrecy rules of the enterprise and as far as clients' data is known to it, the banking and professional secrecy rules of the outsourcing enterprise.

[35] Clients whose data is transmitted to a supplier as a result of an outsourcing solution are to be informed of the outsourcing arrangement before their data is transmitted to a supplier. In case of an outsourcing abroad, clients must be informed by a separate detailed letter and given the possibility to terminate the relationship within a reasonable timeframe and without disadvantages if data is not transferred on an anonymous basis.

[36] The outsourcing enterprise and its internal and external auditors as well as the FINMA must at all times possess complete and unrestricted insight into and control of the outsourced business.

[37] In the event of outsourcing abroad, an enterprise must be capable of demonstrating that the enterprise itself as well as its Banking or Stock Exchange Law auditors and the FINMA may assume and also legally enforce their rights to perform controls.

[38] A written and clear contract is to be concluded between the enterprise and the supplier.

56.8.2   Insurance companies

56.8.2.1   Federal Act on Supervision of Insurance Companies

The Federal Act on Supervision of Insurance Companies of 17 December 2004 (FASIC)[39] requires that significant outsourcing agreements are included in the business plan[40] that must be submitted to FINMA, to obtain a licence to operate as an insurance company in Switzerland (Article 4 para.2 lit. j FASIC).[41] Subsequently, any amendment or new significant outsourcing agreement must be notified to the FINMA before it becomes effective. If no formal examination is commenced by the FINMA, the amendment is deemed to be approved (Article 5 para.2 FASIC).

FASIC also requires that the people entrusted with the administration and management of an insurance company must have a good reputation and thereby ensure the proper conduct of the insurance company's business operations (Article 14 FASIC). The same requirements apply to a supplier being entrusted with core activities, functions or operations under an outsourcing agreement.

56.8.2.2   Explanatory notes to the business plan

The explanatory notes to the requirement to prepare a business plan, as issued by FINMA[42] give further details of the restrictions on and requirements for an outsourcing arrangement by insurance companies.

In principle:

(a)   the outsourcing of activities of an insurance undertaking may not endanger the interests of the insured parties nor be detrimental to supervision by the FINMA; and

(b)   when outsourcing tasks, Article 50 para.4 FASIC must be observed, according to which natural and legal persons assuming tasks of the insurance undertaking are also subject to the duty to provide information to the supervisory authority.[43]

An outsourcing agreement is subject to approval if the following conditions apply cumulatively:

(a)   the arrangement concerns principal functions[44] or processes of an insurance undertaking;

---

[39]   RS 961.01.
[40]   Form J: "Contracts or other agreements by which principal functions are to be outsourced".
[41]   Outsourcing for purposes of Article 4 para.2 lit. j FASIC also includes the transfer of tasks between the Swiss branch of a foreign insurance undertaking and the foreign head office or other unit of the company.
[42]   Explanations on the business plan (issue 01/2012).
[43]   The insurance undertaking shall designate one internally responsible person for each outsourced area.

(b)   the outsourcing is long term; and

(c)   the service provider is granted entrepreneurial discretion in fulfilling its tasks.[45]

Direction, supervision and control by the board of directors, as well as key management responsibilities, may not be outsourced.[46]

56.9   Public procurement

56.9.1   *Outline*

In Switzerland, public procurement is regulated both at a federal and cantonal level. In addition, Switzerland is a signatory to several international treaties which deal with public procurement (the most important are the WTO Government Procurement Agreement and the Bilateral Agreements with the EC). Nevertheless, as Switzerland is not an EU member, the EC public procurement directives do not apply to outsourcing or services contracts in Switzerland.

Swiss procurement regulations provide for a mandatory competitive tender if the price paid for the services provided by the external supplier exceeds a certain threshold.

---

[44]   Principal functions for the purposes of Article 4 para.2 lit. j are those functions necessary for the effective operation of an insurance undertaking. Such functions are:
(a)   Core functions:
(i)   production (product development, distribution, risk underwriting);
(ii)   administration of client base (administration of policies);
(iii)   claims settlement.
(b)   Other principal functions:
(i)   accounting;
(ii)   asset investment/management; and
(iii)   IT.
Outsourcing of principal functions is possible in the following circumstances:
(a)   of the core functions set out in points (a)(i)–(iii), a maximum of two may be outsourced, provided that such outsourcing is sufficiently justified;
(b)   the other principal functions set out in points (b)(i)–(iii) may be outsourced;
(c)   captives may outsource all principal functions set out in points (a) and (b) to specialist captive management companies;
(d)   companies in run-off after renouncing a licence may outsource all principal functions set out in points (a) and (b) as long as this appears useful in a concrete individual case (e.g. if only a few contracts and claims remain to be processed).
[45]   This means in particular that a mere assignment relationship in which the customer insurance company maintains its right of instruction in detail cannot be deemed outsourcing. If, for instance, the processing of some claims is carried out by an external law office, this is not qualified as outsourcing of an entrepreneurial function.
[46]   The explanatory notes expressly mention the following exceptions:
(a)   outsourcing of internal audit;
(b)   outsourcing of the management of captive re-insurers to appropriately specialised captive management companies; and
(c)   outsourcing of certain control functions within an insurance group or insurance conglomerate subject to group supervision.

56.9.2   Procurements of federal authorities

Public procurements of federal authorities are governed by the Federal Act on Public Procurement (FAPP).[47] A procurement is subject to the FAPP if its estimated value reaches or exceeds the thresholds contained in the FAPP.[48]

The FAPP provides for three different kinds of procedures: the open procedure (Article 14 FAPP), the selective procedure (Article 15 FAPP) and the procedure without prior publication (Article 16 FAPP).

56.9.3   Procurements of cantonal and communal authorities

Public procurements of cantonal or communal authorities are regulated by the Inter-Cantonal Agreement on Public Procurement (ICAPP)[49] and by the relevant cantonal public procurement laws of each canton.

According to the ICAPP, an invitation procedure must be followed for procurement of services exceeding CHF 150,000, while a public call of tenders is necessary for procurement of services exceeding CHF 250,000.

56.10   Competition law

56.10.1   Outline

The provisions of the Swiss competition law can be found in the Federal Act on Cartels and Other Restraints of Competition ("FACORC" or "Swiss Cartel Act").[50]

According to article 2 FACORC, the Swiss Cartel Act applies to private and public enterprises[51] that are party to cartels or to other agreements affecting competition, have market power or take part in concentrations of enterprises.

The Swiss Cartel Act applies to restrictive practices that have an effect in Switzerland, even if the respective practice originates in another country.

---

[47] RS 172.056.1.
[48] Currently, the thresholds for services is CHF 230,000.
[49] RS 172.06.5.
[50] RS 251.
[51] As provided in Article 1 bis FACORC, the term "enterprises" shall mean all customers and suppliers of goods or services in the commercial process regardless of their legal or organisational form.

56.10.2   Merger control

56.10.2.1   Concentration of enterprises

"Concentrations of enterprises" are subject to the Swiss merger control. This term is defined in Article 4 as:

(a)   the merger of two or more enterprises previously independent of each other; and

(b)   any transaction whereby one or more enterprises acquire, in particular by the acquisition of an equity interest or conclusion of an agreement, direct or indirect control of one or more hitherto independent enterprises or of a part thereof (i.e. the acquisition of sole or joint control).

In practice, if an outsourcing or services transaction will qualify as a concentration, it will in most cases constitute an acquisition of either sole or joint control over an enterprise or a part of it.

The decisive question is whether the outsourcing or services transaction does entail such an enterprise.

In assessing this, the Swiss authorities are very likely to follow the rules set out in para.25 et seq. of the Jurisdictional Notice of the European Commission under Council Regulation (EC) No. 139/2004 on the control of concentrations between undertakings. A transfer of assets/staff constitutes such an enterprise if the assets constitute a business with access to the market. This requires that the assets previously dedicated to in-house activities of the seller will enable the outsourcing service supplier to provide services not only to the outsourcing customer but also to third parties, either immediately or within a short period after the transfer. This will be the case if the transfer relates to an internal business unit or a subsidiary already engaged in the provision of services to third parties. If third parties are not yet supplied, the assets transferred in the case of manufacturing should contain production facilities, the product know-how (it is sufficient if the assets transferred allow the build-up of such capabilities in the near future) and, if there is no existing market access, the means for the purchaser to develop a market access within a short period of time (e.g. including existing contracts or brands). As regards the provision of services, the assets transferred should include the required know-how (e.g. the relevant personnel and intellectual property) and those facilities which allow market access (e.g., marketing facilities).

56.10.2.2   Turnover thresholds

A concentration has to be notified to the Swiss Competition Commission if it fulfils certain turnover thresholds. A notification has to be made if in the last financial year prior to the concentration (Article 9 para.1 FACORC):

(a) the enterprises concerned had a joint worldwide turnover of at least CHF 2 billion or a turnover in Switzerland of at least CHF 500 million; and

(b) at least two of the enterprises concerned reported turnover in Switzerland of at least CHF 100 million each.

If one of the enterprises involved has previously been found to have a dominant position in a market in Switzerland and the concentration involves either that market or a market up or downstream from there, notification must be made regardless of the turnover of the enterprises involved.

56.10.2.3 Creation or strengthening of a dominant position

Upon notification, the Competition Commission will assess the nature of the enterprises involved and the structure of the relevant market in order to determine whether the concentration creates or strengthens a dominant position (Article 10 FACORC). A concentration will be prohibited or only be permitted under conditions and obligations, if:

(a) it creates or strengthens a dominant position that may eliminate effective competition; and

(b) the competitive conditions are not improved in another market to such a degree that they outbalance the disadvantages of the dominant position.

56.10.3 Unlawful restrictions of competition

According to the Swiss Cartel Act, agreements that eliminate or significantly affect competition are prohibited unless they can be justified on grounds of economic efficiency.[52]

In general, outsourcing or services agreements between non-competitors will not give rise to problems under competition law. In contrast, where the outsourcing or services transaction involves two competitors, it has to be assessed whether the agreement significantly restricts competition and if it does, whether it is necessary to achieve efficiencies. Theoretically, it could be argued that agreement constitutes an agreement on the limitation of output that presumptively eliminate effective competition according to Article 5 para.3 lit. b FACORC. However, there are good arguments that outsourcing and services agreements do not fall under the presumption of Article 5 para.3 lit. b FACORC.

---

[52] Since 1 April 2004, parties that enter into agreements eliminating competition will be subject to financial penalties of up to 10 per cent of their turnover in Switzerland over the previous three years.

56.10.4 Abuse of dominant position

As regards the provisions regarding the abuse of a dominant position, an outsourcing or services agreement concluded with a dominant service supplier by itself should not constitute an abuse of a dominant position.

56.11 Other relevant issues

56.11.1 Transfer of property

In Switzerland, different rules apply for the transfer of title of movable and immovable property. For immovable property the transfer requires:

(a) a contract in writing with public authentication (such authentication can only be made by notaries who have been so empowered under the applicable laws); and
(b) the registration in the real-estate register.

For movable property the transfer requires a (written or oral) contract and the transfer of the possession (*"traditio"*). It is noteworthy that, under Swiss law, an agreement to reserve ownership is operative only if it has been entered in the public register of the transferee's domicile, which is kept for this purpose by the bankruptcy office.

56.11.2 Taxation

If an outsourcing or services arrangement involves the sale of assets from the customer to the supplier, such transactions will be subject to the following taxes:[53]

(a) value added tax if the assets are transferred to a supplier within Switzerland. Under certain circumstances, where the transaction involves the sale of a self-contained part of a business, the transaction may be completed without triggering value added tax by using the notification procedure. The same may apply if the arrangement involves a de-merger or a joint venture;[54]
(b) taxes on profits if the sales of assets gives rise to a profit (e.g. because of the realisation of hidden reserves).

---

[53] Complex outsourcing projects should always be carefully reviewed for tax considerations by tax experts and/or submitted to the tax authorities (tax rulings) at an early stage.
[54] If the companies are sufficiently closely connected after the transaction, they may be eligible for group taxation (intercompany turnover between the companies involved would not be subject to value added tax).

De-mergers and the incorporation of joint venture companies are tax neutral for outsourcing or services arrangements provided that a self-contained business element is transferred and continues to operate unchanged.

56.11.3   Dispute resolution

56.11.3.1   Arbitration

Switzerland, as both a neutral and international venue, has a longstanding tradition of international arbitration.[55] A number of chambers of commerce offer arbitration services for both international and domestic arbitration. These include the chambers of commerce of Zurich, Geneva, Basel, Bern, Vaud, Neuchâtel and Ticino, which in 2004 adopted the "Swiss Rules of International Arbitration" (essentially based on the UNCITRAL Arbitration Rules[56]).

International arbitrations are governed by Chapter 12 of the Federal Act on Private International Law (FAPIL),[57] which applies to all arbitration cases where the arbitral tribunal has its seat in Switzerland and at least one of the parties had no domicile or habitual residence in Switzerland at the time when the arbitration agreement was concluded.

Switzerland is a party to several arbitration conventions, including the Geneva Protocol of 24 September 1923 on Arbitration Clauses,[58] the Geneva Convention of 26 September 1927 on the Enforcement of Foreign Arbitral Awards[59] and the New York Convention of 10 June 1958 on the Recognition and Enforcement of Foreign Arbitral Awards.[60]

Arbitration regarding parties domiciled in Switzerland is governed by the Swiss Federal Civil Procedure Code which came into force on 1 January 2011.

56.11.3.2   State courts

Until recently, every Canton had its own Civil Procedure Code and therefore, 26 different Civil Procedure Codes existed in Switzerland. On 1 Janu-

---

[55] The Chambers of Commerce of Zurich and Geneva are among the world's very first providers of international arbitration services. The first Arbitration Rules of the Zurich Chamber of Commerce were launched in 1911.

[56] The Swiss Rules of International Arbitration are essentially based on the UNCITRAL Arbitration Rules. However, the parties to the arbitration are free to choose the rules governing the arbitral proceedings as well as the law governing the subject matter in dispute. In the absence of a choice of procedural rules, the arbitral tribunal sets up its own rules as far as necessary. The Swiss Rules of International Arbitration have been amended in 2012.

[57] RS 291.

[58] RS 0.277.11.

[59] RS 0.277.111.

[60] RS 0.277.12.

ary 2011, the Swiss Federal Civil Procedure Code[61] came into force and replaced the Cantonal Civil Procedure Codes.[62] According to the Swiss Federal Civil Procedure Code there are several courts of primary jurisdiction (or "district courts" in larger cantons) and one court of appeal. Under given circumstances, the decision of the last cantonal instance may be brought before the Supreme Federal Court, which decides in last instance.

Four cantons (Zurich, Bern, Aargau and St Gallen) have commercial courts, which have often proven very qualified in dealing with complex commercial disputes.[63] In some cantons, specialised courts exist for labour and rent/lease disputes.

---

[61] RS 272.
[62] The organisation of the courts, however, remain in the competence of the Cantons.
[63] The expertise of full-time judges in the commercial courts is supplemented by so-called commercial judges drawn from business and industry, who are chosen for their specialised knowledge in their own field.

Chapter 57

Ireland

Anne-Marie Bohan, Partner

Matheson Ormsby Prentice

57.1   Outline

Parts 1 to 11 of this book describe the key business issues relevant for outsourcing and other services agreements. They also describe the key legal issues under English law. This chapter describes the specific legal and business issues which affect services and outsourcing arrangements in Ireland.

Many of the legal issues identified in Parts 1 to 11 of this Guide, and the resulting business issues, are applicable to outsourcing in and from Ireland, which is unsurprising given the long common legal heritage of Ireland and England prior to 1922. Where there are differences which are relevant to outsourcing contracts, the main issues have been identified below.

57.2   People issues – ARD

57.2.1   *Implementation of ARD in Ireland*

The European Communities (Protection of Employees and Transfer of Undertakings) Regulations 2003 (the "ARD Regulations") implemented the ARD into Irish law. The ARD Regulations give employees certain rights when the whole or part of an undertaking or business is transferred from one employer (transferor) to another employer (transferee) as a result of a legal transfer or merger.

57.2.2   *Application of the ARD Regulations to Services or Outsourcing*

Whether the ARD Regulations apply to a services or outsourcing contract will be a question of fact in each case, and will depend on factors such as whether there has been a transfer of assets (either tangible or intangible), or, in the case of a services agreement involving a labour-intensive part of a business, whether there is a transfer of a significant part of the workforce (whether in terms of numbers or skills (which, in itself, may be described as an intangible asset)). Unlike the position in the UK, there is no automatic application of the ARD Regulations in the event of a "service provision change".

57.2.3   *Effect of application of ARD Regulations*

If the ARD Regulations apply, all employees who are wholly or mainly engaged in the business (or part thereof) transferring have the right to transfer their employment to the supplier, on their existing terms and conditions of employment, with their continuity of service intact. Where a customer contracts out for the first time, if the ARD Regulations apply, the affected employees will therefore have the right to transfer to the supplier. Where a customer changes supplier, the ARD Regulations (if applicable) will normally operate as between the incoming and outgoing suppliers, and should not affect the customer directly (they may indirectly impact on the customer through the new supplier's charges for the services). However, where a customer terminates a services or outsourcing contract and brings the services back "in-house", then if the ARD Regulations apply, the customer would in such case be the transferee for ARD Regulations purposes. In each case, the issues identified in Chapter 31 in respect of identification and indemnification of risks will need to be considered.

57.2.4   *Consultation obligations under the ARD Regulations*

57.2.4.1   *Duty to consult*

The ARD Regulations impose a duty on both the customer (unless the transfer is between two suppliers on a change of supplier) and supplier(s) to inform their respective affected employees (by way of their representatives, whether existing, i.e. a trade union, or specifically elected for the purpose of information and consultation under the ARD Regulations) of various matters in relation to the transfer and consult with them on any measures envisaged in relation to such employees, with a view to reaching an agreement. The ARD Regulations do not specify that an agreement must be reached on all issues, but simply require that the affected employees must be consulted with a view to reaching an agreement.

57.2.4.2   *Information employees must receive*

The information that the affected employees are entitled to receive includes the reasons for the transfer and the legal, social and economic implications of the transfer for them, and must be provided at least 30 days in advance of the transfer or, if this is not reasonably practicable, in good time prior to the transfer. If there are any measures envisaged with regard to the employees (i.e. if there are to be changes to their terms and conditions of employment which are, strictly speaking, prohibited by the ARD Regulations or if redundancies post-transfer are contemplated), then they are entitled to be consulted, again, 30 days prior to the transfer, or if this is not reasonably practicable, in good time prior to the transfer.

57.2.4.3   *Penalty for non-provision of information to employees*

If information provisions and, where applicable, consultation does not take place, or is carried out improperly or late, the affected employees or their representatives are entitled to complain to the Rights Commissioners and an award of up to four weeks' gross remuneration per employee may be made. The supplier would be liable for any successful claim where the ARD Regulations apply.

57.2.4.4   *Information the customer must provide to the supplier*

As an adjunct to the above, and subject always to compliance with data protection legislation, the customer (or transferring supplier, as relevant) must supply all "relevant" employment-related information to the supplier, including information in relation to any outstanding claims that the affected employees might have against the customer (or transferring supplier), to facilitate the supplier in complying with its obligations under the ARD Regulations. If this information is not provided and the supplier incurs liability as a result, it may be in a position to recover any losses against the customer (or transferring supplier).

57.2.4.5   *No obligation on supplier to provide information to customer*

In contrast, unless there are reasons envisaged in relation to the affected employees' employment, there is no equivalent obligation on the incoming supplier to provide information to the customer (or transferring supplier), although in practice, the supplier will commonly request the customer's assistance in disseminating any information about it to transferring employees in advance of the transfer.

57.2.5 Secondment arrangements

Under some services or outsourcing agreements, the parties have seconded employees from the customer to the supplier, rather than have the employees transfer directly. However, this type of arrangement entails a number of inherent risks. There is a risk that the customer and supplier would be held to be co-employers of the employees. In addition, such an arrangement can make it more difficult to deal with the employees on a daily basis. Finally, if assets are transferred as part of the arrangement, there is a risk that the ARD Regulations would in any event be deemed to apply, with the result that the secondment arrangement would not prevent employees claiming that they had a right to transfer. As any provision in any agreement which tries to exclude or limit any provision of the ARD Regulations, or which is inconsistent with any of its provisions, is void, structuring the arrangement as a secondment would not preclude the application of the ARD Regulations.

57.2.6 Offshore outsourcing

Where an Irish customer is entering into an offshore outsourcing arrangement, then while the ARD Regulations will apply in principle to the outsourcing, the supplier will be under no legal obligation to comply with any of the requirements of the ARD Regulations, including the consultation obligations (although they may be required to comply with their own regulations which transpose ARD (if applicable)). The contractual provisions dealing with the implications of ARD, including any indemnifications and the allocation of risk and cost, will therefore be of even greater importance for the customer.

57.3 People issues—other employment issues

57.3.1 Redundancy

57.3.1.1 Permissible redundancies

Employees affected by a services or outsourcing agreement can only be dismissed in the case of genuine redundancy. The ARD Regulations permit dismissals for economic, technical or organisational (ETO) reasons requiring changes in the workforce, which has been broadly defined in relevant case law as redundancy. However, dismissals that occur because of the transfer which are not genuine redundancies or are otherwise unlawful give rise to a risk of unfair dismissal and wrongful dismissal claims against the customer and/or supplier(s). Generally, post-transfer dismissals on ETO grounds are easier to justify than pre-transfer dismissals, as pre-transfer dismissals are more likely to be viewed as arising solely by reason of the transfer.

57.3.1.2   Refusal to transfer

The position of employees who refuse to transfer differs from that in the UK, in that a refusal to transfer is not a deemed resignation. The ARD Regulations are silent on this issue. However, in a High Court decision (which was an appeal from the Employment Appeals Tribunal) it was held that a refusal to transfer does not automatically give rise to a redundancy situation, and the two employees who had refused to transfer under the ARD Regulations to the transferee, in circumstances where there were no changes to the terms and conditions of employment (or the location of their employment) were not entitled to a redundancy payment from the transferor.

57.3.1.3   Statutory redundancy

An employee's statutory redundancy payment will be calculated as two weeks' normal remuneration for each year of continuous and reckonable service (pro-rated), plus the equivalent of one week's normal weekly remuneration. One week's normal remuneration is capped at €600 per week or €31,200 per year. The employee must also be given payment in lieu of notice, any outstanding holidays, bonuses and commissions, and arrears of salary, if any, etc.

57.3.2   Collective redundancies

The Protection of Employment Act 1977 (the "1977 Act"), imposes additional obligations relating to informing and consulting employees' representatives and notifying the Minister for Enterprise, Trade and Employment of proposed collective redundancies. Collective redundancies arise where the numbers being made redundant in any 30-day period, for reasons unconnected with the individual employee, amount to 30 or more individuals, or if fewer, if the number is between approximately 10 per cent and 25 per cent of the workforce (depending on how many people are employed in the organisation). The 1977 Act may be relevant where a services or outsourcing arrangement is likely to result in substantial redundancies.

57.3.3   Unfair dismissals/wrongful dismissals

Where a dismissal arises by reason solely of a services or outsourcing agreement to which the ARD Regulations apply, or is not a genuine redundancy, then it will be deemed to be unfair, and the affected employee may be entitled to reinstatement, re-engagement or up to two years' gross remuneration. In contrast to unfair dismissal claims brought under the Unfair Dismissals Act 1977 to 2011, where a claim in respect of a dismissal is brought under the ARD Regulations, the affected employee need not have a minimum year's service and is not under any duty to mitigate loss.

An employee may also, in these circumstances, institute an action at common law and seek damages for wrongful dismissal. An employee can choose whether he wants to proceed by way of unfair dismissal or wrongful dismissal. However, wrongful dismissal claims are very rare in transfer of undertakings situations.

57.4 Pensions issues

57.4.1 Pensions issues under the ARD Regulations

57.4.1.1 Scope of protection—Martin/Beckmann liabilities

The ARD Regulations do not apply to employees' rights to old age, invalidity or survivor's benefits under company pensions schemes that fall outside the scope of the Social Welfare Acts 2005 to 2011. In essence, therefore, occupational pension scheme benefits will not transfer unless they fall with the *Martin/Beckmann* liabilities exception. In practice, *Martin/Beckmann* liabilities would only be expected to arise in public sector schemes or older defined benefit schemes. Risks associated with *Martin/Beckmann* liabilities are generally addressed in the services or outsourcing contract through appropriate indemnification provisions.

57.4.1.2 No minimum pension protection

There is no Irish law equivalent to the UK's minimum pension protection (outlined in Chapter 31). While it was expected that this position would change, the issue of pensions rights under the ARD Regulations has not yet been addressed in legislation. Furthermore, there is currently no indication of when legislation might be introduced to address and resolve these issues. Notwithstanding this, the absence of legislative requirements has not prevented the replication, or partial replication, of pension arrangements as a result of commercial negotiations in situations where the ARD Regulations apply, particularly in the public sector and in industries with strong union representation.

57.5   Contract law

57.5.1   General principles

For the most part, the principles of Irish contract law will be the same as those applying under the laws of England and Wales. Material differences, particularly with respect to liability issues, are identified in sections 57.5.2 and 57.7 below.

57.5.2   Privity of contract issues

57.5.2.1   No third-party beneficiary legislation

There is no Irish equivalent to the Contracts (Rights of Third Parties) Act 1999. Accordingly, the privity of contract rule continues to apply under Irish law.

57.5.2.2   Implication of privity rule

This means that obligations in an agreement that purport to apply to entities that are not a party to the agreement cannot be enforced against those entities, and similarly benefits that purport to be extended to such entities, cannot be enforced by such entities. This can have significant implications for services or outsourcing arrangements which purport to impose obligations on sub-contractors or group companies of the supplier, or to confer benefits on affiliates or customers of the customer, or replacement suppliers.

57.5.2.3   Addressing privity issues

The issue in relation to imposition of obligations can be overcome by making the supplier prime contractor and fully liable for the acts and omissions of its sub-contractors and agents. Overcoming the inability of third parties to the contract to enforce purported benefits is more difficult, as there has been no judicial analysis as yet of the various contractual provisions which have been used to attempt to circumvent this limitation (such as providing that the customer can enforce on behalf of the third party, or deeming third-party losses to be losses of the customer).

57.6 Limitations of liability

57.6.1 *General approach to liability and limiting liability*

In general, the approach to liability issues and limitation on liability provisions, both from a legal and a commercial perspective, will be the same in Ireland as the position outlined in Chapters 34 and 35 in respect of the UK. However, there has been an increasing trend for customers which are multinationals or subsidiaries of multinationals (particularly US multinationals) to seek to impose "US-style" risk allocation provisions in services or outsourcing contracts, with the customers seeking broad indemnification and unlimited liability under an increasing category of heads. This development is particularly marked in the financial services sector, and poses additional challenges for suppliers in an increasingly competitive market.

57.6.2 *Liability under fund custody and administration arrangements*

The somewhat unusual approach to liability under fund custody and administration agreements which has been identified in Chapter 34 mirrors the approach taken in the Irish funds industry. Events in the international financial markets since the start of the recent global liquidity crisis, including the issues which have arisen as a direct result of the Lehman insolvency and the Madoff fraud, have led to a re-examination by Europe of the approach to liability issues under fund custody agreements in particular, culminating in significant changes which will be implemented under the Alternative Investment Fund Managers Directive (AIFMD) (due to be implemented by 1 July 2013) and the proposed UCITS V Directive, as described in Chapter 41.

57.6.3 *Sale of Goods Legislation*

Under the Sale of Goods Act 1893 and the Sale of Goods and Supply of Services Act 1980 (collectively the "Sale of Goods Legislation"), certain terms are implied into every contract for the sale of goods or the supply of a service.

In the context of services contracts, the implied conditions include conditions that the services will be supplied with "due skill, care and diligence", that where materials are used they will be sound and reasonably fit for the purposes for which they are required, and that where goods are supplied they will be of merchantable quality. Where the agreement is between non-consumers, as would be the case in outsourcing arrangements, these implied terms may be excluded or varied by an express term of the contract, or by the course of dealing between the parties, or by usage, if the usage is such as to bind both parties to the contract. However, it is not possible to exclude the implied condition as to title.

57.6.4   Unfair contract terms

Unlike the position in the UK, the application of the Irish legislation which implemented the Unfair Terms in Consumer Contracts Directive[1] (namely the European Communities (Unfair Terms in Consumer Contracts) Regulations 1995) is limited to consumer contracts, and will therefore not be relevant to any business services or outsourcing agreement.

57.7   Data protection

57.7.1   Implementation of the Data Protection Directive in Ireland

57.7.1.1   Implementing legislation

The Data Protection Directive has been implemented in Ireland through the Data Protection Acts 1988 and 2003 (collectively the "DP Acts").

57.7.1.2   Data Protection Commissioner

The Data Protection Commissioner (the "DPC") is the supervisory authority for the purposes of monitoring the application of the Data Protection Directive in Ireland. The DPC is appointed by the Irish government but is independent in the exercise of his functions, which are essentially to uphold the rights of individuals under the DP Acts, and to enforce against data controllers the obligations specified in the DP Acts. The DPC also exercises certain functions arising from Ireland's membership of the EU, including acting as Ireland's representative on the Article 29 Working Party.

57.7.2   Application of the DP Acts

57.7.2.1   Scope of application

The DP Acts will apply to data controllers "established in Ireland" where data is processed in the context of that establishment, or if the data controller is established neither in Ireland nor in any other EEA state, it makes use

---

[1]   Directive 93/13/EEC of 5 April 1993 on unfair terms in consumer contracts.

of equipment in Ireland for processing the data (otherwise than for the purpose of transit through the territory of Ireland).

57.7.2.2   Meaning of "established in Ireland"

A data controller (not being an individual) will be "established in Ireland" for the purposes of the DP Acts if it is:

(a)   an incorporated entity established under the laws of Ireland, i.e. a company established under the Companies Act 1963 to 2009;

(b)   a partnership or other unincorporated association formed under the laws of Ireland; or

(c)   an entity not falling under the above categories but which maintains in Ireland an office, branch or agency through which it carries on any activity, or a regular practice.

57.7.2.3   Meaning of "data controller"

Whether an entity is a data controller or data processor will be a question of fact in each case. In the majority of services or outsourcing arrangements, the supplier will be a processor acting on behalf of the customer (which will be the data controller).

While in principle all data controllers and data processors to whom the DP Acts apply are obliged to register with the DPC, in practice the obligation will only apply where a controller is not "exempted". Certain "prescribed" categories of data controller, which include financial services institutions and insurance companies, are obliged to register even if they would otherwise fall within the exempt categories.

57.7.3   Implications of the DP Acts for services and outsourcing contracts

57.7.3.1   Applicable guidelines

The DPC has not issued any specific guidelines in relation to outsourcing of data processing functions, or of services which, of necessity, involve data processing. However, several of the more general guidelines which have been issued by the DPC, including in particular with respect to transfers abroad and sharing of information within the public and private sectors, will be of relevance in the context of services or outsourcing arrangements.

57.7.3.2   General compliance

Obviously, in entering into any services or outsourcing arrangement, the customer as a data controller will be obliged to remain in compliance with its general data protection obligations. This includes in respect of disclosure of personal data relating to employees, which will need to be managed so as to ensure compliance with both the DP Acts and the ARD Regulations.

57.7.3.3   Processing agreements

In addition, under the DP Acts, where a customer contracts out services which involve processing of personal data, the customer will be obliged to put in place a written agreement with the supplier which specifies that the supplier will only act in relation to the personal data on the instructions of the customer and which sets out the necessary security measures that the supplier will implement. The customer must then ensure compliance with those security measures.

57.7.3.4   Supplier obligations as data processor

It should not be overlooked that the supplier, where it is a data processor, will be independently subject to the data protection security principle, and may be obliged to register with the DPC.

57.7.4   Data protection issues in offshore outsourcing contracts

57.7.4.1   Prohibition on transfer

Under the DP Acts, personal data cannot be transferred from Ireland to a country or territory outside the EEA unless that country or territory ensures an "adequate level of protection" for personal data. While the DP Acts go on to set out a number of factors to be taken into account in determining whether there is an "adequate level of protection" in the jurisdiction in question, in practice, unless the European Commission or the DPC has indicated that it views a jurisdiction as affording an adequate level of protection, or the transfer falls under one of the exemptions specified in the DP Acts, the prohibition will apply.

57.7.4.2   Applicable exemptions

The exemptions in the DP Acts include the EC Model Contract Clauses and BCRs, and the comments in Chapter 47 in relation to these exemptions are equally valid in an Irish context. There is also the possibility under the DP Acts of having the DPC specifically approve a bespoke form of contract, although in order to obtain approval, the customer would need to be in a position to justify its decision not to use the EC Model Contract Clauses, and the bespoke contract should not result in a reduction in the level of protection afforded to data subjects.

57.7.4.3   Consent issues

While data subject consent is one of the exemptions under which transfers from Ireland to non-EEA jurisdictions will be permitted, the DPC has raised concerns where personal data is transferred outside the EEA based on consent, particularly where the transfer is systematic. The stated preference of the DPC would be reliance on the EC Model Contract Clauses and BCRs, and for the other exemptions to be relied on only where it is genuinely not practicable or feasible to rely on these.

57.7.4.4   Processor to processor transfers

It should also be noted that the EC Model Contract Clauses provide for transfers between controller and transfers from controllers to non-EEA processors (which are permitted to sub-contract the processing subject to certain conditions). However, they do not exempt transfers from EEA based processors to non-EEA based processors, which can give rise to issues where a supplier wishes to subcontract part of the services to a non-EEA sub-contractor, where an EEA based supplier is part of an international group which wishes to leverage internal structures and technologies as part of the arrangement solution, or where the contractual structure is an "offshore/onshore" or "onshore/offshore" model.

57.7.5   Enforcement

57.7.5.1   Powers of the DPC

The DPC is the body with primary responsibility for enforcement of the DP Acts, and has wide-ranging powers under the DP Acts. The DPC will investigate breaches or likely breaches of the DP Acts, either where an individual complains to him of a contravention (in which case the DPC is obliged to investigate, unless he is of the view that it is frivolous or vexatious), or the DPC is otherwise of the opinion that there has been a contravention. The DPC also has the power to carry out "privacy audits" to ensure compliance with the DP Acts or to identify any contraventions of the DP Acts, as well as investigations of the circumstances surrounding a personal data security breach.

57.7.5.2   Offences

Breaches of many of the provisions of the DP Acts are not, of themselves, offences. Rather, the offence arises from failure to comply with a notice issued by the DPC. Breach of the registration obligations, the carrying on of prescribed processing, provision of false or misleading information to the DPC, and unauthorised disclosure, in certain circumstances, are offences under the DP Acts.

57.7.5.3 DPC notices

The forms of notice which may be issued by the DPC include:

(a) enforcement notices, which are served where the DPC is of the opinion that a person has contravened or is contravening a provision of the DP Acts. This type of notice may require the person to take such steps as are specified in the notice within a specified time to comply with the provision concerned; and

(b) prohibition notices, which prohibit the transfer of personal data from Ireland to a place outside Ireland unless such a transfer is required or authorised by or under any enactment, or required by any convention or other instrument imposing an obligation on Ireland.

57.7.5.4 Statutory duty of care

In addition to the above, the DP Acts establish a statutory duty of care owed by both data controllers and data processors, in respect of the collection by them of personal data or their dealings with such data, towards the relevant data subjects.

57.7.5.5 Individual rights

Individuals also have indirect powers of enforcement of the provisions of the DP Acts, including the right to establish the existence of personal data, the right of access to personal data, a right of rectification or erasure of any personal data in relation to which there has been a contravention of the data protection principles, and the right of a data subject to object to processing of personal data which is likely to cause damage or distress. While primary responsibility for enforcement of the DP Acts rests with the DPC, individuals have further indirect enforcement rights through complaints to the DPC.

57.7.6 Security breaches

Providers of publicly available electronic communications networks or services are subject to specific breach notification requirements under the European Communities (Electronic Communications Networks and Services) (Privacy and Electronic Communications) Regulations 2011 (the "2011 Regulations") (which transposed the E-Privacy Directive 2009/136/EC), where there has been a breach of security involving subscriber information. In cases where the 2011 Regulations apply, service providers are required to notify the DPC of every data breach involving a subscriber, as well as notifying any data subjects that may be adversely affected. Service providers are also required to notify subscribers without delay where there is a risk to the security of the network, unless the DPC is satisfied that the data would be unintelligible to third parties. Failure to comply with these obligations could result in fines of up to €5,000 or on indictment of up to €250,000 per offence.

There is otherwise no specific obligation under the DP Acts requiring controllers or processors to notify either the DPC or affected customers or individuals in the event of a security breach. However, the DPC has consistently adopted the view that, even in the absence of an express obligation, notification is arguably required under data protection principles, and that in any event security breaches should be notified to both it and data subjects as a matter of best practice.

In July 2011, the DPC published a personal data security breach Code of Practice (the "Breach Code"), which applies to controllers other than those subject to the 2011 Regulations. The Breach Code provides that all incidents in which personal data have been put at risk should be reported to the DPC as soon as the data controller becomes aware of the incident, unless the full extent and consequences of the incident have been reported without delay directly to the affected data subjects, where they number less than 100 and no sensitive personal data or personal data of a financial nature was put at risk. The DPC may request a detailed report in relation to any breach or risk incident and may launch a detailed investigation of the circumstances surrounding the incident.

In the public sector, guidance published by the Department of Finance on protecting the confidentiality of personal data also recommends that any security breach be notified to the DPC.

57.8   Insolvency issues

57.8.1   *Examinerships*

57.8.1.1   *Overview of examinerships*

Examinerships are the creation of the Companies (Amendment) Act 1990, as amended. The objective of an examinership is to afford to a company a moratorium during which creditors cannot enforce their rights against it, while an independent court-appointed officer, an examiner, examines the company's financial situation. Provided the examiner is of the view that the company can be saved, the examiner will formulate proposals for a compromise or a scheme of arrangement and report to the High Court with a view to the obtaining the approval of the High Court for the proposals in the hope that the business of the company can continue into the future.

57.8.1.2   *Protection of the High Court*

The availability of the examinership procedure could have implications for both customers and suppliers in the event that the other party to a services or outsourcing contract avails itself of the court protection afforded by the procedure, as upon the appointment of an examiner, the company is placed under the protection of the High Court. Court protection lasts for an initial period of 70 days but can be extended by the court for an additional 30 days. During the protection period, no proceedings can be instigated against a company in examinership. The examiner's main function is to propose a scheme of arrangement to the court, which, if approved by the court and a majority of creditors, becomes binding.

57.8.1.3   *Reasonable prospect of survival*

A court cannot appoint an examiner unless there is a reasonable prospect for the survival of the company and the whole or any part of its undertaking. Not only must there be a reasonable prospect of survival of the company but there must also be a reasonable prospect of the survival of the whole or any part of its undertaking as a going concern. If, for example, the company proposed to sell a company's business and assets then there would not be a reasonable prospect of the survival of the undertaking as a going concern.

57.8.1.4   *Restrictions on proceedings against company in examinership*

Once the company is placed under court protection, the creditors of the company are prevented from taking any action to enforce their security. In particular:

(a)   no proceedings for the winding up of the company may be commenced or resolution for winding up passed and any resolution passed shall have no effect;

(b)   no receiver shall be appointed and if appointed shall be unable to act;

(c)   where any claim against the company is secured, no action may be taken to realise the whole or any part of that security except with the consent of the examiner.

(d)   no steps may be taken to repossess goods in the company's possession under any hire-purchase agreement except with the consent of the examiner;

(e)   no attachment, sequestration, distress or execution against the company's assets may be effected, without the consent of the examiner; and

(f)   no attachment, sequestration, distress or execution may be effected against any party in respect of the debts of the company and no proceedings may be commenced against any such party in respect of the debts of the company.

Furthermore, there is a general prohibition barring issuing all other proceedings against a company that is under the protection of the court (except with leave of the court).

57.8.1.5   *Scheme of arrangement*

Where a scheme of arrangement is approved by the court and a majority in number and value of the creditors, it will become binding on all creditors, including those who objected to the scheme, and will generally result in the creditors receiving only a proportion of the amounts due to them.

57.8.1.6   *Implications for outsourcing agreements*

The initiation of an examinership procedure in relation to one party to a services or outsourcing agreement could therefore significantly restrict the ability of the other party to recover costs or damages. For these reasons, the appointment of an examiner to a customer or supplier would generally be treated as triggering a right to terminate (but not automatic termination, in the same way as the appointment of a liquidator or receiver would trigger a termination right), with a view to limiting any further exposure of the unaffected party.

57.9   Financial services regulation

57.9.1   *Financial regulation in Ireland*

The Central Bank of Ireland (the "Central Bank") is the body responsible for authorisation and regulation of credit and financial services institutions and insurance providers in Ireland.

57.9.2   *Implementation of MiFID in Ireland*

57.9.2.1   *Implementing legislation*

MiFID has been implemented in Ireland through the European Communities (Markets in Financial Instruments Directive) Regulations 2007, as amended (the "MiFID Regulations"). Some measures complementary to the MiFID Regulations, such as the imposition of significant penalties for conviction on indictment for major breaches of the MiFID Regulations, required the enactment of primary legislation and were introduced in the Markets in Financial Instruments and Miscellaneous Provisions Act 2007.

57.9.2.2   *No "gold-plating"*

The MiFID Regulations do not contain any "gold-plating" of MiFID, and are a direct transposition of the requirements of MiFID into Irish law. Therefore, the general comments in relation to MiFID in Chapters 38 and 39 apply equally in an Irish context.

57.9.2.3 Formalisation of practice

The introduction of MiFID into Irish law formalised and codified, for MiFID firms, what was already industry practice across a broad range of financial services and insurance outsourcings, as well as introducing an express requirement to document the outsourcing in greater detail than might have been the case prior to MiFID (particularly for intra-group outsourcings).

57.9.3 Implementation of CRD in Ireland

57.9.3.1 Implementing legislation

CRD has been implemented into Irish law through the European Communities (Capital Adequacy of Investment Firms) Regulations 2006 and European Communities (Capital Adequacy of Credit Institutions) Regulations 2006 (collectively the "CRD Regulations"). The Central Bank has also issued an administrative notice on the implementation of CRD, which, together with the CRD Regulations and CEBS CRD guidance, forms the basis of the transposition of CRD in Ireland. The Central Bank's notice cross-refers to the CEBS guidance which, absent an explicit statement to the contrary in the Central Bank's notice, should be also regarded as applicable Central Bank guidance.

57.9.3.2 No "gold-plating"

As is the case with the implementation of MiFID, the CRD Regulations did not impose additional obligations on credit institutions and investment firms. Accordingly, the general comments in Chapters 38 to 42 will equally apply in an Irish context.

57.9.4 Central Bank approach to outsourcing

The Central Bank has not published any specific guidance on outsourcing. In practice, however, the Central Bank has applied, as relevant, the international and sector-specific outsourcing guidelines and criteria identified in Chapters 38 to 42 (namely those of the Joint Forum, IOSCO and CEBS), the outsourcing rules under MiFID, and the governance requirements under CRD. Even where not mandatory in the context of non-material outsourcings, the relevant guidelines and rules should nonetheless be taken into account in the context of non-material outsourcings. Material outsourcings must be notified to the Central Bank in advance.

The Central Bank has also previously published an Assistance Paper on outsourcing, which sets out the views of the Central Bank in relation to certain aspects of outsourcing, and which effectively tracks the provisions of MiFID relating to outsourcing.

In July 2011, the Central Bank introduced specific requirements for outsourcing by fund administration firms (dealt with in section 57.9.6.2 below).

Specific requirements relating to outsourcing by payment institutions are included in the Central Bank's prudential requirements for payment institutions.

57.9.5   General Irish provisions

57.9.5.1   Fitness and probity regime

During 2011, the Central Bank issued a Code on Fitness and Probity Standards ("Code") pursuant to its powers under s.50 of the Central Reform Act 2010 (the "2010 Act"), which applies to all regulated financial services providers (with the exception of credit unions). The 2010 Act created a statutory system for the regulation of persons performing controlled functions (CF) or pre-approval controlled functions (PCF), and the Code specifies the standards of fitness and probity (the "Standards") with which all persons performing these functions must, at a minimum, comply. The Central Bank has also issued guidance on the Standards (the "Guidance"). The Central Bank Reform Act 2010 (ss.20 and 22) Regulations 2011, as amended (the "2010 Act Regulations") specify the functions that are designated CFs (eg, functions providing advice to customers) and PCFs (e.g., directors, chairman, head of finance etc).

The Guidance states that where a financial institution outsources the performance of a PCF, it will not be required to obtain Central Bank approval in respect of the person performing that function, provided there is a written agreement in place and the financial institution to which the function is being outsourced is regulated by the Central Bank or an equivalent authority in another jurisdiction. While the pre-approval requirement does not apply in this case, a person benefitting from this exclusion may still be subject to an investigation, suspension or prohibition notice under the 2010 Act.

Where the performance of a PCF is outsourced to an unregulated entity, the financial institution concerned must obtain the approval of the Central Bank before appointing the unregulated entity to perform the PCF on its behalf. The written outsourcing agreement must also name the person within the unregulated entity who will be responsible for performing the PCF and persons performing a PCF under such an outsourcing agreement must comply with the Standards.

If a CF is outsourced to an unregulated entity, the unregulated entity must be able to identify the individuals who will perform the CFs and assess whether those persons are compliant with the Standards. In such cases, the outsourced service provider should be able to provide written confirmation to the financial institution that the individuals performing CFs are compliant with the Standards and have agreed to be bound by them.

57.9.5.2 Minimum competency requirements

Pursuant to its powers under the 2010 Act, the Central Bank has also updated its minimum competency requirements and has published the Minimum Competency Code 2011 (the "MCC"). The MMC provides that where a regulated firm outsources activities, the regulated firm remains fully responsible under the MCC. The MCC specifies the minimum competency standards with which a person falling within its scope must comply when performing a CF or a PCF, and sets out details on the recognition of qualifications for the purposes of minimum competency standards.

57.9.5.3 Central Bank Consumer Protection Code

The Central Bank has not published general principles or regulations applicable to regulated firms which would be equivalent to the FSA Handbook. In January 2012, however, it updated its Consumer Protection Code (CPC), which is of relevance to an outsourcing by a regulated entity (with some exceptions, including firms providing MiFID services) of functions which might impact on the firm's interactions with its customers.

57.9.5.4 CPC general principles

The CPC sets out a number of general principles to which all firms covered by the CPC must adhere in their dealings with customers and prospective customers (whether or not consumers) and *within the context of their authorisations*. These obligations include:

(a) having and employing effectively the resources and procedures, systems and control checks that are necessary for compliance with the CPC;
(b) full disclosure of relevant material information;
(c) speedy, efficient and fair error correction and complaints handling; and
(d) ensuring that any outsourced activity complies with the requirements of the CPC.

57.9.5.5 Meaning of "consumer" in the CPC

The CPC also contains detailed provisions which apply where a CPC firm is dealing with "consumers" (which for the purposes of the CPC includes businesses other than incorporated bodies having an annual turnover (or being part of a group having an annual turnover) in excess of €3 million). In addition to the general principles outlined above, the provisions dealing with consumer records, and error and complaints handling, may be of potential relevance in the context of outsourcing arrangements.

57.9.6 *Financial services issues in offshore outsourcings*

57.9.6.1 *No prohibition on offshore outsourcings*

In principle, there is no prohibition on regulated entities entering into offshore outsourcing arrangements. Where an outsourcing involves an offshore jurisdiction, the Central Bank will focus closely on the confidentiality, security and business continuity arrangements which are implemented as part of the outsourcing.

57.9.6.2 *Outsourcing by fund administration firms*

In the funds administration sector, the Central Bank had in the past imposed requirements in relation to the minimum administration activities which were required to be undertaken in Ireland where the administration services are provided in respect of Irish authorised funds (both UICTS and non-UCITS). In practice, however, derogations had been granted on a case-by-case basis which had resulted over time in ad hoc derogations from most of the minimum activities restrictions.

Towards the end of 2010, and in light of the then imminent implementation of the UCITS IV Directive, including the management company passport, the Central Bank entered into a formal consultation with industry in relation to the minimum activities regime. The result was the adoption by the Central Bank on 1 July 2011 of outsourcing guidelines for fund administration firms ("Administration Guidelines") and the abandonment of the minimum activities regime. The Administration Guidelines broadly mirror the MiFID outsourcing rules. While in principle, all fund administration activities can now be outsourced by fund administrators, the Guidelines mandate that the "core administration functions" of the final checking and release of net asset value for dealing purposes, and maintenance of the fund shareholder register, must be performed in Ireland.

Overseas hardware and software facilities may also be availed of by Irish management companies/administrators/trustees by means of direct access. The substantive administration and control of the relevant fund must remain in Ireland.

57.9.6.4 *Fitness and probity in offshore outsourcings*

The Code is not limited to control functions performed within Ireland. Where someone performs a CF or PCF outside Ireland, but on behalf of a financial institution that is authorised, licensed or registered in Ireland, that individual will be subject to the Code (including the requirement that PCFs obtain prior approval from the Central Bank). However, the 2010 Act Regulations provide that where the performance of a function is outsourced pursuant to a written agreement to an entity which is regulated either by the Central Bank or by a comparable regulatory authority in another jurisdiction, that function will not be taken to be a PCF.

57.10 Public Procurement Directives

57.10.1 *Implementation of the Public Procurement Directive in Ireland*

57.10.1.1 *Implementing legislation*

The European Communities (Award of Public Authorities' Contracts) Regulations 2006 (the "Public Sector Regulations") implemented the Public Procurement Directive into Irish law. The Public Sector Regulations came into force in Ireland on 22 June 2006 and apply to all public contracts above certain thresholds (other than those entered into by utilities, dealt with in section 57.12 below) entered into after that date.

57.10.1.2 *Effect of implementation*

The Public Sector Regulations give effect to all of the provisions of the Public Procurement Directives described in Chapter 43, including framework agreements, competitive dialogue and electronic auctions.

57.10.1.3 *Remedies*

The European Communities (Public Authorities' Contracts) (Review Procedures) Regulations 2010 (the "Public Sector Remedies Regulations") provide for remedies and enforcement procedures in respect of contracts governed by the Public Sector Regulations.

The Public Sector Remedies Regulations provide that public contracting authorities must observe a standstill period of at least 14 days if the notice to an unsuccessful tenderer is sent by electronic means, or 16 days if by other means. Ireland has opted to exclude contracts awarded on the basis of a framework agreement or a dynamic purchasing system from the requirement to observe a standstill period.

57.10.2 Guidance for other public procurement contracts

57.10.2.1 National guidelines

Public contracts that fall below the thresholds in the Public Procurement Regulations are dealt with at national level. The relevant procedures have been codified in the Department of Finance Public Procurement Guidelines (or the "Green Book") which was last updated in November 2010.

57.10.2.2 Scope of application

The Public Sector Regulations and the Green Book apply to all government departments and offices, local and regional authorities and state-sponsored bodies in the procurement of public building and civil engineering contracts, public supply contracts and public service contracts, as well as to the disposal of public property.

57.10.2.3 Guidance

It is important to note that the Green Book acts only as guidance and is not legally binding on public contracting authorities. Rather, it sets out the general principle that a procedure based on competitive tendering should be used for all government contracts, save in exceptional circumstances when the approval of the Department of Finance is required. Non-compliance with the Green Book may give rise to corporate governance issues for state bodies.

57.10.3 General principles

There is a dearth of sector-specific guidance for public sector projects (other than in relation to PPP projects as described below, and the use of generic technical specifications in the ICT sector). However, public sector bodies must ensure that all procurement, whether above or below the Public Procurement thresholds, complies with certain general principles derived from the Treaty on the Functioning of the European Union (the "**Treaty**"), such as non-discrimination, equality of treatment, transparency, proportionality and mutual recognition.

57.10.4 PPP and PFI contracts

57.10.4.1 Guidance at national level

PFIs are a common form of PPP where the delivery of public services involves private sector investment in infrastructure. Many of the PPP contracts entered into in Ireland in the delivery of infrastructure projects share the characteristics of PFI contracts in the UK which are identified in Chapter 44. PFI specific guidance and best practice notes, akin to the UK HM Treasury guidance on the Standardisation of PFI Contracts, have not been published by the Irish authorities. However, the Guidelines for the Provision of Infrastructure and Capital Investments through Public Private Partnerships: Procedures for the Assessment, Approval, Audit and Procurement of Projects, deal with various forms of public procurement, including "design, build, finance, operate and, maintain" (or "DBFOM") contracts (with deferred annual or unitary payments), which would be the equivalent of PFIs as described. In addition, the National Development Finance Agency has published a template form of project agreement for accommodation PPPs, as well as a compendium of clauses for a DBFOM contract (available at *http://www.ppp.gov.ie* [Accessed 28 September 2012]), which cross-refers in some instances to the UK HM Treasury guidelines.

57.10.4.2 *International practice*

The HM Treasury guidelines would generally be viewed as best practice for DBFOM contracts, and accordingly the approach to risk allocation and key issues such as termination, force majeure, liability, compensation and waiver of damages (other than for breaches of contract not covered by the payment mechanism) will largely mirror the approach in the UK.

57.10.4.3 *Recent developments*

Some forms of DBFOM contracts, which incorporate a "balloon payment" on completion of construction, prior to service commencement, together with a shorter concession period during which the services fees will be paid, are being seen as more attractive investments to third-party financing institutions in the current financial market. It is also anticipated that the current credit market difficulties may lead to increasing focus on the covenant of the financing parties in DBFOM projects.

57.11 Utilities Directive

57.11.1 *Implementation of the Utilities Directive in Ireland*

57.11.1.1 *Implementing legislation*

The European Communities (Award of Contracts by Utility Undertakings) Regulations 2007 (the "Utilities Regulations") implement the Utilities Directive in Ireland. The Utilities Regulations came into force in Ireland on 28 February 2007 and apply to all utilities contracts above certain thresholds entered into on or after that date.

57.11.1.2 *Effect of implementation*

The Utilities Regulations give effect to all of the provisions of the Utilities Directives described in Chapter 46, including framework agreements and electronic auctions. The Utilities Regulations also provide for a standstill period, which is in line with the Remedies Directive, although with Ireland having opted for a 14-day standstill period.

57.11.1.3 *Remedies*

The European Communities (Award of Contracts by Utility Undertakings) (Review Procedures) Regulations 2010 (the "Utility Remedies Regulations") provide for almost identical remedies and enforcement procedures, in respect of contracts governed by the Utilities Regulations, as those applied by the Public Sector Remedies Regulations. The Utility Remedies Regulations came into force on 25 March 2010.

57.11.1.4 *National Guidelines—the Green Book*

The Department of Finance Guidelines will apply to utilities contracts which fall below the thresholds in the Utilities Regulations where the utility is a public sector body covered by the Green Book.

57.12   Competition law

57.12.1 *Merger control*

57.12.1.1 *Irish merger control*

The EU merger control regime described in Chapter 33 may apply to services and outsourcing arrangements involving an Irish customer and/or supplier. Alternatively, the arrangement may be subject to Irish merger control under Part 3 of the Competition Act 2002 (the "Competition Act 2002") (if the EU merger control regime applies, the Irish rules will not be applicable).

57.12.1.2 *Meaning of "merger/acquisition"*

Under the Competition Act 2002, a merger or acquisition will be deemed to have occurred if, inter alia, the result of the acquisition by one undertaking of the assets (including goodwill, or a substantial part of the assets) of a second undertaking is to place the first in a position to replace or substantially replace the second in the business (or the part of the business concerned, as appropriate) in which that undertaking was engaged immediately before the acquisition. Creation of a full-function joint venture (i.e. a joint venture created to perform, on an indefinite basis, all of the functions of an autonomous entity) will also constitute a merger or acquisition for Competition Act 2002 purposes, as would the direct or indirect acquisition by one or more undertakings of the whole (or a part) of another undertaking. A merger or acquisition is understood to occur following the acquisition of direct or indirect control of another undertaking. The relevant test for establishing control of an undertaking under the Competition Act 2002 is that of "decisive influence".

57.12.1.3   *Notification thresholds*

In order for the mandatory notification obligation under the Competition Act 2002 to apply, the transaction must meet the following thresholds in the most recent financial year:

(a)   the worldwide turnover of each of two or more of the undertakings involved is not less than €40 million; and
(b)   each of two or more of the undertakings involved "carry on business" in any part of the island of Ireland (i.e. Ireland and Northern Ireland); and
(c)   any one of the undertakings involved has a turnover in Ireland (i.e. not including Northern Ireland) of not less than €40 million.

57.12.1.4   *Notification is mandatory*

No merger meeting the thresholds can come into effect prior to obtaining clearance from the Competition Authority or the merger benefits from "deemed clearance" (where the Competition Authority has failed to issue a determination within statutorily defined periods). Clearance will cover not only the merger itself, but any ancillary restrictions (i.e. those which are directly related and necessary to the implementation of the merger and which are expressly referred to in the notification).

57.12.1.5   *Substantive test*

The substantive test for assessment under the Competition Act 2002 is "whether the result of the merger or acquisition would be to substantially lessen competition in markets for goods or services" in Ireland. In guidance that the Competition Authority has published in relation to its application of this test, consumer welfare, and in particular likely price increases to consumers as a result of the merger, are emphasised. The Competition Authority has also been sceptical to date in relation to arguments based on efficiencies, although recent indications are that this is changing.

57.12.2   *Prohibited anti-competitive agreements*

57.12.2.1   *Below-threshold mergers*

Where mergers fall below the thresholds for mandatory notification, they may nonetheless give rise to competition issues under ss.4 and 5 of the Competition Act 2002, which prohibit anti-competitive agreements and abuse of dominance respectively (equivalent at national level to Articles 81 and 82 of the EC Treaty). The Competition Act 2002 provides for a voluntary notification procedure in respect of mergers falling below the specified thresholds. The advantage of voluntary notification is that where a merger is cleared by the Competition Authority, it is immune from challenge under ss.4 and 5. However, in practice, voluntary notification is quite rare.

57.12.2.2   *Other anti-competitive agreements*

Similarly, where a services and outsourcing arrangement does not fall within the definition of a merger for the purposes of the EC Merger Regulation or the Competition Act 2002, the agreement itself, or an element of it, might be restrictive of competition contrary to ss.4 and 5 of the Competition Act 2002. Under the Competition Act 2002, the Competition Authority may adopt Declarations in respect of categories of agreements which meet the criteria for exemption under s.4(5) of the Competition Act 2002 (equivalent to Block Exemptions). The Competition Authority has adopted a number of Declarations at national level. Two Declarations are currently in effect, namely a Declaration in respect of vertical agreements and concerted practices, and a Declaration in respect of exclusive purchasing agreements for cylinder liquefied petroleum gas. In other cases, the Competition Authority may follow guidance at EU level, in which case the discussion in Chapter 33 in relation to exemptions and Commission notices will be of relevance in an Irish context.

57.13   Other relevant laws and best practice

57.13.1   *Dealing with disputes*

57.13.1.1   *ADR options*

The various forms of ADR discussed in Chapter 11 are becoming increasingly common in commercial disputes in Ireland, although mini trials/ executive tribunals and early neutral evaluation (ENE) are still rare.

57.13.1.2 The Commercial Court

In the context of litigating any claims in the Irish courts, it is likely that any claim under a services and outsourcing agreement would be initiated before the High Court. Application may then be made to have the matter entered into the commercial list of the High Court (colloquially known as the "Commercial Court"). Entry into the Commercial Court is at the discretion of the judge, but is likely to be granted in any case involving a business contract dispute or dispute in relation to the provision of services where the value of the claim is over €1 million, or in any case where the judge in question considers the dispute an appropriate matter for resolution by the Commercial Court. The major advantages of the Commercial Court are judges who specialise in commercial disputes, and speed, with cases before the Commercial Court taking on average 26 weeks from initiation to listing for hearing. The timelines in the High Court can otherwise be very lengthy.

57.13.2 Taxation

57.13.2.1 Complexity

As is the case in the UK, services and outsourcing arrangements can give rise to a variety of complex taxation issues, and expert taxation advice should be sought at the earliest opportunity to ensure that the taxation implications of the proposals do not undermine the business case for the transaction. A number of the more common Irish taxation issues are highlighted below in more detail.

57.13.2.2 Corporation tax

Several aspects of corporation tax should be considered in the context of services and outsourcings, including:

(a) Capital allowances. Where plant and equipment in respect of which capital allowances are available is transferred, the transfer can trigger a balancing charge or balancing allowance on the books of the customer, depending on the difference between the proceeds received on disposal and the tax written-down value as at the date of disposal.
(b) Tax losses. There may be a loss of the benefit of losses carried forward where the activity the subject of the arrangement is a separate business of the customer, as the customer can no longer be viewed as carrying on that activity. This issue will not arise where the activity was merely a function previously carried on internally within the customer as an inherent part of its overall business.
(c) Tax deduction for service fees. Generally, the customer will be entitled to an Irish tax deduction for any fees which are paid wholly and exclusively for the purposes of a trade carried on by the customer in Ireland.

(d) Transfer pricing. Ireland's transfer pricing rules may apply to a services and outsourcing arrangement where the customer and servicer are connected to each other (eg are part of the same corporate group) and the services or outsourcing arrangement is entered into for the purposes of a trade carried on in Ireland by either the customer or the servicer (or both). Where Irish transfer rules apply, the customer or the service provider (or both) may be obliged to calculate their Irish taxable income in accordance with the 'arm's length' principle. This means that, for the purposes of computing their Irish taxable profits, the customer may be treated for Irish tax purposes as having paid to the service provider, and the service provider may be treated as have received for Irish tax purposes, a servicing fee of an amount which would be paid by independent third parties entering to the same services or outsourcing arrangements.

57.13.2.3   Capital gains tax

In services and outsourcing arrangements to unrelated suppliers, any disposal of assets by a customer may constitute a disposal for Irish capital gains tax purposes. In general, therefore, the customer may be required to account for Irish capital gains tax on any chargeable gain that arises. The customer is usually treated as having disposed of, and the supplier as having acquired, the asset at its market value. The Irish capital taxation analysis can become considerably more complex depending on how the consideration is structured. Transfers of intellectual property may give rise to either Irish capital gains tax or corporation tax liabilities, depending on how the transfer and consideration are structured. Exemptions from Irish capital gains taxation may apply where, as part of a services and outsourcing arrangement, assets are disposed of to a connected supplier who is a company within the charge to Irish capital gains tax.

57.13.2.4   Stamp duty

Irish stamp duty may arise in connection with a number of aspects of services and outsourcing arrangements which involve the transfer of assets. Transfers of land or premises (real property) on commencement and/or on termination may give rise to a charge to stamp duty of up to 2 per cent of the value of the real property.

A transfer of other assets including, for example, goodwill of a business carried on in Ireland, will also result in a charge to Irish stamp duty, although plant and machinery and similar equipment will generally transfer by delivery and therefore stamp duty should not become an issue in such case. Finally, stamp duty will be applicable to assignments of contracts based on the value of the contract, whereas novations will usually not attract a stamp duty charge.

The transfer of most forms of intellectual property rights are exempt from Irish stamp duty.

Exemptions from Irish stamp duty may apply where, as part of a services and outsourcing arrangement, assets are transferred to a supplier which is company that is connected to the customer.

57.13.2.5   *Value Added Tax and Sales Tax*

Most supplies of services which have been contracted out will be subject to VAT and most services will be subject to the standard rate of VAT, currently 23 per cent.

Where the supplier and recipient is located in Ireland, the supplier will be obliged to account for VAT and will issue a VAT invoice charging such VAT to the recipient. Where the supplier is located outside Ireland and makes the supply to an Irish recipient, the services are likely to give rise to an obligation for the recipient to account for Irish VAT on a "reverse charge" basis to the Revenue Commissioners.

In most industries, the recipient should be entitled to fully recover such VAT on its normal VAT return. However, particular attention will be required where the recipient operates in an industry which is generally exempt from VAT such as banking or insurance where such VAT will not be recoverable and will represent a real cost to the recipient. In such scenarios, it may be the case that the services are also capable of classification as exempt from VAT, though professional advice should be sought.

In addition, generally, the broad VAT principles outlined elsewhere in this Guide are also of general application in Ireland.

Chapter 58

France

Mary-Daphné Fishelson, Partner

La Garanderie & Associes

58.1   Outline

This chapter describes the specific legal issues that will be relevant if the services, partnering or outsourcing agreement covers France.

58.2   People issues—ARD

58.2.1   *Application of ARD to outsourcing in France*

The ARD has now been fully transposed into French law. French law already provided similar rules to ARD so that applicable French rules stem mainly from Article L.1224-1 of the Labour Code and relating case law amended to take into consideration the ARD and European Court decisions on the subject.

58.2.1.1   *Article L.1224-1 of the Labour Code*

Article L.1224-1 (formerly L. 122-12) of the Labour Code states:

> "If the employer's legal status changes, particularly by way of succession, sale, merger, conversion of the business, or incorporation of the company, all contracts in progress on the day of the change subsist between the new employer and the company's personnel."

58.2.1.2   *Case law of the French Cour de Cassation (Court of Cassation—Supreme Court)*

Many decisions have been reached in this area, some of which deal with questions unresolved by the legislators. French and European courts have not always seen eye to eye in the past, particularly concerning the notion of "economic entity" and the necessity for a legal link between successive employers. However, this is no longer the case and decisions of both courts concur with and complement each other. The Court of Cassation often refers to Article L. 1224-1 of the Labour Code in the light of ARD.

58.2.1.3   Application of ARD to services and outsourcing

Services or outsourcing arrangements will not automatically result in the application of ARD.

ARD will only apply if the services or outsourcing arrangement entails:

(a)   the transfer of an economic entity that retains its identity; and
(b)   the activity previously carried out by the economic entity is continued or taken over.

The activity must enjoy real autonomy, both with regard to its human resources as well as its organisation and operating resources.

The existence of personnel specially dedicated to operating the transferred entity is a prerequisite. This condition is satisfied in particular if the relevant employees require a special qualification.

The existence of an economic entity also requires tangible or intangible assets. The transfer does not necessarily imply transfer of the ownership of assets. It is sufficient if the new operator of the transferred entity ("the supplier") is loaned the assets needed to run the activity.

Judges assess the conditions for the application of Article L. 1224-1 on a case-by-case basis, very often putting employees' interests first. The transfer of employees also depends in practice on the results of the negotiations between the employer and the works council according to whether the works council considers that it is in the employees' interest to be transferred (particularly depending on the advantages provided or not provided by the new employer). However the opposition of the works council cannot prevent an employer from carrying forward its decision to enter into a services or outsourcing arrangement as long as the arrangements comply with the above conditions.

58.2.1.4   Refusal of the employees to transfer

If Article L. 1224-1 of the Labour Code applies, the employee cannot refuse the transfer of his/her employment contract. His/her refusal constitutes a breach of his/her employment contract. Thus, for instance, if the employee does not show up for work after the transfer, the supplier, who is now the employer, may dismiss him/her for serious misconduct ("faute grave").

58.2.1.5 Modification of the employment contract simultaneously with/after the transfer

Services or outsourcing arrangements may result in a modification of the employment contract of the employee whose employment contract is transferred. They may entail a change in the location of the workplace. If the place of work is specified in the employment contract, or if the new place of work is very far from the old one (in a different geographical sector) and the employee's contract has no mobility clause, the employee will be entitled to refuse the change of his employment contract. Since, in theory, the employment contract is transferred on the day of the transfer, it is, in principle, up to the supplier to dismiss the employee.

Following the transfer, the supplier may propose amendments to the transferred employees' employment contracts, in accordance with the usual rules:

(a) if a simple change in working conditions is concerned, the supplier is free to modify them unilaterally (e.g. change of working hours or of task); and

(b) if a modification of the employment contract is concerned (i.e. a change of essential elements such as compensation, place of work or working time), the supplier must obtain the express written consent of the employee; in the absence of the employee's written consent and if the supplier cannot forgo the modification, he may dismiss the employee for economic reasons if he can prove that real and serious economic grounds exist.

However, there is a limit in the case of fraud as defined in Article L. 1224-1. The purpose of the modification must not be to avoid the effect of the transfer. In practice, if the employment contract is modified after the transfer, the following conditions should be met to avoid the risk of fraud as defined in Article L. 1224-1:

(a) the employment contract must have been in effect with the supplier for some time (evaluated on a case-by-case basis);

(b) the modification must be for economic reasons; and

(c) the dismissal must not be pronounced until after applying the dismissal order criteria and only if there is no possibility of redeployment.

58.2.1.6 Outstanding wages

Under Article L. 1224-2 of the Labour Code, the employment contract of the transferred employees is continued with the new employer, thus the supplier is liable to the transferred employees for:

(a) all sums owed to the employees for the period following the services or outsourcing arrangement; in particular, the employee is entitled to his/her accrued holidays; and

(b) all sums owed and not paid by the previous supplier/former employer for the prior period.

However, the supplier may claim against the previous employer in respect of the sums that he pays to employees that relate to the period prior to the date of transfer, unless:

(a) the previous employer is involved in receivership or winding-up proceedings; and

(b) there is no agreement between the successive employers (for example, if there is a succession of suppliers).

58.2.1.7 *Transfer of part of a contract of employment*

Article L.1224-1 will apply to employees assigned to the transferred activity on a full-time basis. It will also apply for those employees who, before the services or outsourcing arrangement, were assigned partly to the transferred activity and partly to the retained activity. In this case, their employment contracts will be transferred on the same partial basis. This will result in the employees working part time for the new supplier and part time for their former employer.

However, this mechanism, which will modify the employees' employment contracts in that they will be transformed into part-time employment contracts, will require the consent of the employees. Moreover, it is particularly difficult to apply in practice.

After the automatic transfer of the contracts of employment, the former employer, the supplier and each employee concerned may conclude a tripartite agreement where the employee agrees to work full time for either his/her former employer or the supplier instead of part time for each of them.

58.2.1.8 *Transfer of protected employees*

Protected employees are staff representatives (i.e. a member of a work council, union delegate, member of the Committee for Health and Safety at Work, judge at the Labour Court etc.)

The transfer of an entire economic entity according to Article L. 1224-1 of the Labour code involves the automatic transfer of the protected employees' employment contracts.

In the case of a partial transfer of the company (such as in a services or outsourcing arrangement), the transfer of protected employees' employment contracts is subject to the prior authorisation of the labour inspector, whose job it is to ensure that there is no discrimination against protected employees and that the transfer is not an excuse to "get rid" of them. Consequently, the former employer will have to obtain authorisation for the transfer of the protected employees from the labour inspector before the transfer. Authorisation must be requested 15 days prior to the planned date of the transfer.

The protected employees will be transferred on the date of the labour inspector's authorisation.

If the inspector rejects the transfer, the situation will be that the employees' previous jobs will in fact have ceased to exist, so maintaining their employment with their previous employer will require a modification of their employment contracts, which will need their formal approval.

If protected employees are transferred without the labour inspector's authorisation, they will be entitled to request reinstatement with their previous employer. If no position is available the employer can decide to dismiss the protected employee but will need the labour inspector's authorisation.

In case of dismissal without authorisation the employer can be penalised by one year's imprisonment and/or a fine of €3,750.

58.2.1.9   *Mandates of staff representatives*

Concerning the mandates of staff representatives, two situations may apply.

(a) If Article L. 1224-1 of the Labour Code applies, and an autonomous economic entity is transferred with a works council (i.e. a transfer of a full establishment of the company) then the mandates of staff representatives will be transferred to the new supplier as well, provided that the transferred entity remains legally autonomous. Consequently, the protected employees who are transferred will keep their mandates as staff representatives and will have the right to exercise their duties within the supplier company until the expiry of their initial mandate. However, the length of their mandate can be extended or reduced in order to correspond to the date of election of staff representatives at the new supplier by way of a collective agreement concluded between the new employer and the union delegates.

(b) Otherwise, the mandates of the staff representatives will be terminated automatically on the effective date of the services or outsourcing arrangement. However, they will be protected from any dismissal for a period of six months for staff representatives and 12 months for union delegates, unless the prior authorisation of the labour inspector is obtained.

58.2.1.10   Collective benefits

In addition to the advantages provided for in their employment contracts, employees may enjoy collective benefits which apply to all employees or certain employee categories, pursuant to a collective bargaining agreement or an in-house collective agreement[1] applicable to the company or pursuant to custom etc., for example a bonus, or a thirteenth-month salary.

58.2.1.11   Collective bargaining agreements

Pursuant to Article L. 1224-1, there are four different situations:

(a)   Where a different collective bargaining agreement is applied by the former employer and by the supplier. The transferred employees will be entitled, for a maximum period of 15 months (i.e. 12 months and a three months notice period), to claim the most favourable provision in either collective bargaining agreement. After 15 months, only the collective bargaining agreement in force within the supplier will apply to the transferred employees in addition with the transferred employees' personal vested rights (*"avantages individuels acquis"*), unless a specific agreement (*"accord d'adaptation"*) is concluded with the supplier's trade unions.

(b)   Where the former employer and the supplier apply the same collective bargaining agreement. This collective bargaining agreement will remain applicable.

(c)   Where the former employer has no collective bargaining agreement but the supplier has one. The transferred employees will be entitled as from the transfer of their employment contract to benefit from the collective bargaining agreement of their new employer.

(d)   Where the former employer has a collective bargaining agreement and the supplier does not. The transferred employees will be entitled, for a maximum period of 15 months, to claim the application of the collective bargaining agreement of their former employer. After 15 months, only the transferred employees' personal vested rights will apply to the transferred employees, unless a specific agreement is concluded with the supplier's trade unions.

58.2.1.12   In-house collective agreements

Different types of in-house collective agreements may exist.

(a)   Health plans: pursuant to Article L. 1224-1, there are various different

---

[1]   There is a difference in France between:
(a)   collective bargaining agreements (*"conventions collectives nationales"*) negotiated and signed at a national level between the big employers' trade unions and employees' trade unions; and
(b)   in-house collective agreements (*"accords collectifs d'entreprise"*) negotiated and signed between the trade unions of the company and the employer.

situations. If the transferred employees did not benefit from a health plan whilst they were employed by the previous employer, then they will be immediately entitled to the supplier's health plan as from the date of the transfer if one is applied by the supplier.Otherwise, the effect of the services or outsourcing arrangement will depend upon how the previous employer's health plan was set up:

(i) if the health plan was incorporated into the employees' employment contracts, the health plan will be transferred with the employment contracts if Article L. 1224-1 of the Labour Code applies;

(ii) if the health plan was incorporated into a company-wide agreement, the applicable rules relating to the collective bargaining agreements will apply (see section 58.2.1.10); or

(iii) if the health plan was incorporated into an in-house agreement concluded by referendum/unilateral commitment of the former employer/customer, it will still apply after the transfer of the employees until the supplier terminates it according to the applicable procedure set out in the relevant agreement.

(b) Profit-sharing agreements: according to Articles L. 3313-4 and L. 3323-8 of the Labour Code, in the event of the transfer of an activity with its employees to a new company, the following will happen to any mandatory profit-sharing agreement and any optional profit-sharing agreement in force with the previous employer:

(i) if the former employer had profit-sharing agreements but the supplier does not, the employees will no longer be entitled to the benefit of the profit-sharing agreements. If, after the transfer, there are more than 50 employees employed by the supplier, the supplier will have to start to negotiate in order to enter into a mandatory profit-sharing agreement and an optional profit-sharing agreement that would be appropriate for the supplier's business, within six months of the outsourcing; or

(ii) if both the former employer and the supplier have profit-sharing agreements, the agreements with the former employer will no longer be applicable from the date of the transfer. The transferred employees will have the benefit of the agreements in force with the supplier as from this date.

Companies should pay particular attention to the drafting of profit-sharing agreements and consider how they will apply in the event of the company deciding to outsource any of its services.

58.3   People issues—other employment issues

58.3.1   *Unlawful types of outsourcing agreements*

The services or outsourcing contract ("externalisation") must not consist of a service entailing the supply of employees ("sous-traitance") to the customer's site or supply of employees to the supplier's site by a sub-contractor, at the risk of it being considered as:

(a)   the unlawful leasing of a work force ("any operation for profit whose exclusive purpose is the leasing of labour")—this will be punishable by one year of imprisonment and a fine of €30,000 for the company's executive if he is an individual and a fine of €150,000 if it is a legal entity (Article L. 8243-1 of the Labour Code); or

(b)   improper sub-contracting ("any operation for profit entailing the supply of manpower which has the effect of causing prejudice to the employee concerned or eluding the application of legal provisions or the stipulations of an agreement or of a collective bargaining agreement")—this will also be punishable by one year of imprisonment and a fine of €30,000 for the company's executive if he is an individual and a fine of €150,000 if it is a legal entity (Articles L. 8234-1 and 8 of the Labour Code).

If what is envisaged is the supply of a service and not the transfer of an activity or part of an activity the following rules should be followed:

(a)   the parties should precisely define in the contract the services to be rendered and the supplier's special know-how in the performance of the services;

(b)   exclusive supervisory control over and responsibility for staff of the supplier should be left with the supplier as the sole employer;

(c)   the charges should be calculated on the basis of a lump-sum payment and not on the basis of the number of employees assigned to the service provision or their qualifications; and

(d)   the parties should ensure that the supplier/sub-contractor performs its services using its own materials and resources and remains independent.

58.3.2   *Duty to consult*

French law does not contain an obligation to inform employees of the proposed services or outsourcing arrangement in the absence of staff representative. In practice, it is highly recommended that employees are informed individually prior to their transfer.

The works councils of the supplier and that of the customer must be informed and consulted in respect of the planned services or outsourcing arrangement (Article L. 2323-6 of the Labour Code). The works council must be asked to give its opinion on the services or outsourcing t plan sufficiently in advance so that its opinion can be taken into account by the company before any contract is signed with the supplier. However, the project must be sufficiently advanced so that the management of the company can provide the works council with comprehensive information. If the works council is not in favour of the services or outsourcing arrangement, this does not prevent the services or outsourcing arrangement from being pursued, but if the works council refuses to give its opinion, the employer cannot proceed with the transfer, and must obtain an interim order requiring the works council to give an opinion.

Failure to comply with the obligation to inform or consult with the works council constitutes an offence, the maximum penalty for which is imprisonment of one year and a fine of €3,750 for the company's executive if he is an individual and a fine of €18,750 if it is a legal entity (Article L. 2328-1 of the Labour Code).

58.3.3   *Transfer under a collective bargaining agreement*

In some sectors, collective bargaining agreements provide for the transfer of employment contracts in the event of services or outsourcing arrangements, even if there is no transfer of an autonomous economic entity. The sectors concerned are in particular the restaurant, cleaning, security, railway handling and connected work, cleaning and handling of airports, road transport companies and waste companies.

The collective bargaining agreements will usually set out the scope (i.e. the transfer may be limited to some specific category of employees) and the conditions of transfer. They may also impose specific obligations on the former employer or the supplier.

58.3.3.1   *Employees' refusal to transfer*

Unlike the situation where employees transfer under Article L. 1224-1,[2] where employees transfer under a collective agreement, they are entitled to refuse the transfer of their employment contract and their refusal is not a ground for dismissal. If the employer intends to terminate such an employee, it will have to consider another reason (generally an economic reason).

---

[2]   See section 58.2.1.4.

58.3.3.2   Protected employees

The transfer of protected employees under a collective agreement (similar to a transfer under Article L. 1224-1) is subject to the prior authorisation of the labour inspector (see section 58.2.1.8).

Like other employees, protected employees are entitled to refuse the transfer of their employment contracts. If they object, the employer can only notify them of their dismissal after obtaining the opinion of the works council, if any, and obtaining the authorisation of the labour inspector.

For protected employees who accept their transfer, there are two situations:

(a)   Where there is no provision regarding their mandate as staff representatives in the collective bargaining agreement, their mandates will not be maintained. They will be terminated at the date of transfer of the employment contracts. The protected employees only benefit from their protection against dismissal for a period of six months after the termination of their mandates.

(b)   Where the collective bargaining agreement provides for the transfer of their mandates as staff representatives, their mandates will be maintained with the supplier until their date of termination.

58.3.3.3   Consequences for collective benefits

The transfer will be limited to the employment contracts and the collective benefits will not be transferred to the supplier. As a consequence, the collective benefits provided by custom, in a collective bargaining agreement or in in-house agreements will no longer be enforceable from the date of the services or outsourcing arrangement. The sole exception is when benefits have been integrated into the employment contract. In such a case, they will remain in force.

58.3.4   Voluntary transfer

The supplier may still need the employees who previously worked in providing the services or outsourced activity even if no collective bargaining agreement provides for the transfer of the employment contracts and Article L. 1224-1 of the Labour Code does not apply to the outsourcing arrangement, for example because:

(a)   the employees may have worked only occasionally on the activity;

(b)   the activity does not have any tangible or intangible assets; or

(c)   the activity may have been an autonomous economic entity with the former employer, but it will be reorganised by the supplier after which it will cease to be an autonomous economic entity.

In such cases, the former employer, the supplier and the employees will need to agree a voluntary transfer of the employment contracts.

58.3.4.1 Form of the agreement

The transfer of the employment contracts constitutes a modification of these contracts, which will require the prior express consent of the employees affected. The employee's approval must be in writing. The voluntary transfer can be effected by one of the following methods:

(a) amicable termination, or *"rupture conventionnelle"* since the new law dated 25 June 2008, with the former employment contract and conclusion of a new contract with the new supplier: this method should be used very carefully in order to avoid any claim from the employee for wrongful dismissal with the resulting liability for severance pay;

(b) resignation by the employee and signing of a new contract with the supplier: employees are usually reluctant to resign, as they will lose the benefit of unemployment allowances should they be terminated by their new employer in the months following the signing of a new contract; or

(c) a tripartite agreement: this is the easiest and the most secure method. It is concluded between the former employer, the new supplier and the employee. It should set out the conditions for the transfer (date of effect, seniority, applicable collective bargaining agreement etc.); it is neither considered as a resignation nor as a dismissal.

58.3.4.2 Outstanding wages

The parties will agree in the voluntary agreement upon each party's liabilities. Despite the terms of the agreement, the transferred employees will still be able to claim from their former employer for any liabilities due prior to the transfer of the employment contracts and from their new employer for any liabilities arising after the transfer, even if they relate to the period before the transfer—in this case, the new employer will be entitled to claim a reimbursement from the former employer.

58.3.4.3 Consequences for collective benefits

The consequences with regard to collective benefits will be the same as those with regard to the transfer under a collective bargaining agreement (see section 58.3.3.3).

58.4 Pensions issues

In principle, services or outsourcing arrangements, if they entail the application of Article L. 1224-1, will not affect the employees' entitlement to basic old-age insurance benefits, which are paid by the French social security system. However, they may affect the employees' rights to benefits granted under collective bargaining agreements, the content of which will vary from company to company.

58.4.1   *Supplementary pensions*

Every employee in France must be affiliated to a supplementary pension scheme. There are two mandatory regimes:

(a)   the "Arrco" regime: for employees and executives but only for a part of their remuneration ("A bracket"); and
(b)   the "Agirc" regime: for B and C brackets of executives' remuneration.

Levels of annual gross remuneration are divided into three brackets:

(a)   Remuneration A bracket involves the part of remuneration below the ceiling provided by the social security every year, that is, €34,308 for 2009;
(b)   Remuneration B bracket involves the part of the remuneration between the above ceiling and four times that amount, that is, between €34,308 and €137,232; and
(c)   Remuneration C bracket involves the part of the remuneration B bracket and eight times the above ceiling, that is, between €137,232 and €274,464.

Agirc and Arrco pension schemes are provided by several institutions depending upon the location of the company and the nature of the company's activity. Every company created after 1 January 2002 must be affiliated to an Agirc institution and an Arrco institution from the same group of insurance coverage. A company's adherence to a supplementary pension institution (Agirc/Arrco) is, in principle, definitive. That is, the company may change the institution only in limited circumstances, such as in a merger, franchise etc.

It may happen that the pensions schemes provided by the former employer and the supplier or the two successive suppliers belong to different pensions institutions. However, services or outsourcing arrangements do not belong to the limited cases where the change of institution is possible. If the supplier, after the transfer of employees, wants to move to the pension schemes with institutions from the same group, it can still make a request to the Agirc and Arrco, which will be approved under certain conditions (circular 2007-9-DRE).

58.4.2   *Pension schemes*

If the employee benefited from a collective pension fund (a "Perco") with his/her initial employer, two situations are possible:

(a)   if the new supplier has set up a Perco, the employee may request the transfer of his/her entitlements to the Perco of his/her new employer; or

(b)   if the new supplier does not have a Perco, the employee may continue to pay into the Perco of his/her previous employer, but he/she will no longer benefit from the employer's contribution and will have to pay the related management costs (Article R. 3332-13 of the Labour Code).

58.4.3   *Savings schemes*

Concerning savings schemes:

(a)   if the new supplier has implemented a savings scheme the employee may request the transfer of his/her entitlements to the savings scheme of his new employer; or

(b)   if the new supplier does not have any savings scheme the employee's savings will be maintained in the scheme of his/her previous employer until the end of the inalienability period.

58.4.4   *Self-funded pension scheme*

What happens to self-funded pension schemes will depend upon how they were set up by the previous employer:

(a)   if they were part of the employment contract, the scheme will be transferred with the employment contract if Article L. 1224-1 of the Labour Code applies;

(b)   if they were set up under a company-wide agreement or collective bargaining agreement, the rules above will apply relating to the collective status (see section 58.2.1.10); or

(c)   if the agreement was concluded by referendum/unilateral commitment of the former employer/customer, it will still apply after the transfer to the employees concerned until the new supplier terminates it according to the applicable procedure set out under case law.

58.5   Contract law

58.5.1   Formation of contract under French law

According to Article 1108 of the French Civil Code (FCC), there are four requirements essential for a valid agreement:

(a)   the consent of the party who binds himself/herself;
(b)   capacity to contract;
(c)   a definite object which forms the subject matter of the undertaking; and
(d)   a lawful cause in the obligation.

58.5.1.1   Consent

A party's consent can be provided orally or in writing. Some contracts must be formalised in writing to be valid, such as the sale contracts for real-estate properties.

According to Article 1109 of the FCC, there is no valid consent, where the consent was given by error, or where it was extorted under duress or by deception. An agreement entered into by error, duress or deception is not voided by operation of law. Instead it gives rise to an action for annulment or rescission in accordance with Article 1117 of the FCC.

58.5.1.2   Object

According to Article 1126 of the FCC, a contract must have as its object a thing which one party binds himself to transfer, or which one party binds himself to do or not to do.

The thing must be determined at least as to its nature. The quantity of the thing may be uncertain, provided it can be determined (Article 1129 FCC).

For sale contracts (for instance, the sale of IT hardware by the client to the supplier), the price must be determined and stated by the parties, or it may be left to the determination of a third person (Articles 1591 and 1592 of the FCC).

If the provisions of Articles 1591 and 1592 of the FCC are not followed, other than where specifically excepted, the contract becomes automatically void by operation of law.

58.5.1.3   Cause

Article 1129 of the FCC provides that an obligation without cause or with a false cause, or with an unlawful cause, may not have any effect. A cause is unlawful where it is prohibited by law or where it is contrary to public morals or to public policy.

58.5.2 Effects of binding agreements under French law—remedies

According to Article 1134 of the FCC, agreements lawfully entered into are considered like a contract between the parties who have made them and oblige them to respect their terms and conditions. They may be revoked only by mutual consent or on grounds authorised by the law. They must be performed in good faith.

Article 1142 of the FCC provides that if a party to any agreement fails to comply with a contractual obligation to do or not to do something then the other party will be entitled to receive damages. The other party may also have the obligation performed itself, at the expense of the defaulting party (Article 1144 of the FCC).

58.5.3 Interpretation of agreements

The FCC (Articles 1156 to 1164) regulates the interpretation of agreements with the following rules:

(a) in agreements, one must endeavour to ascertain the common intention of the contracting parties, rather than paying attention to the literal meaning of the words in the agreement;
(b) where a clause has two meanings, the meaning shall be favoured that gives the clause effect over that which produces none;
(c) where a term has two possible meanings, the meaning which best suits the subject matter of the contract shall prevail;
(d) any ambiguity shall be interpreted with reference to the meanings in use in the region where the contract was made; and
(e) in case of doubt, an agreement shall be construed against the beneficiary of the obligation and in the favour of the obligor.

58.5.4 Time-limitation/prescription rules

It should be noted that a new law dated 17 June 2008 has fundamentally modified the rules that apply to prescription issues.

Before 17 June 2008, all claims, in rem as well as in personam, were limited to a standard 30-year period which applied unless specific statutory exclusions stated otherwise.

Now, Article 2224 of the FCC provides that all claims, in rem as well as in personam, are limited to a five-year period.

There are some exceptions:

(a) claims in rem regarding real-estate matters are still limited to the 30-year period (Article 2227 of the FCC);
(b) claims for tort liability are barred after 10 years from the date of the damage or of its causation. Where the injury is caused by torture and acts of cruelty, assault or sexual aggression committed against a minor, the action in tort is barred after 20 years; and
(c) the limitation period for real estate is 10 years when the purchaser has a valid title and acts in good faith and 30 years in all other cases.

Prescription may not be excluded in advance but a prescription that has accrued may be (Article 2250 of the FCC).

According to the new provision in Article 2254 of the FCC, parties can agree to either shorten or extend the prescription duration within the respective limit of one year and ten years, except for payment claims regarding yearly or shorter instalment.

58.5.5   Types of contracts

Under French law, the services and outsourcing t contract are classified as a contract for services or work (Articles 1779 and following of the FCC).

A work contract is defined as a "contract relating to work, requested by one person of another without the latter being at the former's service, and most frequently for a fee"[3] or a contract in which "a person (the contractor) undertakes for a fee to independently carry out work to the benefit of another (the client), without acting as the latter's representative".[4]

A work contract differs from an employment contract because of the independence of the parties and the lack of subordination of the supplier to the client.

Although, in principle, the work contract places general obligations of due care on the supplier, in practice the parties are advised to include in the services or outsourcing contract detailed provisions setting out the supplier's performance obligations, including a definition of deliverables, deadlines, definition of performance indicators in the service level agreement, etc., as described in Chapters 1 to 10 of this Guide.

---

[3]   J. Huet, *Les principaux contrats spéciaux*, (L.G.D.J.), 2nd edn, N° 32102.
[4]   Malaurie, Aynès et Gautier, *Les contrats spéciaux*, Edition CUJAS, 14th edn, N° 708 s.

58.5.6 Liability and force majeure

58.5.6.1 Liability

In accordance with statutory contract law (Article 1147 of the FCC) and in the absence of provisions to the contrary, the supplier will be liable for any damages resulting from the non-performance of all or a part of its contractual obligations.

The damages will, as a rule, cover the loss which the other party has suffered and the profit of which it has been deprived, subject to force majeure.

Before the customer can file a liability claim against the supplier, the following conditions must be met:

(a) the loss must be a consequence of the breach of contract by the supplier;
(b) the customer must establish that it suffered a loss which is recoverable at law such as loss of earnings because of the delay in performance;
(c) the supplier must not be able to cite facts that justify the loss (such as that the breach of contract was caused by force majeure or by an act of the customer); and
(d) in the absence of facts that constitute justification, the customer must prove that the loss is caused by the supplier and that there is a causal link between the supplier's fault and the loss incurred.

In order to be recoverable, the loss must be (Article 1151 of the FCC):

(a) certain (actual and not simply potential);
(b) direct (the loss must result directly from the fault); and
(c) personal (only the person that sustained the loss may seek reparation).

In principle, compensation is only available for a foreseeable loss (Article 1150 of the FCC). Whether a loss is foreseeable is evaluated as on the day the contract was signed. Under French law it is possible to provide contractually for compensation for unforeseeable losses. Moreover, compensation for unforeseeable damage is available if the party committed the damage intentionally or as a result of gross misconduct.

58.5.6.2 Force majeure

A debtor is not required to compensate the other party for a loss arising as a result of an event of force majeure (Article 1147 of the FCC).

Case law defines a force majeure event as one which was unforeseeable when the contract was signed and one which makes it impossible to perform the service in question. It is irrelevant whether or not this event is beyond the debtor's control. However, the parties are free to define the scope of force majeure in the contract.

A debtor who proves that non-performance resulted from force majeure will not need to make good the corresponding loss. If the force majeure event renders the performance of the contract impossible, the contract will automatically terminate.

The debtor will also be exonerated from having to offer compensation if the loss is ascribable to a fault of the creditor or the unforeseeable and unavoidable actions of a third party.

58.6   Limitations of liability

The principle of contractual freedom allows the parties to stipulate certain clauses that limit the liability of one or both of the parties in the case of non-performance of the contract, within the limits of good faith and provided that limitation clauses must not:

(a)   exonerate the debtor in the case of non-performance owing to intentional breach[5] (fraud perpetrated against the other party) or gross misconduct;

(b)   exclude liability for bodily injury suffered by the other party;

(c)   exclude the essential obligation of the contract and exonerate the debtor in advance from liability for breach of its obligation;[6] or

(d)   limit possible compensation to an absurdly low amount.

In general, the parties limit their liability by agreeing to a compensation ceiling and/or by limiting themselves to compensating "direct" damage only. It is essential that this notion of direct or indirect damage (loss of custom, damage to image, etc.) is defined in the contract.

---

[5]   Article 1150 C.civ. "A debtor is liable only for damages which were foreseen or which could have been foreseen at the time of the contract, where it is not through his own intentional breach that the obligation is not fulfilled".

[6]   Cass. 1re civ., 28 avr. 1987 : D. 1988, jurispr. p1, note Ph. Delebecque.

58.7 Confidentiality and data protection

58.7.1 *Confidentiality*

There are no specific provisions under French law relating to the duty to safeguard confidential information.

The confidentiality obligation must be for a specific period. As a general rule, it is impossible to contract for a "perpetual" obligation. A perpetual obligation is null and void. Consequently, if there is a confidentiality obligation expressed to survive the services or outsourcing contract, the term of this obligation must be defined. A term of 5–10 years following the end of the contract is customary.

An employment contract can provide an obligation for employees not to reveal confidential information within a specified time limit.

58.7.2 *Data protection*

The protection of personal data has been regulated in France since the Data Protection Act 78-17 of 6 January 1978 was passed. The Act was amended by Act 2004-801 of 6 August 2004 on the protection of natural persons with regard to the processing of personal data, in order to transpose Directive 95-46 of 24 October 1995.

Data Protection Act 78-17 of 6 January 1978 already contained the main principles of the Directive 95-46 of 24 October 1995. Consequently, the Act 2004-801 of 6 August 2004 consists mainly of amendments to the pre-existing French provisions on personal data protection, such as: a simplification of the declarative formalities (the preliminary control of the French Data Protection Authority—Commission Nationale Informatique et Libertés (CNIL)—being henceforth limited to treatments presenting particular risks of infringement of rights and liberties), a consequent increase of the powers of intervention of the CNIL, and the strengthening of the rights of the data subject to their data.

The CNIL is the administrative authority in France responsible for implementing and controlling the application of obligations relating to personal data protection. It has powers to carry out investigations into all companies at any time or following a complaint by any person concerned. It may also impose sanctions, pursuant to the Data Protection Act (no. 78-17 of 6 January 1978, as amended by the Act 2004-801 of 6 August 2004). The CNIL exercises a priori and *a posteriori* control of the automatic processing of personal data.

Its powers to carry out on-site inspections, inspect documents and take measures have been increased and precisely defined. It may order the blocking, erasure or destruction of data at risk.

Depending on the seriousness of the breaches committed, the CNIL may issue warnings likely to be made public, formal notices or injunctions to discontinue the treatment in question and it may impose fines of up to €300,000 for serious breaches of statutory data processing obligations. Since 2004, the CNIL has imposed penalties on several occasions. To date, the highest fine imposed by the CNIL is €40,000 (decision of 11 December 2007 CNIL/SIG).

58.7.3   Data protection issues in offshore outsourcing

Data protection is a particularly sensitive topic in the context of offshore outsourcing, where activities are often outsourced to countries that are not yet recognised as offering adequate protection within the meaning of the Data Protection Directive.

It should be noted that, under pressure from European supervisory authorities, these countries seem to be more and more aware of the need to conform to European data protection regulations. Morocco, for instance, recently passed a law that almost exactly reproduces the French regulations in this area.

58.8   Insolvency issues

58.8.1   General

Bankruptcy and winding-up proceedings in France were governed by the Commercial Code and the Decree of 27 December 1985 until 2006. Law no. 2005-845 of 26 July 2005 (effective as of 1 January 2006) and implementing decree no. 2005-1677 of 28 December 2005 have significantly modified this area, with the aim of simplifying and adapting existing procedures while improving the tools available to prevent French businesses from being wound up. A new procedure, called the safeguard procedure (*procédure de sauvegarde*), has been embodied in the Commercial Code and was inspired, to a certain degree, by the US Chapter 11 proceedings.

The order 2008-1345 of 18 December 2008 (effective as of 15 February 2009) has modified the rules to improve the mechanism of the safeguard procedure and to improve the procedure of judicial winding up.

Cross-border aspects of bankruptcy in France should be reviewed taking into account EC Regulation no. 1346/2000 of 29 May 2000 on insolvency proceedings and the French principles applicable to international private law and case law.

French law provides for voluntary arrangements with creditors, generally before the bankruptcy stage is reached, such as the *mandat ad hoc*(counselling proceedings) or the conciliation (mediation proceedings). A certain overlap exists between the bankruptcy prevention mechanisms and the judicial procedures.

The main objectives of bankruptcy proceedings under French law are, in order of priority:

(a) to preserve the activities of distressed companies and to enhance prospects for recovery;
(b) to save jobs; and
(c) to pay creditors.

From a foreign investment perspective, the importance given in France to the preservation of jobs (and consequently, the unavoidable costs of preserving them) is considered particularly disadvantageous to possible rescue plans.

The traditional bankruptcy proceedings under French law are receivership (*redressement judiciaire*) and judicial winding up (*liquidation judiciaire*).

58.8.2   *Commencement of proceedings*

When a French company reaches the stage where it is unable to meet its liabilities with available (cash or cash equivalent) assets (known as *cessation de paiements*), its representative must file a petition with the local Commercial Court within 45 days of the *cessation de paiements* (if it has not first opted for the conciliation proceedings). The court must then decide either:

(a) to place the distressed company in receivership (*redressement judiciaire*) (for example, if the company has reached the stage of *cessation de paiements*while under the conciliation scheme); or
(b) to liquidate it immediately (*liquidation judiciaire*) if there is no possibility of recovery or if it has ceased its activities.

The court may also seize the assets of all related companies at any moment, should it be proven that the defaulting company was created to defraud creditors or that the assets of the companies within a group (including those of the distressed French company) are intermingled.

58.8.3   Professional bodies

Upon commencement of proceedings, the court appoints the following persons.

In the event of receivership:

(a)   a receiver who will be responsible for:

    (i)   temporarily assisting the management of the company while the debtor remains in possession and continues to manage the company in person; and

    (ii) preparing a recovery plan.

(b)   a creditors' representative who will represent the creditors and record and verify their claims.

In the event of a winding up:

(a)   a liquidator, generally the same person as the receiver;

(b)   the creditors' representative, who will be vested with the power to sell the assets and apportion the funds between creditors; and

(c)   a judge to handle the proceedings (the Judge Commissaire).

58.8.4   Creditors

Secured and unsecured creditors whose claims existed before the company was placed in receivership or liquidation proceedings by the court ("pre-bankruptcy creditors") must file their claims with the creditors' representative within two months of publication of the court's opening judgment in a legal gazette known as the "BODACC".

58.8.5   Insolvency solutions

58.8.5.1   Recovery plan

Since 1 January 2006, the aim of receivership has been solely the continuity of the business through a recovery plan (*plan de continuation*) with its current management. Creditors may be required under the plan to defer payment of their claims for a maximum period of 10 years.

58.8.5.2   Liquidation

Since 1 January 2006, the total or partial sale of the business is one of the objectives of the judicial winding-up proceedings in cases where the debtor himself is no longer capable of managing the business towards recovery (see also Part III, Acquisition of a Bankrupt Company).

58.8.6   *Termination rights*

In practice, to protect a party from the insolvency of the other party, formal clauses are generally inserted into the contract. Such clauses stipulate that if insolvency proceedings are initiated against one party, the other party may terminate the contract. They may even provide for the automatic cancellation of the contract.

However, from a legal point of view, both of these types of clause are null and void on the grounds that they are against public policy.[7]

Therefore, the customer may want to insert an automatic termination clause in the services or outsourcing agreement which comes into effect on the occurrence of an insolvency event (such as non-performance) prior to the commencement of the collective proceedings, as this clause will not be void as being in breach of public policy.

In the absence of a valid automatic termination clause in the services or outsourcing agreement, a party to a contract is obliged to maintain contractual relations with the other party even if non-performance occurs before insolvency proceedings are commenced.

If the contract is in progress, the party who has entered into a contract with the party involved in insolvency proceedings may formally ask the receiver to make a pronouncement on the continuation of the contract. In that case the receiver has one month (in some cases the judge in charge of the procedure may grant him an extra month) in which to make his decision. If no reply is given after that time, the contract is considered terminated.

If the receiver decides to continue with the contract, the principle of contract enforceability applies: the contract is continued with the same terms, conditions and sanctions. The receiver must ensure that the company in receivership complies with its obligations, as promised.

58.9   Financial services regulation

Directives 2004/39/EC and 2006/73/EC on markets in financial instruments were transposed into French law by order 2007-544 of 12 April 2007, Conseil d'Etat decree 2007-901 of 15 May 2007, decree 2007-304 of 15 May 2007, the decision of 15 May 2007 approving the modification of the general regula-

---

[7]   CA Paris, 21 mars 1997, D. Aff. 1997, p.702.

tions of the financial markets authority (*Autorité des Marchés Financiers* ("AMF")), modified by the decree of 22 February 2011.

The French government and the AMF have tried to remain as faithful as possible to the Directives when transposing them, avoiding the addition of specific domestic rules. Whenever possible, the same terminology as in the Directives was used.

The first paragraph of Article 13.5 of Directive 2004/39 was transposed to Articles L. 533-10-4 and 5 of the Monetary and Financial Code. However, the rest of Article 13.5 and all of the provisions of the Directives concerning outsourcing were transposed to subsection 5 of the AMF General Regulations, whose articles almost exactly reproduce the wording of the articles of Directives 2004/39/EC and 2006/73/EC.

The AMF General Regulations only apply to asset management companies. In the case of investment suppliers that are not asset management companies, outsourcing terms and conditions are set out in Chapter II of Regulation 97-02 of the *Comité de la réglementation bancaire et financière* (CRBF), the wording of which is very close to that of the AMF General Regulations.

58.10   Public Procurement Directives

Decree 2006-975 of 10 August 2005 established the new Public Procurement Contracts Code, which adopted into French law Directive 2004/18/EC on the co-ordination of procedures for the award of public works contracts, public supply contracts and public service contracts. The procedure for the award of public procurement contracts defined in Directive 2004/18/EC was reproduced in the Public Procurement Contracts Code.

The Public Procurement Contracts Code applies to contracts concluded with all public entities with the exception of state commercial or industrial public institutions.

The provisions of Directive 2004/18/EC have led to modifications in other codes. Order 2005-645 of 6 June 2005 amended the Local and Regional Collectivity Code in order to harmonise the latter with the provisions of Directive 2004/18/EC.

Directive 2004/18/EC also led to the publication of order 2005-649 of 6 June 2005 on contracts concluded with certain private or public persons not subject to the Public Procurement Contracts Code.

Order 2004-559 of 17 June 2004 modified by the law n° 2008-735 of 28 July 2008 introduced "*contrats de partenariat*" (the French equivalent of PFI projects) which it defines as:

"an administrative contract by which the State or a public institution of the State confers on a third party, for a period determined in accordance with the investment amortisation term or the chosen financing terms and conditions, a global mission the purpose of which is the financing, construction or conversion, maintenance, servicing, operation or management of works, equipment, or intangible assets necessary for the public service as well as their financing to the exception of any participation in the share capital."

The *contrat de partenariat* is not a public contract within the meaning of the Public Procurement Contracts Code. The provisions of the Public Procurement Contracts Code (see public procurement contracts governed by Directive 2004/18/EC) do not apply to it. However, in order to reinforce the legal security of this type of contract, order 2004-559 of 17 June 2004 stipulates that all of the EU rules on the award of public contracts apply to these contracts.

58.11   Utilities Directive

Directive 2004/17/EC was transposed into French law by order 2005-649 of 6 June 2005 and decree 2005-1308 of 20 October 2005 to form the second part of the Public Procurement Contracts Code.

The transposition is only partial, since it only concerns the contracting authorities specified in Article 2 of the Public Procurement Contracts Code (i.e. the state and its public institutions other than those having a commercial and industrial character and regional authorities and local public authorities) if they fall within the scope of the Directive. In fact, the notion of contracting entities as per the Public Procurement Contracts Code is not exactly the same as that used in Directive 2004/17/EC, which specifies that contracting entities are public corporations or private organisations that operate utilities networks.

The Public Procurement Contracts Code only applies to the state and its public institutions, whereas Directive 2004/17/EC applies to a wide range of entities: the state, regional or local authorities, bodies governed by public law, associations formed by one or several such authorities or one or several of such bodies governed by public law. Yet in an annex, it also refers to a list of private companies that operate utilities networks including EDF and GDF.

58.12   Competition law

58.12.1   *Merger control*

58.12.1.1   *Application to services and outsourcing agreements*

Services and outsourcing agreements may lead to the creation of a concentration within the meaning of the merger rules in several circumstances:

(a)   if the agreement causes a transfer of assets and/or employees likely to be considered as being a part of a company, that is, transfer of elements sufficient to have an economic activity and a market presence (providing a service for the customer and also for third parties);

(b)   if the agreement involves the creation of a joint venture which performs all of the functions of an autonomous economic entity on a lasting basis;

(c)   if the agreement involves the control of the management and financial resources of the contracting party, over the long term; or

(d)   in exceptional circumstances, if the agreement creates an economic dependency.

Services and outsourcing agreements do not often lead to a concentration, as they do not often lead to one of the circumstances above.

However, French authorities have had the opportunity to examine transactions in connection with outsourcing activities on few occasions.[8] In particular, a number of companies, which internally manufactured the products that they sold under their trademarks, decided to outsource the manufacture of their products. As a consequence, they sold their production assets (production site, employees dedicated to the production activity) to a third company, and entered into an outsourcing agreement appointing the latter to meet their needs.

It shall be noted that French authorities carry out analysis similar to that undertaken by the European Commission for the implementation of EC merger rules (see Chapter 33) in order to determine whether outsourcing agreements may lead to a concentration under French merger rules.

---

[8]   Letter of the Ministry of the Economy on 29 December 2003 Famar/Aventis: acquisition of a production site of Aventis group, by a pharmaceutical group (Famar/Marinopulos) which the activity consists in offering outsourcing services to pharmaceutical and cosmetic companies (development of products, logistics, production packaging and distribution of products). Letter of the Ministry of the economy on 12 April 2003, case C2006-23 *Favera/ Pfizer*: acquisition by Favera of assets from Pfizer (2 production sites); the transfer of assets came with an outsourcing agreement between the parties according to which Favera should manufacture drugs on Pfizer's behalf.

58.12.1.2   Thresholds

An acquisition, a merger, the setting up of a joint venture or any other last-ing change of control over a company, may fall within the scope of the EU or the French merger control legislation if the applicable thresholds are met.

Pursuant to French merger rules set out in Articles L. 430-1–L. 430-10 of the Commercial Code, the acquisition of a company by another must be notified and authorised by the Competition Authority (that replaces the Ministry of Economy in this function as from March 2009), when it meets all three of the following conditions:

(a)   the combined aggregate worldwide turnover, taxes excluded, of all the concerned undertakings exceeds €150 million;
(b)   the aggregate turnover, taxes excluded, carried out in France by at least two of the undertakings concerned exceeds €50 million; and
(c)   the concentration does not fall within the scope of the EC Merger Control Regulation.

58.12.1.3   Duty to notify or obtain approval

A concentration can be subject either:

(a)   to a prior notification to, and approval by, the European Commission, if the EC Merger Control Regulation applies (i.e. if the EU thresholds are met); or
(b)   to a prior approval by the French government if the EC Merger Control Regulation does not apply *and* the French thresholds are met.

Neither the size of the transaction nor its impact on competition are taken into account while analysing the obligation to notify. This becomes relevant only in the assessment of the situation once notified. The notification obliga-tion is only triggered by the turnover thresholds of the companies involved in the transaction. Thus, even a transaction, which has no impact on competition, must be notified if the turnover of the companies involved meets the above conditions.

If the conditions are met, the Competition Authority must be notified of the transaction, which may not be implemented prior to clearance.

It is possible to notify an intended transaction, i.e. before the conclusion of the purchase agreement, provided that a letter of intent has been signed or a memorandum of understanding (*accord de principe*) has been entered into.

58.12.1.4   Duty of the Competition Authority to respond

The Competition Authority must examine the operation within five to eight weeks after the receipt of the complete notification.

Where the Competition Authority has not rendered any decision within five weeks (or possibly eight weeks if commitments are to be made), the concentration is deemed authorised.

At the end of the period, the Competition Authority may find that the operation is authorised subject to, as the case may be, compliance with the commitments they have entered into.

When they consider that the operation is likely to affect competition and that the commitments are not a sufficient remedy, the Competition Authority will decide to examine more deeply the criteria and the consequences of the operation. The Competition Authority may either authorise the concentration, with or without commitments, or prohibit the concentration.

58.12.1.5   Fines

Fines may be imposed where:

(a)   the concentration is put into effect without notification;
(b)   the concentration is put into effect before a decision is received from the Competition Authority; and
(c)   the notification is not complete or the parties supply incorrect information.

The Competition Authority may also impose periodic penalty payments on the parties to compel them to notify unless they restore the *status quo ante*.

58.12.2   Prohibited anti-competitive agreements

Article L. 420-1 of the French Commercial Code prohibits agreements that have the object or effect of preventing, restructuring or distorting competition in the market. Just as under EU competition law, infringements to those rules may lead the French competition authorities to impose on the companies involved fines of up to 10 per cent of the global turnover of the group to which the company concerned belongs. In case of serious infringements (in particular market shares, bid-rigging, concerted bids), a criminal procedure may follow and lead to penalties of up to €75,000 and four years' imprisonment for any individual having a personal, fraudulent and determining part in the prohibited practice.

Analysis under French competition rules of the exclusivity and non-competition provisions that services and outsourcing agreements may include is similar to that undertaken by the EU competition authorities (see Chapter 33).

58.13   Other relevant laws and best practice

It should be noted that various professional standards exist in France in relation to services and outsourcing arrangement. These standards are not compulsory, but constitute good practice guides. The following standards may be relevant:

(a)   ISO 9000 December 2000 Quality Management Systems; Fundamentals and Vocabulary;

(b)   ISO 9001 December 2001 Quality Management Systems; Requirements;

(c)   ISO 14001-2004 on Environmental Management;

(d)   ISO 14004-2004 on Environmental Management;

(e)   AFNOR Z67-801-1 Facilities Management Specifications;

(f)   AFNOR Z67-801-2 Facilities Management Implementation of Services;

(g)   Security Techniques ISO 27001 (Information Security Management Systems) and ISO 27002;

(h)   Charter for the use of the knowledge base systems of the *Association Française de l'Audit et du Conseil Informatique* (French audit and information technology consulting association (AFAI));

(i)   Charte Cigref-Syntec Informatique (Infogérance et TMA) (facilities management and third-party applications maintenance).

INDEX

Index

Index

Index

Index

834

Index

840

Index

Index

Index

Index

Index

Index